MACWORLD
MW
AUTHORIZED
EDITION

QuarkXPress 3.2/3.3 Bible

by Barbara Assadi and Galen Gruman

Foreword by Fred Ebrahimi
President
Quark Inc.

Preface by Ralph Risch
Product Manager
QuarkXPress for Macintosh
Quark, Inc.

IDG BOOKS

IDG Books Worldwide, Inc.
An International Data Group Company

San Mateo, California ♦ Indianapolis, Indiana ♦ Boston, Massachusetts

QuarkXPress 3.2/3.3 Bible

Published by
IDG Books Worldwide, Inc.
An International Data Group Company
155 Bovet Road, Suite 310
San Mateo, CA 94402

· Library of Congress Catalog Card No.: 93-80873

ISBN: 1-878058-85-1

Printed in the United States of America

10 9 8 7 6 5 4 3 2 1

Distributed in the United States by IDG Books Worldwide, Inc.

Distributed in Canada by Macmillan of Canada, a Division of Canada Publishing Corporation; by Computer and Technical Books in Miami, Florida, for South America and the Caribbean; by Longman Singapore in Singapore, Malaysia, Thailand, and Korea; by Toppan Co. Ltd. in Japan; by Asia Computerworld in Hong Kong; by Woodslane Pty. Ltd. in Australia and New Zealand; and by Transword Publishers Ltd. in the U.K. and Europe.

For information on where to purchase IDG Books outside the U.S., contact Christina Turner at 415-312-0633.

For information on translations, contact Marc Jeffrey Mikulich, Foreign Rights Manager, at IDG Books Worldwide; FAX NUMBER 415-358-1260.

For sales inquiries and special prices for bulk quantities, write to the address above or call IDG Books Worldwide at 415-312-0650.

About the Authors

Barbara Assadi and Galen Gruman have used, taught, and reviewed desktop-publishing technology for many years, on both Macintosh and PC platforms. Fluent in all the major desktop-publishing programs, they have regularly reviewed publishing technology for the computer trade weekly *InfoWorld*, serving as members of the publication's review board.

One of their *InfoWorld* articles, published in 1990, still stands as a landmark and has been much imitated. That article was the first to compare a number of desktop-publishing programs, not by evaluating individual features (hyphenation-exception dictionaries, graphics scaling, and so on), but by actually applying the programs to the process of publishing a complex document. This article caused more than one product developer to reconsider approaches to user needs for desktop-publishing software.

A member of *InfoWorld*'s Software Review Board since 1988, Assadi has authored nearly one hundred articles on desktop publishing and word processing software, and has written two other books on QuarkXPress. Her passion for desktop publishing began in the early 1980s when she became a consultant to businesses interested in automating the publishing process. Her work was the subject of a feature on corporate publishing in *Publish* magazine. She has taught courses on technical publishing techniques at the university level, and has spoken at many conferences on computer publishing in the corporate environment. She has also received several national awards for writing. In 1993, Assadi joined Quark, Inc., where she manages the company's writers and editors. She makes her home in a suburb of Denver, Colorado, where she is a weekend hiking enthusiast.

Gruman was an early adopter of desktop publishing technology, helping bring the then-nascent technology to bear on production of several internationally distributed trade magazines. He has followed the technology's maturation and occasional missteps as an *InfoWorld* desktop-publishing reviewer since 1987, as well as a reviewer for other publications. Gruman also is senior associate features editor at *Macworld*, where he writes and edits articles, and is president of the Computer Press Association, an international association of journalists who cover the computing industry. He has been honored by the Computer Press Awards for his technology news reporting in "A Flaw in the Shield?" (*Science Digest*, May 1986) and shared first-place honors with Lon Poole and Arne Hurty for the three-part series "Your Computer Revealed" (*Macworld*, October-December 1992), which won the American Society of Business Press Editors' best in-depth technical feature article award. When not exploring publishing and computer technology, he can often be found on his bicycle.

About IDG Books Worldwide

Welcome to the world of IDG Books Worldwide.

IDG Books Worldwide, Inc., is a division of International Data Group, the world's largest publisher of computer-related information and the leading global provider of information services on information technology. IDG publishes over 194 computer publications in 62 countries. Forty million people read one or more IDG publications each month.

If you use personal computers, IDG Books is committed to publishing quality books that meet your needs. We rely on our extensive network of publications, including such leading periodicals as *Macworld, InfoWorld, PC World, Computerworld, Publish, Network World*, and *SunWorld*, to help us make informed and timely decisions in creating useful computer books that meet your needs.

Every IDG book strives to bring extra value and skill-building instruction to the reader. Our books are written by experts, with the backing of IDG periodicals, and with careful thought devoted to issues such as audience, interior design, use of icons, and illustrations. Our editorial staff is a careful mix of high-tech journalists and experienced book people. Our close contact with the makers of computer products helps ensure accuracy and thorough coverage. Our heavy use of personal computers at every step in production means we can deliver books in the most timely manner.

We are delivering books of high quality at competitive prices on topics customers want. At IDG, we believe in quality, and we have been delivering quality for over 25 years. You'll find no better book on a subject than an IDG book.

John Kilcullen
President and C.E.O.
IDG Books Worldwide, Inc.

IDG Books Worldwide, Inc. is a division of International Data Group. The officers are Patrick J. McGovern, Founder and Board Chairman; Walter Boyd, President. International Data Group's publications include: **ARGENTINA's** Computerworld Argentina, InfoWorld Argentina; **ASIA's** Computerworld Hong Kong, PC World Hong Kong, Computerworld Southeast Asia, PC World Singapore, Computerworld Malaysia, PC World Malaysia; **AUSTRALIA's** Computerworld Australia, Australian PC World, Australian Macworld, Network World, Reseller, IDG Sources; **AUSTRIA's** Computerwelt Oesterreich, PC Test; **BRAZIL's** Computerworld, Mundo IBM, Mundo Unix, PC World, Publish; **BULGARIA's** Computerworld Bulgaria, Ediworld, PC & Mac World Bulgaria; **CANADA's** Direct Access, Graduate Computerworld, InfoCanada, Network World Canada; **CHILE's** Computerworld, Informatica; **COLOMBIA's** Computerworld Colombia; **CZECH REPUBLIC's** Computerworld, Elektronika, PC World; **DENMARK's** CAD/CAM WORLD, Communications World, Computerworld Danmark, LOTUS World, Macintosh Produktkatalog, Macworld Danmark, PC World Danmark, PC World Produktguide, Windows World; **EQUADOR's** PC World; **EGYPT's** Computerworld (CW) Middle East, PC World Middle East; **FINLAND's** MikroPC, Tietoviikko, Tietoverkko; **FRANCE's** Distributique, GOLDEN MAC, InfoPC, Languages & Systems, Le Guide du Monde Informatique, Le Monde Informatique, Telecoms & Reseaux; **GERMANY's** Computerwoche, Computerwoche Focus, Computerwoche Extra, Computerwoche Karriere, Information Management, Macwelt, Netzwelt, PC Welt, PC Woche, Publish, Unit; **HUNGARY's** Alaplap, Computerworld SZT, PC World; **INDIA's** Computers & Communications; **ISRAEL's** Computerworld Israel, PC World Israel; **ITALY's** Computerworld Italia, Lotus Magazine, Macworld Italia, Networking Italia, PC World Italia; **JAPAN's** Computerworld Japan, Macworld Japan, SunWorld Japan, Windows World; **KENYA's** East African Computer News; **KOREA's** Computerworld Korea, Macworld Korea, PC World Korea; **MEXICO's** Compu Edicion, Compu Manufactura, Computacion/Punto de Venta, Computerworld Mexico, MacWorld, Mundo Unix, PC World, Windows; **THE NETHERLAND'S** Computer! Totaal, LAN Magazine, MacWorld; **NEW ZEALAND's** Computer Listings, Computerworld New Zealand, New Zealand PC World; **NIGERIA's** PC World Africa; **NORWAY's** Computerworld Norge, C/World, Lotusworld Norge, Macworld Norge, Networld, PC World Ekspress, PC World Norge, PC World's Product Guide, Publish World, Student Data, Unix World, Windowsworld, IDG Direct Response; **PANAMA's** PC World; **PERU's** Computerworld Peru, PC World; **PEOPLES REPUBLIC OF CHINA's** China Computerworld, PC World China, Electronics International, China Network World; **IDG HIGH TECH BEIJING's** New Product World; **IDG SHENZHEN's** Computer News Digest; **PHILLIPPINES'** Computerworld, PC World; **POLAND's** Computerworld Poland, PC World/Komputer; **PORTUGAL's** Cerebro/PC World, Correio Informatico/Computerworld, MacIn; **ROMANIA's** PC World; **RUSSIA's** Computerworld-Moscow, MIR, Foty; **SLOVENIA's** Monitor Magazine; **SOUTH AFRICA's** Computing S.A.; **SPAIN's** Amiga World, Computerworld Espana, Communicaciones World, Macworld Espana, NeX I I IDI D, PC World Espana, Publish, Sunworld; **SWEDEN's** Attack, ComputerSweden, Corporate Computing, Lokala Natverk/LAN, Lotus World, MAC&PC, Macworld, Mikrodatorn, I o World, Publishing & Design (CAP), Datalngenjoren, Maxi Data, Windows World; **SWITZERLAND's** Computerworld Schweiz, Macworld Schweiz, PC & Workstation; **TAIWAN's** Computerworld Taiwan, Global Computer Express, PC World Taiwan; **THAILAND's** Thai Computerworld; **TURKEY's** Computerworld Monitor, Macworld Turkiye, PC World Turkiye; **UNITED KINGDOM's** Lotus Magazine, Macworld, Sunworld; **UNITED STATES'** AmigaWorld, Cable in the Classroom, CD Review, CIO, Computerworld, Desktop Video World, DOS Resource Guide, Electronic News, Federal Computer Week, Federal Integrator, GamePro, IDG Books, InfoWorld, InfoWorld Direct, Laser Event, Macworld, Multimedia World, Network World, NetWORLD, PC Games, PC Letter, PC World Publish, Sumeria, SunWorld, SWATPro, Video Event; **VENEZUELA's** Computerworld Venezuela, MicroComputerworld Venezuela; **VIETNAM's** PC World Vietnam

Dedication

To my wonderful father, Dean Garth Seeley.

—Barbara Assadi

To Ingall Bull, who's made sure that I regularly stop to smell the roses along the way.

—Galen Gruman

Credits

Publisher
David Solomon

Managing Editor
Mary Bednarek

Acquisitions Editor
Janna Custer

Production Manager
Beth Jenkins

Senior Editors
Sandy Blackthorn
Diane Graves Steele

Production Coordinator
Cindy L. Phipps

Acquisitions Assistant
Megg Bonar

Editorial Assistants
Patricia R. Reynolds
Darlene Cunningham

Project Editor
Marta Justak Partington

Editors
Tim Gallan

Technical Reviewer
Michael J. Partington
Partington Design

Technical Reviewer of Disk
Michael Cohen

Production Staff
Tony Augsburger
Valery Bourke
Mary Breidenbach
Sherry Gomoll
Drew R. Moore
Gina Scott

Proofreader
Sandy Grieshop

Indexer
Sharon Hilgenberg

Book Design
IDG Production Staff

Photography of Parts Pages
Steve Adams, Staff Photographer at Quark
Charlotte Isoline, Art Director at Quark

Acknowledgments

Many people helped us create this book. We thank them all for their help. For help in getting real-world examples: Angela Burgess of *IEEE Software*; Rob Francisco and John Frick Jr. of Pacific Mutual Life Insurance Company; Charlotte Isoline, Eric Lewallen, Wesley Rittenberry, Jenna Riggs, and Kathy Thompson of Quark, Inc.; Dirk Hagner; and Al Perez. For their advice and encouragement: Deke McClelland, Deborah Fox, Jay McBeth, and Ralph Risch. For their help in getting us XTensions and scripts for the freebies disk: Jennifer Corder of Corder Associates; John Davis of Lepton Technologies; Nathan Dickson of Zaner-Bloser; Marc Grabowski, Kelly Kordes, Sid Little, Dave Shaver, Mark Neimann-Ross, and Peter Warren of Quark; Thomas Müller of CART•Computer+Grafik; Donal O'Connor of CompuSense; Sarah Clancy of Npath Software; and Jim Wiegand of XChange. And for producing the product that so many people benefit from: the developers and staff at Quark, Inc.

(The publisher would like to give special thanks to Patrick J. McGovern, without whom this book would not have been possible.)

Contents at a Glance

Contents

Foreword

In 1988, I became aware of Barbara Assadi and Galen Gruman when I read their product reviews in *InfoWorld*. Early on, I recognized that these two people have an understanding of the desktop-publishing field that goes much deeper than just knowing how to evaluate a program feature by feature. Bringing their own solid publishing backgrounds into play, they were the first to approach product reviews from a basis of understanding the intricacies of the publishing process.

I had the privilege of meeting Barbara and Galen at computer publishing trade shows, and I took advantage of the time to talk with them about the direction of desktop publishing and to get their feedback on some of our own product ideas. To put it simply, when it comes to publishing on the computer, these two know their stuff. You will recognize that as you use this book, which guides you through the process of creating a variety of documents with QuarkXPress. Regardless of whether you are a beginner or expert, you will find value in these pages as these two industry experts share their insights on the best ways to use this program.

— Fred Ebrahimi,
President, Quark, Inc.

Preface

I first met Barbara Assadi and Galen Gruman in my role as product manager, demonstrating the latest round of features to the reviewing press. Most reviewers, for all their knowledge of the software industry, are not experts on publishing. In contrast, Barbara and Galen not only understood the new features, they had anticipated them. Even when shown the surprises we threw in, they immediately recognized their value. There is nothing so satisfying as to show off technology you have created, and to see that spark of understanding as professionals put it to use.

QuarkXPress has changed tremendously with each subsequent version, providing tools for each step of the publishing process. But as the rewards of using QuarkXPress increase, so does the challenge of learning all the features. In this book, Barbara and Galen, through their understanding of publishing, relate the magic of QuarkXPress directly to the needs of the designer or publisher. For the sophisticated user who wants to unleash the power of QuarkXPress right away, this book should prove an invaluable guide.

—Ralph Risch, Product Manager,
QuarkXPress for Macintosh, Quark, Inc.

Introduction

Welcome to the *Macworld QuarkXPress 3.2/3.3 Bible*— your personal guide to a powerful, full-featured publishing program that offers precise control over all aspects of page design. Our goal is to guide you each step of the way through the publishing process, showing you as we go how to make QuarkXPress work for you. You'll also learn tips and tricks about publishing design that you can use in any document, whether it was created in QuarkXPress or not.

QuarkXPress does more than offer a wide range of desktop publishing capabilities to sophisticated designers who develop magazines, books, ads, and product brochures. It also gives the power of the press to individuals and groups who use the program's impressive set of publishing tools to communicate their thoughts, dreams, and philosophies.

The market for QuarkXPress knows no limits in terms of publishing applications. It also knows no national boundaries. The program is sold throughout the world, and its founders take pride in enabling people to communicate. Quark, Inc., takes this responsibility seriously and keeps a wide range of users in mind when developing software to serve them.

Simply put, the philosophy of the people who give us QuarkXPress is to provide the best possible publishing tools to those who strive to educate, inform, and document the world in which we live.

What This Book Offers

Since QuarkXPress comes with good documentation that is chock-full of examples, why do you need this book? In a phrase, "to see the bigger picture." Publishing design involves much more than understanding a particular program's tools — it involves knowing when, how, and, most important, *why* to use them. In this book, we help you realize the potential of QuarkXPress by applying its tools to real-world publishing design needs.

Desktop publishing users in general, and QuarkXPress users in particular, are an interesting bunch of people. Some have years of high-end, creative, design-intensive experience. Others are just getting started in publishing, perhaps by producing simple newsletters or flyers to advertise a community event.

Desktop publishing users fall into several classes:

- ∞ Experienced designers new to desktop technologies
- ∞ Novice designers new to desktop technologies
- ∞ Designers new to QuarkXPress but familiar with other desktop technologies
- ∞ Designers familiar with traditional publishing tools but new to the Macintosh

No matter which class you are in, you'll find that this book addresses your needs. The book is aimed at meeting the needs of those who design publications with QuarkXPress. That doesn't mean a degree in design or 10 years' experience producing national ad campaigns; it means anyone responsible for developing and implementing the look of documents, whether a four-page company newsletter or a four-color billboard ad. The basic techniques and issues are the same for both ends of the spectrum. And we, of course, cover in detail the specialized needs — such as table creation, image control, and color output — of high-end designers. (For those just learning about such advanced techniques, be sure to read the sidebars that explain the underlying issues.)

Regardless of your level of experience with desktop publishing, this book will help you use QuarkXPress. It is written with plenty of detail for experienced designers, while including enough step-by-step introductory material for the newest user. What distinguishes this book from the rest is that it does not attempt to substitute for the documentation that accompanies QuarkXPress. Instead, it guides you through the *process* of publishing a document, regardless of whether that document is your first or your 1000th. If you're new to the Macintosh, you'll appreciate how this book also includes information on getting started with the Macintosh operating environment.

How to Read This Book

If you are a novice publisher or designer, we suggest you read the book in order. The process of page design is presented in increasing levels of sophistication — you first learn how (and why) to create a template, then how to work with common elements such as text, and finally how to use special effects and deal with high-end publishing issues such as output controls and image manipulation.

If you are experienced, read the book in any order you want — pick those chapters or sections that cover the design issues you want to know more about, either as basic design issues or as QuarkXPress implementation issues.

Whether you read the book sequentially or nonsequentially, you'll find the many cross-references helpful. Publishing design is successful ultimately because the result is more than the sum of its parts — and the tools used to create and implement your designs cannot be used in isolation. Because this is true, it is impossible to have one "right" order or grouping of content; the cross-references let you know where to get additional information when what you're seeking to understand or learn doesn't fit into the way we've organized this book.

Conventions Used in This Book

Before we begin showing you the ins and outs of using QuarkXPress, we need to spend a few minutes reviewing the terms and conventions used in this book.

QuarkXPress commands

The QuarkXPress commands that you select by using the program menus appear in this book in normal typeface. When you choose some menu commands, a related pull-down menu or a pop-up menu appears. If we describe a situation in which you need to select one menu and then choose a command from a secondary menu or list box, we use an arrow symbol. For example, *Choose View ➪ Thumbnails to display the pages in thumbnail (reduced) view* means that you should choose the Thumbnails command from the View menu.

Mouse conventions

Because you use a mouse to perform many functions in QuarkXPress, you need to be familiar with the following terms and instructions:

- ➪ **Pointer:** The small graphic icon that moves on the screen as you move your mouse is the pointer. The pointer takes on different shapes depending on the tool you select, the current location of the mouse, and the function you are performing.

- ➪ **Click:** Quickly press and release the left mouse button once. Sometimes, you are instructed to *click the box* or *click the button.* To follow this instruction, use the mouse to move the pointer into position over the box or button before you click.

- ➪ **Double-click:** Quickly press and release the left mouse button twice.

- ➪ **Drag:** Dragging is used for moving and sizing items in a QuarkXPress document. To drag an item, position the mouse pointer on it. Press and hold down the left mouse button and then slide the mouse across a flat surface to "drag" the item.

Icons

You will notice special graphic symbols, or *icons,* used throughout this book. We use these icons to call your attention to points that are particularly important or worth noting. The following icons are used in this book:

The New icon indicates that the feature being described was added to version 3.2 or version 3.3 of QuarkXPress.

The Note icon appears next to an explanation about why QuarkXPress behaves in a certain way.

The Tip icon indicates that the accompanying paragraph includes a tip or an idea about how to use a QuarkXPress feature.

The Caution icon alerts you to a warning about potential unwanted effects of using a QuarkXPress feature.

The Design Tip icon accompanies paragraphs that include information on how to use a publishing technique (this is general publishing advice and is not necessarily specific to QuarkXPress).

The Cross Reference icon means the paragraph includes a reference to information contained in another part of the book.

Closing Remarks

Publishing is an exciting field, and desktop publishing has brought that excitement to the masses, revolutionizing communications and giving deeper meaning to "freedom of the press." We've been excited about desktop publishing from the early days, and we hope that you share that enthusiasm (or that we infect you with it!).

Desktop publishing is an ever changing field. QuarkXPress has evolved significantly since its first version, and its chief competitors (worthwhile programs in their own right for a variety of users) Aldus PageMaker and Ventura Publisher also continue to evolve, as do the computers we all run them on. Despite this evolution, the principles of publishing remain the same, so we hope you'll find this book's advice valuable over the years, even when you're using QuarkXPress 6.0.

QuarkXPress Fundamentals

No one is born a desktop-publishing expert, not even people skilled with using computers or with traditional layout and production techniques. The marriage between the two areas requires a strong foundation in both.

In this section, we cover the fundamentals for publishing, the Macintosh, and QuarkXPress itself. If you're an experienced user in any of these areas, feel free to skip over the relevant text. If you're new, start here. If you're somewhat experienced, go ahead and skim the chapters in this section. No matter who you are, look back to this part if you realize when you're somewhere else in the book that you're just not sure what we're talking about.

QuarkXPress has plenty of features, but it's not difficult to learn — if you take it a step at a time. Some words of advice: use QuarkXPress whenever you can so that you get plenty of practice. The more you use QuarkXPress, the better at using it you will be and the more features you will know how to use. Those tools will give you the power to do ever more creative work.

What Is QuarkXPress?

CHAPTER 1

In This Chapter

- ➡ The QuarkXPress publishing metaphor
- ➡ Publishing terms
- ➡ Controlling aspects of your documents locally and globally

The QuarkXPress Approach _____

Publishing programs, although similar in many ways, differ in their approach to the publishing task. One way to describe a program's approach to publishing is to talk about its *metaphor*, or the overall way that it handles publishing tasks. Some programs use a *pasteboard metaphor*, which means that the method used to assemble a document is based on assembling page elements as you would if they were placed on a pasteboard until ready for use. Other programs approach page layout using a *frame-based metaphor* in which frames (or boxes) hold both the page elements and the attributes that control the appearance of those elements.

QuarkXPress takes a structured approach to publishing. It is frame-oriented or *box-based*, meaning that you build pages by assembling a variety of boxes. First, you set up the basic framework of the document — the page size and orientation, margins, number of columns, and so on. You then fill that framework with text, pictures, and lines.

Before you can put text on a QuarkXPress page, you need a text box. You can tell QuarkXPress to create text boxes automatically for you, or you can draw them with the Text Box tool (the full set of QuarkXPress tools is described in Chapter 2). If you want to add pictures to a page, you need a picture box. You draw picture boxes using one of four Picture Box tools, each of which creates a different shape of box. You can put frames around picture boxes and text boxes; you can also resize, rotate, and apply color to both types of boxes.

If you simply want to put a line on a page, however, you don't need a box. You can draw lines anywhere on a page by using one of two Line tools, and you can specify the style and thickness of the lines you draw.

In simple terms, this box-based approach is the publishing metaphor of QuarkXPress. Although the idea of text boxes, picture boxes, and lines sounds simple and straightforward, in the right hands it can generate truly impressive results (see color instructional gallery).

Who Uses QuarkXPress?

QuarkXPress is used by an impressive list of people. Nearly three-quarters of all American magazines — including *Rolling Stone, US* magazine, *Macworld,* and *Readers Digest* — are produced with QuarkXPress, as are the majority of U.S. newspapers. It's also the best-selling page layout program with professional design firms. In Europe, QuarkXPress is the leading publishing program, and it is sold in 17 languages.

What does this information mean for you? It means that QuarkXPress can handle sophisticated tasks, but its simple approach to publishing also makes it a good choice for smaller projects like flyers and newsletters. It is also a good choice for corporate publishing tasks such as proposals and annual reports. Using QuarkXPress puts you in good company.

Terms You Should Know

Like many specialized functions, desktop publishing tools include their own unique terms. Not too long ago, only a few publishing professionals knew — or cared — what the words *pica, kerning, crop,* or *color model* meant. Today, almost everyone who wants to produce a nice-looking report, a simple newsletter, or a magazine encounters these terms in the menus and manuals of their layout programs. Occasionally the terms are used incorrectly or are replaced with general terms to make nonprofessional users feel less threatened, but that substitution ends up confusing a professional printer or someone who works in a service bureau. Here are definitions, grouped by publishing task, of some of the basics terms that you need to know.

Typography terms

Typography terms include words that describe the appearance of text in a document. These terms refer to such aspects of typography as the size and style of the typeface used and the amount of space between lines, characters, and paragraphs.

Characters

A *font* is a set of characters at a certain size, weight, and style (for example, 10-point Palatino Bold). This term is now used often as a synonym for *typeface*, which is a set of characters at a certain style in *all* sizes, weights, and stylings (for example, Palatino). A *face* is a combination of a weight and styling at all sizes (for example, Palatino Bold Italic). A *font family* is a group of related typefaces (for example, the Franklin family includes Franklin Gothic, Franklin Heavy, and Franklin Compressed).

Weight describes typeface thickness. Typical weights, from thinnest to thickest, are *ultralight, light, book, medium, demibold, bold, heavy, ultrabold,* and *ultraheavy*.

Type can have one of three basic stylings: *Roman* type is upright type; *oblique* type is slanted type; and *italic* type is both slanted and curved (to appear more like calligraphy than roman type). Type also may be *expanded* (widened), *condensed* (narrowed), or *compressed* (severely narrowed). See Figure 1-1 for examples of some of these stylings.

Figure 1-1:
A sample sans serif typeface with different stylings.

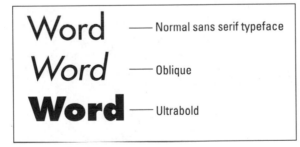

— Normal sans serif typeface

— Oblique

— Ultrabold

The *x height* refers to the height of the average lowercase letter (this is based on the letter *x*). The greater the height, the bigger the letter looks when compared to letters in other typefaces that are the same point size but have a smaller x height. *Cap height* is similar: it refers to the size of the average uppercase letter (based on the letter *C*).

In a letter such as *q*, the part of the letter that goes below the baseline is called a *descender*. The part of a letter that extends above the x height (as in the letter *b*) is called an *ascender* (see Figure 1-2).

A *serif* is a horizontal stroke used to give letters visual character. The strokes on the upper-left and bottom of the letter *p* in a typeface such as Times are serifs (see Figure 1-2). *Sans serif* means that a typeface does not use these embellishments. Helvetica is an example of a sans serif typeface.

Figure 1-2:
A sample showing different elements of a typeface.

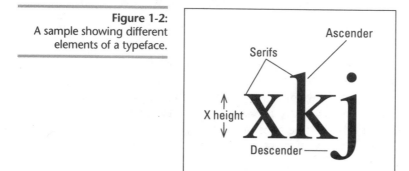

A *ligature* is a set of joined characters, such as *fi*, *fl*, *ffi*, or *ffl*. The characters are joined because the characters' shapes almost blend together by default, so typographers of yore decided to make them blend together naturally.

Measurement units

A *pica* is a measurement unit used to specify the width and depth of columns and pages. A pica is just a little less than ⅙ of an inch (most people round up to an even ⅙ inch). A *point* is a measurement used to specify type size and the space between lines. There are 12 points in a pica, so there are about 72.27 points to the inch — most people round down to 72 per inch. A *cicero* is a unit of measure used in many parts of Europe. One inch equals about 5.62 ciceros.

The terms *em*, *en*, and *punctuation space* (also called a *thin space*) are units of measurement that reflect, respectively, the horizontal space taken up by a capital *M*, capital *N*, and lowercase *t*. Typically, an em space is the same width as the current point size; an en space is ½ of the current point size; and a punctuation (thin) space is ¼ of the current point size. In other words, for 12-point type, an em is 12 points wide, an en space is 6 points, and a punctuation or thin space is 3 points. A *figure space* refers to the width of a numeral, which usually is the same as an en. (In most typefaces, all numerals are the same width so that tables align naturally.)

Spacing

Leading, also called *line spacing*, refers to the space from the base of one line (the *baseline*) to another. (Leading is named after the pieces of lead once used to space out lines.) See Figure 1-3 for examples of leading.

Tracking determines the overall space between letters within a word. If you increase tracking, space increases globally (throughout your entire document). *Word spacing* defines the preferred, minimum, and maximum spacing between words. *Letter spacing* (sometimes called *character spacing*) defines the preferred, minimum, and maximum spacing between letters. QuarkXPress uses your preferred spacing specifications unless you justify the text; if you justify text, the program spaces letters and words within the limits you set for maximum and minimum spacing.

Figure 1-3:
Different point type with different point leading can make a big difference in the way a document looks.

Qieodj elsgjcvmei kdbajieh jdhfla vneu fjeia fjna ienf ajjfiel ah heubs fueh vuena fhel funcceiu
— 14 point type with 14 point leading

Qieodj elsgjcvmei kdbajieh jdhfla vneu fjeia fjna icnf ajjfiel ah heubs fueh vuena fhel funcceiu
— 14 point type with 18 point leading

Kerning refers to an adjustment of the space between two letters. You kern letters to accommodate their specific shapes. For example, you probably would use tighter kerning in the letter pair *to* than in *oo* because *to* looks better if the *o* fits partly under the *t*. *Pair kerning* is a table, called the *kerning table* in QuarkXPress, that indicates the letter pairs you want the publishing program to kern automatically. Kerning is used most frequently in headlines where the letter spacing is more noticeable. See Figure 1-4 for an example of kerning.

Figure 1-4:
An example of kerned versus unkerned letters.

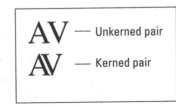

AV — Unkerned pair
AV — Kerned pair

Justification adds space between words (and sometimes between letters) so that each line of text aligns at both the left and right margin of a column or page. *Ragged right* and *flush left* both refer to text that aligns against a column's left margin but not its right margin; *ragged left* and *flush right* text aligns against the right margin but not the left margin. *Centered* text is aligned so that there is equal space on both margins. *Justification* also is used to refer to the type of spacing used: justified, ragged right, centered, or ragged left.

Vertical justification adds space between paragraphs (and sometimes between lines) so that the tops and bottoms of each column on a page align. (This term is often confused with *column balancing*, which ensures that each column has the same number of lines.) *Carding* is a vertical-justification method that adds space between paragraphs in one-line increments. *Feathering* uses fractional-line spaces between paragraphs.

Paragraphs

You typically indicate a new paragraph with an *indent*, which inserts a space (often an em space in newspapers and magazines) in front of the paragraph's first letter. An *outdent* (also called an *exdent*) shifts the first character past the left margin and places the other lines at the left margin. This paragraph alignment is typically used in lists. A *block indent,* a style often used for long quotes, moves an entire paragraph in from the left margin. A *hanging indent* is like an outdent except that the first line begins at the left margin and all subsequent lines are indented.

A *bullet* is a character (often a filled circle like •) used to indicate that a paragraph is one element in a list of elements. Bullets can be indented, outdented, or kept at the left margin. A *drop cap* is a large capital letter that extends down several lines into the surrounding text (the rest of the text wraps around it). Drop caps are used at the beginning of a section or story. A *raised cap* is the same as a drop cap except that it does not extend down into the text. Instead, it rests on the baseline of the first line and extends several lines above the baseline.

Style sheets contain named sets of such attributes as spacing, typeface, indent, leading, and justification. A set of attributes is known as a *style* or *style tag*. Essentially, styles are formatting macros. You *tag* each paragraph with the name of the style that you want to apply. Any formatting changes made to one paragraph are automatically reflected in all other paragraphs tagged with the same style. Note that QuarkXPress uses the term *style sheet* to refer to individual style.

Hyphenation

A *hyphen* is used to indicate the division of a word at the end of a line and to join words that combine to modify another word. *Hyphenation* is determining where to place the hyphen in split words. *Consecutive hyphenation* determines how many lines in a row can end with a hyphen (more than three hyphens in a row is considered bad typographic practice). The *hyphenation zone* determines how far from the right margin a hyphen can be inserted to split a word.

An *exception dictionary* lists words with nonstandard hyphenations. You can add words that the publishing program's default dictionary does not know and override the default hyphenations for a word such as *project,* which is hyphenated differently as a noun (*proj-ect*) than as a verb (*pro-ject*). Placing a *discretionary hyphen* (also called a *soft hyphen*) in a word tells the program to hyphenate the word at that place if the word must be split. A discretionary hyphen affects only the word in which it is placed.

Layout terms

Document layout — the placement of text, pictures, and other items on a page — involves many elements. A brief primer on layout terms follows; you'll find more detailed explanations later in this book, particularly in Chapter 8.

Layout tools

Galleys are single columns of type that are not laid out in any sort of page format. Publishers typically use galleys to check for proper hyphenation and proof for errors. Galleys also are sent to authors for proofreading so that corrections can be made before the text is laid out.

A *grid* is the basic layout design of a publication. It includes standard positions of folios, text, graphics, bylines, and headlines. A layout artist modifies the grid when necessary. Grids also are called *templates*. A *dummy* is a rough sketch of the layout of a particular story. *Guidelines* show the usual placement of columns and margins in the grid. In some programs, guidelines are nonprinting lines that you can use to ensure that elements align.

An *overlay* is a piece of transparent paper or film laid over a layout board. On the overlay, the artist can indicate screens in a different color or overprinted material such as text or graphics. Some programs have electronic equivalents of overlays.

A *knockout* is when one element cuts out the part of another element that it overlaps. A designer would say that one element knocks out the other or that one element is knocked out of the other — in either phrasing, it means the first element covers up the part of the other element under it. This differs from overlaying the other element, since in an overlay, both elements are visible (like a superimposed image).

Design elements

A *column* is a block of text. When you place two or more columns side by side, the space between columns is called the *gutter.* (In newspapers and magazines, gutter space usually is one or two picas.)

The *margin* is the space between the edge of a page and the nearest standard block of text. Some designers allow text or graphics to intrude into the margin for visual effect.

A *bleed* is a graphic element or block of color that extends to the trimmed edge of the page.

A *wrap* refers to a textual cutout that occurs when a column is intruded by graphics or other text. The column margins are altered so that the column text goes around — wraps around — the intruding graphic or text instead of being overprinted by the intruding element. Depending on what the text wraps around and the capabilities of the layout program, a wrap can be rectangular, polygonal, or curved. QuarkXPress supports all three shapes.

A *folio* is the page number and identifying material (such as the publication name or month) that appears at the bottom or top of every page.

White space is the part of the page left empty to create contrast to the text and graphics. White space provides visual relief and emphasizes the text and graphics.

Most desktop publishing programs use *frames* to hold layout elements (text and graphics) on a page; QuarkXPress refers to these frames as *boxes.* Using a mouse, you can delete, copy, resize, or otherwise manipulate boxes in your layout. The boxes that hold layout elements can have ruling lines around them; Quark calls these lines *frames.* You can create a *template* by filling a document with empty boxes and defining style tags in advance; you then can use the template repeatedly to create documents that use the same boxes and styles.

Image manipulation

Cropping an image means to select a part of it for use on the page. *Sizing* an image means to determine how much to reduce or enlarge the image (or part of the image). Sizing is also called *scaling.* With layout programs, you often can *distort* an image by sizing it differently horizontally and vertically, which creates special effects such as compressing or stretching an image.

Reversing (also called *inverting* in some programs) exchanges the black and white portions of an image. This effect is similar to creating a photographic negative.

Color terms

Spot color is a single color applied at one or more places on a page, such as for a screen or as part of an illustration. You can use more than one spot color per page. Spot colors can also be process colors.

A *process color* refers to any of the four primary colors in publishing: cyan, magenta, yellow, and black (known as a group as *CMYK*). A *color model* is an industry standard for specifying a color. The printer uses a premixed ink based on the color model identifier you specify; you look up the numbers for various colors in a table of colors (which is often put together as a series of color samples known as a *swatchbook*). *Four-color printing* is the use of the four process colors in combination to produce most other colors. A *color separation* is a set of four photographic negatives — one filtered for each process color — shot from a color photograph or image. When overprinted, the four negatives reproduce that image. A *build* attempts to simulate a color-model color by overprinting the appropriate percentages of the four process colors.

Color space is a method of representing color in terms of measurable values such as the amount of red, yellow, and blue in a color image. The EfiColor XTension, included with versions 3.2 and greater of QuarkXPress, works with three color spaces: *RGB* (which represents the red, green, and blue colors on video screens), *CIE LAB* (which specifies colors by one lightness coordinate and two color coordinates — green-red and blue-yellow), and *CMYK* (which specifies colors as combinations of cyan, magenta, yellow, and black). *Color gamut* is the range of colors that a device, such as a monitor or a color printer, can produce.

Production terms

Registration marks tell a printer where to position each negative relative to other negatives (the registration marks must line up when the negatives are superimposed). *Crop marks* tell a printer where to cut the negatives; anything outside the crop marks is not printed. Crop marks are used both to define page size and to indicate which part of an image is to be used.

A *screen* is an area printed at a particular percentage of a color (including black). For example, the border of a page may have a 20 percent black screen.

Trapping refers to the technique of extending one color so that it slightly overlaps an adjoining color. Trapping is done to prevent gaps between two abutting colors. Such gaps are sometimes created by the misalignment of color plates on a printing press.

Global Control Versus Local Control

The power of desktop publishing in general, and QuarkXPress in particular, is that it enables you to automate time-consuming layout and typesetting tasks while at the same time letting you customize each step of the process according to your needs. You can use *global* controls to establish general settings for layout elements and then use *local* controls to modify those elements to meet specific publishing requirements. The key to using global and local tools effectively is to know when each is appropriate.

Global tools include:

- General preferences and application preferences (see Chapter 4)
- Master pages (see Chapter 5)
- Style sheets (covered in Chapter 6)
- Sections (see Chapter 11)
- Hyphenation and justification (H&J) sets (see Chapter 13)
- Libraries (see Chapter 23)

Styles and master pages are the two main global settings that you can expect to override locally throughout a document. You shouldn't be surprised to make such changes often because the layout and typographic functions that styles and master pages automate are the fundamental components of any document.

Local tools include:

- Text Box and Picture Box tools (see Chapters 9 and 10)
- Character and paragraph tools (see Chapters 12 and 13)
- Graphics tools (see Part V)

In many cases, it's obvious which tool to use. If, for example, you maintain certain layout standards throughout a document, then using master pages is the obvious way to keep your work in order. Using styles is the best solution if you want to apply standard character and paragraph formatting throughout a document. When you work with special-case documents, such as a single-page display ad, it doesn't make much sense to spend time designing master pages and styles — it's easier just to format elements on-the-fly.

In other cases, it's harder to decide which tool is appropriate. For example, you can control page numbering on a global basis through the Section dialog box (accessed via Page ⇨ Section). But you also can change page numbering within a document by moving to the page on which you want to change a page number, invoking the Section dialog box, and selecting new settings.

Another situation in which you can choose between local or global controls is specifying measurement values. Regardless of the default measurement unit, you can use any unit when entering measurements in a QuarkXPress dialog box. If, for example, the default measurement is picas but you're accustomed to working with inches, go ahead and enter measurements in inches. QuarkXPress accepts any of the following measurement units:

- " (for inches)
- q (for hundredths of an inch)
- p (for picas)
- pt (for points)
- cm (for centimeters)
- mm (for millimeters)
- c (for ciceros)

 You can enter fractional picas in two ways: in decimal format, as in *8.5p*; and in picas and points, as in *8p6*. Either of these settings results in a measurement of 8½ picas. Note that if you use points, you must place them after the *p*.

Summary

- QuarkXPress is box-based, meaning that you build pages by assembling a variety of boxes and then filling the boxes with text or pictures.

- You'll find it easier to use QuarkXPress if you familiarize yourself with basic publishing terminology.

- Use global controls to establish general settings for layout elements.

- Use local controls to modify elements to meet specific publishing requirements.

Basic Elements

In This Chapter

- ◆ Choosing hardware and software to use with QuarkXPress
- ◆ Using QuarkXPress menus and palettes
- ◆ Selecting items to make them active

Hardware and Software Recommendations

For maximum performance, we recommend that you exceed the minimum requirements listed on the QuarkXPress box. For QuarkXPress to work smoothly, you should
have at least the following hardware and software:

- ∞ A Macintosh II or greater; 5 or more megabytes of RAM; a hard disk (we recommend a Centris 610 or faster Mac, one using at least a 20MHz 68040 CPU, with no
  less than 8 megabytes of RAM)

- ∞ A color or gray-scale monitor (we recommend a 16-inch display or larger) with an 8-bit
  video card (if you use lots of high-end color, a color monitor, and a 16- or 24-bit video
  card; most new Macs support 16-bit color with their built-in video circuitry)

- ∞ A mouse

- ∞ System 7 or greater

- ∞ Unless the text portion of your documents is relatively light (for example, if you
  produce graphics-intensive ads that have little copy), or you're budget dictates
  otherwise, you might want to consider a separate word processing program.
  Also, if your documents include cross references — tables of contents, indexes,
  and the like — you can either purchase XTensions to QuarkXPress, or you can use a
  word processor and then import the document into XPress for final formatting.

- ∞ A separate graphics program and, if you will be using a scanner, a separate image-
  editing program

      ⮺　As many type fonts as you can manage — the more the better

 QuarkXPress runs on Mac IIs (or greater) equipped with System 6.0.5 or greater and with 3MB of total RAM, but the setup we've listed will give you the best performance.

The Document Window

The way in which you communicate and work with QuarkXPress is controlled by the program's *user interface*. QuarkXPress has a user interface that is very similar to that used by other Macintosh programs. If you use other Macintosh programs, you are already familiar with such QuarkXPress interface components as file folders, document icons, and the set of menus at the top of the document window. The rest of this chapter explains the basics of using QuarkXPress interface components.

When you open a document in QuarkXPress, the program displays a document window containing the elements shown in Figure 2-1.

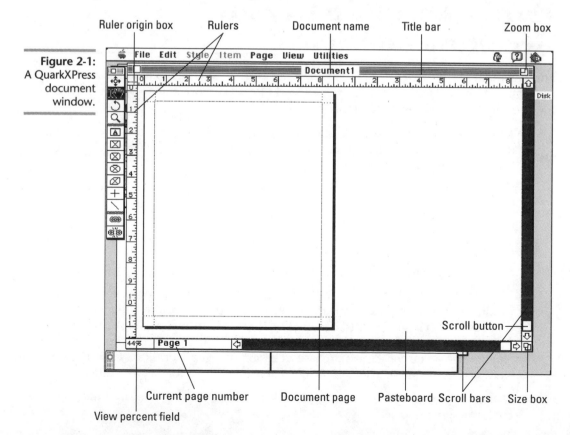

Figure 2-1:
A QuarkXPress
document
window.

- The *ruler origin box* lets you reset and reposition the ruler origin, which is the point at which the side and top rulers are 0 (zero).

- The name of the open document appears on the *title bar*, located at the top of the document window. You can move the document window around in the screen display area by clicking and dragging the title bar.

- If you have reduced or enlarged a document, clicking the *zoom box* at the top right corner of the document window returns it to its previous size.

- The *vertical* and *horizontal rulers* on the left and top of the window reflect the measurement system currently in use.

- The *pasteboard* is a work area around the document page. You can temporarily store text boxes, picture boxes, or lines on the pasteboard. Items on the pasteboard do not print.

- QuarkXPress displays a shadow effect around the document page. The shadow indicates where the pasteboard begins.

- If you select Automatic Text Box in the New dialog box (which you access by selecting New ⇨ Document from the File menu), a text box appears on every page of the new document.

- Clicking and dragging the *size box* resizes the document window as you move the mouse.

- The *View Percent* field shows the magnification level of the currently displayed page. To change the magnification level, enter a value between 10 and 400 percent in the field and then press the Return key or click elsewhere on the screen.

- Use the *scroll bars, boxes,* and *arrows* to shift the document page around within the document window. If you hold down the Option key while you drag the scroll box, the view of the document is refreshed as it moves.

QuarkXPress Menus

The menu bar appears across the top of the document window. To display, or "pull down," a menu, click the menu title and hold down the mouse button.

From the menu, you can select any of the active menu commands; other commands that are not available to you (that is, commands whose functions don't apply to whatever you happen to be doing at a given moment in the program) cannot be selected. QuarkXPress displays inactive menu commands with dimmed ("grayed-out") letters.

To select one of the active menu commands, you simply continue to hold down the mouse button as you slide through the menu selections. As you gain familiarity with the program, you can avoid using menus by using the keyboard equivalents for menu selections. Keyboard equivalents are displayed to the right of the command name.

If an arrow appears to the right of a menu command, QuarkXPress displays a second, associated menu when you choose that command. Sometimes this secondary menu appears automatically when you highlight the first menu command; other times, you must continue to hold down the mouse and slide it to the submenu name in order to activate the menu. Figure 2-2 shows the Style menu and the secondary menu that appears when you select the Font menu command.

Figure 2-2:
Selecting
menu
items in
QuarkXPress.

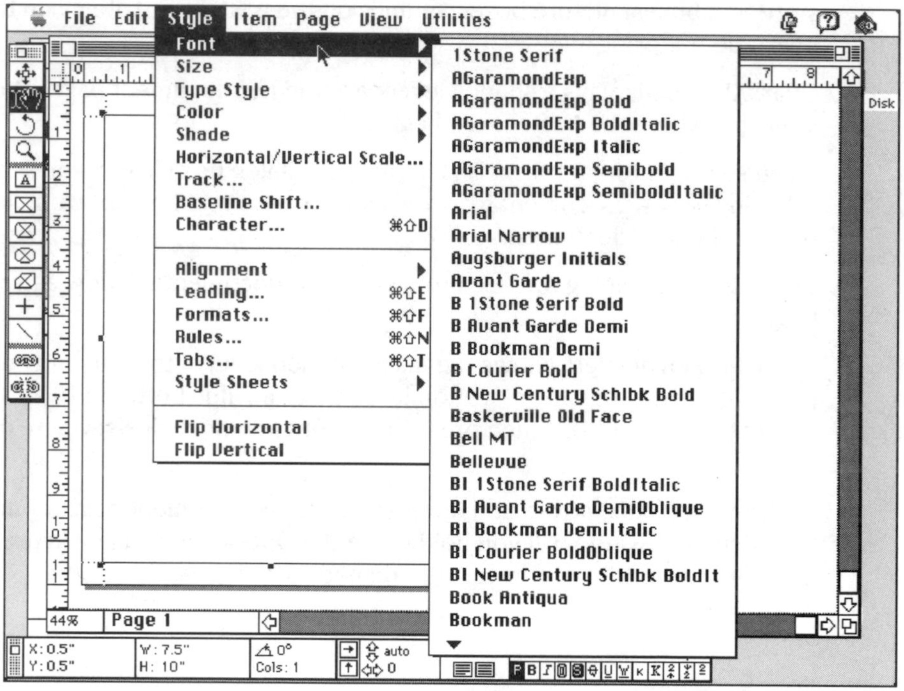

Dialog Boxes

You'll notice that some menu commands are followed by a series of dots, or an ellipsis (. . .). If you choose a menu command whose name is followed by an ellipsis, a *dialog box* will appear. Figure 2-3 shows an example of a dialog box.

Dialog boxes are, in a sense, more powerful than menu commands because dialog boxes let you enter specific information. Dialog boxes give you a great deal of control over how QuarkXPress applies specific features or functions to your document.

But the level of control you have over your document doesn't end with the dialog box; some dialog boxes also contain pop-up menus, which are also called pick lists. Pop-up menus can appear in either of two places: in a pull-down menu or within a dialog box. If a menu has a pop-up associated with it, an arrowhead appears to the right of the menu entry. Figure 2-3 shows a pop-up menu for text justification.

Figure 2-3:
A dialog box and pop-up menu.

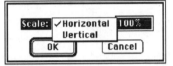

Keyboard Shortcuts

Like many Macintosh programs, QuarkXPress gives you a variety of options in selecting program functions. You can select some functions through pull-down menus, some through palettes, some through keyboard shortcuts, and some through all three options. If you are a new user, you will probably prefer menus at first because they are so readily available. But as you become more comfortable with using the program, you will be able to save time by using keyboard shortcuts.

Suppose, for example, that you want to move from page one of a document to page three. You can change pages by choosing Go To from the Page menu, or you can use the keyboard shortcut: press and hold the Command key while you press the J key. In this book, we present key combinations as follows: Option- ⌘N. We use the same format for all keyboard shortcuts.

Palettes

One of the most innovative features of the QuarkXPress interface is its *palettes*. Palettes let you perform a wide range of functions on an open document without having to access pull-down menus. They are the biggest time-saving feature of the QuarkXPress interface, and using them really speeds up the process of creating documents. You will undoubtedly find yourself using a couple of the palettes — the Tool palette and the Measurements palette — all the time.

The Tool palette

The Tool palette (see Figure 2-4) is one palette you will use often when you build a document in QuarkXPress. When you first open the program, the Tool palette appears along the left edge of your computer's monitor. If it's not there, you can get it to appear by selecting Show Tools from the View menu. This palette contains tools that you use to create, change, link, view, and rotate text boxes, picture boxes, and lines.

Figure 2-4:
The Tool palette.

To use a tool on the palette, you first need to activate it. To do this, use the mouse to place the cursor on the tool icon that you wish to use and click the mouse button. Depending on the tool you select, the cursor takes on a different look to reflect the function the tool performs. When you click the Linking tool, for example, the cursor changes to look like links in a chain.

In the chapters that follow, we explain in greater detail many of the functions you can perform with the Tool palette. In this chapter, we provide brief descriptions of each tool.

Item tool

 The Item tool takes care of the *external* aspects of an item on a page. If you want to change something within an item on the page, you use the Content tool, described next. The Item tool controls the size and positioning of items. When you want to change the shape, location, or presence of a text box, picture box, or line, use the Item tool. The Item tool enables you to select, move, group, ungroup, cut, copy, and paste text boxes, picture boxes, lines, and groups. When you click the Item tool on a box, the box becomes *active,* meaning that you can change or move it. Sizing handles appear on the sides of the active box; you can click and drag these handles to make the box a different size.

Content tool

 As we said previously, although the Item tool controls the external aspects of an item on a page, the Content tool controls its internal aspects. Functions you can perform with the Content tool include *importing* (putting text into a text box or putting a picture into a picture box), cutting, copying, pasting, and editing text.

To edit text in a text box, first select the Content tool. Then select the areas of text that you want to edit by clicking and dragging the Content tool to highlight the text or by using different numbers of mouse button clicks, as follows:

- **To position the cursor:** Use the mouse to move the pointer (it looks like a large capital *I*) to the desired location and click the mouse button once.

- **To select a single word:** Use the mouse to move the pointer within the word and click the mouse button twice.

- **To select a line of text:** Use the mouse to move the pointer within the line and click the mouse button three times.

- **To select an entire paragraph:** Use the mouse to move the pointer within the paragraph and click the mouse button four times.

- **To select the entire story:** Use the mouse to move the cursor anywhere within the story and click the mouse button five times.

 In a picture box, the Content tool cursor changes to a hand shape. You can use this tool in a picture box to move (or crop) the contents of the box. You can also use it when manipulating the picture's contents, such as applying shades, colors, or printing effects. For more information on these functions of the Content tool, see Chapters 20 and 21.

Rotation tool

 By clicking and dragging with the Rotation tool, you can rotate items on a page. Using the Rotation tool, you can click a text box, picture box, or line and rotate it by dragging it to the angle that you want. You can also rotate items on a page using the Measurements palette or the Modify command in the Item menu. See Chapters 9, 10, and 11 for more details.

Zoom tool

As you are working on a document in QuarkXPress, you may want to change the magnification of the page on-screen. For example, you may be making copy edits on text that is set in 8-point type; increasing the displayed size of the text makes it easier to see what you are doing as you edit. The Zoom tool lets you reduce or enlarge the view that you see in the document window. When you select the Zoom tool, the cursor looks like a small magnifying glass. When you hold the cursor over the document window and click the mouse button, QuarkXPress changes the magnification of that section of the screen up or down in increments of 25 percent.

Another way of changing the magnification of the page is to enter a percentage value in the bottom left corner of the document window. When a page is displayed at actual size, that percentage is 100%. QuarkXPress lets you select any viewing amount, including those in fractions of a percent (such as 49.5%), within the range of 10% and 400%. Note that you don't need to enter the % symbol.

Text Box tool

 QuarkXPress is box-based. Although you can import text from a word processor file or enter text directly onto a document page using the word processing features built into QuarkXPress, you need a text box to hold the text. You can instruct QuarkXPress to create text boxes on each page of the document automatically. Or you can create a text box manually — which you do using the Text Box tool.

To create a text box, select the Text Box tool and place the cursor at the approximate location where you want the box to appear. Click the mouse button and hold it down as you drag the box to size.

 See Chapter 9 for more information on creating text boxes.

Picture Box tools

Picture boxes hold graphics that you import from graphics programs. QuarkXPress offers four Picture Box tools. Using these tools, you can draw the following four different box shapes:

 ↪ **Rectangle Picture Box tool:** Use this to create rectangular or square picture boxes.

 ↪ **Rounded Rectangle Picture Box tool:** Use this tool to create picture boxes that are rectangular but have rounded corners. You can change the curve of the corners by using the Modify command in the Item menu.

 ↪ **Oval Picture Box tool:** This tool enables you to create oval or circular picture boxes.

 ↪ **Polygon Picture Box tool:** Using this tool, you can create any shape of picture box you want. The only restriction is that the box must have at least three sides.

You create the first three styles of picture boxes (rectangle, rounded rectangle, and oval) in the same manner as text boxes: place the cursor at the approximate spot that you want the box to appear on the page; click the mouse button and hold it down as you drag the box to size.

To create a polygon picture box, draw the first line in the box and click the mouse button once to end the line. Continue drawing the lines of the box, clicking the mouse button once to end each line. Close the box by connecting the final line to the originating point of the polygon.

Line tools

The two Line tools enable you to draw lines, or *rules*. After you draw a line, you can change its thickness (*weight*) or line style (dotted line, double line, and so on). The Orthogonal Line tool (top) draws horizontal and vertical lines. The Diagonal Line tool (bottom) draws lines at any angle.

QuarkXPress documentation refers to the Diagonal Line tool as simply the *Line tool*. We use *Diagonal Line tool* so that it is not confused with the Orthogonal Line tool.

To use either of the line tools, click the tool to select it and position the cursor at the point where you want the line to begin. Click the mouse button and hold it as you draw the line. When the line is approximately the length you want, release the mouse button. After you draw a line, use the Measurements palette to select the line weight and line style.

For more specifics on drawing lines, see Chapter 11.

Linking and Unlinking tools

The bottom two tools in the Tool palette are the Linking tool (top) and the Unlinking tool (bottom). The Linking tool enables you to link text boxes together so that overflow text flows from one text box into another. You use the Unlinking tool to break the link between text boxes.

Linking is particularly useful when you want to *jump* text — for example, when a story starts on page one and jumps to (continues on) page four. Chapter 9 covers linking in more detail.

The Measurements palette

The Measurements palette was first developed by Quark and is now being widely imitated by other software programs. This palette is certainly one of the most significant innovations to take place in the evolution of desktop publishing, and you will use it all the time. The Measurements palette gives you precise information about the position and attributes of any selected page element, and it lets you enter values to change those specifications. If you want to see the Measurements palette, you need to have a document open as you choose View ⇨ Show Measurements.

The information displayed on the Measurements palette depends on the element currently selected. When you select a text box, the Measurements palette displays the text box position coordinates (X and Y), size (W and H), amount of rotation, and number of columns (Cols), as shown in Figure 2-5. Using the up- and down-pointing triangles on the palette, you can modify the leading of the text box (or you can simply type in a value in the space next to the triangles); use the right- and left-pointing arrows to adjust kerning or tracking for selected text.

You can specify text alignment — left, center, right, or justified — by using the alignment icons. In the type section of the palette, you can control the font, size, and type style of selected text. Chapters 12, 13, and 14 cover these features in detail.

Figure 2-5:
The Measure-
ments palette
when a text box
is selected.

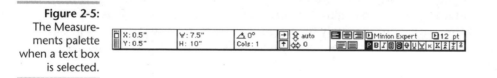

| X: 0.5" | W: 7.5" | 0° | auto | Minion Expert | 12 pt |
| Y: 0.5" | H: 10" | Cols: 1 | 0 | P B I O S ❸ U W K K ² ² | |

If you select a picture box, the Measurements palette displays a different set of information (see Figure 2-6). It shows the position of the box (X and Y), its size (W and H), the amount it is rotated, its corner radius, whether it has a reduction or an enlargement percentage (X% and Y%), its repositioning coordinates (X+ and Y+), the amount of picture rotation within the box, and the amount of slant.

Figure 2-6:
The Measure-
ments palette
when a picture
box is selected.

| X: 1.293" | W: 0.819" | 9° | X%: 90% | X+: −0.075" | 12° |
| Y: 1.124" | H: 0.757" | 0" | Y%: 90% | Y+: 0.5" | 0° |

When you select a line, the Measurements palette displays the location coordinates (X and Y), line width, line style, and endcap (line ending) style (see Figure 2-7). The line style list box lets you select the style for the line.

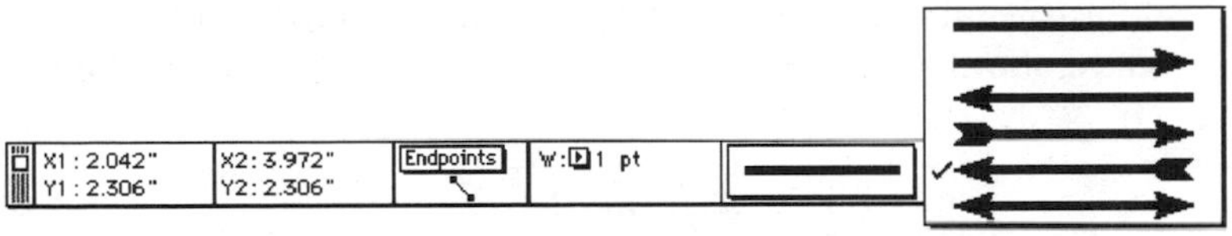

Figure 2-7: The Measurements palette for a line.

The Document Layout palette

The Document Layout palette (see Figure 2-8) lets you create, name, delete, move, and apply master pages. You can also add, delete, and move document pages. To display the Document Layout palette, choose Show Document Layout from the View menu.

Figure 2-8:
The Document Layout palette.

The Colors palette

Figure 2-9 shows the Colors palette. Using this palette, you can designate the color and shade (percentage of color) that you want to apply to text, pictures, and backgrounds of text and picture boxes. You also can produce color blends, using one or two colors, to apply to box backgrounds. To display the Colors palette, choose Show Colors from the View menu. Chapters 21 and 22 cover color in more detail.

Figure 2-9:
The Colors palette.

The Style Sheets palette

The Style Sheets palette displays the names of the style tags attached to selected paragraphs and also enables you to apply style sheets to paragraphs. To display the Style Sheets palette, shown in Figure 2-10, choose Show Style Sheets from the View menu.

Figure 2-10:
The Style Sheets palette.

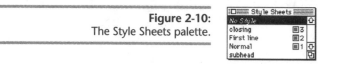

The Trap Information palette

Trapping controls how one color in a document prints next to another color. In the Trap Information palette (see Figure 2-11) you can set or change trapping specifications for selected items. A word of warning: don't use this palette unless you know what you are doing. Trapping is considered an expert feature, and using it without knowing what you are doing can produce uneven results when you print your document. You use the Trap Information palette to set custom trapping for selected items; the range is –36 to 36 points. To display the Trap Information palette, choose Show Trap Information from the View menu. Chapter 22 provides more information about trapping.

Figure 2-11:
The Trap Information palette.

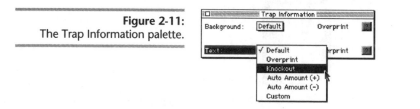

Library palettes

QuarkXPress lets you store layout elements (text or picture boxes, lines, or groups) in a Library palette. To use this feature, you select the element from the document or the pasteboard and drag it into an open Library palette. You then can use items stored in the library in other documents. To open a library palette such as the one shown in Figure 2-12, choose Library from the File menu (File ➪ Open ➪ Library). Chapter 23 covers libraries in detail.

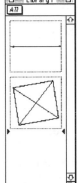

Figure 2-12:
A library palette.

Variations of the Mouse Pointer ____

By changing the mouse pointer (also called *cursor*) to depict the current tool,
QuarkXPress provides a visual cue so that you can tell which tool is active. You'll see
some tool icons all the time and others only occasionally because they are used for
specialized features. This section provides an overview of the various mouse pointers
in QuarkXPress.

Common mouse pointers

You'll frequently come across the following mouse pointers:

▸ ➣ **Standard pointer:** This is the most common pointer. It appears as you move
through dialog boxes, menus, and windows. It also appears as you move over
nonselected elements.

+ ➣ **Creation pointer:** This pointer appears if you have selected a box or line tool. To
create a rectangular or oval box, click and hold down the mouse button at one
corner of the box, drag the mouse to the opposite corner, and then release the
button. (Hold the Shift key to keep the box a perfect square or circle.) For a
polygon box, click each point in the polygon and return to the first point when
done (the creation pointer changes to a rounded box to indicate that you are
over the first point). For a line, click and hold down the mouse button at one end,
drag it to the line's end, and then release the button.

➣ **Sizing pointer:** This pointer appears if you select one of the handles on a text or
picture box (with either the Item or Content tool selected) or on a line. You can
resize the item by holding down the mouse button and dragging a handle.

✥ ☞ **Item pointer:** This pointer appears if the Item tool is selected and you have selected a box or line. You can move the selected item by holding down the mouse button and dragging the item.

☞ **Lock pointer:** This pointer appears if the Item tool is selected and you have selected a locked text box, picture box, or line. This indicates that the box will not move if you try to drag it. (You can move it, however, by changing the coordinates in the Measurements palette or via Item ⇨ Modify.)

☞ **I-beam (text) pointer:** This pointer appears if the Content tool is selected and you select a text box. If the cursor is blinking, any text you type inserts where the cursor appears. If the cursor is not blinking, you must click at the location in the text box where you want to edit text.

☞ **Grabber pointer:** This pointer appears if the Content tool is selected and you have selected a picture box containing a graphic. You can move the graphic within the box by holding down the mouse button and dragging the item.

☞ **Zoom-in pointer:** This pointer appears if you select the Zoom tool, move to your page, and click the mouse button (this zooms in by the predefined amount, which by default is 25 percent). You can also select an area to zoom into by selecting the zoom tool and holding down the mouse button at one corner of the area of interest, dragging the mouse to the opposite corner, and then releasing the button. Chapter 4 covers zoom preference settings; Chapter 8 covers the different views to use while working on layouts.

☞ **Zoom-out pointer:** This pointer appears if you select the Zoom tool and hold the Option key down while clicking the mouse button after the pointer is placed on the page (this zooms out by the predefined amount, which by default is 25 percent). Chapter 4 covers zoom preference settings; Chapter 8 covers using different views while working on layouts.

☞ **Rotation pointer:** This pointer and the rotation guide target appear when you select an item on the page with the Item tool or the Content tool and then select the Rotate tool. Place the target on the page by moving the mouse to the location you want to be in the "center of rotation." Hold the mouse button down and move the pointer around the target until you have achieved the desired rotation on the selected item. The line connecting the target to the pointer can be made larger or smaller by moving the pointer further away or closer to the target; the further away the pointer from the target, the finer the rotation increments that you control. Chapter 10 covers rotation for picture boxes; Chapter 15 covers rotation for text boxes.

☞ **Link pointer:** This pointer appears if you select the Link tool. Click the pointer on the first text box and then on the second text box in the chain of boxes that you want text to flow through. If there are more boxes, select them in the flow order as well. You can switch pages while this tool is active to flow text across pages. Chapter 9 covers linking.

ᗶ **Unlink pointer:** This pointer appears if you select the Unlink tool. If you want to sever the text flow between two text boxes, click the pointer on the first text box and then on the second text box. If there are more boxes to unlink, repeat this process. You can switch pages while this tool is active to unlink text flow across pages. Chapter 9 covers linking.

Specialized pointers

The following pointers are those you'll run across less often:

ᗶ **Library pointer:** This pointer appears in the current library window if you have selected a library element and are moving it either within the window or to another open library window. Libraries are covered in Chapter 23.

The following three pointers appear only in the Document Layout palette, accessed via View ⇨ Show Document layout. For details on master pages, see Chapter 5. When inserting master pages, drag the appropriate master-page icon (facing or single, depending on what type of master page you want) from the top left of the palette into the location where you want the new master page to be inserted.

ᗶ **Insert Master Page Pointer:** This pointer appears in the Document Layout palette when you insert a master page into the palette's master-page list. The arrow will point at the page that the new page isbeing moved in front of.

ᗶ **Facing Master Pages pointer:** When you are inserting a facing master page into the palette, this pointer appears.

ᗶ **Single Master Page pointer:** When you are inserting a singlemaster page into the palette, this pointer appears.

Active and Selected Items _____

Throughout this book, you'll see instructions such as *select the text box* or *apply the change to the active line. Selecting* an item is the same as *activating* it — which you must do before modifying an item in QuarkXPress. If you want to make a change to an entire item, select or activate the item by clicking on it with the Item tool. If you want to make a change to the item's contents, click the Content tool on the item.

When an item is selected or active, you see small black boxes, or sizing handles, on its sides and corners, as illustrated in Figure 2-13.

Figure 2-13:
QuarkXPress displays sizing handles on the sides and corners of an active item.

Summary

➥ When you choose a menu command that has an arrow to its right, QuarkXPress displays a secondary, associated menu.

➥ A dialog box appears when you choose a menu command that has an ellipsis to its right.

➥ Use keyboard shortcuts and palettes to save time when using QuarkXPress.

The Macintosh Environment

3

In This Chapter

➠ Understanding the Macintosh interface

➠ Manipulating files

➠ Installing PostScript and TrueType fonts

➠ Downloading fonts to printers

The Mac Interface

It's been said that the Macintosh was *designed* for desktop publishing. Although that's not exactly true, one thing is certain: the Macintosh makes a near-perfect publishing platform. It handles high-end graphics with ease. It has the ability to run multiple programs simultaneously, to move elements between different documents or programs, and to work with a consistent set of tools, fonts, and device drivers.

If you are an experienced Mac user, you can skip this chapter. But if you are a relatively new Mac user who is now also using QuarkXPress, read on for a very brief review of some of the Macintosh basics you'll need to know. For a comprehensive look at Macintoshes, we recommend *Macs For Dummies 2nd Edition* by David Pogue, *Macworld Macintosh Secrets* by David Pogue, *Macworlds Complete Mac Handbook Plus CD, 2nd Edition* by Jim Heid, and *Macworld Guide to System 7.1, 2nd Edition* by Lon Poole.

Mac Interface Basics

When you turn on your Macintosh, the screen will look something like the screen in Figure 3-1. The Finder program, built into the Macintosh, creates this screen, which is also known as the *desktop*. In the upper right corner is the *icon* for the computer's hard disk.

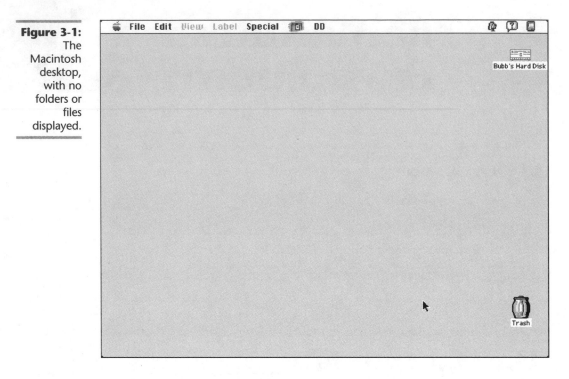

Figure 3-1:
The Macintosh desktop, with no folders or files displayed.

Most of the Macintosh interface is based on icons, which are small graphic illustrations that represent Mac programs, files, or functions. Icons represent applications, such as QuarkXPress; file folders, which help you organize your hard disk by holding things like documents and applications; disks (if you put a disk into the disk drive, a little picture of a disk appears on your desktop); and documents, including QuarkXPress documents and those created by word processing applications.

Menus are another big part of the interface. Across the top of the screen in Figure 3-2 is a menu bar. The menu bar includes the names of menu titles. To see a menu, you move the mouse so that the pointer appears on the menu title; then you hold the mouse button down and the menu appears.

 Pointer refers to the icon that moves on the Mac screen with the movement of the mouse. *Selecting* means using the mouse to get the pointer "on top of" something on the screen and then clicking on the item (or clicking and holding the mouse button down if you are selecting a passage of text, for example). When something is selected, it reverses its appearance (white letters become black, black letters become white). You can also open something by *double-clicking* on it, where you move the mouse to position it on top of the item, and click the mouse button twice with the second click immediately following the first. The difference is that double-clicking opens a document or launches a program. Single-clicking just selects it.

The names of active menu selections and menu titles are darker than inactive ones, which are lighter or "grayed out," as are some of the menu selections in Figure 3-2. An inactive menu selection is one that you can't make given the current circumstances on your Macintosh. For example, if you haven't already selected a section of text and copied it to the Mac clipboard (by selecting Cut or Copy from the Edit menu), the Paste option in the edit menu is inactive because there is nothing on the clipboard to paste; if there is something on the clipboard, the Paste is active.

When you pull down a menu, some menu items have a keyboard shortcut listed to their right. You can use the shortcut keys to access those menu options directly, bypassing the need to select a series of menu options. An ellipsis (. . .) after a menu option means that when you select the option, a dialog box appears offering more options. Dialog boxes have places where you can make selections by either typing in information, or by clicking on buttons that appear in the boxes.

A right-pointing arrow to the right of a menu option means that when you select that option, a submenu appears next to the first menu. Figure 3-2 shows menu options with ellipses, right-pointing arrows, and keyboard equivalents.

Figure 3-2:
The
Macintosh
menu
interface,
shown here in
QuarkXPress.

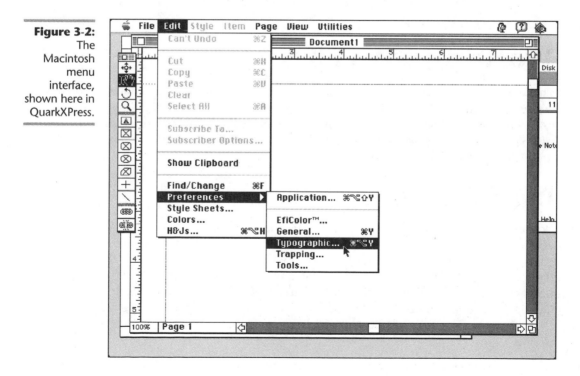

You can resize an open Macintosh window by selecting the sizing box in the lower right corner, holding the mouse button down, and dragging the window to the desired size. You can get the original size back by clicking the sizing box at the upper right corner of the window. If the window is already at full size, clicking that box will change the size to the previous size you made the window.

 Drag means to select an item with the mouse and keep the mouse button pressed while moving the selected item.

A scroll bar at the right and bottom of the window lets you move around within a window. You can click the scroll buttons (the arrows) or drag the scroll slider (small open square) to access elements of a window that may be out of view. You can also click on the scroll bar itself: Clicking above the scroll slider scrolls a window up one page; clicking below the scroll slider scrolls a window down one page.

If you want to move a window around on the screen, use the mouse to position the pointer in the window's title bar (the bar at the top of the window that gives its title), and hold down the mouse button as you move it to the desired location.

Working with Files

The Macintosh interface, with its readily accessible icons of file folders and documents, makes working with files on the Macintosh a relatively easy and straightforward process. This part of Chapter 3 reviews some of the basics of working with Macintosh files, with specific attention paid to how those basics work with QuarkXPress.

Opening a file

Double-click on the file folder or document to open it. If the folder you are opening contains an application, such as QuarkXPress, you can launch the program by double-clicking on its icon. If you double-click on a QuarkXPress document that is outside of the folder containing the application, it may give you a message that the file could not be opened because the application that created it is missing. In this case, first open the QuarkXPress application by double-clicking on its icon. Then open the file by selecting Open from the File menu and locate the file by means of the controls in the Open dialog box.

Saving files

 One of the best habits you can acquire is saving your work. With many Mac applications, you save your work by choosing Save from the File menu (you would use Save As if the file has not previously been saved; Save would usually be grayed out in this case). QuarkXPress makes saving files easier by the addition of its Auto Save feature.

To have QuarkXPress automatically save your documents at intervals you specify, you set up Auto Save in the program's Application Preferences dialog box (see Figure 3-3). To access this dialog box, choose Preferences ⇨ Application from the Edit menu. We set our documents to be saved automatically every five minutes, but you can vary the setting according to your work habits. If you tend to work quickly, every five minutes (the default) is a good interval. If you take your time as you work, you can stretch the interval to every 10 or 15 minutes.

 Also with version 3.2 and later, QuarkXPress has an automatic backup option. This lets you specify how many backup copies of a document to keep. The maximum number of backup copies per document is 100, which is more than you are likely to ever need.

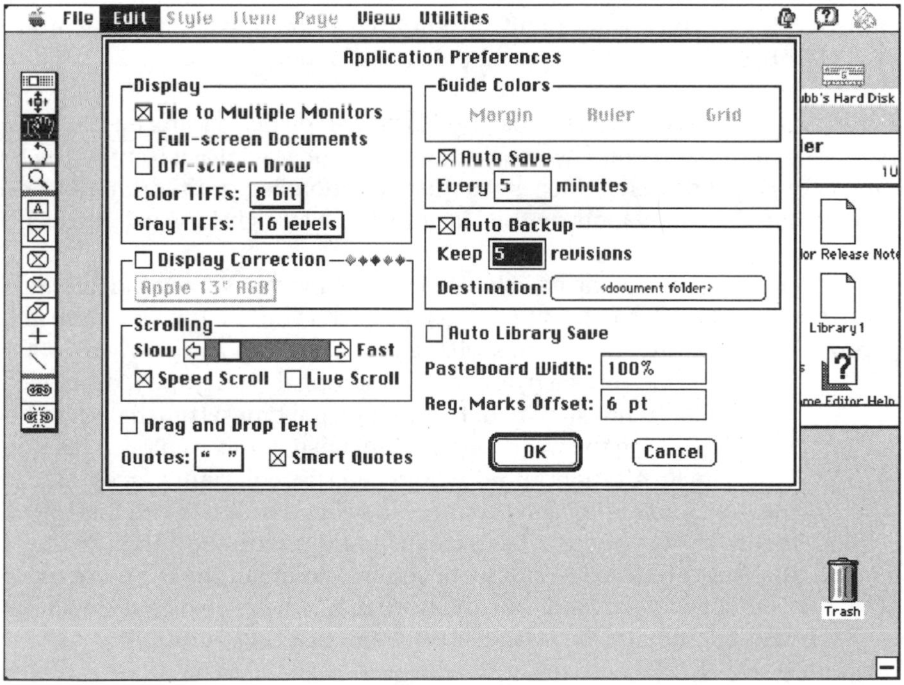

Figure 3-3:
In QuarkXPress's Application Preferences dialog box, you can specify the intervals at which documents are saved and the number of backup versions to keep.

Moving and deleting files

To move a file or document to another folder or disk, click on its icon to select it. Then hold the mouse down as you drag it to its destination. If you move something from one disk to another, the Macintosh copies the item. When you drag an element within a disk, it is simply moved from one location to another. To copy within a disk, hold the Option key down as you drag the element until you have moved the icon to its new location and then release the mouse button.

To delete a file or document, click on its icon to select it and then drag it to the icon that looks like a trash can. Until you choose to empty the trash can by choosing Empty Trash from the Special menu, you can recover the file or document by double-clicking on the trash can icon to open it and then dragging the item back to the desktop or to a disk.

Working with Fonts

QuarkXPress can do wonders with type in either the TrueType or PostScript Type 1 format. But for QuarkXPress to see typefaces, you must install them properly. Even though Adobe Type Manager and System 7 have simplified font installation, there are still a few tricks and cautions you should know about.

For instance with PostScript fonts, the Macintosh displays fonts on the screen differently than it prints them. This means that, for your Macintosh to print the font you see on screen, it needs to have access to the corresponding printer font (also called an *outline font*). Installing fonts on the Macintosh is a straightforward process.

 Desktop publishing has changed the meaning of some fundamental typographic terms, which can lead to confusion. When you see the word *font* in the context of a computer, that means what a traditional typographer would call a *face* — one basic variant of a *typeface*. (In traditional typography, a *font* means a face at a particular point size, a context that digital typesetting has all but eliminated.) Thus, you'll see the word *font* used to mean, for example, Times Roman or Times Italic. A typographer would call these variants *faces*. Many people use the word *font* informally to mean *typeface*, which is the collection of related faces. Thus, your service bureau would understand the phrase "I'm using the News Gothic font in my brochure" to mean that you are using the News Gothic typeface, and that the bureau needs to ensure it downloads the whole family to the imagesetter when printing your job.

QuarkXPress works with System 6.0.5 or better, but we recommend that you upgrade to System 7, which includes the ability to install fonts by simply dragging them into your Mac's System Folder. (With System 6.0.5, you need a utility program to install or delete fonts.) Also, System 7 includes TrueType fonts, which are fonts that include built-in scaling that makes the fonts appear smooth (versus jagged) on your monitor and on the printed page. System 7 also offers features that make it easier to use QuarkXPress, such as better memory handling, a stationery option that lets you turn any file into a template, and a Find command that makes it easier to locate files on your system.

Using TrueType fonts

TrueType fonts can be used with any Macintosh-compatible printer. When used with a PostScript printer, the PostScript driver converts them to PostScript format automatically. (Some printers now support both PostScript and TrueType fonts; TrueType fonts used with these printers are not converted to PostScript.) The way you install TrueType fonts varies slightly according to the version of system software on your Macintosh:

- **If you are using System 6**, install TrueType fonts using Apple's Font/DA mover.

- **If you are using System 7.0x**, open the font suitcase by double-clicking on it. Then select the fonts you want and drag them into the System folder.

- **If you are using System 7.1**, click on the font suitcase icon to select it and drag it into the System folder or into the Fonts folder inside the System folder.

Using PostScript fonts

You install PostScript fonts almost the same way you do TrueType fonts:

- **If you are using System 6**, install TrueType fonts using Apple's Font/DA mover. You'll have to have the TrueType INIT installed on System 6 to use TrueType fonts. The INIT is available from Apple; call (408) 996-1010 for information.

- **If you are using System 7.0x**, open the font suitcase by double-clicking on it. Then select the screen fonts you want and drag them into the Extensions folder in the System folder. The printer fonts go in the System folder.

- **If you are using System 7.1**, click on the font suitcase icon to select it and drag it into the System folder or into the Fonts folder inside the System folder.

Should You Use TrueType or PostScript Fonts?

The most basic question about fonts usually is whether you should use TrueType or PostScript fonts. The answer depends on the work you do. If you produce newsletters, magazines, ads, or brochures that you output on a typesetter or imagesetter, use PostScript, because that is the standard format on these devices. If you output to a laser printer, TrueType is probably the better bet because it prints faster in most cases, especially if you print to a non-PostScript printer. However, you do not have to use one font format exclusively:

- ❧ If you see a TrueType typeface that you want to use in your typeset document, use it — the Macintosh converts TrueType fonts into PostScript format when printing to a PostScript device (or to a file designated for use by a PostScript device). The drawback is that this conversion process may make your files larger because the Macintosh must download the converted TrueType font file into your document.

- ❧ Conversely, if you have PostScript typefaces, there's no reason to give them up if you switch to TrueType. On a PostScript printer, you can use both formats. On other printers, all you need is a program such as Adobe Type Manager to translate PostScript font files into a format the printer can use.

Don't base decisions about whether to use TrueType or PostScript fonts on assumptions about quality. Both technologies provide excellent results, so any quality differences are due to the font manufacturer's standards. If you purchase typefaces from recognized companies, you don't need to worry. (Many smaller companies produce high-quality fonts as well.)

Make sure you install both the screen fonts and the printer fonts for each PostScript font. You may have a suitcase with several screen fonts for your PostScript font, or you may have separate files for each screen font, depending on which option the company decided to use.

If you use PostScript fonts, make sure you also use Adobe Type Manager 2.0 or later. You probably already have ATM, since many companies bundle it with their software. If you don't have it, it's a worthwhile investment. This type scaler makes sure your text displays on-screen cleanly and crisply at all sizes. Without a type scaler, text can look jagged or blocky on-screen, though fonts will print smoothly. The type scaler also lets you print PostScript Type 1 fonts on non-PostScript printers — it automatically converts the PostScript format to the printer's format when printing.

  PostScript fonts come in two versions: Type 1 and Type 3. Type 1 fonts are the most common; they consist of an outline that a type scaler can use to create crisp text at any size. Type 3 is a bitmap version, which means that the type does not scale well.

Working with Font Suitcases

 A font suitcase is basically a special kind of folder that contains only fonts (a suitcase has the icon shown on the left). For TrueType, it contains one file for each face (such as medium, italic, and bold). That file is both the printer font and the screen font. For PostScript, the suitcase contains screen fonts — usually several of them for different sizes and faces. PostScript printer fonts are not kept in the font suitcases. You can have both PostScript and TrueType fonts in the same suitcase. This can be handy for two reasons:

☞ The Macintosh has a limit of 128 font suitcases, so if you have many fonts, you need to combine many suitcases into fewer suitcases. Suitcases are just like folders, and you open and move elements among them as you would for any Macintosh folder.

☞ You want to have several standard font sets, so that you create a suitcase for each standard collection.

Figure 3-4 shows the contents of a System 7.1 Fonts folder and two suitcases. Note the mix of both suitcases and PostScript printer files in the Fonts folder (at right), as well as the two icons:

 for Adobe brand PostScript fonts

 for fonts created with Ares Software's FontMonger program

There are other icons used to designate PostScript printer fonts as well:

 for Bitstream brand fonts and

 for fonts created with Altsys Corp.'s Fontographer program — since different font makers use different icons

At bottom is a suitcase for the PostScript font News Gothic. At left is a suitcase containing several fonts; most are PostScript, although one (Onyx) is TrueType:

 represents TrueType fonts

 represents PostScript screen fonts

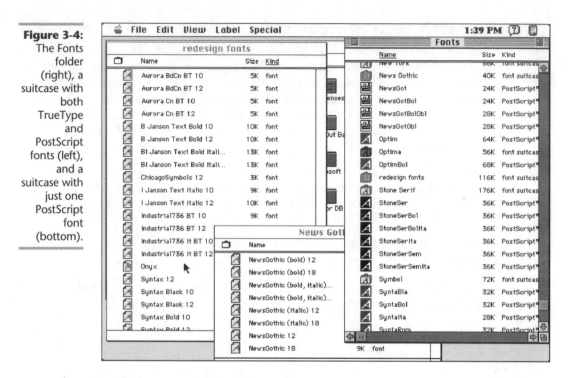

Figure 3-4:
The Fonts
folder
(right), a
suitcase with
both
TrueType
and
PostScript
fonts (left),
and a
suitcase with
just one
PostScript
font
(bottom).

Downloading PostScript fonts

For faster printing, it's best to download PostScript fonts to printer memory. Otherwise, each time you print, your computer must upload the fonts to the printer, which can be time-consuming. Your Mac should have a font downloader utility (called LaserWriter Font Utility) bundled with the system disks. Many printers come bundled with Adobe's downloader utility (called Downloader; an old version is called SendPS). They all work basically the same way: you select the fonts you want to download and then tell the utility to do the work. Figure 3-5 shows the process in Downloader.

The one trick to downloading fonts to printer memory is to not download too many. Each font takes up room in the printer memory that would otherwise go for processing your files. If you put too few fonts in printer memory, you'll waste a lot of time having your Macintosh send fonts repeatedly to the printer. But if you put too many fonts in printer memory, you'll waste a lot of time having the printer process the file under tight memory constraints, which slows it down.

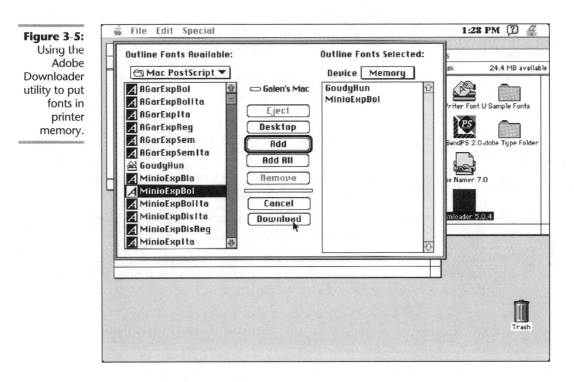

Figure 3-5:
Using the
Adobe
Downloader
utility to put
fonts in
printer
memory.

A good rule of thumb is to download no more than 10 fonts per megabyte of printer memory, after reserving 2MB for the printer's internal processing. For example, if your printer has 4MB of memory, download no more than 20 fonts to it. Keep in mind that "font" in this context means each distinct face, so downloading the News Gothic family — News Gothic Medium, News Gothic Oblique, News Gothic Bold, and News Gothic Bold Oblique — counts as four fonts.

Keep this in mind when deciding which fonts to download. Another rule of thumb: download those that appear on every page of your document, and let your Macintosh itself download those used just occasionally when it needs to.

Note that fonts downloaded to printer memory are removed from memory when you restart or shut down the printer. If you constantly use many fonts, get a printer with a built-in or external disk drive onto which you can download the fonts permanently.

■ ■

Summary

- → The Macintosh interface is based on icons that represent applications, file folders, documents, and disks; menus are another fundamental part of the interface.

- → QuarkXPress can automatically save copies of documents, and it lets you decide how many backup copies to keep.

- → While QuarkXPress works with System 6.0.5 or better, we recommend that you use System 7.0x or System 7.1.

- → Create font suitcases containing multiple typefaces to get around the Macintosh's 128-suitcase limit or to group typefaces by project.

- → Download commonly used fonts to printer memory. If you use many fonts all the time, invest in a printer with a built-in hard drive or hard-drive connector so that you can permanently download fonts to it.

■ ■

PART II

Document Preparation

Publishing is complicated. It's a mix of art and science open to interpretation, experimentation, and boundary-breaking. You can apply a set of publishing tools in many ways, just as you can use a set of woodworking tools in more than one way. And just as in most professions, no matter how varied the applications, tools are best used after the goal is defined and the approach laid out.

This section explains how to set up QuarkXPress and other tools to work in the way you prefer and that is best suited to your document's needs. By setting up document elements and structure wisely, you save yourself a lot of effort down the road without compromising flexibility.

You can read Part II first to get a general understanding of the underlying issues and then follow with Part III to understand the specific details of the various tools. Or read Part III first to understand the tools and then come back to Part II to see how setting up preferences affects how you use the tools.

Customizing QuarkXPress

In This Chapter

- ➥ Which program settings QuarkXPress lets you control
- ➥ How to make your preferences apply only to the current document or to all subsequent documents
- ➥ Preference options for QuarkXPress's user interface, layout tools, image control, output control, and typography

Why Customize QuarkXPress?

Publishing is a big industry, and one with many variables. One of the authors of this book, for example, comes from a newspaper and magazine background. He works with picas as a basic layout measurement unit, and he calls pull-quotes *decks* and titles *heads*. The other author comes from a technical documentation and corporate communications background. She uses inches as her basic layout measurement, and she calls pull-quotes *pull-quotes* and titles *titles*. QuarkXPress lets each of us work in our own style, even when working on common projects such as this book. It can do the same for you.

Even though documents may be different, there are commonalities among them, such as using certain typefaces that form part of your corporate or public identity. However, the program control settings discussed in this chapter are more useful in helping you use QuarkXPress itself rather than establishing standards for your document. (Subsequent chapters on master pages and style sheets will show you how to establish standards.)

QuarkXPress offers many controls that enable you to customize the program to the way *you* work. You establish nearly all QuarkXPress control settings from one menu option: Edit ⇨ Preferences (see Figure 4-1). You can set these settings globally (for use in all future new documents) by entering values in dialog boxes without having a document open, or you can set them for a specific document (by having that document open when you set the preferences). The following sections cover all the various preference settings available, which we divide first by the type of preferences available and then by the dialog boxes that use them.

Figure 4-1:
The Edit
Preferences
menu.

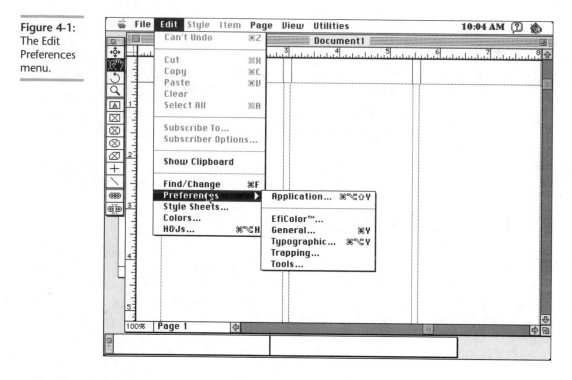

You'll probably set or change most QuarkXPress control settings only occasionally. You'll rarely switch measurement units, for example, because QuarkXPress lets you enter any unit you want in dialog boxes, no matter which default settings you establish. But you may change other settings that apply to specific documents more frequently. As an example of different preference settings, compare the images in Figures 4-2 and 4-3; among the settings that are immediately obvious, they use different measurement units in their rulers, display different types of grids, and treat the display of images and text differently.

Figure 4-2: Some of the obvious preference settings are the display of column grids over the text, the use of picas in the rulers, and the full display of images and text. Compare this to the preferences used in Figure 4-3.

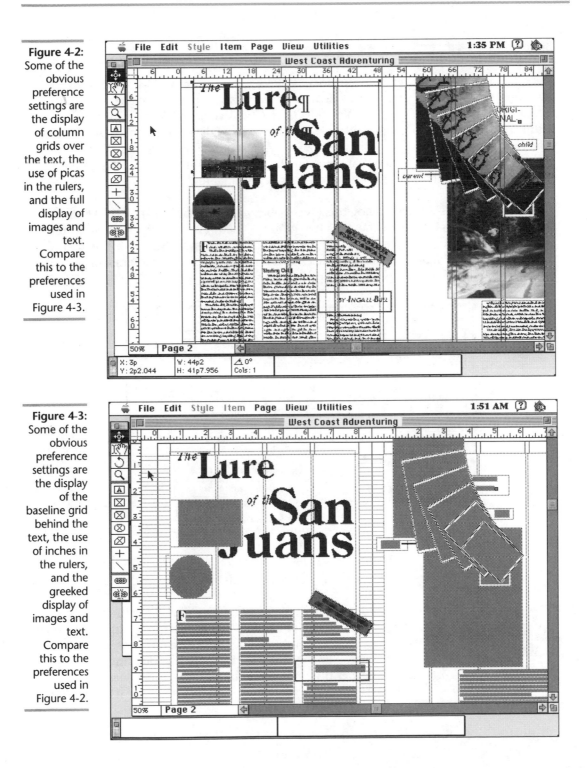

Figure 4-3: Some of the obvious preference settings are the display of the baseline grid behind the text, the use of inches in the rulers, and the greeked display of images and text. Compare this to the preferences used in Figure 4-2.

Program Settings

The most important settings — because they affect your everyday work — are those that affect QuarkXPress itself. They also are the least-used settings, because after you set them, you rarely change them. You tell QuarkXPress your preferences for these settings through three options available when you select Edit ⇨ Preferences: Application, General, and Tools. The other options — Typographic, Trapping, and (if you installed the EfiColor XTension that comes with QuarkXPress) EfiColor — affect your layout and typography; these are covered later in this chapter.

The Application Preferences dialog box (accessible via the keyboard shortcut Option-Shift- Y), shown in Figure 4-4, includes two groups of settings: one for the QuarkXPress user interface and one for output. (Output is covered in a later section.) For the interface, you can control the guide colors, pasteboard width, scroll parameters, image display parameters, and screen display parameters.

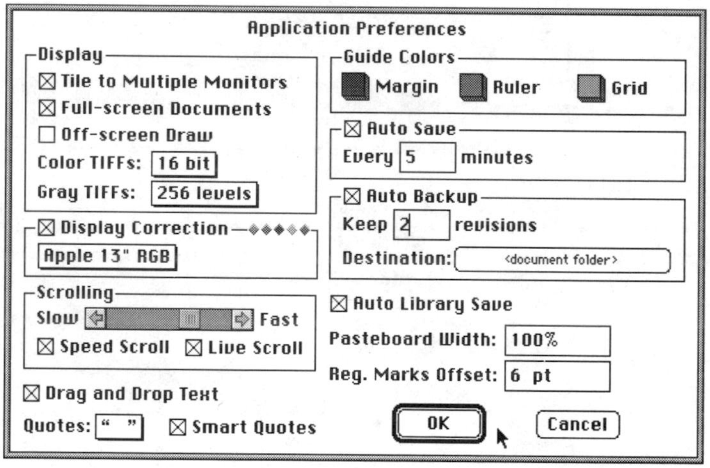

Figure 4-4:
The Application
Preferences
dialog box.

Application Preferences
Display
☒ Tile to Multiple Monitors
☒ Full-screen Documents
☐ Off-screen Draw
Color TIFFs: 16 bit
Gray TIFFs: 256 levels
☒ Display Correction ◆◆◆◆◆
Apple 13" RGB
Scrolling
Slow ◁ ▭ ▷ Fast
☒ Speed Scroll   ☒ Live Scroll
☒ Drag and Drop Text
Quotes: " "   ☒ Smart Quotes
Guide Colors
■ Margin   ■ Ruler   ■ Grid
☒ Auto Save
Every 5 minutes
☒ Auto Backup
Keep 2 revisions
Destination: <document folder>
☒ Auto Library Save
Pasteboard Width: 100%
Reg. Marks Offset: 6 pt
OK   Cancel

The General Preferences dialog box (Y) sets controls for default measurement units, placement and use of layout aids, layout controls, and display of text and pictures.

You can use the General Preferences dialog box (see Figure 4-5) either for the current document or for all new documents. If you change the settings while no document is open, all documents you subsequently create use those settings. If a document is open when you change the settings, only that document is affected. You can tell whether the settings will be global or local because the dialog box's title will be "General Preferences for *document name*" if the settings are local to that document.

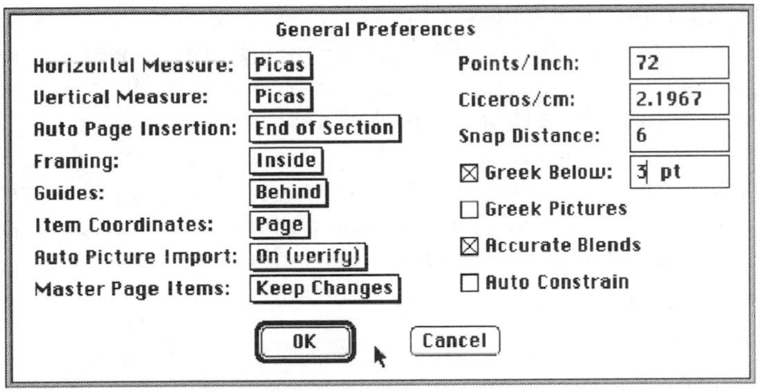

Figure 4-5:
The General
Preferences
dialog box.

General Preferences

Horizontal Measure:	Picas
Vertical Measure:	Picas
Auto Page Insertion:	End of Section
Framing:	Inside
Guides:	Behind
Item Coordinates:	Page
Auto Picture Import:	On (verify)
Master Page Items:	Keep Changes

Points/Inch:	72
Ciceros/cm:	2.1967
Snap Distance:	6
☒ Greek Below:	3 pt
☐ Greek Pictures	
☒ Accurate Blends	
☐ Auto Constrain	

OK   Cancel

Figure 4-5:
The General
Preferences
dialog box.

Environment settings

QuarkXPress offers several controls over environment settings, which let you choose the layout environment most familiar to you. There are three basic components to the environment: the measurement units (and how locations are determined), the use of guides for positioning and alignment, and the pasteboard (working space) on which layout elements reside.

Measurement units

Depending on your training, you may be comfortable using a particular measurement unit for layout. Many people measure column width and depth in inches, while others (particularly those with newspaper or magazine backgrounds) use picas. Europeans use centimeters instead of inches and ciceros instead of picas. QuarkXPress supports them all.

Although you can enter any measurement unit in any dialog box by entering the code for the unit after the number (see Chapter 2), you also can set the default units for layout elements. (QuarkXPress assumes that text size and leading is set in points, which is common in most environments, no matter which unit is used for layout elements.) You can set separate units for horizontal and vertical measurements; QuarkXPress offers this flexibility because many people measure horizontally with picas but vertically with inches. Select Horizontal Measure and Vertical Measure in the General Preferences dialog box to set your layout measurement preferences.

In addition, you can set the number of points per inch and the number of ciceros per centimeter through the Points/Inch and Ciceros/cm options, respectively. QuarkXPress uses a default setting of 72 points per inch and 2.1967 ciceros per centimeter. The reason you may want to change these is that the actual number of points per inch is

72.271742, although most people now round that off to 72. (QuarkXPress requires you to round it to 72.27 if you use the actual value.) Similarly, there are two accepted measurements for a cicero. A cicero, used in France and most of continental Europe, is based on 12 Didot points. But a Didot point has a different measurement in the United States and Britain than it does elsewhere. The QuarkXPress default of 2.1967 ciceros per centimeter matches the standard European cicero size. If you use the American-British cicero, the number should be 2.3723. Most people don't have problems using the default values, but it can make a difference in large documents, such as banners, where registration and tiling of multiple pieces is important.

Coordinate basis

Whichever system of measurement you use, you can control how the coordinates for layout elements are calculated. Select Item Coordinates in the General Preferences dialog box to tell QuarkXPress whether to base your ruler and box coordinates on a page or on a spread. If you treat each page as a separate element, keep the option set to Page, which is the default setting. If you work on a spread as a single unit, change the setting to Spread. If you choose Spread, the leftmost horizontal coordinate of the right page is the same as the rightmost horizontal coordinate of the left page. If you choose Page, both pages begin at 0.

Guides and rulers

Guides and rulers are important tools for a layout artist because they help to position the elements correctly.

In the Application Preferences (see Figure 4-4) dialog box, QuarkXPress provides three types of guides that help you align items: box margins (normally blue), ruler lines (normally green), and the leading grid (normally magenta). The box margin guides show you the column and gutter positions for text boxes, as well as any margins for picture boxes. The ruler lines are lines you drag from the horizontal and vertical rulers so that you can tell whether a box lines up to a desired point. The leading grid shows the position of text baselines (defined in the Typographical Preferences menu, described later).

The color of these guides can be important in helping you distinguish them from other lines and boxes in your layout. Figure 4-6 shows all three guides active at the same time. The two lines that cross at the mouse pointer are the ruler guides, and the lighter horizontal lines are the baseline grids.

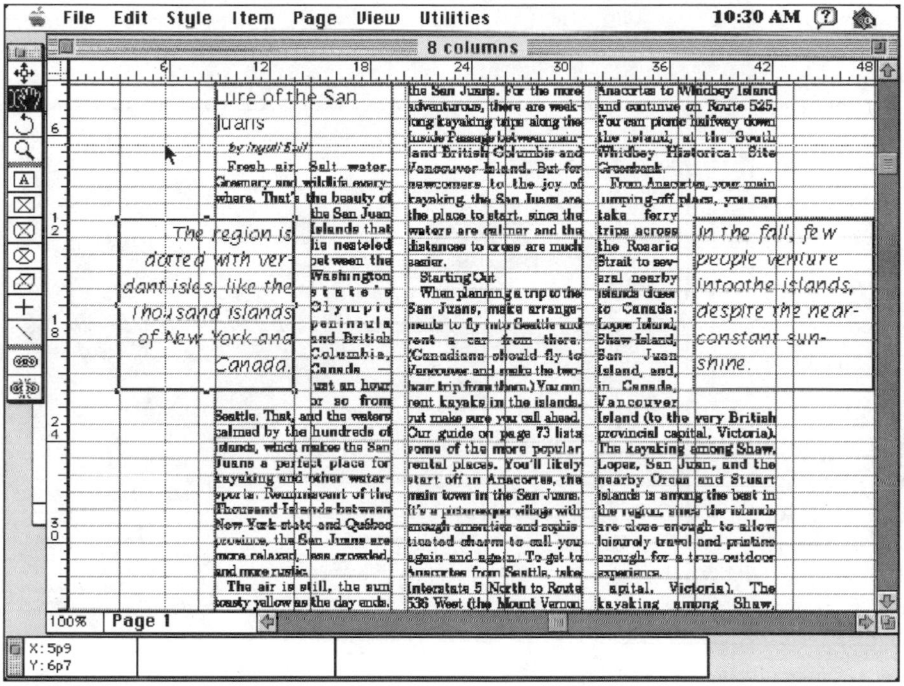

Figure 4-6:
Box
margins,
ruler lines,
and baseline
grid guides.

More often than not, you use margin guides routinely and ruler guides occasionally, particularly when you want to align something within a box to a ruler point. It's easier to use the box coordinates to make sure that boxes or their margins are placed exactly where you want them. But baseline guides help you to estimate column depth and to see if odd text such as a headline causes vertical-alignment problems.

You can change the colors of these guides to any color available by using the Mac's color wheel. Just click the color square for the guide whose color you want to change to bring up the color wheel (see Figure 4-7). The color in the top rectangle shows the new color; the color below it shows the original color. When using the color wheel, select a point in the wheel for the hue you want and use the slider at right to select the intensity (top is most vivid, bottom is darkest).

Although you set colors for guides in the Application Preferences dialog box, select the View menu to display the guides. Select Show Guides to display margin guides and choose Hide Guides to remove them. Likewise, select Show Baseline Grid and Hide Baseline Grid respectively to turn baseline grids on and off.

Figure 4-7:
The color
wheel used
to define the
colors of the
guides.

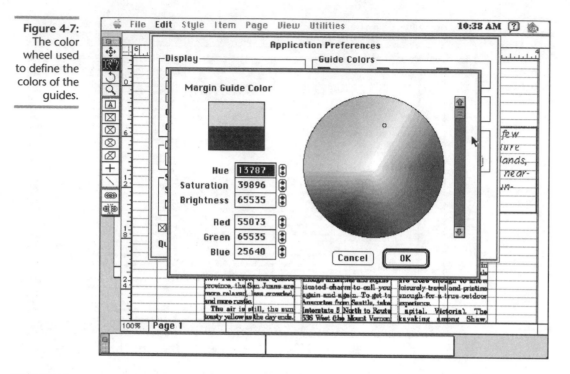

Figure 4-7: The color wheel used to define the colors of the guides.

 Ruler lines display whether or not you activate Show Rulers or Hide Rulers. To get rid of a ruler line, select it and drag it back to the ruler. If the ruler is not displayed, drag it off the page past where the ruler would be.

Use the options in the pick list for Guides in the General Preferences dialog box (see Figure 4-5) to specify whether guides appear in front of boxes (the default setting) or behind them. When guides are behind boxes, it can be easier to see what is in the boxes, but harder to tell if elements within the boxes line up with margins, gutters, or baselines.

 If you select text boxes when guides are set to display behind boxes, the boxes "knock out" the guides. This makes the guides invisible within the box (see Figure 4-8). The guides stay knocked out even when you select other boxes. But guides overprint the contents of text boxes that are not yet selected. When the screen is redrawn, guides again overprint any text boxes that are not currently selected. (Picture boxes always knock out their guides.)

Figure 4-8:
When guides display behind text boxes, guides within a selected text box become invisible.

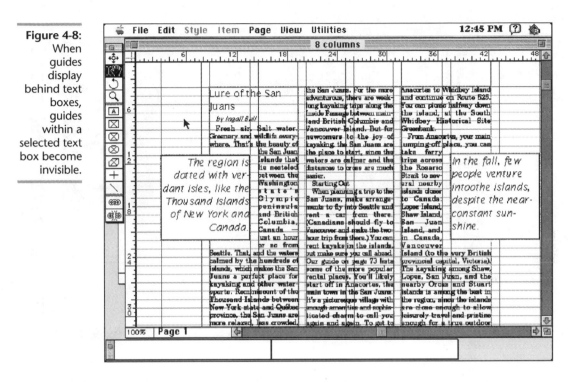

Pasteboard size

The only layout preference set in the Application Preferences dialog box (see Figure 4-4) is the pasteboard size, which applies to all documents until you change the setting again.

The pasteboard is a familiar tool to layout artists who are experienced with manual paste-up — the kind you do when you roll strips of type through a waxing machine and then temporarily tack them to the wall or to the outside of your light table until you need them. QuarkXPress supports this metaphor by creating an area to the side of each page or spread that you can use as an electronic scratch pad for picture and text boxes and other elements.

If you don't use the pasteboard, you may want to reduce its size. Even if empty, the pasteboard takes up space on your screen that affects scrolling because the scroll width includes the pasteboard area. Figures 4-9 and 4-10 show the pasteboard set at the default setting of 100 percent and at 50 percent of page size, respectively. At 100 percent, the pasteboard is equal to one page. If you do reduce your pasteboard, items may extend beyond it and appear to be cut off; they actually remain intact.

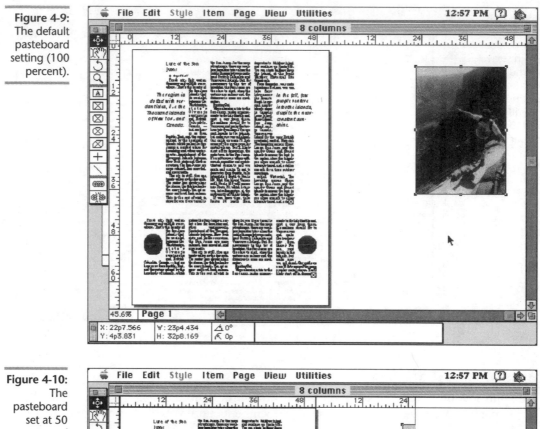

Figure 4-9:
The default pasteboard setting (100 percent).

Figure 4-10:
The pasteboard set at 50 percent of the default size.

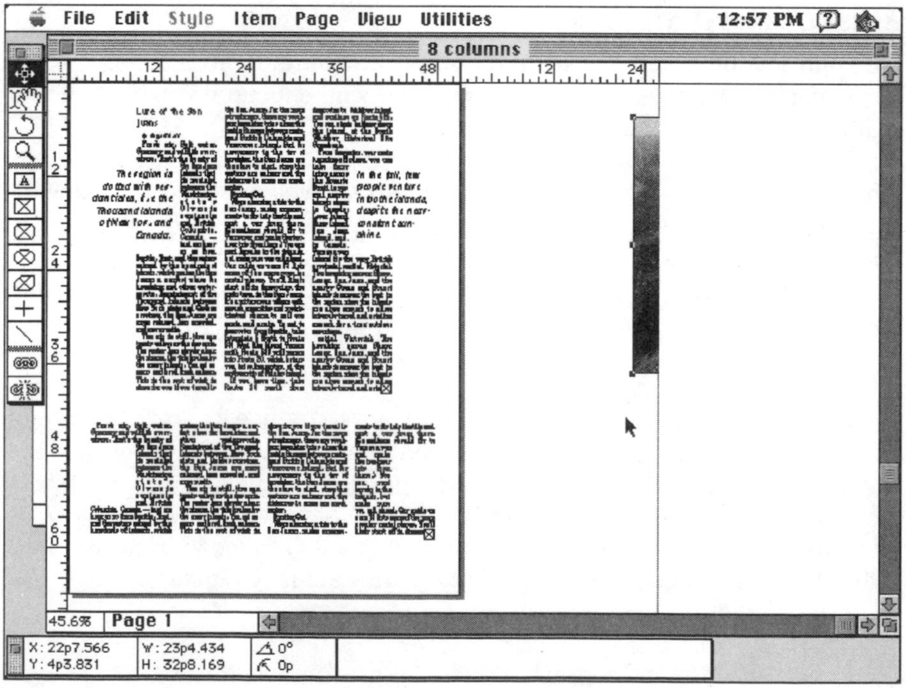

On-screen display

QuarkXPress offers many controls designed to customize the on-screen display of elements. For example, you can customize and manage the way you handle text, images, and color on-screen. These controls typically do not affect the elements themselves, just how the layout artist perceives them. The reason QuarkXPress gives you a choice between, say, seeing an image's full color range or just enough to recognize the image is that the more detail QuarkXPress displays, the more computation is required by QuarkXPress to display them, which slows screen redraw and scrolling speed.

Image display

The image display controls are designed primarily to let you control the balance between speed and image fidelity. Typically, layout artists don't need to see a superior quality image of the images they're placing. They just need to see what the image looks like and what its dimensions are. QuarkXPress lets you determine the trade-off between speed and fidelity through several settings.

Two settings in the Application Preferences dialog box (see Figure 4-4) affect how bitmapped images are displayed on-screen: Color TIFFs and Gray TIFFs. (These replace the Low Resolution TIFF and 256 Levels of Gray check boxes in Version 3.1.) Use these two settings to control how accurately the colors and shades for your TIFF images are displayed on-screen. The more accurate the display, the longer the screen redraw time will be. Unless you are using QuarkXPress's image controls (described in Chapter 20), set these to 8-bit (256 colors) and 16 levels, respectively, for color and gray-scale images. Note that most color images created by scanners and paint programs are 8-bit.

Selecting the 32-bit option for color TIFF files also lets you print 24-bit images to a color QuickDraw printer (normally, PICT files cannot support such great color depth). No matter what color depth or gray level you select, printing to a PostScript printer is not affected. The image will print either at its top resolution or at the best resolution the printer can offer for the image.

If you select a color bit depth greater than your monitor's capabilities, you will see only the color that your monitor can actually display. However, your system will slow down because the higher bit depth makes QuarkXPress perform extra computations.

Understanding Color Depth

A monitor can display a nearly infinite number of colors, but what it actually displays depends on the video signals it receives from the computer. Older Macs use video-display boards to send these signals to the monitor; modern Macs have built-in video circuitry that does the same thing. Most Macs that support color are equipped to generate 8-bit color, which allows the display of 256 colors simultaneously (256 colors is 2^8, thus the term *8-bit color depth*.

Color monitors, not just monochrome ones, can also display 256 levels (shades) of gray simultaneously if they have an 8-bit video board or built-in video that supports 8-bit color.

Using a 16-bit or 24-bit video-display board, or adding enough video RAM (VRAM) to a Mac that has built-in video circuitry (such as an LC III, IIvx, Performa 550, Centris, or Quadra), you can display more colors. High-end scanners and image editors work at higher bit depths, and if you are using images with such bit depths, you'll want a high-color video-display board or extra VRAM.

The figure shows the differences between images displayed in 8-bit and 16-bit modes. The images at top are in 8-bit (256-color) mode; the images at bottom are in 16-bit (32,768-color) mode (shown here as grays).

Note that QuarkXPress's Application Preferences dialog box has an option to display color TIFF files at 32-bit color depth, while most programs and video-display boards offer a maximum of 24-bit color depth. Actually, the two bit depths are the same, and QuarkXPress's 32-bit option for color TIFF files will actually display 24-bit color (16.7 million colors, or 2^{24}) if you have a 24-bit video-display board installed (or are using a Quadra 700, 900, or 950 with sufficient video RAM). The labels for this level of color differ because 24 bits of information are used for the colors themselves and the other 8 bits for the alpha channel, which essentially controls how the colors are managed by the display board or video circuitry. Similarly, what is called 16-bit color (32,768 colors) actually is 15-bit color with a 1-bit alpha channel. (An alpha channel is not needed for 8-bit color.)

Most programs, including QuarkXPress, treat color and gray-scale images separately because color requires more processing. A color file has three constituent colors, compared to one for gray-scale, so color images slow down the system more than gray-scale images.

The General Preferences dialog box (see Figure 4-5) also offers two options that affect the on-screen display of images:

⇨ **Greek Pictures:** Checking this option causes all graphics to appear as gray shapes, which speeds up display considerably. This feature is useful after you position and size your images and no longer need to see them on your layout. When you print, images are unaffected by greeking.

⇨ **Accurate Blends:** If you check this option, blends between two colors (created via the Colors palette) that you place in a box background appear more accurately on monitors using 8-bit (256-color) video boards. However, it slows down screen redraw on pages with blends. (The default setting has this option checked.) If you have a 16-bit or 24-bit video board or enough video RAM on a Mac that supports 16-bit or 24-bit display with its built-in video circuitry, your blends display accurately whether or not you check this option.

Text display

To speed screen display, QuarkXPress offers an option in the General Preferences dialog box (see Figure 4-5) that controls how text appears on-screen. The Greek Below setting tells QuarkXPress at what size to stop trying to display text and simply use bars of gray to indicate it instead. (This feature is called *greeking* because typographers once used Greek text as placeholder text. The gray bars are, in effect, placeholder text, so desktop publishing developers adopted the same term.) The default setting is 7 points, but you can enter values from 2 to 720 points. Greeking small text speeds up screen display, but on faster Macs, the speedup isn't very noticeable. You can turn off greeking altogether by unchecking the box. When you print, text is unaffected by greeking.

Display correction

Whether the EfiColor XTension bundled with QuarkXPress 3.2 or 3.3 is installed determines the options for the Display Correction option in the Application Preferences dialog box (see Figure 4-4).

Without EfiColor, you can select or deselect the Calibrated Pantone box. Checking this box ensures the best possible display of Pantone colors on your display. Note, however, that no monitor can accurately display most Pantone colors, so you should use a Pantone guidebook to select the actual colors used in your document.

 Chapters 21 and 22 explain how to work with colors.

With EfiColor, you can choose from among a set of monitors listed in the Display Correction option's pick list. If your monitor does not appear in the pick list, pick the Apple 13" RGB setting or uncheck the box so that no correction occurs. If this option is selected, QuarkXPress will adjust the hues on color images to compensate for the color cast in your monitor. Apple's monitors tend to be slightly bluish because that makes whites look whiter on-screen.

Document maneuvering

Another critical area related to overall performance is how you maneuver through a document; for example, how scrolling is controlled. QuarkXPress offers several options to optimize performance.

Three settings in the Application Preferences dialog box (see Figure 4-4) affect how you move through your documents: Scrolling, Live Scroll, and Speed Scroll:

- **Scrolling:** Use this slider to control how fast the page scrolls. If you set the slider closer to Slow, QuarkXPress moves more slowly across your document, which is helpful if you want to pay close attention to your document while scrolling. If you set the slider closer to Fast, QuarkXPress zips across the document, which may cause you to move past a desired element. Most people prefer a setting somewhere in the middle range. You may have to adjust the setting a few times until it feels right to you. Generally, it should be slightly closer to Fast than to Slow.

- **Live Scroll:** If you check this box, QuarkXPress automatically scrolls the screen when your cursor moves off the screen. It scrolls the screen until the part of the document you want to access comes into view. Generally, you should check this option.

- **Speed Scroll:** This new option speeds up scrolling in graphics-intensive documents by masking out the graphics as you scroll and not requiring QuarkXPress to redraw the document as you scroll. After you stop scrolling, the graphics are redrawn. Generally, you should check this option.

The Page Grabber Hand option from Version 3.1 no longer exists because this feature is now automatic. To use the page grabber, hold the Option key and move the mouse — the entire page will move. You're not moving the page within the pasteboard, just scrolling your view by moving the page relative to the screen rather than by using the scroll bars.

Three other options control how QuarkXPress documents relate to the monitor's screen area: Tile to Multiple Monitors, Full-screen Documents, and Off-screen Draw:

 ∞ **Tile to Multiple Monitors:** If you have multiple monitors attached to your Mac, this lets QuarkXPress automatically display a large document across several monitors. (Use the Monitors control panel that comes with your System disks to set up multiple monitors. It's installed by default in the Control Panels folder when you install System 7.)

 ∞ **Full-screen Documents:** If you check this box, the document window will appear at the screen's far left, under the default position for the Tool palette. Unless you move the Tool palette down, you'll find that having this option enabled means the document window's close box is obscured. Therefore, we recommend that you not routinely use this option. There is one advantage to using it: it can give your document window enough width to fully display a document. However, when you use it, make sure that you move your Tool palette so that you can click the close box.

∞ **Off-screen Draw:** This option controls how QuarkXPress displays elements on your screen as you scroll through a document. If checked, it redraws each element displayed in order of display. If unchecked, it displays them all simultaneously. Both options take the same amount of time to redraw the screen, so there is no advantage to either setting. Note that with the Speed Scroll option selected, the Off-screen Draw option has no noticeable effect.

Element Controls

QuarkXPress also offers several features designed to control how certain layout elements, like boxes, are handled during layout. The aim of these features is to ease some tasks, like element positioning or typographic substitution, by letting QuarkXPress do the precision work.

Element positioning

Desktop publishing programs automate much of the difficult detail work formerly encountered in layout. You can place an element near its final destination and let the program do the actual positioning or you can set up the rules by which elements are positioned relative to one another. QuarkXPress offers many controls over positioning that you can set in the General Preferences dialog box (see Figure 4-5).

 Keep in mind that any preferences set in the General Preferences dialog box affect only the open document. If no document is open, these settings affect all new documents created.

Snap threshold

To set the threshold for when objects snap to guides (assuming Snap to Guides is selected in the View menu), enter a value in the Snap Distance option box. The default setting is 6 pixels; you can specify any value from 0 to 100 pixels. The larger the number, the further away you can place an object from a guide and still have it automatically snap to the guide.

Box constraints

The last layout control option in the General Preferences dialog box is Auto Constrain, which controls the behavior of boxes that are created within other boxes. If you check the Auto Constrain option, a box that is created within a text box — a picture box, for example — may not exceed the boundaries of the text box. Nor can you move it outside the text box boundaries. Most people should leave this option unchecked, which is the default setting.

 The Item menu offers Constrain and Unconstrain options that can override for any selected box the Auto Constrain setting in the General Preferences dialog box. Constrain appears as an option in the Item menu if the selected box is unconstrained; Unconstrain appears if the selected box is constrained.

Page insertion

Auto Page Insertion tells QuarkXPress where to add new pages when all of your text does not fit into a text box you defined in a master page (see Chapter 5). QuarkXPress creates as many pages as needed to contain all the remaining text. You must define the text box containing the overflow text as an automatic text box in the page's master page. (This is indicated by an unbroken chain icon at the upper left of the master page.)

In the pick list for Auto Page Insertion, your options are:

- **End of Section:** The default setting, this places new pages (which are based on the master page) at the end of the current section (sections are defined via the Page ➪ Section option, described in Chapter 11). If no sections are defined, End of Section works the same as the End of Document option.

- **End of Story:** End of Story places new pages (based on the current master page) immediately following the current page.

- **End of Document:** If you select this option, QuarkXPress places new pages at the end of the document (based on the master page used at the end of the document).

- **Off:** If you choose Off, QuarkXPress adds no new pages, leaving you to add pages and text boxes for overflow text wherever you want. The existence of overflow text is indicated by a checked box at the bottom right of the text box.

Framing position

Selecting a Framing setting in the General Preferences dialog box tells QuarkXPress how to draw the ruling lines (frames) around text and picture boxes (done via the Item ➪ Frame option covered in Chapter 11). You have two choices: selecting Outside places the frame on the outside of the box; selecting Inside places it inside. Figure 4-11 shows how the two differ. At left, the frame is inside the box, and at right, the frame is outside.

Figure 4-11:
The Inside framing option (left) and the Outside setting (right).

If you change the Framing setting while working on a document, only the frames you subsequently create are affected by the change; frames created earlier are unchanged. Thus, you can use both the Inside and Outside settings in the same document.

Drag-and-drop editing

The only positioning setting available through the Application Preferences box (see Figure 4-4) is the Drag and Drop Text option. If checked, it lets you highlight a piece of text and then drag it to a new location (like in recent versions of most word processors), rather than cut it from the old location and paste it to the new one.

Customizing tool specifications

QuarkXPress lets you customize how its basic tools work by changing settings in the Tool Preferences dialog box (see Figure 4-12). To set the defaults, first select the tool you want to modify. Unavailable options are grayed out, as explained in the following paragraphs. After you make changes, choose Save to record the changes or Cancel to undo them.

 If you access the Tool Preferences dialog box with no document open, all defaults apply to all subsequently created documents. Otherwise, the defaults apply only to subsequently created boxes and lines for the current document.

Figure 4-12:
The Tool Preferences dialog box. Settings for the Text Box tool are shown here.

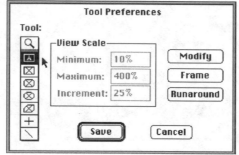

The tools you can customize fall into three groups:

↬ **Zoom tools:** You can change the minimum and maximum zoom views to any value between 10 and 400 percent. You also can specify how much QuarkXPress zooms into your document each time you click the document with the Zoom tool active. To do this, enter any value from 10 to 400 percent, in increments of 0.1, into the Increment option box.

↬ **Box tools:** You can set the item settings for all the box tools: Text Box, Rectangle Picture Box, Rounded-corner Rectangle Picture Box, Oval Picture Box, and Polygon Picture Box. You can establish settings for options normally available for the individual boxes via the Item menu's Modify, Frame, and Runaround options. If you select one of these box tools from the Tool Preferences dialog box, the three buttons corresponding to those Item menu options appear, and you can set them just as you do if you select a box on a document page. The difference is that you are setting them as defaults. Not all Picture Box Specification or Text Box Specification options are available to you; those that affect sizing, for example, are grayed out. But the ability to customize certain settings comes in handy. You can, for example, give oval picture boxes an offset of 1 pica, or set text boxes to have a 3-point frame and a green background. All boxes subsequently created with these tools take on any new preferences you establish in the Tool Preferences dialog box.

⊙ **Drawing tools:** Likewise, you can establish defaults for new lines that you draw with the Orthogonal Line and Line tools. You can set most regular-line options that are normally available through the Item menu, but as with the box tools, options that affect position are grayed out. However, you can set other line-specification and runaround options, such as line color and weight. All lines subsequently created with these tools take on any new preferences you establish in the Tool Preferences dialog box.

Text-box specifications are covered in detail in Chapter 9. Picture-box specifications are covered in detail in Chapter 10. Line specifications are covered in detail in Chapter 11.

Master page overrides

Master Page Items, another setting found in the General Preferences dialog box (see Figure 4-5), lets you control what happens to text and picture boxes that are defined on a master page when you apply a different master page to your document pages. Note that this setting applies only to items used *and* modified on a document page based on a master page's items, not to unmodified items based on a master page. Your options are Keep Changes (the default) and Delete Changes.

Figure 4-13 shows an example of how these settings work. In the example:

⊙ The top two pages shown (pages 6 and 7 in the Document Layout palette) are the two master pages. Master 1 contains the picture of the male backpacker; Master 2, the picture of the female rock climber.

⊙ In the second row (pages 8 and 9), Master Page Items is set to Keep Changes. Page 8 used a modified version of the picture box defined in Master 1, in which a frame was added around the backpacker image. (When we added page 8, we based it on Master 1, so that the backpacker image was automatically copied to it. We then modified that copy.) When Master 2 was applied to page 8, the picture box from Master 2 was added, resulting in a page with the pictures of both people.

⊙ In the third row (pages 10 and 11), Master Page Items is set to Delete Changes. Page 10 also used the modified version of the picture box defined in Master 1. But when Master 2 was applied to page 10, the backpacker picture from Master 1 was deleted from that page while the rock climber picture was added from Master 2 to page 10.

Figure 4-13:
The Master
Page Items
setting
affects how
QuarkXPress
treats
modified
elements
based on
one master
page when a
different
master page
is applied.

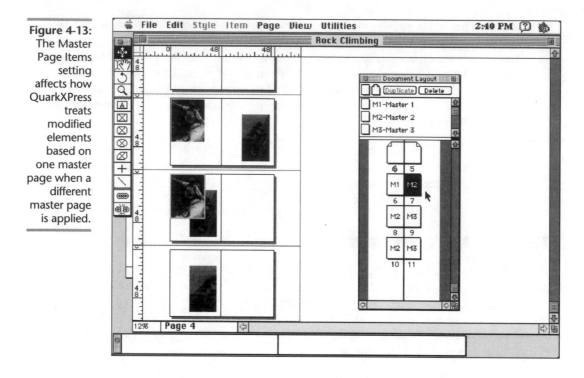

In either row 2 or row 3, if the document page did not use a modified version of the picture box (containing the backpacker image) from Master 1, the backpacker image would be removed no matter which Master Page Items setting was in effect. This is because this setting applies only to elements created in a master page and then *modified* in the document page to which the new master page is being applied.

Because this can be confusing, follow a simple rule of thumb: leave this setting on Keep Changes. Then, after applying a new master page, manually remove any unwanted elements left behind.

Picture linking

Auto Picture Import lets you create links to your source images. This is handy if your picture might change frequently and you don't want to forget to update your layout to accommodate it. You can select from three Auto Picture Import settings in the General Preferences dialog box:

- **On (verify):** If you choose this setting, QuarkXPress checks the graphics files to see if they have been modified (by looking at the file's date and time stamp). It then displays a list of all the graphics files in your document so that you can decide whether or not to update the layout with the newest version.

- **On:** This setting tells QuarkXPress to automatically import the latest version of changed graphics files.

- **Off:** If you select Off, QuarkXPress does not check to see if the source file has been modified.

In most cases, you should use On (verify) or On, depending on whether you expect graphic files to change much. If files may change size, use On (verify), so that you'll know which pictures to check to determine whether layout is affected. If file size is unlikely to change — for example, suppose that a logo incorporates the current month but the logo size doesn't change — use the On setting.

 This option works only with graphics that have been imported through QuarkXPress's File ⇨ Get Picture command. Those pasted into QuarkXPress via the Macintosh clipboard are not affected because the pasted file is copied into your document. Files pasted through System 7's Publish and Subscribe live-link feature are updated automatically. (Publish and Subscribe is covered in detail in Chapter 24.) If you delete or rename a file, the Missing/Modified Picture dialog box appears no matter which automatic import option you select.

Typographic Settings

QuarkXPress lets you define default typographic preferences, which you can then modify for individual styles or for selected text. You specify your preferences in the Typographic Preferences dialog box (see Figure 4-14) which you open by choosing Edit ⇨ Preferences ⇨ Typographic. The shortcut is Shift-⌘Y.

 As with changes you make in the General Preferences dialog box, any changes to the settings in this dialog box affect only the current document. If no document is open, the changes affect all subsequent new documents.

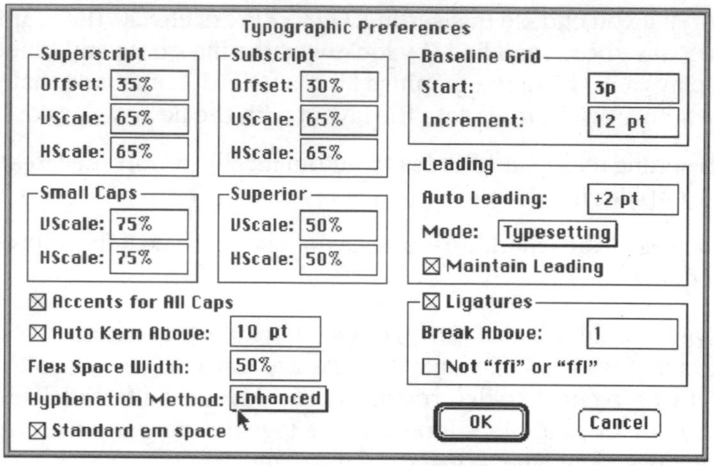

Figure 4-14:
The
Typographical
Preferences
dialog box.

Typographic Preferences

┌─Superscript─────┐ ┌─Subscript─────┐ ┌─Baseline Grid──────┐
Offset: 35%   Offset: 30%   Start: 3p
VScale: 65%   VScale: 65%   Increment: 12 pt
HScale: 65%   HScale: 65%

┌─Small Caps──────┐ ┌─Superior──────┐ ┌─Leading──────────────┐
VScale: 75%   VScale: 50%   Auto Leading: +2 pt
HScale: 75%   HScale: 50%   Mode: [Typesetting]
                                        ☒ Maintain Leading

☒ Accents for All Caps   ┌─☒ Ligatures──────────┐
☒ Auto Kern Above: 10 pt   Break Above: 1
Flex Space Width: 50%   ☐ Not "ffi" or "ffl"
Hyphenation Method: [Enhanced]
☒ Standard em space   [OK   ] [Cancel]

Most of the preferences you define in the Typographic Preferences dialog box need to be set only once, although a few are likely to change for different classes of documents. The preferences are described in detail throughout the chapters in Part IV; they are summarized here.

Character defaults

Several options in the Typographic Preferences dialog box affect character defaults. These include the four boxes labeled Superscript, Subscript, Small Caps, and Superior, all found on the left side of the Typographic Preferences dialog box. (Superiors are a special type of superscript that always align along the cap line, which is the height of a capital letter in the current typeface. They typically are used in footnotes.) These settings define how QuarkXPress creates these attributes. Subscript and Superscript share the same options:

    ↪ **Offset:** The Offset option dictates how far below or above the baseline QuarkXPress shifts the subscripted or superscripted character. The default settings are 33 percent for both Subscript and Superscript. We prefer 35 percent for superscripts and 30 percent for subscripts because those values do a better job of taking into consideration the effects of leading.

    ↪ **VScale and HScale:** These determine scaling for the subscript or superscript. Although the default is 100 percent, this is useful only for typewritten documents; typeset documents typically use a smaller size for subscripts and superscripts — usually between 60 and 80 percent of the text size. The two values should be the same because subscripts and superscripts are typically not distorted along one dimension.

The options for Small Caps and Superior are similar, even though these are very different attributes:

- ⏧ **VScale and HScale:** These determine the scaling for the small cap or superior. The two values should be the same because small caps and superiors typically are not distorted along one dimension. Usually, a small cap's scale should be between 65 and 80 percent of the normal text, and a superior's scale should be between 50 and 65 percent.

Special characters

QuarkXPress has added an Accents for All Caps option. If checked, accented characters will retain their accents if you apply the All Caps attribute to them via the Measurements palette, Shift-⌘K shortcut, Style ⏍ Type Style ⏍ All Caps menu option, or the Character Attributes dialog box (accessed via Shift-⌘D or Style ⏍ Character). In many publications, the style is to drop accents from capitalized letters, and this feature lets you control whether this style is implemented automatically or not. Note that using accents on capitalized letters may change the leading of your text, unless you use the Maintain Leading option described later in this chapter.

By checking the Ligatures box, you enable QuarkXPress to automatically replace occurrences of "fi," "ffi," "fl," and "ffl" with "fi," "ffi," "fl," and "ffl," both when you enter text and when you import it. Some people don't like using ligatures for "ffi" and "ffl"; they can check the Not "ffi" or "ffl" box to prevent these ligatures from being automatically used. When you search for text in the Find/Change dialog box, you can enter "ffi" and QuarkXPress will find the ligature "ffi."

The Break Above option for ligatures lets you set how a ligature is handled in a loosely tracked line. You can enter a value from 0 to 100. That value is the number of units of tracking (each unit is 1/200th of an em space) at which QuarkXPress will break apart a ligature to avoid awkward spacing. For example, if you set the Break Above option to 3, the ligature "fi" will be set as "fi" if the text is tracked looser by 4 or more units.

Not all fonts support ligatures, and most fonts don't support "ffi" and "ffl." For these fonts and occurrences, the standard characters will be retained. Likewise, Windows does not support ligatures at all, so files moved to QuarkXPress for Windows will retain the standard characters. Also, ligatures in many sans serif Mac typefaces look like their nonligature equivalents.

If you uncheck the Ligatures box, all ligatures in your document will be translated to standard character combinations.

Although QuarkXPress has the same controls over ligatures as in Version 3.1, the dialog box you use to implement them has been modified. Gone is the pick list with its three menu items; these have been replaced with the check boxes just described.

Spacing defaults

The Typographic Preferences dialog box also offers options for vertical and horizontal spacing. There are two vertical-spacing options:

- **Baseline Grid:** These options specify the default positions for lines of text. The Start option indicates where the grid begins (how far from the top of the page), while the Increment setting determines the grid interval. Generally, the grid should start where the basic text box starts, and the interval should be the same as body text leading.

- **Leading:** The options here determine the default setting for leading in the Paragraph Formats dialog box, through which you establish paragraph settings for styles and selected text. For the Auto Leading field, which specifies the space between lines, the default is 20 percent, which sets leading at 120 percent of the current text size. A better option is +2, which sets leading at the current text size plus 2 points — a more typical setting among typographers. If you check the Maintain Leading box, text that falls under an intervening text or picture box snaps to the next baseline grid, rather than falling right after the intervening box's offset. This procedure ensures consistent text alignment across all columns. The Mode option is a throwback to QuarkXPress's early years; you should always pick the Typesetting option from the pick list. (Typesetting mode measures leading from baseline to baseline, while Word Processing mode measures from top of character to top of character.)

There are three horizontal spacing controls:

- **Flex Space Width:** This lets you define the value for a flex space, which is a user-defined space. The default is 50 percent, which is about the width of the letter *t*. A better setting is 200 percent, which is equal to an em space (the width of the letter *M*). An em space is used often in typography but is not directly available in QuarkXPress.

- **Standard em space:** This determines how QuarkXPress calculates the width of an em, a standard measurement in typography upon which most other spacing measurements are based. If you check this box, QuarkXPress uses the typographic measurement (the width of a capital "M," which is usually equal to the current point size). Unchecked, QuarkXPress uses the width of two zeroes, which was how QuarkXPress has always calculated an em space. Often, these two values are the same because typographers gave numerals the width of half an em space (an en space) to make alignment easy in tables. If you encounter difficulty in aligning numeral-intensive documents, uncheck this option.

∞ **Auto Kern Above:** Auto Kern Above enables you to define the point size at which QuarkXPress automatically kerns letter pairs. The default of 10 points is fine for laser-printed documents, but typeset documents should be set at a smaller value, such as 8 points.

One other option should be left at its default:

∞ **Hyphenation Method:** Keep this option set at Enhanced. Standard exists only to keep the program compatible with earlier versions, which had a less accurate hyphenation algorithm.

The layout of the Typographic Preferences dialog differs from that in Version 3.1. In addition to the changes described earlier for ligatures, the Auto Leading, Leading Mode (renamed Mode), and Maintain Leading options have been combined into a Leading section of the dialog box, and the Flex Space Width and Auto Kern Above options have been moved to the left side of the dialog box.

Quote settings

The only settings not in the Typographic Preferences dialog box, the Quotes option and the related Smart Quotes check box in the Application Preferences dialog box (see Figure 4-4), add new controls to QuarkXPress.

Use the pick list for the Quotes option to pick the default quotation marks when you type inside QuarkXPress. Figure 4-15 shows the available sets, which handle the needs of most Western languages.

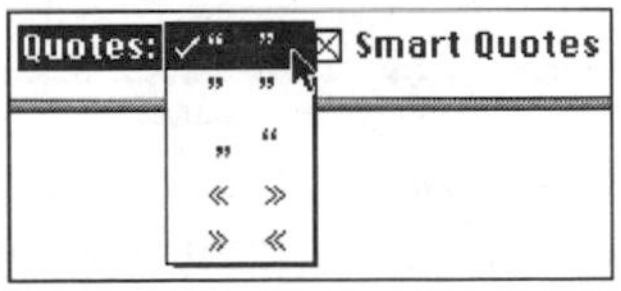

Figure 4-15:
The portion of the Application Preferences dialog box that offers default quotation mark styles.

To have these quotation marks automatically substituted when you type the keyboard " character within text boxes, check the Smart Quotes box. Note that checking this option will also translate the keyboard ' character to ` and ' when typing.

With this option, the Find/Change dialog box (accessed via ⌘F or Edit ➔ Find/Change) will find both the typographic and keyboard quotes when you enter the keyboard quotes in the Find What field. If you enter the keyboard quotes in the Change To field, it will use the typographic symbols.

To use the keyboard quotes, hold the Control key when typing " or '.

When you import text, you can set QuarkXPress to automatically translate keyboard quotes to typographic quotes, as explained in Chapter 7.

Output Settings

Most output settings are handled in the Print dialog box so that you can control your printing as it occurs (see Chapter 26), but a few global options are set elsewhere.

Registration marks

In the Application Preferences dialog box (see Figure 4-4), you control the position of registration marks. Choose Reg. Marks Offset to specify the space between the borders of a page and the registration and crop marks. The default is 6 points, which is fine for most printers; you can enter values from 0 to 30 points, in increments of 0.1 points. Unless your printer asks you to change this value, leave it at the default setting.

Color trapping

In the Trapping Preferences dialog box (accessed via Edit ⇨ Preferences ⇨ Trapping) QuarkXPress offers a set of trap options that define how it prints overlapping colors when you use PostScript printers. If you are unfamiliar with color trapping, leave the defaults as they are. As Figure 4-16 shows, the options are:

Figure 4-16:
The Trapping Preferences dialog box.

Trapping Preferences	
Auto Method:	Absolute
Auto Amount:	0.144 pt
Indeterminate:	0.144 pt
Overprint Limit:	95%
☒ Ignore White	☒ Process Trap
OK	Cancel

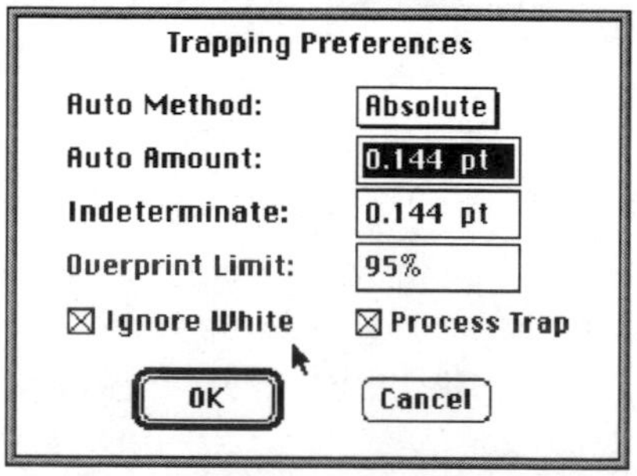

☞ **Auto Method:** This setting determines whether QuarkXPress uses the trapping values specified in the Auto Amount option or whether it adjusts the trapping based on the saturation of the abutting colors. If you choose Absolute, the program uses the values as is; if you choose Proportional, QuarkXPress calculates new trapping values based on the value entered in Auto Amount and the relative saturation of the abutting colors. This applies only to colors set at Auto in the Trap Specification dialog box (access this box by choosing Edit ⇨ Colors ⇨ Edit Trap menu). The default is Absolute.

- **Auto Amount:** Select this option to specify the trapping value for which the program calculates automatic trapping, both for the Auto Method option and for the Trap Specification dialog box (accessed via Edit ⇨ Colors ⇨ Edit Trap). You can enter values from 0 to 36 points in increments of 0.001 points. If you want the amount to be infinite (so colors overprint), enter the word **overprint.** The default setting is 0.145 points.

- **Indeterminate:** The Indeterminate setting tells QuarkXPress how to trap objects that abut multicolored or indeterminate-colored objects, as well as imported color graphics. As with Auto Method, this setting applies only to colors set at Auto in the Trap Specification dialog box. Valid options are 0 to 26 points, in 0.001-point increments, as well as **overprint.** The default is 0.145 points.

- **Overprint Limit:** This value tells QuarkXPress when to overprint a color object. You can specify any percentage from 0 to 100 in increments of 0.1. If you enter 50 percent, QuarkXPress overprints any color whose trap specification is set as Overprint and whose saturation is 50 percent or greater; otherwise, it traps the color based on the Auto Amount and Auto Method settings. This limit affects black objects regardless of whether black is set at Auto or Overprint. The default is 95 percent.

- **Ignore White:** If you check this option box, QuarkXPress traps an object based on all nonwhite objects abutting or behind the object. Otherwise, QuarkXPress calculates a trap based on the smaller of the Indeterminate setting and the trap specification for any other colors (including white) abutting or behind the object. This option is checked as a default because it makes little sense to trap to white (as there is nothing to trap to).

- **Process Trap:** Checking this box tells QuarkXPress to calculate traps for overlapping process colors based on their saturation (for example, it traps 50 percent cyan and 100 percent magenta differently than 80 percent cyan and 100 percent magenta), as well as on all the other trap settings. Otherwise, it uses the same trapping values for all saturation levels. The default setting turns this option on (the box is checked), which makes for smoother trapping.

The Trapping Preferences dialog box is new (see Figure 4-16); its settings resided in the Application Preferences dialog box in Version 3.1.

Color calibration

If the EfiColor XTension is installed, the EfiColor Preferences dialog box will be available via Edit ⇨ Preferences ⇨ EfiColor (otherwise, the option will not appear in the Preferences menu). This bundled XTension calibrates colors of scanned and computer-created images so they will reproduce as faithfully as possible on the target output device or printing press. It also calibrates the on-screen representation.

Figure 4-17 shows the EfiColor Preferences dialog box. The options are:

- **Use EfiColor:** Checking this box enables EfiColor.

- **Color Printer Corrections:** Checking the boxes in this section of the dialog box enables EfiColor's calibration of imported pictures (except for EPS graphics) and colors created within QuarkXPress for the combination of the target printer and the printing press output profile chosen in the Page Setup dialog box. For colors defined in QuarkXPress, you can select any or all of CMYK process colors, RGB colors, and named colors (those defined via the Pantone, Trumatch, or other swatch-based color models). You should check all as the default, unless your printer advises otherwise.

- **Default Profiles:** For RGB and CMYK colors, you select from the pick lists the default color profiles used when importing color images or creating colors. These profiles tell EfiColor how to alter the output files or printer instructions so that the colors output match your expectations. For RGB colors, choose Apple 13" RGB or the appropriate monitor if you created your images on a Mac and want the colors you saw on-screen to be what EfiColor tries to ensure is output to the target printer or is printed on printing press. Use EFI Calibrated RGB or contact Electronics for Imaging directly (the number is 800/285-4565 or 415/286-8600) for a custom profile. For CMYK colors, select the final output device (use SWOP-Coated for standard web offset printing on coated paper stock, such as that used in magazines, brochures, and catalogs). As with RGB profiles, you can contact EFI for other profiles. These profiles can be overridden when you import files that come from other devices (such as scanners or monitors), or you can change them on a case-by-case basis in your layout. You can also change the profile when you print, which is handy if you are printing to a proofing device before creating your final output.

Changes made in the EfiColor Preferences dialog box when no documents are open become the default for all subsequently created documents. Changes made while a document is open affect only the open document.

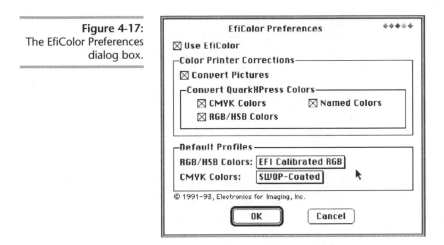

Figure 4-17:
The EfiColor Preferences
dialog box.

Chapter 22 and Chapter 26 cover EfiColor in more detail. Chapter 21 explains color models and how to create colors within QuarkXPress.

Document Management

QuarkXPress's preferences include those that control how a document is managed, particularly how its elements are saved. These options are found in the Application Preferences dialog box (see Figure 4-4). Figure 4-18 shows the section that contains them.

Figure 4-18:
The portion of the Application Preferences dialog box that offers document-management controls.

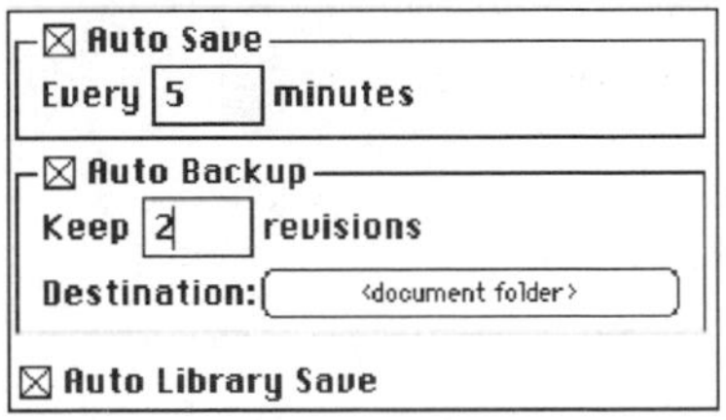

Document save and backup

By checking the Auto Save option, you set QuarkXPress to save all opened documents at regular intervals. You determine that interval through the value you enter in the Every Minutes field.

You can also have QuarkXPress retain backup copies of your document by checking the Auto Backup box. You determine how many previous versions are retained in the Keep Revisions field, and you determine where those backups are stored in the location specified via the Destination button. The default location is in the same folder as the current document, but you can change that by clicking the button and using the Backup Destination dialog box to select a different folder. (It works like a standard Macintosh Open dialog box.) If you want to reset the destination to the document folder, select the Use Document Folder button in the Backup Destination dialog box.

The backup feature is handy if you are experimenting with a layout, since you can go back to prior versions if you don't like how the layout has evolved. You can achieve the same effect by periodically saving your layout with a different name, but using the backup feature is easier.

 The backup and auto-save options are independent. If both backup and auto-save are enabled, backups are created only when you explicitly save with the File ⇨ Save command (or the keyboard shortcut ⌘S).

Automatic library save

QuarkXPress's library feature (described fully in Chapter 23) lets you add common elements to a library that is accessible to multiple documents. When the Automatic Library Save box in the Application Preferences dialog box is checked, it saves the library whenever something is added to or deleted from it. Otherwise, when the box is unchecked, the library is saved only when you close it (including when you quit QuarkXPress).

■ ■

Summary

- ➡ You can customize layout aids such as guide colors and measurement units to fit your work style.

- ➡ You can set different view modes for color and gray-scale TIFF images to speed up screen display, as well as hide all images and set text-size display thresholds for faster screen display.

- ➡ With the Smart Quotes option, you can have QuarkXPress automatically convert keyboard quotes to typographic ones as you type. With the Quotes option, you can select quotation marks from any of several languages that you may want used.

➡ By choosing a setting in the General Preferences dialog box, you can control whether modified elements taken from a master page are retained when you apply a different master page to a document page.

➡ You can specify whether you want boxes that are contained within other boxes to be constrained to the dimensions of the outside box.

➡ You use the Typographical Preferences dialog box to set basic typographic defaults for character attributes (including small cap size and superscript size and position) and for character spacing (including leading).

➡ By making selections in the Trapping Preferences dialog box, you establish basic trapping values for color elements and specify how you want QuarkXPress to handle different trapping situations.

➡ Specify the position of registration marks by entering a value in the Application Preferences dialog box.

➡ The Auto Save and Auto Backup options let you ensure that documents are not lost because of a system crash and that you have earlier iterations of your layout to go back to if you don't like how the design has evolved.

➡ The EfiColor XTension settings let you calibrate how colors print based on the target device and the system on which they were created.

Using Master Pages

■ ■

In This Chapter

➡ Creating master pages

➡ Making changes to master pages

➡ Applying master pages to existing document pages

■ ■

Building a Foundation _____

Part of the challenge of being a professional publisher is creating a consistent look throughout a document. You want what appears on page 5 to look like it is somehow connected to what was on page 1, and so on. The master pages in QuarkXPress can help you achieve this goal.

Master pages hold the elements of a page that you want repeated on other pages. For example, you may want the bottom outer corner of each page to show the current page number. You may want a company logo to appear at the top of each page of an annual report. You may want a picture box to be placed at a specific spot on each page, ready to receive a graphic. These are just a few ideas about how you can make Master Pages work for you.

Creating a new master page

When you create a new QuarkXPress document via the File ➪ New menu option (or by using the keyboard shortcut ⌘N), the main master page is automatically created. QuarkXPress bases the main master page on the settings in the New dialog box, shown in Figure 5-1. You establish default settings — or change to new default settings — by making changes in the New dialog box; if you create a new document, the settings in the

New dialog box at the time you created the new document become the default settings for the next new document. If you leave the Facing Pages box unchecked, QuarkXPress creates a single-sided master page. If you check the Facing Pages box, two master pages are created: one for the left page (named L-Master A), and one for the right page (R-Master-A).

 While master pages help keep documents consistent, they also allow for a great deal of flexibility. You can have up to 127 master pages per document. You can add, modify, or delete master page elements just like you do those elements that are not on master pages. After a master page is modified, those changes automatically apply to any document pages based on that master page.

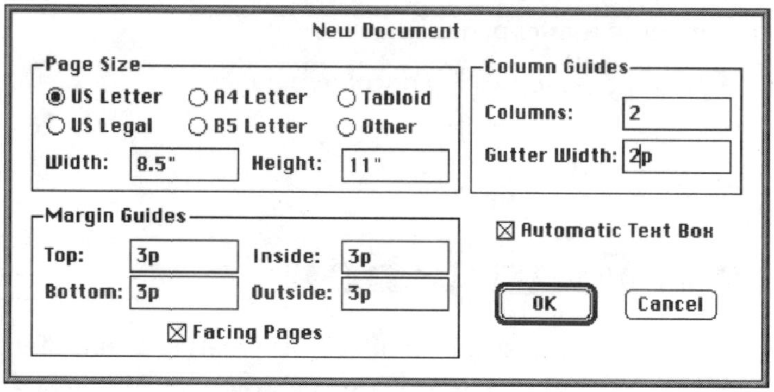

Figure 5-1:
The New dialog box, where the basic specifications for the main master page are established.

New Document	
Page Size	**Column Guides**
◉ US Letter ○ A4 Letter ○ Tabloid	Columns: 2
○ US Legal ○ B5 Letter ○ Other	Gutter Width: 2p
Width: 8.5" Height: 11"	
Margin Guides	☒ Automatic Text Box
Top: 3p Inside: 3p	
Bottom: 3p Outside: 3p	OK Cancel
☒ Facing Pages	

Displaying a master page

After you've created a new document, it's a good idea to set up the master pages right away. To set up master pages, you need to leave the *document* mode and go into the *master page* mode, where you can establish features that you want to be repeated throughout the document.

QuarkXPress lets you "toggle" between document pages (document mode) and master pages (master page mode) by using the Display command in the Page menu. To have the screen on your computer display the actual document page, choose Page ⇨ Display ⇨ Document. To display a master page for the document, choose Page ⇨ Display ⇨ *Master* (after you've established master pages, where we have used *Master*, the display will actually include a list of all master pages associated with the document; hold the mouse button down to select the master page you want to see). Figure 5-2 shows how you select the master page in a new document.

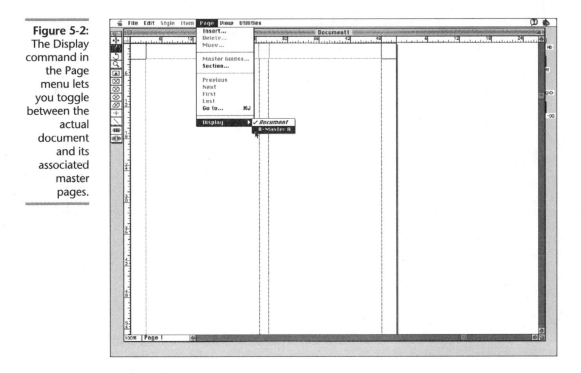

Figure 5-2:
The Display
command in
the Page
menu lets
you toggle
between the
actual
document
and its
associated
master
pages.

Establishing master page items

Although you can put just about anything on a master page, here are some of the items most commonly used on master pages:

- ⌘ Page headers ("running" heads) that you want to repeat from page to page.

- ⌘ Page footers, or the information that repeats across the bottom of pages in a document.

- ⌘ Automatic page numbers, which you create by placing a Current Page Number character (⌘3) at the point on the master page where you want to see page numbers appear.

- ⌘ Page sidebars, or information in the outer side margins of a page that you want repeated on other pages.

- ⌘ Corporate logos, or other artwork that you want to appear throughout the document.

Figure 5-3 shows a facing-page document. Note that we have set the reverse-type box "Outdoor Fun" on the top outer margins of the left and right master pages. When we shift back to the actual document, all left pages based on this left master page will have the "Outdoor Fun" text box on the top left of the page; all right pages based on this right master page will have the text box on the top right of the page.

Figure 5-3:
Left and
right master
pages.

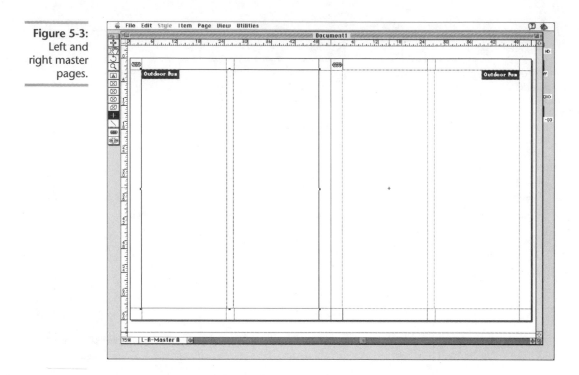

Figure 5-3:
Left and
right master
pages.

Making Changes to Master Pages ___

Even if you have a master page associated with a page in your document, you can make local changes to the page that don't affect the master page. To do this you simply edit the page with the document in *Document* mode (choose Page ⇨ Display ⇨ Document).

After working on a document for awhile, you also might want to make changes to master pages. For example, you might decide to move the page number from the bottom center of the page to the outer margin.

To view a master page so that you can change it, choose View ⇨ Show Document Layout. This displays the Document Layout palette. Double-click on the icon of the master page you want to modify. The master page is displayed. Make any changes that you want to make to the master page, and then return to the actual document by choosing Page ⇨ Display ⇨ Document.

To insert a new page based on an existing master page, choose View ⇨ Show Document Layout to display the Document Layout palette. Click on the icon of the master page you want the new document page to be associated with, and drag the icon into the lower part of the Document Layout palette, which shows the positioning of the master pages. As you drag the page icon into position, the icon will change to an arrow, and then back into a page icon. Release the mouse when you have positioned the icon in the spot you want. In Figure 5-4, you can see what the icon looks like as you drag it into position.

Figure 5-4:
When you
use the
Document
Layout
palette to
insert a new
document
page based
on a Master
Page, the
icon looks
like a box
with an
arrow in it as
you drag the
page into
place.

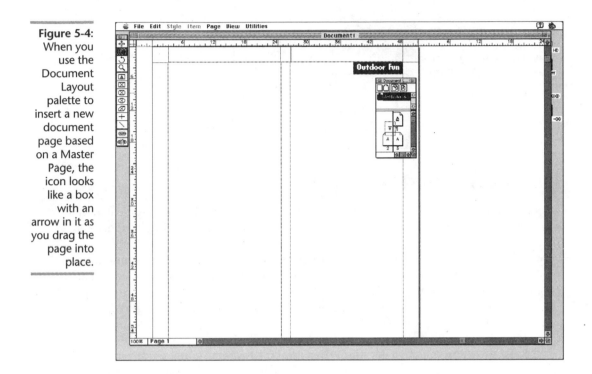

Rather than using the Document Layout palette, you can also insert a new document page based on an existing master page by choosing Page ➪ Insert. This displays the Insert Pages dialog box. You can associate the inserted pages with a master page by choosing one of the master pages shown in the Master Page pop-up menu.

To link the automatic text boxes on pages that you are inserting to the active text box on the page that precedes the insertion of new pages, check Link to Current Text Chain in the Insert Pages dialog box. This option is available only if the text box on the preceding page is active, and if the pages you are inserting are set to include Automatic Text Box.

The QuarkXPress Document Layout palette has been evolving over the past few releases. Both version 3.2 and 3.3 have Document Layout palettes that differ from each other and from the palette in earlier versions. The Document Layout palettes in versions 3.2 and 3.3 function the same, but have different icons for duplicating and deleting master pages. Figure 5-5 shows the difference between the Document Layout palette for the two versions.

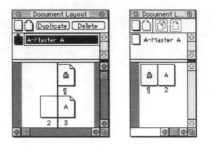

Figure 5-5:
The Document Layout
palette in version 3.2 (left)
and version 3.3 (right).

Deleting master pages

After spending some time working on a document, you may find that you have established a master page that you no longer need. Deleting a master page is a simple operation.

First, display the Document Layout palette by choosing View ➪ Show Document Layout. When the Document Layout palette is displayed, click on the icon of the master page you want to delete. Then click the delete icon at the top of the Document Layout palette (the Delete icon looks like a page icon with an "X" through its center). Figure 5-6 shows a master page that is ready to be deleted.

Be very careful when deleting a master page because you cannot undo the master page deletion without reverting to the last-saved version of the document.

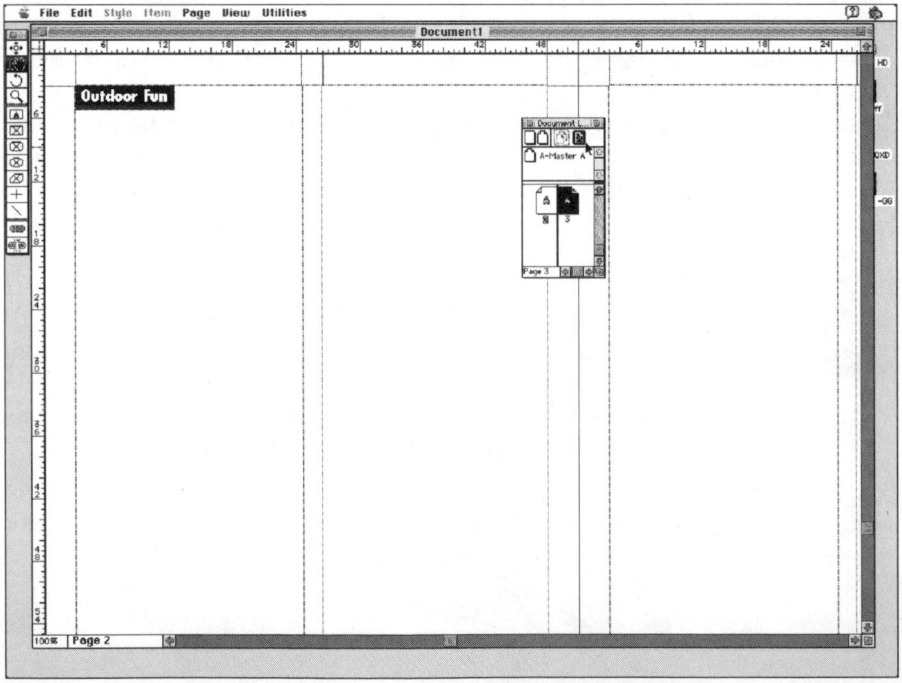

Figure 5-6:
Deleting a
master
page.

Rearranging master pages

Because QuarkXPress allows you up to 127 master pages per document, it is conceivable that — at some point — you may want to rearrange the order of the master pages associated with the document. For example, you might want to have the third master page in a set become the first, or the second master page become the last, and so on.

To rearrange master pages, choose View ⇨ Show Document Layout to display the Document Layout palette. Then click on the icon of the master page you want to move and drag it into position. When you release the mouse button, the master page stays put.

Changing the guides on a master page

It happens to the best of us: you're working on a document when you realize that the margins you established when you first created the document are too wide or too narrow, or that you really need two columns instead of one. You might think that you need to start all over again but, thanks to a nifty Master Guides feature, you can adjust your initial settings without sacrificing all your hard work on the document.

To change the margin or column guides for a master page, follow these steps:

STEPS:	Changing Guides on a Master Page
Step 1.	Choose View ⇨ Show Document Layout to display the Document Layout palette.
Step 2.	Double-click on the icon of the master page you want to modify; this displays the master page.
Step 3.	Choose Page ⇨ Master Guides to display the Master Guides dialog box (see Figure 5-7).
Step 4.	Make any changes you'd like to the Margin Guides or Column Guides fields in the dialog box, and click the OK button. Any changes you make apply to document pages that are associated to the master page.

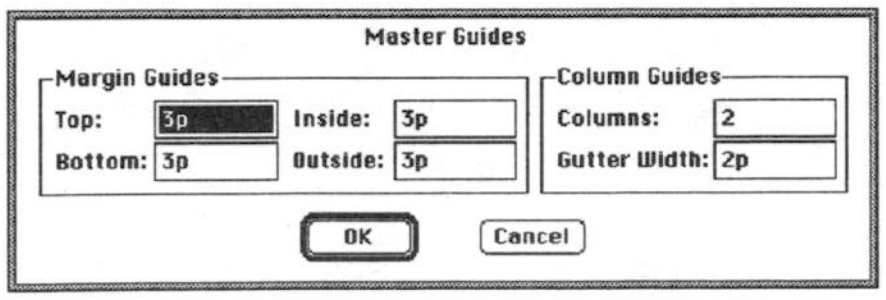

Figure 5-7:
You can make changes to the margins or columns of a master page by using the Master Guides dialog box.

Master Guides

Margin Guides
Top: 3p   Inside: 3p
Bottom: 3p   Outside: 3p

Column Guides
Columns: 2
Gutter Width: 2p

OK   Cancel

Applying a Master Page to a Document Page

You can apply master page settings to existing document pages — but be careful because doing so usually causes text and layout changes. To apply master pages to existing pages, take the following steps:

STEPS: Applying Master Pages to Existing Pages

Step 1. Make sure the Document Layout palette is visible (if it isn't, choose View ⇨ Show Document Layout).

Step 2. Click on the page icon of the page in the Document Layout palette to which you want to apply a master page.

To apply a master page to a contiguous set of pages, press and hold the Shift key as you click on the first and last page in the range of pages; to apply a master page to noncontiguous pages, press and hold the ⌘ key as you click on the icons of the separate pages to which you want to apply the master page.

Step 3. Press and hold the Option key as you click on the icon for the master page you want to apply to the document page(s); then release the Option key and the mouse button.

Summary

- ➡ Master pages hold the elements of a page that you want repeated on other pages.

- ➡ When you create a new QuarkXPress document, the main master page is automatically created.

- ➡ You can have up to 127 master pages per document.

- ➡ You can add, modify, or delete master page elements just like you do those elements that are not on master pages.

- ➡ QuarkXPress lets you "toggle" between document pages and master pages by using the Display command in the Page menu.

- ➡ Even if you have a master page associated with a page in your document, you can make local changes to the page that don't affect the master page.

- ➡ You can apply master page settings to existing document pages.

Creating Style Sheets

C H A P T E R

6

In This Chapter

→ The advantages of using style sheets to create your documents

→ How to create, modify, and apply styles

→ How to import word-processor style sheets

Understanding Style Sheet Basics ___

Style sheets are similar in purpose to master pages. They define basic specifications for your text: typefaces, type sizes, justification settings, and tab settings. As with master pages, you can override style settings locally whenever you want. (See the section "Overriding Styles" later in this chapter.)

By putting this common text-formatting information into styles — which essentially are macros for text attributes — you can save a lot of effort. Instead of applying each and every attribute individually to text, just tell QuarkXPress that you want certain text to take on all the formatting attributes established in a style tag.

The terminology for styles can be confusing because some programs use them differently and many people use these terms interchangeably. Here is a rundown of terms as we use them:

↪ **Style sheet:** The group of styles in a document. It's called a *sheet* because, in times before electronic publishing, typesetters had typewritten sheets that listed the formatting attributes they were to apply to specific kinds of text, such as body copy and headlines. QuarkXPress treats style sheets as an integral part of the document (although you can transfer styles among documents), so there is no style sheet per se in QuarkXPress.

    ⚭ **Style tag** or **style:** These two terms refer to a group of attributes that you apply to one or more paragraphs. You name the group, or style, so that you can apply all the attributes at once. The word *tag* is used because you "tag" selected paragraphs with the style you want to apply. The word *style* also sometimes refers to a character attribute, such as italics or underline, so many people use *style tag* to refer to the group of attributes. This avoids confusion between the two meanings.

You apply styles to whole paragraphs, not to selected words or sentences. For example, headlines can have a headline style, captions a caption style, bylines a byline style, body text a body text style, and so on. You should create a style for all common paragraph formats. What you call those styles is your business, although using standardized labels can help you and your coworkers apply the right formatting to the right text.

You can use styles in two places: on selected paragraphs in your QuarkXPress document or in the word-processing text you plan to import (either by entering a code to indicate the desired style or by using the word processor's own style sheets, as described in "Creating Style Sheets," later in this chapter). The choice you make depends on the type of document you are working on.

 It makes sense to apply styles in your source text for long or routine documents (such as a newsletter, when everyone knows the styles to be used). And it makes sense to apply styles in QuarkXPress for a brochure or other highly designed or nonstandard document.

No matter when you apply styles, you'll find that they are a must for productive publishing of all but a small handful of documents (one-time pieces such as ads are possible exceptions).

Creating Styles

Almost every function you need for defining styles resides in the Style Sheets dialog box, which you access via Edit ⇨ Style Sheets (see Figure 6-1).

Two significant functions are *not* set in the Style Sheets dialog box:

    ⚭ Hyphenation controls are set in the H&Js dialog box, which you access via Edit ⇨ H&Js.

    ⚭ Character- and space-scaling controls are set in the Typographic Preferences dialog box, accessed via Edit ⇨ Preferences ⇨ Typographic.

 Both functions are covered in detail in later chapters. See Chapter 12 for information about word and letter spacing; refer to Chapter 13 for more information on hyphenation.

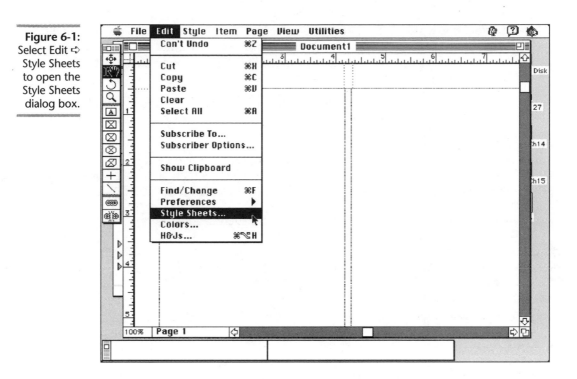

Figure 6-1:
Select Edit ⇨
Style Sheets
to open the
Style Sheets
dialog box.

You can create styles without understanding these options and then later retrofit styles to include them. But if you are experienced in typography and somewhat experienced with style sheets (in any program), consider reading those chapters before continuing with this one.

Style Sheets dialog box

The Style Sheets dialog box provides several options for editing style sheets, as Figure 6-2 shows. Your editing choices are as follows:

◌ **New** lets you create a new style from scratch or create a new style based on an existing style.

 If you define text settings through the Style menu or Measurements palette and decide you want to create a style that contains those attributes, just position your text cursor anywhere on the text that has the desired settings. Then choose New in the Style Sheets dialog box. All settings are automatically included in the new style you create. This is handy if you want to experiment with settings on dummy text before creating a style for future use.

☞ **Edit** enables you to edit an existing style. You can also use Edit to create a style by editing an existing style, changing the style name to a new name, and changing whichever attribute settings you want. This has the same effect as the Duplicate option.

☞ **Duplicate** copies all the attributes of an existing style and gives the duplicate style the name *Copy of style*. You can then change any attribute settings, including the style name.

☞ **Delete** lets you delete existing styles. This option is grayed out when Normal is selected because you cannot delete the Normal style. You are asked to confirm the deletion if you applied the style to text in the current document.

Figure 6-2:
The Style Sheets dialog box.

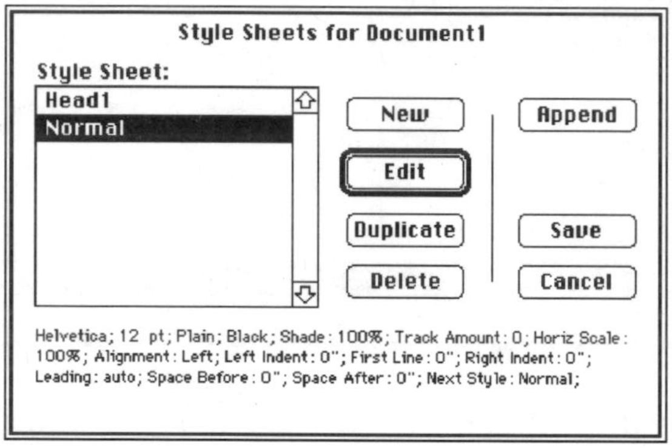

Style Sheets for Document1

Style Sheet:

| Head1 |
| Normal |

[New]   [Append]

[Edit]

[Duplicate]   [Save]

[Delete]   [Cancel]

Helvetica; 12 pt; Plain; Black; Shade: 100%; Track Amount: 0; Horiz Scale: 100%; Alignment: Left; Left Indent: 0"; First Line: 0"; Right Indent: 0"; Leading: auto; Space Before: 0"; Space After: 0"; Next Style: Normal;

If you attempt to delete a style sheet that has been applied to text, an alert is displayed (see Figure 6-3). With version 3.2, you can then choose a replacement for the style sheet you want to delete, or you can delete the style and have the No Style tag attached to the affected paragraphs.

Figure 6-3:
The delete existing style warning box.

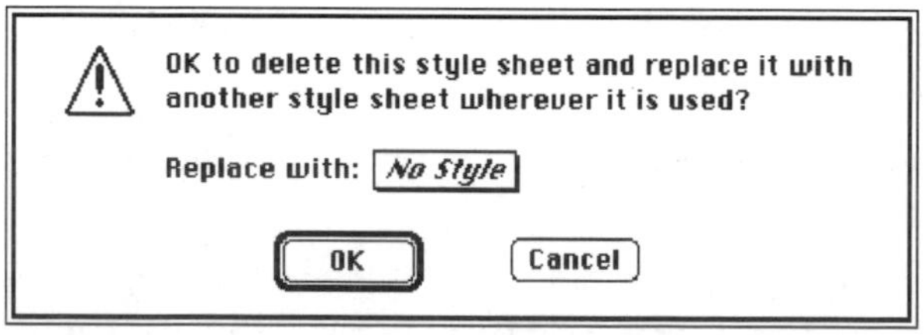

⚠ OK to delete this style sheet and replace it with another style sheet wherever it is used?

Replace with: [*No Style*]

[OK]   [Cancel]

While QuarkXPress lacks a find and replace function for style sheets, in a pinch you can use the Delete option to change the style sheets of several paragraphs at once. Of course, this is an "all or nothing" choice — you must change all the paragraphs with the style applied, or none of them.

Any text using a deleted style retains the style's attributes. But the Style Sheet palette and menu show these paragraphs as having No Style.

- ✎ **Append** enables you to copy a style from another QuarkXPress document.

- ✎ **Save** lets you save all the style additions, deletions, and changes you make in the Style Sheets dialog box. You *must* save your styles when leaving the dialog box for changes to take effect.

- ✎ **Cancel** instructs QuarkXPress to ignore all style additions, deletions, and changes you made in the Style Sheets dialog box.

Whether you choose New, Edit, or Duplicate when you create a style sheet, the next dialog box to appear is Edit Style Sheet, shown in Figure 6-4. This dialog box is the launching pad for the actual definition of style attributes.

Figure 6-4:
The Edit
Style Sheet
dialog box.

```
                        Edit Style Sheet
       Name:
      ┌──────────────────────────────────┐   ┌─────────────┐
      │ Head 1                           │   │  Character  │
      └──────────────────────────────────┘   └─────────────┘
       Keyboard Equivalent:                   ┌─────────────┐
      ┌──────────────────────────────────┐   │   Formats   │
      │                                  │   └─────────────┘
      └──────────────────────────────────┘   ┌─────────────┐
                                              │    Rules    │
       Based on:   │ No Style │               └─────────────┘
                                              ┌─────────────┐
       Next Style: │ Head 1 │                 │    Tabs     │
                                              └─────────────┘

       Helvetica; 14 pt; +Bold; Black; Shade: 100%; Track Amount: 0; Horiz Scale:
       100%; Alignment: Left; Left Indent: 0"; First Line: 0"; Right Indent: 0";
       Leading: auto; Space Before: 0"; Space After: 0"; Next Style: Head 1;

                   ┌──────────┐   ┌──────────┐
                   │    OK    │   │  Cancel  │
                   └──────────┘   └──────────┘
```

The Name field is not filled in if you selected New. The Based On field reads No Style unless you are editing or duplicating a style that uses the based-on option, described later in this chapter. You can enter or change the style name; if you choose the name of an existing style, an error message asking for a new name appears when you choose OK.

The Keyboard Equivalent field lets you set up hot keys that allow you to apply styles to text quickly. For example, you can establish Ctrl-F2 as the hot key for the Normal style. This tells QuarkXPress to apply that style to currently selected paragraphs when you press Ctrl-F2. You can use the function keys and the numeric keypad keys as hot keys. You also can establish keyboard shortcuts for applying styles. To enter keyboard equivalents, press the actual key or keys you want to use, including any combinations with Shift, Option, and ⌘, such as Shift-⌘X.

QuarkXPress includes a keyboard template listing function key equivalents for often-accessed commands. You can override the original commands by assigning function keys to style sheets, but you lose the ability to access the commands assigned to those keys. Simply add the Ctrl key as a modifier and you can assign styles to function keys, maintaining the original command equivalents. For example, assigning F2 as an equivalent keyboard key for a style would take away Quark's F2 Cut Key, so instead assign Ctrl-F2 as the keyboard equivalent keys for your style.

The Based on field allows you to use a base style sheet as a starting point for building a style group. Should you decide to change the group, you only need to change the original base style and those changes will automatically apply to the rest of the group. For instance, if you had five body text styles created using the "Based on" option (and thus using the same font), instead of altering all five style sheets to change your body text font, you merely edit the base style and the remaining group of styles reflects the font change.

 Next Style, new in version 3.2, comes in handy when you need to enter text directly into QuarkXPress because it lets you establish linked styles. For example, you can specify that a body text style is to always follow a subhead style, which is to always follow a head style. Here's how this nifty feature works: As you type text into the QuarkXPress page, every time you enter a paragraph return after typing a subhead, the style automatically changes to your body text style.

You'll find four buttons along the right side of the Edit Style Sheet dialog box: Character, Formats, Rules, and Tabs. These invoke the appropriate dialog boxes for each major part of the style. Select Character for text attributes such as typeface and size; Formats for paragraph attributes such as leading and indentation; Rules for ruling lines associated with paragraphs; and Tabs to define tab stops and tab types. You can use these in any order and ignore ones that don't apply to the current style (typically, Rules and Tabs are ignored).

 The dialog boxes these buttons invoke are identical to the Style menu dialog boxes with the same names. The chapters in Part IV cover these dialog boxes in detail.

A step-by-step guide to creating a style

Before you create a style, start with developing some idea of the basic elements you want to have in your document. For example, elements in a newspaper include body text, headlines, bylines, captions, and page numbers (folios). In addition, lead text, pull-quotes, biographies, subheads, sidebar heads, bulleted lists, and other more specialized types of formatting may be necessary. Don't worry about knowing in advance all the types of formatting you need to assign styles to — it's very easy in QuarkXPress to add a new style at any time.

Start with the body text because this is the bulk of your document. You can create a style called something like Body Text, or you can modify the Normal style that QuarkXPress defines automatically for each new document and use that as your body text style.

You can create a default Normal style that each new document uses. This is handy if, for example, most of your documents use the same typeface or justification or point size (or any combination of these) for body text.

The initial setting for Normal is left-aligned, 12-point Helvetica with automatic leading. To change any attributes of Normal, close all open documents, access the Style Sheets dialog box by selecting Edit ⇨ Style Sheets, and edit the Normal style in the usual way, described next. These settings are saved as the new defaults for all future new documents. When creating this default Normal style, you don't need to use real text because real text is used only to gauge the effects of the style formatting. Similarly, any style created with no document open becomes part of the default style sheet for all new documents.

The following example illustrates the process of creating styles. For the example, we imported a text file to be used in a newsletter whose style has not yet been defined. When loaded, the text took on the attributes of the Normal style because we did not use style options in the original word processor. This text has five main elements: the body text, the body lead (which has a drop cap but otherwise is like the body text), the byline, the headline, and the kicker (the small headline above the headline that identifies the type of story — in this case, a commentary). Our newsletter also needs styles for captions, folios (page numbers), the publication name, and the publication date, all of which typically run at the top or bottom of each page. In addition, we need styles for subheads and sidebar heads (for simplicity, we decided that sidebar text will be the same as the body text).

Our first step in defining styles was to invoke the Edit Style Sheets dialog box, as described earlier in this chapter. We then selected the Character button to open the Character Attributes dialog box, shown in Figure 6-5. Then we changed the Font to Stone Serif, the Size to 9, and the Track Amount to negative two; -2. We left the other attributes alone because they were appropriate for body text. We clicked OK to return to the Edit Style Sheets dialog box.

Several QuarkXPress dialog box options offer pop-up menus to help you make selections faster. For example, in the Character Attributes dialog box, Font, Size, Color, and Shade all offer pop-up menus. You can also enter the value you want in the field directly. In the Font field, QuarkXPress displays the first typeface it finds that begins with the letter you type in. This enables you to jump quickly to or near a particular typeface — convenient if you have a long list of typefaces to scroll through. Figure 6-6 shows the pop-up menu for the Font field.

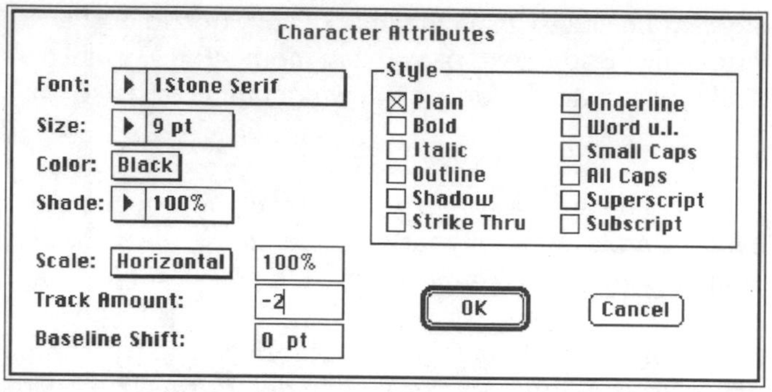

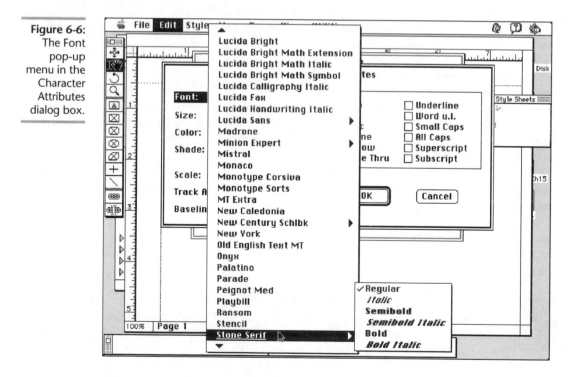

Figure 6-5:
The Character
Attributes dialog
box.

Then we opened the Paragraph Formats dialog box (see Figure 6-7) by selecting the Formats button in the Edit Style Sheet dialog box. We changed the First Line field so that the first line of each paragraph was indented 9 points. We also changed Alignment to Justified and Leading to +2 points, which tells QuarkXPress to make the leading 2 points more than the point size; the default is Auto, which makes leading 120 percent of the point size.

Figure 6-6:
The Font
pop-up
menu in the
Character
Attributes
dialog box.

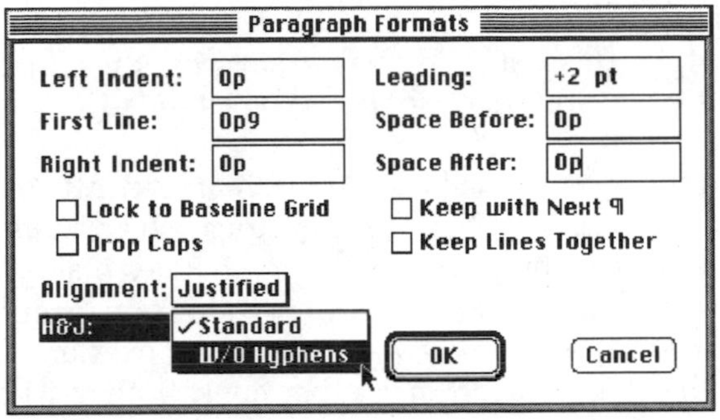

Figure 6-7:
Setting style sheet
specifications in the
Paragraph Formats
dialog box.

In Figure 6-7, you also see the pop-up menu for the H&J field; we included this to show where you select hyphenation and justification (H&J) settings. You define H&J sets separately via the Edit ➪ H&Js menu option, which is described in Chapter 13.

We then chose OK to leave the Paragraph Formats dialog box, OK to leave the Edit Style Sheets dialog box, and Save to save all our changes to the Normal style. Figure 6-8 shows the sequence of two of these dialog boxes. You use this same process to create styles for your documents.

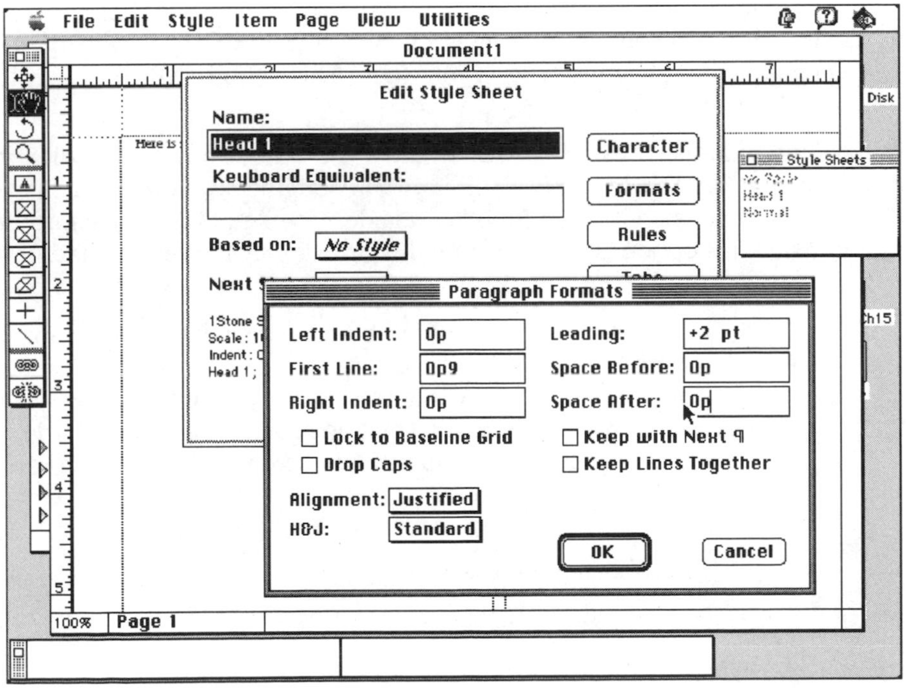

Figure 6-8:
You move
through
several
dialog boxes
to save style
attributes.

At the bottom of the Style Sheets dialog box is a description of the attributes for the selected style. This is a handy way to see what the current settings are, as well as to verify that you set the options you intended.

 For details on the options available via the Character Attributes dialog box (accessed via the Character button), the Paragraph Formats dialog box (accessed via the Formats button), the Paragraph Rules dialog box (accessed via the Rules button), and the Paragraph Tabs dialog box (accessed via the Tabs button), see the chapters in Part V. These dialog boxes are identical to those available via the Style menu, because they apply both to whole paragraphs and to selected groups of characters.

Applying Styles

To apply a style, you have three options, as illustrated in Figure 6-9:

- **Option 1:** Use the Style ⇨ Style Sheet menu option. This option is the least efficient way to apply styles to text.

- **Option 2:** Use the Style Sheet palette, shown in the upper-right corner of the figure, which you invoke through the View ⇨ Show Style Sheets option. (You can resize and move the palette if you want.) This option is the best way to apply styles in most cases.

- **Option 3:** Use the keyboard shortcut, if you defined one in the Edit Style Sheet dialog box. The shortcut key is shown in both the Style Sheet palette and Style ⇨ Style Sheet menu option (in this example, we did not invoke a shortcut key). While this option is the fastest method, use it only for very commonly used styles because it requires memorizing the keyboard shortcuts that you assigned.

 A quick way to select all the text in a document so that you can apply the Normal (or other) style to it is to choose Select All from the Edit menu. Pressing ⌘A achieves the same effect without requiring you to use pull-down menus. To use this feature, you must select a text box containing text with the Text tool. All text in that text box, as well as any text box linked to it, will be selected.

Figure 6-9:
QuarkXPress
offers several
avenues for
applying
styles.

Figure 6-9:
QuarkXPress
offers several
avenues for
applying
styles.

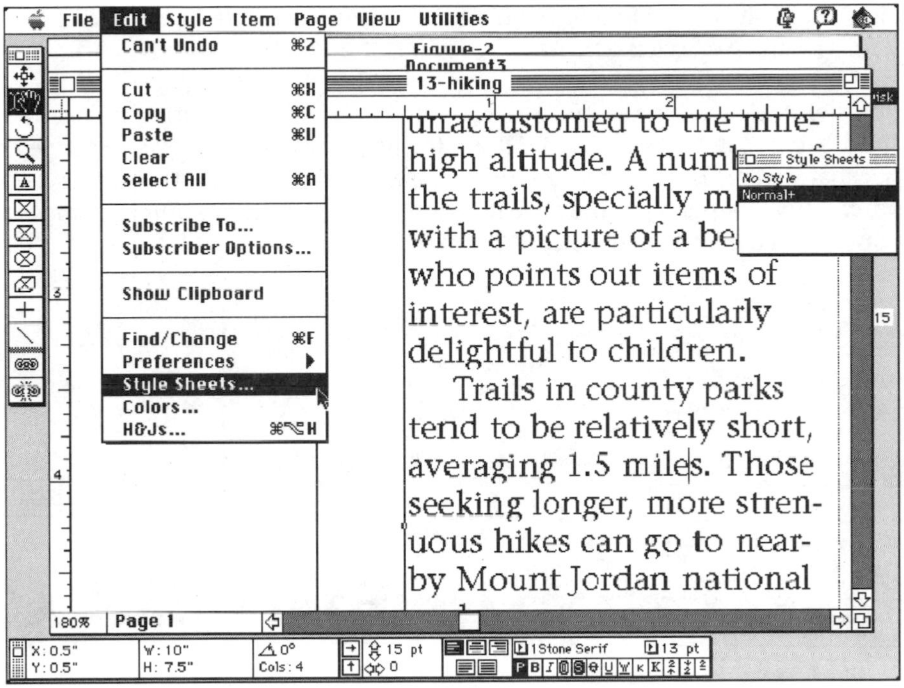

Editing Styles

To make edits to styles, you open the Style Sheets dialog box and select Edit. You can then change attributes as you want. You can also use this approach to create new styles that are based on current ones.

When you create styles for a document, you'll probably have several similar styles, and some may be variations of others. For example, you might have a body text style plus a style for bulleted lists that is based on the body text style.

Fortunately, QuarkXPress uses a technique called "based-on formatting" in its styles. You can tell QuarkXPress to base the Bulleted Text style on the Body Text style, in which you defined typeface, point size, leading, justification, hyphenation, indentation, tabs, and other attributes. You then modify the Bulleted Text style to accommodate bullets — by changing the indentation, for example. The great thing about based-on formatting is that later, if you decide to change the typeface in Body Text, the typeface automatically changes in Bulleted Text and in all other styles that you created or edited based on Body Text — saving you a lot of work in maintaining consistency of styles.

Figure 6-10 shows the Edit Style Sheet dialog box for a style named Head 1, which is based on the No Style style.

Another modification technique is simply to duplicate an existing style and then edit the attributes in that duplicate. Alternatively, you can edit an existing style and give it a new name. This is similar to creating a based-on style, except the new style is not automatically updated if the style it is duplicated from is modified — unless the style you duplicated or edited is based on another style.

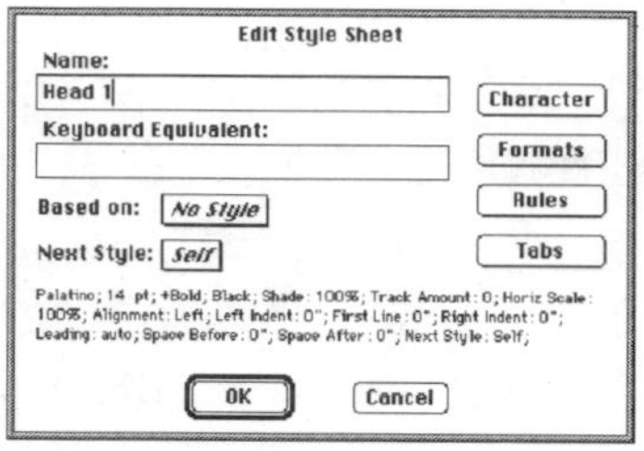

Figure 6-10:
The style description lists differences between the "Head 1" style and the "No Style" style on which it is based.

Importing Styles from QuarkXPress Documents

QuarkXPress lets you copy styles from one document to another. You do this by selecting the Append button in the Style Sheets dialog box. When you select Append, you open the Append Style Sheets dialog box (see Figure 6-11). This dialog box is similar to the dialog box for opening a QuarkXPress document. You can change drives and directories as needed to select the QuarkXPress document that has the style sheet you want.

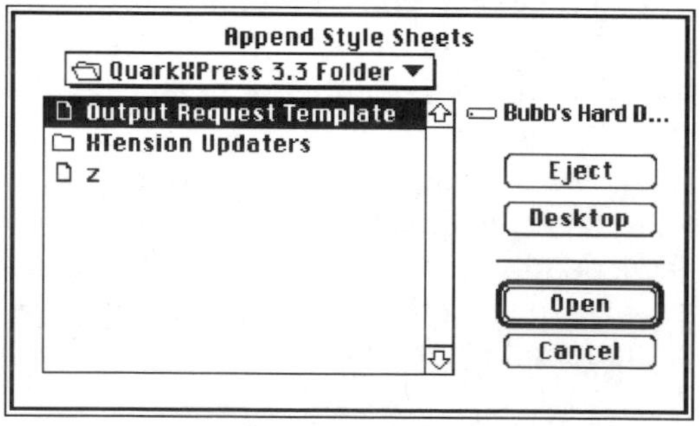

Figure 6-11:
The Append Style Sheets dialog box.

When you select a document and choose OK, QuarkXPress copies all of its styles into your current document. You cannot choose individual styles to import.

 If a style in the current document has the same name as a style you are importing, QuarkXPress preserves the current document's style and ignores the style in the other document. The program does not display an error message to tell you that a conflict occurred and was avoided.

 QuarkXPress cannot copy H&J sets associated with imported styles. If imported styles use H&J sets that are undefined in the current document, QuarkXPress displays an error message telling you that some style sheets to be appended use H&Js not defined in the current document. You then have the option to use the Standard H&J set in your current document or to cancel the style import. To avoid this error message, first use the Append button in the H&Js dialog box (Edit ⇨ H&Js, or Shift-⌘H) to import the H&J sets from the other document; then use the Append button in the Style Sheets dialog box to import the styles.

Importing Styles from Your Word Processor

QuarkXPress lets you import styles created in several word processors: most Macintosh word processors, including Microsoft Word and WordPerfect are included. When importing files with style sheets, make sure the Include Style Sheets box is checked, as shown in Figure 6-12.

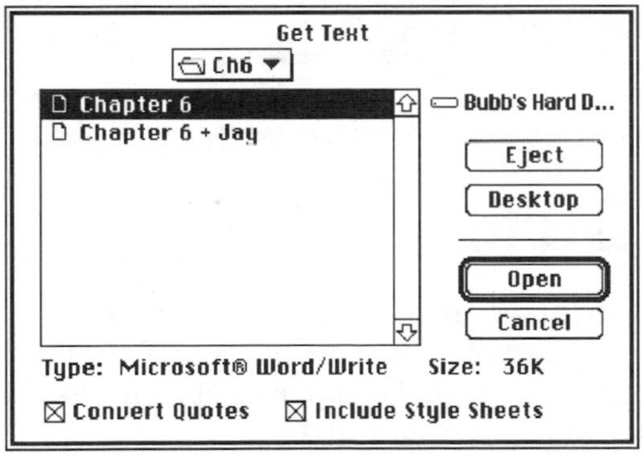

Figure 6-12:
Checking Include Style Sheets when you do a Get Text operation imports the word-processor document's style sheets as well as its text.

Get Text
🖿 Ch6 ▼
🗋 Chapter 6
🗋 Chapter 6 + Jay
▭ Bubb's Hard D...
Eject
Desktop
Open
Cancel
Type: Microsoft® Word/Write   Size: 36K
☒ Convert Quotes   ☒ Include Style Sheets

You also want to use the Include Style Sheets option if you are importing text saved in the XPress Tags format (described in the next chapter). Although the purpose of the XPress Tags format is to embed style tags and other formatting information in your text, you still must explicitly tell QuarkXPress to read those tags during import. Otherwise, QuarkXPress imports your text as an ASCII file, and all the embedded tags are treated as regular text and are not acted upon.

If you check the Include Style Sheets check box for formats that have no style sheets, QuarkXPress ignores the setting. Thus, if you typically import style sheets with your text, it's good to get in the habit of always checking this box; checking the box does not cause any problems when importing other text formats.

Unlike the Convert Quotes check box, the Include Style Sheets check box in QuarkXPress version 3.2 does not remain checked after you leave the Get Text dialog box. This is another reason to get in the habit of always checking this box if you use word processing style sheets routinely. (In version 3.3, the box does remain checked until you uncheck it.) Figure 6-13 shows a list of styles that we imported from a Microsoft Word document.

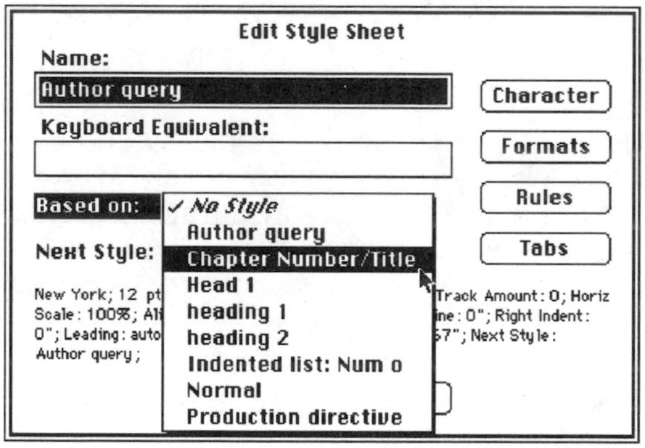

Figure 6-13:
Use the Based On option to make an imported word-processor style tag take on the attributes of a QuarkXPress style tag.

> **Edit Style Sheet**
>
> **Name:**
> Author query
>
> **Keyboard Equivalent:**
>
> **Based on:** ✓ *No Style*
> **Next Style:** Author query
>   **Chapter Number/Title**
>   Head 1
>   heading 1
>   heading 2
>   Indented list: Num o
>   Normal
>   Production directive
>
> New York; 12 pt
> Scale: 100%; All
> 0"; Leading: auto
> Author query ;
>
> Character
> Formats
> Rules
> Tabs
>
> Track Amount: 0; Horiz
> ine : 0"; Right Indent:
> 7"; Next Style:

Style Conflicts

The names of imported style tags are listed in the Style Sheets palette and can be edited like any other style. If the imported style sheet has a style tag that uses a name already in use by the QuarkXPress document, the imported style tag is renamed. The new name takes the form of the old name plus an asterisk (*).

This renaming feature ensures that you don't lose any formatting. But what if you want to use an existing QuarkXPress style tag on text that uses a word processor's style tag that is formatted differently? Consider this example:

℞ The QuarkXPress document has a style called Normal that, among other things, sets the text to 9-point Janson Text with a leading value of +2 points and uses a H&J set called 4 Hyphens Max that limits consecutive hyphens to four and sets the minimum character space to –5 percent.

℞ The text you want to import was created in Microsoft Word, and has a style called Normal that, among other things, sets the text to 12-point Courier and has a leading of 1.5 lines. There is no such thing as additive leading in a word processor, much less an H&J set. Even if the person who created the document could change the other style tag settings to match those in the QuarkXPress style, some tags simply will be different.

When you import your Word text with the Include Style Sheets box checked, QuarkXPress renames the Word style to Normal* because QuarkXPress has its own Normal style defined. But your goal is to have the text that was tagged Normal in Word take on the attributes of the QuarkXPress tag called Normal.

Before QuarkXPress 3.2, synchronizing these two styles was an awkward process: you could not rename the Normal* tag to Normal because the Normal tag already exists. If you deleted the Normal tag so that you could rename Normal*, you would lose Normal's definitions. But you could edit Normal* so that it was *based on* Normal. While this meant that you ended up with two tags in your document that do the same thing, you wouldn't have to tag each imported paragraph individually. But with QuarkXPress 3.2 and later, you can just delete the *Normal style in the Style Sheet dialog box and tell QuarkXPress to substitute Normal.

 You can quickly turn formatted text into styles by selecting any formatted text and using the New button in the Style Sheets dialog box; QuarkXPress transfers that formatting to a style, as described earlier in this chapter.

Overriding Styles

QuarkXPress is designed to give you the maximum control over typography; as a result, there are few global settings but many local settings. You can create several variations on global settings when creating style sheets or H&J sets, and you can override these styles at any time.

Most of your settings are contained in your style sheet, which the chapters in Part II explain in more detail. Because a style is the publishing equivalent of a macro, all paragraphs tagged with the Headline style, for example, take on the characteristics defined in the Headline style. But sometimes you want to override style settings. One example is when you want to italicize some text for emphasis. You must apply the italics locally to just those words you want italicized. The same is true for other font changes and spacing attributes, as well as special effects such as rotation and color. QuarkXPress offers several ways to override style settings:

- **Option 1:** You can define many font attributes — such as boldface, small caps, underline, and italics — in your word processor. QuarkXPress preserves this formatting in imported text even as it applies the styles. You can even define much formatting — such as typeface, type size, and justification — in Microsoft Word or a word processor that can save files in RTF format; when importing files into Quark, you check the Include Style Sheets option in the Get Text dialog box.

- **Option 2:** You can highlight text you want to change attributes of and then select the Style menu and pick from its many options. Alternatively, you can use the keyboard shortcuts that invoke commonly used dialog boxes and menus. These shortcuts are listed to the right of menu options that have them. For example, the Character Attributes dialog box shortcut is ⌘D.

- **Option 3:** You can use the QuarkXPress Measurements palette to change text options. (This powerful feature also lets you change text-box and picture-box settings. The box settings are on the left side of the palette.) If the palette is not on-screen, use View ⇨ Show Measurements to turn it on. Notice that the settings in the palette reflect whichever text is currently selected, providing a handy way to see what your settings are without using menus and dialog boxes.

- **Option 4:** You can create new styles on-the-fly as you discover you need them. For example, you may decide while creating a document that you want the first paragraph in each section to have a drop cap (a large letter set in several lines of text) to draw attention to it. Except for the fact that it has a drop cap and the first line is not indented, this lead paragraph is no different than body text. So simply create a new style (under Edit ⇨ Style Sheets ⇨ New), basing the new style on the body text style. Using the Based On option provides another advantage: If you later change the settings for, say, the typeface in your body text, all styles based on body text are instantly updated.

If you format text locally and then decide to create a new style from it, you can simply position the text cursor anywhere in the formatted text and use Edit ⇨ Style Sheets ⇨ New. This automatically applies all your local settings in the selected text to the new style you are creating.

If you format text locally (through the Style menu or Measurements palette) rather than through a style tag, and you later apply a tag to that locally format- ted text, your text may not take on all of the tag's settings. Because local formatting is designed to override global formatting, any formatting applied locally to the text is not overridden by the new style tag, even though that tag was applied after the local formatting. But any formatting not specifically applied locally reflects the style tag's settings. For example, if you apply font attributes locally but do not apply justification settings locally, justification changes when you apply a style tag with different H&J settings, but the font does not change.

■■

Summary

➡ Style sheets automate the application of a range of character and formatting attributes.

➡ All but two style sheet controls reside in the Edit ⇨ Style Sheets menu option. Hyphenation controls reside in Edit ⇨ H&Js, and character and space defaults are set in Edit ⇨ Preferences ⇨ Typographic.

➡ You can assign keyboard shortcuts for commonly used styles.

➡ The Based On feature lets you create a style that uses attributes defined in another style. If the source style changes, any unmodified attributes in the new style are automatically updated.

➡ QuarkXPress can import styles from other documents. But H&J sets are not copied across documents, and a style whose name is the same in both documents is not overridden. QuarkXPress preserves the style in the document to which styles are being imported.

➡ You cannot selectively import styles from a document — all nonduplicate styles are imported.

➡ Be sure to check the Include Style Sheets box in the Get Text dialog box before importing Word for Windows, WordPerfect, or RTF text whose style sheets you want to import. This box must be checked each time you enter the Get Text dialog box.

➡ By using QuarkXPress's Based On feature, you can have text tagged in a word processor take on the attributes of a QuarkXPress style tag instead of the word processor's style tag. Just edit the imported style tag so it is based on the QuarkXPress style.

➡ You can override global elements by selecting them and applying new formatting through the Style menu (for text) and Item menu (for picture boxes and text boxes).

■■

Preparing Files for Import

7 CHAPTER

- -

In This Chapter

- ➡ Determining which formatting tasks to do in QuarkXPress and which to handle in other programs

- ➡ Preparing files for import from word processors and graphics programs

- ➡ Working with special file formats

- -

Determining Where to Do Document Formatting _____

You can import text and graphics into your QuarkXPress documents in several ways. QuarkXPress is particularly adept at importing documents created in Macintosh formats. And through the Publish and Subscribe features described in Chapter 2, you can import file formats not directly supported by QuarkXPress.

QuarkXPress import capabilities may tempt you to do a lot of your text and graphic formatting outside the program; however, it's not always wise to do so. Here are some reasons why you shouldn't work outside the program:

- ➶ Because a word processor's style sheets won't match all QuarkXPress typographic features, it's often not worthwhile to do extensive formatting in your word processor. This is particularly true of layout-oriented formatting. Multiple columns and page numbers, for example, will be of a much higher standard in your final QuarkXPress document than you could hope to create in a word processor. After all, even the sophisticated formatting features in today's word processors don't begin to approach those needed for true publishing. (For more information on this subject, review the preceding chapter.)

⇘ Similarly, formatting tables in your word processor or spreadsheet is typically a wasted effort because you have to re-create the tables using QuarkXPress tab settings (see Chapter 16) or using a table-creation XTension like Npath's Tableworks Plus (see Chapter 27). If you turn your spreadsheet or chart into a graphic before importing it, you cannot edit the data. Nor can you resize the picture to fit a changing layout without winding up with different-size numbers among at least some charts — a definite no-no.

⇘ Some graphics tasks, including setting line screens and other halftone settings, background colors, and frames, are best-suited to QuarkXPress, since they relate to how the image is printed as part of the QuarkXPress document. For creating the actual artwork, of course, it does make sense to do extensive work in the originating program. After all, no desktop publishing program offers the kind of graphics tools that an illustration program or photo editor does.

Preparing Text Files

What preparation can you possibly need to do for your word processor files? They should just load into QuarkXPress as is, right? Not necessarily, even if your word processor supports one of the QuarkXPress text-import formats. Actually, the key to preparing text files is to not *over*-prepare them.

Most of today's major word processors include basic graphics and layout features to help users format single-document publications. Avoid using these features in files you intend to bring into QuarkXPress. Do your sophisticated formatting in QuarkXPress — that's one of the reasons you invested in such a powerful tool. This approach also enables you to do formatting in the context of your layout, rather than in a vacuum. Much of the graphics and layout formatting you do in a word processor is all for naught anyway because such nontextual formatting does not import into QuarkXPress. Remember, you're importing text, not documents.

Limit your word processor formatting to the type of formatting that enhances reader understanding or conveys meaning. Such formatting may include using italics and boldface to emphasize a word, for example, or using style sheets to set headlines and bylines in different sizes and typefaces. (See the preceding chapter for tips on using style sheets in word processor text.) Let your editors focus on the words; leave presentation tasks to your layout artists.

Translating Text Files

One type of file preparation you may need to do is to translate text files into formats supported by QuarkXPress. The following tips can help you work with popular word processors:

- ꙮ QuarkXPress supports the major Macintosh word processors — Microsoft Word 3.0 and later, WordPerfect 1.0 and later, WriteNow 3.0, Microsoft Works 2.0, and Claris MacWrite and MacWrite II.

- ꙮ QuarkXPress does not support the Rich Text Format used by most Microsoft programs, as well as by some other word processors and publishing programs.

- ꙮ QuarkXPress does not support DOS or Windows versions of Word, Works, or WordPerfect; you must save these files in the Mac format before importing them into QuarkXPress. (The Mac versions of Word and WordPerfect can read their DOS and Windows counterparts.)

- ꙮ QuarkXPress supports ASCII (text-only) files, however you should avoid using them. ASCII files cannot handle any character formatting, so you must do a lot of clean-up work in QuarkXPress. Although programs must continue to support ASCII text because it is the only universally supported format, use ASCII as a last resort.

Preserving Special Features in Text Files

Today's word processors let you do much more than enter and edit text. You also can create special characters, tables, headers and footers, and other document elements. Some of these features work when imported into a publishing program, but others don't. Table 7-1 shows which character formatting is preserved for the two most popular Mac word processors: Word and WordPerfect.

Table 7-1		
Imported Character Formatting		
Format	*Word*	*WordPerfect*
Character Formatting		
All caps	yes	NA
Boldface	yes	yes

(continued)

Table 7-1 *(continued)*

Format	Word	WordPerfect
Color	yes	yes
Condense/expand	yes	NA
Font change	yes	yes
Hidden	no	NA
Italics	yes	yes
Outline	yes	yes
Overlays	NA	no
Point size	yes	yes
Shadow	yes	yes
Small caps	yes	yes
Strikethrough	yes	yes
Subscript	yes	yes
Superscript	yes	yes
Underline	yes[5]	yes[5]
Word-only underline	yes	no[5]
Other formatting		
Annotations	no	NA
Date/time	yes	no
Drop caps	yes[3]	yes
Footnotes	yes[2]	no
Overlays	NA	no
Page breaks	yes	no
Pictures	yes[6]	no
Redlining	NA	no
Section breaks	yes[1]	NA
Special characters	yes	yes
Subscribed items	no[7]	no
Tables	yes[4]	no

NA = Not available in this program.

[1] = Treated as a page break.   [2] = Placed at end of text.   [3] = Drop cap is made into its own paragraph.

[4] = Converted to tabbed text.   [5] = All underlining converted to single underlines.

[6] = Document's internal preview of the placed image is converted to PICT; the original file itself is not imported into QuarkXPress.

[7] = Text items are converted to plain text; picture items are removed.

Tables

We stated before that you should do table formatting in QuarkXPress, not in your word processor. But there is an exception to the rule: If you use style sheets to format a table with tabs in your word processor, by all means, import the formatted table into QuarkXPress — you can then modify the styles, if necessary, as your layout changes. If, however, you create tables with the word professor's table feature, expect the table to be stripped out during import into QuarkXPress.

Headers and footers

Headers and footers are a layout issue, not a text issue, so there is no reason to include these elements in your word processor document. Because page numbers will change based on your QuarkXPress layout, there's no point in putting the headers and footers in your word processor document anyway. Note that if you do use them, they will not import into QuarkXPress. Chapter 11 explains how to add these elements to your layout.

Footnotes

If you use a word processor's footnote feature and import the text file, the footnotes are placed at the end of the imported text. The superscripted numerals or characters in the footnotes may or may not translate properly.

In-line graphics

Mac word processors typically support in-line graphics, enabling you to import a picture into your word processor document and embed it in text. Word and WordPerfect for Mac both let you import graphics, and QuarkXPress, in turn, can import the graphics with your text. Graphics embedded in your word processor document via Publish and Subscribe or via OLE (a similar scheme from Microsoft) will not import into QuarkXPress.

Using Special Characters

The Mac has built-in support for special characters, such as symbols, accented characters, and non-English letters. There are several ways to access these characters:

- ✎ Using keyboard shortcuts.

- ✎ Using Apple's KeyCaps program, which comes with the System and is accessible via the Apple menu. The figure below shows the program. The two sets of special characters are found by holding Option and Option-Shift (each results in a different set).

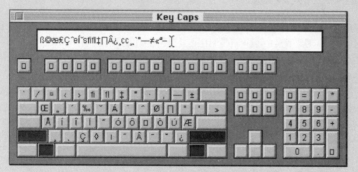

- ✎ Using a shareware utility like Gunther Blaschek's PopChar control panel (called a cdev in System 6), which is available on several bulletin boards, including the DTP Forum on CompuServe (see figure below). Notice how the keyboard shortcut for each special character is shown at the upper right as a character is highlighted.

- ✎ Using a utility like the KeyFinder program supplied with Symantec's Norton Utilities 2.0. The figure on the next page shows the program. Like KeyCaps, this is usually installed in the Apple menu.

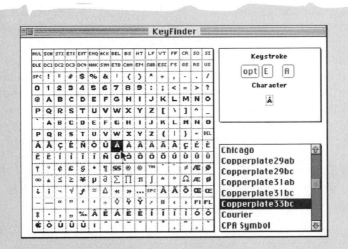

- Using a word processor's own feature for special-character access. The most popular Mac word processor, Microsoft Word, has such an option via Insert ⇨ Symbol or via the toolbar (look for the icon with the ¿á characters). WordPerfect has a similar dialog box accessed via Font ⇨ Character Map (see the figures below).

Note that not all fonts may have all special characters available. Typically, fonts from major type foundries like Adobe and Bitstream have all the characters in each font, but custom-made fonts and those from other foundries may use different characters or have fewer. Also, fonts translated from Windows through a program like Altsys's Fontographer or Ares Software's FontMonger will likely have special characters in different locations than a native Mac font, and will generally have fewer special characters in the font.

In-line graphics will import as their PICT previews, not as the original formats. This means that you'll get a lower-resolution version in your QuarkXPress layout.

Despite their limitations, the use of in-line graphics in your word processor can be helpful when putting together a QuarkXPress document: Use the in-line graphics whose PICT previews are imported into QuarkXPress as placeholders so that the layout artist knows you have embedded graphics. He or she can then replace the PICT previews with the better-quality originals. If you find yourself using several graphics as characters (such as a company icon used as a bullet), use a font-creation program like Altsys's Fontographer or Ares Software's FontMonger to create a symbol typeface with those graphics. Then both your word processor and layout documents can use the same, high-quality versions.

Avoiding Other Text-file Pitfalls

Sometimes, issues not related to the contents of a word processor file can affect how files are imported into QuarkXPress.

Fast save

Several programs (notably Microsoft Word) offer a fast-save feature, which adds information to the end of a word processor document. The added information notes which text has been added and deleted and where the changes occurred. You can use this feature to save time because the program doesn't have to write the entire document to disk when you save the file. When you use the fast-save feature, however, text-import into publishing programs — including QuarkXPress — becomes problematic. We suggest that you turn off fast save, at least for files you import into QuarkXPress. With today's speedy hard drives, the time you gain by using fast save is barely noticeable, anyway.

Figure 7-1 shows the dialog box for Word 5.1 (Tools ⇨ Preferences ⇨ Open and Save). You turn fast save on and off in this dialog box. You don't need to worry about whether fast save is enabled if you use Save As or Export options to save the file either in a format other than the word processor's native format or to a different name or location.

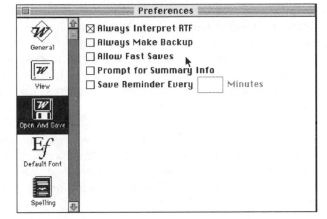

Figure 7-1:
Uncheck the Fast
Save option in
Microsoft Word files
you import into
QuarkXPress.

Software versions

Pay attention to the version number of the word processor you use. This caution may seem obvious, but the issue still trips up a lot of people. Usually, old versions (two or more revisions old) or new versions (newer than the publishing or other importing program) cause import problems. The import filters either no longer recognize the old format (something has to go to make room for new formats) or were written before the new version of the word processor was released. QuarkXPress is compatible with Claris MacWrite 5.0 and MacWrite II, Microsoft Works 1.1 through 2.0, Microsoft Word 3.0 through 5.1, WordPerfect 1.0 through 2.1, and WordStar (formerly T/Maker) WriteNow 2.0 through 3.0.

Using XPress Tags

QuarkXPress offers a file format of its own: XPress Tags. XPress Tags actually is ASCII (text-only) text that contains embedded codes to tell QuarkXPress which formatting to apply. You embed these codes, which are similar to macros, as you create files in your word processor.

Most people do not use this option because the coding can be tortuous. You cannot use XPress Tags in conjunction with your word processor's formatting. If you create a file in Microsoft Word, for example, you cannot use XPress Tags to apply a style to a paragraph while using Word's own boldface and italics formatting for text. You either code everything with XPress Tags and save the document as an ASCII file, or you don't use XPress Tags at all. This either-or situation is too bad because the ability to combine a publishing program's formatting codes with a word processor's formatting features adds both power and flexibility — as users of Corel Ventura Publisher and Aldus PageMaker know.

So why have XPress Tags at all? Because this format is the one format sure to support all the formatting you do in QuarkXPress. Its usefulness is not in creating text for import, but in transferring files created in QuarkXPress to another QuarkXPress user (including someone using the Windows version) or to a word processor for further work. You can export a QuarkXPress story or piece of selected text in the XPress Tags format and then transfer the exported file to another QuarkXPress user or to a word processor for further editing.

Exporting an XPress Tags file into a word processor makes sense if you want to add or delete text without losing special formatting — such as fonts, kerning, or style tags — that your word processor doesn't support. After you edit the text, you can save the altered file (make sure that it is saved as ASCII text) and reimport it into your QuarkXPress layout.

Appendix C of the QuarkXPress manual defines the 61 XPress Tags codes and their variants that you embed in your text file. These codes range from the simple, such as <I> for italicized text, to the moderately complex. The following code is for a 2-point, 100-percent red rule that uses line style 1, is indented 18 points to the right and left of the column, is offset 25 percent, and is placed above the current paragraph:

```
<*ra(02,1,"Red",100,18,18,25%>
```

Basically, you can use as many of the 61 XPress Tags codes as needed, and place them between < and > characters. In the preceding example, we are using the *ra code (which stands for right aligned) and filling in the parameters it expects.

Some codes are programming-level codes, for which you define the style tags by combining as many of the 61 basic XPress Tags codes as appropriate. The following example defines a style called *Lead* as black, 9.5-point Cheltenham Book Plain with a four-line drop cap, 12 points of leading, a 10-point first-line indent, no left or right indents, no space above, 100-percent shade and scale, full justification, and locked to the baseline grid:

```
@Lead=<*J*p(0,10,0,12,0,0,G)*d(1,4)f"Cheltenham Book"j"black z9.5s100h100P>
```

The = after @Lead in the preceding example signals QuarkXPress to *define* the Lead style with the codes between the angle brackets.

To use that style, you type **@Lead:** at the beginning of the paragraph you want to format; the colon tells QuarkXPress to *use* the style tag. (You can't apply a style tag that you did not define earlier in your text file.)

In practical terms, you may not mind editing XPress Tags slightly or leaving them in a file when you alter its text. But you're not likely to forgo the friendly formatting available in your word processor and in QuarkXPress to apply XPress Tags coding to everything in your text files.

Preparing Tabular Data for Import

QuarkXPress has no filters to accept files in formats such as Lotus 1-2-3, Microsoft Excel, Claris FileMaker Pro, or Microsoft FoxBase Pro. That means you have two basic options for preparing files that contain tabular information (usually spreadsheets or databases) for import:

- **Option 1:** Save the files as tab-delimited ASCII text. Then import them and apply the appropriate tab stops (either directly or through styles) to create the desired table. Or paste the data (into a QuarkXPress text box) into your document through the Mac clipboard; it will be pasted as tab-delimited ASCII text.

- **Option 2:** Use the file as a graphic by using a charting tool (such as that in Excel or Lotus 1-2-3). Paste the chart via the Mac clipboard or use Publish and Subscribe (see Chapter 24).

If you choose the latter option, make sure that you size all charts and tables the same way so that the size of the numbers in them, when imported and placed, is consistent throughout your QuarkXPress document. Use a vector format like PICT or EPS whenever possible to ensure the best reproduction quality no matter what size you scale the chart graphics to.

Preparing Graphics Files

QuarkXPress offers support for all major formats of Mac graphics files. Some formats are more appropriate than others for certain kinds of tasks. The basic rules are as follows:

- Save line art in a format such as EPS or PICT. (These object-oriented formats are called *vector* formats. Vector files are composed of instructions on how to draw various shapes.)

- Save bitmaps (photos and scans) in a format such as TIFF, MacPaint, Photo CD, RIFF, or PICT. (These pixel-oriented formats are called *raster* formats. Raster files are composed of a series of dots, or pixels, that make up the image.)

QuarkXPress imports the new Kodak Photo CD format, which is used on CD-ROM discs containing digitized photographs. The filter to import Photo CD is not automatically installed when you install QuarkXPress; if you intend to work with this format, be sure to add the XTension when installing or to move it from the Other XTensions subfolder to the main QuarkXPress folder.

 PICT files can be in vector or bitmap format depending on the original image and the program in which it was created or exported from. If you enlarge a PICT image and it begins to look blocky, it is a bitmap.

 The Mac version of QuarkXPress supports fewer graphics formats than the Windows version because of the de facto standardization by Mac users around a core set of formats. If you are working in a multiplatform environment, standardize on EPS and TIFF formats so that your images are usable by both versions of QuarkXPress. Most programs export or save in these formats.

 If you output to high-end PostScript systems, make EPS and TIFF formats your standards. EPS files can use PostScript fonts; can be color-separated if produced in a program such as Adobe Illustrator, Aldus FreeHand, or Deneba Canvas; and can support an extremely large set of graphical attributes. You also can manipulate gray-scale TIFF files in QuarkXPress to apply custom contrasts, line screens, and other photographic effects.

EPS files

EPS files come in several varieties — not every EPS file is the same. You see the most noticeable differences when you import EPS files into QuarkXPress.

Preview headers

The preview header is a displayable copy of the EPS file; because the Mac doesn't use PostScript to display screen images, it can't interpret a PostScript file directly — which is why many programs add a preview header to the EPS files they create.

First, you may not see anything but a big gray rectangle and the words `PostScript Picture` when you import an EPS file. The file either has no preview header or its header is in an unreadable format. This condition is typical for EPS files transferred from the Mac, which uses a different header format. Although the image prints correctly, it's hard to position and crop because you must repeatedly print your page to see the effects of your work.

When you first get the picture, you can see whether there is a preview by checking the Picture Preview box. As you click on a file, a preview will appear; if the preview is gray, that means there is no preview. The Type field under the list of file names will tell you what sort of file the image is.

If your picture lacks a usable preview header, use this workaround: After you print an EPS graphic, use the Item ⇨ Constrain option to add a polygon picture box inside the picture box containing the EPS file. Edit the polygon so that it becomes an outline of the EPS graphic. (This method ensures both that the outline is the right size and that it moves with the picture box as the layout changes.) Then use this outline as a guide to wrap text around or otherwise manipulate the EPS file. (See Chapter 11 for details of the Constrain option; Chapter 10 covers picture boxes.)

To generate an acceptable image header in an EPS file created on the Mac, save the file with a Mac header. This is the default for most Mac programs. In Adobe Illustrator 5.0, the default is to have no header; change that to Color Macintosh when saving. (Illustrator's native format is EPS, so don't look for an export or save-as option.)

None of the major Windows programs can generate the appropriate header. CorelDRAW generates a low-resolution black-and-white preview (even with the high-resolution option selected) for its color files. Adobe Illustrator 4.0 generates no Mac-compatible preview. Like CorelDRAW, Computer Support Corp.'s Arts & Letters Graphics Editor generates only a black-and-white preview, and then only if you select TIFF for the preview format (use the Setup button in the Export dialog box).

Color values

To take advantage of QuarkXPress color-separation features for imported EPS files, you need to create the colors correctly. (If you intend to print your file on a color printer rather than have it separated, don't worry about the following instructions.)

If you create color images in an illustration program, make sure that you create them using the CMYK color model or using a named spot color. If you use CMYK, the color is, in effect, preseparated. With QuarkXPress 3.3, any colors defined in an EPS file are automatically added to the Colors palette for your document and set as a spot color (you can change it to a process color via Edit ⇨ Colors; see Chapter 21 for details). If you are using an earlier version of QuarkXPress and are importing an EPS file that uses a spot color, define the same color with the same name in QuarkXPress — either as a process color, if you want it separated into cyan, magenta, yellow, and black plates, or as a spot color, if you want it to print on its own plate. (Defining colors is covered in Chapter 21.)

If your program follows Adobe's EPS specifications (Aldus FreeHand and Adobe Illustrator both do), QuarkXPress will color-separate your EPS file, no matter whether it uses process or spot colors. Canvas automatically converts Pantone spot colors to process colors in your choice of RGB and CMYK models. For other programs, create your colors in the CMYK model to be sure they will print as color separations from QuarkXPress.

 The *CV* after the Pantone Matching System color number in the Illustrator and QuarkXPress dialog boxes means *computer video,* which is Pantone's way of warning you that what you see on-screen may not be what you get in print. Because of the different physics underlying monitors and printing presses, colors cannot be matched precisely, even with color calibration. This is true for other color models, such as Focoltone and Trumatch.

 Most artists use Pantone to specify desired colors, so keep a Pantone swatch book handy to see which CMYK values equal the desired Pantone color. (One of the available Pantone swatch books — *The Pantone Process Color Imaging Guide CMYK Edition* — shows each Pantone color next to the CMYK color build used to simulate it.)

If you don't have the Pantone swatch book, you can define the color in QuarkXPress as a Pantone color and then switch color models to CMYK. QuarkXPress immediately converts the Pantone color to CMYK, and then you know which value to use in your illustration program (if it doesn't support Pantone itself). Many high-end illustration programs, including Adobe Illustrator, support Pantone and can do this instant conversion as well. If available (as it is in QuarkXPress), use the Pantone Process color model because that is designed for output using CMYK printing presses.

 For more information on defining colors and working with color images, see Chapter 21 in Part VI.

Calibrated color

 With the bundled EfiColor XTension installed, QuarkXPress will color-separate non-CMYK files. (Version 3.2 of QuarkXPress will not color-separate non-CMYK EPS files unless you define all the colors used in that EPS file in QuarkXPress as process colors.) It will also calibrate the output colors (whether printed to a color printer or color-separated for traditional printing) based on the source device and the target output device.

When importing color files, be sure to change the color profile assigned by EfiColor (if you are using this XTension) for images created by devices other than the source. For example, your default profile for RGB images may be Apple 13" RGB because the TIFF and PICT files you usually use were created on a Mac with this type of monitor. But if you are importing a scanned image, you should change the profile to match that particular scanner. You do so by choosing the appropriate file from the pick list at the EfiColor Profile option (under the list of files). Note that it may take a moment for QuarkXPress to display that pick list because first it scans the image to see if it contains a profile of its own (called a Metric Color Tag, or MCT). You can also change an image's profile after it is imported (via Style ⇨ Profile).

 Chapter 20 explains how to work with gray-scale images, while Part VI explains how to work with color images. Chapter 26 covers issues involving outputting such images.

Fonts

When you use fonts in text included in your graphics files, you usually have the option to convert the text to curves (graphics). This option ensures that your text will print on any printer.

If you don't use this conversion before making an EPS file, make sure that your printer or service bureau has the fonts used in the graphic. Otherwise, the text does not print in the correct font (you will likely get Courier or Helvetica instead). Remember that QuarkXPress does not show fonts used in graphics in its Font Usage dialog box, so your layout artists and service bureau have no way of knowing which fonts to have available.

DCS

The Document Color Separation variant of EPS is a set of five files: an EPS preview file that links together four separation files (one each for cyan, magenta, yellow, and black). Use of this format ensures correct color separation when you output negatives for use in commercial printing. These files are often preferred over standard EPS files by service bureaus that do color correction.

PICT

The standard Macintosh format for drawings, PICT (which stands for *Picture*) also supports bitmaps and is the standard format for Macintosh screen-capture utilities. QuarkXPress imports PICT files with no difficulty. Colors cannot be color-separated unless the EfiColor XTension is installed. Because fonts in vector PICT graphics are translated to curves, you need not worry about whether fonts used in your graphics are resident in your printer or available at your service bureau.

Bitmap formats

Bitmap (also called *raster*) formats are simpler than vector formats because they are made up of rows of dots (*pixels*), not instructions on how to draw various shapes. But that doesn't mean that all bitmaps are alike.

TIFF

The most popular bitmap format for publishers is TIFF, the *Tagged Image File Format* developed by Aldus Corp. and Microsoft Corp. TIFF supports color up to 24 bits (16.7 million colors) in both RGB and CMYK models, and every major photo-editing program supports TIFF on both the Macintosh and in Windows.

But TIFF comes in several variants, and no program, including QuarkXPress, supports all of them. You should have no difficulty if you use the uncompressed and LZW-compressed formats supported by most Mac programs (and increasingly by Windows programs). If you do have difficulty, we recommend that you use uncompressed TIFF files.

The biggest advantage to using TIFF files rather than other formats that also support color, such as PICT, is that QuarkXPress is designed to take advantage of TIFF. QuarkXPress can work with the contrast settings in gray-scale TIFF images to make an image clearer or to apply special effects — something QuarkXPress can't do with any other bitmap format (see Chapter 20).

If you want to color-separate your QuarkXPress document, you must save your TIFF file in CMYK format (Adobe Photoshop supports this format) because QuarkXPress cannot color-separate non-CMYK files unless the EfiColor XTension is installed.

RIFF

This compressed relative of TIFF is a rarely used format (Fractal Design Painter is an exception). It works similarly to TIFF.

PCX

Version 3.3 of QuarkXPress added support for the PCX (PC Paintbrush) format popular on PCs. Like TIFF, PCX supports color, gray-scale, and black-and-white images.

PICT

PICT, the standard Macintosh format for drawings, also supports bitmaps and is the standard format for Macintosh screen-capture utilities. QuarkXPress imports PICT files with no difficulty. With the EfiColor XTension installed, QuarkXPress will color-separate PICT files.

Photo CD

Like other bitmap formats, no special preparation for this file format is necessary — which is great, considering that users have no control over the image format because it is created by service bureaus converting 35mm film to digital images via Kodak's proprietary process. With the EfiColor XTension, QuarkXPress can color-separate Photo CD files.

If you are using Photo CD files, keep in mind that you need two extensions installed in your System folder: Apple Photo Access and QuickTime, neither of which comes with a Mac's System disks. Both are usually included on Photo CD products, however. (You need QuickTime because Photo CD files are saved using a compression method that QuickTime supports.) Note that you need these extensions even if you are importing Photo CD images copied from a CD onto a hard disk or other medium, not just if you are accessing the images directly from a CD-ROM drive (see Figure 7-2).

Figure 7-2:
The Apple Photo Access and QuickTime extensions are needed to open Photo CD files.

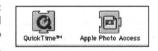

Also, Photo CD images are stored in five resolutions on the CD. If you import the image from the CD's Images folder, you will get the highest-resolution image, which can take several megabytes. It's better to go into the subfolders and select a lower-resolution version, such as 768 by 512 or 192 by 128. The smaller you print the image, the less resolution you need.

JPEG

Version 3.3 of QuarkXPress added support for the JPEG (Joint Photographers Expert Group) compressed color-image format, which is used for very large images and the individual images comprising an animation or movie. Images compressed in this format may lose detail.

Summary

→ Don't apply layout-oriented formatting in your word processor document — that's what QuarkXPress is designed to do.

→ Use style sheets if your word processor supports them.

→ Don't format tables in your word processor unless you do it by defining tab stops in a style sheet that you can import into QuarkXPress and modify further.

→ Create complex graphics in a graphics program, not in QuarkXPress.

→ Avoid using ASCII format for your text because it does not support character formatting.

→ The preview images for in-line graphics in your word processor file import into QuarkXPress, but embedded Publish and Subscribe and OLE graphics do not.

→ Turn off any fast-save feature in your word processor for files you intend to import into QuarkXPress (or elsewhere).

→ Use the XPress Tags format to transfer heavily formatted QuarkXPress stories to other QuarkXPress users (Mac or Windows). Also use XPress Tags if you need to edit a heavily formatted story in your word processor and reimport it into QuarkXPress. (You can export stories in the XPress Tags format from your QuarkXPress layout.)

→ Save spreadsheet and database data as tab-delimited ASCII files; then, in QuarkXPress, use a style with appropriate tab-stop definitions to format the data.

→ EPS and TIFF are the preferred formats for line art and bitmaps, respectively.

→ EPS files without a preview header recognizable to QuarkXPress appear on-screen as a gray box, but they will print correctly.

→ With the EfiColor XTension installed, QuarkXPress can color-separate most graphics. In version 3.2, a major exception was EPS; if you have color EPS files, make sure they are saved in the CMYK or DCS variants. Version 3.3 removes this exception.

→ Make sure that fonts used in EPS graphics are in your printer or available to your service bureau. Alternatively, convert text to curves.

→ QuarkXPress can manipulate gray-scale values only in TIFF images.

Page Layout

III

Whether you do so consciously or not, the first thing you notice when you look at a document is its layout. Even before you perceive what a document is all about, assimilate the contents of a graphic, or scan the text, you form an impression of the document based on its construction — particularly the arrangement of text and graphics on each page.

Effective layout is critical to how well readers receive the rest of your document — the text, the typographic effects, the headlines, the photos, the graphic, and even the content. Skill with layout takes time, training, and an eye for good design. QuarkXPress can give you the tools but not the talent. By taking the time to think through the design process, you'll continue to develop your skills at designing layouts that complement the document's content and are inviting to the reader.

This section first discusses good layout strategies and approaches and then shows how to use QuarkXPress's layout tools to implement those layouts.

Getting Started with Layout

CHAPTER 8

In This Chapter

- ➡ Tips on how to design a document layout
- ➡ How to set measurement preferences
- ➡ Ways of viewing the document on-screen
- ➡ How to use guides and rulers
- ➡ How to group, constrain, and lock layout elements

Seven Basic Tips for Good Design

Like other desktop publishing programs, QuarkXPress lets you control how a document will look when you have finished creating it. But to really make the most of this powerful tool, you need to understand some basic ideas about page design. Of course, if you are a trained graphic designer, you already know the basics; you can immediately put QuarkXPress to use, creating effective layouts. But if you are new to the field, try keeping the following Seven Basic Tips in mind as you begin learning about layout:

1. **Keep an idea file.** As you read magazines, books, newspapers, annual reports, ads, and brochures, pick the page layouts you like, and also keep copies of those you dislike. Keep these layouts — good and bad — in a file, along with notes to yourself about which aspects of the layout work well and which work poorly. As you build your layout file, you educate yourself on layout basics.

2. **Plan your document.** It sounds corny, but it's true: laying out a document is a lot like taking a journey. If you know where you're headed, it's much easier to find your way. Because QuarkXPress makes it easy to experiment as you design a document, it's also easy to end up with a messy conglomeration of text and pictures. You can avoid this pitfall by knowing ahead of time what you are trying to accomplish with the document's layout.

3. **Keep it simple.** When it comes to page layout, simple is better. Even the most experienced, trained graphic designers can tell you that this rule applies at least 99 percent of the time. If you are just beginning to learn how to lay out pages, you'll make far fewer design mistakes if you follow this rule. Regardless of the application, simple layouts are appealing in their crispness, their readability, and their straightforward, no-gimmicks approach.

4. **Leave some white space on the page.** Pages that are crammed full of text and pictures tend to be off-putting — meaning that the average, busy reader is likely to skip them. Keep some space between text columns and headlines and between page edges and layout elements. White space is refreshing and encourages the reader to spend some time on the page. Regardless of the particular document type, readers always appreciate having a place on every page to rest their eyes, a place that offers an "oasis in a sea of ink."

5. **Don't use every bell and whistle.** QuarkXPress is powerful, yes, but that doesn't mean that it is necessarily a good idea to push the program to its limits. You can, for example, lay out a page with 30 columns of text, but would you want to try reading such a page? With QuarkXPress, you can achieve an amazing number of special effects: You can rotate text, skew text and graphics, make linear blends, add colors, stretch and condense type, and bleed photos or artwork off the edge of the page. But using all of these effects at once can overwhelm readers and cause them to miss any message you are trying to convey. A good rule: Use no more than three special typographic or design effects per two-page spread.

6. **Lay out the document so that someone looking at it can get an idea of what it is.** This sounds like a common-sense rule, but you'd be surprised at how often this rule is broken. If you are laying out an ad for a product, make sure the layout *looks* like an ad, not like a technical brochure.

7. **Don't break rule number 6 unless you know what you are doing.** Creativity is OK, and QuarkXPress helps you express your layout ideas creatively. But don't get carried away. If you are laying out a technical brochure, for example, don't make it look like a display ad unless you understand that this may confuse readers, and you are doing it for a reason.

Figure 8-1 shows two pages that contain the same information but use different layouts. The page on the left has body text set close to the headline. The leading is tight, and except for a spot around the illustration, the white space is in short supply. Notice how the page on the right has a lighter look. Which page are you more inclined to read?

Figure 8-1:
To make your documents more inviting, try to include ample white space, as in the example on the right.

Types of Layouts

Documents come in a variety of shapes and sizes. The most successful documents are those with an appearance that complements their content. In many kinds of documents, you can use several layout styles. Within a multipage document, the layout of any single page typically depends on the overall purpose of the document and on where the individual page appears in relation to other pages.

Some pages have a *stand-alone layout* because the document itself consists of a single page, or because that particular page falls into a layout type that is either not used elsewhere in the document or is used sparingly. An example of a stand-alone layout is the title page of a book or a similar document. Because that page is unique, its layout is not repeated on subsequent pages.

Some pages include elements that are *linked* to other elements on the same page or to elements on other pages in the document. (We'll get to an explanation about how to link text boxes later.) For an example of linked elements, consider a typical magazine (or newsletter) article, in which some of the body copy appears within one column or page and the rest appears within another column or page. The two pieces of body copy are linked elements.

Other layout elements, such as headlines, sidebars, and tables, are related to each other. Still other elements are repeating elements; examples include page numbers and folios.

 If your document has a title page or another page with a stand-alone, nonrecurring layout, in the interest of time, you can choose not to develop a style sheet or master page for the page. Master pages and style sheets are covered in Chapters 5 and 6.

Although a full discussion on types of layout is beyond the scope of this book, a brief overview is useful as a background for explaining some of the steps involved in developing layout types. Let's look briefly at some of the most commonly used approaches to layout: horizontal layouts, vertical layouts, facing pages and spreads, and bleeds.

Horizontal layouts

Horizontal layouts often include elements in a variety of widths, with the overall effect being one that moves the reader's eye from left to right. A horizontal layout is often used in announcements, product flyers, and other marketing collateral pieces. In the sample brochure (see Figure 8-2), the landscape orientation, placement of the columns, and location of the illustration all contribute to draw the eye from left to right.

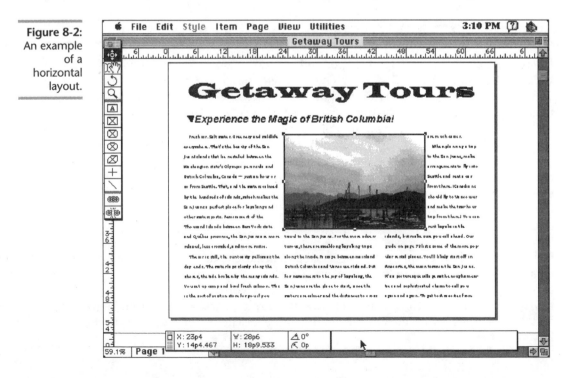

Figure 8-2:
An example
of a
horizontal
layout.

We devised the layout in Figure 8-2 by first setting up an 8½ × 11-inch page (in landscape orientation) with three columns, and then running the masthead logo and headline across the width of the columns. The picture starts at the second column so that the eye can easily find the text at the top of the first column.

Vertical layouts

Layouts with a vertical orientation are typical of what you find in most traditional newspapers. The text is presented in long, vertical sections, often with headlines or subheads that are the width of a single column. In addition to newspapers, newsletters and other common corporate documents lend themselves to a vertical orientation (see Figure 8-3).

We created the layout in Figure 8-3 by setting up a letter-size page with three columns. The masthead runs across the width of the three columns, one kicker and headline run across the width of the first two columns, and one headline on a secondary article runs across the width of the third column.

Figure 8-3:
Example of a
vertical
layout,
typically
used in
newspapers,
newsletters,
and other
corporate
documents.

Facing pages and spreads

Facing pages are commonly used in multipage documents that have material printed on both sides of the paper, such as newsletters and magazines. Whenever you open a new document, even if you select Automatic Text Box in the New dialog box (File ➪ New), QuarkXPress creates one new master page for the document's right-hand page. If you select Automatic Text Box, QuarkXPress allows you to create master pages in addition to the single new master page.

If you are creating a facing-pages document that is longer than two pages, it's worth taking the time to set up the master pages for right- and left-side pages. As you read in Chapter 5, master pages for facing-pages documents let you specify elements (text, graphics, page numbers, and so on) that you want to repeat on similarly oriented pages throughout the document.

It's easy to find out whether a document has right and left master pages. From the View menu, select Show Document Layout to display the Document Layout palette. Figure 8-4 shows a two-page, facing-pages document and its Document Layout palette. The bent upper corner for the page icons in the palette indicates a left or right page master.

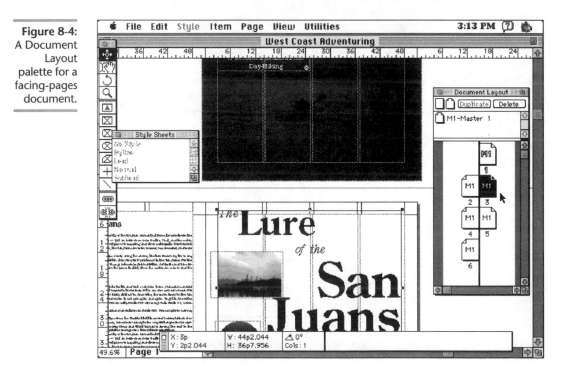

Figure 8-4:
A Document Layout palette for a facing-pages document.

Documents with facing pages tend to have one or both of the following characteristics:

⍟ Alternating headers and footers on even- and odd-numbered pages. An example of an alternating footer is a page number; if you want the page number to print on the outside bottom corner of the page, the footers on right and left master pages differ from each other.

⍟ An inside margin large enough to accommodate the binding or the spreading of pages as the reader reads the document.

What happens if you work on a facing-pages document for a while and then decide you want to lay it out single-sided? The answer is easy: turn off Facing Pages by choosing File ⇨ Document Setup, which displays the Document Setup dialog box. Then click the Facing Pages box to deselect it.

QuarkXPress allows you to create layouts that span two or more side-by-side pages, or *spreads.* Spreads are made up of pages that are adjacent to each other and span a fold in the final document. A set of left- and right-hand facing pages is a spread, as is a set of three or more adjacent pages that appear in a folded brochure.

Refer to Chapter 5 for additional information on setting up master pages for documents with facing pages.

Bleeds

A *bleed* consists of a layout element (such as text, a background screen, a picture, or a line) that extends off the edge of the page after the page is trimmed. A bleed can also be a *crossover* — a layout element that spans two or more pages in a document. QuarkXPress easily accommodates bleeds, which can be an effective element for page design.

Figure 8-5 shows a page containing an image that bleeds off the page. We created this effect by drawing a picture box, filling it with the turtle illustration, and then using the Item tool to move the box so that part of the illustration extends beyond the page boundary.

Although you can bleed pictures to span the fold between two pages in a document, keep in mind that this may not a good idea, particularly if you are producing the document without the assistance of a professional printer. The reason? A folded page has to match up with an adjacent page that is physically printed on another sheet. Unless the adjacent pages that hold the bleed form

Figure 8-5:
An example
of an
illustration
that bleeds
off the page.

the centerfold of the document, you can end up with a graphic that is misaligned from one page to the next, a problem known as being *out of register*. This registration problem is one that a professional printer can sometimes manage during the printing process (depending on the type of printing press used), but aligning split images is almost impossible in documents that are laser-printed and then photocopied. Unless you are having your document professionally printed, the best advice is to avoid bleeds between pages unless they form a centerfold or fall in a similar setup where the flow of ink is unbroken by a page edge.

QuarkXPress Building Blocks _____

Layout in QuarkXPress is a matter of arranging the program's basic building blocks, which include boxes that hold text — *text boxes* — and boxes that hold graphics — *picture boxes*. These boxes, along with rules, form the program's primary *layout elements*.

You arrange these elements to produce a layout in QuarkXPress. But before you begin building a page, it's a good idea to understand some components of the document's foundation, including the measurement units you use to position elements on the page and the view format you need to perform various layout tasks.

Measurement systems

To position elements on the page during the layout process, you have to use a measurement system. You need to select a measurement system you feel comfortable with; QuarkXPress lets you select a measurement system for both the horizontal and vertical rulers you employ to lay out a document.

No matter what you choose, you can use any measurement in any dialog box: just enter the code (in parentheses below) that tells QuarkXPress what the system is.

The measurement system choices are as follows:

- ↷ **Inches:** Inches (") in typical inch format (¼-inch, ½-inch, and so on).

  - ↷ **Inches Decimal:** Inches (") converted to decimal format (.25 inches, .50 inches, and so on).

  - ↷ **Inches Hundredths:** Hundredths (Q) of an inch (850 is 8.5 inches).

  - ↷ **Picas:** One pica (p) is about .166 inches. There are 6 picas in an inch.

- ↷ **Points:** One point (pt) is approximately ½nd of an inch, or .351 millimeters.

- ↷ **Millimeters:** A metric measurement unit — 25.4 millimeters (mm) equals one inch; 1 mm equals 0.03937 inches.

- ↷ **Centimeters:** A metric measurement unit — 2.54 centimeters (cm) is an inch; 1 cm equals 0.3937 inches.

- ↷ **Ciceros:** This measurement unit is used in most of Europe; one cicero is approximately .01483 inches. This is close in size to a point, which is .01388 inches.

Although most people in the publishing industry are in the habit of using picas and points, don't feel that you must conform to their standard. There is no "right" or even preferred measurement unit. QuarkXPress offers you a wide range of measurement system choices so that you can select a measurement unit you can relate to. To set or change QuarkXPress's measurement specifications, use the General Preferences dialog box (see Figure 8-6). In the figure, the options for Horizontal Measure are selected; the same options are available for Vertical Measure.

You can use a different measurement unit for the horizontal and vertical rulers. Many publishers use picas for horizontal measurements but inches for vertical (as in the phrase "column inch").

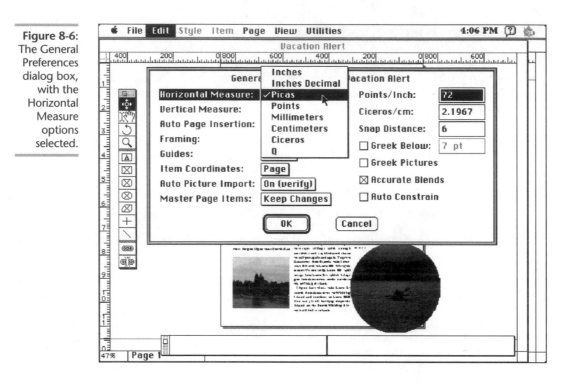

Figure 8-6:
The General
Preferences
dialog box,
with the
Horizontal
Measure
options
selected.

If you open the General Preferences dialog box when a document is open and active, your selections affect the settings for just that particular document. If you open the dialog box when no document is open, any selections you make become QuarkXPress's defaults.

To set measurement preferences, select Edit ➪ Preferences ➪ General (or use ⌘Y). Use the Horizontal Measure and Vertical Measure pop-up list boxes to select the measurement unit you want to use. Make any other desired selections in the General Preferences dialog box and choose OK. Preferences are covered in Chapter 4.

Views

The page view, which you select from the View menu, determines how much of the page you see at one time. The default view, which appears each time you start up the application or open a new document, is Actual Size (100 percent).

As you become more accustomed to working with QuarkXPress, you'll find yourself changing the View selection from time to time, based on the specific task you are trying to accomplish. To change the document view, choose View and then select from one of the six available preset view options. You can change views by a variable amount (between 10 percent and 400 percent) at any time. To do so, enter a percentage value in the box at the corner of the open document window (lower-left side, next to the page number). Preset view options from the View menu are

- **Fit in Window (⌘0 [Command zero]):** This view "fits" the page into your computer's screen area.

- **50%:** This view displays the document page at half its actual size.

- **75%:** Choose this setting to display the document page at three-fourths of its actual size.

- **Actual Size (⌘1):** This setting displays the document page at actual size, which may mean that only part of the page is displayed on-screen.

- **200%:** If you choose this setting, QuarkXPress displays the document page at twice its actual size; this view is useful if you are editing text that is 10 points or smaller, or if you are trying to use the visual method to position an item precisely on a page.

- **Thumbnails:** This view displays miniature versions of the document pages. Figure 8-7 shows a thumbnail view with page 2 (the first page in the first spread) selected (highlighted). You can drag a selected page to a position elsewhere in the document by clicking the mouse button and holding it down as you drag the page. In the bottom right of the figure, you can see the insert-page icon and an outline of a page. This indicates that page 2 is being moved to the new location.

Figure 8-7:
A thumbnail view of a document with the selected page being moved to a new location.

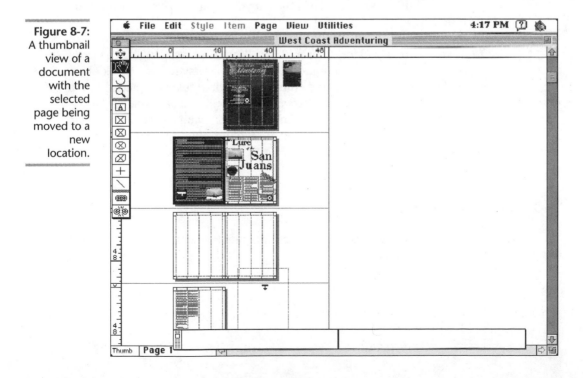

QuarkXPress offers another way of changing views, and it's one we find particularly useful. To increase the page view in 25-percent increments, select the Zoom tool (it looks like a magnifying glass). When you place the pointer over the document with the Zoom tool selected, the pointer changes to a magnifying glass. Each time you press the mouse button, the view increases in 25-percent increments, up to a maximum of 400 percent. To decrease the page view in 25-percent increments, hold down the Option key as you click the mouse button. (Note how the plus in the Zoom tool's pointer changes to a minus.)

For increasing the view by 25 percent, an even easier method is to hold the Control key and click the mouse — you don't have to have the Zoom tool selected.

To zoom in on a specific area, you can click the Zoom tool and select a corner of the area you want, hold the mouse button down, drag to the opposite corner of the area, and release the mouse button.

For all these options, you can change the increment from its default of 25 percent to any other amount by using the Tool Preferences dialog box (Edit ⇨ Preferences ⇨ Tools) for the Zoom tool.

Another easy way to change your view is through a new keyboard shortcut, Ctrl-V, that highlights the view percentage at the bottom left of your QuarkXPress window. Just enter the new percentage (you don't need to enter the % symbol) and press Enter or Return. If you want to go to the thumbnail view, enter T instead of a percentage.

Different views are useful for different tasks. If you are rearranging the order of pages in a document, the Thumbnail view makes it easy to keep track of your actions. If you are doing final copy edits on a block of text you placed into a QuarkXPress document, the 200-percent view setting makes it easier to see your edits, thereby reducing errors. And if you just want to get an overall look at the page to check its balance, the position of graphics in relation to the margins, and so on, the 75-percent and Fit in Window views work well.

Element display

The View menu (see Figure 8-8) also contains commands that enable you to control the display of other items on-screen:

The first section of the menu holds the view option commands.

The second section (new to Version 3.2) lets you control how multiple documents are displayed on the screen, as well as switch among several open documents. Figure 8-9 shows the result of selecting the Tile Documents option. This option is particularly useful if you have multiple monitors (which gives you enough room to see several documents at once). The Stack Documents option simply keeps the windows offset slightly so that all the document names are visible.

The third section offers commands that control the display of positioning aids: guides, baseline grid, rulers, and invisibles (tabs, returns, and so on).

The fourth section contains commands that display or hide QuarkXPress palettes.

In the third through fourth sections of the menu, you toggle features on or off; if a command is active, a check appears next to its name. In the list of open documents in the second section (bottom of the menu), the currently selected document's name has a check next to its name.

Figure 8-8:
Use the View menu to select commands for controlling items on-screen.

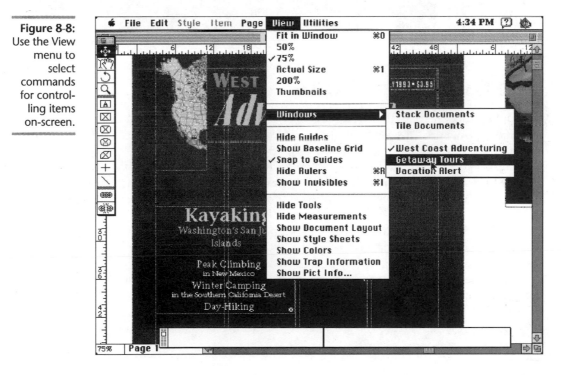

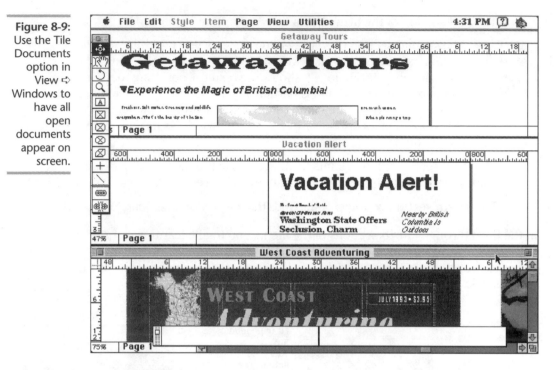

Figure 8-9:
Use the Tile
Documents
option in
View ⇨
Windows to
have all
open
documents
appear on
screen.

The Greeking feature

One option closely related to views is *greeking*. When you use greeking, QuarkXPress displays a gray area on-screen to represent text or pictures on the page (see Figure 8-10).

Turning on greeking speeds up the screen-refresh time needed to display your QuarkXPress document. In fact, greeking — particularly when used for pictures — is one of the best ways to save screen redraw time.

The General Preferences dialog box (Edit ⇨ Preferences ⇨ General) contains two greeking specifications. One field, Greek Below, tells QuarkXPress to greek the text display when text is a certain point size or smaller. The default value is 7 points, but you can enter a value between 2 and 720 points. If you check the Greek Pictures option, QuarkXPress displays pictures as gray boxes.

For more information on greeking, see the section on text and picture display in Chapter 4.

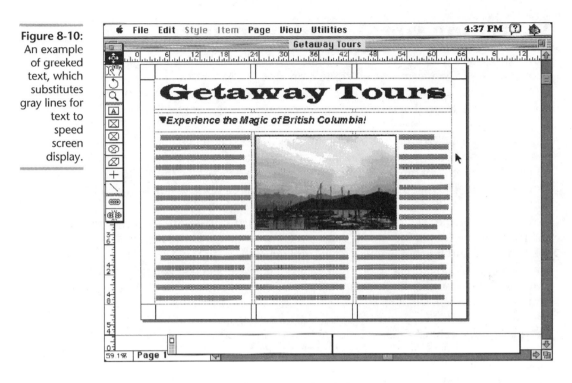

Figure 8-10:
An example
of greeked
text, which
substitutes
gray lines for
text to
speed
screen
display.

Page Setup

The best way to ensure an effective layout is to start with a well-executed plan, always reflected in the final look of the document. If you spend sufficient time planning the layout of the document, you'll need fewer revisions later on.

In other words, think of the first step in layout as the planning phase, or the time you allot to planning and developing your layout ideas. Planning ahead isn't nearly as much work as it sounds. In fact, for most simple documents, you need no more than several minutes to design a basic plan for how elements appear on the pages. For a complex document, you need more time. Keep in mind that the more familiar you become with general layout principles and the more you learn how to best apply QuarkXPress to the task, the quicker you'll be in the planning phase.

Sketching your layout on paper

How do you start to develop a layout plan? If you are still thinking about what the pages should look like, you can develop some more specific ideas by spending a few minutes sketching out the layout before you sit down to produce the document on the computer. One way to do this is to create a *dummy document*, a valuable layout-planning aid.

Let's say you want to create an eight-page newsletter that has standard, 8½ × 11-inch pages. You can create a dummy by taking two sheets of blank, 8½ × 11-inch paper, aligning one on top of the other, and folding them in half across the width of the paper. This technique gives you a miniature version of your eight-page newsletter.

Next, use a pencil to sketch the dummy's masthead, the cover art and/or stories, and the running headers or footers for each page. Form an idea about how wide you want the top, side, and bottom margins to be, and mark them on the pages. Then indicate which pictures and stories go on each page. Of course, because you will be using QuarkXPress to format the document, you can make changes right up to the point when you produce camera-ready pages.

 After you have a general idea of how to structure your document, you can start developing a QuarkXPress style sheet, as described in Chapter 6.

You should find all this planning — which actually doesn't take that much time in relation to the other publishing tasks involved — to be time well spent. The process of sketching out the layout helps clarify your thoughts about the basic layout of your document. You can make preliminary decisions about such things as where to put each illustration and section of text on a page, how many columns of text to use, and whether to use any repeating elements (such as headers and footers). Figure 8-11 shows a typical rough sketch.

Sketching your layout in QuarkXPress

If you are already comfortable using QuarkXPress, you may decide to forego the paper-and-pencil sketching of a new document and use QuarkXPress to do the rough design instead. There are some obvious advantages to this approach:

- ↪ When a document has a set number of text and graphic elements, you can use QuarkXPress to make a series of "sketches" of the document. If you like, you can save each sketch as a separate file with a distinct filename. In each sketch, you can use different element positioning, type styles, masthead placement, and so on. Then you can print a copy of each file and use the copies to assist you in finalizing the look of the layout.

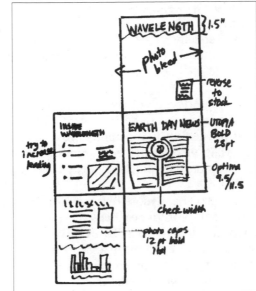

Figure 8-11:
A rough layout sketch is helpful in planning your document.

↪ If you are considering many different layout possibilities, you can develop them quickly on QuarkXPress and then print the series in thumbnail (miniature) size (check the Thumbnails box in File ➪ Print). Seeing the pages in thumbnail view makes it easier to evaluate the overall balance between page elements because you are not distracted by the text or the graphics in such a reduced view.

↪ Printed QuarkXPress copies of rough sketches have a cleaner look, which is especially helpful if you are designing a layout for a client. The advantage to presenting rough sketches that look more "final" is that it tends to make the client approval process go more smoothly, and it can make it easier for you to sell the client on your design. At the same time, slick-looking rough drafts do have a disadvantage: they make it more difficult for clients to understand that what they are seeing is just a rough draft and not a final copy.

How to Start a New Document ____

After you do your preliminary planning, it's time to begin building the QuarkXPress document. You might have noticed that we keep referring to creating a layout as "building." This is a fair analogy for what's involved in laying out a new document because document layout encompasses steps similar to those used for building a house. You start with the foundation (the page dimensions), build the rooms (the text and picture boxes), and fill the rooms with furniture (the actual text and illustrations or graphics). When the house is built and furnished, you add decorative final touches (lines, frames, color, and other graphic effects).

The first step, then, in laying out a document is to establish the foundation by setting up the basic dimensions of the document page. To do this, make the appropriate selections in the New dialog box to specify page size, margins, number of columns, gutter width between columns, and whether you want QuarkXPress to automatically generate text boxes.

Before you begin setting up a new document, decide on the number of text columns you want to use in all (or most) of the pages in the document. You can always make changes later, but you'll save time if you decide on the number of columns before you start. For a typical newsletter or magazine, using two, three, or four columns is the norm, but you can certainly vary from this standard if doing so helps you achieve a desired effect.

If you are worried that you have more text than will fit on the document's pages — for example, you want to produce a two-page newsletter but you have two-and-a-half pages worth of text — consider using one more column than you originally planned. Use three columns instead of two, for instance. Depending on the hyphenation and justification you use, this strategy can make it possible to fit an extra paragraph or two onto the page.

Create a new document

First, open a new document by selecting File ➪ New ➪ Document, or use ⌘N. This displays the New Document dialog box (see Figure 8-12).

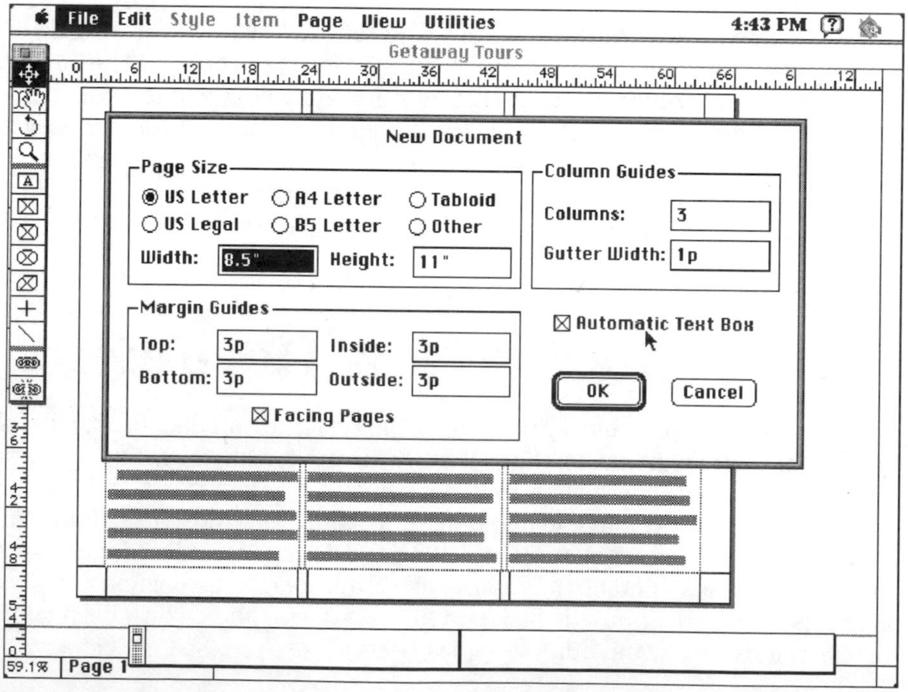

Figure 8-12:
The New
Document
dialog box.

🍎 **File** Edit *Style* Item **Page** View Utilities	4:43 PM ⑦

Getaway Tours

New Document

┌─Page Size─────────────────┐
● US Letter   ○ A4 Letter   ○ Tabloid
○ US Legal   ○ B5 Letter   ○ Other

Width: `8.5"`   Height: `11"`

┌─Column Guides──────────┐
Columns: `3`

Gutter Width: `1p`

┌─Margin Guides──────────┐
Top: `3p`   Inside: `3p`
Bottom: `3p`   Outside: `3p`

⊠ Facing Pages

⊠ **Automatic Text Box**

[OK]   [Cancel]

59.1%   Page 1

When using File ⇨ New, Version 3.2 adds a step to creating a new document: selecting Document or Library. This makes it easier to create a library document (in earlier versions, you created and opened libraries via the Utilities menu). You can get past the extra step by using the shortcut keys: ⌘N for documents, Option-⌘N for libraries. Likewise, you open libraries now from the File menu. Because QuarkXPress now supports multiple open documents, all the open and creation options can be placed within one menu: File. (Libraries are covered in depth in Chapter 23.)

Set the page size

Next, in the Page Size area of the dialog box, select the size of your final pages by clicking the button next to your selection. (The size you choose, by the way, need not necessarily be exactly the same size as the paper your printer can hold; we'll discuss this more in Chapter 26.) QuarkXPress offers five standard page size selections in the dialog box and also gives you the opportunity to specify a custom page size. The standard page sizes are as follows:

- **US Letter:** width 8.5 inches, height 11 inches
- **US Legal:** width 8.5 inches, height 14 inches
- **A4 Letter:** width 8.268 inches, height 11.693 inches
- **B5 Letter:** width 6.929 inches, height 9.843 inches
- **Tabloid:** width 11 inches, height 17 inches

QuarkXPress also lets you create custom page sizes. Select Other and enter any page dimensions ranging from 1 inch x 1 inch to 48 inches x 48 inches.

If you set the page size in the New Document dialog box and change your mind later on, you can modify it. Select Document Setup from the File menu and enter the new page dimensions in the appropriate fields in the Document Setup dialog box. Entering the new page dimensions works as long as the new page size is sufficient to accommodate any elements you already placed; if not, a dialog box appears explaining that the page size you are proposing will force some items off the page. To prevent this, you must enter a page size sufficiently large to hold those items. Move them temporarily from the edge of the current page or onto the pasteboard and then try changing the page size again.

QuarkXPress always displays page width and height in inches, even if you select a different measurement unit in the General Preferences dialog box (which you access when a document is open by selecting Edit ⇨ Preferences ⇨ General or by using ⌘Y). You can specify page dimensions to .001 of any measurement unit, and QuarkXPress automatically makes the conversion to inches in the Page Width and Height fields.

 If you are outputting your document directly to negatives and you want crop marks to be automatically printed at the page margins for a trimmed page (such as the 8½ × 10⅞-inch page size used by many magazines), select Other as the page size and enter the page dimensions in the corresponding field.

How do you know which page size is best? The answer to that question is really up to you, but it's useful to note which page sizes are typically used. Many magazines and newsletters use letter size, which is a convenient size for mailing and for fitting into a standard magazine-display rack. Newspapers and larger-format magazines frequently use tabloid size.

Set the margins

Next, in the Margin Guides area of the New Document dialog box, enter measurement values (to .001 of any unit of measurement) for the top, left, bottom, and right margins of the document. If you are using ragged-right text in the document, you can set right margins a bit smaller than you need for justified text. (To create ragged-right text, you actually set the text to be left-aligned.)

Keep in mind that after you set up the document specifications in the New Document dialog box, QuarkXPress gives you no way to redefine the margins other than by manually expanding the boxes on the page. Unless you are sure about the document's margin dimensions, you may want to consider creating and printing a test page (a single, sample page of the document) to verify margins before you invest the effort necessary to lay out the entire document.

Margin measurements determine how far from the outside edges of the paper you can place the document's text and picture boxes. The margins are for the underlying page, but are by no means set in concrete; for example, you can place individual text boxes or picture boxes anywhere on the page, even into these preset margins. One situation in which a page element may cross over into the margin is when you create a bleed, an illustration that ends past the edge of the physical page.

Be careful not to make margins too large because doing so can give the text and pictures on the page an appearance of insignificance. By the same token, don't make margins too small, which can produce the equally unappealing look that results from having too much information on a page. Also, you may consider having one margin bigger than the margins on the other three sides of a page. For example, if you plan to saddle-stitch or three-hole punch a document, make the inside margin larger so that it can accommodate the staples or holes.

Set the page sides

Next, in the Margin Guides area of the dialog box, check the Facing Pages option box if the document pages will be printed two-sided, with the right and left pages facing each other when the document is open. Turning on the Facing Pages option tells QuarkXPress to set right and left pages that mirror each other in terms of right and left margins. If you select Facing Pages, consider making inside margins larger than those on the outer edges of the page to allow room for the binding. Margin guides appear as lines on-screen, but the lines do not print. You can also turn their display off via View ⇨ Hide Guides.

 You set the measurement unit used for margin and column guides in the General Preferences dialog box (Edit ⇨ Preferences ⇨ General, or ⌘Y). The default measurement unit is the inch.

Set the number of columns

Next, in the Columns option box (in the Column Guides area of the New Document dialog box), enter the number of text columns you want to use on most pages. (The reason we say "most" pages is that you can, for example, select three columns in this dialog box, and then, within the document, use two or some other number of columns on a particular page.)

You can specify as many as 30 columns per page, although you won't often need that many, particularly on a standard 8½ × 11-inch paper. As with margins, column guides appear as lines on-screen, but the lines do not print.

 Just because you plan to have a certain number of text columns in a document doesn't necessarily mean you should enter that exact number in the Columns field of the New Documents dialog box. Suppose that your publication has three columns, plus pull-quotes that are set out of alignment with the text margins.

You may want to try using an 8-column grid and use some of the column grid lines to align the pull-quotes. Of course, if you use this design tip, you don't want text to flow through all columns, so you need to disable (uncheck) Automatic Text Box in the New dialog box.

Figure 8-13 shows a QuarkXPress document that was set up in the New Document dialog box to have eight columns. We did not select Automatic Text Box, so we used the text box tool to create each of the text boxes. Note how we use the column markers as alignment guides in setting up a variety of column treatments, which include pull-quote boxes and columns that vary in width from the top part of the page to the bottom.

Figure 8-13:
You can use column markers as alignment guides.

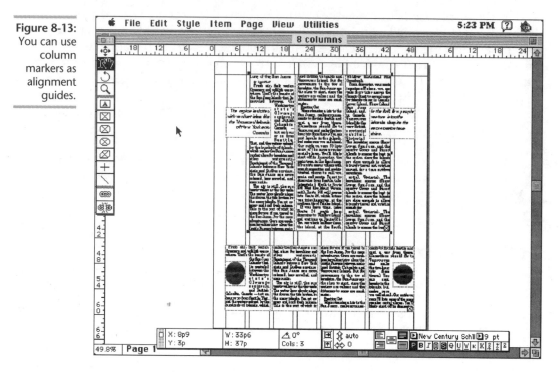

Set the column gutter

Next, in the Column Guides area of the dialog box, enter a measurement value in the Gutter Width field to specify the amount of space between columns of text. Gutters can be as small as 3 points or as large as 288 points. If you enter a Gutter Width value that is too large or too small, QuarkXPress displays a dialog box showing you the range of values from which you must select. We recommend keeping columns to a reasonable width — generally no wider than 21 picas. Otherwise, the columns may become tiring on the reader's eyes.

Don't make gutters too small. This causes the columns of text to appear to run together and makes the document difficult to read. A rule of thumb is that the wider the columns, the wider the margins need to be to give the reader a clear visual clue that it's time to move to the next line. If you *must* use narrow gutters (between 0p9 and 2p0, depending on the page width and number of columns), consider adding a thin (0.5 point or smaller) vertical rule in the center of the gutter. To draw the rule, use the Orthogonal Line drawing tool and draw the line from the top of the gutter to the bottom, midway through the gutter width.

Set the automatic text box

Next, activate Automatic Text Box (by placing a check mark in the option box) if you want a text box on the master page that automatically flows text to other pages inserted into the document. If you don't select Automatic Text Box, you must use the Text Box tool to draw text boxes before you place text with the File ⇨ Get Text command.

After you finish making selections in the New dialog box, choose OK to open the new page.

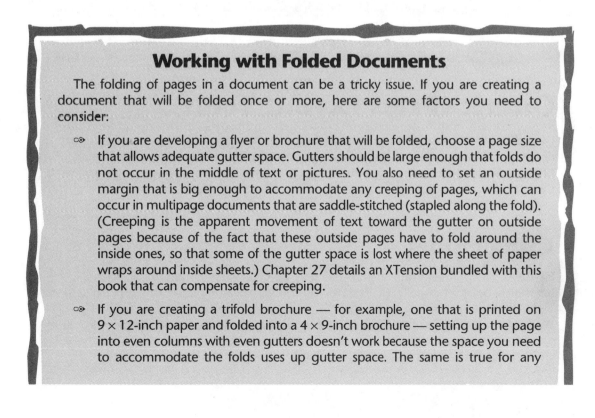

Working with Folded Documents

The folding of pages in a document can be a tricky issue. If you are creating a document that will be folded once or more, here are some factors you need to consider:

⤷ If you are developing a flyer or brochure that will be folded, choose a page size that allows adequate gutter space. Gutters should be large enough that folds do not occur in the middle of text or pictures. You also need to set an outside margin that is big enough to accommodate any creeping of pages, which can occur in multipage documents that are saddle-stitched (stapled along the fold). (Creeping is the apparent movement of text toward the gutter on outside pages because of the fact that these outside pages have to fold around the inside ones, so that some of the gutter space is lost where the sheet of paper wraps around inside sheets.) Chapter 27 details an XTension bundled with this book that can compensate for creeping.

⤷ If you are creating a trifold brochure — for example, one that is printed on 9×12-inch paper and folded into a 4×9-inch brochure — setting up the page into even columns with even gutters doesn't work because the space you need to accommodate the folds uses up gutter space. The same is true for any brochure or document that is folded more than two times. If possible, work with your commercial printer to find out what page and column size to use to accommodate the folds. If you are designing a multifold brochure that will not be commercially printed, allow time to experiment with column widths, margins, and folding.

↪ The paper on which a folded brochure is printed is a major factor in the success of the document. Your paper choice also plays a large role in how you need to set up the document during layout. Obviously, thick paper reacts differently to folding than thin paper, and thick paper also has a different effect in terms of the amount of page creeping that results in a multipage document. Depending on the weight and texture of the paper, a ¼-inch margin set on the first page of a 36-page, saddle-stitched document could be gradually reduced on each page, shrinking to ¹⁄₁₆th of an inch by the centerfold. We recommend talking with your printer ahead of time if your document has multiple folds or if you are planning a document with 24 or more folded pages and saddle stitching.

A good commercial printer should be experienced in handling the issues related to paper weight and can give you some important guidelines about how to lay out a folded document. If your document will be folded, take the time to talk with your printer before you get too far into the layout process.

QuarkXPress Layout Tools

QuarkXPress offers several layout tools that make it easier for you to produce your document. These tools include guides that help you align text and graphics, a pasteboard area that gives you a convenient way to store document elements until you need them, and a feature that allows you to position elements in layers.

Using guides

Laying out a document often means lining up objects with columns, illustrations, headlines, or other objects. Guides are nonprinting lines that make this process easier.

We've already covered two types of guides: margins and columns. And you've seen how you can actually use column guides as alignment aids. QuarkXPress also offers ruler guides, which you "pull out" from the vertical and horizontal document rulers. Of course, you can always use the numeric values displayed in the Measurements palette to precisely position elements, but the ruler guides are handy tools for visually lining up elements on a page. Guides are useful if you want to align an element to another element within a box — such as a part of a picture — and the location is not identified in the Measurements palette (the Measurements palette shows the box's values, not those of its internal elements). You should, however, rely on the numeric values shown in the Measurements palette rather than the pull-out ruler guides when you are concerned about placing boxes and lines precisely on a page.

Controlling how guides display

You can control whether QuarkXPress places ruler and page guides in front of or behind objects on the page. You can select either In Front or Behind in the Guides field of the General Preferences dialog box (to open the dialog box, select Edit ⇨ Preferences ⇨ General, or use ⌘Y).

The default setting for guide position is Behind, for good reason. If you have many elements on the page, selecting the In Front setting tends to make the guides difficult to locate and control. Placing guides behind other objects becomes more and more important as your document increases in complexity.

Because ruler guides don't print, you can use as many of them as you like. To obtain a ruler guide, simply use the mouse to position the cursor within the vertical or horizontal ruler. Then hold down the mouse button as you pull the ruler guide into place.

When to use the snap-to feature

Another handy feature for lining up elements on a page is the Snap to Guides feature, which you access through the View menu. When you select this feature, guides have an almost magnetic pull on objects you place on the page, making them "snap" into alignment with the closest guide. You'll appreciate this feature for some layout tasks, but you'll want to disable it for others.

When do you want the snap-to feature enabled? Imagine that you are creating a structured document containing illustrations framed with a 0.5-point line and aligned with the left-most margin. In this case, select Snap to Guides so that the illustrations snap into position on the margin. If, on the other hand, you have a document containing design elements that are placed in a variety of locations on the page, you may want to position them visually or by means of the Measurements palette instead of having them automatically snap to the nearest guide line.

You can control the distance within which an item snaps to guides by entering a value in the Snap Distance field in the General Preferences dialog box (Edit ⇨ Preferences ⇨ General, or ⌘Y). Snap distance is specified in pixels, and the range is 1 to 100. If the Snap distance is set to 6 pixels, any element within 6 or fewer pixels of a guide will snap to that guide.

If you have a document open, you can also display another set of grid lines. Selecting View ⇨ Show Baseline Grid displays horizontal grid lines that do not print. The actual purpose of these grid lines is to lock the baselines of text onto them, but we find them very useful as positioning guides as well. Chapters 4, 5, and 13 provide more detail on this feature.

You specify the spacing of these grid lines in the Typographic Preferences dialog box (Edit Í Preferences Í Typographic, or Option-⌘Y). In the Start field of the dialog box, enter a value to tell QuarkXPress how far from the top of the page you want the first line. In the Increment field, enter the size of the interval you want between grid lines. Figure 8-14 shows a document page with the baseline grid displayed.

In Figure 8-14, you'll notice that the grid lines appear inside the main text box but not in the pull-quotes' text boxes. To do this, we have given the pull-quotes' text boxes a background of White (in Item ⇨ Modify); the main text box has a background of None.

If you want elements to snap to lines in the baseline grid, be sure that the baseline grid is visible (select View ⇨ Show Baseline Grid). If the baseline grid is not visible, elements snap to the closest visible guide.

Using the pasteboard

In the old days of publishing, people who composed document pages often worked at a large table (or pasteboard) that held not only the documents on which they were working, but also the odds and ends associated with its layout. They might put a headline, a picture, a caption, or a section of text on the pasteboard until they were ready to place the element on the page.

Even though QuarkXPress has automated the page composition process, it includes a tremendously useful pasteboard. You'll find yourself using it all the time. QuarkXPress's pasteboard is an area that surrounds each document spread (one or more pages that are side by side). Each and every spread has its own pasteboard. Figure 8-15 shows the pasteboard, which is holding some layout elements, as it appears around a single-page spread.

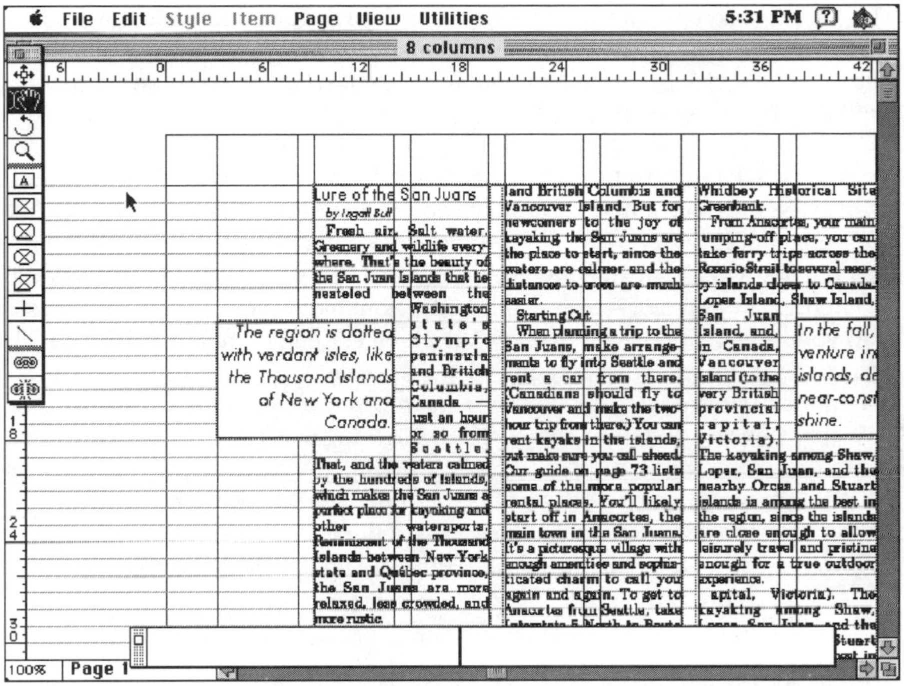

Figure 8-14:
A document
with the
baseline grid
displayed.
Note that
text is not
aligned with
baselines
because
Lock to
Baseline is
not selected
in the
Paragraph
Formats
dialog box
(Style ⇨
Formats).

Figure 8-15:
The
QuarkXPress
pasteboard
holds items
for future
use.

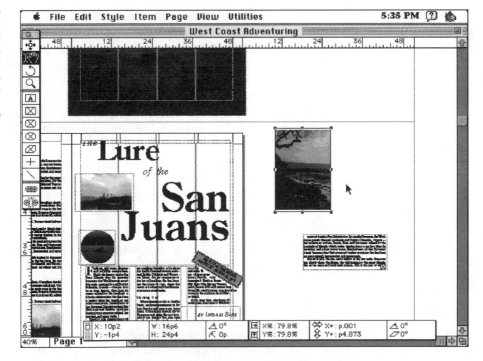

The pasteboard appears on the sides of the spread. You can maneuver around the spread and the pasteboard by using the scroll controls. The default size of the pasteboard is the width of the document page, but you can change the pasteboard size if you want it to be larger or smaller.

Usually, the default pasteboard width is sufficient. But you may want to modify it if you need more or less room on-screen. Choose Edit ⇨ Preferences ⇨ Application to display the Application Preferences dialog box. Enter a percentage value in the Pasteboard Width field. A value of 100 percent means that the pasteboard width is equal to — or 100 percent the size of — the width of the document page. When the pasteboard width is to your liking, choose OK to save the change. Keep in mind that the larger the pasteboard, the more memory is required. If you're not short on computer memory, use the default pasteboard width. If you are running short of computer memory, consider reducing the size of the pasteboard to something less than 100 percent.

The maximum width and height of the combined pasteboard and document spread is 48 inches. QuarkXPress reduces the pasteboard size, if necessary, in order to keep the pasteboard and spread at or below the 48-inch maximum width.

Working with layers

QuarkXPress arranges text boxes, picture boxes, and rules in *layers*. You can control the order of these layers, which means you can stack and restack text boxes, picture boxes, and lines on a page, as if each were on its own separate sheet of paper. QuarkXPress does the layering for you, actually placing every element on the page on its very own layer.

If your document is fairly simple, and its elements do not overlap, you don't need to be concerned with layers. But if you are laying out complex pages with multiple elements, you need to know how to rearrange the layers.

To rearrange the layers in a document, select the page element you want to shift and locate the appropriate command in the Item menu. The full list of layer commands is available only when the open document contains layout elements in multiple layers. The layer commands are

- **Send to Back:** Sends the selected element to the back of the pile

- **Bring to Front:** Brings the selected element to the front of the pile

Unless you need them for special effects, avoid overlapping too many elements. If you have more than four or five layers, the screen refresh time (the time it takes to redraw the screen after you make changes) slows down almost exponentially, meaning that you need to allow yourself extra time to sit and wait while the layered page reappears on-screen.

Figure 8-16 shows how layers work. In the top example, the text is moved to the front with the Bring to Front command (Item menu), the gray box is moved to the back with the Send to Back command, and the black box is sent to the back of the pile with the Send to Back command, which means the gray box is now between the other two boxes. In the bottom example, the order is rearranged.

When you move an element in a layered relationship, it retains its place in the stacking order. In other words, if an element is on a layer third from the top of the stack, it stays on that layer even if you move it elsewhere in your layout. If you need to change the stacking order of elements, use the commands in the Item menu.

As you can see in Figure 8-16, the ability to layer elements can be a powerful layout tool. You can overlap a filled box with another box of text, for example, creating a shadowed or multidimensional effect.

Figure 8-16:
Examples of layered elements.

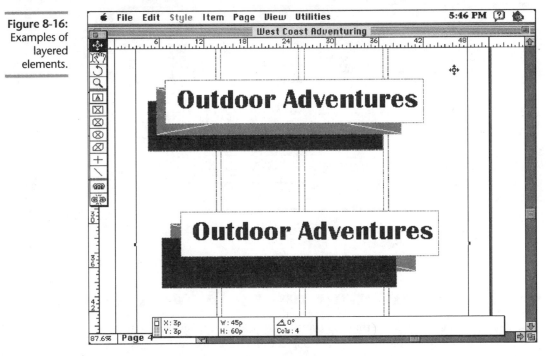

Locking elements in place

Suppose that you've been working on a page layout for some time, and you've positioned an element — for example, the masthead — exactly where you want it to be. Knowing that you still have a number of elements to place on the page, how can you prevent yourself from accidentally moving or resizing the masthead with an errant mouse click?

The answer: Lock the element into position. To lock an element, select it and choose Item ⇨ Lock. Figure 8-17 shows a locked byline. You can tell if an element is locked because the pointer changes to a lock icon when you position it over a locked element, as shown in the figure.

You can still move and resize a locked element, but you must do so either from the Measurements palette or through options in the Item menu. Essentially, what locking buys you is protection from accidental changes. To unlock a locked element, select the element and choose Item ⇨ Unlock.

Figure 8-17:
An example of a locked element (the selected text box with the lock symbol).

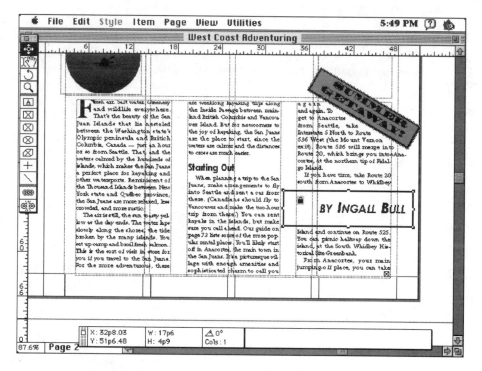

Grouping and ungrouping layout elements

QuarkXPress offers a feature that is common to drawing programs. The program lets you select two or more elements and *group* them. Grouping means associating multiple items with each other so that QuarkXPress treats the group as a single item during moves, resizing, and edits. Grouping is useful if you want to move related items together while keeping their spatial relationship intact.

To group multiple elements, hold down the Shift key while you use the mouse to select the items to be grouped. Choose Item ⇨ Group. When items are grouped, they are bounded by a dotted line (see Figure 8-18). Note that the Measurements palette for grouped items has only X, Y, and rotation coordinates available because these are the only Measurements palette controls that can be applied to the entire group.

 Just because elements are grouped doesn't mean you can't size or edit them independently. Just select the Content tool and choose the individual element. Then resize the element by dragging its handles, or edit it as you would if it were not part of a group.

You can perform actions (Cut, Copy, Paste, Lock, and so on) on groups that you normally perform on singular elements. You also can modify groups of like elements (groups of text boxes, groups of picture boxes, and so on) by using the Item tool and selecting the group, and then choosing Item ⇨ Modify to display the Group Specifications dialog box. To Ungroup previously grouped elements, select the group and choose Item ⇨ Ungroup, as shown in Figure 8-18. What you can't do is resize the entire group at once.

Figure 8-18:
A dotted-line box indicates grouped elements.

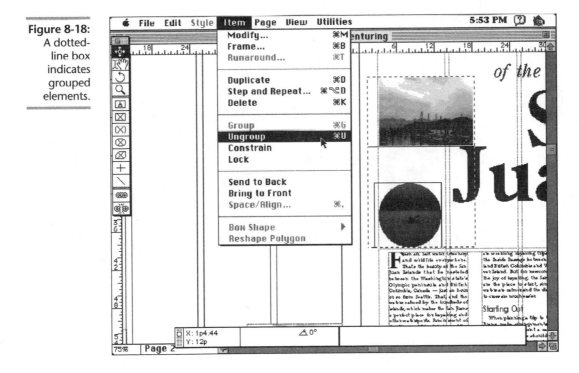

Constraining boxes

Unique to QuarkXPress is the ability to *constrain* a box: you can specify that any new box placed over an existing box cannot be sized or moved beyond the limits of the existing box. Constraining boxes can be considered a subset of grouping, but the two processes actually differ. Constrained boxes behave more like a "parent and child" relationship: the child box is unable to leave the confines of the parent box. In a hierarchy of boxes, the constraining box "parent" is the rear-most box in the hierarchy. It must be large enough to hold all the "child" boxes you want to constrain within it (see Figure 8-19).

Applications that can take advantage of constraining usually are highly structured. One such application is a product catalog. You might set up a large text box that holds descriptive text to constrain a smaller picture box that holds a product illustration. If you develop such a document, and you know ahead of time that you need constrained boxes, you can specify that all boxes in the document are to be constrained. To do this, choose Edit ⇨ Preferences ⇨ General to display the General Preferences dialog box. Check the Auto Constrain box, located just above the OK button.

Figure 8-19: The parent and child relationship of constrained boxes.

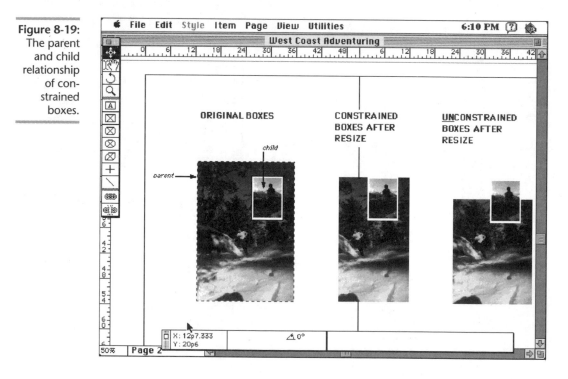

To constrain a particular box, first make sure that all items in a selected group are on a layer in front of the box that is to be the parent in the constraining relationship. With the group and the parent simultaneously selected, choose Item ⇨ Constrain.

After a set of boxes is constrained, you can move and resize individual elements within the constrained group as long as the child elements still fit within the parent box. If you move a constrained box, all elements constrained within it also move.

Summary

- ⇨ Before you begin layout, plan your document by sketching it or by developing a rough version on QuarkXPress.

- ⇨ If you are new to page layout, keep your documents simple, use lots of white space, and keep special effects to a minimum.

- ⇨ The vast majority of documents are printed on 8½ × 11-inch pages, but QuarkXPress lets you create pages as big as 48 inches x 48 inches.

- ⇨ If you create a facing-pages layout, remember to leave enough room on the inside margins to accommodate binding.

- ⇨ QuarkXPress lets you choose from a wide assortment of measurement systems — inches, millimeters, points, and so on. Don't feel pressured to use points and picas if you are more comfortable using inches.

- ⇨ Using guides and grids makes it easier to position elements on the page. And, if you have it selected, Snap to Guides positions elements exactly to the closest guide.

- ⇨ The pasteboard is a handy place for storing elements temporarily until you are ready to use them in the layout.

Working with Text Boxes

9

In This Chapter

- ➡ Creating text boxes
- ➡ Setting text box specifications
- ➡ Adding text to text boxes
- ➡ Linking text boxes
- ➡ Creating special effects with text boxes

Creating Text Boxes

Using text boxes is the basic method for placing text and controlling its position and format throughout a document. By combining QuarkXPress's two ways of creating text boxes — using the automatic text box feature and drawing your own text boxes — you create the layout structure your document uses.

QuarkXPress creates automatic text boxes when you create a new document. These boxes follow the size and column parameters you set in the New dialog box (File ➪ New ➪ Document). For example, if you specify two columns in the New dialog box and also check Automatic Text Box, text from a text file you place on the page automatically fills two columns and flows into two columns per page as you insert other pages into the document.

Manual text boxes are created with the Text Box tool, which lets you draw boxes of any size at any position. You later apply attributes to these boxes such as, for example, number of columns and margins.

STEPS: Using the Text Box Tool to Create Text Boxes

Step 1.   With the document open to the page on which you want to draw the text box, select the Text Box tool. When you use the mouse to move the pointer onto the page, the pointer changes to look like a crosshair.

Step 2.   Position the crosshair pointer where you want to locate one corner of the text box.

Step 3.   Press and hold the mouse button as you draw the text box to the approximate size that you want it to be. If you want to size the box precisely, watch the W (Width) and H (Height) measurements on the Measurements palette, which change to reflect the size of the box as you draw it.

 If you want the text box to be exactly square (instead of rectangular), hold down the Shift key as you draw the box.

Step 4.   Release the mouse button.

The fastest way to size and position a text box — or to resize and reposition it — is to use the Measurements palette after you draw an arbitrarily sized and positioned text box somewhere on the page. The X and Y numbers respectively display the horizontal and vertical coordinates of the text box location. The W and H coordinates show the size of the text box. The measurement unit used for all these measurements is whatever unit you select in the Edit ⇨ Preferences ⇨ General dialog box.

Text Box Specifications

You control the layout of text in the text box. After you create a text box, you can set many of its specifications by using the Text Box Specifications dialog box. This dialog box is useful for accomplishing the following tasks:

- ⇨ Precisely sizing and positioning the text box
- ⇨ Rotating the text box
- ⇨ Placing multiple columns within the text box (as opposed to multiple columns within the page)
- ⇨ Setting text in from the borders of the box
- ⇨ Setting the parameters for the first baseline

∞ Performing vertical alignment

∞ Adding color to the text box

 A number of the settings that you specify within the Text Box Specifications dialog box, such as size and position, can be changed without having to use the Text Box Specification dialog box. To change the text box size or position, for example, you can click and drag the text box, or you can change the settings in the Measurements palette. There is no single, correct way to modify text boxes in QuarkXPress: the program simply provides a variety of ways to accomplish this and many other tasks.

To modify Text Box Specifications, use either the Item tool or the Content tool to select the text box. Then choose Item ➪ Modify to display the Text Box Specifications dialog box shown in Figure 9-1.

Use ⌘M as a shortcut to get the Text Box Specifications dialog box.

 Measurement-related specifications in the Text Box Specifications dialog box reflect the measurement preferences you establish in the General Preferences dialog box.

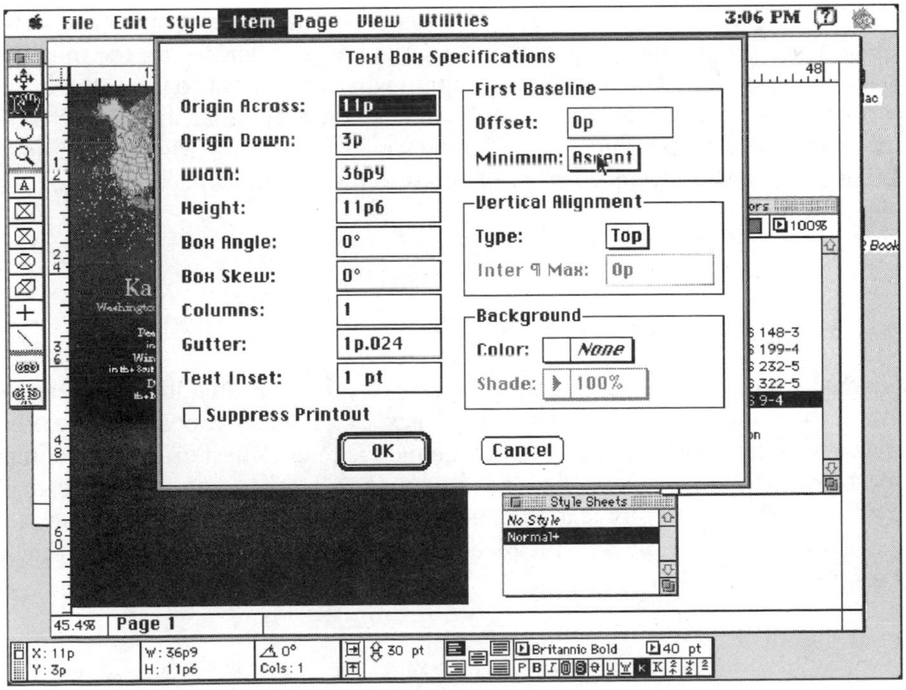

Figure 9-1:
The Text
Box
Specifica-
tions dialog
box.

Positioning the text box

After you create and size a text box, you can move it around on the page. When placing and sizing a single text box precisely, your best bet is to use the QuarkXPress Measurements palette.

STEPS:	Fine-Tuning a Text Box Position
Step 1.	Create the text box. With the Item tool selected, click the text box to activate it.
Step 2.	Enter the X and Y coordinate values in the Measurement palette's X and Y fields. (X is the horizontal coordinate; changes you make to the X value move the text box side to side. Y is the vertical coordinate; changes you make to the Y value move the text box up and down.)
Step 3.	Press Enter or click anywhere outside of the Measurements palette to apply the new position coordinates.

Instead of following these steps to use the Measurements palette, you can also use the Text Box Specifications dialog box (choose Item ⇨ Modify to display this dialog box) to position the text box. In the dialog box's Origin Across field, enter the measurement that corresponds to the horizontal position where you want to place the origin (upper-left corner) of the box. In the Origin Down field, enter the measurement that corresponds to the vertical position where you want to place the origin (upper-left corner) of the box. If you want to make other changes to the text box specifications, do so; otherwise, choose OK.

Sizing the text box

QuarkXPress lets you easily change the size of a text box. In addition to setting the box size in the Width and Height fields of the Text Box Specifications dialog box, you can change it in two other ways: by using the mouse to click and drag the "handles" of the text box to size, or by using the Measurements palette to change the size. In Figure 9-2, the handles on the empty text box on the right page are the eight small squares on the corners and sides of the box; the Measurements palette is positioned at the bottom of the screen.

Figure 9-2:
You can use text box handles or the Measurements palette to resize the box.

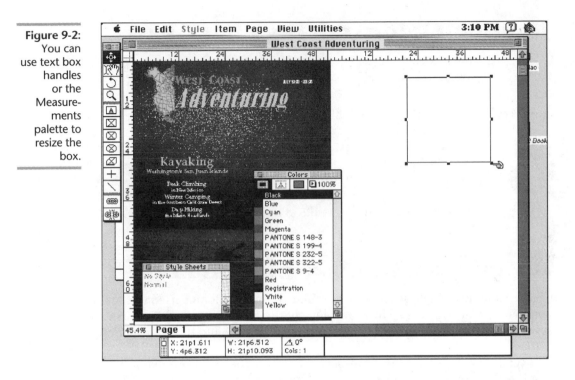

Each of these methods carries an advantage. The click-and-drag method is interactive: you watch as the box changes size. This method is useful if you are still figuring out how you want the page to look because this approach allows for plenty of free-form experimenting.

The Measurements palette method is helpful because it offers precision, as does the Text Box Specifications dialog box. If, for example, you know that the text box should be precisely 4 inches square, you can enter those coordinates in the W and H fields of the Measurements palette.

If you hold the ⌘ key while resizing a text box, the text inside will be resized as well. This is particularly handy if you are working with ads, brochures, and other documents in which the text size is not predetermined based on a standard style (unlike magazines and newsletters). Instead of highlighting the text and trying different sizes, this new resize-with-the-box feature lets you quickly make text fit the appropriate space.

Layout-Oriented Text Settings

After you have placed and sized your text box, you'll want to add the text. Of course, you can add the text at any time during the layout process. You may want to first determine layout-oriented, text-flow attributes (the number of columns) or create special effects (rotation) before adding text.

 The best policy is to add text to your text box *after* you have set the text box's basic text-flow attributes. Why? Because as you change attributes, any text in the box must reflow to fit the new settings, and this process takes time. Of course, if you are experimenting with different settings, it helps to have text in the text box to see what the results of the various settings look like.

Dividing the text box into columns

On occasion, you may want to vary the number of text columns used within a single page. For example, you may have a document that is set in two columns. For variety's sake, you decide to divide one of two columns on a page into three smaller columns.

You can perform this task easily using the Text Box Specifications dialog box. Select the text box that you want to break into more columns. Then choose Item ⇨ Modify (or press ⌘M). In the Columns field, enter **3.** This procedure divides the selected text box into three columns. Figure 9-3 shows such a text box (on the right page). The left-hand column is a text box that is subdivided into three narrower columns.

A simpler way to make the same formatting changes is to use the Measurements palette: select the text box whose number of columns you want to change and replace the entry for Cols in the Measurements palette with the new number of columns. In Figure 9-3, the current entry (3) is highlighted.

Setting text inset

The amount of text inset determines the distance between the text and the boundary edges of the text box. Entering a Text Inset value of 1 point (which, by the way, is the default setting) insets the text 1 point from the borders of the box.

 For most applications, there is really no reason why you need any text inset at all — particularly for text that makes up the body of the document. But QuarkXPress defaults to an inset of 1 point. You can permanently override this setting by using the Edit ⇨ Preferences ⇨ Tools menu to set the Text Box tool's inset to 0 points (refer to Chapter 4 for details on modifying default settings).

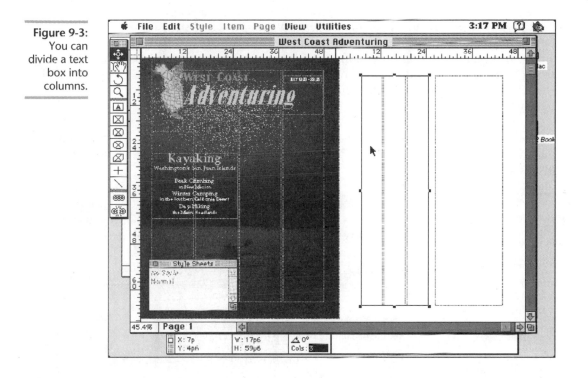

Figure 9-3:
You can
divide a text
box into
columns.

Adding Intercolumn Rules

A common design device is to put thin lines — usually a hairline (¼ point) — between columns. But QuarkXPress offers no feature to add these rules automatically. However, you can add them easily by following the following steps.

First, create your standard multicolumn text boxes — the ones you will use throughout your document. You'll likely have several such standard boxes — your master page will probably have your basic text box for body text, and you'll probably put sidebar boxes and the like either in libraries or on the pasteboard for use when needed.

Second, make sure column guides are visible (View ⇨ Show Guides).

Third, use the Orthogonal Line tool to draw the lines between the columns. (You may have to turn off the snap-to-guides feature, via View ⇨ Snap to Guides.) Use the Measurements palette to specify the line width, color, and other settings.

Fourth, group the lines and the text box (Item ⇨ Group). For boxes on master pages, lock them as well (Item ⇨ Lock).

Fifth, for occasionally used standard text boxes in libraries or on the pasteboard, ungroup the rules and box, resize them as needed, and regroup them.

Text inset comes in handy if you have a text box *within* a text box. Suppose that you have a full page of text, and you use a pull-quote (a portion of the text that is copied into a box and enlarged to create a graphic element) or other text element, such as a byline, that you place so the body text wraps around it. Suppose that you place a frame around the text. A text inset allows some white space around the text. Figure 9-4 shows an in-text byline with a 1-point frame that has a text inset of 10 points.

To modify text inset for a text box, select the text box and then choose Item ⇨ Modify to display the Text Box Specifications dialog box. Enter the text inset value in the Text Inset field.

As useful as Text Inset is, you might expect that QuarkXPress would provide a number of ways to specify it. But this is one QuarkXPress command you can access in one way only: through the Text Box Specifications dialog box.

Figure 9-4:
A byline with a 10-point text inset that provides white space between the byline and the frame.

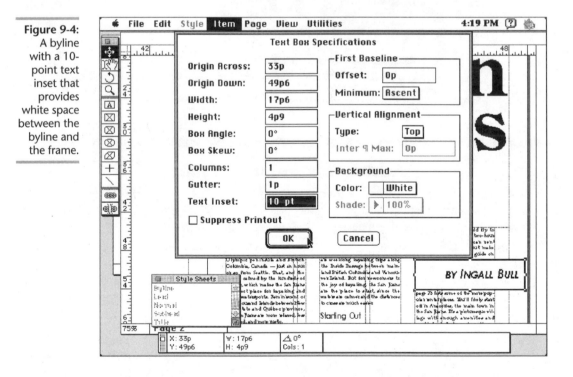

Text runaround

A *runaround* is an area in a page's layout where you don't want text to flow. *Text runaround* allows you place copy around an active element (text box, picture box, or line), fitting the text as close to the contours of the element as you want.

Text runaround is often used in advertisements and other design-intensive documents. Like other special effects, text runaround is most effective when not over-used. Done correctly, this technique can add a unique, polished look to a page layout.

To set the specifications for text runaround, select the text box, picture box, or line that holds the contents that you want the text to run around. Choose Item ⇨ Runaround to display the Runaround Specifications dialog box, shown in Figure 9-5. (There's more space around the byline here than in Figure 9-4 because we've increased the runaround value to 6 points.) In the dialog box, you can control the type of runaround as well as the distance between the object and the text running around it. The effects of the options available in the dialog box depend upon the type of element you select.

Use ⌘T as a shortcut to getting the Runaround Specifications dialog box.

Figure 9-5:
The
Runaround
Specifica-
tions dialog
box.

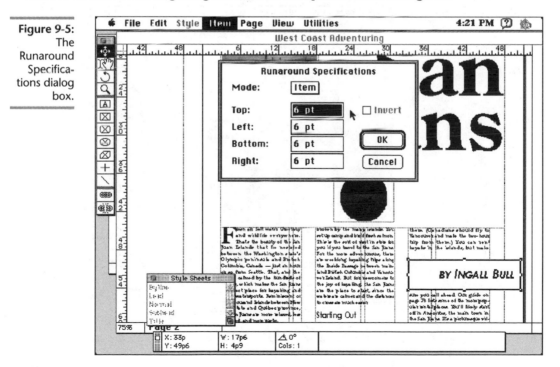

QuarkXPress offers a variety of runaround options. They are determined by both the type of active element and by what you enter in the Mode field. You have a choice of modes that varies depending on whether you run text around boxes or lines. The choice of modes are as follows:

- **None:** This setting causes text behind the active item to flow normally, as if there were no object in the way. Figure 9-6 shows the overprint that occurs when you select None.

- **Item:** Choosing Item as the runaround mode causes text to flow around the box that holds the active element. Figure 9-7 shows the effect of Item runaround. This page includes a line, text box, and picture box. Note how the background text flows around the item by a set amount of offset; in this figure, the offset is 6 points. (The default is 1 point, but you usually want a larger offset than this; we tend to use 6 points or more.)

- **Auto Image:** Used only for picture boxes, this mode automatically determines the shape of the image in the picture box and how text flows around it. The runaround follows the shape of the active item while maintaining the offset that

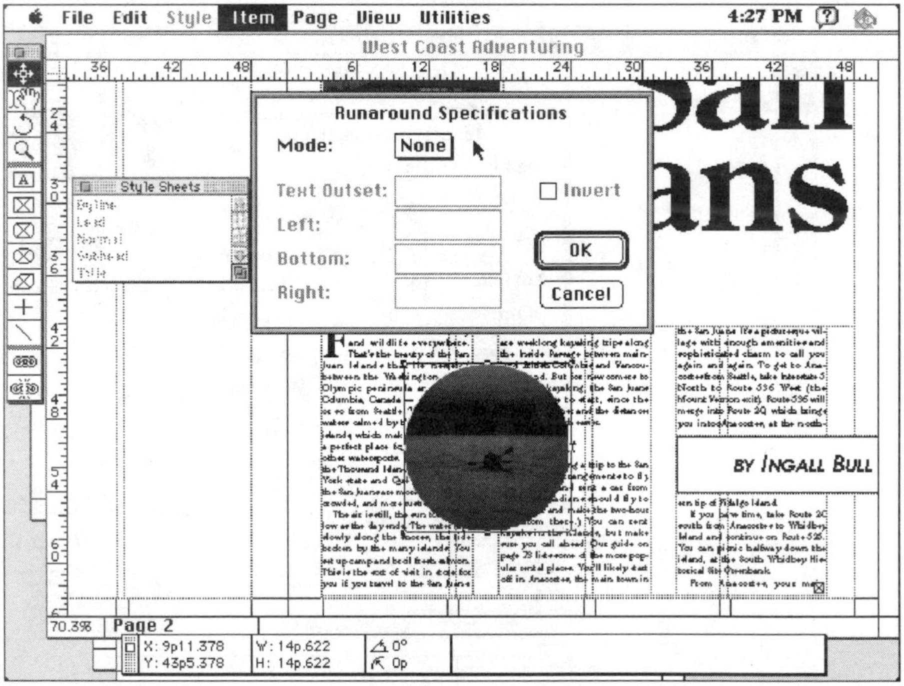

Figure 9-6: Selecting None as the runaround mode creates this overprint.

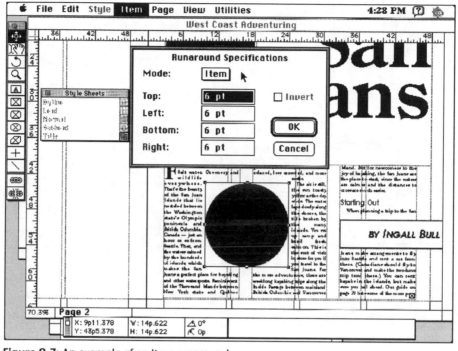

Figure 9-7: An example of an Item runaround.

you specify. Figure 9-8 shows how the program flows text around the picture. In this example, we used a 4-point text offset (the distance between the text and the picture). This offset is also set in the Runaround Specifications dialog box.

∽ **Manual Image:** Also used only for picture boxes, this setting automatically draws a polygon around the active element and then lets you modify the shape of the polygon by clicking and dragging the black handles on the points of the polygon. You can also move line segments in the polygon by clicking on the line and dragging it into place. In Figure 9-9, the runaround follows the lines around the picture shape that are established by the Manual Image polygon.

When you choose Manual Image, you may want more handles for shaping the polygon than the number QuarkXPress automatically gives you. To add a polygon handle to a line, hold down the Ctrl key as you click the line; a new handle appears at that point on the line.

You can also check the Invert box in the Runaround Specifications dialog box. This option causes the text to fill the picture box and conform to its shape. Figure 9-10 shows an example of a story's lead text placed in a circular frame.

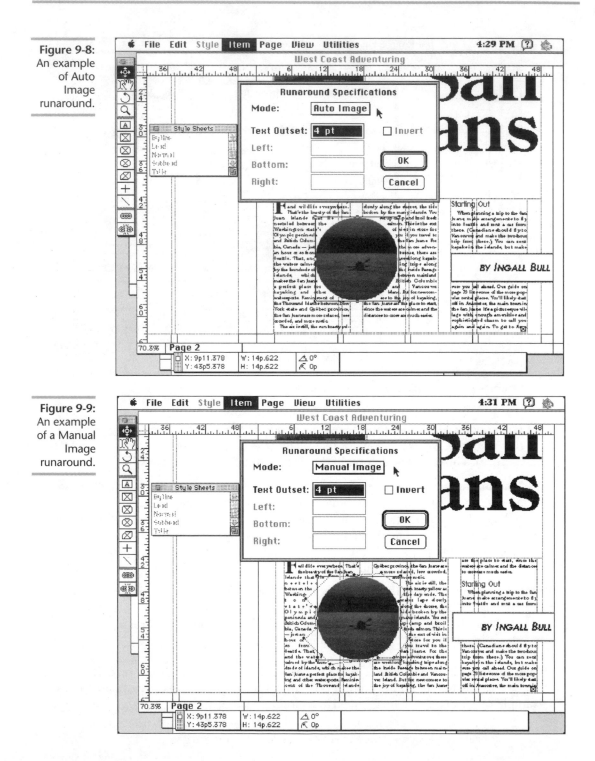

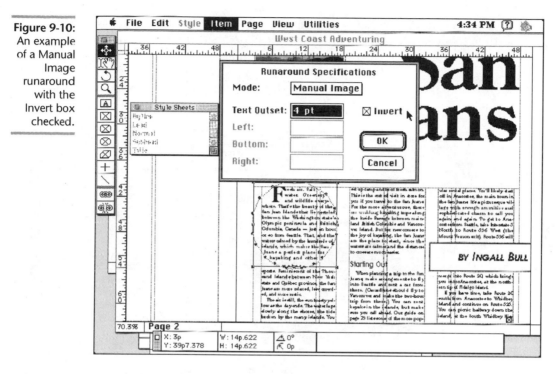

Figure 9-10:
An example
of a Manual
Image
runaround
with the
Invert box
checked.

Irregularly shaped text boxes

QuarkXPress version 3.3 introduced nonrectangular text boxes, so you can have text within polygonal boxes. However, you'll notice that there is no polygon or oval text-box tool — you still have to start with the standard text box and then modify it. Follow these steps to create an irregular text box:

STEPS: Creating an Irregular Text Box

Step 1. Select the text box to be changed.

Step 2. Use Item ⇨ Box Shape to choose the new shape.

Step 3. If you have chosen the polygon shape, use Item ⇨ Reshape to add or delete points. To move control points or line segments, hold the Shift key (the pointer changes to a chevron,   when selecting a control point or line segment. To add new control points, hold the ⌘ key (the pointer changes to a squared open circle,   and select a spot on the text box's boundary; a new control point is created there that you can now move. To delete control points, hold the ⌘ key as you move the mouse over an existing control point; the pointer will change to a squared open circle with an X through it   to indicate you can delete that point (click it to delete it).

To create an irregular curved box, first convert the text box to a polygon and then to an ellipse. This creates the control points that you can then move, delete, or add to. Figure 9-11 shows an example.

You can revert to the original text box shape by using Item ➪ Box Shape and choosing the rectangle.

Figure 9-11:
By reshaping a text box first to an ellipse and then to a polygon, you can create irregular curved text boxes.

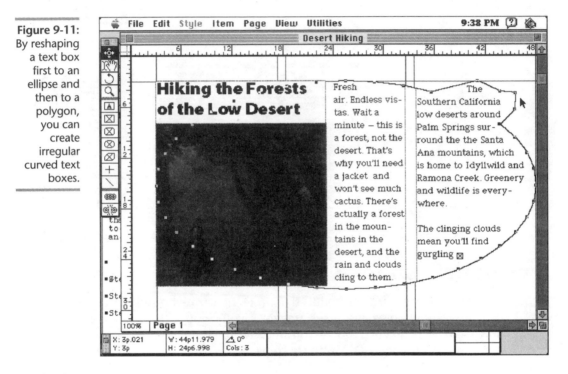

Adding Text to Text Boxes

The text portion of your document is important because it conveys the thoughts that you are communicating to your audience. The appearance of the text — its type style, size, and so on — can determine how well readers receive your message. The specifics of controlling the various characteristics of text are covered in Part IV of this book. This chapter tells you how to get the text into the text boxes.

After you create some initial text boxes in your document, it's time to fill them with text. Because QuarkXPress has a built-in text editor, you can, if you like, enter text directly into the text box. The advantage to using the built-in text editor is that you can perform all text-related activities within one program. The disadvantage is that you miss out on using the more sophisticated features of a dedicated word processing program because the built-in QuarkXPress text editor is relatively simple.

Using the built-in text editor

We definitely recommend using a separate word processor for creating most of your text so that you have access to the word processor's greater set of features. If you just have a small amount of text to enter, you can manage with QuarkXPress's built-in text editor. This tool is useful for creating headlines or the copy in brochures and ads. Use the text editor by following these steps.

STEPS: Entering Text with the Built-In Text Editor

Step 1. With the document open, select the Content tool.

Step 2. Use the mouse to place the I-beam pointer at the top of the text box (the I-beam pointer may already be at this location).

Step 3. Click the mouse button. A blinking I-beam cursor appears, indicating that you can begin typing.

Step 4. Type the text. Figure 9-12 shows how the text box looks when you are typing text into it.

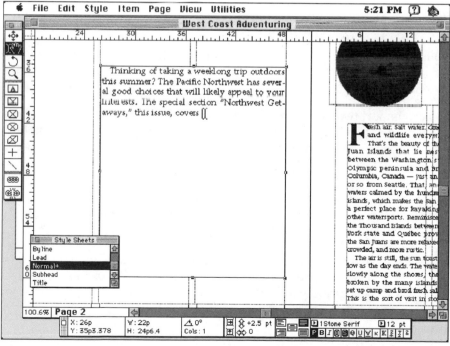

Figure 9-12: Typing text into the text box.

If you use the built-in text editor to enter text, wait until you complete several lines of text before adjusting the font or spacing so that you can better see the effects of any typographical changes you make.

Importing text

Instead of using the built-in text editor, you may want to import text from a word processing program. Before importing text into the text box, read about how to prepare your files for import in Chapter 7. Then take the following steps to import your text.

STEPS:	Importing Text into a Text Box
Step 1.	With the document open, select the Content tool.
Step 2.	Use the mouse to place the I-beam pointer at the top of the text box (the I-beam pointer may already be at this location).
Step 3.	Choose File ⇨ Get Text to display the Get Text dialog box, shown in Figure 9-13.
Step 4.	Use the controls in the dialog box to locate the text file that you want to place into the text box.
Step 5.	After you locate the text file, choose OK. The text flows into the text box.

You can import text any place in a text box even if the text box already contains text. The imported text flows into the text box at the location of the I-beam pointer. Importing text does not remove text that is already in the text box; it just bumps the existing text (following the I-beam pointer) to the end of the inserted text.

Before you import text from a word processor, it's a good idea to open the word-processed file and change the type size to 10 points or smaller. There are two reasons for doing this:

 ✍ Because text typically imports at 12 points, it's likely that you'll need to change it within QuarkXPress anyhow, and it's easier to make changes in your word processor before you import the text.

 ✍ If you select the Automatic Text Box when you create the document, text from the word processor flows in and QuarkXPress automatically adds as many pages as necessary to accommodate the imported text. If the text flows in at 12 points and you actually want to use 10-point type, you must delete the excess pages in the QuarkXPress document later on.

Figure 9-13:
The Get
Text dialog
box.

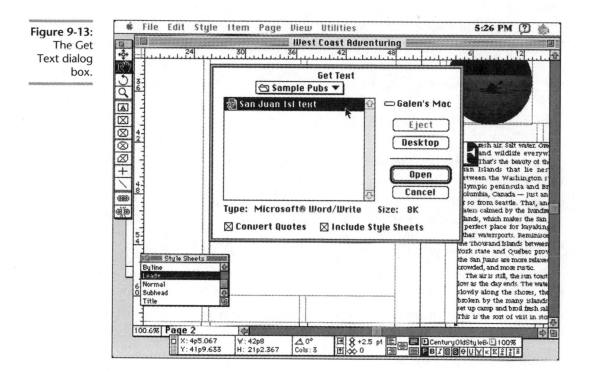

Similarly, another thing you can do before importing text is to select the font you want to use in the word-processed file so that it imports in the font you want to use in the QuarkXPress document.

Linking Text Boxes

Suppose that you have a text box on page 1 of your document. You fill it with text and find that you need to jump (or continue) the text to page 4. How do you handle it? Link two text boxes together.

When you think of linking, think of a metal chain with links connected to other links. The only difference is that in QuarkXPress, you are not linking pieces of metal, but boxes that hold text.

Linking is one of the most useful features in QuarkXPress. Use it whenever you want text to flow between text boxes in a continuous stream that is maintained during the editing process. You can unlink boxes when your layout doesn't need text to flow from one text box to another.

You can always link and unlink boxes after they are filled with text. But linking is easier when the text boxes are created but not yet filled with text.

STEPS: Linking Two Text Boxes

Step 1.   Open the document to the page that contains the *first* text box that you want in the linked chain of text boxes.

Step 2.   Click the Linking tool (second tool from the bottom of the Tool palette) to select it.

Step 3.   Place the pointer in the text box that is to be the first box in the chain. The pointer changes to look like a chain link. Click the mouse button. You'll see an animated dashed line around the selected text box, indicating that it's the start of the link.

Step 4.   Go to the page containing the text box that will be the next link in the chain. (To go to that page, you can either press ⌘J or choose Page ⇨ Go to.)

Step 5.   Place the pointer in the next text box that you want in the chain and click the mouse button. The text box is now linked with the first text box. The text flow will bypass the unlinked text box, continuing on to any others in the text chain.

Step 6.   Repeat steps 2 through 5 until all text boxes you want in the chain are linked.

The order in which you link text boxes is the order in which text will flow. If you start with a text box at the bottom of the page and link to another text box above it or on a previous page, then you will create an unnatural order (and probably nonsensical text as well).

In Figure 9-14, you see two linked text boxes. Links are indicated by an arrow that shows the end of one link and the beginning of the next link.

On occasion, you may want to unlink text boxes that were previously linked. To split one story that spans two linked text boxes into two separate stories, for example, you use the program's Unlinking tool.

Figure 9-14:
Two linked
text boxes.

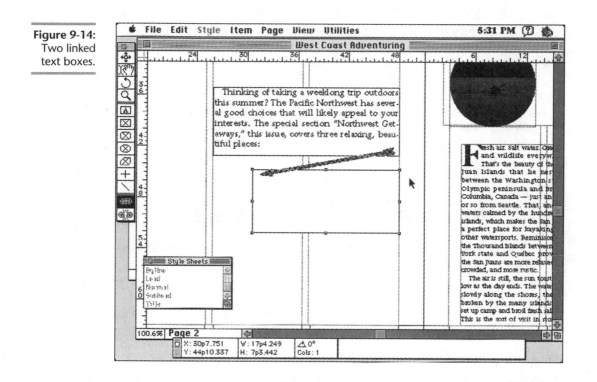

STEPS: Unlinking Two Text Boxes

Step 1. Open the document to the page that has the first text box in the linked chain.

Step 2. Click the Unlinking tool to select it.

Step 3. Place the pointer in the first text box in the chain. Click the mouse button.

Step 4. Go to the page containing the next text box in the chain. (To go to that page, either press ⌘J, or choose Page ⇨ Go to.)

Step 5. Place the pointer in the next text box in the chain and — while holding the Shift key — click the mouse button. The text box is now unlinked from the first text box.

Holding down the Shift key ensures that you won't accidentally unlink text boxes.

Step 6. If you have additional text boxes to unlink, repeat steps 2 through 5.

As a safety feature, the Link and Unlink tools change to the Content tool each time you use them to prevent you from linking or unlinking more boxes than you intend to.

You can break the text chain at the point of the selected box by using the Unlink tool to select the arrowhead or tailfeather of the link to or from the selected box. (If you hold the Shift key while doing so, the Unlink tool works normally: removing the selected text box from the chain, and rerouting the text flow on to the next box in the chain.)

Special Positioning Features

Computer technology brought with it new layout possibilities for text. Instead of placing text in rectangular boxes, you can slant text, rotate it, and even have it flow into many kinds of shapes — all to create a dynamic impact on the reader. QuarkXPress offers several such tools.

Rotating the text box

One of the nicest features of QuarkXPress is the way that it lets you rotate elements, including text boxes, in precise increments. You can control the amount of rotation in three ways:

∽ **Option 1:** Select the text box and choose Item ➪ Modify (or press ⌘M) to display the Text Box Specifications dialog box. You can then enter a rotation amount (between 0 and 360 degrees, in units as small as .001 degrees) in the Box Angle field. If you want to make other changes to the text box specifications, continue making them; otherwise, choose OK.

 To rotate a text box counter-clockwise, use a positive rotation number; use a negative number to rotate a text box clockwise.

∽ **Option 2:** You can rotate a text box on-the-fly by using the Rotation tool and selecting the text box. Then drag the box to the rotation angle that you want by holding down the mouse button as you move the mouse. Objects rotate around the center of their bounding box (an invisible box that holds objects), which is not always where you think it is.

∽ **Option 3:** Enter a rotation degree in the rotation field ⚒ of the Measurements palette.

Most users find the two numerical methods of rotating text boxes (using the Text Box Specifications dialog box or Measurements palette) to be superior. This is because the on-the-fly method involves more trial and error and requires a greater amount of visual skill. Also, it takes a good deal of time to learn how to control the amount of the rotation with the on-the-fly method.

Figure 9-15 shows a newsletter with a text box placed off to the side on the pasteboard. We then rotated the same text box by −30 degrees. We accomplished this rotation by entering −30 in the rotation field of the Measurements palette. Figure 9-16 shows the rotated text after we placed it into the newsletter.

 A positive number rotates the text box counterclockwise; a negative number rotates it clockwise. You don't need to put a + to indicate a positive number (+30 and 30 are treated the same), but you do need to use a hyphen to indicate a negative number (−30).

 Although rotated text is effective for banners, mastheads, and other display type, it is generally not considered the best approach for body text.

Figure 9-15:
The text box on the pasteboard is about to be rotated −30 degrees and then dragged into the document page.

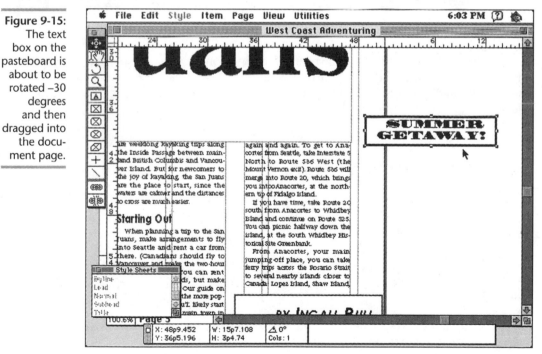

Figure 9-16:
The text box
has been
rotated −30
degrees and
dragged
into position
on the
document
page.

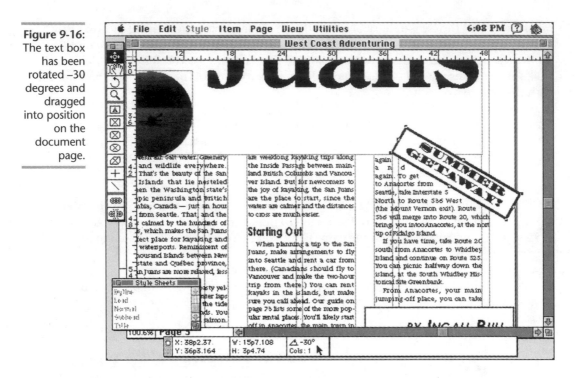

As you can see, rotated text is a powerful effect that you should use sparingly. Because angles do not conform to the standard orientation of text, rotated text calls attention to itself and immediately catches the reader's eye. Reserve rotated text for achieving this effect.

Slanting the text box

QuarkXPress also lets you slant or skew the text box, which is an effect akin to pushing a rectangle to the side: the vertical sides get slanted while the horizontal sides remain untouched.

To use this feature, you must use the Box Skew option in the Text Box Specifications dialog (in Item ⇨ Modify, or via ⌘M). Text is slanted to the same degree as the box that contains it.

Enter the degree of slant as a number between 75 and −75. A positive number slants the box to the right; a negative number to the left.

You can combine slanting and rotation to create unusual layouts, as Figure 9-17 shows. (Here, we rotated the story's main text box by 20 degrees.) But be careful: it's easy to go so overboard that the text becomes hard to read.

Figure 9-17:
A text box
skewed 20
degrees.

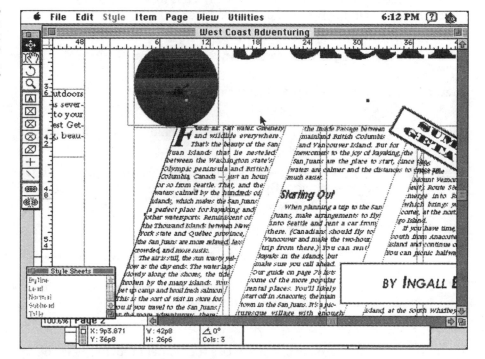

Adding Special Effects to Text

We've covered the bread-and-butter basics of how to work with text. Now it's time to explain some of the more creative text effects that you can achieve with QuarkXPress. These effects include those that layout artists once had to tediously create by hand.

Color and shading

The background of a QuarkXPress text box is normally neutral, meaning that when you print your document, the background is the same color as the color of your paper stock. You can add a background color to a text box, and you can specify the percent shade of the color.

Even if the document is to be printed in a single ink color, you can still add texture to a text box by applying a color (including black) and then specifying a light shade of the color — in the 10 to 40 percent range. We have found many occasions where this technique added to the appearance of a newsletter masthead or a sidebar in a magazine article, even though the text was printed in black.

STEPS:	**Applying Color and Shading to a Text Box Background**
Step 1.	Select the text box and choose Item ⇨ Modify to display the Text Box Specifications dialog box.
Step 2.	In the Background Color field, select a color from the list box (something other than white or None).
Step 3.	In the Shade field, select a shade percentage from the list box. Or enter a shade percentage in the field. (You can specify this value to three decimal places and choose any value between 0 and 100 percent.)
Step 4.	Choose OK to close the dialog box.

 When you shade a picture box, check the shading level by printing the page. How dark the shading appears on the printout depends on the printer device and its resolution.

You also can add color to the text itself. Use the Content tool to select the text and then choose Style ⇨ Color. Select a shade percentage for the text color by choosing Style ⇨ Shade.

The easiest way to apply color to a text box or text is via the Colors palette. Figure 9-18 shows the Colors palette engaged for the "Summer Getaway!" text box. We have selected the text box background icon and applied a 60 percent shade of the spot color Pantone S 199-4. By using the frame and text icons, you can also change the colors of the text and the text box's frame. Note that to change the text's color, you must select the text box with the Text tool. The other two icons work whether you use the Item tool or the Text tool to select the text box. If you have installed the Cool Blends XTension, you can also apply special color gradients (called blends). In Figure 9-18, we have used the default setting of Solid.

Figure 9-18:
Applying
colors to
text boxes
via the
Colors
palette.

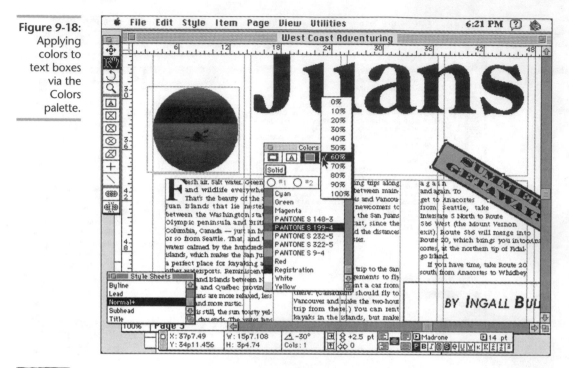

 For more information on applying color to text, refer to Chapter 15. For more information on the Colors palette, color creation, and blends, refer to Chapter 21.

Vertical alignment

You can align text within text boxes with the top, bottom, or middle of the text box. Or you can space text evenly from top and to bottom of the text box. Figure 9-19 shows four different ways of vertically aligning text in text boxes. From left to right, the vertical alignments shown in the figure are: top, centered, bottom, and justified.

To change the vertical alignment of text, select the text box and choose Item ⇨ Modify to display the Text Box Specifications dialog box. Choose an alignment type from the list box in the Vertical Alignment section of the dialog box.

 If you plan to use justified vertical alignment, keep in mind that you need to place pictures outside of the text box that holds the vertically justified text. The presence of a picture disables vertical justification.

Figure 9-19:
Four ways of
vertically
aligning text
in text
boxes.

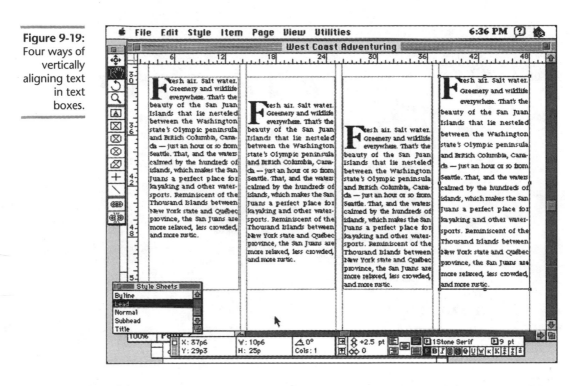

Figure 9-19:
Four ways of
vertically
aligning text
in text
boxes.

Vertical justification spaces text evenly between the first baseline and the bottom of the text box. As long as there are no hard returns in the text, leading adjusts to make each line space the same size as the others in the box. However, if text contains a hard return, you need to specify an interparagraph spacing value in the Inter ¶ Max field. This value tells QuarkXPress the maximum amount of space it can insert between vertically justified paragraphs. If you want the leading to remain constant between paragraphs, set Inter ¶ Max to 0.

Mirroring text

QuarkXPress lets you mirror text — make it read from right to left or bottom to top (or both). There are two ways to apply this effect:

✏ Use the Style ⇨ Flip Horizontally and the Style ⇨ Flip Vertically pull-down menu options. If either of these effects had been previously selected for the current text box, a check mark will appear to the left of the menu item. Make sure that you use the Text tool, or the Style menu will not pull down.

⊛ Use the reading-direction arrows in the Measurements palette. If you click one of the two arrows, the text direction in the selected text box gets reversed from its current setting. If the horizontal arrow ▣ is pointing to the right (text reads left-to-right), clicking it makes the text read right-to-left, and the arrow will change direction. The vertical arrow ▣ likewise toggles between top-to-bottom and bottom-to-top.

 When the reading direction is nonstandard, the arrow goes from being black in a white box to being white in a black box, giving you an added indication that a special effect is activated.

Figure 9-20 shows some sample effects. The "Summer Getaway!" text has been mirrored horizontally and the byline has been mirrored vertically. Note that in the Measurements palette the horizontal text-direction icon for the "Summer Getaway!" text box is selected (white arrow on black background) to indicate that its text has been mirrored horizontally. The vertical text-direction icon remains unselected (black arrow on white background).

When would you want to use this effect? Simply to create graphical effects with type. More pragmatically, you can use this effect for answers to puzzles and quizzes. You can combine mirroring along both axes to create truly confusing text.

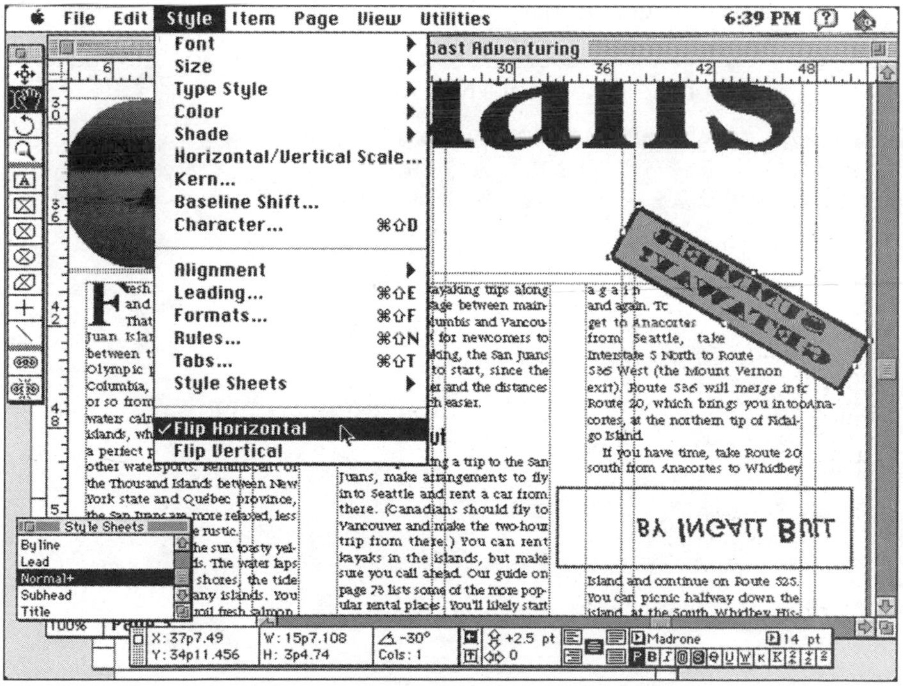

Figure 9-20:
The Flip
Horizontal
and Flip
Vertical
mirroring
controls.

Summary

- You can choose whether a document has automatic text boxes.

- QuarkXPress offers a variety of methods for sizing and positioning text boxes.

- Positive rotation values, which you specify in degrees, rotate a text box counter-clockwise; negative rotation values rotate the box clockwise.

- Rotated text is effective, but only if it is not overused in a document.

- Not all pages need to have the same number of columns. To vary the page layout in a document, you can vary the number and width of text columns on a page.

- Text inset is useful if you are setting a text box near or within another text box and you want some space between them. It is also a good idea to use text inset for text boxes that have frames around them.

- You'll want to use a separate word processor for creating text to be placed in text columns. But in a pinch, the built-in QuarkXPress text editor can handle simple jobs.

- QuarkXPress's linking feature is helpful if you have text that starts on one page and continues on another.

- New features include the creation of irregularly shaped text boxes, the slanting of text boxes, and the ability to mirror text.

Working with Picture Boxes

- -

In This Chapter

➤ Creating picture boxes

➤ Sizing, positioning, and rotating picture boxes

➤ Adding graphics to picture boxes

➤ Suppressing graphic printout

➤ Adding background color to picture boxes

- -

Creating Picture Boxes

Although text is the bread and butter of publishing — the essential message a document contains is almost always textual — graphics are an important part of publishing for two reasons. First, graphics convey some information more easily than text — a photo, chart, or drawing can truly be worth a thousand words if properly used. Second, graphics attract readers and keep them interested in the overall concept of the document. You may need to convince readers that what you have to say is interesting, and graphics can be the initial lure.

In the preceding chapter, you learned how to place, size, and position text boxes. Now it's time to learn to do the same with picture boxes. Picture boxes can contain several types of graphics including photographs, charts, illustrations, and diagrams. In this chapter, we cover the mechanics of the picture box. Later in this book (see Part V), we explain how to modify the graphics that you place into picture boxes, and we describe how to create simple graphics within QuarkXPress.

When you create text boxes in QuarkXPress, you are limited to a rectangular shape (although you can change these boxes, once they have been created, to other shapes with QuarkXPress version 3.3). When creating picture boxes, you have more choices:

rectangle, rounded-corner rectangle, oval, and polygon. You can use the rectangle and oval shapes to create, respectively, perfect square and circles. Polygon picture boxes, the least used of the four options, are useful if you are importing a graphic that has an irregular shape. Experienced designers sometimes use polygon picture boxes to create unique effects, such as placing a graphic into an unusually shaped box.

To create a picture box, you *draw* it using one of four picture box tools in the Tool palette. Figure 10-1 shows picture boxes created with the four tools. Note the *handles* on the polygon picture box in Figure 10-1. Picture boxes created with the polygon or oval tool have handles in a rectangle surrounding the picture box. The handles around the polygon or oval are always in a rectangular pattern, regardless of the shape of the polygon or oval. The following steps guide you through the process of drawing picture boxes.

Figure 10-1:
Four types of picture boxes.

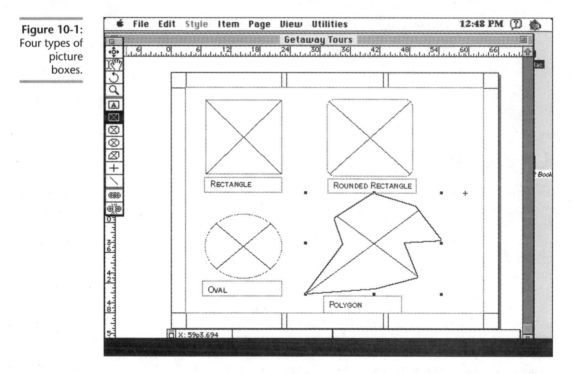

STEPS: **Drawing a Picture Box**

Step 1. Open the document to the page on which you want to draw the picture box and click one of the Picture Box tools. When you use the mouse to move the pointer onto the page, the pointer changes to look like a crosshair (see the right of the polygon picture box in Figure 10-1).

Step 2. Place the crosshair pointer at the location where you want to position one of the corners of the picture box.

Step 3a. For all boxes but the polygon, press and hold the mouse button. Where you pressed, the mouse button becomes a corner of the picture box. As you drag your mouse away from that point, you will see the picture box grow and take shape. When it has the desired dimensions, release the mouse button.

Step 3b. For polygon picture boxes, press the mouse button at the start point and then release it. Move the mouse to the next point on the polygon (you'll see a line extend from where you started to the current mouse position) and press the mouse button again. Do this for each line segment. A polygon picture box must be closed, so you must end at the point where you began. When you get to that point, you'll see the pointer change from a crosshair to a rounded rectangle (the close-polygon pointer). Click the mouse button to complete the polygon. Polygon picture boxes must have at least three sides. At the right side of Figure 10-2 is a set of images that show a polygon being drawn.

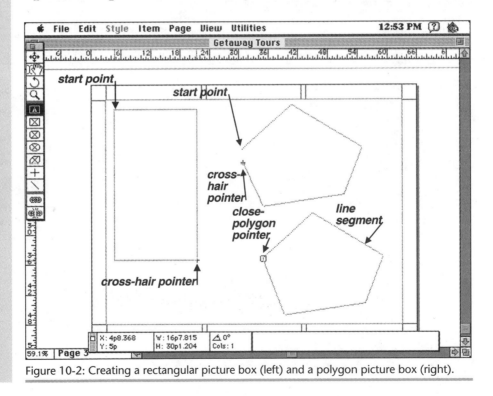

Figure 10-2: Creating a rectangular picture box (left) and a polygon picture box (right).

To cancel a polygon box during creation, use ⌘. (Command-period).

Setting Picture Box Specifications

As with text boxes, you can establish a number of specifications for picture boxes. For picture boxes, you use the Picture Box Specifications dialog box, shown in Figure 10-3. This dialog box is useful for precisely sizing and positioning a picture box, rotating it, scaling it, skewing (slanting) it, and adding color to the graphic's background. You can also use this dialog box to move a graphic within its picture box, so you can crop (offset) an image. (Part V of this book covers in detail the options available in the Picture Box dialog box.)

You can apply these picture-box specifications to a box before importing a graphic, and the settings will be applied to the imported graphic. If, however, you reimport the picture into the box (for example, the image was updated or its location on the disk changed), the settings will be lost.

Figure 10-3:
The Picture
Box
Specifica-
tions dialog
box.

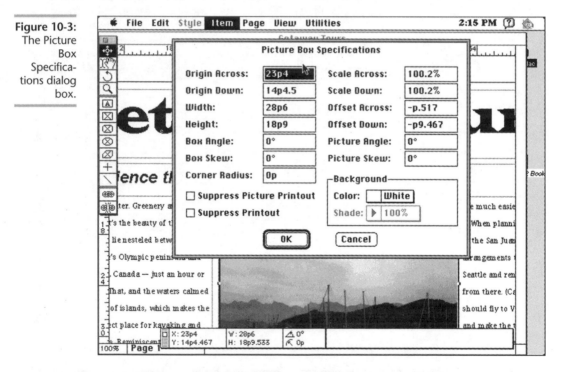

Sizing and positioning picture boxes

If you want to be precise about your picture box's dimensions, the W (Width) and H (Height) measurements on the Measurements palette change to reflect the size of the box as you draw it. The X and Y coordinates in the Measurements palette display, respectively, the vertical and horizontal coordinates of the text box location.

When you create a picture box, draw it at the approximate size and then use the Measurements palette to resize it by changing the X, Y, W, and H dimensions as appropriate. You can resize or reposition a polygon picture box this way, but you can't reposition individual line segments within it.

 If you want the picture box to be perfectly square, hold down the Shift key as you draw the box with the Rectangle Picture Box tool. If you want the picture box to be a perfect circle, hold down the Shift key as you draw the box with the Oval Picture Box tool.

You can control the size and position of a picture box in a number of ways.

- **Option 1:** Enter numerical values in the Picture Box Specifications dialog box (select Item ⇨ Modify). The Origin Across and Origin Down fields control the placement of the box, and the Width and Height fields control its size. (The origin is the upper-left corner of the box.) The Offset Across and Offset Down fields control the position of the graphic within the picture box — you can use these fields to crop an image. Using this dialog box is great for precisely placing and sizing picture boxes, but it has one drawback: the dialog box blocks your view of the actions you take so that you can't see the results until you exit the dialog box.

- **Option 2:** Change the settings in the Measurements palette. X is the horizontal coordinate; changes you make to the X value move the graphic side to side. Y is the vertical coordinate; changes to the Y value move the picture box up and down. The W and H fields control the box's width and height. Like the dialog box method, this option offers precision, but it also allows you to view the results of any changes as they occur.

- **Option 3:** Use the Item tool to drag the entire box into position or to resize the box by clicking and dragging on the box handles. You also can use the Content tool (which, for graphics, becomes a grabber hand) to move the graphic within the box. With this tool, you can see your actions on-screen.

 The easiest way to resize polygon and oval picture boxes is to click and drag the box handles, which appear in a rectangle around the polygon or oval shape.

Special sizing options

QuarkXPress offers several ways to control a picture box and its contents while resizing:

- Just dragging a handle resizes the box but does not alter the graphic's size or scale.

- Holding down Option-Shift while you resize a box causes both the box and the graphic to resize proportionally.

- Holding down Shift keeps a rectangular box square or an oval box circular as you resize it. (For a polygon picture box, this option works the same as Option-Shift — it keeps the polygon proportional.)

- Holding down ⌘ scales the graphic to fit in the new box shape, distorting the graphic if necessary. If you also hold down Shift, the box stays a perfect square or circle, and the graphic will be scaled to fit in it.

It's nice that QuarkXPress gives you such a variety of ways to modify picture boxes. You'll probably use all of them at some point.

 The measurement units used for specifications in the Picture Box Specifications dialog box reflect the settings that you establish in the General Preferences dialog box.

Changing the shape of the picture box

After working on a layout for a while, you may decide that the shape of a particular picture box is not right. You might be tempted to just delete the picture box, along with its contents, and start again. Such measures aren't necessary, though, because QuarkXPress offers a couple of ways to change the shape of a picture box, even if it already contains a graphic.

Rounded corners

If you created the picture box with the rectangle tool or the rounded rectangle tool, you can change its shape by modifying its corner radius. The corner radius is the radius of an invisible circle inside the corner of the picture box. The sides of the invisible circle touch the sides of the picture box.

Rectangular picture boxes have a corner radius of 0 (zero), and if you change the corner radius enough, you can turn rectangular boxes into rounded rectangles or ovals. In fact, a rounded-corner picture box actually is a rectangular box that has a corner radius of 0.25 inches (1.5 picas). Figure 10-4 shows the effects of enlarging the corner radius of a rounded rectangle picture box. The larger the corner radius number, the closer the box gets to becoming an oval. The maximum radius is 12 picas (2 inches).

There are two ways to change the corner radius: through the Picture Box Specifications dialog box's Corner Radius field or through the Measurements palette's corner radius setting (to the right of ⌒ icon).

Figure 10-4:
The corner radius affects the shape of a rectangular picture box.

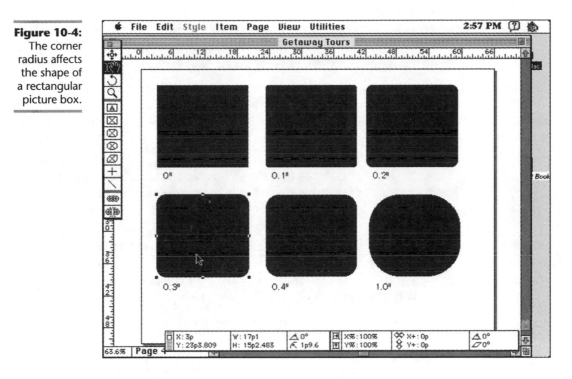

Picture box shape

Another way of changing the shape of a picture box is to select the picture box and choose the Item menu. As you can see in Figure 10-5, the last section of the Item menu has a Picture Box Shape command, which in turn offers a list box that lets you select a new shape for the picture box.

This list has one picture box shape not available through the Tool palette: an inverted, rounded rectangle picture box. Figure 10-6 shows rounded rectangle picture boxes (the same as those in Figure 10-4) with the inverted, rounded rectangle shape applied.

If you want to change the shape of a polygon picture box, select the box and choose Reshape Polygon from the Item menu. You then can change the shape of the polygon by clicking and dragging its handles and lines.

Predefining Picture Box Settings

Chances are that your publication has a house style for standard elements. For example, you may always place a hairline rule around photos. You can set QuarkXPress to automatically add such attributes to new picture boxes by using the Tool Preferences dialog box (Edit ⇨ Preferences ⇨ Tools).

For example, to add a hairline rule, select the Rectangular Picture Box tool icon and then the Frame button in the Tool Preferences dialog box. Choose the frame style from the scroll list at the left side of the Frame Specifications dialog box, and the width, color, and shade of the rule (a hairline is 0.25 points).

You can likewise modify the runaround for all picture boxes (most magazines and newsletters use a standard value, like 6 points or 1 pica) by clicking the Modify button to invoke the Picture Box Specifications dialog box. Likewise, you can change the box background to a color or to None (so that any underlying colors are guaranteed to come through any part of the picture box not containing a graphic).

Chances are that you have multiple types of house styles for standard elements: picture boxes for photos may use a hairline rule around them, but picture boxes for illustrations may have a 1-point frame, and picture boxes for logos and icons may have no frame but need a white background. If these boxes are all rectangular, you can't set up multiple preferences for the Rectangular Picture Box tool, right? Well, only sort of right.

If you rarely use rounded-corner picture boxes, set the preferences for that tool to match one of your standard element's needs. Make the corner radius 0 picas (use the Modify button to invoke the Picture Box Specifications dialog box) — that will make it a rectangular picture box. That gives you two standardized styles for boxes. If you need more, you can set the oval picture box and polygon picture boxes with the desired settings. But you will have to take one extra step if you use these for rectangular boxes: you'll have to reshape each box (using Item ⇨ Box Shape). Still, that's faster than changing all the box's settings for a commonly used box style.

Note that if you make changes via the Tool Preferences dialog box while no documents are open, the preferences will be in effect for all future documents. If you make changes while a document or template is open, the preferences will be in effect only for that document or template, or for documents using that document or template.

The Tool Preferences dialog box invokes the standard picture box dialog boxes, which are covered in this chapter. Any options that can't be set globally are grayed out.

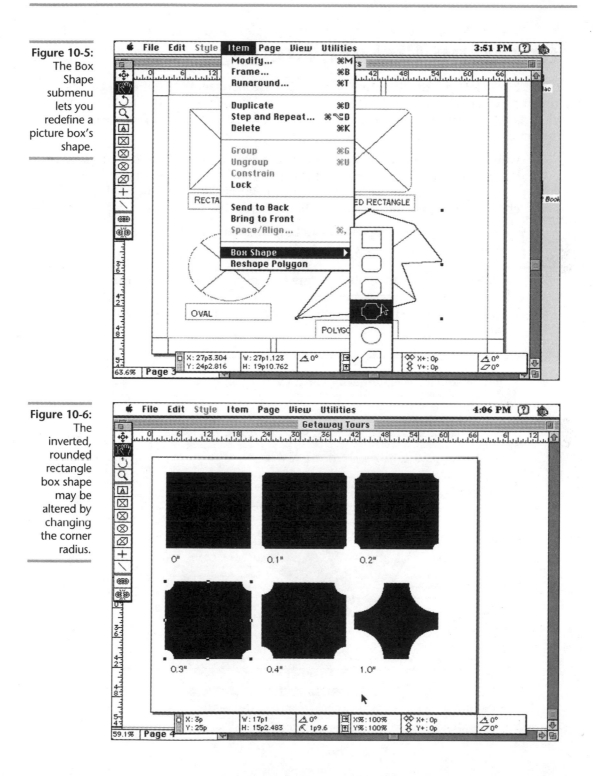

Figure 10-5:
The Box Shape submenu lets you redefine a picture box's shape.

Figure 10-6:
The inverted, rounded rectangle box shape may be altered by changing the corner radius.

Rotating Picture Boxes

QuarkXPress lets you rotate picture boxes in precise increments of .001 degrees. Figure 10-7 shows a picture box that is rotated 30 degrees. The text box with "Greetings from Victoria!" is also rotated 30 degrees, to create the effect of a postcard. You can control the amount of rotation in three ways:

- **Option 1:** Select the picture box and choose Item ➪ Modify to display the Picture Box Specifications box. Then enter a rotation amount (between 0 and 360 degrees, in increments of .001 degrees) in the Box Angle field. If you want to make other changes to the picture box specifications, do so. Otherwise, choose OK.

  To rotate a picture box counter-clockwise, use a positive rotation value; use a negative value to rotate it clockwise.

- **Option 2:** You also can rotate a picture box on-the-fly. To do this, use the Rotation tool. Select the picture box and rotate it by dragging it and holding down the mouse button as you move the mouse. Figure 10-8 shows the picture box being rotated this way.

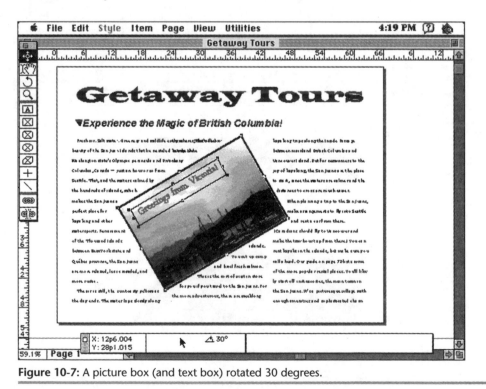

Figure 10-7: A picture box (and text box) rotated 30 degrees.

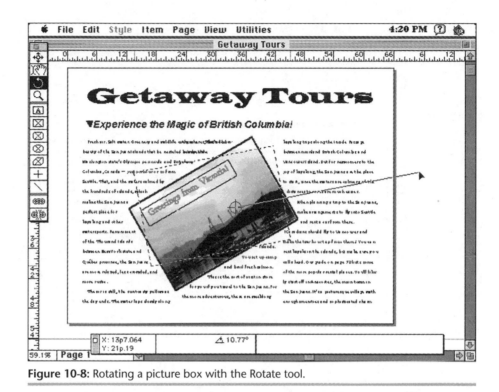

Figure 10-8: Rotating a picture box with the Rotate tool.

∽ **Option 3:** Use the Measurements palette to rotate the text box. Simply enter a rotation degree in the rotation field.

You might want to rotate the picture box but keep the graphic itself at its original orientation. To do so, rotate the picture box and then open the Picture Box Specifications dialog box (via ⌘M). In the Picture Angle field, enter the reverse value of the picture box's rotation angle. For example, if the picture box is rotated 33 degrees, set the Picture Angle at –33 degrees. Figure 10-9 shows a picture box with these rotation settings.

Figure 10-9:
You can
rotate
picture
boxes
indepen-
dently of the
graphics
inside them.

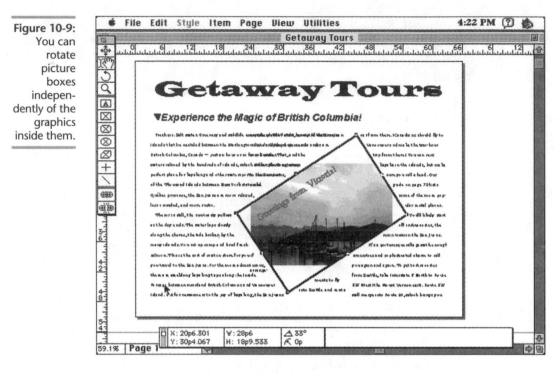

Suppressing Graphic Printout

As you develop a document layout, you may want to print rough-draft copies of it from time to time. Consider printing them without the contents of any picture boxes. Suppressing graphic printout saves considerable printing time.

QuarkXPress gives you two options for suppressing graphic printout. The first, Suppress Picture Printout, prevents the graphic from printing but prints any frame or background color for the box. The second — and quickest — option, Suppress Printout, prevents the graphic *and* its background from printing. To choose either option, choose Item ⇨ Modify to display the Picture Box Specifications dialog box and select the Suppress Picture Printout box or the Suppress Printout box by putting a check mark in the box next to the desired option.

Part VIII details other printing considerations and techniques.

If you select one of these options, remember to go back into the Picture Box Specifications dialog box and uncheck the box before printing final copies of the document.

Adding Graphics to Picture Boxes __

After you create a picture box, you're ready to fill it with a graphic. The following steps detail how.

STEPS: **Placing Graphics in Picture Boxes**

Step 1. With the document open and the picture box selected, click the Content tool.

Step 2. Choose File ⇨ Get Text to display the Get Picture dialog box.

Step 3. Use the controls in the dialog box to locate the graphic file you want to put into the picture box.

Step 4. After you locate the graphic file, choose OK. The graphic appears in the picture box.

After you import the graphic, you probably will need to make some modifications to it. Figure 10-10 shows an example of how an imported graphic first appeared. As you can see, the graphic is off center and too big for the picture box.

Figure 10-10:
How an imported graphic first appears. The image can be resized and repositioned.

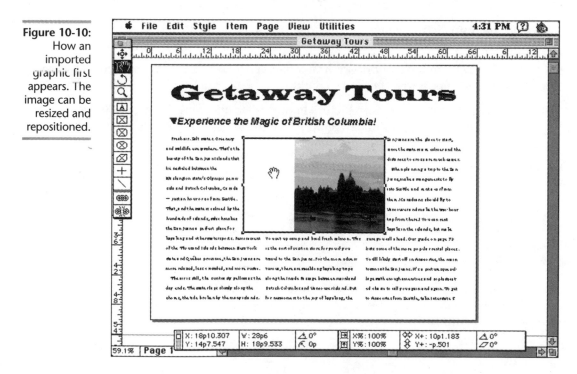

Part V, which covers the details of working with graphics, explains how to change a graphic's size.

To move the graphic around so that it is positioned where you want it to be, click the Content tool. When you position the pointer over the picture box, it becomes a grabber hand (it actually looks like a little hand, as shown in Figure 10-10). Click the mouse button again and keep it pressed as you drag the graphic into position.

QuarkXPress has three shortcuts to simplify graphics sizing and positioning:

- ∞ Shift-⌘M centers the graphic in the picture box,

- ∞ Shift-⌘F fits the graphic to the box's dimensions, distorting the graphic if necessary.

- ∞ Shift-Option-⌘F fits the graphic to the box but maintains the aspect ratio of the graphic. If the picture box and graphic have different aspect ratios, QuarkXPress will make the best fit it can, leaving white space around the image as necessary.

When you open a document, you can tell QuarkXPress to automatically update any graphics that were changed in another program since the last time you opened the document. Choose Edit ➪ Preferences ➪ General to display the General Preferences dialog box. You have three choices:

- ∞ In the Auto Picture Import field, choose On to have QuarkXPress automatically use the latest version of all graphics.

- ∞ If you prefer to have QuarkXPress notify you before it imports graphics that were modified, choose the On (verify) option.

- ∞ The default setting for Auto Picture Import is Off, meaning that QuarkXPress does not automatically update graphics to the latest version unless you tell it to.

See Chapter 4 and Chapter 24 for more details.

Adding Background Color and Shade

As with text boxes, you can add a background color to a picture box, and you can specify the percent shade of the color. To apply color and shade to a picture box background, follow these steps:

STEPS:	**Using the Picture Box Specifications to Add Color**
Step 1.	Select the picture box and choose Item ⇨ Modify to display the Picture Box Specifications dialog box.
Step 2.	In the Background Color field, select a color from the list box.
Step 3.	In the Shade field, select a percentage from the list box or enter a percentage. You can specify a value between 0 and 100 percent, in increments as small as .001 percent.
Step 4.	Choose OK to close the dialog box.

It's easier to use the Colors palette to apply colors and shades:

STEPS:	**Using the Colors Palette to Add Color**
Step 1.	Select the picture box with the Content tool.
Step 2.	Then open the palette via the View menu.
Step 3.	Select the box-background icon, frame icon, or content icon (your selection tells QuarkXPress what you want to color).
Step 4.	Finally, drag the color you want onto the picture box. You can also adjust the shade and apply a blend. Figure 10-11 shows an example.

 Here's an application where the ability to add color and shade to a picture box really comes in handy: If your document will include halftone photos to be stripped in by the printer, you can draw a picture box to mark the position where a halftone will be placed. You then fill the picture box with 100 percent black, creating a black box that marks the spot where your printer is to strip in a photographic halftone.

 For more details on the Colors palette and using color with graphics, see Chapter 21.

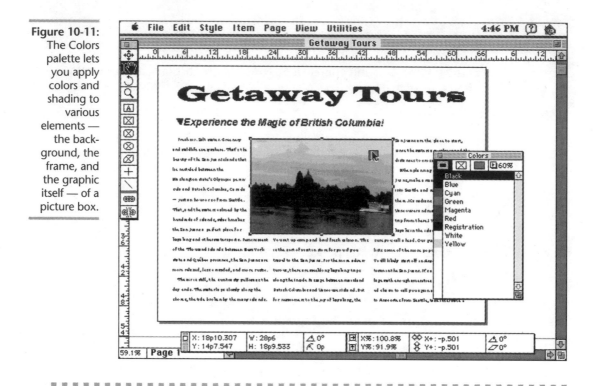

Summary

- ➥ QuarkXPress lets you draw picture boxes in a variety of shapes, including the versatile polygon.

- ➥ After you create and fill a picture box, you can easily change the box's shape, even if it is a polygon.

- ➥ To create a perfect square or circle picture box, hold down the Shift key as you draw with the rectangular picture box tool or the oval picture box tool.

- ➥ Resize picture boxes by using the Measurements palette or by dragging their sizing handles.

- ➥ You can rotate a picture box in one direction and its contents in another.

- ➥ To save time when printing rough drafts of your document, suppress the printout of graphics.

- ➥ QuarkXPress can automatically use the most current version of a graphic created in another program, but only if you so specify.

Additional Layout Features

11

═══

In This Chapter

➡ Aligning and spacing layout elements

➡ Adding rules or arrows to the layout

➡ Adding decorative frames to text and picture boxes

➡ Copying elements and pages from one document to another

➡ Saving pages as EPS files

═══

Aligning Multiple Elements _____

It's not at all uncommon to have a set of two or more layout elements that you want to line up to a certain X or Y coordinate. You may also want to line up these elements with a certain amount of space between them. QuarkXPress lets you align items according to their left, right, top, or bottom edges, or to their centers. You can also control the amount of space between multiple items, and you can specify whether these items are evenly spread across the page or staggered horizontally or vertically.

Space/Align

The Space/Align Items dialog box is a powerful feature that allows you to control the spacing and alignment of elements in your layout.

How does Space/Align work? Showing an example is the best way to illustrate it. Say you have four picture boxes on a page, and you want the boxes to be precisely aligned by their left edges with one-half inch between the boxes. Figure 11-1 shows the settings that you specify in the Space/Align Items dialog box to accomplish this layout. To establish a layout like the one shown in the example, use the following steps.

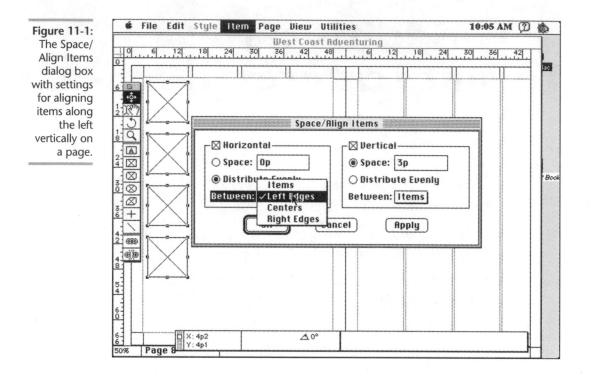

Figure 11-1:
The Space/
Align Items
dialog box
with settings
for aligning
items along
the left
vertically on
a page.

STEPS: Aligning Multiple Elements

Step 1. With the Item tool selected, hold down the Shift key and click each of the four boxes to select them.

Step 2. Choose Item ⇨ Space/Align (or use ⌘, [Command-comma]) to display the Space/Align Items dialog box.

Step 3. Click the Vertical box to select it. Choose Space (which is below the Vertical box) and enter 3p in the Space field.

Step 4. Select Distribute Evenly and then Items from the Between list box.

Step 5. Click the Horizontal box to select it. Choose Space (which is below the Horizontal box) and enter 0p in the Space field.

Step 6. Select Distribute Evenly and then Left Edges from the Between list box.

Step 7. Select Apply to see what the settings will result in (to make sure that you've entered the right settings), and then choose OK to implement the changes.

If you are new to QuarkXPress and want to increase your layout expertise, do some experimenting. Draw a few text boxes and apply different X and Y coordinates to them in the Measurements palette. Also, try using different settings in the Space/Align Items dialog box. This is a great way to learn how these features work.

Step and Repeat

Whenever you can, it's a good idea to let the computer do the work for you, and QuarkXPress makes it easy for the computer to do extra work. As an example, the program has the ability to create multiple copies of selected elements and to space them horizontally or vertically at regular intervals. This powerful feature is called *Step and Repeat.*

Suppose that you want to create a table of contents in which there are six sets of elements (each element contains a group made up of a picture box that has a photo or drawing, a text box overlaid on it to hold the page number, and a text box next to it to list the title, author, and description) from top to bottom.

Figure 11-2 shows an example of this type of layout along with the Step and Repeat dialog box, which you access by choosing Item ⇨ Step and Repeat or via Option-⌘D. The boxes to be repeated are at the top of the page.

Figure 11-2:
The Step
and Repeat
dialog box.

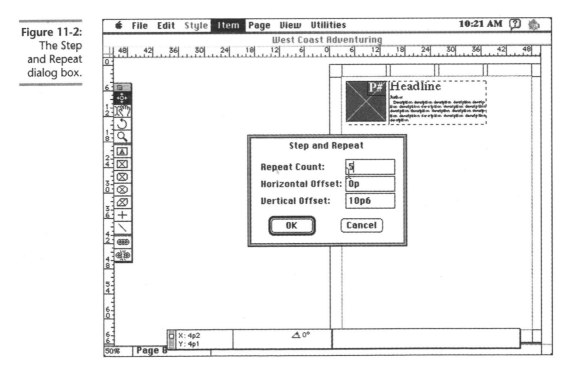

☞ **To select a rule type and line end:** To select a rule type (dotted, doubled, solid, and so on) and line end (arrow point, and so on), select the rule to make it active. Choose Item ➪ Modify to display the Line Specifications dialog box (shown in Figure 11-5) and make the selections you want. Another way of selecting a rule type is to choose one of the line selections in the Measurements palette (see Figure 11-4). This palette also offers a drop-down list box (at far right) that lets you pick from a variety of line endings, including arrows.

If you select a rule composed of two or more lines, keep in mind that the multiple lines may not appear if the line weight is too small. This is because the line weight you specify is the *total* line weight for the double or triple line. A line weight of 1 point for a double or triple line is so small that the line appears as a single, 1 point line.

☞ **To reposition a line:** Select the line and then drag it into position. You can also reposition a line by entering new X and Y coordinates in the Measurements palette or by entering position coordinates in the Line Specifications dialog box (choose Item ➪ Modify to display the dialog box).

☞ **To rotate a line:** Enter a value (in degrees, in .001-degree increments) in the Angle field of the Line Specifications dialog box (Item ➪ Modify). Or enter a value in the rotation field of the Measurements palette.

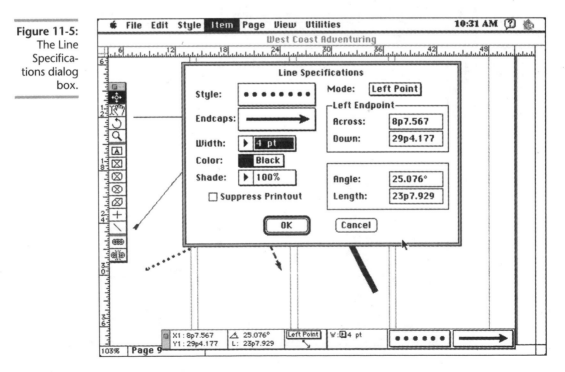

Figure 11-5:
The Line
Specifica-
tions dialog
box.

As we emphasized in earlier layout chapters, simplicity is almost always better. This axiom applies to rules as well. Some of the most obnoxious layouts you'll ever see are those that use a variety of rule types and widths on the same page. Avoid creating a bad page design — don't use too many rules and arrows. If you do use rules and arrows, keep them simple and keep their weights on the light side. Even for a double or triple line, anything more than about 8 points is just too heavy and overpowers the page.

Line Mode

With a feature called line mode, QuarkXPress lets you control the positions of lines in four ways:

- ☞ Endpoints, which shows the coordinates for the beginning and end of the line.

- ☞ Midpoint, which shows the coordinates for the center of the line.

- ☞ Left point, which shows the coordinates for the leftmost point of the line.

- ☞ Right point, which shows the coordinates for the rightmost point of the line.

By changing modes, you change the coordinates that appear in the Measurements palette or Line Specifications dialog box. Figure 11-6 shows the Measurements palette for each of the four modes. Note how the labels for X and Y coordinates change depending which mode is selected: X1 and Y1 indicate the left point; X2 and Y2 indicate the right point; and XC and YC indicate the midpoint.

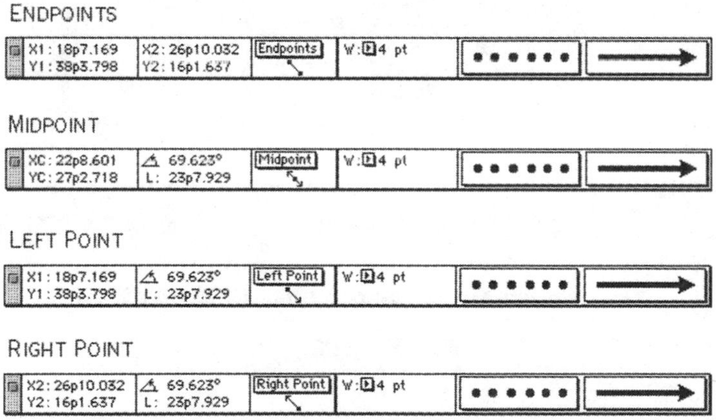

Figure 11-6:
The four modes for selecting line coordinates.

ENDPOINTS

| X1:18p7.169 | X2:26p10.032 | Endpoints | W:4 pt |
| Y1:38p3.798 | Y2:16p1.637 | | |

MIDPOINT

| XC:22p8.601 | 69.623° | Midpoint | W:4 pt |
| YC:27p2.718 | L: 23p7.929 | | |

LEFT POINT

| X1:18p7.169 | 69.623° | Left Point | W:4 pt |
| Y1:38p3.798 | L: 23p7.929 | | |

RIGHT POINT

| X2:26p10.032 | 69.623° | Right Point | W:4 pt |
| Y2:16p1.637 | L: 23p7.929 | | |

You can rotate a line no matter what its line mode is. The Rotate icon in the Measurements palette will not appear, however, if you are using Endpoints as the line mode. (You can still use the Rotation tool or the Line Specifications dialog box to rotate it.)

Framing Text or Picture Boxes

Framing is a QuarkXPress option that lets you add a plain or fancy line around the edge of a single box or around each of the boxes in a group. Most of the time, the text and picture boxes that you use to lay out a page will be unadorned, but you may occasionally want to add a frame. To add a frame, use the Frame Specifications dialog box, accessible via Item ⇨ Frame or ⌘B.

Figure 11-7 shows the Frame Specifications dialog box and a text box surrounded by a double-lined frame. Notice that we kept the line type simple and the line weight light to create a better visual effect.

Figure 11-7:
The Frame Specifications dialog box along with an example of a framed box.

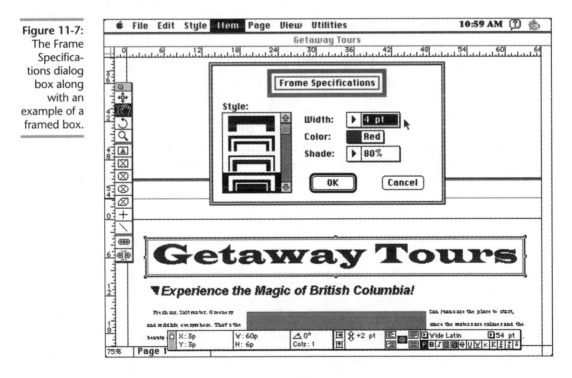

Just because you create a frame around a box, it doesn't necessarily follow that you want the frame to appear on the final, printed document. For one of our applications, a newsletter, we use a 0.5-point frame as a keyline to indicate to our commercial printer which boxes we want to have photos added into. During the actual printing process, the printer removes the frame line, and all that's left is the photo.

Sometimes you might want to draw the frame inside the margins of the box, and other times you might want it outside the margins. To control whether the frame is inside or outside the box, choose Edit ⇨ Preferences ⇨ General to display the General Preferences dialog box. In the Framing field, select either Inside or Outside.

After you've created a frame around a box, you cannot change whether the frame occurs outside or inside the box. A workaround, (if you change your mind in the middle of a layout) so that all framed boxes appear to be similar, is to make smaller the boxes that have a frame on the outside so that they appear to be the same size as the other boxes. For example, if you have a 6-point frame, make the box 12 points smaller in both width and height (this change takes care of the extra 6 points at the left and right and at the top and bottom).

Here are the steps to follow when adding a frame to a box. You can use the same steps to add a frame to all the boxes in a group.

STEPS: Framing a Box

Step 1. Use the Item tool to select the box or group and then choose Item ⇨ Frame (⌘B) to display the Frame Specifications dialog box, shown in Figure 11-7.

Step 2. From the Style scroll box, select one of the seven available frame styles. To give you a preview of what the frame style looks like, QuarkXPress displays the style that you select on a box surrounding the title of the dialog box.

Step 3. In the Width field, enter a line width for the frame line. You can enter a value or pick one from the list box. You can enter values not shown in the list box as well. You can make the frame as wide as you want as long as it is not too big to fit the bounds of the box. Remember that the width you select is the total width of the frame line.

If you choose one of the frame styles that has more than one line, you must make the lines wide enough to accommodate the frame style. For example, for the lines in Figure 11-7, the total width of the frame is 4 points. Because we used a thick/thin combination, the thick line is 2 points and the thin line 1 point (there's 1 point of space). Had we used an 8 point total width, the widths of the two lines and the space between them would be double. Had we used a single line in Figure 11-7, that line would be the full 4 points.

Step 4. In the Color field, select a color from the list box. The default setting is black.

Step 5. In the Shade field, select a shade percentage from the list box or type a percentage value (up to 100 percent, in 0.1 percent increments) in the field. You may enter a value or select one of the values from the list box. You can enter values that do not appear in the list box.

 When you use framing, keep in mind that understatement is an art. The difference between a simple, narrow frame and a complicated, larger one often is the difference between speaking quietly and shouting. Understatement works to your advantage by keeping the reader's attention — as opposed to losing it by bombarding the reader's visual senses. Be careful not to make the frame line too wide or complex, which can upset the balance of a page. For simple framing, we prefer using a single-line frame between 0.5 and 2 points.

Creating Frame Styles

QuarkXPress includes a stand-alone utility called the Frame Editor to edit and create frames. It lets you create more options than the seven default ones within QuarkXPress. The Frame Editor has eight of its own frame styles that you can use or modify. Figure 11-8 shows the Frame Editor menu. After you open the Frame Editor, its styles are added to the list that QuarkXPress displays in its Style scroll box in the Frame Specifications dialog box. These new styles can include ones that you design.

Figure 11-8:
Create a new style in the Frame Editor utility with the New Style option. You can edit existing styles by double-clicking from the scroll list.

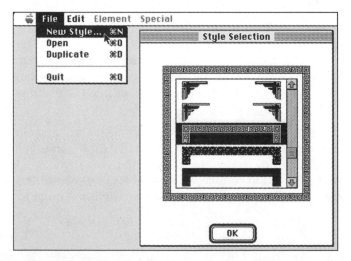

Note that you must quit QuarkXPress before running the Frame Editor; otherwise, an error message will appear and the Frame Editor will not be loaded.

STEPS: Editing or Creating a Style

Step 1. To edit, double-click the style in the Frame Editor or use File ⇨ Open (or ⌘O) after selecting a style. To create, use File ⇨ New Style or ⌘N.

Step 2. Double-click the Size *xx* entry to define the width of the frame (the *xx* indicates the frame size in points). You can also use File ⇨ New Size (or ⌘N). Figure 11-9 shows the dialog box. Click OK if you accept the current size. Note that the size in the Frame Editor is not what appears when you apply the frame style in QuarkXPress — you choose the frame's actual width there. Instead, the size chosen in the Frame Editor determines how finely detailed the frame is — the larger the size, the more bits you have to work with.

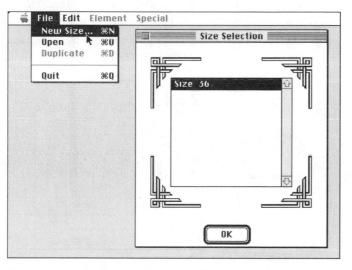

Figure 11-9: Selecting the size of the frame, which determines how fine the details are.

Step 3. You can work with as many as eight areas of the frame (the lengths of each side plus each corner). Figure 11-10 shows the top length being selected. Click an area to select it.

Step 4. Then you will be asked for the frame's width (in points), which tells the Frame Editor how large a cell to use in creating the frame. (Each cell is repeated as many times as needed to create the frame.)

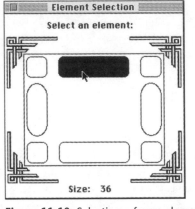

Figure 11-10: Selecting a frame element (lengths and corners) to create or edit.

Step 5. After entering the size, you will have a split dialog box. The left side is where you create the border pattern by holding down the mouse and dragging the pointer throughout the grid or clicking individual grid elements. You deselect a grid element by clicking it again. The right side shows both the pattern at a reduced size and within the current frame style. Figure 11-11 shows the dialog box.

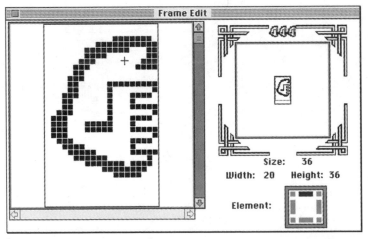

Figure 11-11: The bitmap comprising the frame is edited at left; the panels at right show the results.

Step 6. After creating or selecting a pattern within a frame style, you can use the Copy Elements feature (Element ⇨ Copy Elements) to move the pattern to another frame element. Thus, you need to create a length or corner only once and then copy it to the other lengths or corners. Figure 11-12 shows the dialog box. As you'll see, this dialog box works in a less-than-intuitive way. First, click the From button. Next, move to the frame display at top and select the desired length or corner. Then click the To button and go back to the top display to select the destination. Finally, select either the Copy or the Copy & Flip button, depending on whether the pattern needs to be flipped (mirrored) when used on another segment. Note that you cannot copy a length onto a corner or vice versa.

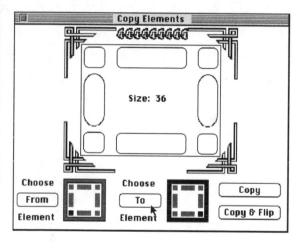

Figure 11-12: The Copy Elements dialog box lets you reuse frame elements, which speeds creation.

Step 7. Close the dialog box and click the Yes button when prompted to save the changes. You will get the same message if you use File ⇨ Quit or ⌘Q.

To remove a frame style, select it and choose Edit ⇨ Clear.

 QuarkXPress 3.1 for Windows does not support these bitmapped frame patterns. If you use them, they will be replaced with solid lines when the document is transferred to Windows. (QuarkXPress 3.3 for Windows *does* support these bitmapped frames.)

Anchoring Boxes

QuarkXPress lets you select a text box or a picture box and *anchor* it (attach it) to the text that surrounds it. You may want to do this to keep a graphic with a certain passage of text. Anchored items *flow* with the text to which they are anchored, even during the most massive edits. One common application of anchored boxes is to create a page that incorporates icons as small graphic elements in a stream of text. A movie guide that uses a different graphic to indicate the critic's opinion and a design that uses icons as paragraph breaks are examples of layouts that would benefit from using anchors. Figure 11-13 shows an example of the latter.

Figure 11-13:
An example of a graphic used in-line with text. Here it is used as a separator between sections of text.

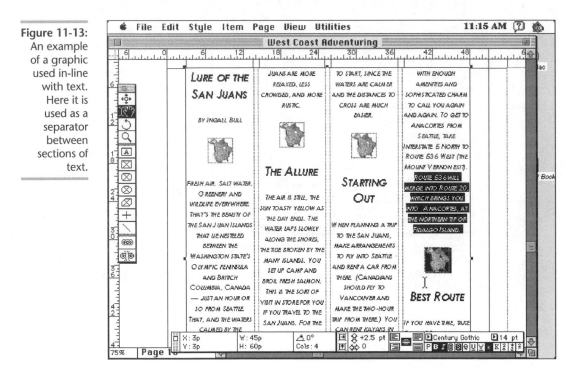

QuarkXPress treats anchored elements as individual characters of text. After you anchor them, you can cut, copy, paste, and delete these items just as if they were single characters of text. To anchor a text box or a picture box, just follow these steps:

STEPS: **Anchoring a Text or Picture Box**

Step 1. Using the Item tool, select the box.

Step 2. Cut or copy the box in the same way that you cut or copy any single text character (use Edit ⇨ Cut or Edit ⇨ Copy or the keyboard shortcuts ⌘X or ⌘C).

Step 3. Using the Content tool, position the cursor at the location where you want to anchor the box and paste in the box (select Edit ⇨ Paste, or ⌘V).

After the box becomes an anchored box, you can modify it by selecting it and then choosing Item ⇨ Modify to display the Anchored Text Box Specifications or Anchored Picture Box Specifications dialog box, shown in Figure 11-14. Because the anchored box is considered a text character, you can also modify it using the Measurements palette. In the figure, you can see the Measurements palette settings for the selected anchored picture box as well as those in the Anchored Picture Box Specifications dialog box.

Note that handles on an anchored box are different along certain edges because of how the box is anchored; you can use the sizing handles to make the box bigger or smaller in one direction but not in others.

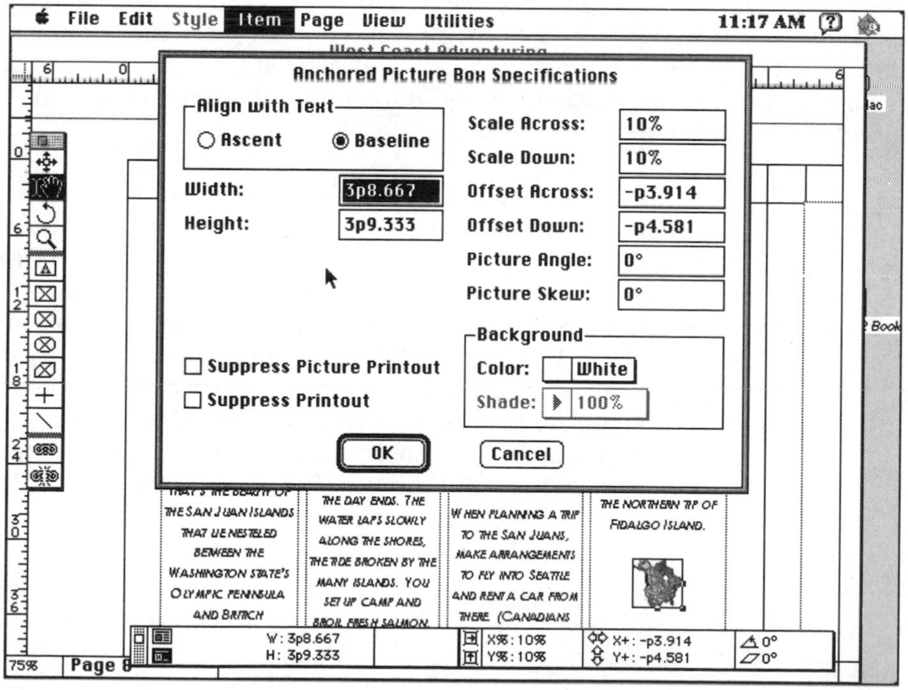

Figure 11-14:
The
Anchored
Picture Box
Specifications
dialog box.

If you anchor a polygon picture box, the box itself takes on the rectangular shape of the polygon's sizing handles.

Managing the Layout

Sometime during the layout process or after you place all the text boxes, picture boxes, and rules, you may want to make some structural changes to the document. For example, you may decide that an element on page three should be moved to page six. You may edit the copy so that what initially occupied nine pages fits on an eight page spread. Or you may realize that, because the document has grown larger than you first anticipated, you need to add page numbers or break the document into sections.

We call this category of document changes *managing the layout*. QuarkXPress has a full set of features that let you easily handle the tasks associated with managing the layout.

Adding and deleting pages

In the early stages of the document layout process, you don't need to think much about adding pages, provided that you enable Auto Page Insertion in General Preferences. If you do, QuarkXPress automatically inserts enough pages to hold the text files you import. At any point in the layout process, you can change the specifications that dictate where those new pages occur. The initial default location is the end of the document, but you may prefer to change it to the end of the story (the current set of linked text boxes) or to the end of the section.

To change the location where pages are automatically inserted, choose Edit ➪ Preferences ➪ General to display the General Preferences dialog box. Choose End of Story, End of Section, or End of Document and then choose OK to close the dialog box.

 If you include a prefix in the document page numbers (an example of a prefix is the *20-* in page *20-1*), be sure to include the prefix when you specify pages to insert, delete, or move. You can also specify absolute page numbers by using a plus sign (+) before the absolute page number. For example, if the page you want to move is numbered 20-1, but it is actually the 30th page in the document, you can use either 20-1 or +30. Figure 11-15 shows an example of such prefixed page numbering (look for the page number SJ-1).

After you place most of the text and pictures in a document, you may decide to insert one or more additional pages. To do this, choose Page ⇨ Insert to display the Insert Pages dialog box, shown in Figure 11-15. In the Insert field, enter the number of pages to insert. Then click the button that corresponds to the location where you want the pages to be inserted. QuarkXPress automatically renumbers the inserted pages and those that follow.

To delete one or more pages, choose Page ⇨ Delete to display the Delete Pages dialog box and then enter the numbers of the pages to be deleted. After the deletion, QuarkXPress automatically renumbers the pages.

Figure 11-15:
The Insert Pages dialog box.

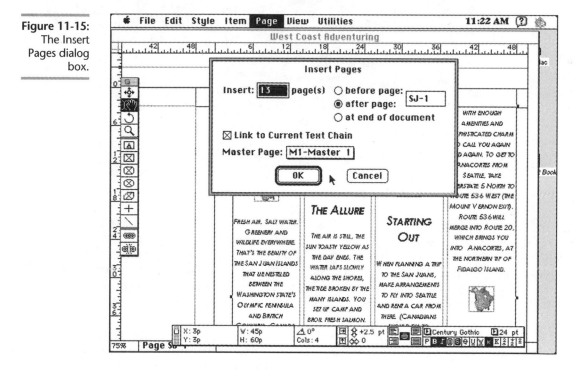

Rearranging pages

Rearranging pages involves moving them to different locations in the document. One way to move pages is to choose Page ⇨ Move to display the Move Pages dialog box shown in Figure 11-16. If you want to move just one page, enter its page number in the Move page(s) field. If you want to move a range of pages, enter the first page in the range in the Move page(s) field and the last page in the thru field. The buttons in the dialog box let you select where you want the pages to end up. You can choose one of the following: before a specified page, after a specified page, or at the end of the document.

Figure 11-16:
The Move
Pages dialog
box.

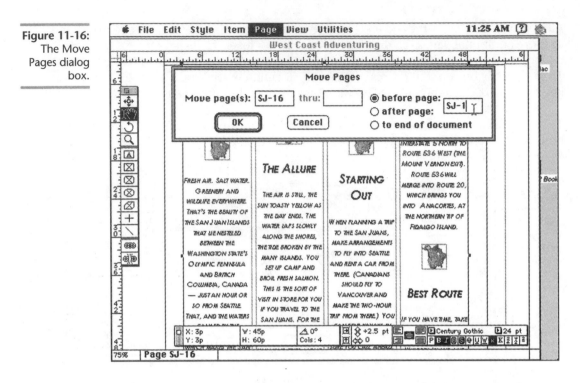

You can also rearrange pages by reducing the document to thumbnail view (choose View ⇨ Thumbnails; or use Ctrl-V, enter T, and press Return) and then dragging the thumbnails into the new page order. After the document is displayed in thumbnail mode, select the page you want to move and then drag it to its new place in the document. When the pointer changes to an arrow, you can release the mouse button to finalize the placement of the page. Figure 11-17 shows such a page move.

One advantage to the thumbnail method is that you can more easily visualize the effects of your page moves; you can actually see them occurring in thumbnail view. Another advantage is that during a page move, the pointer indicates how the move affects other pages in the document:

- ☞ If the pointer looks like a miniature page, it means that the move does not change the placement of other pages in the document.

- ☞ If the pointer looks like a left-pointing or right-pointing arrow, it means that moving that particular page bumps pages to the left or to the right.

- ☞ If the pointer looks like a down-pointing arrow, it means that succeeding pages will be moved.

Figure 11-17: Moving a page by dragging it in thumbnails view. The arrow pointer indicates the new location.

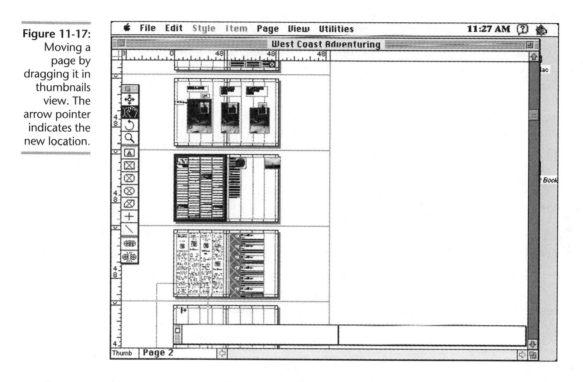

If you want to move a set of adjacent pages (for example, pages three through six) in thumbnail view, hold down the Shift key while you select the first and last pages in the range. To select several, noncontiguous pages, hold the ⌘ key and click each page.

Numbering sections and pages

Sometimes you may want to number pages in a QuarkXPress document consecutively, from first page to last. Other times, such as when the document grows to an unwieldy size or when you are required to do so because of prescribed formatting standards, you may want to break the document into sections. Technical manuals or books with chapters are often broken into sections to make it easier for the reader to locate information.

If the document is divided into sections, you generally want the page numbers to reflect the document's structure. For example, give the 11th page in section 5 the page number *5-11* so that readers can easily determine where pages and sections are in relation to the rest of the publication.

Breaking the document into sections

To break a document into sections, open the document to your intended first page in a section. Choose Page ⇨ Section to display the Section dialog box, shown in Figure 11-18. Check the button next to Section Start to make the current page the first page of the section.

You can then select the numbering format that you want applied to the section. You can enter a prefix (in the page number 5-1, the prefix is 5-) up to four characters long in the Prefix field. In the Number field, enter the number that you want assigned to the first page in the section.

 If you want a space, hyphen, or other separator between the section prefix and the page number, you must enter that separator as part of the prefix name, as we did in Figure 11-18.

The default Number setting is 1, but you may want to change it to a different number. For example, if you are producing a book that already has pages 1 and 2 preprinted, you want your QuarkXPress pages to begin with a page number of 3.

Figure 11-18:
The Section
dialog box.

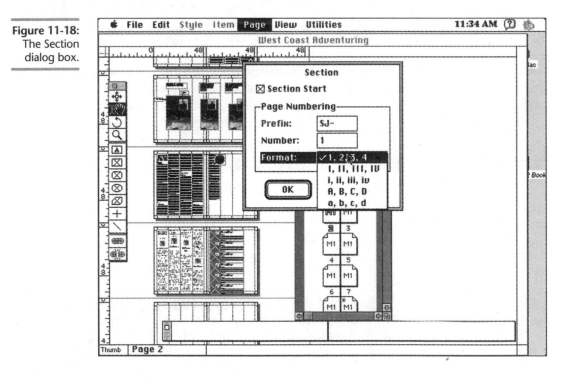

The Format field offers a list box showing the possible formats for automatic page numbering. These include:

- ✑ Arabic numerals (1, 2, 3).

- ✑ Uppercase or lowercase Roman numerals (I, II, III or i, ii, iii).

- ✑ Uppercase or lowercase letters (A, B, C or a, b, c).

The format that you select applies to all page numbers that are automatically generated in this section of the document. You can then use QuarkXPress's automatic page numbers in your documents' headers and footers (called *folios* in magazines and newsletters).

Automatically numbering the pages

The typical way of instructing QuarkXPress to automatically number all pages in a document is to place the Current Text Box Page Number character on the master page (refer to Chapter 5). If, however, the document is divided into sections, you may want to add automatic page numbers on regular pages in text boxes that have more specific text. For example, the text box for a footer might include the chapter name or current topic, as well as the page number.

STEPS:	Adding Automatic Page Numbers on Regular Pages
Step 1.	To enter the Current Text Box Page Number character, create a text box of the approximate size necessary to hold the page number.
Step 2.	Position the text box where you want the page number to appear.
Step 3.	Using the Content tool, select the text box and enter ⌘3 to insert the automatic page number. You can then modify the font, size, and attributes of the page-number character. Automatic page numbers take on the modified attributes.

Creating automatic *Continued on . . .* markers

Whenever your document contains a *jump* (where text that cannot fit entirely on one page is continued on another, linked page), consider adding automatically generated *Continued on. . .* and *Continued from. . .* markers to the document.

Custom Footers and Headers

Magazines and newsletters usually have straightforward headers and footers (or folios), composed of the page number, publication title, and issue date, or some combination of these three elements. Typically, these folios are implemented on master pages (typically, with one folio on the left master page and one folio for the right master page), since the text doesn't vary from page to page except for the current page number (which QuarkXPress can insert automatically). The figure below shows a typical folio setup.

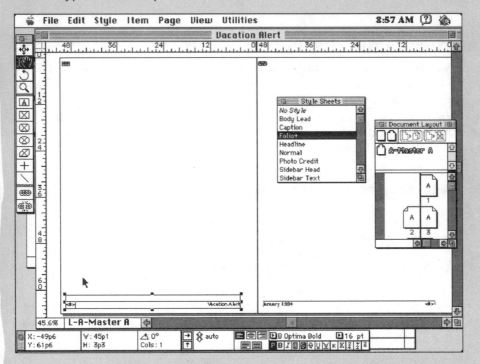

But other documents — such as manuals and books — often have more detailed headers and footers. Often, the header or footer includes information specific to the current chapter or even page. If you do want a header for each section that includes the page number and chapter name, you need to decide whether you can put this header on a master page (so that it automatically appears on each page) or whether you copy the appropriate text box to each page in the section manually. The answer depends on how you use master pages. If you have a different master page for each

section, you'd have a header text box appropriate for each section on that section's master page. If you have only one master page, you'll need to copy the text box customized for a certain section to each page in that section.

You may in fact use both methods if you need further customization. For example, perhaps the footer uses the chapter name, so that it can be implemented in the section's master page, but the header uses the page's current topic, so you'll have to manually edit that on each document page in the section. The figure below shows an example of such a document.

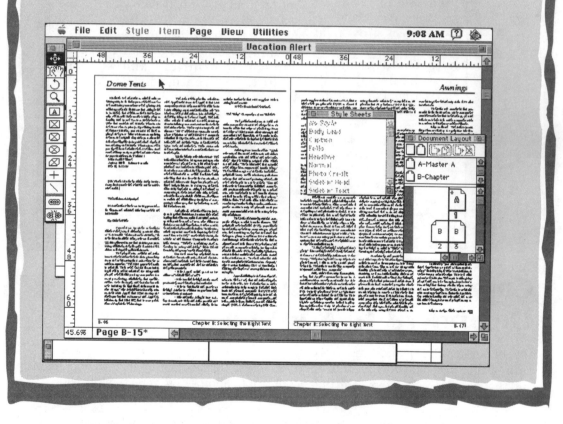

To use this feature, draw a text box at the location in the document where you want the *Continued on...* or *Continued from...* markers to appear. Press ⌘2 (in a *Continued from* box) to have the page number for the previous box holding the story to automatically appear. Press ⌘4 (in a *Continued on* box) to place the marker for the next text box's page-number character.

Figure 11-19 shows the *Continued on. . .* marker which says *None* because we haven't yet added pages to hold the overflow text. After we do, the marker will automatically reflect the continued-on page number.

Figure 11-19:
The Contin-
ued on . . .
marker

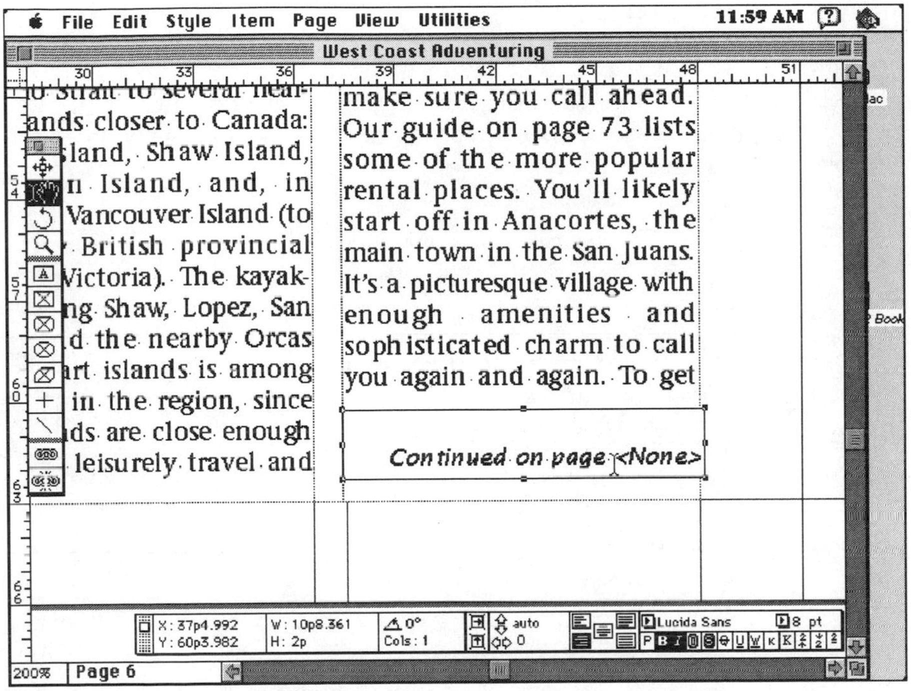

Copying Elements from One Document to Another

One of our favorite QuarkXPress features enables copying layout elements or even entire pages from one document to another. To use this feature, open both documents and then drag-copy the item from one document to another by using the following methods:

    ↵ To copy a *layout element* from one document to another, open both documents. Display them next to each other by choosing Window ➪ Tile. (You can resize the windows using the resize handle at the windows' lower-right corner.) Select the item that you want to copy in the source document and hold the mouse button as you drag the element to the destination document. Figure 11-20 shows the photo from the document at left being copied into the document at right.

You must use the Item tool to select the item to be copied. The page view must not be thumbnail.

↬ To copy a *page* from one document to another, open both documents. Display them next to each other by choosing Window ⇨ Tile. Select the page that you want to copy in the source document and hold the mouse button as you drag the page to the destination document. Figure 11-21 shows the result of a page being copied from the document at left to the document at right.

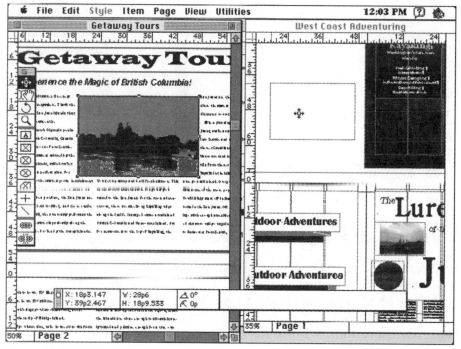

Figure 11-20: Display documents side by side (in any view *but* thumbnail) to copy elements from one to another.

The page view for both documents must be thumbnail.

Drag-copying layout elements or entire pages from a source document to a destination document has no effect on the source document.

You cannot copy a page into a document whose page dimensions are smaller in either direction than those of the source document. If the page sizes do differ, the (larger) size of the destination document's page will be used.

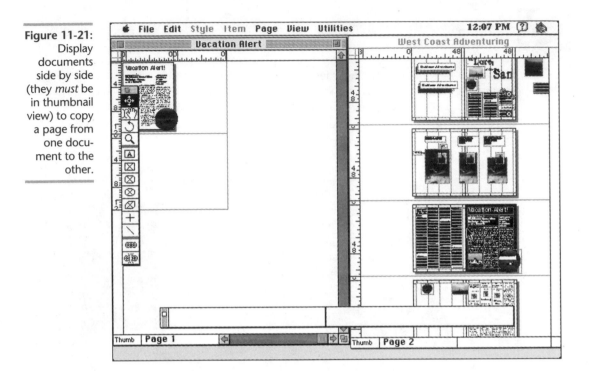

Saving a Page as an EPS File

QuarkXPress has a nifty feature that lets you, in effect, take a picture of a page in a document and turn the picture into an EPS file. You can then use the EPS file as an illustration for another document. A catalog of brochures is a good examples of an application of this feature. You might create several brochures, make an EPS file of each brochure cover, and then create a marketing piece that shows all the brochure covers.

STEPS: Saving a Page as an EPS File

Step 1.   Open the document that contains the page that you want to save.

Step 2.   Choose File ➪ Save Page as EPS to display the Save Page as EPS dialog box, shown in Figure 11-22.

Step 3.   Enter a name for the new EPS file in the File Name text box.

Step 4.   Click the appropriate format for the file type in the Format list box. Choices include — with options for both Macs and PCs — B&W (black-and-white), Color, DCS (the Document Color Separation form of EPS, used when outputting negatives for four-color printing), and DCS 2.0 (a new version of the DCS format).

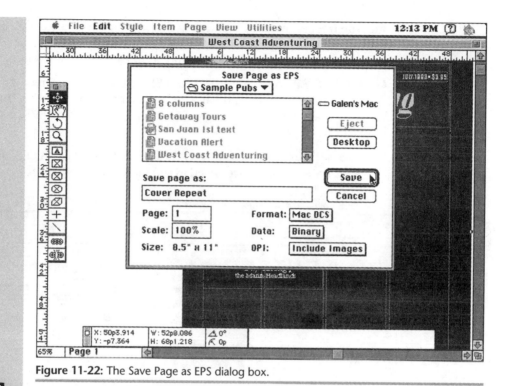

Figure 11-22: The Save Page as EPS dialog box.

The DCS and PC formats are new to QuarkXPress.

Step 5. In the Page text box, enter the page number of the page you want to save as an EPS file.

Step 6. If you want to modify the scale of the page as you save it, enter a percentage value in the Scale text box; 50% (which is the default) reduces the page to half its original size.

Step 7. Unless your service bureau has specifically asked for the output files to be in ASCII format, make sure that the Data field is set to Binary, not ASCII. (ASCII format takes much more disk space, but it can be easier to work with if there are errors when printing.)

The Data field is new to QuarkXPress.

Step 8. If you are using Open Prepress Interface, choose one of the following options in the OPI drop-down list. Your selection determines how pictures and comments are included with a page saved as an EPS file. (If you're not using OPI, don't worry about this step.)

Include Images includes pictures in TIFF and EPS formats and substitutes the low-resolution TIFF if the higher-resolution printing file for the pictures cannot be found. This option is the one used most often.

Omit TIFF & EPS omits both TIFF and EPS pictures in the file but includes OPI comments in the file for both types of pictures. If you are printing to an OPI prepress system that replaces TIFF and EPS pictures, choose this option.

The picture on the left page in Figure 11-23 is a page saved as an EPS file — in this case, a repeat of the cover used in the table of contents.

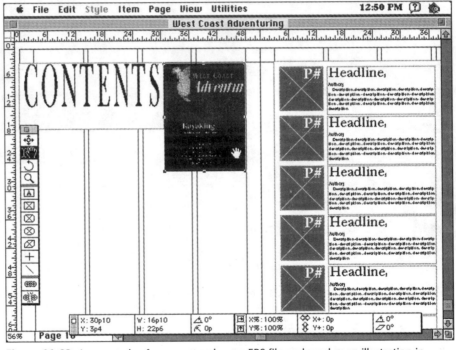

Figure 11-23: An example of a page saved as an EPS file and used as an illustration in another document.

Summary

- ➴ Whenever you can, let the computer do the work for you, as it does when you use the Step and Repeat feature.

- ➴ If you add arrows or rules to a layout, keep them simple — light in line weight and plain in line type.

- ➴ Framing is useful for indicating keylines that a commercial printer uses when placing screens and halftones.

- ➴ As with rules, the best frames are simple and understated.

- ➴ Anchoring text or picture boxes makes them behave the same as individual characters of text.

- ➴ Consider breaking a document into sections if it gets too long. When you do break it into sections, use the Section feature in the Page menu to apply section references to page numbers.

- ➴ Use the automatic page number feature in headers or footers.

PART IV

Typography and Text

Typographic treatment of text can be a subtle, yet powerful, part of your presentation. Although you define the basic look of your document with layout and styles, you give it texture and richness through the way you handle text. Until desktop publishing nearly eliminated the profession, typographers were artists who determined the details of how words looked on a printed page. They dealt with color, weight, and other subtleties that made text inviting and gave it added meaning.

QuarkXPress gives desktop publishers those tools that typographers used to enhance document aesthetics and content. With a little experimentation and a few guiding principles, you can use these typographic tools to improve the aesthetic appeal and clarity of your documents.

This section explains the art of typography and shows how to use the many QuarkXPress tools to turn theory into practice. The section then explains how to use QuarkXPress's built-in text-handling features to produce tables, edit text, and make text fit within your layout's confines.

Controlling Character Spacing

- -

In This Chapter

➦ How to track and kern text

➦ Changing the appearance of text by modifying word and letter spacing

➦ When and how to use character scaling and special fixed spaces

- -

What Is Character Spacing?

Unless you are someone who publishes for a living, you probably don't pay much attention to the space around individual text characters. Yet space around characters has a profound effect on the ease with which a reader understands the text and the message it conveys. No doubt about it, character spacing is a significant contributor to the quality (or lack thereof) of a printed document.

Long before desktop publishing, professional typographers have enhanced the look of documents by increasing or decreasing character spacing. When done correctly, character spacing gives text a "finished" look.

Character spacing — the space around and between characters — is what provides the "mood" of a document. Words set in characters that are surrounded by generous amounts of space have a light, airy feel; words set in characters that are close together feel heavier and more serious. Character spacing gives a psychological boost to the thought conveyed by the text itself.

Character spacing includes several aspects: kerning, tracking, scale, and hyphenation. As a group, these four aspects determine what typographers call *color*, simply another way of describing the appearance of text on a page.

If you want to see a document's typographic color, you need to look at a page until you make yourself cross-eyed, or do whatever else it takes to make your eyes go slightly out of focus. Here's a good way to understand the concept of typographic color: find a magazine page that has a good amount of text on it. Stare at the page for two minutes or so. Then focus on something half way between you and the page. You'll see the text blur. The resulting gray level and consistency is color.

A document's color is important because it affects both its mood and its readability. For most publishing applications, a light to medium color is preferable because it is easier on the eye.

Factors in addition to character spacing influence color. The most fundamental factor is the typeface. An airy, light typeface such as New Baskerville has a light color, while an earthy, heavy typeface such as Tiffany Heavy has a dark color. Figure 12-1 shows the same text in these two typefaces. Notice how the text on the left, in New Baskerville, looks lighter than the Tiffany Heavy text on the right.

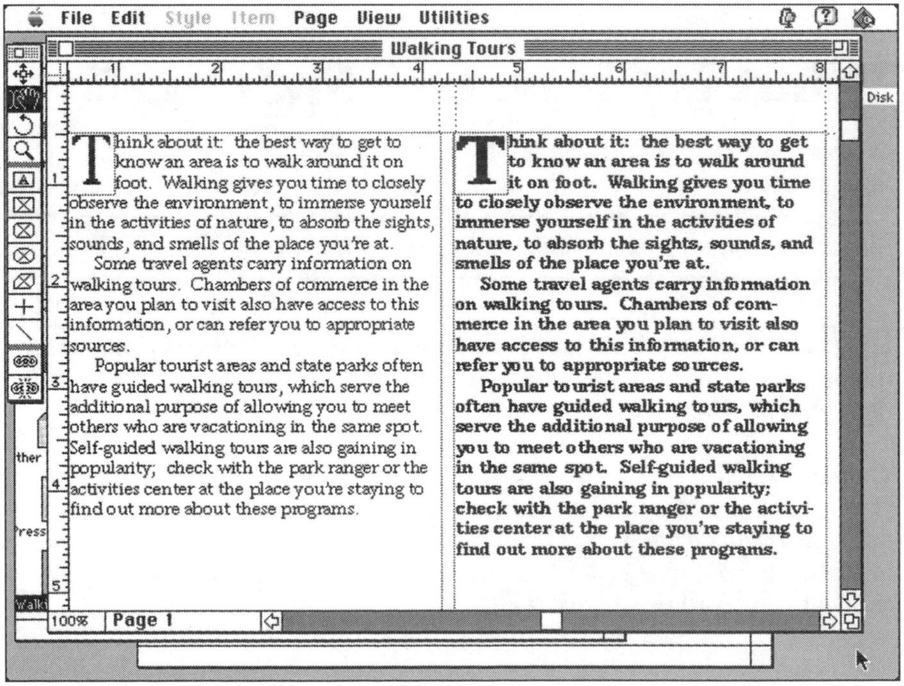

Figure 12-1:
Different typefaces produce different shades of typographic color.

Adjusting Character Spacing _____

As you can see, type fonts are major contributors to typographic color. Some faces are light, some are heavy. Regardless of a typeface's intrinsic weight, QuarkXPress includes character spacing controls that let you modify a font's effect on typographic color.

Tracking

Tracking has the greatest effect on typographic color. Also called *letter spacing*, tracking is a setting for a section of text that defines how much space is between individual letters. The more space between letters, the looser the tracking and the lighter the color. When tracking is loosened excessively, text becomes airy and loses color.

QuarkXPress sets the defaults for tracking at 0. This tells the program to use the letter spacing that the typeface's font file dictates in its width table.

In QuarkXPress, you can set tracking for each style and override tracking for any selected text.

STEPS:	Setting Tracking in a Style Sheet
Step 1.	Access the Edit Style Sheet dialog box by selecting Edit ⇨ Style Sheets ⇨ New, or Edit ⇨ Style Sheets ⇨ Edit, depending on whether you are creating a new style or editing an existing one.
Step 2.	Select Character in the Edit Style Sheet dialog box to access the Character Attributes dialog box.
Step 3.	Enter the tracking amount (in units from –100 to 100) in the Tracking blank. Use a minus sign (–) to reduce spacing (for tighter tracking).

Understanding Ems

QuarkXPress sets tracking in increments of 200ths (one-half percent) of an em, which is the width of a capital letter M in the current type size. In most typefaces (decorative and symbol fonts are the main exceptions), an em is the same width as the current point size. So in 10-point Desdemona or 10-point Bookman, an em is 10 points wide. Thus, reducing tracking by 20 units (or 10 percent) makes characters set in 10-point type 1 point closer together, 9-point type 0.9 points closer, 15-point type 1.5 points closer, and so on.

NEW QuarkXPress has always defined an em as equal to the width of two zeroes. In most cases, that's the same as a traditional em, but not in all. QuarkXPress now supports both types of em spaces. You decide which definition the program uses in the Typographic Preferences dialog box (Edit ➪ Preferences ➪ Typographic) by checking the Standard Em Space box to use the traditional method or unchecking it to use the double-zero method.

Decreasing tracking is fairly common. Increasing it is not. You'll rarely need to increase tracking. But increasing tracking is a good idea in two situations. One is in headlines that use heavy fonts. The letters in a headline can look too close to each other unless you open up some space between them (typographers call this space *air*). Another reason to increase tracking is to achieve a special effect that is increasingly popular: spreading out letters in a word or title so that letters are more than one character apart. This often is used with text that is short, all on one line, and used as a kicker or other secondary label. Figure 12-2 shows an example of such a type treatment. Tracking in the highlighted text is set at 100 units, a very loose tracking setting.

Remember that the "best" amount of tracking is a decision based not on "right" or "wrong," but on personal aesthetics and the intended overall feel of the document. But here are some guidelines that we like to use: If you're using small type (12 points or smaller) and placing it in narrow columns (16 picas or narrower), consider using tighter tracking. The eye more readily sees gaps between small forms and in narrow columns than it does between large forms and in wide columns. Settings from –2 to –10 should work for most common typefaces.

Editing tracking tables

QuarkXPress includes sophisticated tools that let you edit the tracking that comes built into a font. This is handy if you find that, with some fonts, you seem to be adjusting tracking often; if so, you may want to consider editing the font's tracking table. To do this, you need to access the QuarkXPress tracking editor, which appears under the Utilities menu as Tracking Edit.

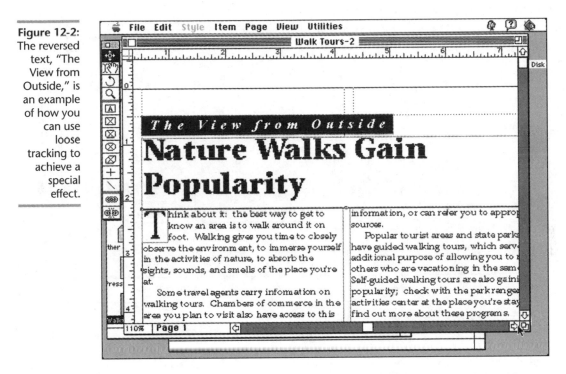

Figure 12-2:
The reversed text, "The View from Outside," is an example of how you can use loose tracking to achieve a special effect.

With the tracking editor, you edit a curve on a graph that establishes the relationship between point size and tracking value. When you click on a point in the curve, you create a turn point at which the direction of the curve can change. Figure 12-3 shows a tracking setting that loosens tracking for headline text (above 48 points in this example) to 20 units.

Since the tracking editor treats each face of a typeface — such as plain, bold, italic, and bold italic — separately, remember to make tracking adjustments in all faces of the typefaces you alter. Appropriate tracking values may be different for each typeface, especially for heavier faces like bold and ultra.

If you make tracking table edits and decide that you don't like the results, you can reset them to the default setting, which is defined in the typeface's font files (it is usually 0), by clicking the Reset button in the Tracking Values dialog box. This works even if you already saved your settings and exited the track editor.

If you want tracking changes to affect all your documents, invoke the tracking editor with no document selected. Any future document uses the new settings. If you want the tracking edits to apply to just one specific document, make the changes when that document is open and active. Since QuarkXPress associates an edited tracking table with the document that was active when you invoked the tracking editor, when you give a service bureau your QuarkXPress document to output to negatives on an imagesetter, your tracking changes remain intact.

Figure 12-3:
To edit
tracking
values for a
font, adjust
the curve in
the Tracking
Values
dialog box.

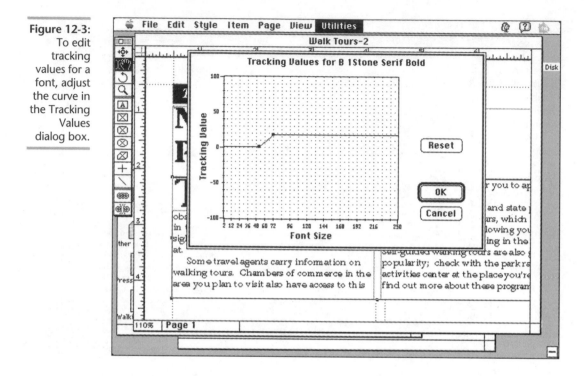

Sometimes you may want to abandon the tracking changes that have been made to a document. Since QuarkXPress detects whether a document's settings match the defaults for that copy of the program, when you open the document, you are given the choice shown in the dialog box in Figure 12-4. The dialog box also shows you which settings differ. Select Use XPress Preferences to apply the default settings.

Changing tracking on the fly

You can use the tracking editor to set tracking values permanently or use QuarkXPress style sheets to establish values for all text that uses a particular style. But there are several situations in which you may want to apply tracking on a case-by-case basis:

Copy fitting: Squeezing or stretching text to make it fit into a fixed amount of space is called *copy fitting*. You can do this to an entire story, but it is more common to retrack widows and any lines that have only a few characters (fewer than six or so), because you gain a whole line by forcing those characters to move into previous lines.

Removing widows and orphans: When the last line of a paragraph consists of only a few characters, it is called a *widow*. This is considered typographically unsightly, particularly on a line that begins a column. How many characters constitutes a widow is personal judgment. We tend to consider anything shorter than a third of a line a widow. An *orphan* refers to the first line of a paragraph (which is indented) that begins at the bottom of a column. Orphans are less taboo than widows. We tend to not worry about them.

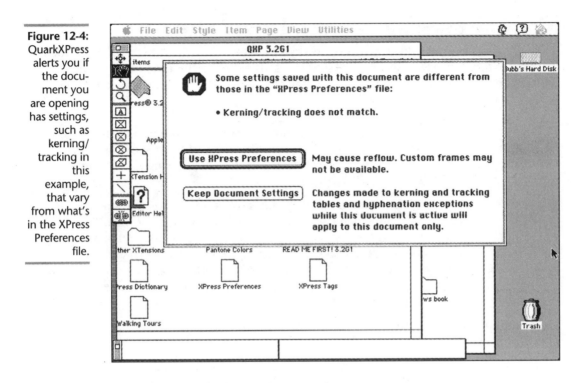

Figure 12-4:
QuarkXPress alerts you if the document you are opening has settings, such as kerning/tracking in this example, that vary from what's in the XPress Preferences file.

Even if fitting text within a certain space is not an issue, widows and orphans are frowned upon in serious publishing because they can look awkward.

You can also copy-fit by cutting out some text, but this requires the involvement of an editor, not just a production person, because the meaning of the text might be affected. Generally, you highlight one or two lines that seem to have excess space and reduce the tracking settings.

Creating special effects: Sometimes stretching a word by increasing its tracking is a good idea, especially if you are trying to achieve a special effect. Often, stretched-out text is formatted in all caps or small caps. If you use this effect in labels or kickers that comprise a self-contained paragraph, it's wise to create a style with these settings rather than apply the tracking manually.

Altering ellipses (. . .): Many people find the ellipsis character too tightly spaced, so they use three periods instead. If you don't like the amount of spacing QuarkXPress provides when you type three periods with default tracking settings, you can change the spacing through tracking. You cannot retrack the ellipsis character itself — spacing within the character doesn't change — so if you want to define the ellipsis via tracking, use three periods instead of the ellipsis character.

Applying tracking values to selected text

To apply new tracking values, select the text you want to retrack. (If you want to retrack all text in a story, use Edit ⇨ Select All to select all the text, rather than highlighting it with the mouse.) After you select the text, you can change the tracking values in three ways:

- **Option 1:** The fastest method is to use the appropriate keyboard shortcut. Press ⌘-Shift-} to increase tracking by $\frac{1}{20}$ em; press ⌘-Shift-{ to decrease it by $\frac{1}{20}$ em. Pressing ⌘-Shift-Option-} increases tracking by $\frac{1}{200}$ em; pressing ⌘-Shift-Option-{ decreases it by $\frac{1}{200}$ em.

- **Option 2:** You can also change tracking values by using the Measurements palette, which is also shown in Figure 12-5, at the bottom of the screen. The number to the right of the left and right triangles shows the current tracking value. Highlight that number and enter a new value. Or click the triangles to change the values incrementally. Clicking the left-pointing triangle decreases the value, while clicking the right-pointing triangle increases the value. The triangles work only in multiples of 10 units.

- **Option 3:** Select Style ⇨ Track and enter the tracking value in the Tracking dialog box (see Figure 12-5).

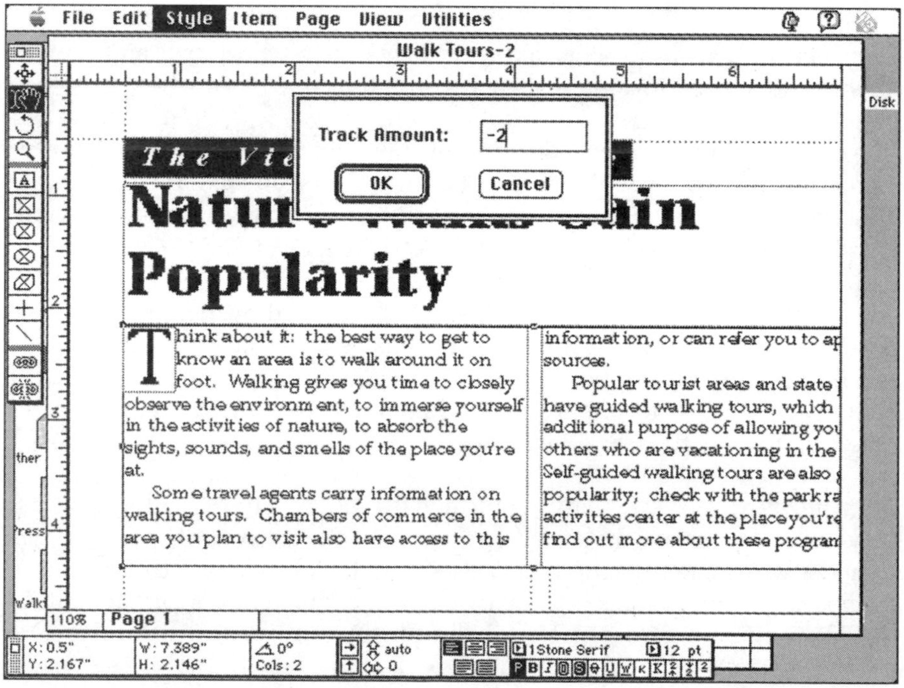

Figure 12-5:
The Tracking
dialog box.

Since tracking in QuarkXPress affects the space to the right of each character, you should select all but the last character in the section of text you want to track; otherwise, you could get some variation in the tracking of the last character in the selection.

Tracking justified text

Justification settings also play a role in character and word spacing. If you justify documents (aligning text against both left and right column margins), QuarkXPress adds space between words and characters to create that alignment. If tracking settings were the sole determinant of character spacing, QuarkXPress would be unable to justify text.

When you apply tracking to justified text, you need to know the sequence that is followed by the program. QuarkXPress applies justification first, and then adjusts the tracking according to your specifications. That means if you specify tracking of –10 (equivalent to 5 percent tighter spacing) and QuarkXPress adds 2 percent more space on a line to justify it, the net spacing on that line is 3.1 percent (102 percent width for justification times 95 percent tracking: 1.02 .95 = 96.9 – 100 – 96.9 = 3.1 percent), or a tracking value of about –6. Nonetheless, the Tracking menu and the Measurements palette both show a tracking value of –10.

This is simply a reflection of how justified text has always been handled, even in type-setting systems that predate desktop publishing.

 Keep in mind that any publishing system ignores tracking settings if that's the only way to justify a line.

You should realize that justification settings influence actual tracking, so set them to work in conjunction with tracking settings to meet your overall spacing goals.

Word spacing

Word spacing — the space between words — is another important contributor to the aesthetics of a document. Think about it: If the words in a sentence are too close to one another, comprehension may be affected because of the difficulty in telling where one word ends and another begins. If the words are too far apart, the reader might have a difficult time following the thought that is being conveyed.

Here's a design rule we like to follow: The wider the column, the more space you should put between words. This is why books tend to have more word spacing than magazines. Like all other typographic issues, there's a subjective component to picking good word spacing. Experiment to see what works best in your documents.

QuarkXPress puts its word spacing features in its Edit Hyphenation and Justification menu, not with its other character spacing options. You access this menu through the Edit ➪ H&Js menu option. The default settings are stored as Standard. Make sure you modify Standard with your preferred word-spacing settings (called H&J sets) before creating other H&J sets, because they are based on Standard's settings.

Figure 12-6 shows the Edit Hyphenation and Justification dialog box. The Space and Char settings let you control how QuarkXPress adds spacing between characters and words to justify text. Space settings control word spacing; Char settings control letter spacing. The QuarkXPress default establishes the same value for the minimum and optimum settings, but they do not have to remain the same. However, you cannot set the optimum setting at less than the minimum or more than the maximum.

The *Min.* (minimum) setting tells QuarkXPress the smallest amount of space allowed between words or characters. The *Opt.* (optimum) setting defines the amount of space you want between words and characters, and QuarkXPress sets spacing as close to that setting as possible. The *Max.* (maximum) setting sets the upper limit on space between words or characters.

As you can see from our settings in Figure 12-6, we prefer minimum settings that are less than the optimum because that helps text fit more easily in narrow columns. Also, we have found that desktop publishing programs tend to add more space than we prefer, so we typically tighten the word and letter spacing to compensate. At the same time, we usually leave the maximum word spacing at 150 percent.

The settings shown in Figure 12-6 — 85 percent minimum, 100 percent optimum, and 150 percent maximum for word spacing and –5 percent minimum, 0 percent optimum, and 10 percent maximum for letter spacing — work well for most newsletters and magazines output on an imagesetter. For material destined for final output on a 300-dpi laser printer, you may want to keep the defaults because laser printers have coarser resolution and thus cannot make some of the fine positioning adjustments our settings impose. In some cases, they move characters closer together than desired, even when the same settings work fine on a higher resolution imagesetter.

Figure 12-6:
The
Justification
Method
portion of
the Edit
Hyphenation
& Justifica-
tion dialog
box has
controls that
let you set
up the
spacing
between
characters
and words
in justified
text.

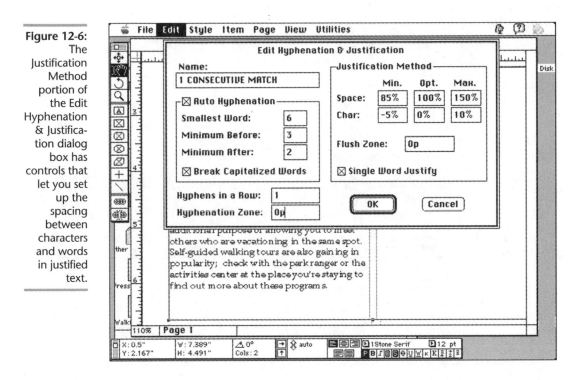

Figure 12-7 compares the default settings to our preferences. The paragraph that uses the settings we recommend has fewer awkward gaps and takes up one less line of page space.

If your text is justified, QuarkXPress never places characters closer together than the minimum setting. But it may exceed the maximum setting if that's the only way to make the line fit. If your text is not justified (if it is left-aligned, right-aligned, or centered), QuarkXPress uses the optimum settings for all text.

The "Hyphenation and Justification" chapter later in this section describes how to use hyphenation settings in concert with letter and word spacing.

Figure 12-7:
Default
word-
spacing
settings (left)
vs. the
authors'
recom-
mended
settings
(right).

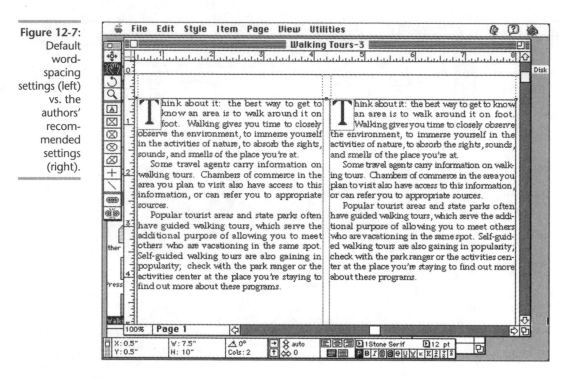

Kerning

The space between certain *pairs* of letters needs to be adjusted so that it looks good. This adjustment of the space between two specific letters is known as *kerning*. Kerning tells the output device — such as a laser printer, typesetter, monitor, or film recorder — to add or, more typically, subtract, a certain amount of space between specific pairs of letters any time those pairs occur in a document, so that their spacing seems natural. The information on which pairs of letters to kern and how much to kern them by is stored in the font file as a kerning table.

Without kerning, some letters may appear to be farther apart than other letters in the same word, tricking the eye into thinking they are, in fact, in different words. You can see an example of this in Figure 12-8. On the top line of the figure, the unkerned letter pairs *AW* and *to* appear far enough apart that the eye may perceive them as belonging to separate words. Kerning adjusts the spacing to prevent this problem, as shown in the bottom line of the figure.

Kerning is important for all large type. The larger the characters, the larger the space between them, and thus any awkward spacing becomes more noticeable. For smaller type, kerning is often not noticeable because the space between letters is already so small.

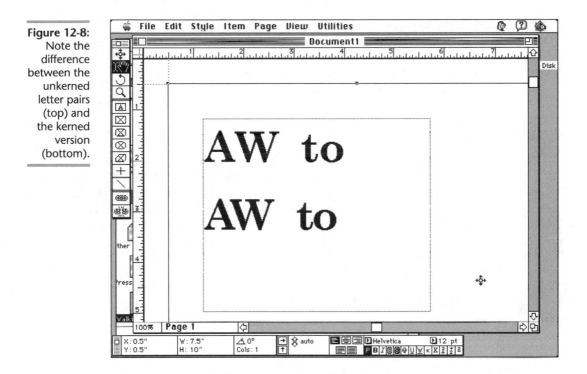

Figure 12-8:
Note the difference between the unkerned letter pairs (top) and the kerned version (bottom).

Because kerning requires QuarkXPress to look at every pair of letters to see whether they have special kerning values, turning on this feature for all text can slow down screen display considerably. To get around this problem, QuarkXPress offers the Auto Kern Above feature, which you turn on and off through the Edit ⇨ Preferences ⇨ Typographic dialog box. This option tells QuarkXPress to stop kerning when text reaches a certain size. Any text at or below the size you specify is not kerned.

With version 3.3, Quark included a Kern to Space feature. This lets you use an en space as one of the characters in a kerning pair. This kern-to-space feature comes in handy when you want to tighten the space between two items. These pairs (a character and an en space) are used just like other kerning pairs. To set up a kern-to-space pair using the Kern/Track Editor, first enter the space in a text box (Option-Space), copy it, and paste it into the Pair field.

The cut-off size you choose for Auto Kern Above is both a personal choice, based on aesthetic judgment, and a technical choice, based on the output device. The relatively low resolution on a 300-dpi laser printer limits how fine you can adjust spacing between characters. But on a 1270- or 2540-dpi imagesetter, there is practically no limit to how much control you have over spacing, so you should take advantage of it.

A rule of thumb is to set Auto Kern Above between 8 and 12 points. It makes sense to set Auto Kern Above to your basic body text size, and for most people, basic body text size falls between 8 and 12 points. If your base text is 9 points, set Auto Kern Above to 9 points. However, use a small value (8 or 9) for any text you output to a 600-dpi or finer device, regardless of the size of your body text.

Editing kerning tables

Often, the kerning table for a font may not match your preferences for some letter pairs. In some cases, the table may not include kerning information for certain letter pairs that cause you trouble. QuarkXPress includes a function that lets you edit kerning information for any TrueType or Adobe Type 1 PostScript typeface. It appears under the Utilities menu as Kerning Table Edit. You can modify existing settings, add new pairs, or remove existing pairs.

QuarkXPress associates an edited kerning table with the document that was active when you invoked the kerning editor. This means that if you give your QuarkXPress document to a service bureau to output to negatives on an imagesetter, your kerning changes remain intact.

If you want kerning changes to affect all documents, invoke the kerning editor with no document selected. Any future document uses the new settings.

Figure 12-9 shows the kerning table editor. Predefined kerning values are displayed in the Kerning Values window, through which you can scroll to select pairs whose values you want to change.

You can delete kerning pairs by highlighting them in the kerning pairs list in the dialog box and clicking the Delete button. Deleting a kerning pair is the same as setting its kerning value to zero.

To add your own kerning pairs, enter the two letters at the Pair prompt. In either case, enter the kerning value at the Value prompt. If you are modifying existing kerning values, select Replace; if you are adding a kerning pair, the button will be labeled Add. As with tracking, the unit of measurement is ½₀₀th of an em, or roughly one-half percent of the current point size. Negative values decrease space between the letters, positive numbers add space.

Clicking the Reset button undoes any changes made to the kerning values in this session (changes made and saved earlier are not reset). Import and Export buttons let you import kerning values from another file or export current ones to a new file.

To save changes, select OK. To cancel changes, select Cancel. (The difference between Reset and Cancel is that Reset leaves you in the dialog box to make other changes, while Cancel closes the dialog box and returns you to your document.)

Figure 12-9:
You can modify kerning values in the Kerning Table Edit dialog box.

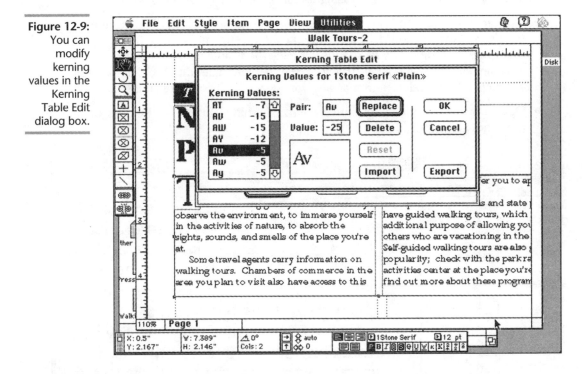

The kerning editor treats each face of a typeface — such as plain, bold, italic, and bold italic — separately, so be sure to make kerning adjustments in all faces of the typefaces you alter. And keep in mind that the appropriate kerning values are different for each face because characters are shaped differently in each face.

Changing kerning on the fly

At times, you may want to manually kern specific letter pairs. For example, your document may incorporate typefaces you use so rarely that it's not worthwhile to modify the kerning table. QuarkXPress enables you to modify kerning on the fly for any letter pairs you select. Put your text cursor between the two letters. You now have three ways to change the kerning values:

↪ **Option 1:** The fastest way to change kerning values, especially when you want to experiment, is to use the keyboard shortcuts. Press ⌘-Shift-} to increase kerning by ⅟₂₀ em; press ⌘-Shift-{ to decrease it by ⅟₂₀ em. Pressing ⌘-Shift-Option-} increases kerning by ⅟₂₀₀ em; pressing ⌘-Shift-Option-{ decreases it by ⅟₂₀₀ em.

↪ **Option 2:** A faster method is to use the Measurements palette. The number to the right of the left and right triangles shows the current kerning value. Highlight that number and enter a new value. Or click the triangles to change the values incrementally: the left-pointing triangle decreases the value while the right-pointing one increases the value. Both triangles work only in multiples of ten units.

↪ **Option 3:** Select Style ⇒ Kern and enter the kerning value in the Kerning dialog box, shown in Figure 12-10.

Figure 12-10: Kerning adjusts the space between two characters.

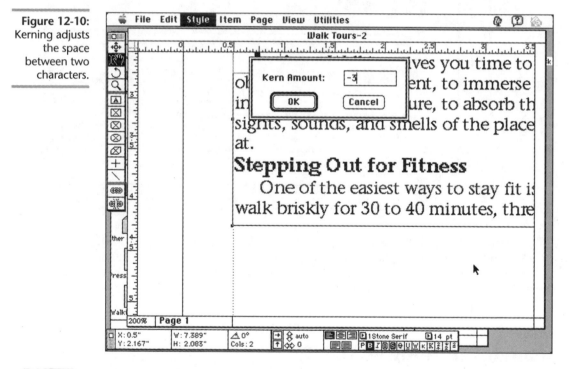

If you highlight characters rather than place the text cursor between the two characters you want to kern, QuarkXPress displays Track instead of Kern in dialog boxes and menus. Tracking is discussed in detail earlier in this chapter.

Horizontal and vertical scale

One unusual but occasionally effective way to influence typographic color is to change the typeface's horizontal or — a new QuarkXPress feature — vertical scale. This compresses or expands the actual characters (rather than the space between the characters) to a percentage, ranging from 25 to 400 percent, in 0.1 percent increments. The Horizontal and Vertical Scale option is available from the Style menu when a text box is active and the Content tool is selected. Figure 12-11 shows the dialog box that appears when you choose Horizontal or Vertical Scale.

Scaled text can be useful in several applications:

- ➣ To fit text in the available space.

- ➣ To call attention to display type, such as drop caps, headlines, or other type-as-design elements.

- ➣ To create a different feel for an existing typeface that might otherwise not be appropriate for the use intended. An example is compressing wide typefaces for use as body text.

QuarkXPress allows you to apply only one kind of scaling to a selected section of text: vertical *or* horizontal. If you want to scale text in both directions, try changing the point size first and then applying a horizontal or vertical scale

You do not need to enter the percent symbol (%) when you enter the scaling value. QuarkXPress automatically assumes the value is a percentage.

A traditional typographer would blanche at the thought of scaling type because each typeface is designed to be displayed optimally at a certain weight and size. (That's why the hinting pioneered by Adobe in its Type 1 PostScript fonts, and adopted by Microsoft and Apple in their TrueType fonts, was such a breakthrough: it automatically adjusts the typeface's characteristics for various sizes. And that's why boldface is more than just fatter characters and italics is more than slanted characters.) When you change a typeface's scale, you distort the design that was so carefully crafted. Instead, a traditional typographer would argue, use existing expanded or compressed (also called condensed) versions of the typeface because they were designed to be used at their percentage of horizontal scaling.

If you don't go overboard, you can use horizontal or vertical scaling effectively. Scaling a typeface to 50 percent or 150 percent of its size will likely destroy its character. But scaling a typeface between 90 and 110 percent often works well, and staying between 95 and 105 percent results in type that is not noticeably different, yet distinct.

Figure 12-11:
The Horizontal and Vertical Scale dialog box.

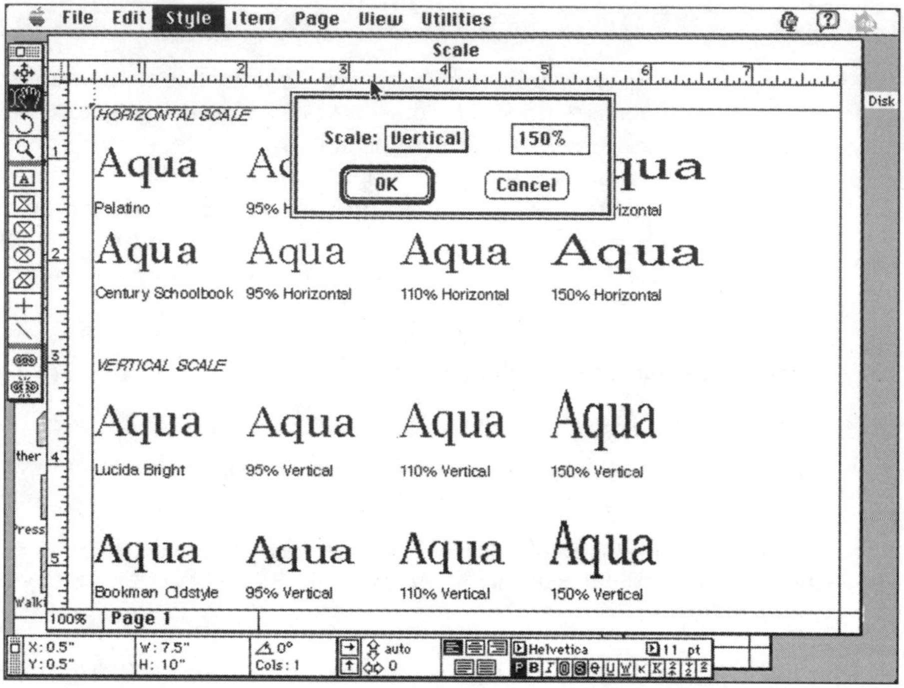

[Screenshot of a Macintosh application window]

File Edit **Style** Item Page View Utilities

Scale

HORIZONTAL SCALE

Aqua   Aq   qua
Palatino   95%

Scale: Vertical   150%
OK   Cancel

rizontal

Aqua   Aqua   Aqua   Aqua
Century Schoolbook 95% Horizontal   110% Horizontal   150% Horizontal

VERTICAL SCALE

Aqua   Aqua   Aqua   Aqua
Lucida Bright   95% Vertical   110% Vertical   150% Vertical

Aqua   Aqua   Aqua   Aqua
Bookman Oldstyle 95% Vertical   110% Vertical   150% Vertical

100% | Page 1

X: 0.5"   W: 7.5"   ∠ 0°   auto   Helvetica   11 pt
Y: 0.5"   H: 10"   Cols: 1   0

Pay attention to the kind of typeface you scale:

- Typefaces that have darker vertical strokes (the constituent components) than horizontal strokes can look odd when expanded too much. Optima is an example of such a typeface. A sans serif typeface such as Eurostile, Helvetica, or Univers works best because its generally even shape has fewer intricate elements that might get noticeably distorted.

- Many serif typefaces work fine if horizontally scaled only slightly. Squarer typefaces such as Melior and New Century Schoolbook lend themselves best to scaling without perceived distortion. When you slightly compress wide typefaces such as Tiffany, which are normally used for headlines and other display type, they can acquire a new feel that makes them usable as body text. Finer typefaces such as Janson Text more quickly become distorted because the differences between the characters' already shallow horizontal strokes and already thicker vertical strokes become more noticeable — especially when expanded.

- Avoid scaling decorative typefaces such as Brush Script, Dom Casual, and Park Avenue. However, Zapf Chancery can be scaled slightly without looking distorted.

Figure 12-12 shows sample horizontal and vertical scaling on four common typefaces.

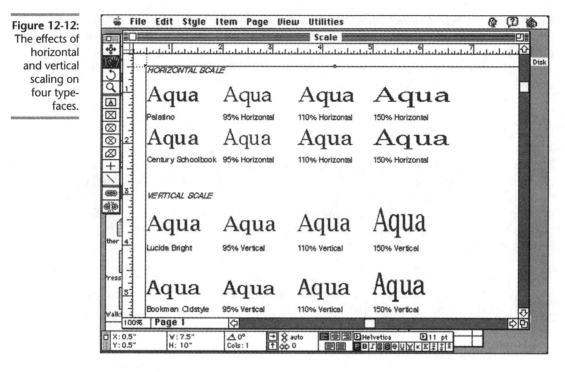

Figure 12-12:
The effects of
horizontal
and vertical
scaling on
four type-
faces.

Special Spaces

In some cases, you may want to impose specific kinds of spacing, rather than rely on the normal spaces whose width is affected by tracking and justification settings. QuarkXPress provides several special space options:

Nonbreaking space: This space ensures that a line does not wrap between two words if you do not want it to. The command is ⌘space.

En space: An en space (press Option-space) is typically used in numbered lists after the period following the numeral. An en space makes a number more visible because the number is separated more from the following text than words in the text are separated from each other. En spaces also are used before single-digit numerals when a numbered list includes both single- and double-digit numerals. (In most typefaces, a numeral occupies the width of an en space. So putting an en space before numerals 1 through 9 aligns them with the 0 in the number 10.) A variation of the en space is the nonbreaking en space, accessed by pressing Option-⌘space.

Punctuation space: A punctuation space, accessed via Shift-space, is the width of a period or comma. It is typically used to ensure alignment of numerals when some numbers have commas and others don't — as in 1,083 and 612. To align the last three digits of both numbers, you place an en space and a punctuation space before 612. A variation is the nonbreaking punctuation space, accessed via Shift-⌘space.

Some people call a punctuation space a thin space; regardless, it is generally half the width of an en space.

Flexible space: A flexible space (Option-Shift-space) is a space you define as a certain percentage of an en space. If you define a flexible space as twice the width (200 percent) of an en space, you create an em space. You define the flex space width in the Typographic Preferences dialog box, accessed via Edit ⇨ Preferences ⇨ Typographic. Specify the width in percentages from 0 to 400, in increments of 0.1. For the nonbreaking variant of the flex space, press Shift-Option-⌘space.

A common fixed space available in most desktop publishing programs, but not in QuarkXPress, is an em space. You can create an em space by using two en spaces or by defining a flex space to be the width of an em.

Summary

➻ Tracking determines spacing between all characters in a selection to optimize overall appearance. Kerning determines spacing between two specific characters to optimize their appearance. QuarkXPress uses the same menu option for both, although the label changes depending on whether multiple characters are highlighted (tracking) or the text cursor is between two characters (kerning).

➻ Use tighter tracking for small text in narrow columns as opposed to wide columns. Use loose tracking for large text set in dark or heavy typefaces.

➻ Use more word spacing for wide columns, less for narrow columns. Set the minimum word spacing to be less than the optimum word spacing, giving QuarkXPress sufficient flexibility when justifying text.

➻ Use Utilities ➪ Tracking Edit to globally change tracking for a particular typeface throughout a document, regardless of which style tag is applied. You can set the typeface's tracking to be different for different text sizes. Tracking values set in style tags and those applied locally will augment the document's global tracking settings, not replace them.

➻ Use Utilities ➪ Kerning Table Edit to permanently change kerning-pair values for a particular typeface in your document. These values may be exported for use in other documents.

➻ Use interactive tracking as the first option to fix widows and orphans.

➻ If necessary to properly justify text, QuarkXPress will override maximum word-spacing and tracking settings by adding more space. But, in an effort to justify text, it will not bring text closer together by overriding minimum word-spacing settings.

➻ Set automatic kerning to 8 points if you intend to typeset your document; leave it at 10 points if you intend to use a 300-dpi laser printer.

➻ Use horizontal and vertical scaling sparingly.

➻ An en space is usually the same as the width of a numeral, so it makes a good placeholder when aligning numbers. Likewise, a punctuation space makes a good placeholder when aligning numbers that contain commas or decimal points.

➻ By defining a flex space to be 200 percent, you create an em space, which is often used as the paragraph indent value in multicolumn layouts.

Controlling Paragraph Spacing

■ ■

In This Chapter

➥ How to control paragraph spacing using hyphenation and justification

➥ How to apply leading to text

➥ When and how to use align text vertically

■ ■

The Importance of Paragraph Spacing

This may sound obvious, but it's important: when you create a document, you usually want someone to *read* it. You want to present information in a manner that moves the reader through the text. To do this, you use the tools in QuarkXPress to give the document contrast, to create visual divisions, and to create uniformity and cohesion.

Particularly in longer documents, paragraph spacing plays an important role in determining how accessible text appears column after column, page after page. Although you can use character spacing to create blocks of text that have good typographical color, you can spoil the overall effect if paragraph spacing is not up to par. Bad paragraph spacing can be serious enough to keep readers from reading that well-colored text. Note that "color" here means typographic color, not a color like red or blue; see Chapter 12.

Effective paragraph spacing is more than simply having adequate spacing between paragraphs. It includes several other factors, from the length of paragraphs (make them too deep and readers skip them) to the way they are justified. Balancing these paragraph spacing attributes is critical to good overall document design, and is essential if you want to keep your readers interested.

Hyphenation and Justification _____

Hyphenation and justification contribute to paragraph spacing by helping to fit text within a certain space, while keeping an attractive appearance to the copy. Both hyphenation and justification have a great impact on the shape of text and its typographic color, which are important parts of the impression the text conveys.

Because professional typesetters almost always use hyphenation and justification together, it comes as no surprise that QuarkXPress treats hyphenation and justification features — or "H&Js" as being closely related. Although you set justification for individual styles through the Edit Style Sheets dialog box, you set the justification method in a more basic setting, through H&J sets defined in the Edit Hyphenation and Justification dialog box, accessed via Edit ⇨ H&Js.

In the Edit Hyphenation and Justification dialog box (see Figure 13-1), you set up H&J sets that control hyphenation and justification parameters for any styles based on them. A document can have different H&J sets, which lets you combine several typographic and layout approaches in the same document.

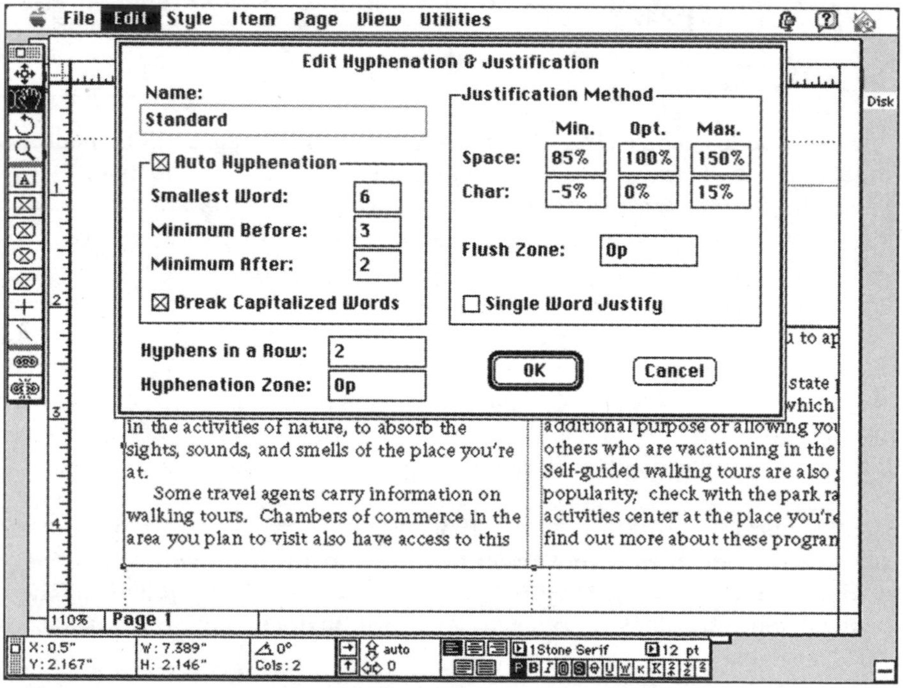

Figure 13-1:
The Edit Hyphenation and Justification dialog box.

To use H&J sets from another document in your current document, select the Append option in the H&Js dialog box. Also choose this option if you establish master settings when no document is open. This lets you append (copy) all the H&J sets from existing documents and templates. Note that any H&J sets in the current document (or master settings) that have the same name as sets you append from the other document are not altered.

You can tell you are editing master H&J sets when the dialog box title is Default H&Js instead of H&Js for *filename*.

Justification methods

In the Edit Hyphenation and Justification dialog box, the two main justification methods — Space and Char — control how QuarkXPress spaces words and letters to align text against both margins of a column. Because justification requires QuarkXPress to figure out where and how much space to add line by line, it needs some guidance on how to do so. That's where the three options — *minimum, optimum,* and *maximum* — of the two justification methods come into play.

Minimum justification settings tell QuarkXPress how much it can squeeze text to make it fit in a justified line, while the *maximum* settings tell the program how much it can stretch text to make it fit. QuarkXPress does not squeeze text more than the minimum settings allow, but it does exceed the maximum settings if it has no other choice. If text is not justified, QuarkXPress uses the *optimum* settings for all text. The Space and Char options that control these settings are discussed in more detail in Chapter 12, "Controlling Character Spacing."

When you use justified text, QuarkXPress gives you two more options: Flush Zone and Single Word Justify.

ᑲ The Flush Zone setting, measured from the right margin, tells QuarkXPress when to take the text in the last line of a paragraph and force it to justify against both margins. (Normally, the last line of a justified paragraph is aligned to the left.) If text in the last line reaches the *flush zone,* it is justified; otherwise it remains left-aligned.

We recommend that you do not use the Flush Zone feature. When the last line in a justified paragraph is left-aligned, it gives the reader a needed clue that the paragraph is complete.

ᑲ Selecting Single Word Justify tells QuarkXPress it is OK to space out a word that is long enough to take up a single line if needed to justify that line.

We recommend that you always turn on Single Word Justify, even though words that take up a full line are rare. When they do occur, having them left-aligned (which is what happens if this option is not selected) in a paragraph that is otherwise justified is confusing because readers might misinterpret them as the end of the paragraph.

Hyphenation settings

Hyphenation settings determine the "raggedness" of unjustified text (text that is left-aligned, right-aligned, or centered) and the size of gaps in justified text (where text is aligned against both the left and right margins of a column). By varying the hyphenation settings, you can achieve a significantly different feel, as illustrated in Figure 13-2.

In the figure, the two left columns appear the same, even though the leftmost is set at unlimited hyphenations and the second is set at three consecutive hyphens maximum, because there are not enough long words in the text to force many consecutive hyphenations. But column 3, where hyphenation is turned off, has some gaps and takes an extra line of page space. The rightmost column is set as justified text with unlimited hyphenation, showing the difference between left-aligned and justified text.

Check the Auto Hyphenation box to turn on hyphenation.

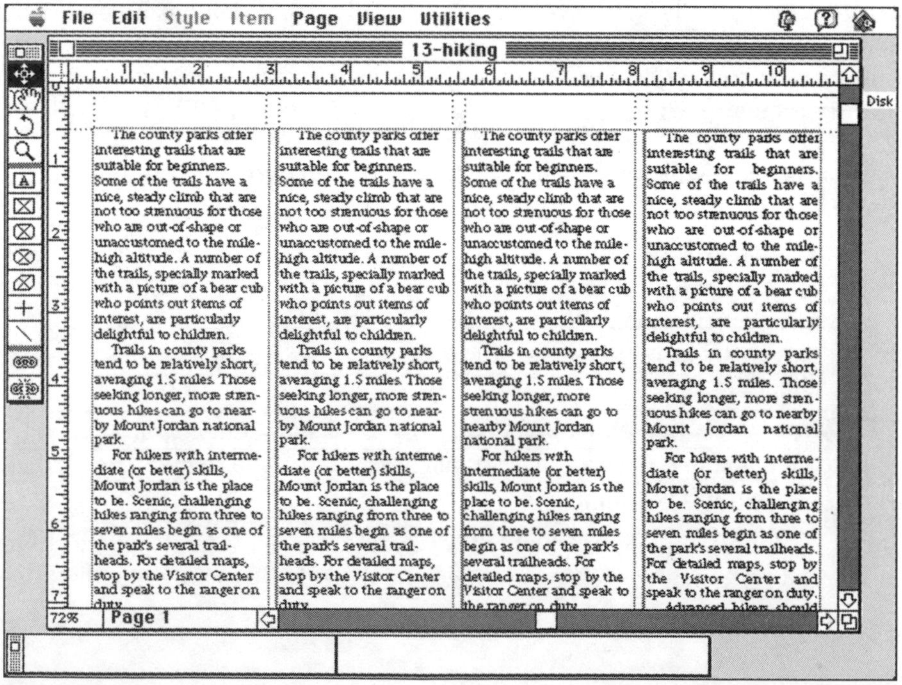

Figure 13-2: Changes to Hyphenation settings can alter column appearance.

Should you turn on Break Capitalized Words? We think so. True, some traditionalists argue against hyphenating proper names, and some pragmatists don't check this feature because most hyphenation dictionaries make mistakes with many proper names. Still, there is no compelling reason not to treat proper names as you do any other text. If the program improperly hyphenates proper names, add them to your document's exception dictionary rather than prohibiting their hyphenation.

Setting word hyphenation parameters

How a publishing program hyphenates is determined in large part by *word hyphenation parameters*. There are three such parameters, and they are set in the Edit Hyphenation & Justification dialog box:

⇨ Smallest Word determines how small a word must be before QuarkXPress hyphenates it. The default of six letters is a reasonable default, although five is acceptable as well.

⇨ Minimum Before determines how many characters must precede a hyphen in a hyphenated word. The default of three characters is a typical typographer's threshold. Consider changing the setting to 2 if you have narrow columns or large text. Although many typographers object to two-letter hyphenation — as in *ab-dicate* or *ra-dar* — it often looks better than text with large gaps caused by the reluctance to hyphenate such words. Hyphenation also makes sense for many words that use two-letter prefixes such as *in-*, *re-*, and *co-*.

⇨ Minimum After sets the number of characters that must follow a hyphen in a hyphenated word. The default setting of two characters is common for newspapers and is most often seen in words ending in *-ed*, such as *blanket- ed*. While we advocate two-letter hyphenation at the beginning of a word, we prefer three-letter hyphenation at the end. Except for words ending in *-ed* and sometimes *-al*, most words don't lend themselves to two-letter hyphenation at the end of the word. Part of this is functional — it's easy for readers to lose two letters beginning a line. We prefer two-letter hyphenations at the end of a word only when the alternative is awkward spacing. As with all typography, this ultimately is a personal choice.

Words broken using minimum settings of 1 look awful in print. They also go against reader expectations because the norm is to have several letters after a hyphen. *Never* use a minimum setting of 1 for Minimum Before. If you do, you get hyphenations such as *A- sia*, *a- typical* and *u- niform* that simply look terrible in print. They also don't provide enough context for the reader to anticipate the rest of the word. Likewise, never use a minimum of 1 for Minimum After because you get hyphenations such as *radi- o*.

Limiting the number of consecutive hyphens

Too many hyphens in a row result in text that is hard to read. The eye gets confused about which line it is on because it loses track of which hyphen represents which line.

How can you avoid having an excessive number of hyphens in a row? Avoid them by selecting a setting in the Hyphens In A Row box in the Edit Hyphenation & Justification dialog box.

The more hyphens you allow, the more easily QuarkXPress can break lines to avoid awkward gaps (in justified text) or awkward line endings (in nonjustified text). A good setting for Hyphens In A Row is 3 consecutive hyphens. This gives the eye enough context to keep lines in sequence. Avoid having fewer than two consecutive hyphens as your maximum because that typically results in awkward spacing.

Controlling the hyphenation zone

When text is not justified (that is, when it's set flush left or flush right), you still need to be concerned about the overall appearance of the justified text. It's a good idea to have some consistency in how lines of text end. Typographers call the uneven line endings *rag*, and tend to manually modify the rag to give it a pleasing shape. This is done by retracking some lines or manually inserting hyphens. A "pleasing shape" is usually defined as one that undulates and has few consecutive lines of roughly the same width.

QuarkXPress lets you partially control the rag of nonjustified text through Hyphenation Zone control, found in the Edit Hyphenation and Justification menu. A setting of 0 tells QuarkXPress to hyphenate whenever it can. Any other setting specifies the range in which a hyphen can occur; this number is measured from the right margin. You won't often need this feature because QuarkXPress does a decent job of ragging text on its own. But if you do use it, a setting no more than 20 percent of the column width usually works best. No matter which settings you use, expect to occasionally override QuarkXPress through manual hyphenation to make the rag match your preferences.

Overriding hyphenation settings

Occasionally, you may want to override hyphenation settings for a paragraph. For example, you might want to disallow hyphenation in a particular paragraph without affecting the rest of the text. To override hyphenation settings for a paragraph, use the Paragraph Formats dialog box (see Figure 13-3). You can apply a different H&J set to the currently selected paragraphs by selecting a new set in the dialog box.

To access the dialog box, press Style ⇨ Formats or the keyboard shortcut Shift-⌘F, and then change the H&J setting to an appropriate H&J set (defined in the Edit ⇨ H&Js dialog box). To turn off hyphenation for a specific paragraph, insert your text cursor anywhere on the paragraph and go to the Paragraph Formats dialog box. Select None (or whatever you named the H&J set that disallows hyphenation) as the new H&J setting. Other paragraphs using the same style are unaffected by this local override.

No doubt there will be times when you don't want to override the style settings for a particular paragraph. Instead, you will want to change the place in a particular word where QuarkXPress inserts the hyphen. QuarkXPress lets you do this through its soft hyphen feature.

To manually insert a soft hyphen, type ⌘- between the letters you want the hyphen to separate. This soft hyphen "disappears" if the word moves (due to the addition or deletion of text, for example) to a place where a hyphen is not appropriate. Should the word and its soft hyphen move to a spot where a word break is appropriate, the hyphen reappears.

You might wonder what happens if a word that is already hyphenated contains a soft hyphen. If a word is already hyphenated, the soft hyphen overrides QuarkXPress's hyphenation of the word. The program uses the soft hyphen rather than the setting in the hyphenation dictionary.

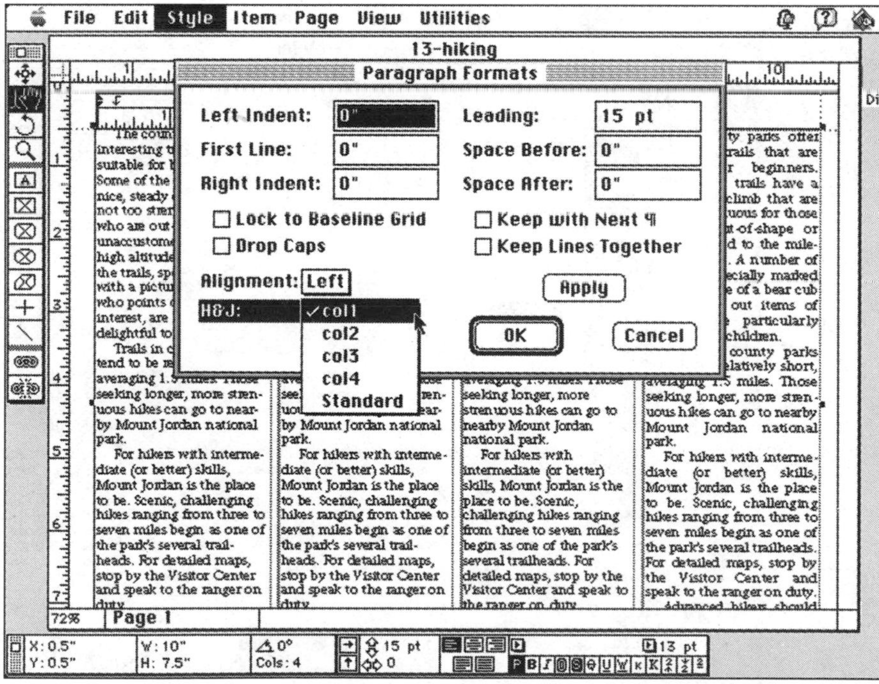

Figure 13-3:
Choose
hyphenation
settings
through the
Paragraph
Formats
dialog box.

Prevent a word from being hyphenated by putting a soft hyphen at the beginning of it.

It's not easy remembering how to hyphenate every word. If you need prompting, select the word in question and then use QuarkXPress's Suggested Hyphenation feature. To access the Suggested Hyphenation dialog box (see Figure 13-4), select Utilities ⇨ Suggested Hyphenation or use the keyboard shortcut ⌘H. QuarkXPress shows the recommended hyphenation settings for the current word (or, if more than one word is selected, for the first word in the selection).

Although handy as a quick reference, the Suggested Hyphenation feature does not replace a dictionary as the final authority on where a word should break. The feature takes into account the current H&J set. If the set specifies that no hyphen can be inserted until after the first three letters of a word, the Suggested Hyphenation dialog box does not show any legal hyphenations that may exist after the second letter in the word.

If you find yourself inserting manual hyphens repeatedly into the same words, you're doing too much work. Instead, add your own hyphenation preferences to QuarkXPress through the hyphenation-exception dictionary feature. You do this through the Hyphenation Exceptions dialog box (see Figure 13-5). To access the dialog box, select Utilities ⇨ Hyphenation Exceptions.

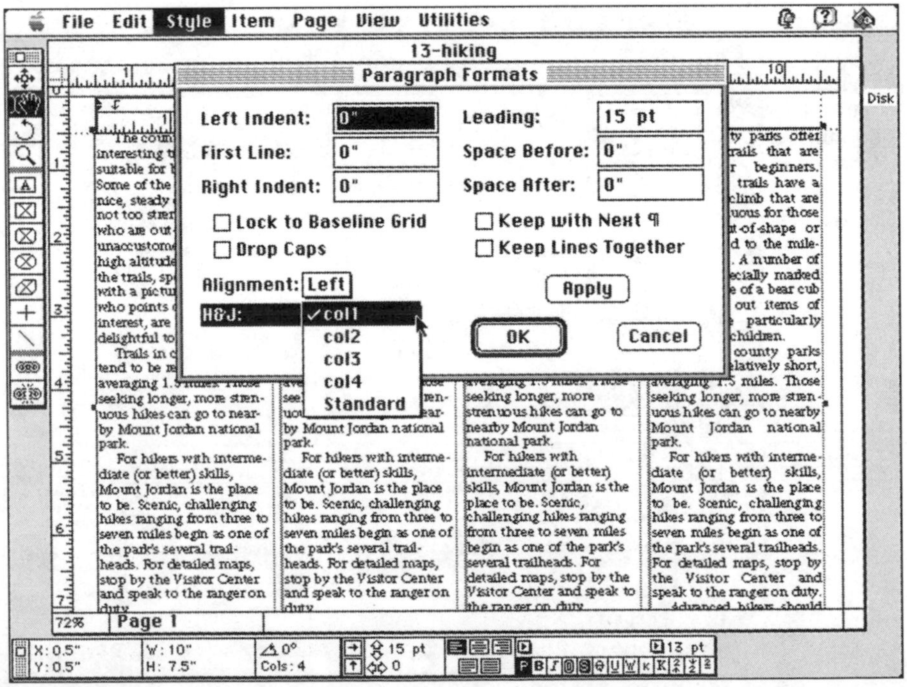

Figure 13-4: Use the Suggested Hyphenation dialog box whenever you have trouble remembering how to hyphenate a particular word.

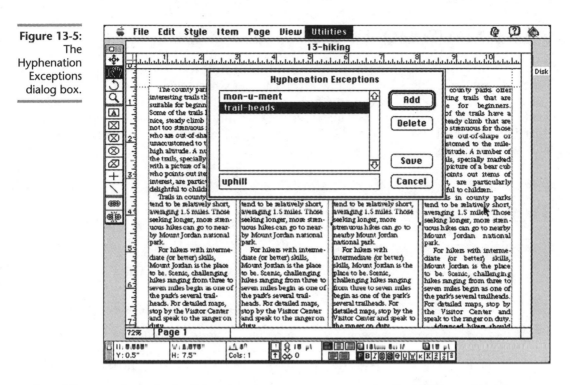

Figure 13-5:
The
Hyphenation
Exceptions
dialog box.

By adding words to the hyphenation dictionary, you can give QuarkXPress hyphenation instructions for words the program does not know, hyphenates incorrectly, or hyphenates differently than your stylebook specifies. Additionally, you can prevent hyphenation of specific words by adding them to the dictionary. This dictionary can be global, affecting all documents, or local, affecting only the current document.

As you add words to the hyphenation dictionary, indicate allowable hyphenation points by inserting hyphens. To prevent a word from hyphenating, type it in without hyphens. You can change existing hyphenation exceptions by clicking on the word you want to change. The Add button is replaced by the Replace button, and whichever word you type in replaces the one highlighted.

If you are in a document that does not use the standard QuarkXPress preferences, any hyphenation exceptions you enter affect only that document. To define hyphenation exceptions you want to use globally, close all active documents (to be sure that your changes are saved in the standard preferences file).

You can tell QuarkXPress to prevent a line of text from wrapping after a hyphen. To do so, use the *nonbreaking hyphen character*, ⌘= to create this character. It is generally used when the text following a hyphen is short, as in words such as *follow-up,* or when a hyphen indicates a range of numbers or a score, such as *4-6* or *14-1*. True, not everyone worries about whether text breaks at such points. But it's nice that QuarkXPress lets it matter if you want it to.

Making the Most of Leading

In traditional typesetting, *leading* (pronounced *ledding*) is the space between lines of type. Although tracking, kerning, and word spacing let you establish good typographic color horizontally, leading lets you do the same vertically. Named for the thin strips of lead that printers used to separate metal type in early printing presses, leading varies based on several elements: column width, type size, whether text is justified or ragged, and total amount of text.

Determining leading settings

There are several ways to set leading:

- **Option 1:** Use the Paragraph Formats dialog box to access the Edit Í Style Sheet option.

- **Option 2:** Another is through the Style Í Leading menu (the shortcut is Shift-ÔE).

- **Option 3:** A third is through the Measurements palette. The number to the right of the up and down triangles reflects the current leading setting, which you can highlight and change or raise or lower incrementally by clicking on the up or down triangles.

The width of a column is the most important factor affecting good leading. The wider the column, the more space you need between lines to keep the reader's eye from accidentally jumping to a different line. That's why books have noticeable space between lines while newspapers and magazines, which use thin columns, have what seems to be no space at all.

A related concern is whether type is justified or ragged-right. Justified text usually requires more leading than nonjustified text because the ragged margin gives the eye a distinct anchor point for each line.

 For text set in multiple columns, we recommend that you set leading at the current point size plus 2 points for text 9 points and larger. For example, if the point size of the text is 12 points, set leading at 14. For text 8 points and smaller, use the current point size plus 1 point; 7-point type would get 8-point leading. This rule of thumb fluctuates somewhat according to column width. Add another 1 point or half point, respectively, if your column width is greater than 16 picas but less than 27 picas; add at least 2 more points if your text is wider than 27 picas.

Small changes in leading and point size alter the feeling of text, as you can see in Figure 13-6. This creative use of leading lets you subtly but effectively differentiate between sections or elements without resorting to extreme use of typefaces or layout variations. Even though the typeface and justification are the same, the text on the left, set at 9.5-point with 11-point leading, has a very different texture than the text on the right, set at 9-point text with 11.5-point leading.

Figure 13-6:
Minor changes in leading and point size make a dramatic difference.

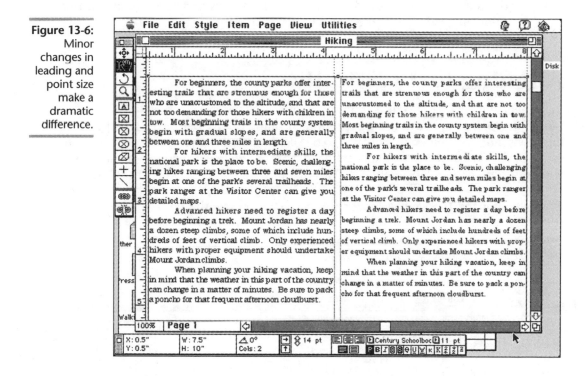

QuarkXPress includes an automatic leading option, which usually sets leading at 120 percent of text size. This is fine for 10-point type because it results in 12-point leading. But for 9-point type, it results in 10.8-point leading, which is an awkward size on which to base a layout grid. And at larger type sizes, leading becomes too large; for example, 43.2-point leading is set for 36-point text.

Although it provides an auto leading option (enter **0** or **auto** as the leading value), QuarkXPress also offers a better alternative. You can set leading to be a certain number of points more than the current type size, no matter what the type size. Enter **+2**, for example, for leading 2 points more than the current type size. This *additive leading* option also ensures that any line that has larger-than-normal type (such as a drop cap) won't overprint other lines.

Additive leading has a drawback. If you use superscripts (perhaps for foot-notes), subscripts, or special text or symbols that extend beyond the body text's height or depth, you get uneven spacing. This is because some lines have more leading than others to accommodate the outsized or outpositioned characters. QuarkXPress bases the additive leading on the highest and lowest character in a line, not on the body text's normal position. If you can't alter your text so that none of it extends beyond the body text range, don't use this option. Instead, specify the actual leading you want in each style tag.

Aligning text vertically

Vertical alignment — the vertical distribution of lines of text in a text box — is as impor-tant to the look of a page as using appropriate leading values. Before desktop publish-ing, it was not uncommon for columns to be slightly out of alignment because lining up strips of text by hand is nearly impossible to do precisely. Being within a point or two was considered adequate. No longer. Uneven type columns today look unprofessional.

Two settings in the Typographic Preferences dialog box prevent this problem. If set properly, QuarkXPress's Baseline Grid Increment and Maintain Leading controls eliminate such slight misalignments. You access these settings through the Typographic Preferences dialog box (select Edit ➪ Preferences ➪ Typographic), shown in Figure 13-7.

Figure 13-7:
The Typographic Preferences dialog box lets you set leading specifica-tions that apply to all documents produced using QuarkXPress.

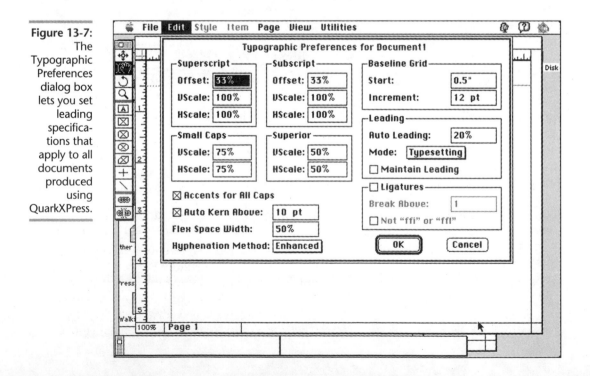

Used with the Lock to Baseline Grid option in the Paragraph Formats dialog box (accessed by selecting Style ⇨ Formats), the Baseline Grid Increment feature enables you to ensure that the baselines — the bottoms of your letters — lock onto the grid lines you set for a document. Any text tagged with a style that has the baseline grid locked is automatically positioned to align with the document grid, ensuring that text aligns across columns.

The text you use the most in a document is body text, which is also where misalignment is most noticeable. To avoid this kind of misalignment, set your baseline grid to be the same as the leading for body text and check the Lock to Baseline Grid option in the paragraph style for that body text (usually called *Normal*).

Do *not* use the Lock to Baseline Grid option on text whose style has different leading settings, as this could result in awkward spacing between lines in text of that style. For example, if your body text has 11-point leading but your subheads have 15-point leading, turning on the baseline lock option forces QuarkXPress to move the subhead to the next grid point, which is either 11 or 22 points below the previous line of body text. This occurs even though you set the leading for the subhead style to place the subhead 15 points after the previous line of body text.

If you put some thought into your styles when you create them, you can ensure consistent vertical alignment. If you do this, you won't have to worry if you have styles with different leading amounts or if additive leading causes some lines to have different leading than others. You also won't need to use the Lock to Baseline Grid option.

Here's an example of how to plan for consistent vertical alignment. When you pick 11.5 points as body-text leading, make sure other text elements add up to multiples of 11.5. If subheads are 14 points, give them 16-point leading and put 7 points of space above them (a total of 23 points, or two body-text lines) or 18.5 points of space above (a total of 34.5 points, or three body-text lines). If the byline is 8 points, give it a leading of 9.5 with 2 points of space above or below it. In both cases, make sure that these other elements do not take more than one line. Otherwise, the leading from the second line means that their total vertical space is no longer a multiple of 11.5. If you cannot ensure this, create a tag with the same leading but different space above (and maybe below) to use when the text in these paragraphs takes two lines.

If you check the Maintain Leading option in the Typographic Preferences dialog box, the line following a text box is positioned an even multiple of lines under the last line above the text box, ensuring vertical alignment across all columns. If you turn this option off, text is positioned immediately after the text box, which may not be the right position to align it with other columns. Using this option maintains proper leading for text that falls under an intervening text box, such as one that contains a sidebar, picture, or pull-quote.

Selecting the leading mode

In the Typographic Preferences dialog box (select Edit ➪ Preferences ➪ Typographic), Leading Mode tells QuarkXPress which technique to use in controlling leading. With very few exceptions, you should set this at Typesetting, which measures leading from baseline to baseline. The first version of QuarkXPress measured leading from top of text to top of text, which Quark calls Word Processing mode. This mode is not used in professional publishing, and even many old word-processing templates were based on measuring leading from the baseline. Unless you have a specific reason to select Word Processing mode, leave this setting at the default Typesetting mode.

Additional Paragraph Spacing _____

Another way to control the appearance of a document is to specify the amount of space above or below paragraphs, as well as the indents from the right and left margins. You do this in the Paragraph Formats dialog box (see Figure 13-8). To access the dialog box for individual paragraphs, press Style ➪ Formats (keyboard shortcut is Shift-⌘F). For styles, access the dialog box via the Formats button in the Edit Style Sheet dialog box (accessed via Edit ➪ Style Sheets).

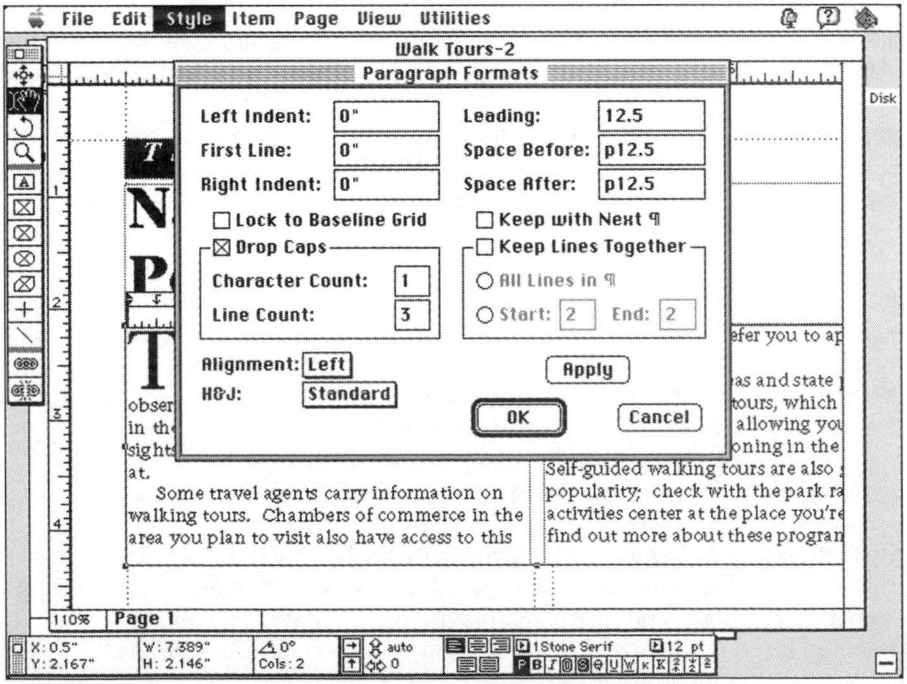

Figure 13-8:
The
Paragraph
Formats
dialog box.

By using the indent and space options, you can call attention to a paragraph by offsetting it from surrounding paragraphs. In Figure 13-8, we selected Left Indent, Right Indent, Space Before, and Space After to frame the paragraph with extra space on all four sides.

 Don't overdo extra paragraph spacing. The effect's success depends on its being used rarely. Common uses include indenting a long quotation or highlighting a recommendation. You need not alter all four options as we did in the example in Figure 13-8; typically, a left indent is sufficient to offset a paragraph from surrounding text.

The Space Before and Space After options are also useful in positioning elements such as bylines, pull-quotes, and subheads that don't follow the same leading grid as the body text. In addition, you can use these options to ensure that the grid is maintained despite the use of larger or smaller type sizes for these elements, as discussed in "Aligning text vertically," earlier in this chapter.

Summary

- Avoid using the flush zone feature to force justification of the last line in a paragraph. This effect can confuse readers.

- Use the single-word justification feature. Although frowned on by many typographers, it is better to justify a long word that takes a full line or more than to have that line unjustified and thus appear different from surrounding text.

- Likewise, use the Break Capitalized Words option.

- For most text, keep the maximum number of consecutive hyphens between 2 and 4.

- Create different H&J sets; have at least one with standard hyphenation settings and another with hyphenation turned off (for elements like headlines, bylines, and pull-quotes).

- Don't allow hyphens before or after a single letter.

- Use the Utilities ➪ Hyphenation Exceptions feature to add specialized words to the hyphenation dictionary.

- The wider the column width, the more leading you should have.

- Justified text requires more leading than ragged or centered text.

- Use the additive leading option rather than the Auto leading option; this avoids fractional point sizes for leading. An exception is if subscripts or other nonbaseline characters extend beyond the leading's setting.

- Use the Lock to Baseline Grid and Maintain Leading options in documents where leading of various elements are multiples of each other; this ensures consistent vertical alignment with minimal manual effort.

- Use the Space Before and Space After options to highlight elements like bylines and subheads by giving them enough space to be visually separate from surrounding elements.

Working with Typefaces

▪▪

In This Chapter

➥ How typefaces differ and how those differences affect document creation in QuarkXPress

➥ Effective ways to use type styles and type variants

➥ How to use ruling lines

▪▪

Types of Type

A typeface usually has several variations, the most common of which are *roman, italic, boldface,* and *boldface italic* for serif typefaces; and *medium, oblique, boldface,* and *boldface oblique* for sans serif typefaces. Other variations that involve type weight include *thin, light, book, demibold, heavy, ultrabold,* and *black. Compressed, condensed, expanded,* and *wide* describe type scale.

Each of these variants, as well as each available combination of variants (for example, compressed light oblique), is called a *face.* Some typefaces have no variants; these are typically *calligraphic typefaces,* such as Park Avenue and Zapf Chancery, and *symbol typefaces,* such as Zapf Dingbats and Sonata. In Figure 14-1, you see samples of several typefaces and some of their variants. By using typeface variants wisely, you can create more attractive and more readable documents.

Figure 14-1:
Some
sample
typefaces.

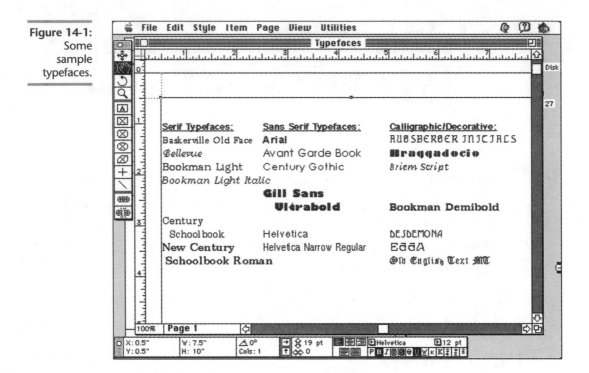

 Desktop publishing programs popularized the use of the term *font* to describe what traditionally was called a *typeface*. In traditional terms, a typeface refers to a set of variants for one style of text, such as Times Roman. A *face* is one of those variants, such as Times Roman Italic. A font, in traditional terms, is a face at a specific point size, such as 12-point Times Roman Italic. (Until electronic typesetting was developed, printers set type using metal blocks that were available only in a limited range of sizes.) Throughout this book, we use the traditional terms.

Selecting the Best Typefaces _____

If you've ever seen a type chart, you already know that thousands of typefaces are available, each with a different feel. Matching the typeface's feel to the effect that you want for your document is a trial-and-error process. Until you are experienced at using a wide variety of typefaces (and even then), experiment with different typefaces on a mock-up of your document to see what works best.

Understanding Typeface Names

The many variants of typefaces confuse many users, especially because most programs use only the terms *normal* (or *plain*), *italic, bold,* and *bold italic* to describe available variations. When a typeface has more than these basic variations, programs usually split the typeface into several typefaces.

For example, in some programs, Helvetica comes as Helvetica, with medium, oblique, boldface, and boldface oblique faces; Helvetica Light/Black, with light, light oblique, black, and black oblique faces; Helvetica Light/Black Condensed, with condensed light, condensed light oblique, condensed black, and condensed black oblique faces; Helvetica Condensed, with condensed medium, condensed oblique, condensed boldface, and condensed boldface oblique faces; and Helvetica Compressed, with compressed medium and condensed oblique faces. (Figure 14-1 shows two of these variations.) When there are this many variations, you have to choose from among several Helvetica typefaces, and you have to know that, for example, selecting bold for Helvetica Condensed results in Helvetica Condensed Bold type.

For some typefaces, the variants are even more confusing. For example, in text, Bookman is usually printed in light face, which is lighter than the medium face. So when you select plain, you really select Bookman Light (shown in Figure 14-1). And when you select bold, you really select Bookman Demibold. Bookman Medium and Bookman Bold are too heavy for use as body text, which is why the typeface comes in the light/demi combination of faces.

Fortunately, the issue of what face a program designates as plain, italic, and the rest rarely comes into play. You usually encounter a problem in one of the following situations:

- ➷ When you are exchanging files between PCs and Macs — because some vendors use slightly different names for their typefaces on different platforms. The Utilities ➪ Font Usage option enables you to correct this problem by replacing one typeface name with another in your document.

- ➷ When you are working with a service bureau that has typeface names that are different, or whose staff uses the traditional names rather than the desktop-publishing names.

- ➷ When you are working with artists or typesetters zto match a typeface. Typically, the problem is a lack of familiarity with the different names for a typeface. The best way to reach a common understanding is to look at a sample of the typefaces being discussed.

We recommend that you take the time necessary to define a standard set of typefaces for each group of publications. You may want all employee newsletters in your company to have a similar feel, which you can enforce by using common body text and headline typefaces, even if layout and paragraph settings differ.

The key to working with a standard set of typefaces is to avoid limiting the set to only a few typefaces. Selecting more typefaces than any one document might use gives you enough flexibility to be creative while providing an obviously standard appearance. You also can use the same typeface for different purposes. For example, you might use a newsletter's headline typeface as a kicker in a brochure. A consistent — but not constrained — appearance is a good way to establish an identity for your company.

You may have noticed that many people use serif typefaces for body copy and sans serif typefaces for headlines, pull-quotes, and other elements. But there is no rule you should worry about following. You can easily create engaging documents that use serif typefaces for every element. All-sans-serif documents are possible, but they are rare because sans serif typefaces tend to be hard to read when used in many pages of text. (Exceptions include typefaces such as News Gothic and Franklin Gothic, which were designed for use as body text.) No matter which typefaces you use, the key is to ensure that each element calls an appropriate amount of attention to itself.

If you're feeling confused about which typeface is right for you, here are some basic guidelines:

- ☞ Use a roman, medium, or book weight typeface for body text. In some cases, a light weight works well, especially for typefaces such as Bookman and Souvenir, which tend to be heavy in the medium weights.

 Output some samples before deciding on a light typeface for body text because many light typefaces are hard to read when used extensively. Also, if you intend to output publications on an imagesetter (at 1200 dpi or finer resolution), make sure that you output samples on that imagesetter because a light font may be readable on a 300- or 600-dpi laser printer but too light on a higher resolution printer that can reproduce thin characters more faithfully than a laser printer. (The laser printer may actually print a light typeface as something a bit heavier: because the width of the text's stroke is not an even multiple of the laser printer's dots, the printer has no choice but to make the stroke thicker than it should be.)

- ☞ Use a heavier typeface for headlines and subheads. A demibold or bold usually works well. Avoid using the same typeface for headlines and body text, even if it is a bolder variant. On the other hand, using the same typeface for subheads and headlines, even if in a different variant, helps ensure a common identity. (And if you mix typefaces, use those that have similar appearances. For example, use round typefaces with other round typefaces and squared-off typefaces with other squared-off typefaces.)

❧ If captions are long (more than three lines), use a typeface with the same weight as body text. If you use the same typeface as body text, differentiate the caption visually from body text. Using a boldface caption lead-in (the first words are boldface and act as a title for the caption) or putting the caption in italics distinguishes the caption from body text without being distracting. If captions are short (three lines or fewer), consider using a heavier face than body text or a typeface that is readily distinguished from your body text.

❧ As a general rule, avoid using more than three typefaces (not including variants) in the main document elements (headlines, body text, captions, pull-quotes, and other elements that appear on most pages). However, some typefaces are very similar, so you can use them as a group as if they were one. Examples include Helvetica, Univers, and Arial; Futura and Avant Garde; Times and its many relatives (including Times New Roman and Times Ten); Galliard and New Baskerville; Souvenir and Korinna; and Goudy Old Style and Century Old Style. You can treat the individual typefaces within these groups almost as variants of one another, especially if you use one of the individual typefaces in limited-length elements such as kickers, pull-quotes, and bylines.

❧ Italics are particularly appropriate for kickers, bylines, sidebar headlines, and pull-quotes.

Type Styles

Typefaces have several faces — such as boldface and italics — to give publishers visual variety and content guides. Publishing programs (as well as some word processors) also offer special *typeface attributes*, such as small caps, shadows, and underlines, to provide even more design and content tools.

How to change typeface attributes

QuarkXPress lets you change typeface attributes in several ways:

❧ **Option 1:** Use the Measurements palette (this is the easiest method). To select a typeface quickly, double click the typeface name in the list of typefaces in the palette or enter the first letter of the typeface's name. The list jumps to the first typeface that begins with that letter. This method is faster than scrolling if you have many typefaces available. Below the typeface list is a row of type style attributes: plain, boldface, italics, outline, shadow, strikethrough, underline all, word underline, small caps, all caps, superscript, subscript, and superior. Any current style settings for the selected text are highlighted.

Figure 14-2 shows the Measurements palette, from which you can control almost every typographic specification, including leading, tracking, paragraph alignment, typefaces, type size, and type style.

✑ **Option 2:** Use the Style menu. Options available in this menu include Font, Size, Type Style, Color, Shade, Horizontal/Vertical Scale, Kern or Track (depending on whether text is selected), Baseline Shift, and Character (which lets you define several attributes at once). You can see the menu in Figure 14-3.

✑ **Option 3:** Use the Character Attributes dialog box, which you access with the shortcut key Shift-⌘D. Figure 14-4 shows the dialog box. You can set several type settings at once.

✑ **Option 4:** Use keyboard shortcuts. Use the codes in Table 14-1 in combination with Shift-⌘. For example, for plain text, press Shift-⌘P.

Plain refers to the basic style for the selected typeface. Most commercial typefaces come with a roman or medium face as the basic style. But many typefaces created by do-it-yourselfers or converted via programs, such as Altsys's Fontographer and Ares Software Corp.'s FontMonger, come with each face as a separate typeface. So, for example, you may have Magazine Roman, Magazine Italic, Magazine Bold, and Magazine Bold Italic as separate typefaces in your fonts menu. If you select Magazine Bold Italic, QuarkXPress's palettes and dialog boxes show its style as plain, but it appears and prints as bold italic. This discrepancy is not a bug in QuarkXPress, but simply a reflection of the fact that the basic style for any typeface is called "plain" no matter what the style actually looks like. In some programs, like FontMonger, you can set a typeface such as Magazine Bold Italic so that it is listed as bold italic in QuarkXPress's palettes and dialog boxes.

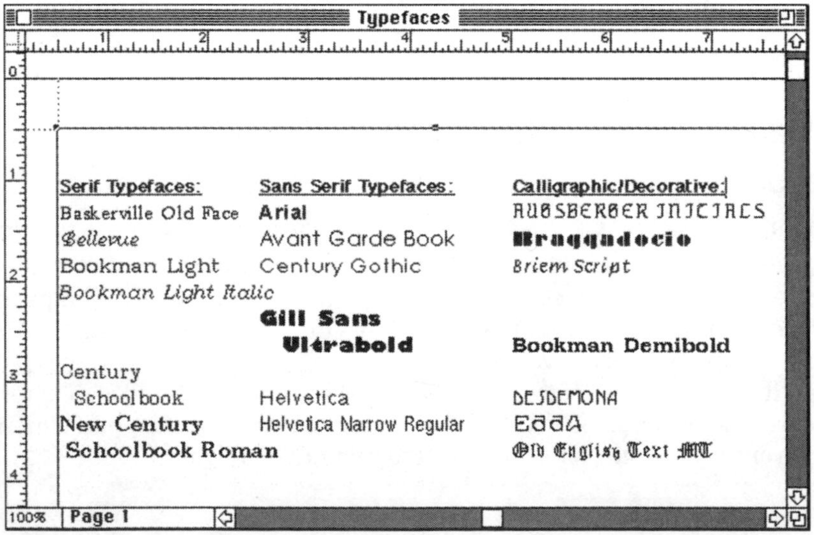

Figure 14-2:
Change type attributes easily by using the Measurements palette

Serif Typefaces:	Sans Serif Typefaces:	Calligraphic/Decorative:
Baskerville Old Face	**Arial**	AUGSBERGER INICIALS
Bellevue	Avant Garde Book	**Braggadocio**
Bookman Light	Century Gothic	*Briem Script*
Bookman Light Italic		
	Gill Sans Ultrabold	**Bookman Demibold**
Century School book	Helvetica	DESDEMONA
New Century	Helvetica Narrow Regular	Edda
Schoolbook Roman		Old English Text MT

100%   Page 1

Figure 14-3:
The
QuarkXPress
Style menu.

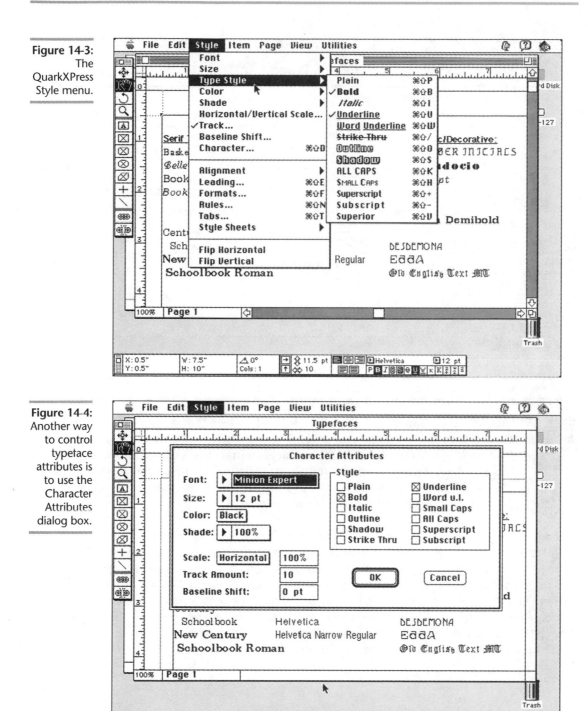

Figure 14-4:
Another way
to control
typeface
attributes is
to use the
Character
Attributes
dialog box.

Table 14-1
Shortcut Keys for Typeface Attributes

Use the following key codes to set typeface attributes.

Attribute	Shortcut Key
Plain	Shift-⌘P
Bold	Shift-⌘B
Italic	Shift-⌘I
Underline all	Shift-⌘U
Word underline	Shift-⌘W
~~Strikethrough~~	Shift-⌘/
Outline	Shift-⌘O (letter O)
Shadow	Shift-⌘S
ALL CAPS	Shift-⌘K
SMALL CAPS	Shift-⌘H
Superscript	Shift-⌘+
Subscript	Shift-⌘- (hyphen)
Superior	Shift-⌘V

QuarkXPress cannot apply a bold style to a typeface that does not have one. If the typeface has a bolder face, QuarkXPress is likely to use that one, assuming the typeface uses the correct internal label so that QuarkXPress knows to do this. Similarly, QuarkXPress cannot apply an italic style to a typeface that does not have one. But QuarkXPress does recognize that when you select italics for a sans serif typeface, oblique face is what you want.

If you change the face of selected text to a face (boldface or italics) not supported by the text's typeface, QuarkXPress may appear to have applied that face successfully. However, when you print, you will see that the face has not really been changed (although the spacing has changed to accommodate the new face). What has happened is that QuarkXPress and the type scaler (such as TrueType or Adobe Type Manager) mistakenly create a screen font based on your request for a face change. When the text with the nonexistent face is printed, the Macintosh finds no printer file for that face and uses the closest face it has for the typeface used.

Basic text styles

Most people are familiar with basic text styles such as boldface and italics. After all, we see them routinely in newspapers, magazines, ads, and television. Despite that familiarity, these styles can be misused, especially by people experienced in producing reports on typewriters and word processors rather than creating published (typeset-quality) documents in which these basic styles are used differently.

The following is a primer on the use of basic text attributes in body text. (Other effects are covered later in this chapter.) Of course, these and other guidelines are meant to be ignored by those purposely trying to create a special effect.

Italics

Italics are used to emphasize a word or phrase in body text — for example, "You *must* remember to fully extinguish your campfire." Italics are also used to identify titles of books, movies, television and radio series, magazines, and newspapers: "Public TV's *Discovery* series had an excellent show about the Rocky Mountains." Italics can also be applied to lead-in words of subsections or in lists (these instances are described in Chapter 15).

In typewritten text, people often use underlines or uppercase as a substitute for italics, but do not substitute these effects in published text.

Boldface

Boldface is seldom used in body text because it is too distracting. When it is used, boldface is typically applied to the lead-in words in subsections. As a rule, do not use it for emphasis — use italics instead. However, when you have a lot of text and you want people to easily pick out names within it, boldfacing the names may be appropriate. If, for example, you create a story listing winners of a series of awards or publish a gossip column that mentions various celebrities, you may want to boldface people's names in order to highlight them.

Small caps and all caps

Capital letters have both functional and decorative uses. Functionally, they start sentences and identify proper names. Decoratively, they add emphasis or stateliness.

Capital letters have a more stately appearance than lowercase letters most likely because of the influence of Roman monuments, which are decorated with inscribed text in uppercase letters (the Romans didn't use lowercase much). These monuments and the Roman style have come to symbolize authority and officialism. Most government centers have a very Roman appearance, as a visit to Washington, D.C., quickly confirms.

Using all capital letters has two major drawbacks:

- ☞ Text in all caps can be overwhelming because uppercase characters are both taller and wider than lowercase. In typeset materials, as opposed to typewritten, all caps loom even larger because the size difference between a capital letter and its lowercase version is greater than it is in typewriter characters, which are all designed to fit in the same space. All caps can be thought of as the typographic equivalent of yelling: "READ THIS SENTENCE!" Now, read this sentence.

- ☞ People read not by analyzing every letter and constructing words but by recognizing the shapes of words. In all caps, words have the same rectangular shape — only the width changes — so the use of word shape as a reading aid is lost. All caps is therefore harder to read than regular text.

The use of small caps can result in elegant, stately text that is not overwhelming. The smaller size of the caps overcomes the yelling problem of all caps. Figure 14-5 shows an example of effective use of small caps. In the example, the kicker and byline are set in small caps.

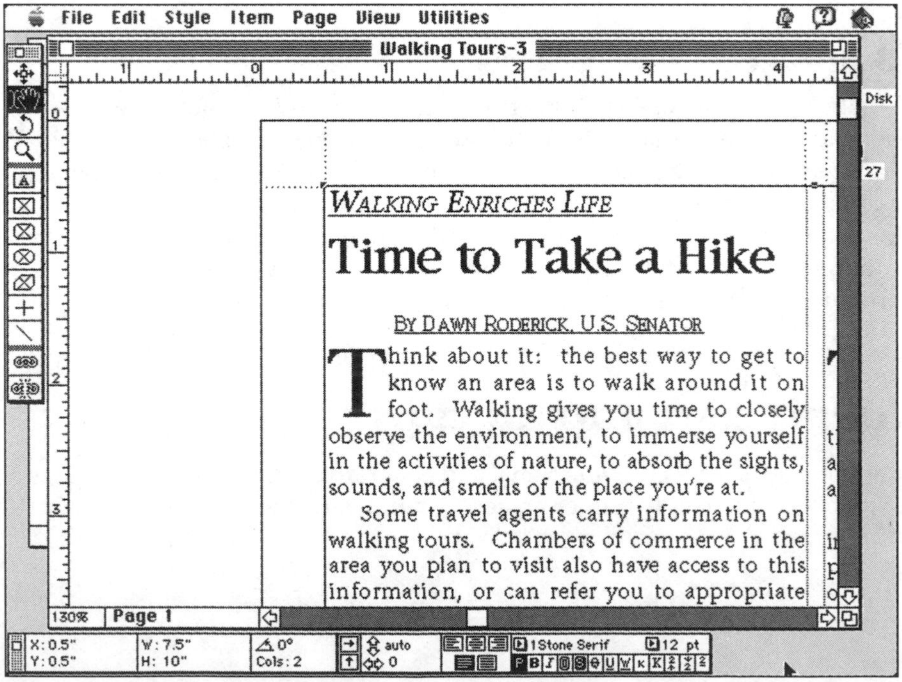

Figure 14-5: Small caps are shown in the kicker (above the headline) and byline.

The key to using small caps is to limit them to short amounts of text where it's OK not to give readers the aid of recognizable word shapes. Small caps are effective in kickers, bylines, and labels.

QuarkXPress lets you set the proportional size of small caps (compared to regular caps) in the Typographic Preferences dialog box, as shown in Figure 14-6. (You can also set the relative size and position of superscripts, subscripts, and superiors in this dialog box.) To access the dialog box, select Edit ⇨ Preferences ⇨ Typographic. You can set the horizontal and vertical proportions separately, although they are usually the same. QuarkXPress's default setting is 75 percent, and most small caps should be set between 70 and 80 percent.

If you want typographic settings to affect all documents, invoke the Typographic Preferences dialog box with no document selected. Any future documents use the new settings as the default settings.

To apply default settings to a document with altered preferences (including typographic settings), open the document and select Use XPress Preferences when QuarkXPress asks whether to use the default settings or the document's settings. (QuarkXPress automatically detects whether a document's settings match the defaults for that copy of QuarkXPress.)

Figure 14-6:
Set the size of small caps in the Typographic Preferences dialog box.

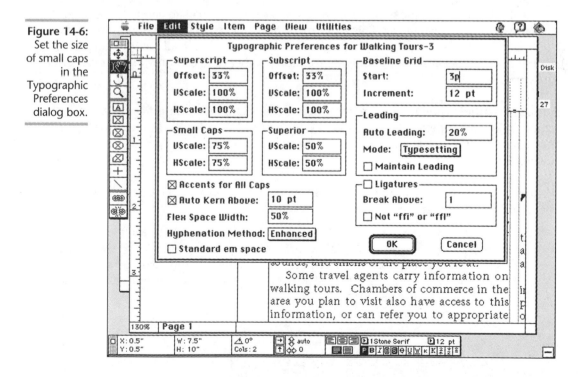

Some typefaces have a version — sometimes called an *expert collection* — that includes specially designed small caps. These caps are not merely proportionally scaled; their strokes are also modified to make them a bit darker. When you scale a character to be smaller, you make its strokes smaller, which makes the character lighter than the equivalent lowercase letter. Simulated small caps can look weaker than true small caps. This difference is usually not a problem, but for design-intensive work such as advertising, the quality difference often makes it worthwhile to get the expert-collection typeface. Keep in mind that using the small caps option in QuarkXPress does not access the expert-collection typeface; you must explicitly apply the expert-collection's small cap typeface to the characters in question using the Measurements palette, Menu, or Character Attributes dialog box described earlier in this chapter.

Traditional numerals

If you look at books published early in this century or in previous eras, you'll notice that the numerals look very different than the ones you see today in books, magazines, and newspapers. Numerals used to be treated as lowercase letters, so some, such as the number 9, had *descenders*, just as lowercase letters such as *g* do. Others, such as the number 6, had *ascenders*, as do lowercase letters such as *b*. But this way of displaying numerals changed, and most modern typefaces treat numerals like capital letters: no descenders and no ascenders. This style keeps numerals from sticking out in headlines, but it also can make numerals too prominent in some text, especially in type-intensive documents such as ads, where individual character shapes are important to the overall look.

Adobe and other type foundries resurrected the old-fashioned numerals as part of expert collection typefaces. As you can see in Figure 14-7, which shows the two types of numerals, the traditional numerals are more stylized and have the typographic feel of lowercase letters.

Although they often look more elegant, old-fashioned numerals have three drawbacks that you should consider before using them routinely:

 ☞ They reside in a separate font, so you must change the font for each and every numeral (or groups of numerals). Even if you code this in your word processor, it can be a lot of extra work. In tables and other numerals-only text, using old-fashioned numerals is less of an issue because you can have a separate style for text that uses the expert font.

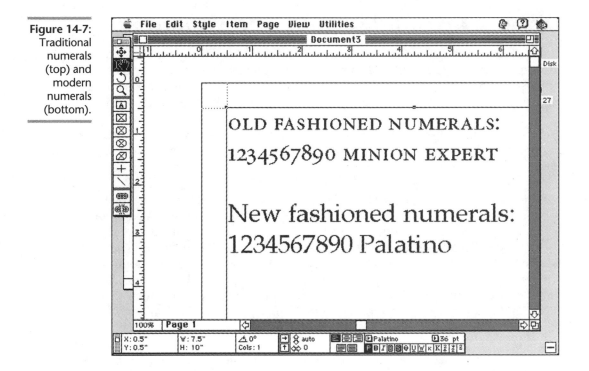

∞ They do not have the same width. Modern numerals are almost always the same width (that of an en space), so typographers and publishers don't have to worry about whether columns of numbers align. (Because all numerals are the same width, they align naturally.) But the old-fashioned numerals in expert fonts have variable widths, just like most characters, so they can look awkward in columns of numbers even if you use decimal or comma alignment.

∞ They are unusual in modern typography, so they can call more attention to themselves than is appropriate. For design-intensive work, this extra attention is usually not an issue, but in commonplace documents such as reports and newsletters, they can look out of place. As their popularity grows, people may grow more used to seeing them.

Superscripts, subscripts, and superiors

Superscripts, subscripts, and superiors let you indicate notes in your text and set some mathematical notations. Although numerals are typically used for these notes, you can also use special symbols such as asterisks and daggers. These notes are in a smaller size than the rest of the text and are positioned above or below the regular baseline.

Superscripts and subscripts are typically used in math and other sciences. A superscript can indicate an exponent, such as a^2 for *a squared,* or a notation, such as U^{235} for *uranium-235.*

Superscripts are commonly used for footnotes, too, but QuarkXPress also offers *superiors*, the traditional typographic method of indicating footnotes. A superior is similar to a superscript, except that the top of a superior always aligns with the top of the text's cap height. A superscript, by contrast, need not align with anything. The advantage to using a superior is that you don't have to worry about the footnote (or whatever) bumping into the text in the line above. This problem is particularly acute if you have tight leading and the superscript is positioned below a character that has a descender (such as a *g* or *p.*) Another potential problem is uneven leading, which is explained later.

Footnotes set via your word processor to be superscripted import as superscripts. If you want to use superiors, you must manually change superscripts to superiors. You cannot use the Edit ➪ Find/Change option to search for superscripts and replace them with superiors because superior is not an option in the Find/Change dialog box.

As it does for small caps, QuarkXPress lets you set the relative size and spacing for superscripts, subscripts, and superiors. You specify these sizes in the Typographic Preferences dialog box, accessed via Edit ➪ Preferences ➪ Typographic. You may need to experiment to derive a setting that works for all paragraph styles.

We prefer the following settings: superscripts offset 35 percent and scaled 60 percent; subscripts offset 30 percent and scaled 60 percent; and superiors scaled 50 percent.

If you use additive leading (discussed in Chapter 13) and your superscript or subscript settings cause the superscripts or subscripts to extend beyond the text's height or depth, you get uneven spacing. The uneven spacing occurs because some lines have more leading than others to accommodate the outsized or outpositioned characters. (QuarkXPress bases the additive leading on the highest and lowest character in a line, not on the text's normal position.) If you can't alter your text — by changing either its leading or the subscript and superscript settings — so that none of it extends beyond the text's range, don't use the additive-leading option.

If you want typographic settings to affect all documents, invoke the Typographic Preferences dialog box with no document selected. Any future document uses these new settings as the default.

To apply default settings to a document with altered preferences (including typographic settings), select Use XPress Preferences (it appears when you open the document) when QuarkXPress asks whether to use the default settings or the document's settings. QuarkXPress automatically detects whether a document's settings match the defaults for that copy of QuarkXPress.

Baseline Shift

Baseline Shift is similar to superscripting and subscripting. Baseline Shift lets you move text up or down relative to other text on the line. The biggest difference between baseline shifting and super- or subscripting is that with Baseline Shift, the text size does not change. This effect is rarely needed, but it can come in handy when you position text for ads and other design-intensive text or when you use it with effects such as ruling lines to create reverse text.

If you need to do so, you change baseline shift through the Baseline Shift dialog box, shown in Figure 14-8, which you access via Style ⇨ Baseline Shift. Entering a positive number moves the text up; a negative number moves it down.

The Baseline Shift feature lets you change the text size to create superscripts or subscripts that differ from the normal settings in a document. Most people won't need this feature; among those who may are scientists and engineers whose documents require several levels of subscripting or superscripting.

 Unlike superscripts and subscripts, baseline shifts do not cause uneven leading when used with additive leading. Instead, QuarkXPress lets text overprint lines the text shifts into.

Underlines and rules

Underlines and rules are not typically used in body text in published documents. In fact, underlines are used in typewritten text as a substitute for italics. But underlines do have a place in published materials as a visual element in kickers, subheads, bylines, and tables. When used in such short elements, underlines add a definitive, authoritative feel.

Figure 14-8:
The Baseline
Shift dialog
box.

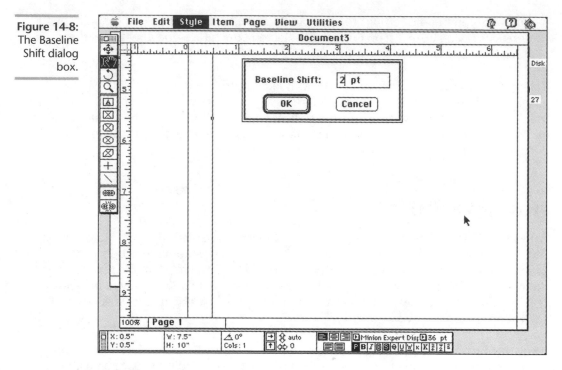

Using underlines

QuarkXPress offers two types of underlines: *regular underline* (Shift-⌘U), which affects all characters, including spaces; and *word underline* (Shift-⌘W), which underlines only nonspace characters (letters, numerals, symbols, and punctuation). When choosing which underline type to use, there is no right or wrong — let the aesthetics of the document be the determining factor.

Using ruling lines

Underlines are limited in line size and position — all underlines are fixed by QuarkXPress. But you can create underlines and other types of lines meant to enhance text with the ruling line feature. QuarkXPress offers a wide range of ruling lines through the Paragraph Rules dialog box, which you access via the keyboard shortcut Shift-⌘N or by selecting Style ⇨ Rules. When this dialog box first appears, it has only two options: Rule Above and Rule Below. If you check either (or both) of these options, the dialog box expands to offer more choices. Figure 14-9 shows the dialog box with both Rule Above and Rule Below checked and with the Style option selected for Rule Below.

Figure 14-9:
The
Paragraph
Rules dialog
box.

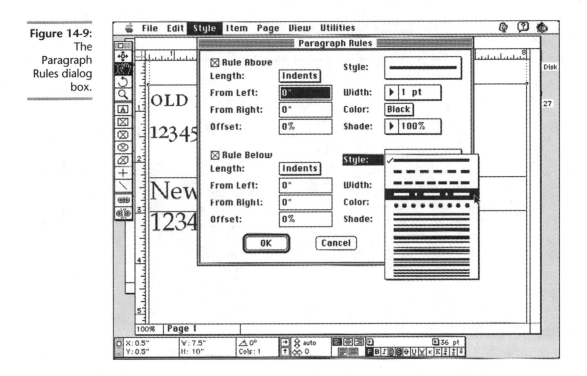

The first option available for the Rule Above and Rule Below is the Length option. You have two choices: Indents and Text. Selecting Indents makes the rule the width of the current column, minus the settings in From Left and From Right. Figure 14-10 shows a ruling line set this way under the byline of the sample article.

When you select Text for Length, the rule is the width of the text it is applied to. In Figure 14-11, you see how the kicker (text above the headline) rule appears when you choose Text instead of Indents.

Use Indents when you want a rule to be a standard width, no matter what the length, of the text it is associated with. An example is a series of centered labels in a menu — *Appetizers, Salads, Pasta,* and so on — whose lengths vary greatly. By making the rules the same width, you call more attention to the rules and to the fact that they indicate a major heading.

By selecting the Offset feature, you can specify the position of the rule relative to the text in the paragraph above it (for Rule Above) or in the paragraph below it (for Rule Below). You can use percentages from 0 to 100, or you can use units of your default absolute measurement (picas, inches, centimeters, etc.) from a negative value of half the rule's width to 15 inches (90 picas or 38.1 cm).

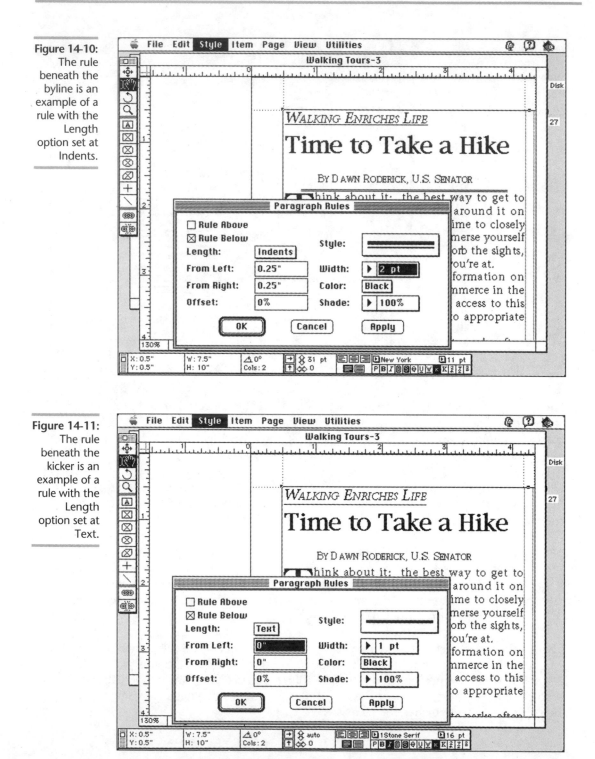

Figure 14-10:
The rule beneath the byline is an example of a rule with the Length option set at Indents.

Figure 14-11:
The rule beneath the kicker is an example of a rule with the Length option set at Text.

Moving a rule up or down via the Offset feature does not affect leading, so QuarkXPress may move the rule into unrelated text. If you want a 2-point ruling line to be 6 points below the text associated with it, and you want the next paragraph to be another 6 points below that, you must set the leading on the paragraph with the ruling line at 14 points (6 + 2 + 6).

You can use the Offset feature to create reversed type, as illustrated in the byline treatment in Figure 14-12. To do this, you essentially move the rule into the text line associated with it. The key is to make the rule larger than the text. In Figure 14-12, the text is 10 points, so we set the rule (shaded at 40 percent black) to be 14 points, which provides a margin above and below the text. (Make your rule at least 2 points larger than the text to get an adequate margin.) We then offset the rule by –6 points (the maximum allowed, or half the rule size). That was not enough, so we selected the text and used the Baseline Shift feature (described earlier in this chapter) to shift the text down 2 points, which centered it in the gray rule. We also changed the text color to white via Style ➪ Color (described in Chapter 15). Last, by selecting the Style ➪ Formats dialog box, we added 6 points of space below the byline so that the gray rule does not touch the text below it.

Figure 14-12: The byline is an example of how you can create reversed type with the Offset feature.

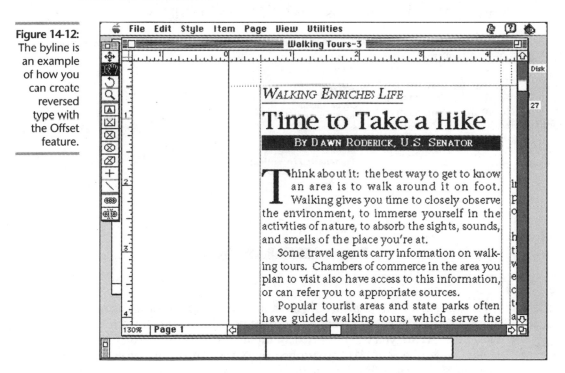

Using Font Creator and Multiple Master Fonts

Adobe Systems has created a special type of PostScript font called Multiple Master. Multiple Master fonts are designed to be elastic, so you can change their characteristics — such as thickness, width, and optical scaling — on the fly by creating new versions (such as semicondensed semibold). Thus, a Multiple Master font like Minion or Myriad may have a dozen versions, not just the usual normal, bold, italic, and bold italic.

 Normally, you use Adobe's Font Creator utility or a font editor like Altsys's Fontographer to create these variations. But QuarkXPress comes with an XTension (also called Font Creator) that lets you create these variations from within QuarkXPress. That lets you create exactly the style of type you need while doing your design.

To use the Font Creator XTension, make sure of two things:

- ❧ You have the XTension installed in your QuarkXPress folder. (The XTension's file name is MMU, for Multiple Master Utility.)

- ❧ You have Multiple Master fonts installed in your System folder.

If both are not installed, the Font Creator menu item (shown in Figure 14-13) will not display in the Utilities menu.

Figure 14-13:
The Font Creator menu item appears if the Font Creator XTension and Multiple Master fonts are installed.

Utilities

Check Spelling ▶
Auxiliary Dictionary...
Edit Auxiliary...
Suggested Hyphenation... ⌘H
Hyphenation Exceptions...
Font Usage...
Picture Usage...
Profile Usage...
Tracking Edit...
Kerning Table Edit...
Font Creator

 If you have installed Adobe's SuperATM font scaler (also known as Adobe Type Manager 3.5 or higher) or Adobe's Acrobat portable-document software (which uses SuperATM), you will have two Multiple Master fonts automatically installed — Adobe Serif MM and Adobe Sans X MM. The QuarkXPress Font Creator XTensions will see these fonts and display the Font Creator menu. However, these fonts are designed for use only with SuperATM (they are what SuperATM uses to simulate fonts not installed on your System; they are installed even if you have turned the Substitute for Missing Fonts feature off in the SuperATM control panel), and if you select the Font Creator menu, QuarkXPress 3.2 may quit unexpectedly (this was fixed in version 3.3). If it does not quit, it will display no Multiple Master fonts to work with.

Adding Font Variations

When you select the Font Creator menu, you will be shown the first available Multiple Master font with the normal style displayed. Figure 14-14 shows an example for the font Minion. At the bottom of the dialog box (above the sample text) are two pick lists, one for the font and one for the variation. Load the font and variation that you want to work from.

Figure 14-14:
The Font Creator dialog box.

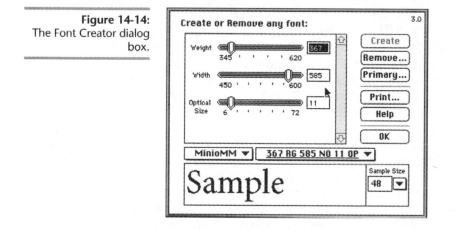

Depending on the font loaded, you will see two or more sliders that let you adjust font attributes. By changing these attributes, you create new variations. In Figure 14-14, the Minion font has three changeable attributes: weight (thickness), width, and optical size (the clarity of the font at different point sizes, which is used to make small type readable while letting larger type be detailed; this feature is often found only on serif fonts).

Figure 14-15 shows a newly created variant of Minion, a condensed semibold version. After you have used the sliders to make a new variant, click the Create button to generate the new variant. If you don't want to create a new variation, click the OK button to leave the Font Creator utility. There is no Cancel button because you must click Create to generate a new variant.

Note that creating a new variant in a roman typeface does not create the equivalent variant in the italic typeface. Thus, for example, creating a semibold variant in Minion does not automatically create a semibold variant of Minion Italic.

Figure 14-15:
A newly created variant
of the font in
Figure 14-14.

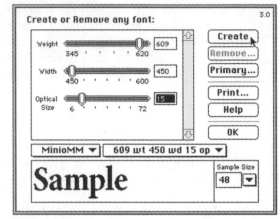

Note the name of the default font in Figure 14-16. The underline is how QuarkXPress indicates which variant is the normal variant. The numbers and codes let you know what the attribute settings are. The numbers show the actual settings from the slider bars. The uppercase codes indicate standard variants. Typical codes include RG for regular weight, SB for semibold weight, BD for bold weight, BL for black weight, LT for light weight, NO for normal width, CN for condensed width, SC for semicondensed width, SE for semi-expanded width, EX for expanded width, and OP for normal optical scaling. When you create new variants, the codes change to lowercase. Typical codes include wt for weight, wd for width, and op for optical scaling. These conventions help you know which variants are normal (those available from standard font-oriented dialog boxes and the Measurements palette) and which are user-created variants. Figure 14-16 and 14-17 shows the codes used in the serif font Minion and in the sans serif font Myriad, respectively.

Removing Variations

You can remove a variant by selecting it and clicking the Remove button. If you remove a variant that was not one of the variants supplied with the Multiple Master font in which the displayed codes are in lowercase, you must re-create it if you want to restore it. But if you remove a variant that came with the Multiple Master font (these are called primary variants), use the Primary button to restore it. Figure 14-18 shows the resulting dialog box, which lists the removed primary variants (in black). Select the removed variants that you want to restore and click the Create button.

Figure 14-16:
A list of the available variants for a serif font.

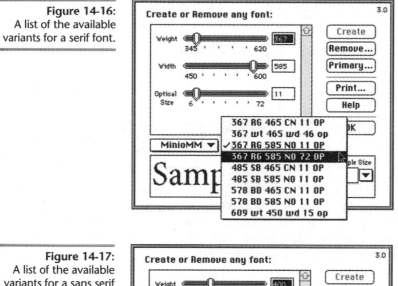

Figure 14-17:
A list of the available variants for a sans serif font.

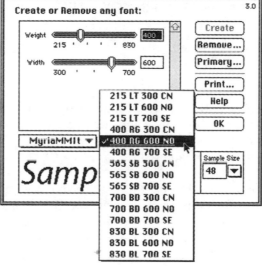

Figure 14-18:
This list shows primary font variations that were removed; you can restore the removed primary variants.

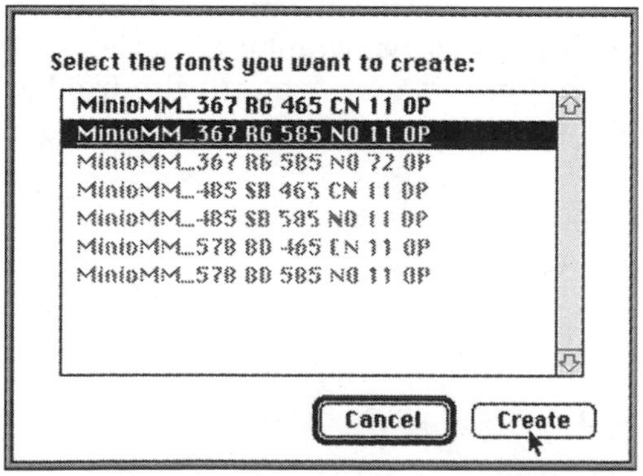

You can use the Primary button to list all the variants that came with your Multiple Master font. Although these names also appear in the Font Creator dialog box's pick list, the list displayed after clicking the Primary button shows only the primary variants, not every variant available.

Typographic Characters and Symbols

Several characters that are not used in traditionally typed business documents are used routinely in typeset documents. Do not ignore these symbols because readers expect to see them in anything that appears to be published, whether on the desktop or via traditional means. If you're used to working only with typewritten or word-processed documents, pay careful attention to the proper use of these characters.

Quotes and dashes

The most common of these characters are *true quotation marks* and *em dashes* (so called because they are the width of a capital *M* when typeset). The typewriter uses the same character ((")) to indicate both open and closed quotation marks, and most people use two hyphens (--) to indicate an em dash when typing. Using these marks in a published document is a sign of amateurism.

Fortunately, a new option in QuarkXPress lets you turn on a feature that inserts typographically correct quotes. It even lets you choose from a variety of quote formats including those used by some foreign language. Figure 14-19 shows show how you specify smart quotes — and their formats — in the Application Preferences dialog box (Edit ⇨ Preferences ⇨ Application).

QuarkXPress also offers an option during text import that automatically changes typewriter dashes and quotes to their typographic equivalents. When you get text, make sure that you check the Convert Quotes box (it also handles em dashes) in the Get Text dialog box, as shown in Figure 14-20.

Figure 14-19:
The Application Preferences dialog box lets you choose from a variety of smart quote formats.

Figure 14-20:
Select Convert Quotes in the Get Text dialog box when you import text.

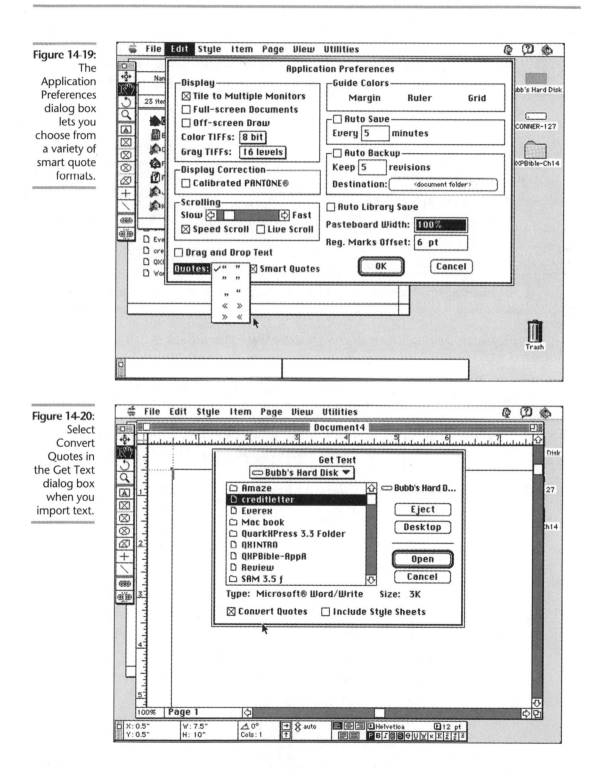

Do not use the keyboard apostrophe (') as an open single quote — use the open single quote key (') instead. QuarkXPress does not translate apostrophes that begin a word into open single quotes. This is not a bug: English allows an apostrophe to begin a word — such as "'tis the season" — so automatic translation of apostrophes as quotes would create errors.

When you type text directly into QuarkXPress, you need to type in a command to get typographic quote marks because they are not available on a standard keyboard. The commands are as follows:

" (open double quote)	Option-[
" (closed double quote)	Option-Shift-[
' (open single quote)	Option-]
' (closed single quote)	Option-Shift-]

Punctuating text with quotes confuses many people, but the rules are not complicated.

- Periods and commas always go inside the quotation.

- Semicolons and colons always go outside the quotation.

- Question marks and exclamation marks go inside if they are part of the quote, outside if not. When the main clause is a question, but the quote is a declaration, the question mark takes precedence over the period, so it goes outside the quotes. When the main clause is a question, and the quote is an exclamation, the exclamation takes precedence, and it goes within the quotation. Look at the following examples:

   Did he really say, "I am too busy"?

   She asked, "Do you have time to help?"

   I can't believe she asked, "Do you have time to help?"

   He really did yell, "I am too busy!"

- When a single quote is followed immediately by a double quote, separate the two with a nonbreaking space (⌘spacebar).

   He told me, "She asked, 'Do you have time to help?' "

   He told me, "Bob heard him say, 'I am too busy.' "

   She asked me, "Can you believe that he said, 'I am too busy'?"

For more information on these rules, refer to a grammar guide.

If you want to enter dashes in text while typing directly into a QuarkXPress document, you must also use special commands:

— (em dash)	Option-Shift-hyphen
— (nonbreaking em dash)	Option-⌘=
– (en dash)	Option-hyphen

Typographers are divided over whether you should put spaces around em dashes — like this — or not—like this. Traditionally, there is no space. But having space lets the publishing program treat the dash as a word, so that there is even space around all words in a line. Not having a space around dashes means that the publishing program sees the two words connected by the em dash as one big word, so the spacing added to justify a line between all other words on the line may be awkwardly large because the program doesn't know how to break a line after or before an em dash that doesn't have space on either side. Still, whether to surround a dash with space is a decision in which personal preferences should prevail.

A nonbreaking em dash does not let text following it wrap to a new line. Instead, the break must occur at a spot preceding or following the dash.

The en dash, so called because it is the width of a capital *N,* is a nonbreaking character, so QuarkXPress does not let a line break after it. Traditionally, an en dash is used to:

- Separate numerals, as in a range of values.
- Label a figure.
- Indicate a multiple-word hyphenation (*Civil War – era*).

Symbols and special characters

A typeface comes with dozens of special symbols ranging from bullets to copyright symbols. The most common ones are accessible from QuarkXPress through the following commands:

- (•) **En bullet:** Press Option-8. A bullet is an effective way to call attention to issues being raised. Typically, bullets are used at the beginning of each element in a list. If the sequence of the elements is important, as in a series of steps, use numerals instead of bullets.

Keep in mind that you have many alternatives to using the regular en bullet (so called because it is the width of a lowercase *n*). Using special characters such as boxes, check marks, triangles, and arrows, you can create attractive bulleted lists that stand out from the crowd. More information on how to select such characters is provided later in this chapter.

(©) **Copyright:** Press Option-C. A copyright symbol signifies who owns text or other visual media. The standard format is *Copyright © 1993 IDG Books Worldwide. All rights reserved.* For text, you must include at least the © symbol, the word *Copyright,* or the abbreviation *Copr,* as well as the year first published and the name of the copyright holder. (Note that only the © symbol is valid for international copyright.) Works need not be registered to be copyrighted — the notice is sufficient, but registering is best.

(®) **Registered trademark:** Press Option-R. This is usually used in advertising, packaging, marketing, and public relations to indicate that a product or service name is exclusively owned by a company. The mark follows the name. You may use the ® symbol only with names registered with the U.S. Patent and Trademark Office. For works whose trademark registration is pending, use the ™ symbol.

(™)**Pending trademark:** Press Option-2.

(§) **Section:** Press Option-6. This symbol is typically used in legal and scholarly documents to refer to sections of laws or research papers.

(¶) **Paragraph:** Press Option-7. Like the section symbol, the paragraph symbol is typically used for legal and scholarly documents.

(†) **Dagger:** Press Option-T. This symbol is often used for footnotes.

When you want a long portion of text to run so that it appears as one visual block — a tactic often used for article openers in highly designed magazines — consider using symbols such as § and ¶ as paragraph-break indicators. (Frequently, they are set in larger or bolder type when used in this manner.) The symbols alert readers to paragraph shifts. *Rolling Stone* magazine is particularly partial to this effect. Figure 14-21 shows an example of how it can be used. Other common symbols are ₤ (Option-3), ¥ (Option-Y), and ° (Option-Shift-8).

Figure 14-21:
You can use
the ¶ symbol
to signify
paragraph
breaks in
text.

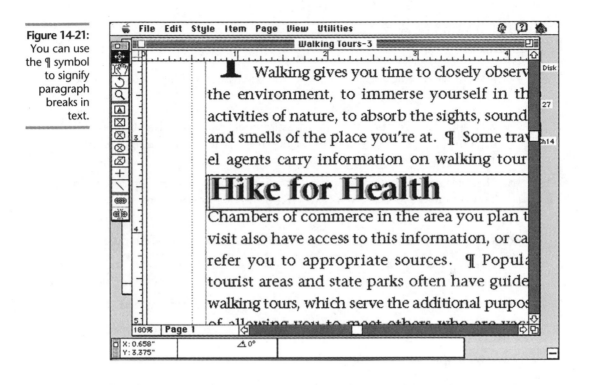

Figure 14-21:
You can use the ¶ symbol to signify paragraph breaks in text.

Summary

- Keep in mind that some typefaces come with groups of faces — usually normal (plain), italic, boldface, and boldface italic — while others come as separate typefaces for each face. For the former, such as Times, you can change the face by using the style options in the Measurements palette or the Style menu options. For the latter, you must change the typeface (for example, from Tiffany Bold to Tiffany Bold Italic).

- The Utilities ⇨ Font Usage option lets you replace typefaces with new ones. This feature is especially handy when moving documents from machines with different sets of typefaces.

- The Measurements palette is usually the fastest way to change type attributes.

- Use italics for emphasis and titles of intellectual works (like books, movies, and plays). Use boldface as lead-in labels or, less frequently, for special emphasis.

- Avoid using all caps. Consider using boldface or small caps instead.

- Superiors are often better for use with footnotes, but all word processors use superscripts instead, and QuarkXPress offers no way to search and replace superscripts with superiors.

- Use a combination of baseline shifting and point-size changes to create multiple levels of superscripts and subscripts.

- QuarkXPress offers two underline options: one that underlines all text, including spaces, and one that underlines only nonspace characters. The first option is usually preferred.

- You can define your own ruling lines and associate them with paragraphs. This feature is particularly helpful when used for headings and other design-oriented display text.

- Make sure you use typographic quotes and dashes, not the typewriter equivalents.

Using Special Typographic Effects

15

In This Chapter

- ➡ When and how to use indentation, bulleted lists, and other types of lists
- ➡ Typographic techniques that aid text organization
- ➡ How to enhance text with drop caps and related effects
- ➡ How to apply effects such as rotation, shadows, and outlines

---

As you've seen in the three preceding chapters, typographic controls over spacing — between words, lines, and letters — help determine a document's overall "color." In addition to spacing controls, you can use several typographic features to enhance your presentation. These features include drop caps and other attention-grabbers, organizational aids such as bulleted lists, and visual labels such as small caps. What all these effects have in common is that they enable you to add meaning or provide reader guidance by changing the appearance of individual characters or small groups of characters.

Using Typography to Organize Text __

Typographic effects create visual signposts that guide the reader through a document. The effects most commonly used for this purpose fall into four basic groups: indents and outdents, bullets and lists, visual labels, and dingbats.

Indents and outdents

Indents and outdents come in a number of variations, but share one goal: to break up a document's solid left margin. These breaks give the reader variances to notice — variances that signify a change in elements. It's less important to break up the right margin of a document because people read from left to right and thus pay more attention to the left margin. In languages that are read from right to left, such as Hebrew and Arabic, the opposite is true.

To set indents, either for a selected paragraph or when defining styles, use the Paragraph Formats dialog box (see Figure 15-1). To open the dialog box, select Edit ➪ Style Sheets to access the Edit Style Sheets dialog box and then select the Formats button. Or select Style ➪ Formats (keyboard shortcut is Shift-⌘F).

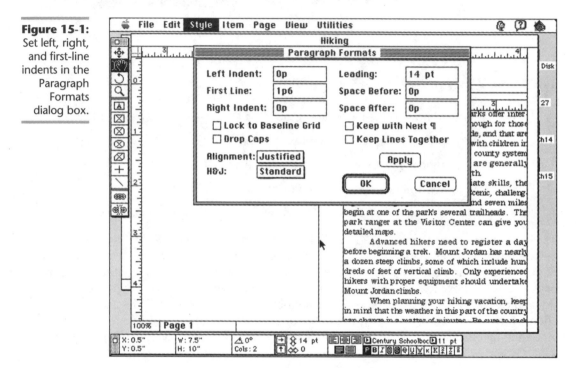

Figure 15-1: Set left, right, and first-line indents in the Paragraph Formats dialog box.

The most basic use of an indent is to offset the first line in a paragraph. This is particularly true in multicolumn publications that use first-line indents rather than blank lines between paragraphs to indicate the start of a new paragraph.

Make sure your first-line indents aren't too small. Usually, indents should be between one and two ems in size. An em is as wide as your current point size, so if text is 9 points, the first-line indent should be between 9 and 18 points. If columns are thin (more than three columns to a standard page), make indents closer to 9 points than 18 points. This avoids gaping indents or awkward justification in the first line of a paragraph.

An *outdent*, also called an *exdent* or a *hanging indent*, achieves the same function as a first-line indent, but moves the first line out into the margin, rather than indenting it. It usually is reserved for bulleted lists because it takes up space that otherwise might be used for text. Some people use outdents for sidebars to provide a visual counterpoint to standard text; this works if the sidebars are not too long.

If you read newspapers or magazines, you're used to seeing sidebars, or those small chunks of information that appear alongside the body of a document while being separate from it. Sidebars are an effective way of visually breaking up what could otherwise be heavy blocks of text. Don't think that sidebars should be reserved for high-end, commercial publications; they are also very effective in making proposals, memos, annual reports, and technical papers more interesting to the reader. Breaking up long sections of text with sidebars is often a good idea, and makes the text seem less formidable.

Another form of indenting is called *block indenting*. In a block indent, the entire paragraph is indented from the left margin, right margin, or both. A typical use of block-indenting — usually from the left, but sometimes also from the right — is to indicate extended quotations. Typically, these are also set in a smaller type size. Use the Left Indent and Right Indent fields of the Paragraph Formats dialog box to set block indents.

You can indent text other than body text. For example, you might indent bylines or credit lines. You can indent headlines, so that the kickers overhang a little bit, or you can indent subheads. As long as you don't go overboard and end up with a seesaw pattern, using indents on a variety of elements helps keep a page visually active, even when it is filled primarily with text.

If you indent several elements in the same document, use only a few different levels of indentation — two or three at most. For example, it works well to use the same amount of indentation on bylines and kickers, even if the indentation amount differs from the amount used for the first line of body-text paragraphs. If you have too many levels of indentation, there is no pattern to help guide the reader's eye, and the resulting document appears jumbled.

Bullets and lists

Lists are an effective way to organize information so that discrete elements are treated individually, with each clearly visible as a separate entity and yet obviously part of a bigger grouping. The two most popular ways to indicate lists are to use bullets or sequential labels (either numerals or letters).

Depending on the length of list items and the width of columns on the page, you may be content simply putting a bullet or label at the beginning of each item. This works best when your itemized text takes many lines (more than five or six) in multicolumn text. Otherwise, you'll probably want to have a hanging indent in itemized paragraphs with the bullet or label hanging over the text's left margin, which is itself brought in from the column's left margin. The two right columns in Figure 15-2 show examples of hanging-indent lists while the leftmost column shows a list that uses only first-line indents.

Figure 15-2:
Different
types of
indented lists.

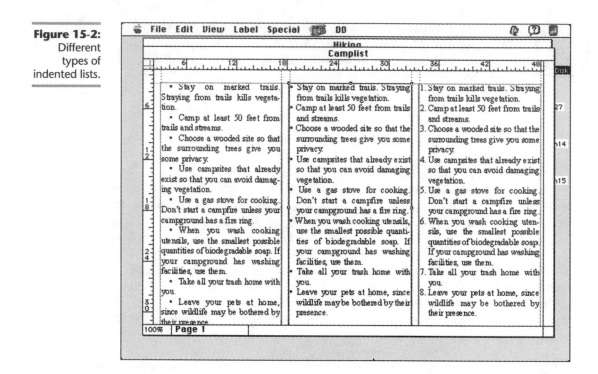

QuarkXPress does not offer a feature that automates the creation of bulleted or labeled lists, but you can cut out most of the work involved by creating a style with the proper settings. After you create the style, all you have to do is apply it to the appropriate paragraphs and add the bullets or labels to the text. Figure 15-3 shows the settings for a bulleted list style. These settings create the proper indentation for a hanging-indent bulleted list. (We also could have applied these settings directly to a single paragraph through Style ⇨ Formats; the dialog box is the same.)

Hanging-indent bulleted lists are most effective when the left indent and the first-line indent are the same amount, but in different directions. What this means is that you use a positive setting for the left indent and a negative setting for the first-line indent. The negative setting creates an outdent. Using the same setting for the outdent as for the left indent ensures that the bullet starts at the column margin because the two values in essence cancel each other out for the first line. The indent amount should equal the space needed for the bullet or label character.

Here is how we determined the settings:

1. We decided to use a regular en bullet as the text character, rather than a square or other shape.

2. We created a new style for the bullet. We based the style on the Normal style used for the body text, so that our typeface, leading, size, and other settings were already set for the bulleted text.

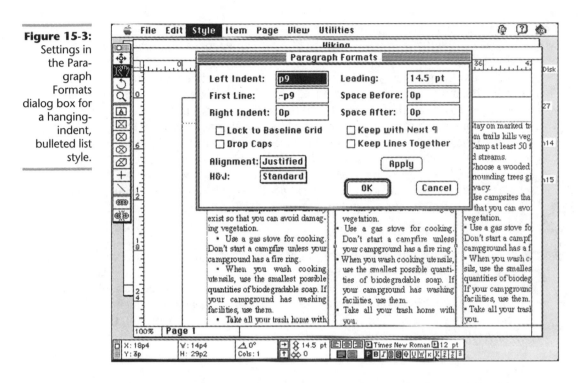

Figure 15-3:
Settings in
the Para-
graph
Formats
dialog box for
a hanging-
indent,
bulleted list
style.

3. We opened the Paragraph Formats dialog box by selecting Edit ⇨ Style Sheets and then selecting the Formats button. We changed the settings in the Paragraph Formats dialog box so that the left indent is 9 points (0p9, or 0 picas and 9 points), which is the width of an en bullet and its trailing space — the 0 before the *p* is optional. That shifts the entire paragraph margin in from the left margin 9 points.

 An en bullet and its trailing space usually take as much room as the current point size, which makes it easy to figure out the indentation settings needed to achieve the correct alignment for the hanging indent.

4. We set the first line's indent at –0p9. Using a negative number as the First Line setting moves the first line *out*, creating an outdent instead of an indent. The left indent and first-line indent settings cancel each other out, ensuring proper alignment of the bullets, as explained earlier.

 For a different visual effect, you might want to use a character other than an en bullet as a bullet. Some of the Zapf Dingbat characters are good for this, as are Wingdings. If you do use another character as a bullet, you'll need to experiment with left-indent and first-line-indent values to get the right settings.

5. We saved the style and applied it to the paragraphs we wanted bulleted.

6. The last step was to enter the bullets, which we did by using the shortcut Option-8. We could also have used a placeholder character (such as an asterisk) in our original text file and then used the find-and-replace feature to change the place-holder to a bullet after importing the text file into QuarkXPress.

To use numerals instead of bullets in the list, we would first determine whether there would be one or two digits in the numerals. In most typefaces, a numeral is the width of an en, which is half the current point size. After factoring in the space taken by the period and the trailing space, you typically need 1.2 ems of space for a hanging indent. An em space is equivalent to the current point size. If we needed two digits, that space would be 1.2 ems (one digit, the period, and the trailing space) plus an en (0.5 ems), or 1.7 times the current point size. Note that the amount of space taken by the period and the trailing space will vary based on the typeface and whether the text is justified, so you will have to experiment with settings for your own text.

 To ensure proper alignment of the single-digit numerals in a list that contains some two-digit numerals, put an en space (Option-space) before the single-digit numerals.

 Consider using a fixed space after a bullet or label to ensure that text always starts in the same position on each line with such a label. If your text is not justified, the normal space will always be the same width, so alignment will not be a problem. However, you may want to use an en space so that there is a bit more space after the bullet or label than there is between words in the text. This will help set the bullet or label apart a bit from the rest of the text.

Visual labels

Some lists use another mechanism for separating elements: in-text labels that highlight the first few words of each new element. These highlighted words may be a few words that act as a miniheadline, or they may simply be the first few words of the paragraph.

You can use any of several type attributes to define in-text labels. To help you see how each looks, we've used the attributes within the following descriptions. Unless otherwise noted, these effects are available from both the Style menu and the Measurements palette. You also can access many of them by using the keyboard shortcuts listed in Chapter 14.

- **Boldface:** The "strongest" attribute, boldface often is used as a second-level subhead when the first-level subhead is a stand-alone headline set in a larger size and perhaps in a different typeface. It also can be used to indicate a first-level subhead in reports or newsletters when strong design is not a priority.

- *Italics:* This is a favorite choice. If you use boldface as a second-level subhead, italics is a natural option for third-level subheads. It also can be used after a bullet when each bulleted item contains a narrative description that benefits from a label summarizing its content.

- <u>Underlines or rules:</u> A common choice for documents that are meant to look like word-processed or typewritten documents, underlines or rules convey a "no frills" feel. They fall between boldface and italics in terms of visual impact. If you use rules, avoid using rules thicker than 2 points (anywhere from 0.5 to 1.5 is usually sufficient), and stay away from special rules such as dotted or thick-and-thin rules. Stick with single or double rules so that you don't distract readers from the text you're trying to emphasize.

- SMALL CAPS: This is a classy choice for text that doesn't need a strong visual label. Small caps appear no stronger visually than regular text, so they are *not* effective if you want to make labels more visible than the surrounding text (for example, so a reader can scan the labels to see which text is relevant). But small caps provide a way to add text labels that summarize content without interfering with the overall look of the document. As with italics, small caps work well in conjunction with bullets. Combining small caps with italics or boldface is an effective way to create labels that have more impact and yet retain the classy look of small caps.

- **Typeface change:** By changing to a typeface that is distinctly different from the current text, you can highlight labels very effectively. If you choose this option, try to pick a typeface used elsewhere in the document, so you avoid the ransom-note look. When body text is set in a serif typeface, it's typical and appealing to use a sans serif typeface for the label, but the reverse is often less effective. We used Univers as the typeface for the label of this paragraph.

Vertical text scaling in the next paragraph is a new 3.2 feature.

- Scaled text :By scaling text horizontally or vertically, you can create a subtle label that has more visual impact than small caps and about the same impact as italics. (To access scaling features, select Style ➪ Horizontal/Vertical Scale.) Be careful not to scale text too much (we used a horizontal scale of 125 percent here), or it will look distorted. A less-effective variation is to scale the label text vertically, so that it is narrower. This technique can work if you combine it with another attribute — for example, small caps and/or boldface — to counteract the reduced visual impact of the vertically-scaled text.

- Size change: By making text a few points larger, you can subtly call attention to labels without being too explicit about it. Don't set the label size more than a few points more than the size of the body text, and never make label text smaller than body text. (We made the label text 2 points larger than body text here.) As with scaling text, this technique can be combined with other techniques effectively.

Changing the horizontal scale, vertical scale, or text size generally are the least effective of the methods used to indicate labels, and they can easily be misused. If you do decide to scale text or change its size, consider carefully the settings you choose.

Choosing Bullets Wisely

The en bullet (•) is the bullet character used most often, but feel free to experiment with other characters as bullets.

A solid square makes the bullet appear bolder and more authoritative. A hollow square gives a "strong but silent" feel. A triangle appears more distinct without being as heavy as a solid square. Arrows reinforce the bullet's basic message of "Look here!" Geometric shapes are great alternatives to the traditional bullet, and typefaces such as Zapf Dingbats and Wingdings offer several options.

Several typefaces have whimsical characters that can function as bullets when placed in the proper context. Another possibility is to use symbols with specific meanings. For example, you can use astrological signs for a horoscope column, religious symbols for a church or temple newsletter, or check marks and check boxes for election materials.

It's likely that your typeface has special symbols or *diacritical marks* (language symbols) that may work as bullets, too. You also can use a logo as a symbol if you create a typeface that uses it. (You can do this with such programs as Altsys's Fontographer.) Using a logo is particularly effective if it is simple and readily identified with your organization.

The accompanying figure shows some potential bullet characters.

Dingbats

A *dingbat* is a special character used as a visual marker, typically to indicate the end of a story in a multistory document like a magazine. A dingbat is especially useful if you have many stories on a page or many stories that "jump to" (continue on) later pages because it may not be readily apparent to readers whether a story has ended or has jumped elsewhere.

As with bullets, you can use almost any character as a dingbat. Squares and other geometric shapes are popular choices, as are logos or stylized letters based on the name of the publication or organization.

The easiest way to create a dingbat is to set a tab in your body-text paragraph style (or in whatever style you use for the last paragraph in a story). Set this tab to be right-aligned to the column's right margin; this is usually where dingbats are placed. If columns are 14 picas wide, set the tab at 14 picas, as shown in Figure 15-4. After you set the tab, go to the final paragraph in the story and add a tab after the last letter. Then add your dingbat character (and change its typeface, if necessary).

If you define the dingbat tab in the style used for your body text, you don't have to worry about remembering to apply the right style to the final paragraph after the layout has been completed and text edited, added, or cut to fit the layout.

Figure 15-4: Set a tab to align dingbats to the column margin.

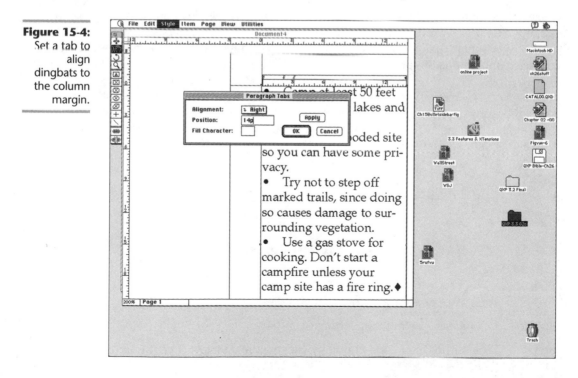

A dingbat need not be aligned against the right margin. You may want to place it one em space after the last character in the paragraph, in which case you simply add two nonbreaking en spaces (Option-   space) before the dingbat. Or you can use the flex space feature explained in Chapter 12.

Drop Caps

Using *drop caps* (a large letter set into several lines of normal-size text) is a popular way to guide readers through changes in topics. Drop caps also are frequently used to identify the introduction and conclusion of a story. When drop caps are used in this manner, the introduction and conclusion usually do not have subheads, but the sections between may have subheads.

Some people consider drop caps and titles to be display type while others consider them to be merely body type. How you treat them depends on how design-intensive your publication is. If all your titles and drop caps follow the same format, you're treating them as body type. But if you make the title of each chapter or story distinct, and perhaps make the drop caps for opening pages different as well, you're treating those elements as display type.

QuarkXPress automates most of the steps involved in creating a drop cap. To set a drop cap, open the Paragraph Format dialog box by selecting the Formats button in the Edit ⇨ Style Sheets dialog box or by choosing the Formats option in the Style menu (the keyboard shortcut is Shift-   F).

Because you are likely to use this effect more than once, it is best to create a style for any paragraphs that use it. In most cases, the settings for a drop-cap paragraph are the same as those for body text, except that the paragraph's first line is not indented and a drop cap is defined. Rather than repeat all the settings for the body text when creating a drop cap style,you can simply follow these steps.

QuarkXPress 3.2 added the ability to have drop caps that are 16 lines deep.

STEPS: Creating a Drop Cap Style Sheet Item

Step 1.   Select Based On from the Edit Style Sheet dialog box and select the body text style as the basis for the new style.

Step 2.   Change the Left Indent setting to 0.

Step 3.   Select the Drop Caps option by clicking the check box next to it.

Step 4. Specify the number of characters (usually 1) to be set as drop caps in the Character Count dialog box.

Step 5. Set the Line Count to specify how many lines deep you want the drop cap to occupy (a typical setting is 3, but it can be as many as 16).

Step 6. Choose OK to get back to the Edit Style Sheets dialog box and select Save to store the new style.

Figure 15-5 shows the settings described in the preceding steps. In our example, we did not select the Keep Lines Together option, but it would be a good idea to do so if you want to prevent a paragraph that begins with a drop cap from breaking in the middle of the cap. By the way, if you decide to set a one-time drop cap by choosing Style ⇨ Formats instead of creating a style, the Paragraph Formats dialog box you see is identical to that in Figure 15-5.

After you create the drop-cap style, you can apply it easily. Position your cursor anywhere on the appropriate text. Then select the new style from either the Style ⇨ Style Sheets option or the Style Sheets palette (if the palette is not visible, use View ⇨ Show Style Sheets to turn it on).

Figure 15-5:
Sample settings used to create a style for a paragraph beginning with a drop cap.

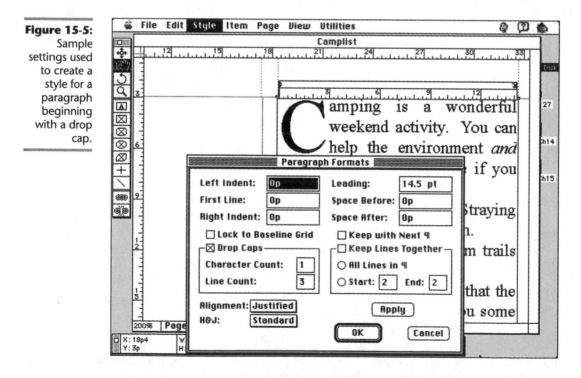

One more thing you might want to consider is a change in the drop cap's typeface. This is optional — there is no reason that a drop cap can't have the same typeface as the rest of the paragraph. But typically, a drop cap is either set in boldface or in a completely different typeface, which gives the drop cap higher visibility and usually results in a more interesting design. It's common for drop caps to be set in the same typeface as the headline or subhead. To change the drop cap's typeface, select it with the mouse and use the Measurements palette's font list or the Style ⇨ Fonts menu. In the example shown in Figure 15-6, Times is selected as the drop-cap typeface.

Figure 15-6:
You can vary the look of a drop cap by changing its typeface.

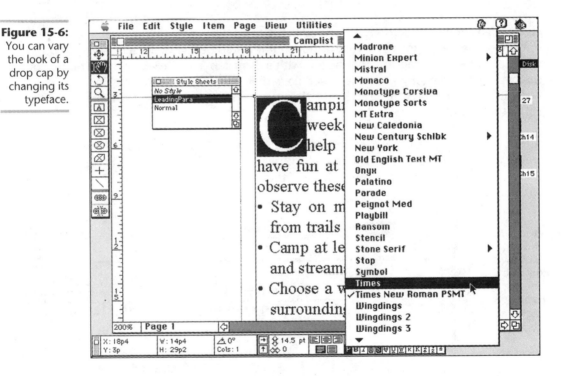

Should you use the open quotation character ("), the open single-quote character ('), or no character at all to indicate the start of a quote? Most typographers choose the last option to avoid having overly big quotation marks, and traditionalist stylebooks agree. (Do, however, use the close-quotation mark (") at the end of the quotation.) Although this is an accepted practice, some people find it confusing because they don't realize they've been reading a quote until they get to the end of it. If you insist on indicating an open quote, use the single quote (') — it distracts the eye from the actual first letter less than the double quote ("). Be sure to set the drop cap's Character Count setting to 2, not 1. Otherwise, you wind up with a large quotation mark only!

A similar effect to a drop cap is a *raised cap,* which is simply a large first letter on the first line of a paragraph. A raised cap does not drop into the surrounding paragraph but rises above it instead. To create this effect, simply select the first character and change its point size and, optionally, its typeface.

You also can create a hybrid between a drop cap and a raised cap. For example, you can add a drop cap that is four lines tall and drops in two lines of text. To do this, make the drop cap's line count 2, select the drop-cap character, and then change its size. Note that when you do this, the Measurements palette options change from displaying actual point sizes to percentages, such as 200%. You are not limited to the choices you see on-screen; you can highlight a percentage shown and type in your own number. Alternatively, you can use the Style ⇨ Size menu to accomplish the same thing (select Other to get the percentage options).

 When you use a larger point size for a raised cap or a hybrid drop cap, the cap may extend into the text above. It's likely that you will need to insert extra returns above the cap to keep text from overprinting. One way to avoid this is to use additive or automatic leading options in your style tag. For information on these leading options, see Chapter 12.

You can create yet another variation of a drop cap by moving the drop cap away from the text to make it more pronounced. Use the Style ⇨ Kern menu or enter a kerning value in the Measurements palette to move the drop cap. In addition, you can compress or expand the drop cap with the Style ⇨ Horizontal/Vertical Scale menu option.

Figure 15-7 shows several variations of a drop cap. Reading from the top of the figure to the bottom and starting at the left column, you see: a traditional three-line drop cap; a three-line raised cap (the point size is three times the leading); a five-line drop cap in a typeface different from body text; and a three-line drop cap that has both a different typeface and extra kerning.

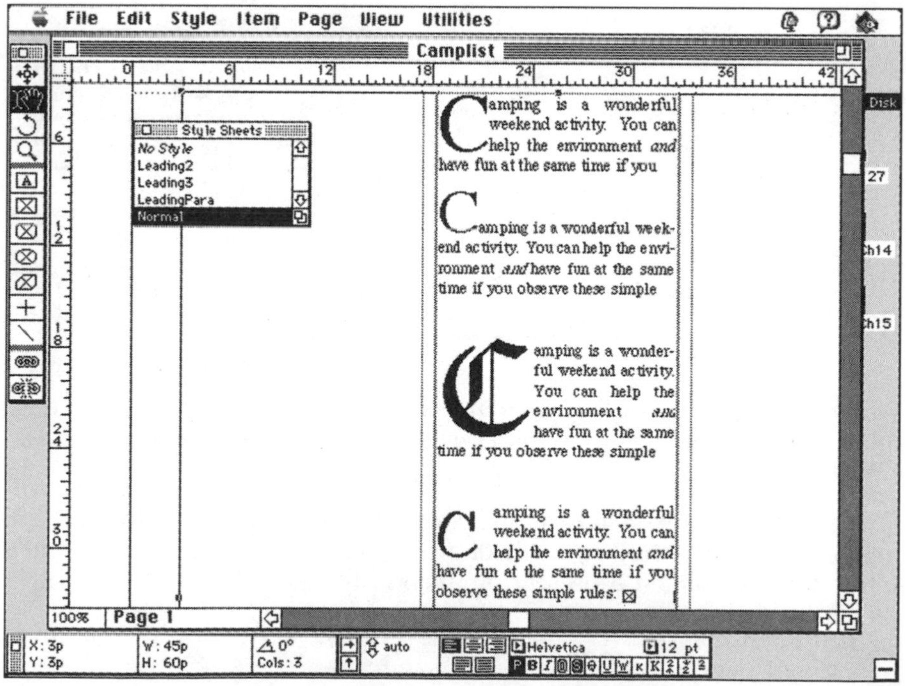

Figure 15-7:
Drop cap
variations.

![QuarkXPress document window titled "Camplist" showing four drop cap variations in a text column, with Style Sheets palette and toolbox]

Text Rotation

Instead of limiting you to display-type treatments that involve changes in font and size only, desktop publishing lets you also move type to different angles of rotation, adding another weapon to your design arsenal. QuarkXPress offers rotation in any angle, giving you maximum flexibility. Text rotation is a popular and effective way to treat *display type*, or type used as art.

In addition to being used for story titles, rotated text is sometimes employed to create angled pull-quotes, banners, and flags on ads and covers, and identifiers at the outside of a page. Figure 15-8 offers examples to give you an idea of some of the potential of this design tool.

Figure 15-8:
Examples of
rotated text.

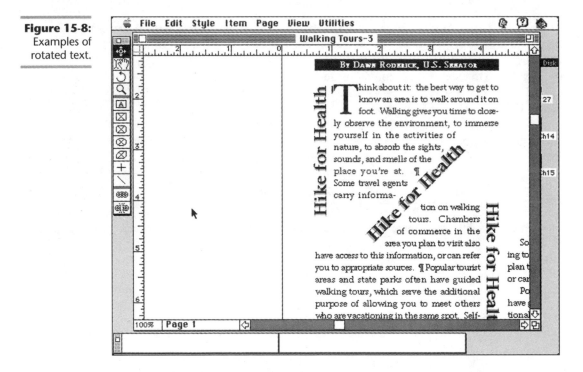

To rotate text, you must first put it in its own text box. After you put the elements to be rotated in their own text boxes and switch to the Item tool, you can rotate them in any of three ways:

- **Option 1:** Use the Measurements palette to enter the rotation amount (the top option on the third column, indicated by a geometric-angle symbol). This is the simplest method, especially if you know what angle of rotation you want in advance.

☞ **Option 2:** Use the Rotation tool (the curved arrow), as shown in Figure 15-9. The advantage to this tool is that it is free-form, letting you eyeball the angle as you turn the text. This comes in handy when, for example, you want to match the text's rotation to a graphic element. The disadvantage is that it takes time to learn to control the rotation tool accurately. You can always fine-tune the angle later through the Measurements palette, however.

Figure 15-9:
Using the
Box Angle
option to
rotate text.

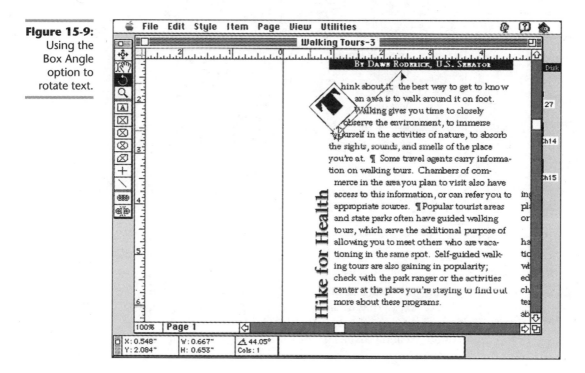

☞ **Option 3:** Use the Box Angle option in the Text Box Specifications dialog box (see Figure 15-10). To open the box, select Item ⇨ Modify or use the keyboard short-cut ⌘M. This is the most cumbersome approach, but it is the fastest method if you also want to modify other settings, such as background color and text-frame position.

Figure 15-10:
We rotated the
drop cap 45° by
entering 45° in
the Box Angle
field of the Text
Box Specifica-
tions dialog
box.

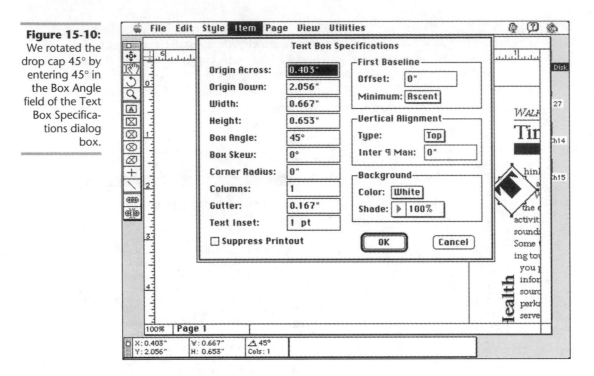

It's likely that you will need to set runarounds for rotated text boxes so they don't interfere with other text and graphics. You also may need to reposition the rotated text box so that its new angle works with other elements on the page. This requires using the Item tool, as described in Chapter 9. Remember, you are in effect treating text as graphics, so layout and graphic techniques now come into play.

Text rotation works well when combined with other features. For example, you can scale the text horizontally or vertically. You can change the color or shade of the text or its background. Fancier rotation techniques, such as having text follow an arc, can also be effective. To use them, however, you need a graphics program that can manipulate text as part of a graphic, such as Adobe Illustrator or Aldus FreeHand.

Colored and Shaded Text

As with most special effects, you should apply color or shading to text sparingly, and reserve these treatments for elements that serve as text-as-art. Good places to use color or shading include titles, bylines, pull-quotes, and ancillary elements such as page numbers.

QuarkXPress lets you apply color or shading (or both) to any selected text or to any paragraph whose style uses color or shading settings. You can access these effects in several ways:

- **Option 1:** Make selections in the Style ➪ Color and Style ➪ Shade menus.

- **Option 2:** Select a color through the Colors palette (made visible by choosing View ➪ Show Colors and invisible by choosing View ➪ Hide Colors).

- **Option 3:** Make a selection in the Character Attributes dialog box. To apply effects to selected text, open the dialog box by selecting Style ➪ Character or by using the keyboard shortcut Shift-⌘D. To apply effects to a style, select Edit ➪ Style Sheets and then select the Character button.

Figure 15-11 shows examples of both shading and color. The byline is shaded at 30 percent black, which complements the drop shadow in the rotated text.

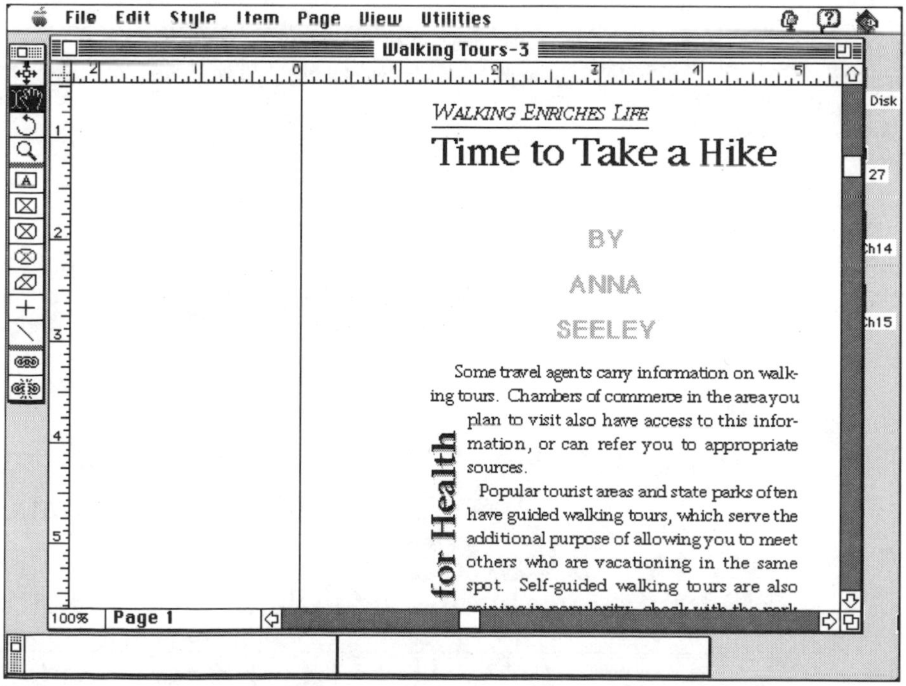

Figure 15-11:
Examples of
shaded type.

Light colors and shades are best used with bold, large type because this keeps them from getting lost in the layout. They also work well when combined with other effects, as is done in the example. Darker colors, such as blues and reds, work well in borders or as the colors of large outlined text.

Shadows and Outlines

Desktop publishing made it easy to create shadowed and outlined text — tasks that were difficult in traditional typesetting because they required manual intervention through darkroom or paste-up techniques. In the early days of desktop publishing, you could identify most desktop-published work because it usually used one or both of these effects. Unfortunately, the effects were so overused that many professionals sneered at the "ransom note" look produced by computer-based publishing novices.

QuarkXPress offers options to create shadows or outlines from any typeface. Figure 15-12 shows a sample of text that incorporates these effects.

Shadows and outlines generally work best with bold type. With lighter type, the characters become obscured because their strokes are not wide enough to be distinguished from the shadow or outline.

Figure 15-12:
Examples of shadowed and outlined text.

You cannot alter the shadow's position and percentage of gray. If you want a different type of shadow, you can duplicate the text box that contains your text, turn off text runaround, and apply the color or shade you want to the duplicate text box. Place the duplicate text box under the original text box. The original text box acts as the "non-shadow" text while the duplicated text box becomes the "shadow." You can position the shadow wherever you prefer to create the effect you want. Figure 15-13 shows this technique.

A particularly stylish effect is to apply a shadow to the text. This effect simulates raised lettering, as the phrase "Time to take a hike" in Figure 15-14 illustrates.

Figure 15-13: You can use QuarkXPress's default shadows (top) or create your own by overlapping text boxes (bottom).

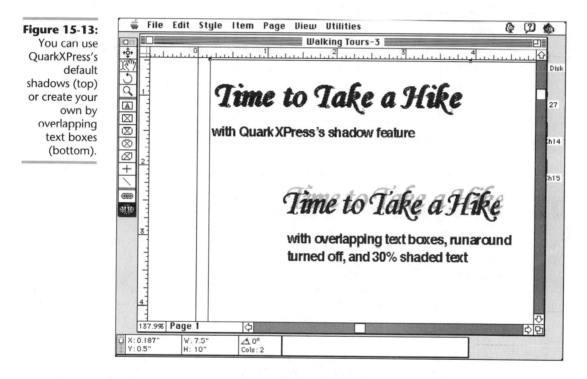

Interactive Text Resizing

Since its earliest days, QuarkXPress has allowed you to click on the handles outside a picture box and resize the picture by holding the mouse button down as you "drag" the picture box to the size you need. Now, since 3.2, you can perform a similar function on text. To resize text on-the-fly, you select it while holding down the Command key; then you hold the mouse button down as you resize it. Figure 15-14 shows the effects you can achieve with interactive text resizing.

Figure 15-14:
Results of
interactive text
resizing.

Hanging Punctuation

A technique used often in advertising is *hanging punctuation,* in which periods, commas, hyphens, and other punctuation marks fall outside the right margin. This technique is used in text that is either aligned right or justified — it does not make sense to hang punctuation in centered or left-aligned text because the punctuation would be too far away from the accompanying text.

Hanging punctuation keeps letters aligned along the right margin, but gives the text some visual flow by using the punctuation as an exterior decoration. Figure 15-15 shows an example of right-aligned text in which the punctuation hangs off the right margin.

QuarkXPress (or any other program) offers no tool to handle this effect. For right-aligned text, you can create hanging punctuation by using tabs, either in a style sheet or through the style menu for the selected text. Here is how we created the hanging punctuation shown in Figure 15-15:

1. We right-aligned the text.

2. We created a tab that aligned right at 43 picas, 3 points. This tab was used at the beginning of each line. For text that took more than one line, we used a line break (Shift-Enter) instead of a normal paragraph (Enter) so that all lines of text aligned together. We chose an alignment value that placed the tab far enough from the

text box's right margin (here, 45 picas) that any punctuation character would fit between that tab and the text box's right margin. (A rule of thumb is to use between one-third and one-half of the current point size because the biggest punctuation symbol — the question mark — usually is about that size.)

3. We added a second tab that aligned right at 43 picas, 4 points. (This value could have been anything more than the first tab's value. At the text's point size, 1 point was comparable to the natural letter spacing. Print out sample text at various tab settings before determining a final value.) We used this tab between the text and the punctuation. If there is no punctuation on a particular line, no tab is needed.

Figure 15-15:
An example of hanging punctuation.

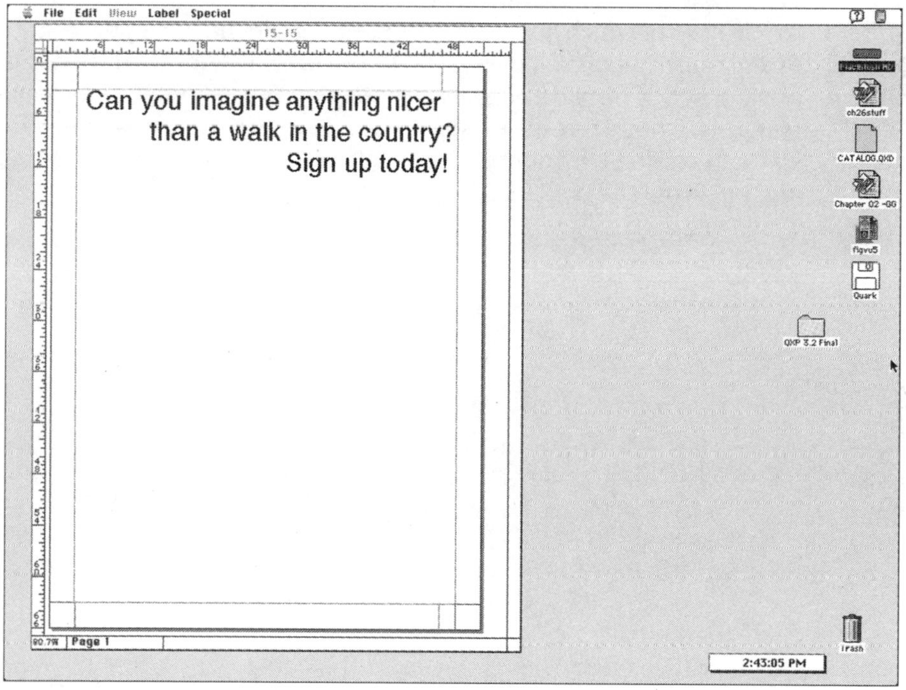

Can you imagine anything nicer
than a walk in the country?
Sign up today!

When setting tabs, use the ruler in the Paragraph Tabs dialog box, not the document ruler at the top of the screen.

The advantage to this approach is that you can use the same tab settings (usually through a style sheet) for all text in which you want this effect. The disadvantage is that it does not work on justified text.

The other method of accomplishing this effect — and the method you must use if text is justified — is to create two text boxes, one for the text and one for any punctuation marks that end a line. You'll probably need two styles as well: one for the text (either right-aligned or justified) and one for the punctuation (left-aligned). The simplest way to handle this is to create a style for the punctuation based on the style for the text, so that if the style for text changes, so does the punctuation style. You can then change the alignment in the punctuation style.

After creating the two text boxes, align them so that the punctuation appears properly spaced after its corresponding text. Then use QuarkXPress's lock feature (Item ⇨ Lock or   L) to prevent the two frames from moving accidentally.

Regardless of which approach you use to create hanging punctuation, if your text changes, you must manually change the line endings or punctuation positions. But because hanging punctuation is used only in small amounts of text, this is not a terrible burden. Also make sure that you turn off hyphenation, so that you don't get double hyphenation (one from the hyphenation feature and one from the punctuation you enter manually).

Summary

- ➤ A rule of thumb for proper first-line indentation value is to keep the indent between one and two ems — or between the text point size and twice that size. Use smaller values in this range for narrower columns than for wider columns.

- ➤ Keep the total number of indentation levels to a maximum of three for most documents.

- ➤ Use a style tag to ease the creation of bulleted lists.

- ➤ Consider using bullet characters other than the standard en bullets.

- ➤ When using enumerated lists that have ten or more items, be sure to precede single-digit numbers with an en space so that all the numbers align on the decimal.

- ➤ Use typeface attributes, such as boldface and small caps, and typeface changes as visual labels.

- ➤ By using dingbats to end stories in multistory documents like newsletters, you let the reader know for sure whether a story has ended or continues elsewhere.

- ➤ Drop caps can come in several forms. Don't lock yourself into only one drop-cap format.

- ➤ Use light colors on bold, large text. Dark colors can also be used on small, thin text and as text outlines.

- ➤ QuarkXPress's shadows cannot be altered. But you can create your own shadow effects by having text boxes that overlap slightly (runaround must be turned off).

- ➤ Interactive text resizing lets you achieve some interesting effects.

- ➤ You can create effects like hanging punctuation through tab settings or by having two independent text boxes locked together.

Using Tabs

In This Chapter

- ◆ Ways to use different types of tabs
- ◆ When and how to use tab leaders
- ◆ How to use tabs to format tables

Reviewing Your Options: Tab Styles __

Tab stops make it possible to align text within columns, which is handy for lists, tables, and other columnar data. You can also use tabs to align single characters, such as dingbats, which are described in Chapter 15. Tabs can be tricky because there are so many tab options and because it is often hard to predict how much space you need between tabs to make the tab fit nicely.

What happens if you just hit the tab key without having set the value for the tab? The tab key will move the cursor along the line by a half inch. Half-inch tabs across the width of the document are the QuarkXPress default.

Typewriters usually offer left-aligned tabs only: you press the tab key and that moves the carriage to a new left margin. But QuarkXPress offers a wide variety of tab alignments, which are available through the Paragraph Tabs dialog box (see Figure 16-1). Each type of tab has its own tab mark on the tab ruler to help you remember which tab is set which way.

Figure 16-1:
Tab styles
available
through the
Paragraph
Tabs dialog
box.

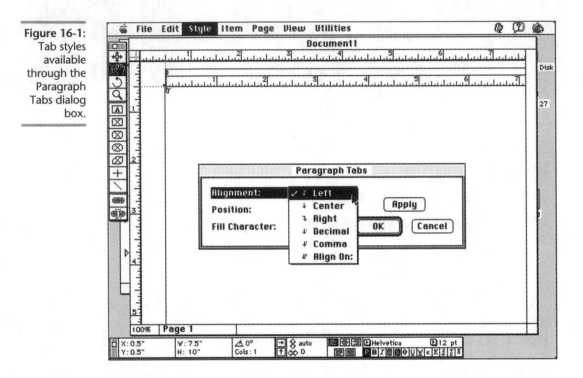

You have the following tab options:

- **Left:** Text typed after the tab will align to the tab as if the tab were a left margin. This is the most popular alignment for text.

- **Center:** Text will type in after the tab is centered, with the tab location serving as the center mark. This is almost as popular as left alignment for text and symbols (such as check boxes in a features table).

- **Right:** Text types in after the tab; it aligns to the tab as if the tab were a right margin. This alignment is typically used with tables of numbers because, regardless of the number of digits, you want the "ones" digit (the rightmost digit) in all numbers to align with the ones digit of all other numbers in a list, the tens digit (the next digit to the left) in all numbers to align, and so on.

- **Decimal:** Numbers with a decimal (.) that are typed in after the tab will align on the period. This is handy if you have data with varying numbers of decimal places, such as 10.2 and 40.41. If there are no decimals in a number, the number aligns as if there were a decimal *after* the number. When the data is a mix of numerals and text, it aligns at the first numeral. If the data consists of text only, with no numerals at all, the text aligns left (see Figure 16-2 for examples).

- **Comma:** Numbers with a comma (,) that are typed in after the tab will align on the comma. This is convenient if you have some data with decimal places, such as 5,210.2, and some without, such as 10,240. If the data is a mix of numerals and letters, it aligns at the first numeral. If there are no numerals in data, the text right-aligns to the tab location.

If a number does not contain commas, it aligns as if a comma *followed* the number, which is usually not what you want. A decimal tab is usually a better option, unless you are using numbers that have no decimals but do have commas.

- **Align on:** With this option, you specify which character the text aligns on. You can specify any letter, number, punctuation, or symbol in the current typeface. The align-on tab handles mixed text (in which some text has the alignment character and some does not) in the same manner as the comma tab.

Figure 16-2 shows how the decimal, comma, and align-on tabs work when used in a variety of text. As the figure illustrates, the QuarkXPress decimal alignment feature is smart enough to handle any kind of number, but the comma alignment can deliver unwanted alignments when numbers don't have commas.

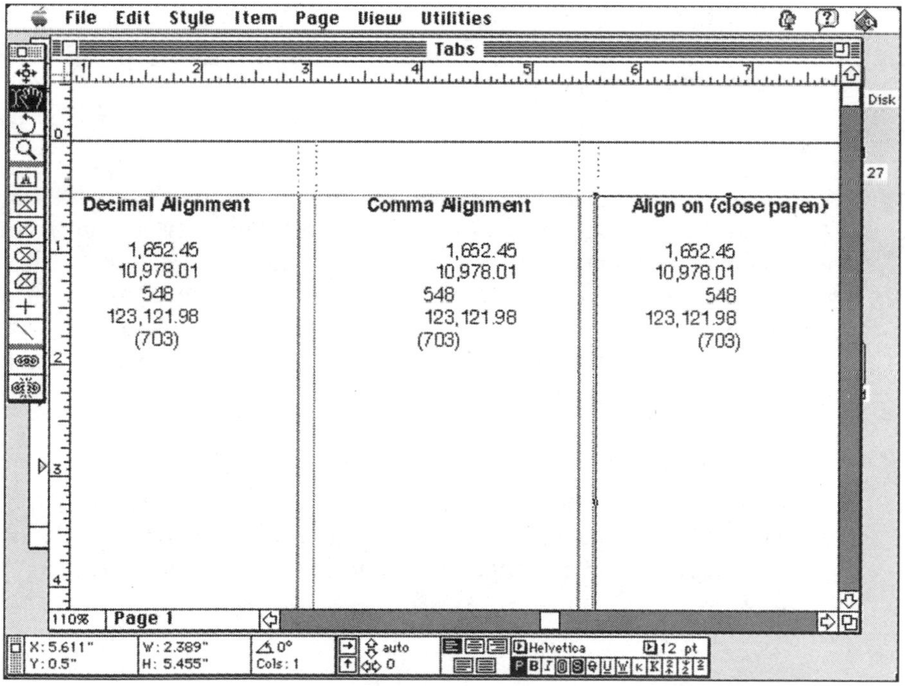
File Edit Style Item Page View Utilities
Tabs
Disk
27
Decimal Alignment
1,652.45
10,978.01
548
123,121.98
(703)
Comma Alignment
1,652.45
10,978.01
548
123,121.98
(703)
Align on (close paren)
1,652.45
10,978.01
548
123,121.98
(703)
110%
Page 1
X: 5.611"
Y: 0.5"
W: 2.389"
H: 5.455"
0°
Cols: 1
auto
0
Helvetica
12 pt

Figure 16-2: Decimal, comma, and align-on tabs have varying effects on text.

Specifying Tabs

As we've already noted, the default tab settings in QuarkXPress place a left tab every half inch. To set up other tabs, you use the Paragraph Tabs dialog box.

To create or modify a style that has tab settings so that you can use them throughout a document, select the Tabs button in the Edit Style Sheets dialog box (select Edit ⇨ Style Sheets ⇨ Tabs). If you are working only on a specific paragraph or want to override a style locally, select Style ⇨ Tabs or use the keyboard shortcut Shift-⌘T to access the Paragraph Tabs dialog box.

Up to 20 tab stops can be set for each paragraph. After you are in the dialog box, set tabs as follows:

STEPS:	**Setting Your Own Tabs in the Paragraph Tabs Dialog Box**
Step 1.	Select the alignment you want (Left, Center, Right, Decimal, Comma, Align On) from the Alignment option.
Step 2.	Either type in the position in the Position text box or move your mouse to the tab ruler in your currently selected text box and click the location of the tab. If you click the tab with the mouse and keep the mouse button pressed, you can move the tab.

All measurements in the tab ruler are relative to the text box's left margin, not to the absolute page or text-box coordinates. That way, in multicolumn text, tabs in each column appear as you would expect. For example, when a tab stop is defined at 3 picas, a tab used in column 1 will occur at 3 picas from column 1's left margin, while a tab used in column 3 will occur at 3 picas from column 3's left margin. Thus, when figuring out where tab stops should be, be sure to use the tab ruler, not the document ruler.

It's just as easy to change tab settings:

- ☞ **To change a tab's alignment:** Single-click the tab in the text box's tab ruler (its position shows up in the Position option in the Paragraph Tabs dialog box) and then move to the Alignments option and select a new alignment.

⌦ **To change a tab's position:** Single-click the tab in the text box's tab ruler (its position shows up in the Position option in the Paragraph Tabs dialog box) and then hold the mouse button down and slide the tab to a new position on the text box tab ruler.

⌦ **To copy a tab to a new location:** Single-click the tab in the text box's tab ruler (its position shows up in the Position option in the Paragraph Tabs dialog box) and then move your cursor to the Position option and enter a new tab-stop location. When you click on the OK button to exit the dialog box, you set both tabs.

⌦ **To delete a tab:** Single-click the tab on the tab ruler, keep the mouse button pressed, and drag the tab out of the tab ruler.

⌦ **To remove all tabs:** Hold the ⌘ key and click the tab ruler. Tab settings revert to the style's settings if you are working locally. If you are working in a style definition, tab settings revert to QuarkXPress's defaults.

Using Leaders

A *tab leader* is a series of characters that runs from text to text within tabular material. Usually, a period is used as the tab leader character. A leader's purpose is to guide the reader's eye, especially across wide distances. For an example, look at the table of contents in this book: a dot leader appears between the section and chapter names and their page numbers.

QuarkXPress calls a tab leader a *fill character*. To define a leader, enter up to two printing characters in the Fill Character text box, which you find in the Paragraph Tabs dialog box. (Note that the 2-character leader is new to 3.3.) If you enter two characters, they will alternate to fill the space between the defined tab stop and the place where you pressed the tab key. In Figure 16-3, a space and an asterisk are selected as the Fill Character.

Figure 16-3:
Select a tab
leader
character in
the Fill
Character
text box.

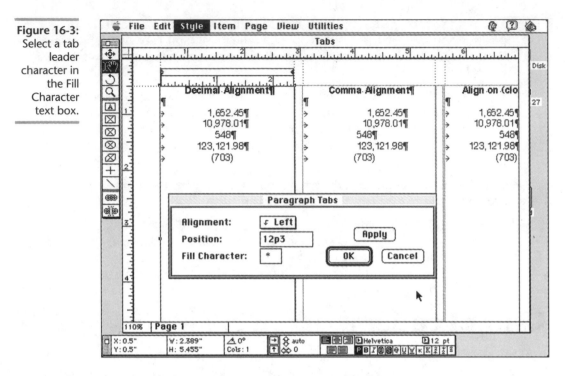

Creating Tables with Tabs

If you need to create complex tables, we recommend that you consider buying the Tableworks Plus XTension, which is described in Chapter 27. But if your table requirements are light, you may be able to get by with using tabs to create tables. By combining various tab settings with other typographic features — and by first thinking through the look you want for your table — you can create nice-looking tables in QuarkXPress. Figure 16-4 shows an example of a relatively simple table.

The table incorporates a mix of tab settings defined in two styles, one for the table text and one for the table headline.

To avoid creating separate styles for each table, consider deriving standard tab settings that apply to groups of similar tables. Then use local tab settings (through Style ⇨ Tabs) to modify styles for individual tables when necessary or to create completely new tabs for a table that is unlike others.

Figure 16-4:
A table
created with
tabs.

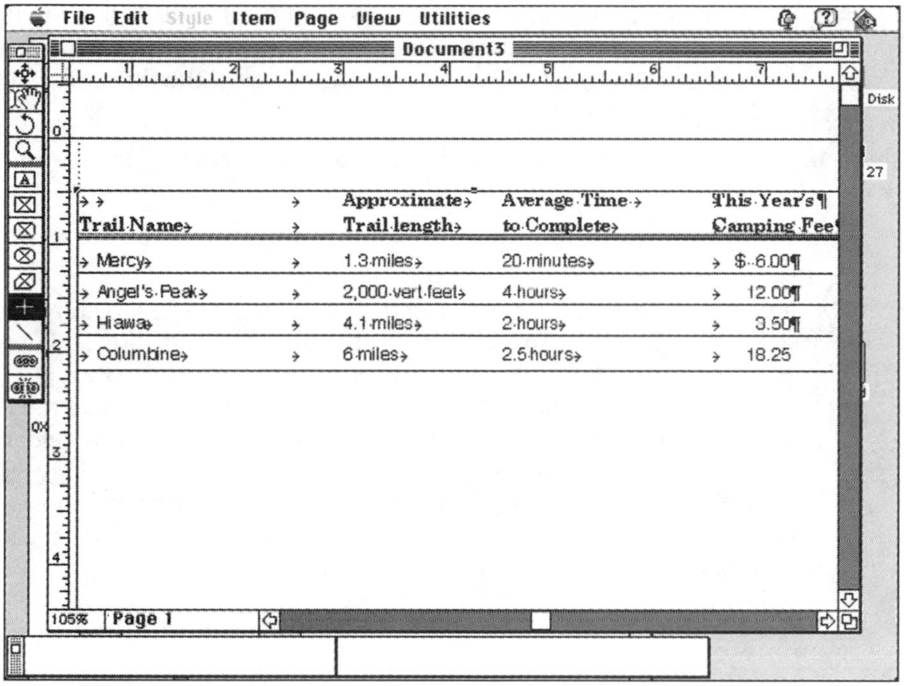

		Approximate	Average Time	This Year's¶
Trail Name		Trail length	to Complete	Camping Fee¶
Mercy		1.3 miles	20 minutes	$ 6.00¶
Angel's Peak		2,000 vert feet	4 hours	12.00¶
Hiawa		4.1 miles	2 hours	3.50¶
Columbine		6 miles	2.5 hours	18.25

STEPS: Creating A Table

Step 1.   We typed in a sample line of text, placing tabs between each column.

Step 2.   We used the Style ⇨ Tabs feature to define tab stops. We determined tab stops by guessing where columns should be, based on text length for each column. We determined alignment based on the type of data. We chose left alignment for regular text and decimal alignment for numbers with decimals. After making educated guesses, we chose Apply to see the result. We moved our tab stops and selected Apply until we were satisfied.

When planning a table, set tabs to accommodate the longest text that you expect to include in each column, so that the tabs work with all rows in your table.

Step 3.   We wrote down the tab stops and repeated step 2 for the table's title row. The tab stops for the title row are different than those of the table body. All tabs in the title row align left because the titles do not contain any numbers with decimals or commas to align elements on.

Step 4.   We chose Cancel so that none of our locally set tabs would take effect.

Step 5.	We created two new styles — Table Body and Table Title — that used the tab stop settings we determined earlier. We also set our typeface, size, and ruling-line settings. We used a ruling line below the title and a ruling line between the rows.
Step 6.	We applied the new styles to the table text as we entered the rest of the table.

 If you want vertical lines between table columns, create a picture box for them the size of the table. Then turn off text wrap for the text box and use the Line tool to draw the lines. (How to set text boxes is covered in Part III.) Next, select the text box containing the text and the picture box containing the lines (hold down Shift when clicking the second box, so that the first one remains selected). From the Item menu, select Group, so the two boxes stay together if the layout later changes. Keep in mind, however, that if the text reflows, the lines do not move with the table text unless the table is in its own text box, independent of the rest of the story.

Summary

●◆ Tabs set with comma alignment or with alignment on a user-defined character will not work as expected for text that does not contain the alignment character. But tabs set with decimal alignment will work as expected in these cases.

●◆ Tab stops are relative to the text box's left margin, not to the page's ruler.

●◆ Tab stops are limited to 20 per paragraph.

●◆ You can create tables by defining tab stops for tabular text. If tables share common formats, you can define a style tag for tables and then locally override it for tables that need fine-tuning.

Editing Text

CHAPTER 17

In This Chapter

●● How to insert, delete, and move text

●● Ways to search and replace text and text attributes

●● How to use the spell checker and make changes to the spelling dictionary

----

Using Basic Editing Techniques ____

Those who use QuarkXPress are divided into two camps: some use the built-in word processor to do basic editing while others do most of their text editing in a separate word processing program. Even though you may be part of the latter group, it's very likely that you do at least minor editing within QuarkXPress.

QuarkXPress's editing tools are sufficient for most basic tasks such as adding or deleting text. If you want to add or delete text, first position your text cursor (which appears if you are using the Content tool) at the spot where you want to make changes and click the mouse button. You then can start typing or deleting text.

STEPS:	Selecting a Block of Text
Step 1.	Position the text cursor at one end of the text block.
Step 2.	Press and hold the mouse button as you drag the cursor so that it is at the other end of the text box.
Step 3.	Release the mouse button. The selected text is highlighted.

To select all text in a text box, or in a series of linked text boxes, place the cursor within the box and choose Edit ➪ Select All (the shortcut is ⌘A).

As in most other Macintosh programs, in QuarkXPress you can also replace text by selecting it and typing in new text or pasting in text from the Clipboard (Edit ➪ Paste, or ⌘V). The new text that takes the place of the old can be from another part of your document, from another QuarkXPress document, or from another Macintosh program. The new text can be a copy of text (Edit ➪ Copy, or ⌘C), or it can be text cut from another document (Edit ➪ Cut, or ⌘X).

Cut text and *deleted* text are different. QuarkXPress inserts cut text automatically into the Clipboard, but it does not insert deleted text onto the Clipboard. (You delete text by using the Delete key or Backspace key.) The only way to recover deleted text is via Edit ➪ Undo Typing. Cut text remains in the Clipboard until you cut or copy other text.

You move text by cutting it from one location and pasting it into another. You duplicate text by copying it from one location and pasting it into another.

With release 3.2, QuarkXPress now supports drag-and-drop editing, which lets you drag text from one place and drop it into another. To use drag-and-drop editing, select the text that you want to move, hold the mouse button down as you drag the selection to the new location, and then release the button. (To enable this feature, turn on drag and drop editing in the Edit ➪ Preferences ➪ Application dialog box.)

Replacing Text and Text Attributes

Basic editing tools are fine for doing simple editing, but you may want to replace one piece of text with another throughout your document. Suppose, for example, that you create a catalog, and you need to change a product's version number in every place that it is referenced throughout the manual. You can make the changes in the original word-processor document and then replace the text in your QuarkXPress document with the updated text. Or you can use QuarkXPress's built-in replace function, which you access through the Find/Change dialog box, shown in Figure 17-1.

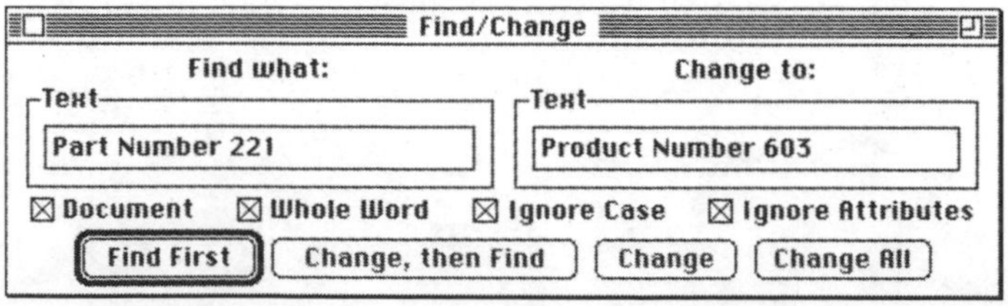

Figure 17-1:
The Find/
Change dialog
box.

Find/Change
Find what: **Change to:**
┌Text─────────────┐   ┌Text─────────────┐
│ Part Number 221 │   │ Product Number 603 │
☒ Document   ☒ Whole Word   ☒ Ignore Case   ☒ Ignore Attributes
[Find First]   [Change, then Find]   [Change]   [Change All]

Replacing text

To replace text throughout the current story — which is defined as text in the currently selected text box plus all those linked to it — use the Find/Change dialog box (Edit ➪ Find/Change, or ⌘F). You also can replace text throughout the entire current document. The QuarkXPress replace function works like the standard search and replace tool found in Macintosh word-processing programs. You can search for whole words or for words whose capitalization matches the words or characters that you type in the Find What field. In Figure 17-1, QuarkXPress is instructed to replace Part Number 221 with Product Number 603.

As you can see, the controls in the Find/Change dialog box let you choose whether QuarkXPress should look for a whole word (if the Whole Word box is unchecked, the program finds the string wherever is appears). You can also have the program search and replace a word — regardless of its capitalization — by selecting Ignore Case. If the Document box is checked, the replace affects all stories and text in your document. The other buttons, such as Find Next, work as they do in word-processing programs.

Changing text attributes

Find/Change also lets you find and replace text attributes, typefaces, and sizes. This feature is useful if, for example, you want to change all instances of 10-point Times New Roman to 12-point Palatino. To access this option, uncheck Ignore Attributes in the Find/Change dialog box. When Ignore Attributes is deselected, the dialog box expands and offers you attribute replacement options, as Figure 17-2 shows.

Figure 17-2:
The Find/
Change dialog
box lets you
search for and
replace text that
has specific
typeface
attributes.

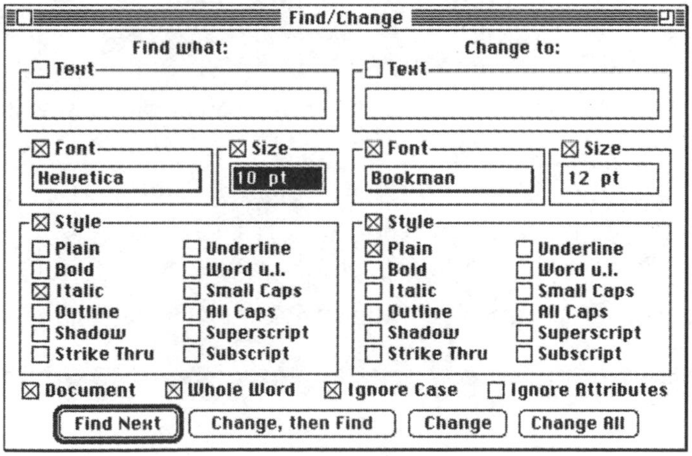

In the example shown in Figure 17-2, we replace any text set in 10-point Helvetica italic text with 12-point Bookman plain text. We also left Ignore Case checked. This example shows how you can select specific text, typeface, and styles for both the search and replace functions. You specify these attributes by checking the Text, Font, Size, and Style check boxes in the Find What and Change To columns of the dialog box.

If you leave an option unchecked in the Find What column, QuarkXPress includes any variant (such as style) in the search. If, for example, we did not check Size in the Find What column but did check it in the Change To column, QuarkXPress would change all Helvetica italic text of any size to 12-point Bookman plain text.

If you leave an option unchecked in the Change To column, QuarkXPress applies the formatting of the text that was searched to the replacement text. If we did not check Size in the Change To column, the size of the replacement text would be the same as the text it was replacing.

When you leave Text unchecked in the Find What column, you replace attributes only. You might do this to change all underlined text to word-underlined text, all bold text to small cap text, all News Gothic bold text to News Gothic bold italic, or all 8-point text to 8.5-point text.

How to Quickly Change Point Size

Here's a quick way to change type size by one point or to the next highest or next lowest preset type size (the preset type sizes are all sizes besides Other in the Measurements palette's font list).

First, select the text whose size you want to change.

- ↪ To increase the selected text to the next highest preset size (for example, increasing from 12 to 14 points), press Shift-⌘period.

- ↪ To increase the selected text by one point, press Option-Shift-⌘period.

- ↪ To decrease the selected text to the next lowest preset size (for example, decreasing from 12 to 10 points), press Shift-⌘comma.

- ↪ To decrease the selected text by one point, press Option-Shift-⌘comma.

Check an attribute box in the Style section of the dialog box if you want to use an attribute. Remove the check mark if you don't want to use an attribute (such as bold) in your search and replace. Make the box gray to tell QuarkXPress to retain whatever attribute is set. (Clicking a box once unchecks it if checked or checks it if unchecked. Clicking a box twice makes it gray.) In the example shown in Figure 17-3, the replacement text will be plain but not bold or italic, but any text that is in outline, shadow, strikethrough, underline, word underline, small caps, all caps, superscript, or subscripts will retain those attributes.

Figure 17-3:
The Font Usage dialog
box.

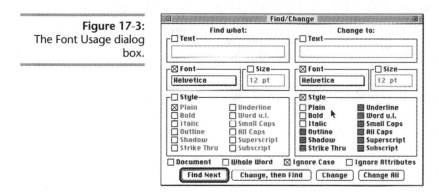

You can search and replace all character attributes available in the Measurements palette, with the exception of superiors.

Using the Font Usage utility

Another way to change text attributes is to use the QuarkXPress utility called Font Usage. Available through Utilities ➪ Font Usage, this utility lists text style and typeface combinations used in the current document. In the example shown in Figure 17-3, we search for Helvetica, and Font Usage highlights where this type style appears in the document. We can now replace it with another typeface and/or style attribute.

Font Usage is designed primarily to help you determine which typefaces are used in a document so that you or your typesetter will know which typefaces you need for printing. The utility also comes in handy if you open a document that uses a typeface not available on your Macintosh; you can replace that typeface with another.

Checking Spelling

A finished document loses credibility when it includes words that are spelled incorrectly. So it's always a good idea to check for spelling errors. QuarkXPress has a built-in spelling checker that catches errors as well as a tool that enables you to specify the proper spelling of words that the program does not recognize.

To invoke the spelling checker, select Utilities ⇨ Check Spelling. This menu item drops down the submenu shown in Figure 17-4, which offers you three spell-checking choices:

- **Word** checks the current word (or the first word in a group of selected words).

- **Story** checks the current story (all text in the current text box, as well as any text in text boxes linked to it).

- **Document** checks every word in the current QuarkXPress document.

Figure 17-4:
The QuarkXPress Check Spelling submenu, accessible through the Utilities menu.

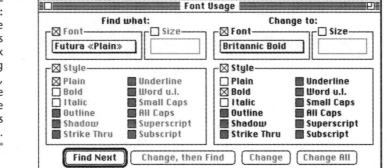

 You can quickly check spelling for the current word by pressing the shortcut keys ⌘L.

The spelling checker displays words that it does not recognize (calling them "suspect" words) one at a time, giving you an opportunity to correct or ignore (skip) the word. The spelling checker can suggest correct spellings for words that it believes are misspelled. Figure 17-5 shows the spelling checker displaying a suggested correction. To ask QuarkXPress to suggest a word, click the Lookup button. To accept a suggested replacement, click the word and the Replace button. You can also type in the correct word yourself, whether or not you use Lookup.

If you're not content with the 80,000-word dictionary in QuarkXPress, you can add additional words to an auxiliary dictionary. Words of a technical nature specific to your company or industry are good candidates for an auxiliary dictionary, as are proper names. If an auxiliary dictionary is open, you can add a word while in the spelling checker by selecting Keep when QuarkXPress displays a suspect word.

Figure 17-5:
The Check
Document
dialog box
gives you
the option
of replacing
suspect
words.

Setting up auxiliary dictionaries

An auxiliary dictionary can be shared by multiple documents, or you can establish a dictionary specific to a particular document. Use Utilities ⇨ Auxiliary Dictionary to invoke the Auxiliary Dictionary dialog box, shown in Figure 17-6. Use this dialog box to create a new dictionary or open an existing one.

If you open an auxiliary dictionary when a document is open, QuarkXPress associates them together so that, when you open the document, the program has access to the auxiliary dictionary. If you don't want the auxiliary dictionary tied to a specific document, open the auxiliary dictionary when no documents are open.

Figure 17-6:
The Auxiliary
Dictionary
dialog box.

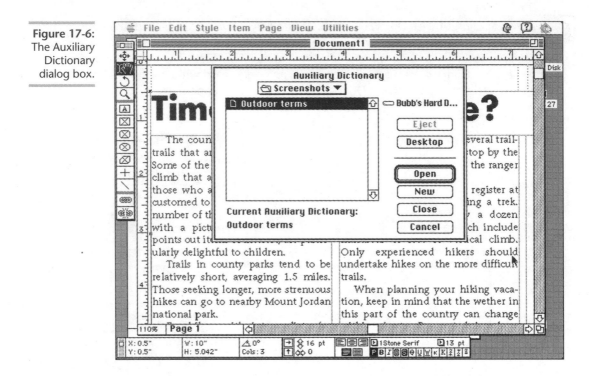

One thing that's nice about auxiliary dictionaries is that you can pretty much put them where you want them. In other words, auxiliary dictionaries do not have to reside in the same file as the documents accessing them.

- **To create an auxiliary dictionary for a specific document:** Open the document and access the Auxiliary Dictionary dialog box (Utilities ⇨ Auxiliary Dictionary). Use the controls in the dialog box to locate the folder in which you want to keep the dictionary. Click the New button.

- **To create a default auxiliary dictionary for all new documents:** Make sure that no documents are open before invoking the Auxiliary Dictionary dialog box.

- **To use an existing dictionary for the current document:** Open your document and then open an existing dictionary from the Auxiliary Dictionary dialog box.

- **To use an existing dictionary as the default for all new documents:** Make sure that no documents are open and then open an existing dictionary from the Auxiliary Dictionary dialog box.

- **To detach an auxiliary dictionary from a current document:** Open the document and select Close in the Auxiliary Dictionary dialog box.

- **To detach an auxiliary dictionary as the default dictionary for all new documents:** Make sure that no documents are open. Select Close in the Auxiliary Dictionary dialog box.

If a dictionary is associated with the current document or is selected as the default auxiliary dictionary, its name appears at the bottom of the Auxiliary Dictionary dialog box as Current Auxiliary Dictionary.

Making changes to an auxiliary dictionary

You can continue to customize an auxiliary dictionary by adding or deleting words from it through the Edit Auxiliary Dictionary dialog box (accessed via Utilities ⇨ Edit Auxiliary), shown in Figure 17-7. The Edit Auxiliary Dictionary dialog box displays its contents alphabetically.

- **To add a word:** Type the word in the field below the list of current words. Click the Add button. You'll note that you can't use the Shift or Caps Lock keys to add capital letters. That's because QuarkXPress doesn't check capitalization, just the sequence of letters (since you'd want it to realize that, say, "TPO," "tpo," and "Tpo" are all misspellings of "top." For proper nouns (like "Quark"), simply enter the text in lowercase.

- **To delete a word:** Use the mouse to highlight the word from the word list, or enter it in the field below the current list of words (typing the word also highlights it in the list). Click the Delete button.

Figure 17-7:
You can continue
customizing an auxiliary
dictionary by making
changes in the Edit
Auxiliary Dictionary dialog
box.

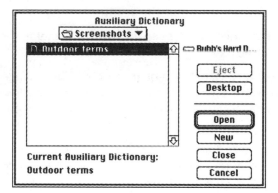

Remember to click the Save button before you exit the Edit Auxiliary Dictionary dialog box. Otherwise, changes that you make are not saved. If you do not want to save your changes, choose Cancel.

Copy Fitting

Copy fitting is just what it sounds like: the process of fitting text into the layout, often by altering the spacing. If your original, unmodified text fits the layout the first time through, consider it a stroke of luck because that's not what usually happens.

Besides making pages look better, copy fitting can be a real business concern. In magazines, newsletters, and newspapers, the number of pages is set in advance, so you don't have the option of adding or removing pages to fit the lack or abundance of copy.

Because copy fitting involves several spacing factors, you might want to review the techniques described in Chapters 12 and 13 before applying the techniques outlined here.

It's sometimes necessary to take a number of actions, often in concert, to make text fit in the available space. Because the usual problem is having more text than space, the following tips assume that the goal is to shorten text. But you can use the same procedures in reverse to expand text. Note that we give these tips in order of preference, so use the last tips only if you can't make text fit using the first few suggestions.

- **Edit text** to remove extra lines. Be on the lookout for lines at the end of a paragraph that have only a few characters. Getting rid of a few characters somewhere else in the paragraph may eliminate these short lines, reducing the amount of page space needed while keeping the amount of text removed to a minimum.

- **Track text** so that it occupies less space and it eliminates short lines. Chapter 12 explains how to track text.

- **Tighten the leading** by a half or a quarter point. This change is so small that the average reader won't notice it, and it may save you a few lines per column, which can add up quickly. See the section on leading in Chapter 13.

- **Reduce the point size** by a half point. This reduction saves more space than is first apparent because it allows you to place a few more lines on the page and put a bit more text in each line. Change point size in the style sheet or select text and use the type size controls in the Measurements palette.

- **Reduce the horizontal scale** of text to a slightly smaller percentage (perhaps 95 percent) to squeeze more text in each line. The section on horizontal and vertical scale in Chapter 12 explains how to make this alteration.

- **Vary the size of columns** by setting slightly narrower column gutters or slightly wider margins.

Try applying these copy-fitting techniques globally to avoid a patchwork appearance. You can, however, change tracking on individual lines without ruining the appearance of your document. If you limit tracking changes to no more than 20 units, the text won't appear obviously different to your readers.

Summary

- Cut and paste works with individual QuarkXPress documents, across multiple QuarkXPress documents, and across Macintosh applications.
- The Find/Change dialog box lets you search and replace not just text but text attributes. You can replace just text, just attributes, or just text with certain attributes.
- The Font Usage dialog box shows you which typefaces are used, and it lets you replace typefaces and type attributes throughout the document.
- QuarkXPress's spelling checker lets you check the spelling of the current word, the current story, and the entire document.
- Auxiliary dictionaries can contain special words that are not in the main dictionary.
- When copy-fitting, try the following techniques in the order presented: edit text; interactively track text to get rid of short lines; tighten leading slightly; reduce point size slightly; condense the text slightly; and widen text margins or narrow column gutters.

Graphics and Images

Whether drawn with QuarkXPress tools, created electronically in separate illustration programs, or captured electronically with scanners, graphics are a vital part of page design. Often the most glamorous parts of a document, pictures and other graphics add an important visual element and play a major role in attracting the reader's eye.

But graphics do much more than make a document look better; graphics convey meaning and tone. It's important to treat the visuals with the same care as you use with the text or the layout itself. To help you do so, QuarkXPress offers a solid set of graphics tools to enable you to import, create, and modify pictures.

This section explains how to manipulate imported images, create simple graphics with QuarkXPress's own tools, and work with bitmapped images like scanned photos. In Chapter 20, look for several sidebars that explain the theory behind gray-scale publishing. These sidebars will help you get the best output that QuarkXPress can deliver.

Modifying Graphics

CHAPTER 18

In This Chapter

➡ Using the Measurements palette to make changes to a picture box

➡ Modifying the contents of a picture box by using the Picture Box Specifications dialog box

➡ Sizing and positioning a picture correctly within a picture box

➡ Speeding up the printing of review pages that contain graphics

In Part III, we explained how to create a picture box and fill it with an imported picture. We also explained how to make changes to the size and position of a picture box.

After you create, position, and size a picture box, you may want to make some changes to its contents — the picture itself. You can alter the contents of an active picture box by using the Style menu, by changing the values in the Measurements palette, or by adjusting the controls in the Picture Box Specifications dialog box (which you open by selecting Item ➪ Modify). This chapter shows you how to use the Measurements palette and the Picture Box Specifications dialog box to modify graphics. You'll learn how to use the Style menu options in Chapter 20.

Using the Measurements Palette to Modify Graphics

To use the Measurements palette to modify the contents of a picture box, you must first make the picture box active. (If the box is active, its sizing handles are visible around the edge of the box.) You also must display the Measurements palette. (To display the palette, choose View ➪ Show Measurements.)

In Figure 18-1, you see a page containing a picture box. The figure shows the page just after we filled the picture box with a picture. We used the Rectangular Picture Box tool to draw the picture box, and we filled the box with the picture by choosing File ⇨ Get Picture (or press ⌘E). Note the sizing handles on the borders of the box: they indicate that the box is active.

Note also that the image doesn't quite fit the picture box's dimensions — it's a bit smaller than the picture box. QuarkXPress loads an image in its actual size and does not try to fit the image to the picture box size. In Figure 18-1, we had QuarkXPress resize the image to fit proportionally within the box's constraints. We explain later in this chapter how to perform this task.

The Measurements palette appears at the bottom of the screen in Figure 18-1. You can make several changes to the box through the Measurements palette, which is the simplest way to manipulate picture boxes and their contents.

> ☞ Entering new values in the X and Y fields changes the distance of the picture box border from the page edge. The boundaries of the picture box shown in Figure 18-1 are 3 picas (½ inch) from the left side of the page.

Figure 18-1:
An active picture box with a graphic placed in it.

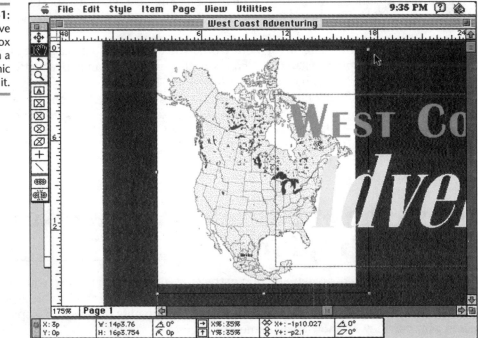

- Entering new values in the W and H fields changes the width and height of the picture box. In the figure, the current dimensions are 14 picas, 3.76 points × 16 picas, 3.754 points. Those exacting coordinates indicate that the picture box was drawn by hand — if we had sized the box via the Measurements palette, we would have rounded off the coordinates to something like 14p × 16p.

- Entering a value in the ⟳ field rotates the picture box. Because the box in Figure 18-1 is not rotated, the value in the field is 0 (zero) degrees.

- Entering a value in the ⫽ field changes the shape of the picture box corners. For example, entering a value of 2 picas causes the picture box corners to become rounded.

- The setting in the X% and Y% fields in Figure 18-1 is 35 percent. Changing the percentage values in the X% and Y% fields reduces or enlarges the picture in the picture box. To keep the proportions of the picture the same, enter the same value in the X field as you enter in the Y field. Unfortunately, you cannot link the two so that if you change one, the other automatically changes with it to keep the picture's proportions consistent. (But you can use the keyboard shortcuts ⌘-Option-Shift-< and ⌘-Option-Shift -> to scale an image smaller and larger, respectively, along both axes simultaneously. This shortcut scales the image 5 percent at a time.)

- Entering any value except zero in the ⟳ field located at the right side of the palette rotates the picture *within* the picture box. (The ⟳ field on the left side of the palette rotates the entire picture box.) The current value for the picture box in Figure 18-1 is zero, which means the box is not rotated. Likewise, the value for the image is zero, so it is also not rotated.

- Entering any value except zero in the ▱ field slants the contents of the picture box. In Figure 18-1, the picture-box contents are not slanted.

- Clicking the shift handles (◇◇ and ⬘⬙) moves an image within the picture box. Each click moves the image in 0.1 increments (0.1 inches, 0p1, and so on). To move the image in coarser increments, choose the Content tool, move the pointer to the image (the grabber icon will appear), hold the mouse down, and reposition the image within the picture box. You can also enter values for the image to be shifted within the picture box in the Measurements palette: enter the numbers in the fields to the right of ◇◇ X+: and ⬘⬙ Y+:.

- Clicking the flip icons (→ and ↑) flips the image along the X and Y axes, respectively. The arrow's direction changes in the icon to let you know whether a picture has been flipped (← and ↓). You can also use the Flip Horizontal and Flip Vertical items in the Style menu.

After you use the Measurements palette to make changes to the picture box, press Return or click the mouse to apply the changes.

Using the Picture Box Specifications Dialog Box

You also can modify a picture contained in an active picture box by using the Picture Box Specifications dialog box, shown in Figure 18-2. To display the dialog box, select the picture box to make it active and then choose Item ⇨ Modify (or use the shortcut key combination ⌘M or simply double-click on the picture box).

Values in the Origin Across, Origin Down, Width, and Height fields control the position and size of the picture box. You can specify these values in units as small as .001 in any measurement system. In Figure 18-2, the origin (the upper-left corner of the picture box) is 3 picas from the left and 0 picas from the top of the page. The picture box width is 14 picas, 3.76 points, and the height is 16 picas, 3.754 points.

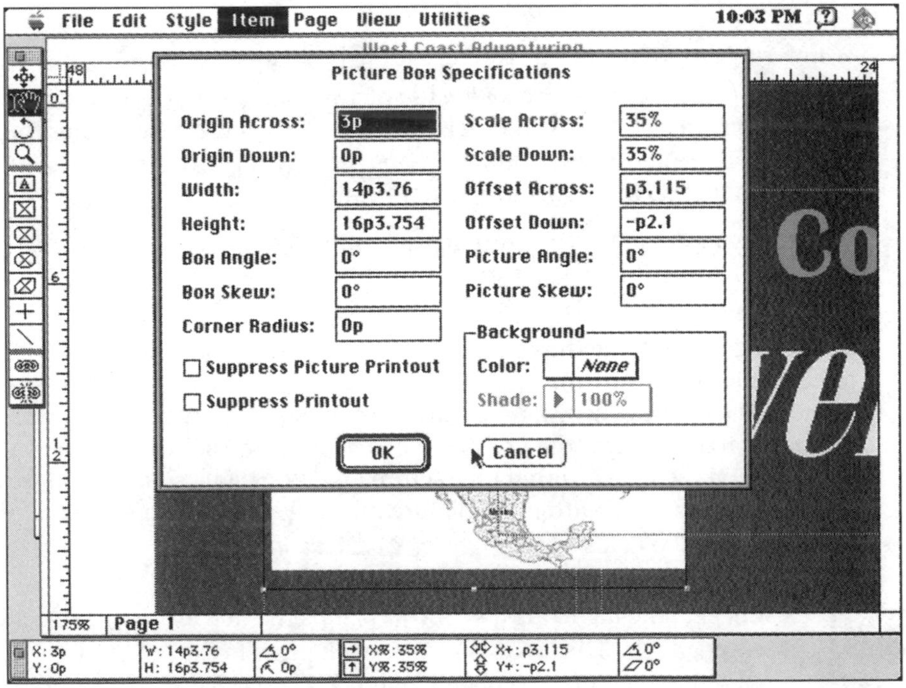

Figure 18-2:
The Picture
Box
Specifica-
tions dialog
box.

The following sections describe the remaining fields in the Picture Box Specifications dialog box and explain how to apply them to an active picture box. You can make changes in one or all of these fields. When you finish making selections in the dialog box, choose OK to save your changes.

As we show examples of these effects, note how the Measurements palette at the bottom of the screen changes to reflect the new values. You can bypass the Picture Box Specifications dialog box for any function displayed in the Measurements palette by entering the appropriate values in the palette itself.

Box Angle

Entering a value in the Box Angle field rotates the picture box around the center of the box. Box angle values range from –360 to 360 degrees, in increments as small as .001 degrees. Figure 18-3 shows the effect of rotating the picture box 5 degrees.

Figure 18-3:
A picture box rotated 5 degrees.

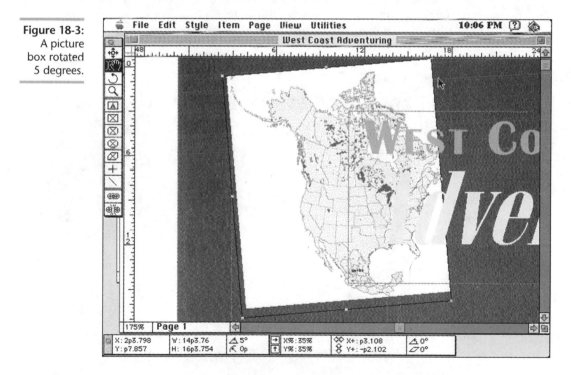

Corner Radius

Entering a value in the Corner Radius field changes the shape of a picture box's corners. The reason this field contains the word *radius* is that invisible circles exist in the corners of boxes drawn in QuarkXPress. These circles are located within the bounds of the box corners and touch the two sides of the box next to them. The radius is the size of the circle used to form rounded edges to the box.

The Corner Radius field is not available when the picture box is an oval or polygon.

When you first create a rectangular picture box, its corner radius values are 0 (zero). You can enter a measurement value from 0 to 2 inches (0 to 12 picas), in .001 increments of any measurement system. Figure 18-4 shows the effect of selecting a corner radius of 2 picas.

We don't recommend changing the corner radius of a picture box unless you are certain that it adds to the design of the page. Rounded-corner picture boxes are typically not effective and can make a layout appear amateurish.

Figure 18-4:
A picture box with a corner radius of 2 picas.

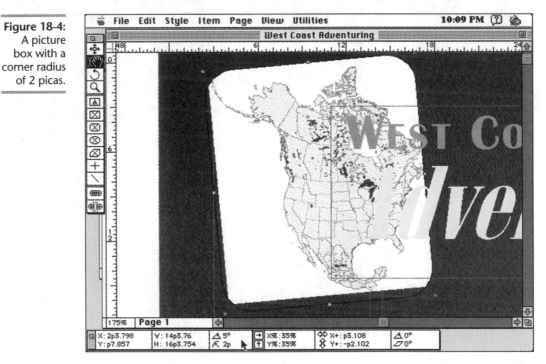

Scale Across and Scale Down

As you work with QuarkXPress, you'll probably use the Scale Across and Scale Down feature frequently. In fact, it's one of the handiest items in the entire program, especially if you create documents that include graphics.

When you first fill a picture box with a picture (by choosing File ⇨ Get Picture or by using the shortcut ⌘E), QuarkXPress places the picture in the text box at 100 percent scale. It's not at all uncommon for the picture to be larger or smaller than you would like, and you can change its size by entering new values in the Scale Across and Scale Down fields. You can specify a size from 10 to 1,000 percent of the picture's original size. You can enter scale values in increments as small as .1 percent. You don't have to enter the same values for Scale Across and Scale Down; you can enter different values for each field to distort the picture.

In the first illustrations presented in this chapter, we used a picture at 35 percent scale across and down. Figure 18-5 shows the same illustration scaled 70 percent along both dimensions, which is twice as large as the size used up until now.

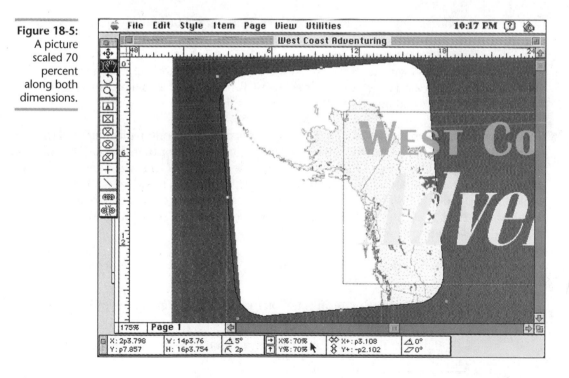

Figure 18-5:
A picture scaled 70 percent along both dimensions.

As mentioned earlier, you can use keyboard shortcuts to increase or decrease both Scale Across and Scale Down values simultaneously:

    ⊙ Press ⌘-Option-Shift-< to decrease Scale Across and Scale Down values by 5 percent.

    ⊙ Press ⌘-Option-Shift-> to increase Scale Across and Scale Down values by 5 percent.

Offset Across and Offset Down

Often, imported pictures are not positioned within the box as you want them to be. The focal point of a picture might be too far to the left, too far to the right, or too high or low within the box.

One easy way to position a picture within the picture box is to use the Content tool. First, select the Content tool. If you then place the cursor over the active picture box, it turns into a grabber hand that lets you shift the picture into place.

You can do the same thing — but in a more precise, numerical fashion — by entering values in the Offset Across and Offset Down fields in the Picture Box Specifications dialog box. Figure 18-5 shows the picture box with the picture offset as it was when originally imported. In Figure 18-6, we adjust the offset to the left by entering an Offset Across value of –6 picas. This change moves the picture box contents 6 picas to the left. (A positive number would move it to the right.)

The change we made in Figure 18-6 improved the *across*, or horizontal, placement of the picture within the picture box (to focus on western Canada, rather than Alaska), but the top of the picture still has extra space at the top of the box. To fix this, we enter an Offset Down value of –2 picas. You see the result in Figure 18-7. A positive number would move the picture down. A negative value moves the picture up because the 0 (zero) on the ruler is at the top of the screen, so to move toward zero, the picture has to be moved in a negative direction.

Keyboard methods for positioning a picture within a picture box include the following:

    ⊙ ⌘-Shift-F stretches or shrinks the picture to the borders of the picture box without keeping the picture's aspect ratio.

    ⊙ ⌘-Option-Shift-F fits the picture as close as it can to the picture box but maintains the picture's aspect ratio.

    ⊙ ⌘-Shift-M centers the picture in the middle of the picture box.

Figure 18-6:
Adjusting
the Offset
Across value
to −6 picas
shifts the
picture to
the left of
the picture
box.

Figure 18-7:
Adjusting
the Offset
Down value
to −2 picas
moves the
picture up to
the top of
the box.

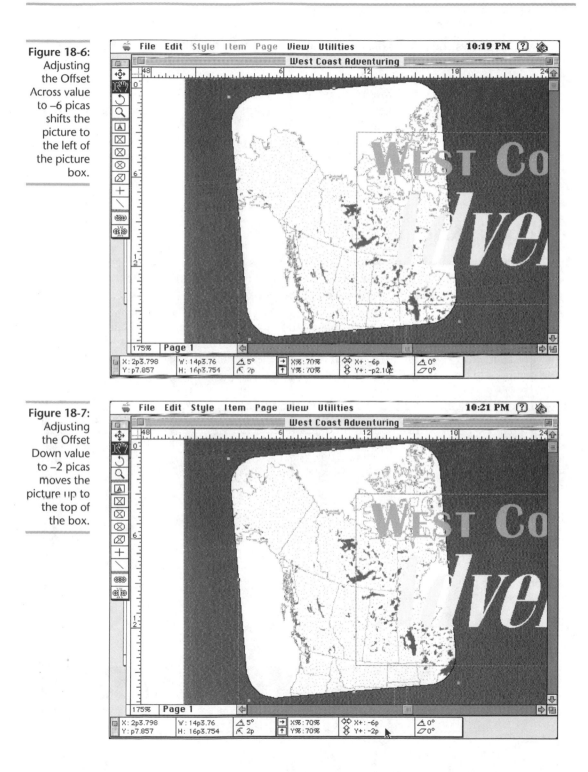

Figure 18-8 shows the results of all three operations. Note that the image at right was fit to the picture box before being centered, as centering does not fit an image to its box

If you keep a picture's aspect ratio, it means that you keep its proportions the same as you enlarge it or reduce it. Keeping aspect ratio means keeping equal scale-across and scale-down percentages, such as 50%, 50%, and so on. You may occasionally want to place a graphic when you aren't sure what shape the picture box should take. What you should do is create the picture box, import the picture, and then resize the picture box to fit the graphic.

Picture Angle

When you first place a picture into a picture box, it is oriented in the same angle it had in its source graphics program. Occasionally, you may want to change the angle of the picture without changing the angle of the picture box itself.

Entering a value in the Picture Angle field of the Picture Box Specifications dialog box rotates the picture within the box. The picture is rotated around the center of the picture as it was created in the original graphics program. The angle of the box stays the same; only the contents rotate.

Figure 18-8:
The effects (left to right) of non-proportional fitting (⌘-Shift-F), proportional fitting (⌘-Option-Shift-F), and centering (⌘-Shift-M) after a proportional fit.

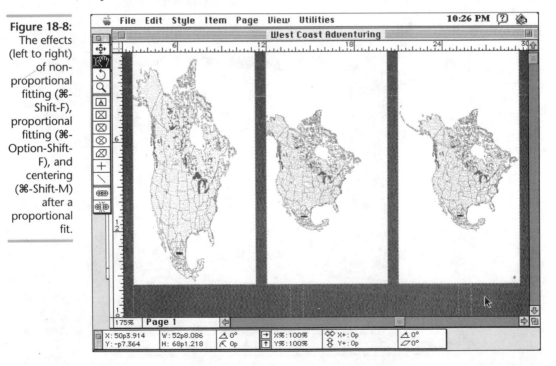

You can enter Picture Angle values from –360 to 360 degrees, in increments as small as .001 degrees. Figure 18-9 shows the effect of changing the Picture Angle from 0 degrees to 40 degrees.

Figure 18-9:
The picture box contents are rotated 40 degrees; the box itself is not rotated.

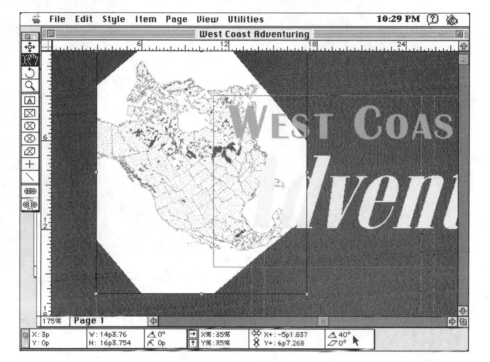

Picture Skew

Another special effect you can try with QuarkXPress is *skewing,* or slanting, a picture within its box. You do this by entering a value in the Picture Skew field of the Picture Box Specifications dialog box. You can enter values from –75 to 75 degrees, in increments as small as .001 degrees. If you enter a positive value, the picture skews to the right; if you enter a negative value, the picture skews to the left. Figure 18-10 shows the effect of skewing our picture 40 degrees. Skewing changes the angle formed by the left and bottom edges of the picture. Normally, that angle is at 90 degrees; the number you enter is the amount by which this 90 degrees is changed (thus, setting the skew angle to 40 degrees makes the angle 130 degrees clockwise or an acute angle of 50 degrees).

Figure 18-10:
This picture is
skewed 40
degrees.

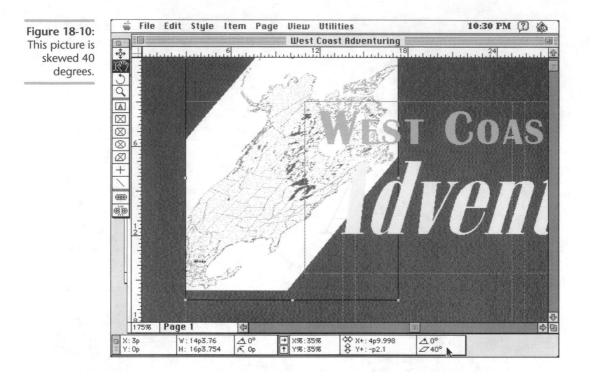

Figure 18-10:
This picture is
skewed 40
degrees.

Suppress Picture Printout and Suppress Printout

In these two fields, you can select options that speed document printing — something you may want to consider when you print proofs or rough copies. If you select Suppress Picture Printout, the frames or backgrounds of picture boxes print, but the contents of the picture boxes do not. Selecting Suppress Printout takes this option one step further. It prevents picture box frames, backgrounds, and contents from printing.

To choose either option, check the box next to the option label. If you select one of these options, remember to go back into the Picture Box Specifications dialog box and uncheck the box before printing final copies of the document.

 If you use frames around picture boxes, we recommend that you print proof copies with Suppress Picture Printout selected. This lets you see the size and placement of the frames.

Background Color

QuarkXPress lets you add color to the background of a picture box and control the depth (*saturation*) of the color. To add color to the background of an active picture box or to change an existing background color, select a color from the Color list box in the Picture Box Specifications dialog box or use the Colors palette (if not visible, use View ⇨ Show Colors to make it appear).

One of the selections available in the Color list box is None. If you select None, the picture box background is transparent.

The new drag-and-drop feature lets you select a color from the Colors palette and drag it onto the box.

If you don't find the background color that you want in the Colors palette, you can create it. Choose Edit ⇨ Colors and use the color selection screen that appears to create the color you want.

See Chapter 21 for more information on applying colors and creating custom colors.

After you select the background color that you want to apply to the picture box (and you select a color other than None or White), you can specify the saturation level of the color. Select a predefined shade (0 to 100 percent) in the Shade list box or enter a custom shade value (in increments as small as 0.1 percent) in the Shade field. There's a pop-up pick list for shade increments in the Colors palette as well (at the top right), in which you can use your own values or choose from the existing ones.

Keyboard Shortcuts for Modifying Graphics

Here is a summary of some keyboard shortcuts you can use to modify graphics within active picture boxes:

- ⌘M opens the Picture Box Specifications dialog box.

- ⌘-Shift-F fits the picture to the picture box (this shortcut does not keep the picture's aspect ratio).

→ ⌘-Option-Shift-F fits the picture to the picture box, maintaining aspect ratio.

→ ⌘-Shift-M centers the picture in the picture box.

→ ⌘-Option-Shift-< decreases both the Scale Across and Scale Down values by 5 percent.

→ ⌘-Option-Shift-> increases both the Scale Across and Scale Down values by 5 percent.

Summary

→ You can modify the contents of a picture box in the following ways: using the Measurements palette, entering values in the Picture Box Specifications dialog box, or using certain keyboard shortcuts.

→ QuarkXPress lets you change the corner radius of a picture box to round the box corners. We recommend avoiding this unless you need to do so for specific design requirements.

→ If you print review or rough-draft copies of your document, consider using Suppress Picture Printout or Suppress Printout. These options prevent graphics from printing and thus speed up printing time. If you use frames around picture boxes, print the review pages with Suppress Picture Printout selected so that you can see the size and position of the box frames.

Creating Graphics in QuarkXPress

CHAPTER 19

In This Chapter

- ➡ Using QuarkXPress tools to create simple graphics
- ➡ Creating a basic organization chart
- ➡ Creating a bar chart

Creating Simple Graphics

Why create graphics in QuarkXPress? That's a good question. True, this powerful program lets you accomplish amazing feats with documents. But let's face it, QuarkXPress is not — nor does it claim to be — a graphics program. Given the choice and sufficient resources, you most likely will use a separate graphics program to create graphics and then import those graphics into QuarkXPress picture boxes.

On the other hand, you may not have the budget for a separate graphics program. In addition, if your graphics needs are on the order of simple boxes, shades, and lines, a graphics program is overkill. Even if you do have Adobe Illustrator or Aldus FreeHand, sometimes it's simpler to create a basic graphic in QuarkXPress, rather than switch to an illustration program, create the artwork, export it, and place it in QuarkXPress. If you have been dealing with any of these tasks, you'll be pleased to know that, given some patience and ingenuity, you can design a decent range of simple graphics within QuarkXPress. The program is particularly adept at handling bar charts, organizational charts, and simple flow diagrams. Here's some techniques you can use:

- ↪ With the assorted picture box tools (rectangular, rounded rectangular, oval, and polygon), you can create a range of simple shapes.

- ↪ With the rotation and skewing tools, you can create even more shapes based on those offered via the picture box tools.

- ↪ You can add background color and shade (saturation) to a text or picture box to spice up the shapes you create.

- ∾ Using the Frame feature, you can add one of seven possible frame patterns to the boundaries of a picture box, and you can specify the width of the frame. You can also create your own frame patterns. Chapter 11 has more information on frames.

- ∾ You can create a variety of lines and arrows, and you can specify the width of the lines.

- ∾ Because QuarkXPress places each layout element on its own layer, you can arrange all of the items on a page by bringing them forward or sending them backward in a stack of elements.

Creating a Simple Organizational Chart

The process of producing a basic organizational chart demonstrates how you can put some QuarkXPress tools to use in creating simple graphics. This section details a step-by-step process we used to create an organizational chart.

STEPS: Creating an Organizational Chart

Step 1.   **Drawing a text box**

First, we opened a new document (File ⇨ New ⇨ Document, or ⌘N). Using the Text Box tool, we drew the text box shown in Figure 19-1. We adjusted the size of the text box by selecting and then dragging the box's sizing handles. Another way of sizing the text box is to enter values in the W and H fields (Width and Height) in the Measurements palette.

Step 2.   **Entering and formatting text**

With the text box still active, we selected the Content tool and typed the text into the first text box, as shown in Figure 19-2. We used the Measurements palette to select the font, boldface the name, and center the text horizontally. We used the Text Box Specifications dialog box (Item ⇨ Modify, or ⌘M) to make the vertical alignment centered as well.

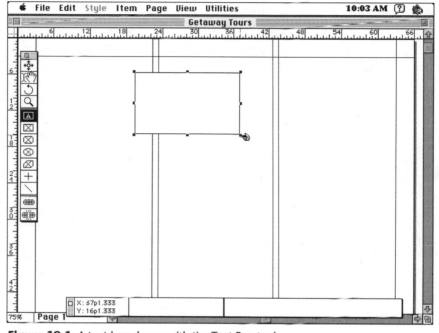

Figure 19-1: A text box drawn with the Text Box tool.

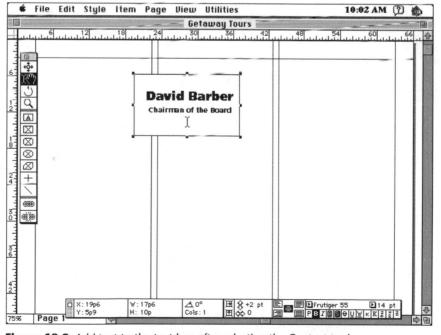

Figure 19-2: Add text to the text box after selecting the Content tool.

Step 3.   **Duplicating the text box**

To add the other two boxes for the chart, we could have drawn them to match the size and style of the first box. Instead, we made two copies of the first text box. To do this, we chose the Item tool, selected the text box to make it active, and selected Edit ⇨ Copy (the shortcut is ⌘C). We then pasted the copied box twice by choosing Edit ⇨ Paste (the shortcut is ⌘V).

Next, we positioned the two new text boxes, as shown in Figure 19-3. We used the Item tool to drag them into their approximate positions and then refined their positions by entering values in the X and Y fields in the Measurements palette.

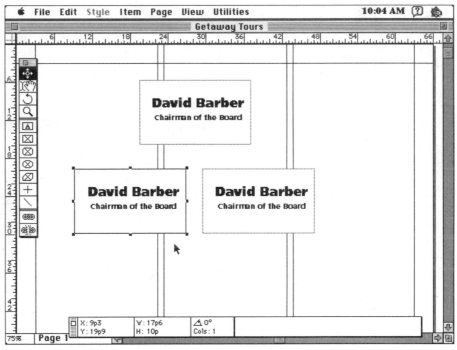

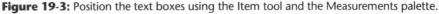

Figure 19-3: Position the text boxes using the Item tool and the Measurements palette.

Step 4.   **Changing text in copied text boxes**

Our next step was to replace the duplicated text in the two new text boxes. We used the Content tool to select the duplicated text and typed in the correct names in each text box. By doing this one line at a time (name line and then title line), we were able to maintain the type attributes we established in the first text box. Figure 19-4 shows the three boxes positioned correctly and containing the proper text.

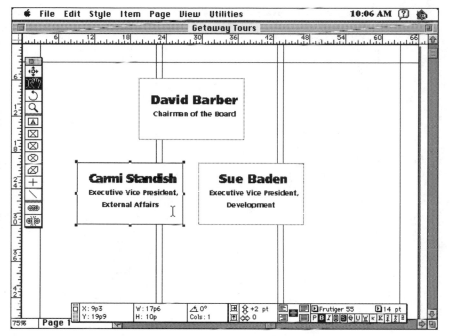

Figure 19-4: Replace the text in the two new text boxes with the correct names and titles.

Step 5. **Adding circles to the chart**

To indicate the next level of subordinates in the organizational chart, we chose to use circles instead of rectangles, as you can see in Figure 19-5. To draw a circle, we used the Oval Picture Box tool. To create a true circle instead of an oval, we held down the Shift key while we drew the shape. After we made the initial circle the correct size, we duplicated it three times by selecting the Item tool, clicking the circle to make it active, and choosing Edit ⇨ Copy (the shortcut is ⌘C). We then pasted the copies by choosing Edit ⇨ Paste (⌘V). To have text appear in those circles, we placed text boxes (with runaround turned off and no background color) on top of the circles, as shown in the rightmost circle in Figure 19-5.

Step 6. **Adding drop shadows for effect**

To create a shadowed effect behind the text boxes, we copied the text boxes, deleted their text, and repositioned them slightly offset from the original text boxes. Then we used Item ⇨ Send to Back to move them behind the original text boxes. Next, we filled the copied boxes with 100 percent black by choosing Item ⇨ Modify (⌘M) to open the Text Box Specifications dialog box where we selected a Background Color of Black and a Shade of 100 percent. Then, we selected the original (foreground) text boxes and changed the background color to white so that the text would knock out of the backgrounds. Figure 19-6 shows the result.

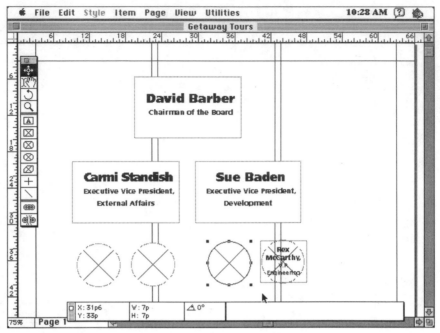

Figure 19-5: The circles with the overprinting text boxes indicate the next level of organization.

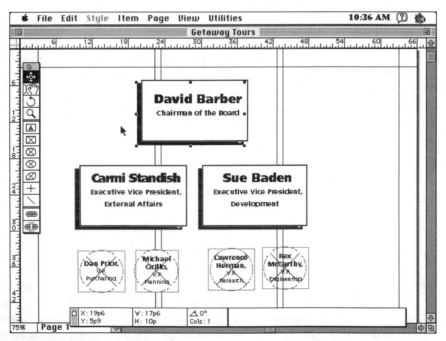

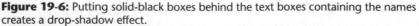

Figure 19-6: Putting solid-black boxes behind the text boxes containing the names creates a drop-shadow effect.

Step 7.

Shading the circles for effect

To give the circles a more distinctive appearance, we added a 20 percent black shade to them. To do this, we used the Colors palette (View ➪ Show Colors) and selected the background icon. We set the background color to black and set the shade to 20 percent. We repeated this process for each circle. The results are shown in Figure 19-7. (You can also use the Item tool to select a circle. Choose Item ➪ Modify (⌘M) to display the Picture Box Specifications dialog box. Then select a Background Color of Black and a Shade of 20 percent.)

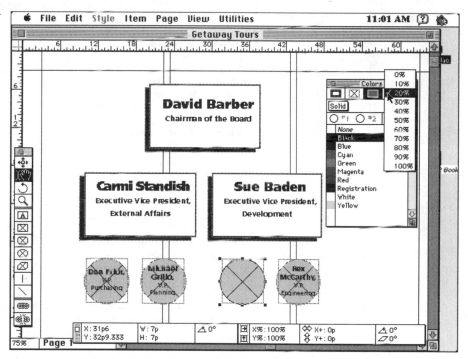

Figure 19-7: Using shades gives the second-level items a different feel from the first-level items.

Step 8.

Connecting elements with arrows and lines

To finish our simple organizational chart, we needed to add lines and arrows (see Figure 19-8). To add the arrows and lines that connect the top box with its two subordinate boxes, we used the Orthogonal Line tool to draw the horizontal sections of the lines. Then we drew the vertical sections. (We used the line-sizing handles to drag the lines to the correct size.) We used the line settings in the Measurements palette to set the line widths at 3 point in the Measurements palette and to add the arrowheads to the vertical sections of both lines. Note that the size we selected, 3 points, does not appear in the pick list of point sizes that would appear if you clicked the arrow button next between the W field and the current size (3 points). As with all QuarkXPress pick lists for point size, you can enter your own size rather than be limited to the common sizes displayed.

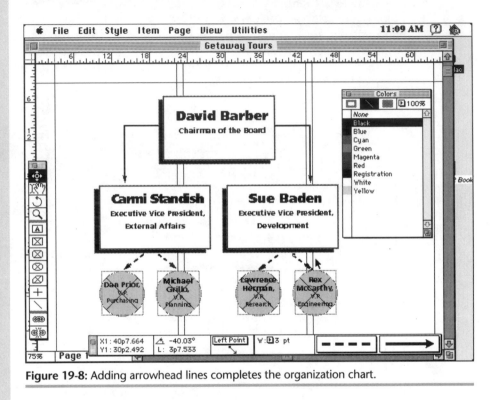

Figure 19-8: Adding arrowhead lines completes the organization chart.

To connect the elements in our simple organizational chart, we used the Diagonal Line drawing tool to draw the slanted lines. Then we used the line settings in the Measurements palette to select a dashed line with arrowheads and a width of 3 points.

If you use QuarkXPress to create simple graphics, you may occasionally want to group boxes and lines so that you can move them around on the page without altering their arrangement. To temporarily group items, hold down the Shift key and select the items you want to activate. This groups them together. To keep the selected items grouped, choose Item ⇨ Group, or ⌘G.

Creating a Bar Chart

With some of the same tools used to create the organizational chart in the preceding example, you can also create a bar chart.

To create the bar chart in Figure 19-9, we followed the Step and Repeat function (Item ⇨ Step and Repeat, or Option-⌘D), which is described in greater detail in Chapter 11. After duplicating the original picture box five times, we resized each picture box as appropriate using the Measurements palette to control the size. We also could have used vertical and horizontal guides from the ruler. (To drag guides from rulers, position the cursor in the vertical ruler and hold down the mouse button as you pull the guide into place. Do the same for the horizontal ruler. Then visually align the boxes to those guides or use the snap-to-guide feature — View ⇨ Snap to Guides — to have QuarkXPress help you ensure the correct alignment.) We then filled each picture box with a different shade percentage, from 10 to 60 percent.

To create the rest of the chart, we drew a text box to hold the years (1988, 1989, and so on). We added and formatted the text, used the Step and Repeat function to make five more copies, edited the text, and rotated the text boxes (individually, not as a group) 35 degrees before dragging them into position. Then we added the rules and text boxes for the values (at left). Figure 19-9 shows the final result.

 It can be difficult to line up small items — like the lines used as tick marks — with a mouse. Using the Measurements palette can also be cumbersome because you're often not sure of the precise X or Y coordinate to enter. QuarkXPress offers a third option: After you have selected a line or box with either the Content or Item tool, use the keyboard cursor keys to move the object one point at a time — up, left, right, or down. If you hold the Option key, you'll move the object a tenth of a point at a time.

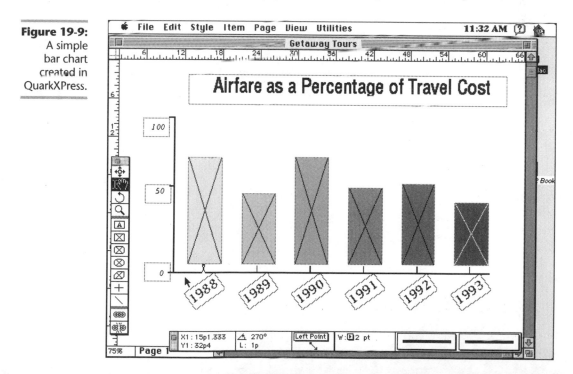

Figure 19-9:
A simple
bar chart
created in
QuarkXPress.

Summary

- You can create simple shapes using the QuarkXPress picture box tools (rectangular, rounded rectangular, oval, and polygon).

- You can use Background Color and Shade settings in the Picture Box Specifications dialog box to add color or texture to shapes.

- You can create lines and arrows, and you can specify the width and pattern of the lines.

- You can arrange elements in a layered stack and then bring elements forward or backward in the stack.

- For fine positioning control, you can use the keyboard's cursor keys to move objects one point at a time; hold down the Option key to move them a tenth of a point at a time.

Working with Bitmap Images

In This Chapter

- ⇥ Applying special effects to bitmap images
- ⇥ Changing the output of grays in bitmap images
- ⇥ Changing the line-screen settings of bitmap images
- ⇥ Choosing line-per-inch settings for output
- ⇥ Dithering an image
- ⇥ Changing the color and shade of bitmap images

Using Contrast Controls

QuarkXPress offers sophisticated ways of controlling bitmap images, and this is particularly true for gray-scale images. An important part of traditional publishing, gray-scale images are usually scanned photographs, but they can also be original artwork created by paint programs.

Through the Style menu, QuarkXPress offers the full contrast controls over gray-scale images that traditional publishers expect. But there's a catch: QuarkXPress offers these controls only for image files in the bitmap version of the Macintosh's native PICT format and in the TIFF format (Tagged Image File Format, originally developed by Aldus and Microsoft for Aldus's PageMaker software). For both file formats, the gray-scale control is available only if the image is an 8-bit gray-scale image (256 levels of gray). If the bit depth is less than 8 bits, you will not be able to alter the gray-scale output settings — such as posterizing the image or changing its brightness or contrast — from within QuarkXPress. For PICT files, you cannot create a negative image if the bit depth is less than 8 (256 levels) and more than 1 (black and white). This limitation does not apply to TIFF files.

Gray-scale TIFF and PICT files

When you work with 8-bit gray-scale TIFF and PICT bitmap files, you can apply any of several contrast filters that affect the levels of gray in the image. You also can create your own filter effects. In addition, you can control the output line screen, screen angle, and screen element (described in detail later in this chapter). You can apply colors and shades to your image, exchanging black for another color or shade. Figure 20-1 shows the options available for an 8-bit gray-scale TIFF or PICT file. The Style menu has a separate set of options for bitmap images when the Content tool is active and a picture box containing an image is selected.

The ability to apply shades to gray-scale TIFF images is new with version 3.3.

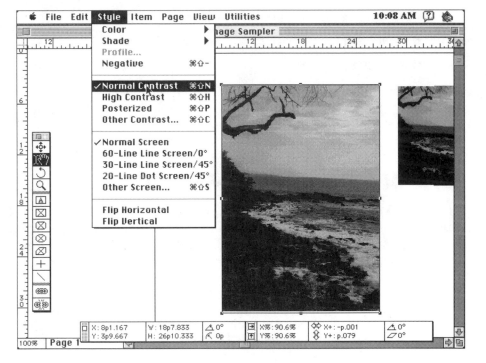

Figure 20-1: Image-control options for 8-bit gray-scale TIFF and PICT files.

Other bitmap files

With black-and-white bitmap files or those with a bit depth of less than 8 (including those in TIFF and PICT formats), you have no control over gray levels because there aren't any or there aren't enough. You do have the ability to create a negative image (exchange black for white and vice versa), but you cannot alter contrast. Other controls — including line screen, colors, and shades — are available, however. Figure 20-2 shows the image-control options available for black-and-white bitmap and low-gray-level images. As with non-8-bit gray-scale images, when you use color bitmap files, only one control is available in the Style menu: QuarkXPress allows you to create a negative image.

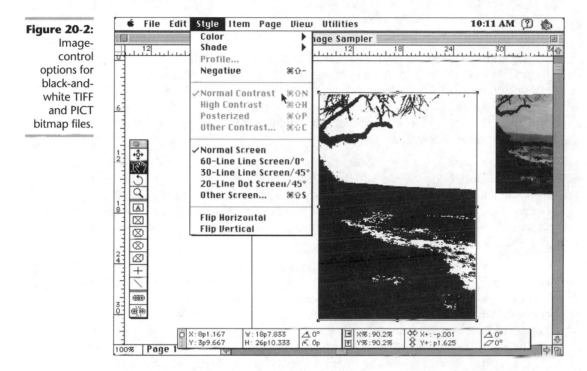

Figure 20-2: Image-control options for black-and-white TIFF and PICT bitmap files.

Getting the right file format

When you work with gray-scale images in formats other than TIFF or PICT, you must translate them to one of these formats. If you want to use any of QuarkXPress's image controls on, for example, PCX (PC Paintbrush) or BMP (Microsoft Windows bitmap) files from a PC, you must first convert them (through a program like DataViz's MacLinkPlus) or save them as 8-bit TIFF format in the originating application (such as Adobe Photoshop or Fractal Painter on either a Mac or PC, or PC-only applications such as Corel Photo-Paint or Aldus PhotoFinish) before bringing them into QuarkXPress. You can also use programs like Photoshop to read in some of these formats and then save them as TIFF or PICT. (You probably don't need a separate translation program if you use an image-editing program like Photoshop that support many formats for import.) This is true even for formats like PCX and JPEG that QuarkXPress can import directly, since these image controls are not available in QuarkXPress for other formats.

What's in a Gray Level?

The number of gray levels determines how natural an image looks. Each level is a percentage: the more levels there are, the more percentages of gray are used to display an image.

Having two levels means the image is black-and-white. Having 16 levels means that there is enough shading to make an image recognizably detailed. Having 256 shades is enough to make an image look realistic. Another way to think of it is like this: With 16 levels of gray, you can represent 0% black, 6.7%, 13.3%, 20%, and so on, up through 100% black. With 256 levels, you can represent 0% black, 0.4%, 0.8%, 1.2%, and so on, up through 100% black.

The human eye can barely detect such subtle jumps, which is why 256 levels is the most you'll find for gray-scale, whether it be for the images themselves or for the levels a monitor (even a color one that supports millions of colors) will display. The figure below shows the same images at several popular gray levels to make the differences apparent. You'll see the subtleties that higher gray levels allow in the clouds and along the shore.

The maximum number of levels corresponds to the image's bit depth, or color depth. Having 8 bits gives the computer 2^8 possible shades, or 256 levels. Having 4 bits gives it 2^4, or 16 levels. Note that an image in 8-bit format, such as a TIFF file saved in gray-scale mode in Adobe Photoshop, may have fewer than 256 levels of gray if effects like posterization were applied to it. In other words, if some gray levels are unused in an 8-bit file, the file nonetheless remains an 8-bit file. The bit depth determines the maximum number of levels; the image's visual characteristics determine how many levels are actually used.

256 LEVELS (MAXIMUM) 16 LEVELS 8 LEVELS 4 LEVELS 2 LEVELS (BLACK-AND-WHITE)

TIFF files come in many varieties. For best results, use an uncompressed TIFF format if it is available in your scanning or paint application. Files in this format can take a lot of disk space, so many users prefer to use a compressed version. The best of these is called LZW; QuarkXPress reads files in this format reliably (Version 3.1 of Windows QuarkXPress had some difficulties with this format, but the Mac version seems to have none).

PICT files also come in several varieties. Most PICT files are bitmaps with bit depths of 2 (black-and-white), 4 (16 levels of gray), or 8 (256 levels). Some are vector files (line art), similar to EPS files. PICT files created by image editing programs like Photoshop or by screen-capture programs like Mainstay's Capture are bitmap files.

Files in vector formats, such as EPS, can also contain bitmap images. These files print to the best resolution of the printer or to the resolution set in the program that created them. You must control output resolution and effects in the original illustration program because the publishing program cannot control these attributes for bitmaps embedded in vector files.

Table 20-1
Image Controls Available for Graphics

Image	Type	Negative	Contrast	Screen	Profile	Color	Shade
EPS, DCS	no	no	no	yes	no	no	
JPEG	no	no	no	no	yes	no	no
MacPaint	no	no	yes	yes	yes	yes	
PCX	no	no	no	no	yes	no	no
Photo CD	no	no	no	yes	no	no	
PICT							
color bitmap	yes	yes	no	yes	no	no	
vector	no	no	no	yes	no	no	
8-bit gray-scale bitmap	yes	yes	yes	yes	yes	no	
low-gray bitmap	no	no	no	yes	no	no	
black-and-white bitmap	no	no	yes	yes	yes	yes	
TIFF, RIFF							
color	no	no	no	yes	no	no	
8-bit gray-scale	yes	yes	yes	yes	yes	no	
low-gray	yes	yes	yes	yes	yes	no	
black-and-white	yes	no	yes	yes	yes	yes	

NOTE: A low-gray image is one with fewer than 256 levels of gray (8-bit) but more than black-and-white (1-bit).

Save bitmap files — whether gray-scale, color, or black-and-white — in the size that you intend to use for layout. Enlarging a bitmap more than 20 to 50 percent can result in a blocky-looking image, as illustrated in Figure 20-3, which shows two images (one black-and-white, one gray-scale) enlarged by 235 percent. The poor image results because the pixels that make up the image are enlarged along with the image itself. Reducing a bitmap doesn't cause such problems, but this reduction wastes disk space and processing time because the file contains more information than is needed when printed.

Figure 20-3:
These bitmapped images, enlarged to 235 percent, look blocky because the pixels that make up the images are enlarged along with the images themselves.

For more information on TIFF and other file formats, see Chapter 4 and Chapter 7.

Contrast controls explained

All controls over bitmap images reside in the Style menu. To access these options, activate the Content tool, select the picture box containing the image you want to alter, and then select Style. The Style menu displays a different set of options when a picture box is selected than it does when a text box is selected (described in Chapters 12 through 17).

The Style menu offers five controls — called contrast filters — over gray levels. In all of the following examples, the Figures display both the image and the Picture Contrast Specifications dialog box. In reality, this dialog box appears only if you select Other Contrast. We included the dialog box in the Figures to clarify how to create or modify a filter and to show you the actual settings used for each filter.

- **Negative (Shift-⌘– [Shift-⌘hyphen]):** This swaps black with white, causing a photographic-negative effect. Figure 20-4 shows how an image appears with the Negative filter applied.

Figure 20-4:
A gray-scale image with the Negative filter applied.

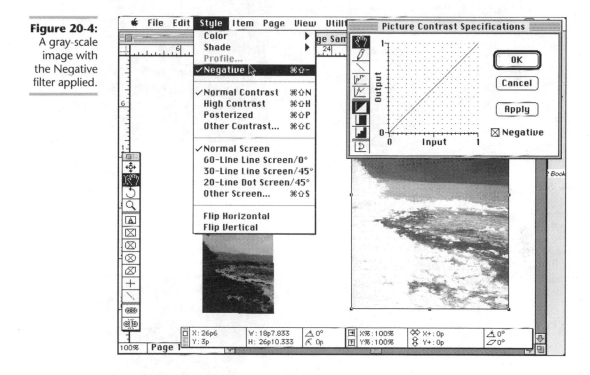

- **Normal Contrast (Shift-⌘N):** Selecting this setting returns an image to the original settings defined in the source file. Figure 20-5 shows how the image in Figure 20-4 appears normally. Use this option if you change the settings and decide that you don't like the results.

- **High Contrast (Shift-⌘H):** If you choose the High Contrast setting, QuarkXPress turns any part of the image that is 30 percent gray or darker into 100 percent black. It makes anything lighter than 30 percent gray into 0 percent black — in other words, it makes that part of the image transparent (it usually appears as white unless the picture box has a background color). Figure 20-6 shows how the image in Figure 20-5 appears with the High Contrast filter applied.

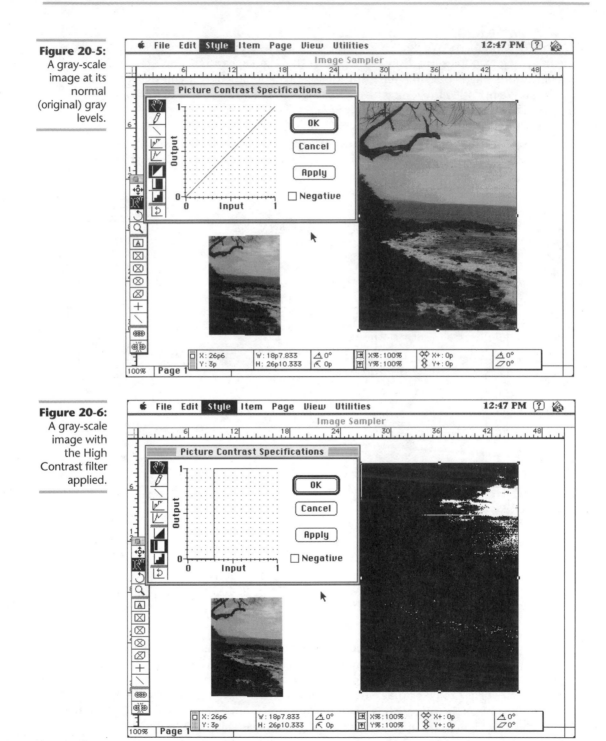

Figure 20-5:
A gray-scale image at its normal (original) gray levels.

Figure 20-6:
A gray-scale image with the High Contrast filter applied.

⌒ **Posterized (Shift-⌘P):** This setting gathers groups of gray levels and makes them all the same level. In effect, this reduces the number of different gray levels and creates a banding effect. Figure 20-7 shows how the original image shown in Figure 20-5 appears with the posterization filter applied. The figure in the sidebar "What's in a Gray Level?" shows the same image at different gray levels, which also lets you compare different amounts of posterization.

Figure 20-7:
A gray-scale image with the posterization filter applied.

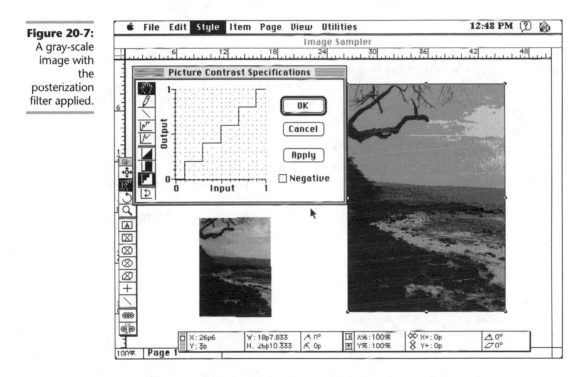

⌒ **Other Contrast (Shift-⌘C):** The Other Contrast setting lets you create your own filter or modify one of the previously mentioned filters. When you use this setting, the Picture Contrast Specifications dialog box appears.

Make sure the Content tool is selected; otherwise, these filter options will be grayed out.

How filters work

Essentially, a contrast filter tells QuarkXPress how to print each level of gray. When you set the gray-level control to Normal Contrast, the program prints each level of gray as it exists in the original graphic. In the Picture Contrast Specifications dialog box, you see a diagonal line when you choose the Normal Contrast setting (refer to Figure 20-5). That line, technically called a *gamma curve,* describes the relationship between the input gray level and the output gray level — the difference between what QuarkXPress *sees* when it reads the original graphic and what it actually prints.

If you refer again to Figure 20-6, you see that when you choose High Contrast, the line in the dialog box goes abruptly from 0 percent black (for all gray values up to 30 percent) to 100 percent black (for all values greater than 30 percent).

Similarly, when you choose Posterized (see Figure 20-7), the line appears as a series of steps. These steps correspond to the banding that results when QuarkXPress groups a range of grays into one gray level for output (everything from 0 to 10 percent prints as 0 percent black; everything from 10 percent to 30 percent prints as 20 percent, and so on).

The line for the Negative filter (see Figure 20-4) appears to be the same as for the Normal Contrast filter. The difference is that the Negative box (at the bottom right of the Picture Contrast Specifications dialog box) is checked. Selecting the Negative box tells QuarkXPress to reverse the gray-scale relationships — to use the opposite, or negative, of the line displayed in the picture box. You can achieve the same effect by drawing the gamma curve line from the upper left of the grid to the bottom right and deselecting the Negative box.

Custom gray-level settings

The Picture Contrast Specifications dialog box, which you open by selecting Style ➪ Other Contrast, includes several icons along its left side. Using these icons, you can establish custom gray-level settings by drawing your own gamma curve line. From top to bottom, the icons and their uses are as follows:

➪ The grabber (hand) icon lets you move the entire line in any direction, which is useful for shifting all gray-level mappings at once. For example, shifting the line upward darkens the entire image because lighter input values are mapped to darker output values. Moving the line with the grabber hand results in a consistent image even though gray levels are shifted.

➪ The pencil icon lets you draw your own line, which is handy if you want to experiment.

➪ The line icon causes node points on the line to appear so that you can move them. It works similarly to an arrow tool applied to points on a polygon or curve in a graphic program. This is useful for editing existing lines, especially those that have discontinuities between points (such as in the high-contrast filter).

- The modified-step icon lets you select increments on the line and move them as a group. The selected segment between two points on the line moves. This icon is helpful when editing posterization settings.

- The modify-line icon lets you select any point on the line and move it. Like the line icon, this icon is helpful for editing existing lines, particularly if the changes are not discontinuous.

- The Normal, High Contrast, and Posterized line icons all reset the gray-level settings to the defaults for those standard options.

- The swap-axis icon lets you put the input axis at the left of the grid and the output axis at the bottom. This is beneficial if you are used to editing gamma curves oriented in the transverse direction of QuarkXPress's default orientation.

You can use several different tools to edit the same line. You also can use the Negative check box with any kind of line. Even though the line appears the same on-screen, checking the Negative box has the effect of flipping the gray-level map horizontally (so that left and right are swapped).

The section "Contrast Settings" in the "Advanced Color Techniques" full-color insert shows the effects of applying these settings on colored images.

Because you can fundamentally alter the character of an image by editing its gray-level map, QuarkXPress lets you preview the effects of your edits via the Apply button. Figure 20-8 shows the use of several effects, mostly by modifying the gamma curve with the modify-line and modify-step tools at various points on the curve. Use the Apply button to preview your changes before deciding whether to implement them. QuarkXPress actually implements your changes only if you choose OK.

Photo-editing programs like Photoshop offer many more sophisticated options for image manipulation. Most people use Photoshop and an excellent resource is *Macworld Photoshop 2.5 Bible* by Deke McClelland.

If, after editing a gray-level map, you want to return the image to a more common gray-level map, you can use the standard options on the Style menu or reenter the dialog box and use one of the default-setting icons (Normal, Posterized, or High Contrast). This kind of change is possible because QuarkXPress does not actually modify your source image but simply retains a set of instructions generated by your contrast settings. It applies these settings to the output image while printing but never applies them to the source image itself.

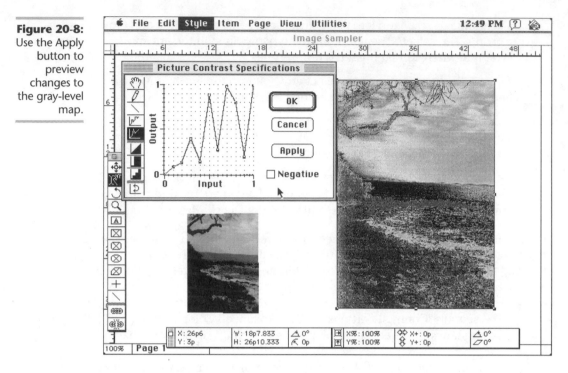

Figure 20-8:
Use the Apply
button to
preview
changes to
the gray-level
map.

Using Line-Screen Controls

Most people never worry about line screens (in fact, many desktop publishers don't know what they are), but they can have a profound effect on how your bitmap images print. Many artists use line-screen controls to add a whole new feel to an image.

In traditional printing, a line screen is an acetate mask covered with a grid of spots. Printers use such a device to convert a continuous-tone image like a photograph into the series of spots, called a *halftone*, which is required to reproduce such an image on a printing press. (Color images use four sets of spots, one each for cyan, magenta, yellow, and black. The process of filtering out each of these colors is called *four-color separation,* which is described more fully in Chapters 21 and 26.) Take a magnifying glass to a photo — either color or black-and-white — in a newspaper or magazine, and you'll see the spots that the photo is made of. These spots are usually dots, but they can be any of several shapes.

When making a halftone in the traditional way, a line-screen mask is placed on top of a piece of photographic paper (such as Kodak's RC paper, used for decades in traditional photography). The continuous-tone original is then illuminated in a camera so that the image is projected through the mask onto the photographic paper. The photographic paper is exposed only where the mask is transparent (in the grid holes, or spots), producing the spots that make up the image to be printed. The size of each spot depends on how much light passes through, which in turn depends on how dark or light each area of the original image is. Think of a window screen through which you spray water: the stronger the spray, the bigger the spots behind the screen's holes.

The spots that make up the image are arranged in a series of lines, usually at a 45-degree angle (this angle helps the eye blend the individual spots to simulate a continuous tone). The number of lines per inch (or *halftone frequency*) determines the maximum dot size as well as the coarseness (*halftone density*) of the image (thus the term *line screen*). The spots in the mask need not be circular — they can be ellipses, squares, lines, or more esoteric shapes like stars. These shapes are called *screen elements*. Circular dots are the most common type because they result in the least distortion of the image.

When your source image is electronic, how do you create the series of black spots needed to mimic continuous gray tones? Desktop publishing programs use mathematical algorithms that simulate the traditional piece of photographic line screen. Because the process is controlled by a set of equations, desktop publishing programs such as QuarkXPress offer more options than traditional line screens, which come in a fixed set of halftone frequencies and with a limited set of elements.

Effects of line-screen settings

Seeing is believing when it comes to special graphics effects, so you'll want to experiment with line-screen settings before going to press with your document.

 Special graphics effects are available only for PostScript printers because other types of printers (such as QuickDraw printers) do not have the correct controls in their internal computers to do the calculations required to achieve these effects.

In most cases, you should use Normal Screen, which is the default for all imported images. The default line-screen frequency for Normal Screen is set in the File menu's Page Setup dialog box through the Halftone Screen option. The default screen angle is 45 degrees, and the default screen element is a dot; neither of these defaults can be changed.

Understanding lpi

Lines per inch (lpi) and dots per inch (dpi) are not related because the spots in a line screen are variable-sized while dots in a laser printer are fixed-sized. (Because newer printers using techniques like Hewlett-Packard's Resolution Enhancement Technology or Apple Computer's FinePrint and PhotoGrade use variable-sized dots, the distinction may disappear one day.) Lines per inch specifies, in essence, the grid through which an image is filtered, not the size of the spots that make it up. Dots per inch specifies the number of ink dots per inch produced by the laser printer; these dots are typically the same size. A 100-lpi image with variable sized dots will therefore appear finer than a 100-dpi image.

Depending upon the size of the line-screen spot, several of a printer's fixed-sized dots may be required to simulate one line-screen spot. For this reason, a printer's or imagesetter's lpi is far less than its dpi. For example, a 300-dpi laser printer can achieve about 60-lpi resolution; a 1270-dpi imagesetter can achieve about 120-lpi resolution; a 2540-dpi imagesetter about 200-lpi resolution. Resolutions of less than 100 lpi are considered coarse, and resolutions of more than 120 lpi are considered fine.

But there's more to choosing an lpi setting than knowing your output device's top resolution. An often overlooked issue is the type of paper the material is printed on. Smoother paper (such as *glossy-coated* or *super-calendared)* can handle finer halftone spots because the paper's coating (also called its *finish)* minimizes ink bleeding. Standard office paper, such as that used in photocopiers and laser printers, is rougher and has some bleed that is usually noticeable only if you write on it with markers. Newsprint is very rough and has a heavy bleed. Typically, newspaper images are printed at 85 to 90 lpi; newsletter images on standard office paper print at 100 to 110 lpi; magazine images are printed at 120 to 150 lpi; calendars and coffee-table art books are printed at 150 to 200 lpi.

Other factors affecting lpi include the type of printing press and the type of ink used. Your printer representative should advise you on preferred settings.

If you output your document from your computer directly to film negatives (rather than to photographic paper that is then shot to create negatives), inform your printer representative. Outputting to negatives allows a higher lpi than outputting to paper because negatives created photographically cannot accurately reproduce the fine resolution that negatives that output directly on an imagesetter have. (If, for example, you output to 120 lpi on paper and then create a photographic negative, even the slightest change in the camera's focus will make the fine dots blurry. Outputting straight to negatives avoids this problem.) Printer representatives often assume that you are outputting to paper and base their advised lpi settings on this assumption.

But when you want to do something special, you can. As a rule, most people using line-screen effects prefer coarser halftone frequencies to make the image coarser but bolder. They usually also change the screen element to a line or other shape to alter the image's character. In acknowledgment of this tendency, QuarkXPress predefines three line-screen settings that you can apply directly from the Style menu:

- **Normal Screen:** This setting uses the defaults defined via File ⇨ Printer Setup (see Chapter 26).

- **60-lpi Line Screen/0°:** This setting creates a 60-line-per-inch (lpi) halftone frequency, using lines aligned at 0 degrees (horizontal) as the screen element.

- **30-lpi Line Screen/45°:** This sets a 30-lpi halftone frequency using lines aligned at 45 degrees as the screen element.

- **20-lpi Dot Screen/45°:** This sets a 20-line-per-inch halftone frequency using dots aligned at 45 degrees.

None of these options has a keyboard shortcut.

 If one of the line-screen settings has already been applied to an image, a check mark appears to the left of the appropriate icon.

The last option available from the Style menu is Other Screen, which lets you define any combination of frequency, element, and angle you want. Selecting this option (also available via the shortcut Shift-⌘S) opens the Picture Screening Specifications dialog box. Figure 20-9 shows this dialog box; behind it is a view of an image set at 30 lpi with a line screen element at 45 degrees. (You cannot preview your settings; here we applied the settings and reinvoked the dialog box to show the settings and their effects simultaneously.)

 If a user-defined screening specification is applied to an image, a check mark appears to the left of the Other Screen option in the Style menu.

You can see on-screen the effects of the settings you make. If you check the Display Halftoning box in the Picture Screening Specifications dialog box, QuarkXPress displays the image with the screening specifications applied. This helps you see how your settings affect the image, and it also helps you remember which images have special screening affects applied to them. If this box is unchecked, the image will not change on-screen, but it will print with the new screening specifications.

 Because of limits in monitor resolutions, QuarkXPress cannot display halftone frequencies finer than 60 lpi, which is the default setting for 300-dpi laser printers. If you use a finer halftone frequency, QuarkXPress displays the image at the best resolution available for your monitor. You can tell if a special line screen is applied, even if you can't exactly determine the setting.

To gauge the effects of different line-screen elements, compare Figures 20-9 through 20-12. All are set at 30 lpi, and all are viewed at 300 percent so that the differences are magnified. Figure 20-10 shows the effects of using dots as the screen element. Figure 20-11 shows a line screen with ellipses as the screen element. In Figure 20-12, squares are used as the screen element. In all four figures, the screen elements are arranged at a 45-degree angle.

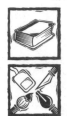

The section "Screening Controls" in the "Advanced Color Techniques" full-color insert shows other examples in color of how these controls affect output.

We recommend that you create a sample page that has a series of strips set for different line screens and line elements. You can accomplish this by taking the steps that follow after these figures.

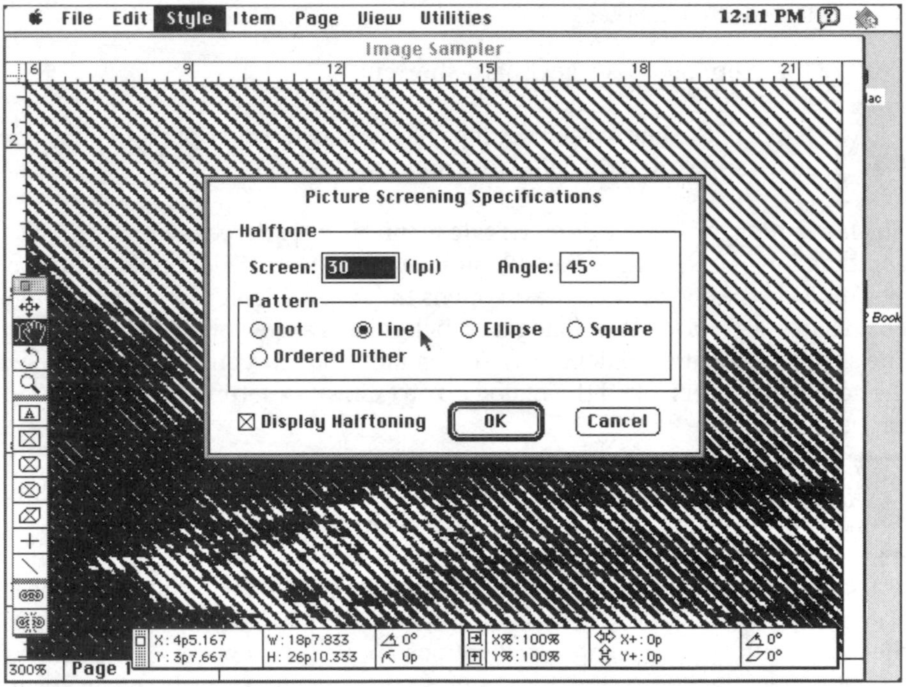

Figure 20-9:
The Picture Screening Specifications lets you set all screen controls. Here, the image is set at 30 lpi, with lines arranged at 45 degrees used as the screen element.

Figure 20-10:
A screen that uses dots as the screen element.

Figure 20-11:
A screen that uses ellipses as the screen element.

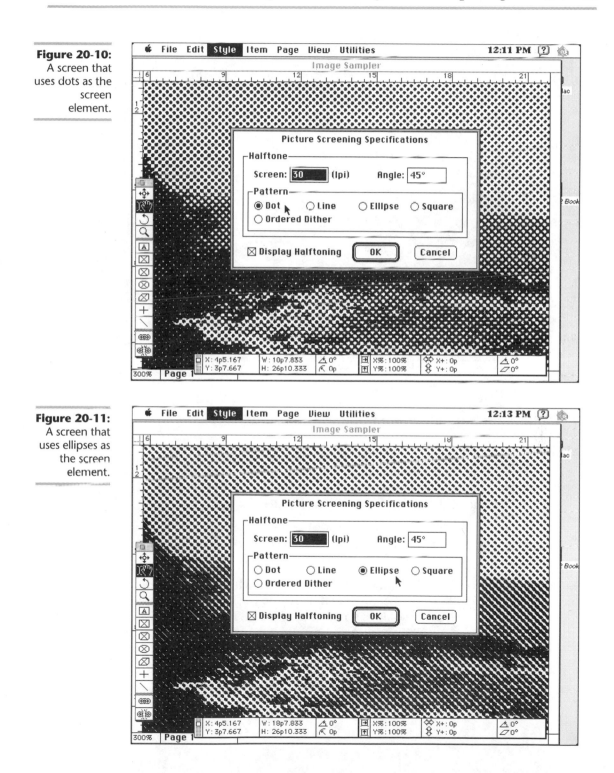

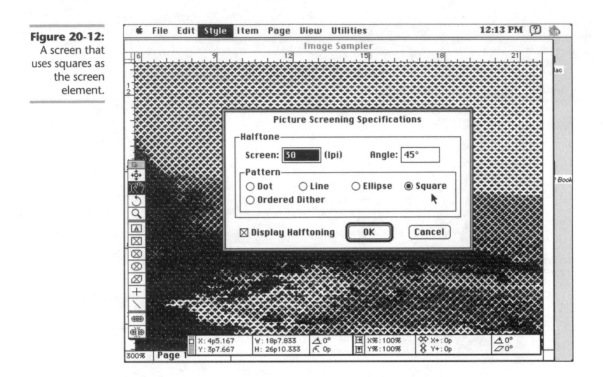

Figure 20-12:
A screen that
uses squares as
the screen
element.

STEPS: Creating a Sample Page of Lines and Screens

Step 1. In an image-editing program, create a gray-scale TIFF file that has a smooth gradient from white to black. The image in this file should be shaped like a long rectangle, either horizontal or vertical, with the gradient going from one end to the other along the longest axis.

Step 2. Import this object into a QuarkXPress document's picture box and then duplicate that box several times, placing each duplicate next to the previous one. You now have a series of gradient strips.

Step 3. Use the Style ⇨ Other Screen option to set each strip at a different line-screen setting. We recommend that you do this at least for common line-screen frequency settings (such as 20, 30, 60, 85, 110, 120, 133, and 150). You can then copy all these picture boxes to a new page and change the screen element for each (which you must do one at a time). Likewise, you can do the same for different screen angles.

Step 4. Output these pages on a 2540-dpi imagesetter.

Calculating Halftone Scans and Output

One of the most difficult concepts in black-and-white publishing to implement is picking the right dpi setting when scanning gray-scale (and color) artwork. You scan in fixed-size dots per inch (dpi), but you output to film in lines per inch (lpi) composed of variable-sized dots. There's also a relationship between both the dpi and the lpi and the number of gray levels you can scan and print, respectively.

First, here's how to figure out the right scan resolution (*dpi*) for your scans: The simplest way is to multiply the screen frequency (*lpi*) you plan to output to by 2: $lpi \times 2 = dpi$. This assumes that you're scanning the image in at the same size it will be reproduced. If you intend to change the size, the math gets trickier: Multiply the longest dimension of the final size (*lf*) by the screen frequency (*lpi*), and multiply this result by 2. Divide the result by the longest dimension of the original size (*lo*): $(lpi \times lf \times 2) \div lo = dpi$. (If the number is not a whole number, round up to the nearest whole number; for example, treat a dpi result of 312.32 as 313.) Note that if you're outputting to coarse paper, such as newsprint, you can use a smaller multiplier than 2. But don't go lower than $\sqrt{2}$ (equal to about 1.4).

Second, here's how to figure out the needed resolution from your imagesetter to achieve the output screen frequency (*lpi*) your printing press is set for: $lpi \times 16 =$ imagesetter's required dpi. Thus, for magazine-quality frequencies of 133 and 150 lpi, you would need to ensure the imagesetter outputs at 2540 dpi (the 133-lpi setting requires an output dpi of 2128 dpi — that's $133 \times 16 = 2128$ — and the 150-pi setting requires 2400). So why 2540 dpi? Because that's the standard high-resolution setting for most imagesetters; the other standard setting, used mostly for text-only documents, is 1270 dpi. At 2540 dpi, the highest lpi you can achieve is 158¾.

Last, here's how to figure out how many gray levels you'll actually get when printing, based on the imagesetter's output resolution (*dpi*) and output screen frequency (*lpi*): $(dpi \div lpi)^2 + 1 =$ gray levels. Thus, an imagesetter set for 2540 dpi and a QuarkXPress document setup for 133 lpi screening frequency can produce 365 — more than enough for most images. (To get that number, the math is $(2540 \div 133)^2 + 1$, or $19.1^2 + 1$, or $364.7 + 1$, or 365 after rounding.) At 150 lpi, that means 287 gray levels. At an output resolution of 1270 dpi, you would get 92 gray levels at 133 lpi and 72 gray levels at 150 lpi. It may seem counterintuitive that the higher lpi setting results in fewer grays, but it's true. The trade-off you make is that at the higher lpi settings, the image seems smoother, but lower lpi settings give you greater gray-scale fidelity.

 Two other sidebars in this chapter — "What's in a Gray Level?" and "Understanding lpi" — cover related issues.

You can use the resulting guide to see the effects of various line-screen settings on the entire range of gray values, from white to black. You can also create a similar guide using a sample gray-scale photo.

Dithering

An effect related to halftone screening is called *dithering*. Dithering means replacing gray levels with a varying pattern of black and white. This pattern does not attempt to simulate grays; instead, it merely tries to retain some distinction between shades in an image when the image is output to a printer that does not have fine enough resolution to reproduce grays (through the fine grid of dots used in screening to reproduce each gray shade). In other words, dithering uses coarse patterns of dots and lines to represent the basic details in a gray-scale image. A set of mathematical equations determines how the dithered pattern appears for each image. The basic technique is to replace dark shades with all black, medium shades with alternating black and white dots or lines, and light shades with a sparse pattern of dots or lines.

There are many such sets of equations; QuarkXPress uses one called *ordered dithering*, which you select by choosing Ordered Dither in the Picture Screening Specifications dialog box. Figure 20-13 shows the dialog box and an image to which ordered dithering is applied. We've placed the normal image (using the default settings for screen frequency and elements) at the left; the dithered version is at right. To apply other dithering equations, you must dither the image in a paint or graphics program that supports dithering before importing the image into QuarkXPress.

Figure 20-13:
The Ordered Dither option converts gray-scale images (left) into coarse patterned black-and-white images (right) for output to low-resolution printers.

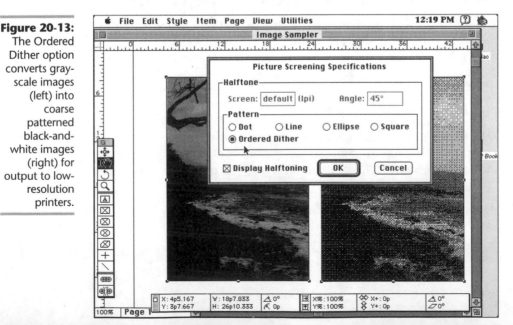

With dithering, there are no controls available for halftone frequency or screen-element angle because these elements are determined by the dithering equations.

You can use dithering to simulate a wood-cut or pointillism effect. Otherwise, use dithering only if your printer has less then a 300-dpi resolution.

Using Color and Shade Controls ____

Even if you don't alter gray levels or screening, you can still alter the way in which gray-scale and black-and-white bitmap graphics print by using QuarkXPress color and shade controls, available through the Style menu.

Color and shade controls do not work with color images or with vector images (such as EPS and some forms of PICT) because they are meant to add color and shades to black-and-white and gray-scale images. The assumption is that such color changes should be done in a color graphics program. The shade controls work only with black-and-white bitmap images and with gray-scale TIFF images.

Through the Style menu's Color option, you can replace the black parts of an image — including grays, which after all are simply percentages of black — with a color. Figure 20-14 shows the secondary menu that appears when you highlight the Color option on the Style menu. Any colors defined in the document appear in the list of colors. (Chapter 21 describes colors in depth.)

Likewise, you can make the image lighter by applying a shade through Style ➪ Shade. Figure 20-15 shows how a black-and-white image appears with a 40 percent shade applied. You are not limited to the shade percentages displayed in the Shade drop-down menu. By choosing Other, you can set any percentage from 0 to 100, in 0.1 percent increments.

The section "Using Color Tints" in the "Advanced Color Techniques" full-color insert shows the use of different tint settings on final output.

Figure 20-14:
Through Style
⇨ Color, you
can apply
colors to black-
and-white or
gray-scale
images. In this
figure, the
image is being
colored as
Pantone 148-3.

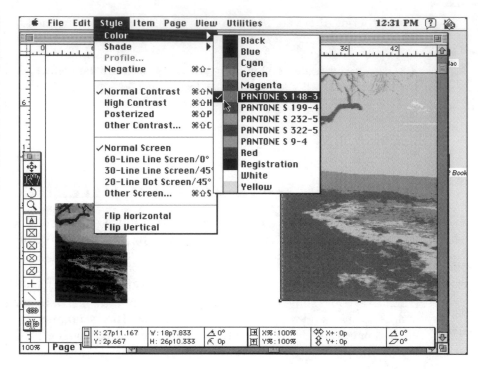

Figure 20-15:
A black-and-
white image
with a 40
percent shade
applied via
Style ⇨ Shade.

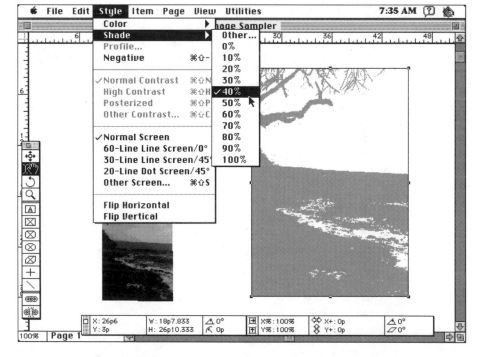

Version 3.3 of QuarkXPress allows you to apply a shade to a gray-scale TIFF image. For example, if you applied a 40 percent shade to a scanned photo, each gray level would appear at 40 percent of its original level, so the image remains faithful to the original value ratios, even though it prints that much lighter. This effect is handy when you want to have text overprint a photograph or other image. In earlier versions of QuarkXPress, you can't apply a shade to a gray-scale image in earlier versions. But there is a workaround: define a color that is simply the percentage of black you want (what shade of gray) and then apply that gray "color" to your image. Figure 20-16 shows the result of this technique, with a 40 percent shade applied to the photo used throughout this chapter's examples.

Figure 20-16:
A gray-scale image with a 40 percent black shade applied via Style ⇨ Color. With QuarkXPress version 3.3, you can use Style ⇨ Shade to achieve the same effect.

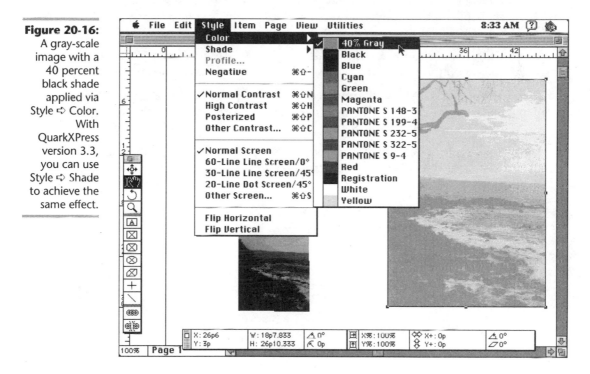

You can combine the Color and Shade options. You can print an image at 30 percent magenta, for example, over a solid cyan background (for the picture box), which would give you a surrealistic blend of magenta and cyan. You can also apply other effects, such as gray-level filters and screen settings, to the same image.

A new Style menu option, Profile, lets you apply a different color profile to an image to enhance its output based on the type of production and printing process to be used. This feature is covered in detail in Chapter 22. Like the other features covered in this chapter, it affects only the output, not the original image. However, the Profile feature (part of the EfiColor XTension) applies to both bitmap and vector images, unlike the other features covered in this chapter.

Summary

➡ You can modify gray levels for 8-bit gray-scale TIFF and PICT files only.

➡ You can apply only the Negative filter to color bitmaps and to bitmaps whose bit depth is less than 8.

➡ Images that have gray-level filters applied can be reset to their original settings or to other settings at any time.

➡ You can modify line-screen settings for any gray-scale or black-and-white bitmap files. Line-screen settings are available only if you use a PostScript printer.

➡ Your monitor cannot display line-screen frequencies finer than 60 lpi, so be sure to output samples before using finer screens on final documents.

➡ The appropriate lpi settings for a document depend on the printer, the paper, and other press-related factors. Make sure the representative at your printing plant knows how you create your negatives, as this affects the advice you get.

➡ Shade controls affect an image uniformly. Typically, shading is used to lighten an image so that text can be overprinted on it. Color controls, whether used alone or with shade controls, often are used for the same effect.

Color Publishing

Color adds a dimension to the printed page that should not be underestimated. Although you can create highly pleasing documents with just black and white, people react viscerally to color. Color is what they see every day; color in a document suggests a stronger sense of reality.

With version 3.2, QuarkXPress made a huge leap in color publishing by offering the color calibration features of Electronics for Imaging's EfiColor XTension. This program helps ensure the truest possible reproduction of color images on all sorts of output devices with images created on all sorts of monitors or scanners.

Using color can be tricky, and many of the QuarkXPress features are best left to experienced professionals. Understanding the program's capabilities, however, will help even a novice work effectively with illustrators and service bureaus to ensure the best possible output.

This section covers the whole range of the QuarkXPress color features, beginning with those capabilities that most users will work with. The second chapter covers the high-end features — trapping and EfiColor calibration — in a way that explains the concepts to beginners but provides a lot of detail and advice for professionals. In both chapters in this section, you'll find sidebars offering advice on how to work with color across the publishing process, not just within QuarkXPress. Also look for the 8-page full-color instructional gallery that shows the effects of using the QuarkXPress high-end color tools.

Defining and Applying Color

In This Chapter

- ➭ Setting QuarkXPress color controls
- ➭ Understanding process color vs. spot color
- ➭ Defining colors
- ➭ Applying colors to pictures and layout elements
- ➭ Creating color blends

Although color is most widely used by high-end publishers — people producing magazines and catalogs — color is becoming more accessible to all publishers, thanks to the recent emergence of color printers, color copiers, and leading-edge desktop publishing programs. Whether you want to produce limited-run documents on a color printer, create newsletters using spot colors, or publish magazines and catalogs using process colors and special inks, QuarkXPress offers the tools that you need to do the job well.

You can either use color in your graphics or apply colors to text and layout elements (such as bars along the edge of a page). Or you can use color in both ways. To a great extent, where you define and apply color determines what you can do with it.

 If you're doing professional-quality color production, such as a color catalog printed on a standard web offset printing press, QuarkXPress includes the EfiColor XTension from Electronics for Imaging that lets you calibrate the output against the input source (such as monitor or scanner) and the output target (such as the printing press or color printer). Chapter 22 covers EfiColor and other high-end color issues in depth. This chapter concentrates on how to create and apply colors within QuarkXPress.

Process Color Versus Spot Color

Several forms of color are used in printing, but the two basic ones are *process color* and *spot color.*

Process color refers to the use of four basic colors — cyan, magenta, yellow, and black (known as a group as *CMYK*) — that are mixed to reproduce most color tones the human eye can see. A separate negative is produced for each of the four process colors. This method, often called *four-color publishing,* is used for most color publishing.

Spot color refers to any color — whether one of the process colors or some other hue — used for specific elements in a document. For example, if you print a document in black ink but print the company logo in red, the red is a spot color. A spot color is often called a *second color* even though you can use several spot colors in a document. Each spot color is output to its own negative (and not color-separated into CMYK).

 Using spot color gives you access to special inks that are truer to the desired color than any mix of process colors can be. These inks come in several standards, with Pantone being the most popular. (The Pantone system is also called *PMS color* — the full name is *Pantone Matching System.* Pantone has several variants, each designed for different types of paper, such as coated and uncoated.) Trumatch, Focoltone, Toyo, and DIC (Dainippon Ink & Chemical) are less popular but still common standards, with Trumatch used mainly in the U.S., Focoltone in Europe, and Toyo and DIC (added in QuarkXPress version 3.3) in Japan. QuarkXPress supports all five standards. For Pantone, it supports four variants (these variants are new to QuarkXPress 3.2).

Spot-color inks can produce some colors that are impossible to achieve with process colors, such as metallics, neons, and milky pastels. You even can use varnishes as spot colors to give layout elements a different gleam than the rest of the page. Although experienced designers sometimes mix spot colors to produce special shades not otherwise available, it's unlikely that you will need to do so.

Some designers use both process and spot colors in a document — known as *using a fifth color.* Typically, the normal color images are color-separated and printed via the four process colors while a special element (such as a logo in metallic ink) is printed in a spot color. The process colors are output on the usual four negatives; the spot color is output on a separate, fifth negative and printed using a fifth plate, fifth ink roller, and fifth ink well. You can use more than five colors; you are limited only by your budget and the capabilities of your printing plant.

QuarkXPress can convert spot colors to process colors. This handy capability allows designers to specify the colors they want through a system they're familiar with, such as Pantone, without the added expense of special spot-color inks and extra negatives.

Conversions are never an exact match, but there are now guidebooks that can show you in advance the color that will be created. With Pantone Process variation (which QuarkXPress supports), designers can now pick a Pantone color that will color-separate predictably.

If you use Pantone colors, we suggest that you get a copy of the *Pantone Process Color Imaging Guide: CMYK Edition* swatchbook, available from several sources, including art and printing supply stores, mail order catalogs, and Pantone itself. This swatchbook shows each Pantone color and the CMYK equivalent so that you can see how accurate the conversion will be and thus, whether you want to use the actual Pantone ink on its own negative or convert to CMYK.

You can set QuarkXPress to convert some spot colors in a document to process colors while leaving others alone. Or you can leave all spot colors as spot colors.

Working with Color Pictures

When you work with imported graphics, whether they are illustrations or scanned photographs, color is part of the graphic file. So the responsibility for color controls lies primarily with the creator of the picture. It is best to use color files in CMYK EPS or DCS format (for illustrations) or CMYK TIFF format (for scans and bitmaps). RGB EPS and RGB TIFF files also work, but the RGB-to-CMYK conversion may result in color shifts. (RGB is color created by combining red, green, and blue. This is the standard color model used by scanners and graphics software because monitors use red, green, and blue electron guns to display images.) These standards are de facto for color publishing, so QuarkXPress is particularly adept at working with them. (See Chapter 7 for details on preparing graphics files for import.)

If you create files in EPS format, do any required color trapping in the source application. (Trapping for elements created in QuarkXPress is covered in Chapter 22.)

 If you're using QuarkXPress version 3.2, be sure to define any Pantone or other spot colors used in your graphic in your QuarkXPress document as well (this process is explained later in this chapter). Otherwise, the spot colors will not be color-separated when you output color separations. An alternative, if you intend to separate process colors as CMYK, is simply to define your colors as CMYK colors in the program that you use to create the EPS file. (Version 3.3 automatically imports color definitions from EPS files, so this step is not necessary. Also, the ColorManager XTension bundled with this book can import EPS color definitions in QuarkXPress 3.2; Chapter 27 details this XTension.)

Not all programs encode color information the same way. If you create EPS files in some illustration programs, colors may not print as expected. One of three things can happen:

℞ Each color prints on its own plate (as if it were a spot color), even if you defined it as a process color.

℞ A spot color is color-separated into CMYK even when you define it as a spot color in both the source program and in QuarkXPress.

℞ A color prints as black.

Color TIFF files do not cause such peculiarities; however, only those files saved in CMYK TIFF format can be color-separated. (If you have installed the EfiColor XTension, you can color-separate RGB TIFF files as well.)

After you import a color graphic, you can do little to it other than resize or crop it. For all graphics files, you can change the EfiColor profile. In addition, for PICT bitmaps, you can create a negative of the image and apply various contrast filters using the options in the Style menu, as described in Chapter 20.

 Color files pasted via the clipboard should print properly after they are pasted into a QuarkXPress picture box. But problems do sometimes occur, such as dropped colors or altered colors, depending on the applications involved and the amount of memory available.

Working with Color Layout Elements

More color controls exist for layout elements that you create in QuarkXPress than for imported graphics. You can do the following:

℞ Apply color to specific text

℞ Apply colors to imported gray-scale and black-and-white bitmaps (see Chapter 20)

℞ Add color backgrounds to text and picture boxes

℞ Add color borders to boxes

℞ Apply color to ruling lines associated with text and to lines drawn with the line tools

In addition, by using empty picture boxes (boxes with no pictures imported into them) as shapes, you can create simple graphics to which you can apply colors.

Defining Colors

Before you can apply any colors — to bitmap images or to layout elements — you must first define the colors. You can also define their trap values (covered in the next chapter). To define colors, select Edit ⇨ Colors to open the dialog box shown in Figure 21-1. From this dialog box, you can

- ⊛ Select New to add colors.

- ⊛ Choose Edit to edit any color you add.

- ⊛ Select Duplicate to duplicate an existing color for editing purposes.

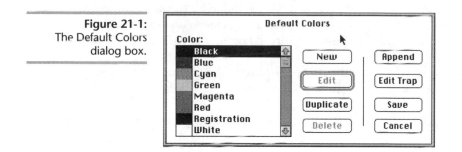

Figure 21-1:
The Default Colors
dialog box.

QuarkXPress comes with several predefined colors: black, blue, cyan, green, magenta, red, registration, white, and yellow. (Registration is a color that prints on all negatives and is primarily used for crop and registration marks.) You cannot edit cyan, black, magenta, yellow, or white. You can duplicate any of the predefined colors *except* registration and then edit the duplicates. (You can, for example, use green as both a spot color and as a process color, perhaps with each version named Green Spot and Green Process.)

 As with most basic attributes, QuarkXPress lets you open the Default Colors dialog box when no document is open. If you do this, the dialog box is titled Default Colors; any changes to the color settings are automatically reflected in all subsequently created documents. If a document is open when you open the dialog box, the dialog box title is Colors for *filename*, and any color settings apply only to the open document.

You can import colors defined in other QuarkXPress documents or templates by selecting the Append button, which opens the Append Colors dialog box shown in Figure 21-2. All colors defined in the specified document or template are imported; you cannot selectively import colors. The color trap values are imported with the colors.

Figure 21-2:
The Append Colors
dialog box.

Any color in the current document with a name that matches that of a color in the second document or template is not overridden by the append operation. The color in the current document is preserved. QuarkXPress does not display a message saying a name collision occurred and was avoided.

For your changes to take effect, you must choose Save in the Colors dialog box after you finish defining colors. Choose Cancel to undo any changes you make.

The Edit Trap options in the Default Colors dialog box are covered in the next chapter.

Because regular black can appear weak when it's overprinted by other colors, many designers create what printers call *superblack* by combining 100 percent black and 100 percent magenta. You can define superblack as a separate color or redefine the registration color as 100 percent of all four process colors, and use that as a superblack.

Color models

QuarkXPress supports several color models, which are ways of representing colors. The supported models include the following: Pantone (of which four variants are supplied); Trumatch; Focoltone; Toyo; DIC (Dainippon Ink & Chemical); process (CMYK); RGB (red, green, blue), which is used in monitors; and HSB (hue, saturation, brightness), which is typically used in creating paints. You can convert a color defined in any model to CMYK, RGB, or HSB models simply by selecting one of those models after defining the color.

Advanced Color Techniques

QuarkXPress offers sophisticated color features and controls, as shown over the next eight pages. Chapters 21 and 22 detail how to apply these effects. This color insert was produced in QuarkXPress and, where noted, in Adobe Photoshop. The sample covers on the last page were scanned in from artwork produced with QuarkXPress and Photoshop.

COLOR MODELS

QuarkXPress supports a range of color models, including CMYK and several variants of the industry-standard Pantone Matching System. Shown here are the color wheels for CMYK and RGB, as well as sample swatches for the other color models supported by QuarkXPress.

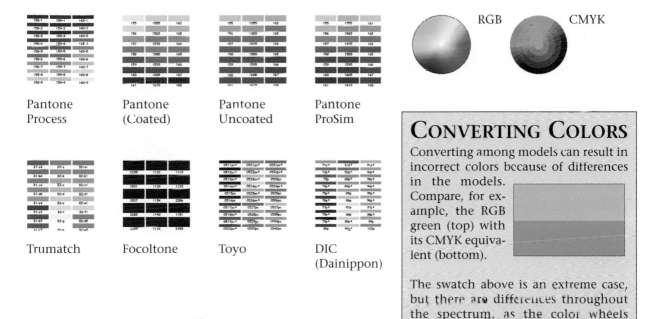

Pantone
Process

Pantone
(Coated)

Pantone
Uncoated

Pantone
ProSim

RGB

CMYK

Trumatch

Focoltone

Toyo

DIC
(Dainippon)

CONVERTING COLORS

Converting among models can result in incorrect colors because of differences in the models. Compare, for example, the RGB green (top) with its CMYK equivalent (bottom).

The swatch above is an extreme case, but there are differences throughout the spectrum, as the color wheels below show. The wheel at left is the original RGB wheel; the one at right was converted to CMYK.

HOW PRINTERS HANDLE COLOR

Different types of printers handle different ranges, or gamuts, of color. A printing press uses CMYK, so it can handle any CMYK color, including any color model based on CMYK (like Trumatch). Such CMYK-based presses have problems with the RGB colors used in computer-generated art — including scanned images.

QuarkXPress can show the gamut for a particular printer in its Edit Colors dialog box. As the color wheels at right show, the gamut depends on the color intensity. Both color wheels are RGB; their difference is the color saturation (brightness). The brighter the RGB color, the less likely it can be reproduced on a CMYK printer. (The areas inside the red lines indicate the color gamut the target printer can handle.) An RGB printer would have similar difficulty reproducing some CMYK colors.

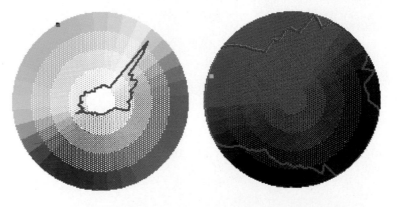

THE EFFECTS OF USING EFICOLOR PROFILES

The heart of the EfiColor XTension is a set of translations from one color model, or space, to another. These translations have been optimized to provide the truest possible output for the colors in an image within the constraints of the originating device and the output device. The samples on these two pages show output on a standard web offset printing press (SWOP).

❮ Original, uncorrected RGB TIFF image

RGB TIFF image, using EFI Calibrated RGB profile ❯

❮ RGB TIFF image, using SuperMac SuperMatch 20•T monitor profile

RGB TIFF image, using Hewlett-Packard ScanJet IIc scanner profile ❯

Original, uncorrected RGB TIFF image

RGB TIFF image, using EFI Calibrated RGB profile

RGB TIFF image, using SuperMac SuperMatch 20•T monitor profile

RGB TIFF image, using Hewlett-Packard ScanJet IIc scanner profile

‹ Original,
uncorrected
CMYK TIFF image

CMYK TIFF image,
using SWOP-
Coated printing
press profile ›

‹ CMYK TIFF
image, using
Euroscale printing
press profile

CMYK TIFF image,
calibrated with
EfiColor for
Photoshop for
SWOP output ›

OUTPUT ON PROOFING PRINTERS

These samples show the effects of EfiColor on various proofing devices.

Without
EfiColor

With
EfiColor

Tektronix Phaser IISD

Fiery/Canon CLC500

QMS ColorScript 100

Fiery/Xerox 5775

OUTPUT SAMPLES COURTESY QUARK, INC.

CONTRAST SETTINGS

QuarkXPress's controls over image contrast let you apply special effects to low-resolution (less than 300 dpi) PICT images. (To use these effects with TIFF or EPS images, you must apply them in a program like Photoshop before importing the images into QuarkXPress.)

Original image (normal contrast)

High contrast

Posterized

All colors inverted

Blue component inverted

Green component posterized, blue component given high contrast

Negative

Blue component modified so that the output heightens the original image's blues

PHOTOGRAPHIC VS. SOLID RENDERING STYLE

QuarkXPress lets you print images with two rendering styles: photographic, for photos and other such finely detailed elements, and solid, for text, frames, rules, and diagrams. See how they compare below.

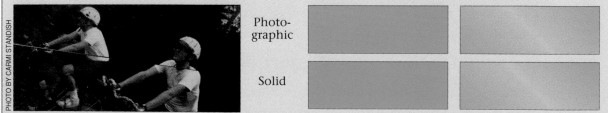

PHOTO BY CARMI STANDISH

Photo-graphic

Solid

DESIGNERS' COLOR TECHNIQUES

By applying colors, shades, and blends to various parts of images, to type, and to boxes and lines, you can add dimension to a document, as these examples show.

COMBINING ELEMENTS

QuarkXPress works well with other design tools, as the example to the left shows. The logo was created with Adobe Illustrator and exported as a PICT file with no background box. The sunburst in the logo was added in QuarkXPress as text in a TrueType dingbats typeface (Wingdings); the polygon picture box. The text at the bottom left uses QuarkXPress's own drop shadow and is set in small caps. The buff color is achieved by applying 5 percent yellow to the text which presents a softer feel than pure white. The image was scanned into Photoshop and exported as an RGB TIFF file so that QuarkXPress's EfiColor XTension could calibrate its output.

MATCHING IMAGE COLORS

By sampling a color in Photoshop (immediately below) and using its values to define a color in QuarkXPress (bottom right), you can create display type using colors that match colors in your images (bottom left). This effects helps tie in elements visually.

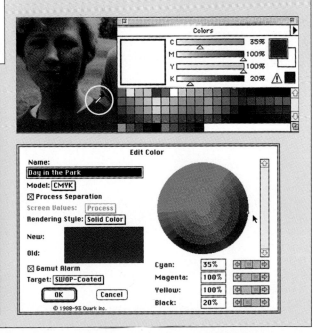

SCREENING CONTROLS

QuarkXPress lets you change the line-control settings for monochrome images, such as the gray-scale photo below that has been tinted in QuarkXPress (with various Trumatch colors). A swath of the original image remains on each altered image to make the results of the effects clearer.

30-lpi screen, with line screen element set at 45°. The color is Trumatch 7-b2.

60-lpi screen, with square screen element set at 30°. The color is Trumatch 1-a7.

75-lpi screen, with ellipse screen element set at 0°. The color is Trumatch 41-a5.

15-lpi screen, with dot screen element set at 15°. The color is Trumatch 18-a6.

USING COLOR TINTS

By applying color shades and/or colored backgrounds to gray-scale images, you can introduce rich subtlety. The use of colors behind the images simulates the use of color paper, while the use of color on the images makes what could appear as dull gray come to life. The combination of the effects adds a sophisticated touch.

TOP: Original gray-scale TIFF image.
BOTTOM: 50 percent Trumatch 49-d2 background.

TOP: 100 percent Pantone ProSim 3425 tint for image.
BOTTOM: 20 percent Trumatch 29-a background.

TOP: 100 percent Pantone Process S 322-5 tint for image.
BOTTOM: 40 percent Trumatch 41-a5 background.

TOP: 100 percent Focoltone 1096 tint for image.
BOTTOM: 7 percent yellow background.

THE EFFECTS OF TRAPPING SETTINGS

Trapping settings can prevent — or create — disastrous alignment of color elements. The examples on this page show the results of different settings. The top set of images shows the effects of traps on borders, backgrounds, and photos. The bottom set of images shows the effects on solid colors over a mixed-color background (a linear blend). Note that the letters not rotated use the default trapping settings, as does the arrow at upper left.

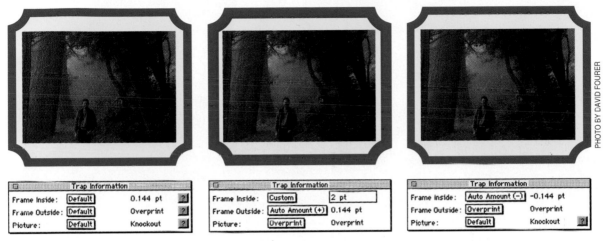

Normal settings: 0.144 points of spread of the blue onto the yellow, overprinting the white page, with the picture knocked out of the yellow.

Modified settings: 2 points of spread of the blue onto the yellow, 0.144 points of spread onto the white, with the picture overprinting the yellow.

Modified settings: 0.144 points of spread of the blue away from the yellow, overprinting the white page, with the picture knocked out of the yellow.

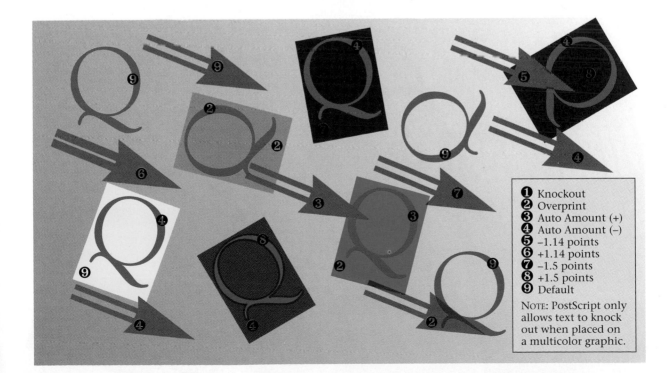

❶ Knockout
❷ Overprint
❸ Auto Amount (+)
❹ Auto Amount (−)
❺ −1.14 points
❻ +1.14 points
❼ −1.5 points
❽ +1.5 points
❾ Default

NOTE: PostScript only allows text to knock out when placed on a multicolor graphic.

COLOR COVER GALLERY

Covers are perhaps the most critical part of a publication's color content because it is what the reader first sees. Below is a small sampling of covers produced with QuarkXPress, courtesy of *Macworld*, *IEEE Software*, *Aquarium Fish Magazine*, and Quark. Enjoy!

The four Pantone color-model variants added since the release of QuarkXPress Version 3.1 should be used differently:

☞ **Pantone:** Use this when your printer will use actual Pantone inks (as spot colors) when printing to coated paper stock. Colors in this variant will have the code *CV* (Computer Video) appended to their names.

☞ **Pantone Uncoated:** This is the same as Pantone but for uncoated paper. Colors in this variant will have the code *CVU* (Computer Video Uncoated) appended to their names.

☞ **Pantone Process:** Use this when you color-separate Pantone colors and your printer uses the standard Pantone-brand process-color inks. Colors in this variant will have the code *S* (SWOP, or single-web offset printing) prefixed to their names.

☞ **Pantone ProSim:** Use this when you color-separate Pantone colors and your printer uses other manufacturers' brands of process-color inks. Colors in this variant will have the code *CVP* (Computer Video Process) appended to their names.

The two major Japanese color models — Toyo and DIC — are new to QuarkXPress 3.3.

When printing on uncoated stock with any colors designed for use on coated stock, you will usually get weaker, less-saturated color reproduction.

Colors defined in one model and converted to another may not reproduce exactly the same because the physics underlying each color model differ slightly. Each model was designed for use in a different medium such as paper or a video monitor.

The sections "Color Models" and "Converting Colors" in the "Advanced Color Techniques" full-color instructional gallery show different color models and the effects of converting colors.

Where to Get Swatchbooks

Anyone who uses a lot of color should have a color swatchbook handy. You probably can get one at your local art-supply store or from your commercial printer (prices typically range from $50 to $100, depending on the color model and the type of swatchbook). But if you can't find a swatchbook, here's where to order the popular color models' swatchbooks.

- **Pantone.** There are several Pantone swatchbooks, including ones for coated and uncoated paper, and those for spot-color output and process-color output. If you are converting (called *building* in publishing parlance) Pantone colors to CMYK for four-color printing, we particularly recommend the *Pantone Process Color Imaging Guide CMYK Edition* or the *Pantone Process Color System Guide* swatchbooks. Pantone, 55 Knickerbock Rd., Moonachie, NJ 07074; phone (201) 935-5500, fax (201) 896-0242.

- **Trumatch.** Based on a CMYK color space, Trumatch suffers almost no matching problems when converted to CMYK. There are variants of the swatchbooks for coated and uncoated paper. Trumatch, 25 W. 43rd St. #802, New York, NY 10036; phone (212) 302-9100.

- **ANPA.** Designed for reproduction on newsprint, these colors also are designed in the CMYK color space. Newspaper Association of America, 11600 Sunrise Valley Dr., Reston, VA 22091; phone (703) 648-1367.

- **Focoltone.** Like Trumatch, this color model (used primarily in Europe) is based on the CMYK color space. Focoltone Ltd., Springwater House, Taffs Well, Cardiff CF4 7QR, U.K.; phone 44 (222) 810-940, fax 44 (222) 810-962.

- **Toyo.** Similar to Pantone in that it is based on spot-color inks, this model is popular in Japan. Toyo Ink Manufacturing Co. Ltd., 3-13 2-chome Kyobashi, Chuo-ku, Tokyo 104, Japan; phone 81 (3) 2722-5721.

How to define colors

You define colors in the Edit Color dialog box, which appears when you choose New, Edit, or Duplicate in the Colors dialog box. Figure 21-3 shows a color being defined through the CMYK model, which is the standard model used in the publishing industry. After selecting the model from the Model list box, we entered values in the Cyan, Magenta, Yellow, and Black fields. If you prefer, you can define the color values by using the slider bars or by moving the black spot on the color wheel to the desired color. Or you can use any combination of these three techniques.

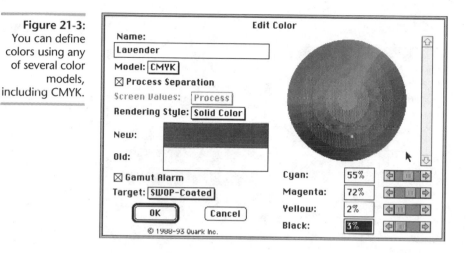

Figure 21-3:
You can define colors using any of several color models, including CMYK.

In Figure 21-3, the bar to the right of the color wheel is grayed out. You use this bar to control brightness when you define colors through the HSB color model. When you use RGB and HSB color models, the arrangement of the slider bars is different from what you see in the figure. All three of the mix-based color models (RGB, HSB, and CMYK) use a color wheel to show the range of allowable mixtures.

You can name a color anything you want, provided that you stay within the character limit of the Name field. To make it easier to remember what a defined color looks like, either use descriptive names (such as *lavender*, as we did in Figure 21-3) or use names based on the color settings. For example, if you create a color in the CMYK model, give it a name based on its mix, such as *55C 72M 2Y 3K* for our lavender color — composed of 55 percent cyan, 72 percent magenta, 2 percent yellow, and 3 percent black. (Believe it or not, this naming convention is how professionals specify colors on paste-up boards.) The same system applies to the RGB and HSB models. That way, you can look at the Colors palette and immediately tell what color you'll get.

If you edit an existing color, the old color is displayed in the box to the right of the word *Old* in the Edit Color dialog box (shown in Figure 21-3). As you define the new color, you see the new color to the right of the word *New*. If you define a color for the first time, no color appears in the field named *Old*.

Figure 21-4 shows a Pantone color being added to the QuarkXPress color list. As you can see, the fields in the Edit Color dialog box change depending upon which color model you use. When you use a spot-color model such as Pantone, QuarkXPress replaces the color wheel with a series of color swatches and their identifying labels. If you know the label, you can enter it in the field at the bottom right; alternatively, you can scroll through the list of labels.

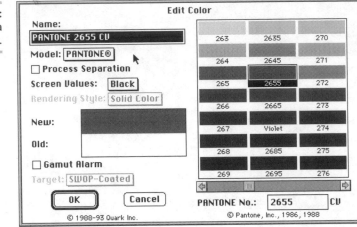

Edit Color

Name:
PANTONE 2655 CU

Model: **PANTONE®**

☐ Process Separation

Screen Values: **Black**

Rendering Style: **Solid Color**

New:

Old:

☐ Gamut Alarm

Target: **SWOP-Coated**

263	2635	270
264	2645	271
265	2655	272
266	2665	273
267	Violet	274
268	2685	275
269	2695	276

[**OK**]   [Cancel]

PANTONE No.: **2655**   CU

© 1988-93 Quark Inc.   © Pantone, Inc., 1986, 1988

Keep in mind that the colors displayed are only on-screen representations; the actual color may be different. The difference will be particularly noticeable if your monitor is running at 8-bit (256 hues) resolution. Check the actual color in a color swatch book for the model you are using. (Art and printing supply stores usually carry these swatch books. The sidebar "Where to Get Swatchbooks" lists other sources.)

Color-separation controls

No matter what color model you select, you have the option of checking the Process Separation box in the Edit Color dialog box, as shown in Figure 21-5. QuarkXPress then color-separates the color when you output negatives. If you do not check this box, the color outputs as a spot color on its own negative — even if you enable color separation in the Print dialog box. If you build a color using the CMYK model, the Process Separation box remains available because the color could be output as a spot color even if defined via the CMYK method. Although printing a color defined via CMYK as a spot color is rare for professional publishing, it may be used for other color output methods, such as thermal-wax or laser printers.

You can select or define a color in one of the swatch models (like Pantone and Trumatch) and then convert it to CMYK (or RGB) by changing the color model to CMYK (or RGB). You can likewise convert between CMYK and RGB color models. However, converting a swatch color to CMYK with this method may result in unexpected color shifts when using the EfiColor XTension because EfiColor cannot calibrate colors converted in this way for optimal output to the target printer. If you are using EfiColor, check the Process Separation box instead after selecting a swatch color. Then, when you output your document, EfiColor will be able to calibrate the color as it is converted to CMYK.

How to Simulate Other Color Models

While QuarkXPress 3.3 supports many color models — Trumatch, DIC, Toyo, Focoltone, and several variants of Pantone — there are other color models in use, such as the ANPA color model. (*ANPA* stands for the American Newspaper Publishers Association, which recently renamed itself the Newspaper Association of America, but the color model's name hasn't changed.) You can still use these color models in QuarkXPress by following these techniques.

If you are using spot color, in which the ANPA color prints on its own plate, just define a color with the ANPA name you want the printer to use. The printer doesn't care if you actually had the right color on screen — the fact that he knows what color you want and you have a plate for that color is all that's needed.

If you are using process (CMYK) color, you'll need to create the ANPA colors using the CMYK color model. That means you'll need to know the CMYK values for the ANPA colors you want to use; you can get these values from the swatch book you use to select colors or from your commercial printer. (You can also use RGB values to enter the colors and then switch the model with QuarkXPress to CMYK. That may result in some altered colors, since you are converting colors twice: once to RGB and then again to CMYK. Any conversion between color models may result in color differences because of the physics involved in reproducing color.)

If there are certain ANPA colors you use repeatedly, create them in the Colors dialog box (Edit ⇨ Colors) with no document open — they'll then be available for all future documents. If different types of documents use different sets of colors, define them in the template for each type of document. Doing so will save a lot of redefinition.

This technique works with any color model for which you have the CMYK or RGB equivalents.

In process-color printing, each color prints at a slightly different angle so that the overlap of the four colors produces evenly mixed colors. Although spot colors rarely mix with process colors, QuarkXPress needs to orient the angle of the line screen that prints the spot color, just in case there is mixing with process colors or other spot colors.

The Screen Values option in the Edit Color dialog box lets you define the screening angle for spot colors. You can pick any of the process color plates — cyan, magenta, yellow, or black — to define the screening angle. We suggest that you use the yellow plate's angle for light spot colors; darker colors can use any of the others. (See the sidebar "Special Considerations for Spot Colors" for advice on mixing process and spot colors.)

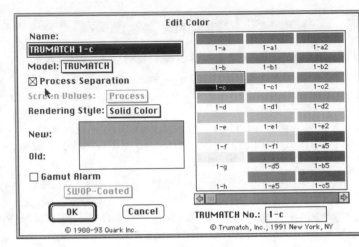

Figure 21-5:
Check Process Separation to tell QuarkXPress to reproduce a color using CMYK process-color values.

When the Process Separation box is checked, the Screen Value option is automatically grayed out. Because no separate negative is produced, you do not need to assign a screening angle for it.

The EfiColor-specific options in the Edit Color dialog box — Rendering Style, Gamut Alarm, and Target — are covered in the next chapter. If EfiColor is not installed, these options will not display in the Edit Color dialog box.

Applying Colors

After you define colors, you can apply them. Most dialog boxes for text and items contain a color list option, as do many options in the Style menu. All colors defined in a document appear (in alphabetical order) in any of these color lists.

When working with picture boxes, text boxes, and lines, you can apply colors by using the Colors palette (accessible through the View menu's Show Colors option) rather than invoking the dialog boxes. Figure 21-6 shows the Colors palette. This palette gives you a handy way to quickly apply colors to lines and to picture and text box backgrounds, frames, and, in some cases, contents. (Chapter 20 includes a table showing which types of images can have colors applied to them.) In the figure, we've applied Pantone S 6-6, which has the look of aged newsprint, to the background of the gray-scale image inset into the color image at left.

Figure 21-6:
The Colors
palette.

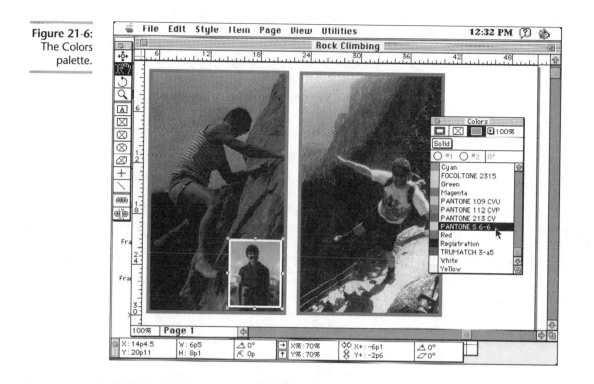

Special Considerations for Spot Colors

In most cases, you need not worry about spot-color output, since most users of these colors apply them to solid objects or text. However, some designers use them more demandingly, such as mixing them with black to produce many variants or such as using them with scanned images. In these cases, the way that QuarkXPress outputs them may result in displeasing results.

Many designers use spot colors because they cannot afford four-color (CMYK) printing. But they want more than just black and their color. Thus, many will create new colors by mixing the spot color with shades of black. If you do this, make sure you change the spot color's screening angle, since the default angle for spot colors is the same as for black. By choosing a different screening angle, you ensure that the dots making up the two colors don't overprint, resulting in a muddy image.

Choose either the magenta or cyan angles, not yellow (see Figure 21-1). The reason is complex, but it basically boils down to the fact that the angle for yellow was chosen because the other colors overpower it when viewed by the human eye, and so it's OK if it is overprinted with stronger colors. The screen angles for other colors overprint each other less. If you choose the yellow values for your screening angle, there's a bigger chance your spot color will have many of its dots overprinted by black, changing the mix of the two colors. The rule of thumb is that darker colors should be at least 30 degrees apart from each other, while lighter colors should be at least 15 degrees apart from other colors.

To change the angle for a spot color, select the process color whose angle values you want to use from the Screen Values pick list in the Colors dialog box (accessed via Edit ⇨ Colors). What that angle is for your output device is defined via File ⇨ Print (see Chapter 26).

When you are working with both process and spot colors, picking the right screening angle is tougher. Pick a process color that is never or rarely used with the spot color, or that the spot color knocks out (see Chapter 22). If that can't be avoided, consult your printer or service bureau for advice.

When working with scanned images, use black as the screening angle, since that results in a 45-degree angle that often avoids moiré patterns. If you must use a different screening angle (perhaps because you have other spot colors defined or you are using black mixed with the spot color), consult your service bureau or printer.

You or your service bureau may have to manually edit your screen angle settings in the PostScript file. To create a PostScript file with a Level 1 driver (LaserWriter or PSPrinter 7.0), select PostScript File as the Destination in the Print dialog box (File ⇨ Print). To create a PostScript file with a Level 1 driver (LaserWriter or PSPrinter 8.0), select File as the destination, and make sure (in the dialog box that appears after you click the Save button) that you have chosen the PostScript Job option from the Format pick list and selected the ASCII option. Editing settings in a PostScript file requires a fairly intimate knowledge of the PostScript language. Don't expect your service bureau or printer to automatically do this work for — consult with them first.

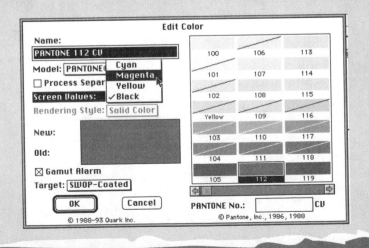

The Colors palette displays a list of available colors. The palette also contains icons that let you direct how QuarkXPress applies colors to the selected box. From left to right, the Colors palette icons are as follows:

- **Frame:** If you select this icon, QuarkXPress applies the selected color to the box frame. (If no frame is defined in the Item ⇨ Modify option for the box, no color appears. As soon as a frame is defined, it takes on the color you applied.)

- **Contents:** The contents icon changes depending upon which element is currently selected. The icon looks like a picture box if the selected item is a picture; like a text box if the selected item is text; and like a line if the selected element is a line. Choosing the icon applies the selected color to the contents of the box or line. Figures 21-7 and 21-8 show how the palette looks when you apply colors to different types of elements. Note that the Content tool must be selected for this option to be available. If the Item tool is selected, the icon is grayed out.

You can apply colors to any contents except color pictures. If you apply color to the contents of a text box, any text you subsequently enter into the text box takes on the applied color. Existing text is unaffected.

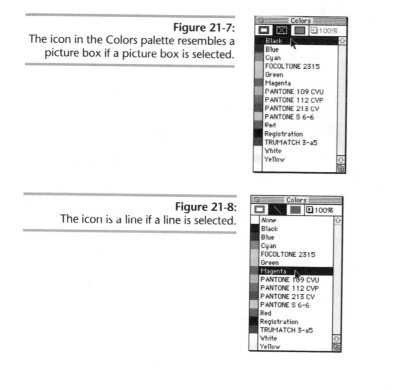

Figure 21-7:
The icon in the Colors palette resembles a picture box if a picture box is selected.

Figure 21-8:
The icon is a line if a line is selected.

   ◈ **Background:** Selecting this icon applies the selected color to the box background. Figure 21-9 shows how the palette looks when this icon is selected. (The palette's pick list of predefined shades is also selected.)

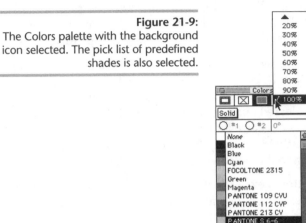

Figure 21-9:
The Colors palette with the background icon selected. The pick list of predefined shades is also selected.

If an option is not available for the selected item (for example, a background for a line), its icon is grayed out.

You can apply the color at different shades by editing the number in the field located at the upper right of the Colors palette. Enter any value from 0 to 100 percent, in 0.1 percent increments. You can access common percentages (multiples of 10) through the pick list to the right of the field. Figure 21-9 shows this pick list enabled.

There are two ways to apply a color:

   ◈ Select the box or line, select the icon in the Colors palette, and then select the color you want to apply by clicking on its name.

   ◈ Use the new drag-and-drop technique to apply a color (see Figure 21-10). Click the mouse on the color sample for the color you want to apply from the Color palette. Drag the color sample icon to the box or line; the color will change when the icon passes onto the box or line. For a box, dragging a color onto it changes only the background color, no matter which Colors palette icon is selected.

If you delete a color (through the Delete button in the Edit Color dialog box) that is used in your document, you will get the dialog box shown in Figure 21-11. This dialog box lets you substitute any other color for the removed one. If the color being deleted is not used in your document, this dialog box does not appear.

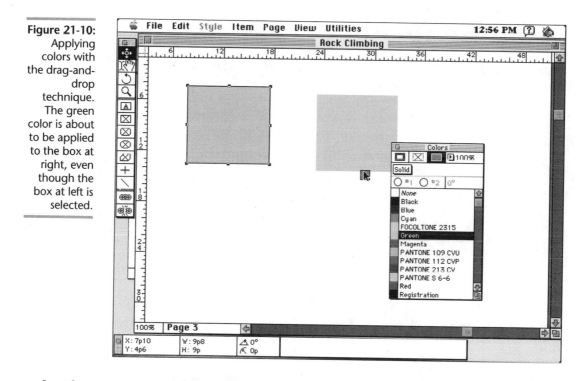

Figure 21-10:
Applying colors with the drag-and-drop technique. The green color is about to be applied to the box at right, even though the box at left is selected.

In either case, you also have the option of canceling the delete operation by picking the Cancel button in the Colors dialog box (you would click Save to go through with the change). When removing a color used in your document, you can also click the Cancel button in the dialog box asking you if it's OK to delete the color.

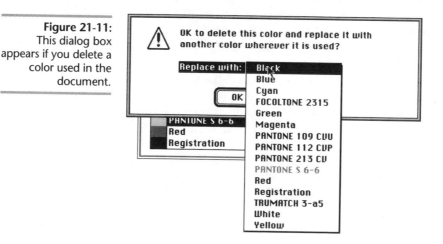

Figure 21-11:
This dialog box appears if you delete a color used in the document.

Creating Blends

Using the Colors palette, you also can apply a *blend,* which is a smooth transition from one color to another. QuarkXPress comes with a linear blend built-in. If you install the Cool Blends XTension, you have five other choices: mid-linear, rectangular, diamond, circular, and full circular. Figure 21-12 shows the pick list enabled.

The Cool Blends XTension is now bundled with QuarkXPress.

Figure 21-12:
The pick list of blends when the Cool Blends XTension is installed.

You can apply a blend to a selected picture or text box. To perform this task, select the background icon from the Colors palette and then invoke the pick list of blend options below the row of icons (the current list selection will likely be Solid, which is the default). The two radio buttons and a numeric field are where you specify the blend's colors and angle (see Figure 21-13).

The #1 radio button is selected by default, and the current background color is highlighted. (The color is White if you did not apply a color to the box). You create the blend from the selected color; change the color if necessary. Then click the #2 radio button and select the color you want to blend into. In the field to the right of the #2 button, enter the angle of the blend. You can enter any value from –360 to +360 degrees, in increments of 0.001 degrees. A setting of 0 degrees blends the two colors from top to bottom; a setting of 90 degrees blends the colors from left to right.

Figure 21-13 shows eight examples of the use of six blends. For the top six, an angle of 30 degrees was chosen to show the effects of this feature. The bottom two show the effects of the angle on circular blends: a smaller angle results in a more compact circle.

Figure 21-13:
The top six
boxes show
examples of
the six blend
options
available with
the Cool
Blends
XTension.
These six are
set at
30-degree
angles. The
bottom two
boxes show
how a smaller
angle (0, in
this case)
makes the
circular
blends more
compact.

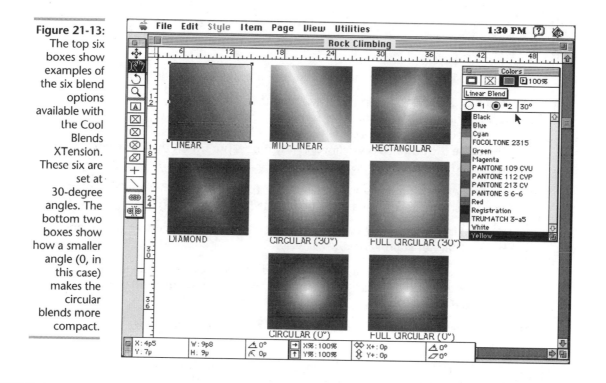

Summary

- ⊶ TIFF and EPS formats are the best choices for imported color images.

- ⊶ You can define colors using any of several color models. Colors defined in one model and translated to another sometimes print differently than the original colors because of differences between the color models that defy translation. The same is true for colors defined in any model but CMYK that are color-separated via process colors.

- ⊶ Colors defined in models other than CMYK (process) are color-separated only if you check the Process Separation box in the Edit Color dialog box.

- ⊶ You can import colors defined in other documents into the current document, but you cannot import colors selectively.

- ⊶ Creating a superblack color, perhaps based on the registration color, can result in stronger blacks, especially when printing over color images and other colored elements.

- ⊶ Using the Colors palette is a handy way to apply colors and shades to boxes and lines.

- ⊶ The Colors palette includes a blend feature for picture box and text box backgrounds. If the Cool Blends XTension is installed, there are six options; otherwise, there is just one (linear).

Color Prepress

■ ■

In This Chapter

➥ Setting color traps and defining global trapping defaults.

➥ Applying EfiColor profiles on imported images.

■ ■

Color Prepress on the Desktop_____

Since their invention in the mid-1980s, desktop publishing programs have broadened their features to cover more and more color publishing needs. Many of the color-oriented features have caused consternation among professional color separators and printers who have seen amateurs make a tough job worse or ruin an acceptable piece of work. This situation is familiar to anyone in desktop-publishing in the early years when the typographic profession looked on in horror at amateurs publishing documents without understanding tracking, hyphenation, and many other fundamental areas.

After years of user education and efforts by software developers like Quark to build in some of the more basic typographic assumptions into their programs, most desktop publishers now produce decent typographic output. QuarkXPress's color prepress features — notably its trapping tools and EfiColor calibration tools — offer amateur color publishers the same basic fallback. To really use these tools effectively, you should understand color printing. But if you don't, you can be assured that the default settings in QuarkXPress will produce decent quality color output.

If you're printing to a color laser, dye-sublimation, ink-jet, or thermal wax printer, don't worry about trapping. You're not getting the kind of output resolution at which this level of image fine-tuning is relevant. But if you're outputting to an imagesetter (particularly if you are outputting to negatives) for eventual printing on a web offset or other printing press, read on. In either case, you'll also want to understand the color calibration features in the EfiColor XTension (covered later in this chapter) because it will help you get the best color fidelity possible with your images and output devices.

Please note that the illustrations and figures in this chapter are in black and white. You'll need to look at your color monitor to see the effects of what's described here. See the full color instructional gallery for examples.

Working with Color Traps _____

Color trapping — which controls how colors overlap and abut when printed — is one of the most powerful features available in QuarkXPress. It's also one that novice users can abuse terribly. If you don't know much about trapping, leave the features of the program at the default settings. Before you use QuarkXPress trapping tools, study some books on color publishing, talk to your printer, and experiment with test files that you don't want to publish. If you are experienced with color trapping — or after you become experienced — you'll find QuarkXPress trapping tools a joy to use.

 You'll still want to use the trapping tools within the illustration product with which you create your EPS graphics because these tools will help you to finely control the settings for each image's specific needs. Also, if you are using a service bureau that does high-resolution scanning for you and strips these files into your layout before output, check to make sure that the bureau is not also handling trapping for you with a Scitex or other high-end system. If it is, make sure you ask whether and when you should be doing trapping yourself.

So what is trapping, anyway? Trapping adjusts the boundaries of colored objects to prevent gaps between abutting colors. Gaps can occur because of misalignment of the negatives, plates, or printing press — all of which are impossible to avoid.

Colors are trapped by processes known as *choking* and *spreading*. Both make an object slightly larger — usually a fraction of a point — so that it overprints the abutting object slightly. The process is called choking when one object surrounds a second object, and the first object is enlarged to overlap the second. The process is known as spreading when you enlarge the surrounded object so that it leaks (bleeds) into the surrounding object.

The difference between choking and spreading is the relative position of the two objects. Think of choking as making the hole for the inside object smaller (which in effect makes the object on the outside larger), and think of spreading as making the object in the hole larger. The one made larger depends on the image, but you generally bleed the color of a lighter object into a darker one. If you did the opposite, you'd make objects seem ungainly larger.

Figure 22-1 shows the two types of trapping techniques. Spreading (at left) makes the interior object's color bleed out; choking (at right) makes the outside color bleed in, in effect making the area of the choked element smaller. The dashed lines show the size of the interior object; as you can see in the image at right, when you choke a darker object into a lighter one, the effect is to change its size (here, the interior object gets smaller).

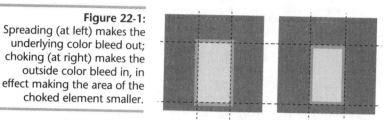

Figure 22-1:
Spreading (at left) makes the underlying color bleed out; choking (at right) makes the outside color bleed in, in effect making the area of the choked element smaller.

In practice, trapping also involves controlling whether colors *knock out* or *overprint*. The default is to knock out — cut out — any overlap when one element is placed on top of another. If, for example, you place two rectangles on top of each other, they print like the two rectangles on the right side of Figure 22-2. If you set the darker rectangle in this figure to overprint, the rectangles print as shown on the left side of the figure. Setting colors to overprint results in mixed colors, as on the left, while setting colors to knock out results in discrete colors, as on the right.

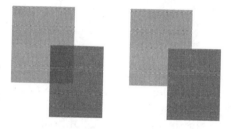

Figure 22-2:
Setting colors to overprint results in mixed colors (left); setting them to knock out results in discrete colors (right).

Setting traps

You define trapping settings for separate documents and colors in the Trap Specifications dialog box, shown in Figure 22-3 (to open the dialog box, select Edit ⇨ Colors ⇨ Edit Traps). However, you define default trapping settings in the Trapping Preferences dialog box, accessed via Edit ⇨ Preferences ⇨ Trapping. Figure 22-4 shows this dialog box.

The title of the Trap Specifications dialog box shows the color for which you are defining trapping values. (In Figure 22-3, trapping values are being defined for black.) In the Background Color list box, you see all defined colors except registration, black, and white. You do not need to trap these three colors as background colors because black and registration completely obscure any color spread into them. Also, white does not "mix" with other colors — it's just paper with no ink on it — and thus causes no unsightly gaps or color artifacts due to misregistration.

Figure 22-3:
The Trap Specifica-
tions dialog box.

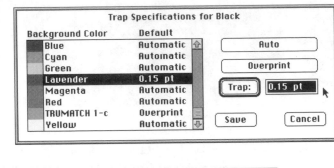

The list of background colors includes one color not defined via Edit ⇨ Colors: Indeter-minate. This item is not exactly a color but a special case used by QuarkXPress to handle multicolored backgrounds (such as a color picture or multiple color objects abutting) for which trapping information is unavailable or is conflicting.

You can choose three basic options in the Trap Specifications dialog box by selecting the corresponding button:

- **Auto:** This is the default setting for all colors; it applies whatever trapping values are set in the Trapping Preferences dialog box.

- **Overprint:** Overprint sets the color named in the dialog box title to overprint the color selected in the color list. (Except for black, colors always knock out unless you choose overprint.)

- **Trap:** Trap lets you specify an actual trapping value, which you enter in the field to the right of the button. You can enter any value from –36 to +36 points, in 0.001-point increments.

Entering a negative trapping number chokes the object that has the background color. Entering a positive number spreads the background color. The difference between the two is subtle (as described earlier and shown in Figure 22-1) and usually comes into play for fine elements such as text and lines. If the object using the background color is thin or has a light hue, a good rule of thumb is to spread; otherwise, choke.

Figure 22-4:
The Trapping Preferences
dialog box.

Setting trap defaults

In the Trapping Preferences dialog box, you set the defaults that Automatic represents in the Trap Specifications dialog box:

- **Auto Method:** This setting determines whether QuarkXPress uses the trapping values specified in the Auto Amount option or whether it adjusts the trapping based on the saturation of the abutting colors. If you choose Absolute, the program uses the values as is; if you choose Proportional, QuarkXPress calculates new trapping values based on the value entered in Auto Amount and the relative saturation of the abutting colors. The default is Absolute.

- **Auto Amount:** Select this option to specify the trapping value for which the program calculates automatic trapping for both the Auto Method option and the Trap Specification dialog box. You can enter values from 0 to 36 points, in increments of 0.001 points. If you want the amount to be infinite (so that colors overprint), enter the word **overprint.** The default setting is 0.144 points.

- **Indeterminate:** The Indeterminate setting tells QuarkXPress how to trap objects that abut multicolored or indeterminate-colored objects as well as imported color graphics. As with Auto Method, this setting applies only to colors set at Auto in the Trap Specification dialog box. Valid options are 0 to 26 points, in 0.001-point increments, as well as **overprint.** The default is 0.144 points.

- **Overprint Limit:** This value tells QuarkXPress when to overprint a color object. You can specify any percentage from 0 to 100, in increments of 0.1. If you enter 50 percent, QuarkXPress overprints any color whose trap specification is set as Overprint and whose saturation is 50 percent or greater; otherwise, it traps the color based on the Auto Amount and Auto Method settings. This limit affects black objects regardless of whether black is set at Auto or Overprint. The default is 95 percent.

- **Ignore White:** If you check this option box, QuarkXPress traps an object based on all nonwhite objects abutting or behind the object. Otherwise, QuarkXPress calculates a trap based on the smaller of the Indeterminate settings and the trap specification for any other colors (including white) abutting or behind the object. This option is checked as a default because it makes little sense to trap to white (as there is nothing to trap to).

- **Process Trap:** Checking this box tells QuarkXPress to calculate traps for overlapping process colors based on their saturation (for example, it traps 50 percent cyan and 100 percent magenta differently than 80 percent cyan and 100 percent magenta), as well as on all the other trap settings. Otherwise, it uses the same trapping values for all saturation levels. The default setting turns this option on (the box is checked), which makes for smoother trapping.

Overriding traps

Because trapping depends as much on the elements being trapped as their colors, trapping tools based solely on relationships among colors would be insufficient. That's why QuarkXPress offers the ability to override trapping settings for selected objects.

To override trapping locally, you must first invoke the Trap Information palette, which is accessible via View ⇨ Show Trap Information. The contents of this palette depend on the type of object selected, but no matter what the contents, the palette works the same way. Figure 22-5 shows the Trap Information palette for a picture box.

The section "The Effects of Trappings Settings" in the "Advanced Color Techniques" full-color instructional gallery shows how different trap settings affect the printed output.

Figure 22-5:
The Trap Information palette. QuarkXPress explains its trapping rationale when you select the question mark icon.

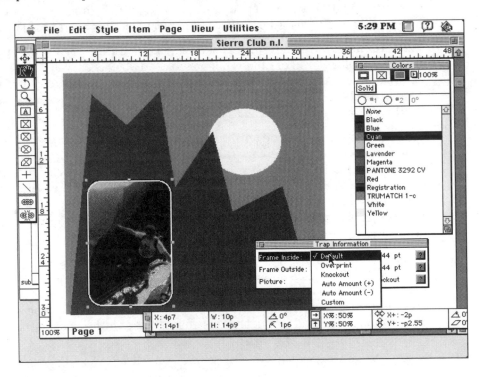

In Figure 22-5, all three picture-box elements for which trapping is appropriate are set at Default (shown in the middle column), which means that they take on whatever settings were made globally in the Trap Specifications dialog box. Because there are so many possible combinations of colors, no one can be expected to remember how every color combination traps. Recognizing this, QuarkXPress displays what the default setting is in the column at right. Thus, in Figure 22-5 the defaults are as follows:

- The default for trapping the frame color with the color of the image inside the frame is 0.144 points (which happens to be the setting for automatic trapping in this document).

- The default for trapping the frame color with the color of the object outside (abutting) the frame is also 0.144 points. Had the frame abutted a white color or no object, the default would have been Overprint because there would have been no color to trap to.

- The default for trapping the picture with the picture box background is Knock-out, which is what you would expect a picture to do. However, as an example of how you can override default settings, Figure 22-5 shows the drop-down list box to change this last trapping setting. The last three options (Auto Amount (+), Auto Amount (-), and Custom) would be grayed out because you cannot trap a bitmap image — it either knocks out or overprints.

To further explain trapping settings, QuarkXPress describes the current trapping rationale if you select the question mark icons in the Trap Information dialog box. Figure 22-6 shows example explanations for the picture box in Figure 22-5. We superimposed all three rationales so that you can see several examples. QuarkXPress can display only one at a time.

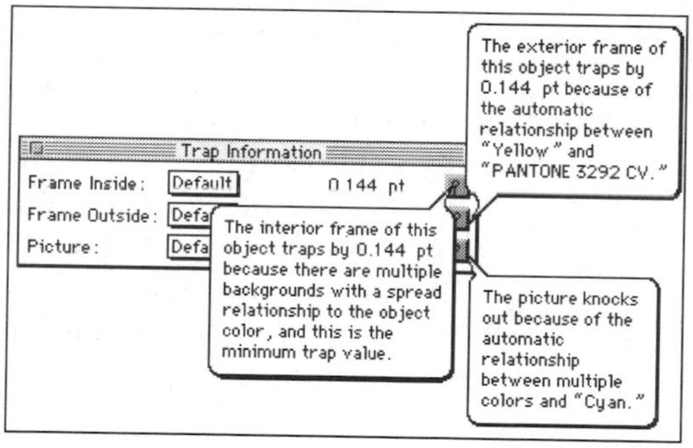

Figure 22-6:
Sample explanations for QuarkXPress's trapping decisions.

The exterior frame of this object traps by 0.144 pt because of the automatic relationship between "Yellow" and "PANTONE 3292 CV."

Trap Information

Frame Inside: Default 0.144 pt

Frame Outside: Defa

Picture: Defa

The interior frame of this object traps by 0.144 pt because there are multiple backgrounds with a spread relationship to the object color, and this is the minimum trap value.

The picture knocks out because of the automatic relationship between multiple colors and "Cyan."

When to Use Independent Trapping Tools

QuarkXPress's trapping tools are great for making sure color elements — lines, type, and backgrounds — created in QuarkXPress print well. But there are some types of elements for which you'll need to go outside QuarkXPress for the right tools.

For example, if you create a logo as an EPS file and place it over a TIFF photo (perhaps for a cover), QuarkXPress's trapping settings won't be applied. That's because QuarkXPress can't work with the EPS file at that level of detail. In many cases, your document will print fine, but if you see the need for trapping when you look at the match print or final output, it's time for a professional trapping tool.

One solution is to use a program like Aldus TrapWise (contact Aldus at 206/628-3230) that lets you do trapping on the EPS or DCS files you create from QuarkXPress. Of course, if you're not a trapping expert, you should have your service bureau do the trapping.

Color Calibration

With the new EfiColor XTension, QuarkXPress can help you ensure accurate printing of your colors, both those in imported images and those defined in QuarkXPress. What EfiColor does is track the colors in the source image, the colors displayable by your monitor, and the colors printable by your printer. If the monitor or printer does not support a color in your document, EfiColor alters the color to its closest possible equivalent. EfiColor can also tell you which colors cannot be accurately produced with the output device chosen.

Note that we do not characterize EfiColor's capabilities as color matching. It is impossible to match colors produced in an illustration or paint program, or via a scanner, with what a printer or other output device can produce. The underlying differences in color models (how a color is defined) and the physics of the media (screen phosphors that emit light versus different types of papers with different types of inks that reflect light) make color matching impossible. But a calibration tool like EfiColor can minimize differences and alert you to unrealistic expectations.

 EfiColor is new to QuarkXPress.

Understanding profiles

The mechanism that EfiColor uses is the profile that contains the information on color models and ranges supported by a particular creator (such as an illustration program or scanner), display, and printer. EfiColor includes several predefined profiles. If your monitor or output device is not included, you can buy profiles directly from Electronics for Imaging (EfiColor's developer), at 800/285-4565 or 415/286-8600. Profiles typically cost between $129 and $329; those for printing presses cost $529, while some monitor profiles are free to registered users.

To better understand a profile, look at the color wheels in Figure 22-7. From left to right, they show the color gamut (the range of colors reproducible) when printing to a standard web offset press (SWOP), QMS ColorScript 100 printer, and Canon CLC500 printer. The outline toward the center of the color wheel shows the gamut's boundaries. Anything within the gamut will reproduce correctly on the target device, but anything outside must be approximated by using the closest match from within the gamut. Every type of color device — whether an RGB monitor, a Pantone color matching book, an ink-jet printer, or an offset web press using CMYK inks — has such a gamut.

Figure 22-7:
Color gamuts (ranges) for three type of printers: standard web offset, QMS ColorScript 100, and Canon CLC500.

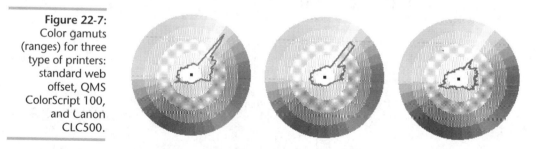

EfiColor uses a device-independent color space to match these gamuts against each other. A color space is a mathematical way of describing the relationships among colors. By using a device-independent model (the CIE XYZ standard defined by the International Standards Organization), EfiColor can compare gamuts from other device-dependent models (like RGB and the others). What this means is that EfiColor can examine the colors in your imported images and defined colors, compare them against the capabilities of your monitor and printer, and adjust the colors for the closest possible display and printing.

An EfiColor profile also contains information on the rendering style, which comes down to choosing whether the colors are solid (as in a color applied as a background) or photographic (in which they mix and their close proximity has an effect on their overall appearance because of the way the human eye reacts to mixed colors).

Monitor color display

The EfiColor XTension comes with profiles for several Mac monitors, including the common Apple 13" RGB and the large SuperMac Technology monitors often used by color publishers. If your monitor does not appear on the list, select the EFI Calibrated RGB option. You select the monitor via Edit ⇨ Preferences ⇨ EfiColor, as Figure 22-8 shows. The monitor that you select will tell EfiColor how to display imported images and colors defined within QuarkXPress.

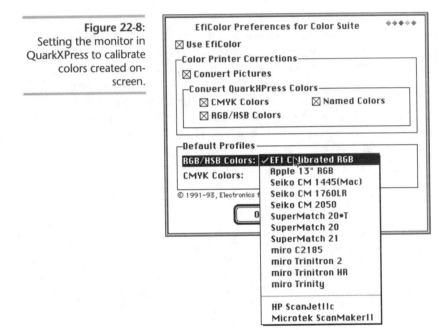

Figure 22-8: Setting the monitor in QuarkXPress to calibrate colors created on-screen.

It's possible to have a different on-screen appearance than EfiColor expects. For example, your brightness and contrast settings affect how colors display, but EfiColor has no way of gauging their settings. Likewise, you can change the color characteristics (the *gamma*) of your display in the Monitors control panel by holding the Option key when clicking the Option button. Figure 22-9 shows the dialog box that lets you change these characteristics. You check the Use Special Gamma box and select an option from the list below it. In the figure, Mac Std Gamma is selected, which is the setting that calibration products like EfiColor expect. But you may want to select Uncorrected Gamma, which makes the monitor display colors as the manufacturer originally intended. Apple's monitors have a slight bluish cast to them (which makes whites appear whiter), but a monitor's display usually appears more vivid without the Mac gamma, so some people change the gamma to Uncorrected Gamma to get a more pleasing display.

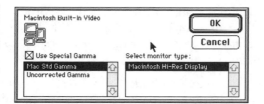

Figure 22-9:
Changing a monitor's color
characteristics via the
Monitors control panel.

Other programs may have similar settings for calibrating their display against your type
of monitor. For example, Adobe Photoshop offers such an option (via File ➪ Preferences
➪ Monitor Setup), as Figure 22-10 shows. If you're creating colors in a program and
importing those colors into QuarkXPress, it's important to have them calibrated the
same way, or at least as closely as the different programs will allow.

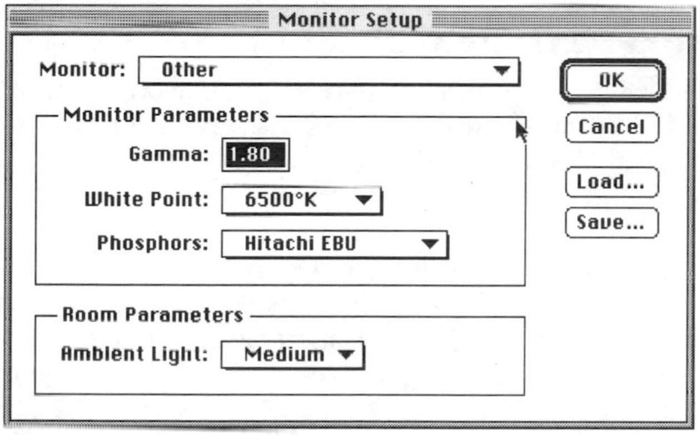

Figure 22-10:
Setting the monitor
in Adobe Photoshop
to calibrate colors
created on-screen.

Defining colors

Whether you define colors in QuarkXPress or in your illustration or paint program, the
method you use to define them is critical to ensuring the best possible output.

It's best to define all colors in the same model as the target output device. Use the
following guidelines:

- ➼ If your printer is RGB, use the RGB model to define colors.

- ➼ If your printer is CMYK (like an offset printer), use CMYK to define colors.

- ➼ If you are using Pantone colors for traditional offset printing, pick the Pantone or
  Pantone Uncoated models if using Pantone inks.

- ➼ If you are using Pantone colors for traditional offset printing, pick the Pantone
  Process or Pantone ProSim models if you will color-separate those colors into CMYK.

☞ Trumatch and Focoltone colors were designed to reproduce accurately whether output as spot colors or color-separated into CMYK. Other models (such as Toyo) may or may not separate accurately for all colors, so check with your printer or the ink manufacturer.

☞ If you're using any Pantone, Focoltone, Trumatch, Toyo, or DIC color and outputting to a desktop color printer (whether RGB or CMYK), watch to ensure that the color definition does not lie outside the printer's gamut, as explained in the next section.

☞ Never use the screen display to gauge any non-RGB color. Even with EfiColor's monitor calibration, RGB monitors simply cannot match most non-RGB colors. Use the on-screen colors only as a guide and rely instead on a color swatchbook from your printer or the color ink's manufacturer.

Colors defined in QuarkXPress

Let's first look at how EfiColor comes into play for colors you define within QuarkXPress. You will essentially use it to work with spot colors for type, box backgrounds, box frames, and lines.

When you define a color (as explained in Chapter 21) make sure you have checked the Gamut Alarm box in the Edit Color dialog box. Figure 22-11 shows the result for the lavender color defined via the RGB model. Note that an exclamation mark in a triangle appears to the left of the New color bar. This alert signifies that the defined color is outside the gamut of the target device (an offset press). If you look at the color wheel, you'll see the gamut boundary and a light spot (bottom center) that shows where the lavender's color definition lies. If you use this color with this printer, EfiColor will substitute the closest match it can. For special inks like Trumatch, QuarkXPress puts a diagonal line through the swatch of the color that falls outside the target device's gamut (as Figure 22-12 shows).

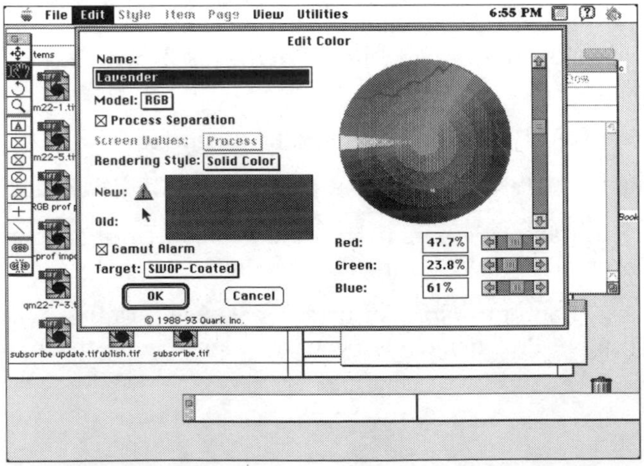

Figure 22-11: An out-of-gamut color alert for an RGB color.

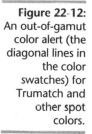
Figure 22-12: An out-of-gamut color alert (the diagonal lines in the color swatches) for Trumatch and other spot colors.

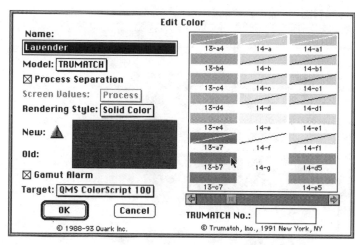

Colors defined elsewhere

Generally, you should follow the same advice when creating colors in another program as we just gave for defining them within QuarkXPress. But there are some important considerations to keep in mind:

- ☞ If your image-editing or retouching software supports Metric Color Tags (like Photoshop 2.5.1), be sure to enable this option when saving your images. EfiColor uses these to retain the color profile for such images.

- ☞ Make sure that any calibration features within your originating program are set to the target device to which you will be outputting your document. Also be sure that the software was calibrated for the monitor that was used. Otherwise, what you print may not match your original expectations. Figure 22-13 shows an example. Although the figure is in gray-scale, you can see that the range of hues is less in the bottom two images in comparison to the top, and even the bottom two differ from each other. The differences between the bottom two images and the original (the top) are caused solely by changing the target output device and monitor for each image to a different combination in Photoshop (where they were created). For example, the middle image was targeted for output on a QMS ColorScript printer; the bottom one was calibrated for a Eurocolor-standard newspaper printing press. Neither supports as wide a range of colors as standard web offset presses, which is what the top image (and this QuarkXPress document) is calibrated to. Figure 22-14 shows an example output calibration dialog box from Photoshop (use File ➪ Preferences ➪ Printing Inks Setup).

- ☞ EfiColor does *not* calibrate color in EPS files. If you use EPS, we strongly recommend that you use the DCS (pre-separated CMYK) variant. If you use RGB EPS files, the color-separated results may not match your needs.

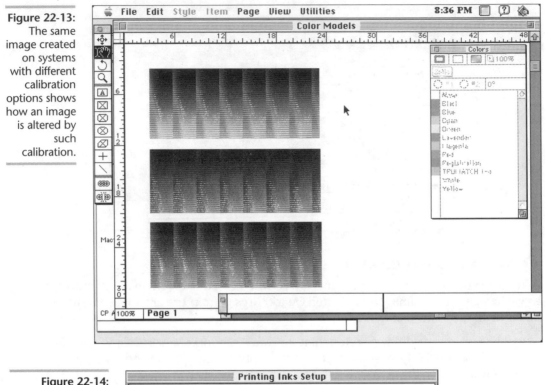

Figure 22-13:
The same image created on systems with different calibration options shows how an image is altered by such calibration.

Figure 22-14:
The Photoshop dialog box is used to calibrate an image's color based on the target printer.

Calibrating imported colors

When you load an image into QuarkXPress, the EfiColor XTension applies the default settings defined in the EfiColor Preferences dialog box (these are described later in this chapter). But you can change those settings as you import each file by using the EfiColor Profile and Rendering Style options in the Get Picture dialog box.

You may need to wait for 10 or more seconds for the pick lists associated with these two options to appear because EfiColor must read the file to determine what options are valid.

EfiColor lets you apply only target-printer profiles, such as SWOP-Coated, to CMYK files. This limitation exists because EfiColor assumes that the image is designed for output to that specific printer and thus will calibrate it with that target in mind. For RGB files, EfiColor lets you apply monitor-oriented profiles such as EFI Calibrated RGB or Apple 13" RGB. EfiColor assumes that the image's output should be matched as closely as possible to the originating monitor's representation. Figure 22-15 shows the pick list for a CMYK file, and Figure 22-16 shows the pick list for an RGB file.

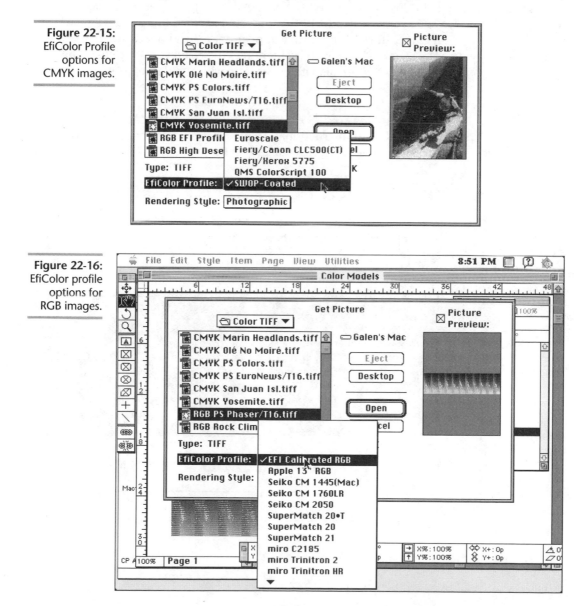

Figure 22-15: EfiColor Profile options for CMYK images.

Figure 22-16: EfiColor profile options for RGB images.

You can also set the rendering option. For bitmap images, you should leave it at Photographic (the default) because this setting optimizes the output of colors that are mixed throughout an image, as in a photograph. For solid colors, such as those used in illustrations, you should leave it at Solid. However, if your illustrations use gradient fills, you will have to choose between the two options. We suggest that you select Photographic in these cases because the color blends in such fills are more characteristic of photographs than of solid colors. Figure 22-17 shows an example of an image imported both ways. The image at right was imported as Solid, even though it was a photograph. Although it is hard to see in gray-scale, the image imported as Solid has a more limited range of colors (which makes the bright blue sky appear darker and the entire image more yellow because the range of blues is more limited in the Solid version than in the Photographic version). Flesh tones are also more realistic with the Photographic setting.

 The section "Photographic versus Solid Rendering Style" in the "Advanced Color Techniques" full-color instructional gallery shows another example, in color, of how the two rendering styles affect final output.

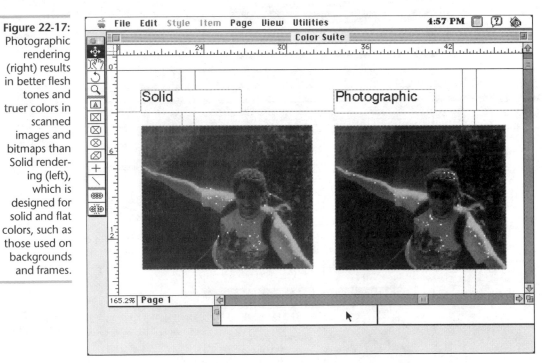

Figure 22-17: Photographic rendering (right) results in better flesh tones and truer colors in scanned images and bitmaps than Solid rendering (left), which is designed for solid and flat colors, such as those used on backgrounds and frames.

You can also change profiles after you import an image by selecting a picture box with the Content tool and selecting Style ➪ Profile. Figure 22-18 shows the resulting dialog box. Note that this option will not appear if EfiColor is not installed. If you open a QuarkXPress chapter with a copy of QuarkXPress that does not have the EfiColor XTension installed, your profile information is retained for the next time you open it in a copy of QuarkXPress that has EfiColor installed.

Figure 22-18:
The Profile dialog box (for a CMYK image).

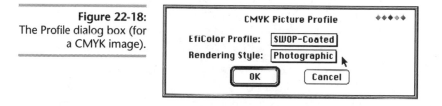

If you are unsure of which profiles a document uses (perhaps someone else put together the document that you are working on), you can use the Profile Usage dialog box (Utilities ➪ Profile Usage). You can also use this dialog box to update any missing profiles or to change to a new profile after you've installed it in your system. Figure 22-19 shows the dialog box. (This dialog box works like the Picture Usage and Font Usage dialog boxes which perform similar functions.)

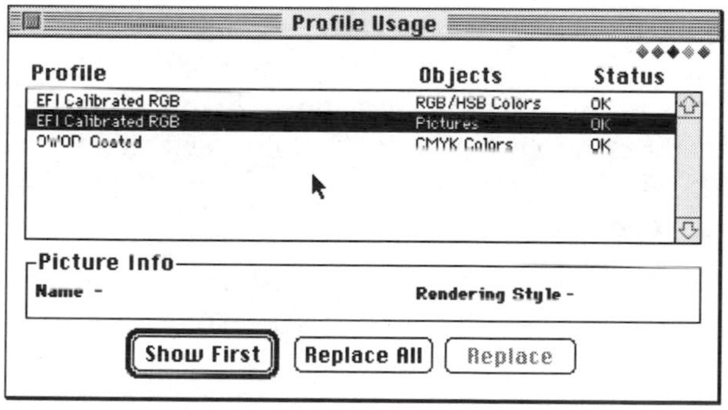

Figure 22-19:
The Profile Usage dialog box.

Calibrating colors for output

By setting the EfiColor profiles when defining colors or importing images, you have done most of the work needed to calibrate your colors for optimal output. Still, you have a few options:

↪ Be sure that the Calibrated Output box is *unchecked* in the Print dialog box (File ⇨ Print, or ⌘P). The EfiColor calibration handles these needs, and having QuarkXPress do its own limited calibration (meant to adjust the dot gain for different output devices, which anticipates the inevitable slight splotching that occurs on a printing press) is unnecessary.

↪ When outputting four-color positives or negatives for eventual output on a printing press, you can change the GCR (gray component replacement) amount in the Page Setup dialog box (File ⇨ Page Setup, or ⌘-Option-P). The amount may vary from printer to printer, but it's usually 75 percent. This option will be grayed out unless you have selected an EfiColor profile and a printer that supports color separations.

What GCR does is replace the grays created by mixing cyan, magenta, and yellow (these grays are created when converting an image from RGB to CMYK) with grays created from shades of black. The higher the GCR level, the sharper the grays. But if you make the level too high, you'll lose some of the soft, naturalistic gray tones that you get from having other colors mixed in. Unless you dislike your output, leave these settings alone. Rely on an image-editing or retouching program to do any serious GCR work — EfiColor's five settings of 0, 25, 50, 75, and 100 percent are insufficient for fine-tuning images.

↪ You can check the Use PDF Screen Values box at the bottom left of the Page Setup dialog box. If the box is unchecked, QuarkXPress uses its own values. If the box is checked, it uses the printer driver's values (PDF is the printer description file) or EfiColor's values. Those values appear in the Halftoning list above the check box. If your printer driver uses special screen angles for optimized color separations (in which moirés are minimized), check the PDF option. Otherwise, leave the box unchecked.

Note that Use PDF Screen Values is replaced with Use EfiColor Screen Values if you have selected a color printer; we suggest you check the box in this case.

Figure 22-20 shows the Page Setup dialog box in which most of the options we've described are available. Note that the dialog box in Figure 22-20 may differ from the one on your Mac because we used the PostScript Level 2 driver (released in late spring 1993), which offers a different layout and a few added options compared to the Level 1 driver.

When printing to a proofing printer (such as to a color thermal printer), set your profile to the final target printer (such as web offset) so that EfiColor can give you a good estimation of what the final output will look like. If you calibrate your output to the proofing printer, EfiColor will adjust the colors accordingly, and those adjustments will likely not represent the adjustments it makes when you do your final output.

Figure 22-20:
The Page Setup dialog box contains several output calibration options including EfiColor profile, gray component removal (GCR), and halftoning screen values.

```
PSPrinter Page Setup                              8.0        [   OK   ]

                    Paper:  [ Letter ▼ ]                     [ Cancel ]
                   Layout:  [ 1 Up   ▼ ]
    ┌──────────┐  Reduce or  [100] %                         [ Options ]
    │    a     │  Enlarge:
    │          │  Orientation:  🛆📄  ▶         ▲             [  Help  ]
    └──────────┘

   Printer Type:   [ Linotronic  ]     Paper Offset:  [ 0p ]
   EfiColor Profile: [ SWOP-Coated ]   Paper Width:   [ 51p ]
   GCR:            [ 75%  ]             Page Gap:      [ 0p ]
   Resolution:     [ 1270 ]  (dpi)    ┌─────Halftoning─────┐
   Paper Size:     [   ]              │ C : 60 lpi, 105°   │
                                      │ M : 60 lpi, 75°    │
   Data Format:    [ Binary ]         │ Y : 60 lpi, 90°    │
                                      │ K : 60 lpi, 45°    │
   Halftone Screen: [ 60 ]  (lpi)    └────────────────────┘
                                      ☐ Use PDF Screen Values
```

Setting EfiColor defaults

You set EfiColor defaults in the EfiColor Preferences dialog box (see Figure 20-21), which is accessed via Edit ➪ Preferences ➪ EfiColor. The options are as follows:

ced **Use EfiColor:** Checking this box enables EfiColor.

ced **Color Printer Corrections:** Checking the boxes in this section of the dialog box enables EfiColor's calibration of imported pictures (except for EPS graphics) and colors created within QuarkXPress for the combination of the target printer and the printing press output profile chosen in the Page Setup dialog box. For colors defined in QuarkXPress, you can select any or all of CMYK process colors, RGB colors, and named colors (those defined via the Pantone, Trumatch, or other swatch-based color models). You should check all as the default unless your printer advises otherwise.

ced **Default Profiles:** For RGB and CMYK colors, you select from the pick lists the default color profiles used when importing color images or creating colors. These profiles tell EfiColor how to alter the output files or printer instructions so that the colors output match your expectations. For RGB colors, choose Apple 13" RGB or the appropriate monitor if you created your images on a Mac and want the colors you saw on-screen to be what EfiColor tries to ensure is output to the target printer or is printed on printing press. Use EFI Calibrated RGB or contact Electronics for Imaging directly (the number is 800/285-4565 or 415/286-8600) for a custom profile. For CMYK colors, select the final output device (use SWOP-Coated for standard web offset printing on coated paper stock, such as what is used in magazines, brochures, and catalogs). As with RGB profiles, you can contact EFI for other profiles. These profiles can be overridden when you import files that come from other devices (such as scanners or monitors), or you can change them on a case-by-case basis in your layout. You can also change the profile when you print (via the Page Setup dialog box, as described in the previous section), which is handy if you are printing to a proofing device before creating your final output.

Figure 22-21:
The EfiColor
Preferences dialog
box.

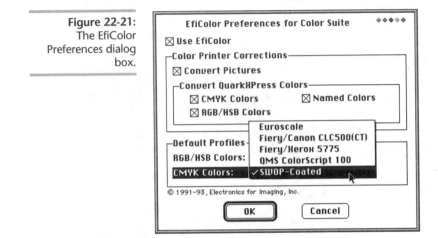

Changes made in the EfiColor Preferences dialog box when no documents are open become the default for all subsequently created documents. Changes made while a document is open affect only the open document.

Summary

•➔ Generally speaking, when you establish trapping values, use spreading (indicated via positive numbers) for light-hued or thin elements; use choking (negative numbers) for darker or thicker elements.

•➔ Use the Trap Information palette to override global trapping settings for selected elements.

•➔ Set your monitor calibration to the same settings in all programs that you use to create images. Make sure colleagues who supply images to you have appropriately calibrated their systems. Make sure any output calibration options are also set for the target printer.

•➔ Whenever possible, define colors with the same color model with which they will be output.

•➔ EfiColor does not calibrate EPS images, so be sure to apply all calibration before importing them into QuarkXPress.

•➔ Use the Solid rendering style for solid colors that you will apply to type, box background, box frames, and the like. Use the Photographic rendering style for imported bitmap files (including scanned photographs) and color blends.

•➔ Set your output profile in the Page Setup dialog to the final target printer even when printing to an intermediary proofing color printer. This technique will let you see more accurately what the final output will be like.

Managing Documents

One of the toughest aspects of publishing — whether done on a desktop computer or via traditional means — is keeping track of the many elements that comprise the document, including the source text, graphics, and style standards.

QuarkXPress offers several tools to help you manage these elements within and across documents. Understanding how to use these tools is critical to using QuarkXPress effectively, especially in an environment in which many people contribute to the final publication. Even if you work in a large organization intent on using a network-wide publishing management system like Quark's own CopyDesk or Quark Publishing System, you'll find that the basic principles covered here are key to understanding how to manage your work flow effectively.

This section covers document management from the successive perspectives of the designer, the people involved in one document, and finally the entire publishing work force. The initial focus is on how you can maintain access to standard elements. The section then explains how to keep your document's elements updated in a changing environment and finally shows how to work with other QuarkXPress users in both a Mac-only and cross-platform environments.

Using Libraries

In This Chapter

➡ Creating and using QuarkXPress libraries

➡ Displaying selected library elements

➡ Moving elements between libraries

➡ Using library elements in documents

A powerful layout-management feature that originated with QuarkXPress is the ability to create *libraries* of text and graphics. This feature is a great aid if you reuse elements throughout a set of publications. For example, you can have a library containing your corporate logos, photos, and such standard text as mastheads and postal statements. QuarkXPress does more than let you create libraries; it lets you create multiple libraries — any or all of which may be open at a time. QuarkXPress also lets you group library elements to make them easy to find.

The libraries themselves are separate files that can reside anywhere on your hard disk (or network). Because the libraries are not part of any document, any document can use them.

QuarkXPress for Mac libraries and QuarkXPress for Windows libraries are not compatible. If you are using QuarkXPress on both platforms, you must create separate libraries for each platform.

Creating Libraries

Before you can use a library, you must create it. Selecting File ➪ New ➪ Libraries (or using the shortcut Option-⌘N) opens the New Library dialog box shown in Figure 23-1. Navigate the folders and disks as you do in any Mac application until you access the folder that you want to use for the library.

Figure 23-1:
The New Library dialog box.

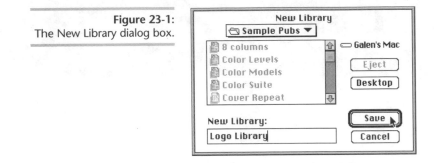

To create a library, enter a name in the New Library field. After you enter a filename, select Save. An empty library appears in your document, as Figure 23-2 shows.

Figure 23-2:
A new, empty library.

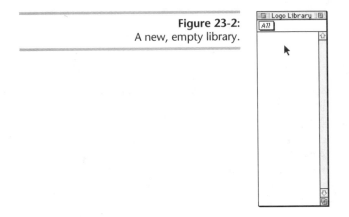

The library filename appears at the top of the library, and the name may be cut off. You can resize the window by selecting the resize icon at the bottom left of the dialog box, or you can click the full-size icon at the upper right to make the library take the full screen space (if you click that icon again, the dialog box returns to the original size). The library elements will flow from left to right (assuming the window is wide enough to hold two or more elements) and then from top to bottom.

Opening libraries

To open a library, use the standard Open dialog box you use for your documents (File ⇨ Open, or ⌘O). You can distinguish libraries from documents by the icon that QuarkXPress displays. Figure 23-3 shows both icons; the one that looks like a stack of books (near the pointer) is the library. We suggest that you use the word "library" in your names or an abbreviation like ".lib" or ".qxl" at the end of your file name to make it easier to distinguish libraries from regular documents.

Figure 23-3:
QuarkXPress uses a different icon for libraries (the books) than for documents (the layout).

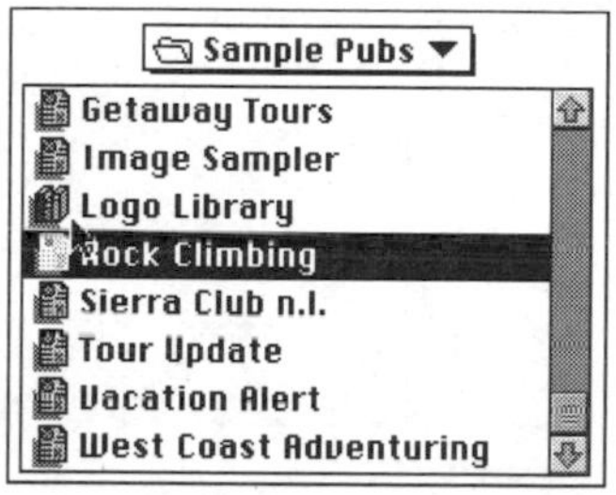

> Sample Pubs ▼
>
> 🖹 Getaway Tours
> 🖹 Image Sampler
> 📕 Logo Library
> **Rock Climbing**
> 🖹 Sierra Club n.l.
> 🖹 Tour Update
> 📕 Uacation Alert
> 🖹 West Coast Adventuring

Adding Elements to Libraries

After you create your library, you can add elements from any open document or library to it. If you want to bring in elements from several documents, you can — the library window stays on-screen as you open and close documents, as well as when you open and close other libraries.

There are two basic ways to add elements to libraries:

- **Option 1:** Use the standard cut, copy, and paste functions, either through the keyboard shortcuts (⌘X, ⌘C, and ⌘V, respectively) or through the Edit menus in the QuarkXPress document and library windows.

- **Option 2:** Drag elements from documents or libraries to the destination library (see Figure 23-4). Notice how the pointer changes to a pair of glasses (the library pointer) and a thin box appears when your pointer is in the library window. Figure 23-4 illustrates this part of the process. Release the mouse button, and the element appears as a box in the library window.

Whichever method you prefer, make sure the Item tool is selected (not the Content tool) because boxes can be moved only with the Item tool.

If you check the Auto Library Save option in the Application Preferences dialog box (open by selecting Edit ➪ Preferences ➪ Application), the library is saved each time that you add or delete an element. Otherwise, the library is saved when you save the current document, close the library, or quit QuarkXPress. (Preferences are covered in Chapter 4.)

Figure 23-4: Dragging an element into the library window.

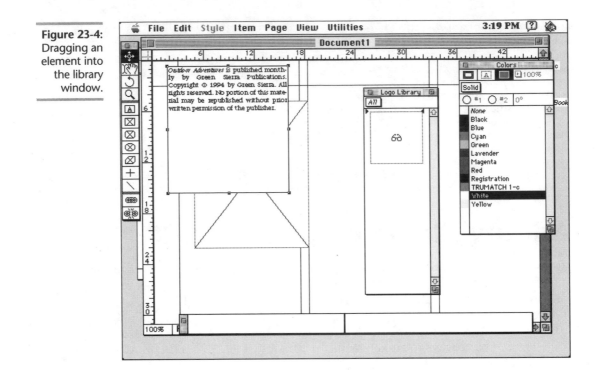

Repeat the copying process for all elements (from all documents) that you want to put in the library. The result is a library like the one shown in Figure 23-5. We opened several documents to get elements for this library. You may find that your libraries evolve over time, too. Figure 23-6 shows the same library resized. Notice how the elements' order changes so that elements go from left to right and then top to bottom.

Libraries will accept only elements that are in text or picture boxes or that are created with one of the line tools. You cannot include a graphics file that is not in a picture box or a text file that is not in a text box. All attributes applied to boxes — including frames, backgrounds, and colors — are retained when you copy the boxes to libraries. Graphics include all cropping, sizing, and other such information; text includes all formatting — including paragraph styles and H&J sets.

If you have a style in a library whose name matches that of a style in the document to which the library element is being moved, QuarkXPress will apply the library's styles to the copied text, but it will not change the document's style definition. (It simply applies the library style's formatting locally to the copied text.) In the case of having H&J sets with the same name in the library and the target document, the H&J settings from the document will be applied to the copied text because QuarkXPress does not allow local application of H&J information. (Chapter 6 explains how to override styles.)

You may use elements linked via Publish and Subscribe in a library. The link to the source document and originating application are retained for the element when copied or moved into a library and when placed into a new document from the library.

Figure 23-5: A library with text and graphics elements from several documents. The library palette's width shown here is the default width; Figure 23-6 shows how a user might resize the palette.

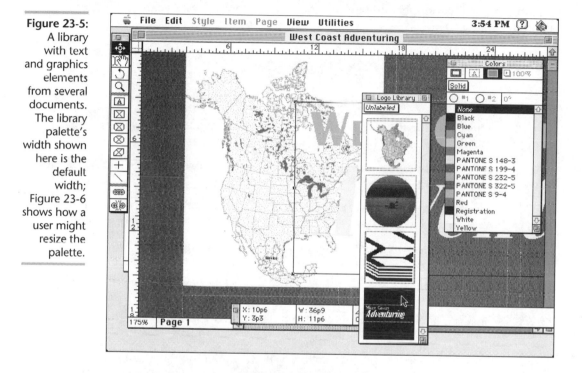

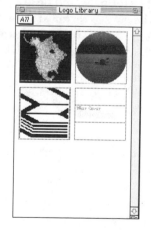

Figure 23-6: The library palette in Figure 23-5 resized.

Adding Master Pages to Libraries ___

Moving master pages from documents to libraries is tricky because QuarkXPress offers no feature explicitly designed to perform this task. But you can move master pages by taking the following steps:

STEPS: **Moving Master Pages to Libraries**

Step 1.   Open or create a library to hold the master pages.

Step 2.   Open the document that contains the master page that you want to copy. Display the master page by selecting Page ➪ Display.

Step 3.   Select the Item tool and then select all items (choose Edit ➪ Select All or use the shortcut ⌘A).

Step 4.   Drag (or copy and paste) the items into an open library and release the mouse. All elements on the master page appear in their own library box.

Step 5.   Open the document into which you want to copy the master page. You don't need to close the other document, but unless you intend to get other elements from it or work on it later, go ahead and close it to reduce clutter both on-screen and in the Mac's memory.

Step 6.   Insert a new blank master page in the second document. (Creating master pages is covered in Chapter 5.)

Step 7.   Drag (or copy and paste) the library item containing the master-page elements to the new master page and position it where you want it. (You may want to change the screen display to fit-to-window view so that you can better position the elements on the new master page. To display this view, select View ➪ Fit in Window or use the keyboard shortcut ⌘0 [zero].)

Step 8.   Use the Document Layout palette to display the master pages and rename the new master page so that you can remember what it contains.

 Master pages are discussed in detail in Chapter 5.

Managing Libraries _____

After elements are in your library, you can manage their order and remove unwanted elements. You can always add elements later using the techniques described in the preceding section, and you can use those same techniques to copy elements from library to library.

Rearranging element order

The order of elements in a library depends on where you drop them or where the pointer is when you paste them. If you want to rearrange the order, select the element you want to move, hold down the mouse button, and move the pointer to the new position in the library window. Release the mouse button when you reach the desired location (the triangles that appear as you move the element are the insertion points).

Labeling elements

Because a library can easily grow so large that there are too many elements to scroll through, QuarkXPress lets you assign labels to elements. You then can tell QuarkXPress to display only those elements that have a particular label. In effect, you create sublibraries within a library. The process of adding a label is simple. Just follow these steps:

STEPS:	Labeling Elements in a Library
Step 1.	Double-click the element you want to label. The Library Entry dialog box appears.
Step 2.	Either type in a label (see Figure 23-7), or select an existing label (a label already used in the current library) from the drop-down list box next to the Label field. Several entries can have the same label.
Step 3.	Choose OK.

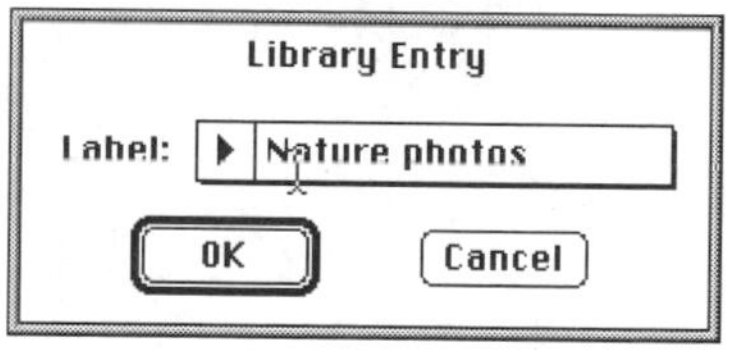

Figure 23-7:
The Library Entry dialog box.

Library Entry

Label: ▶ Nature photos

OK   Cancel

The label does not display with the element image in the library window. To see a label, you must double-click the item to bring up the Library Entry dialog box.

After you create labels, you can use the library window's Labels menu (see Figure 23-8) to select which elements are displayed. Because All is checked, all elements are displayed. If you select Unlabeled, QuarkXPress displays all elements that are not labeled. This option is handy for those odds-and-ends library elements you want to see infrequently but need to access easily.

You can select more than one type of label. To do this, double-click the All label. The label in the pick list will change to Mixed Labels (see Figure 23-9), and all label names will have check marks to their left. You can deselect (or reselect) each label in turn to determine the labels for those elements you want to see.

Figure 23-8:
The labels menu in the library window.

Figure 23-9:
Using the mixed labels option, you can select multiple groups of elements to be displayed.

Using multiple libraries

Although labels are a great way to keep the list of library elements manageable, this method is no substitute for creating different libraries to hold distinct groups of elements. Don't let the label feature be an excuse for having an unwieldy library. When the elements in a library become too diverse, it's time to create a new library and move some elements into it. There are three ways to move elements from one library to another:

- **Option 1:** Drag the element into the new library. This option copies the element from the first library into the second while leaving the original element intact in the first library.

- **Option 2:** Use the copy command in the first library and paste a copy of the element into the second library. This option also copies the element from the first library into the second while leaving the original element intact in the first library.

- **Option 3:** Use the cut command in the first library and paste the element into the second library. The element is removed from the first library.

Another benefit of creating multiple libraries is that you can more easily find the library elements that a specific document requires if you use logical filenames for your libraries, such as Corporate Logos or Kayaking Photos.

Deleting unwanted elements

Your libraries will evolve over time as your document elements change. As a result, you will occasionally need to delete library elements. There are two ways to delete elements:

- **Cut:** Cutting an element removes it from the library but puts a copy in the clipboard so that you can paste it elsewhere, such as into another document or library.

- **Clear:** Clearing an element removes it from the library and does not put a copy in the clipboard. A cleared element is erased permanently from the current library.

You can use QuarkXPress's Edit menu to cut and clear. To cut an element, you also can use the keyboard shortcut ⌘X. There is no shortcut for clear. When you cut or clear an element, QuarkXPress asks you to confirm the edit, as shown in Figure 23-10.

Figure 23-10: QuarkXPress asks for confirmation when you attempt to cut or clear an element from a library.

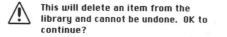

This will delete an item from the library and cannot be undone. OK to continue?

OK

Cancel

Using Library Elements

After you create and fill your libraries, it's easy to move the library elements into your documents. Just drag them or use the cut, copy, and paste commands as you did to put elements in the library in the first place.

Note that library elements always paste into documents in their original size, not the smaller version displayed in the library. After you place an element into a document, you can modify it as you do any other text box, picture box, or line.

Libraries are especially helpful when you work with graphic and text elements that have special effects applied. For example, you might place a text box that has a word rotated, drop-shadowed, and colored. You probably won't want to have that word used in other documents, but you'll probably want to reuse the effect. By placing such special-effects text in the library, you save yourself the work of later applying those special effects. After copying the element into a document, you can easily change the text to something else while retaining all the formatting of the original element. This technique is also handy for special lines like arrowheads and for picture boxes that have intricate frames, special color blends, or odd shapes.

Summary

➻ Libraries let you collect common text, pictures, and lines that are then available to any document with all formatting retained. You can put complex text formatting in a library by applying such formatting to dummy text and putting that text in the library.

➻ Graphics placed into libraries maintain all links — including Publish and Subscribe links — to their source files.

➻ You can enlarge library windows to make their names more readable. You also can reduce library windows so that they do not cover up too much of a document.

➻ Dragging elements to a library is the easiest way to add them to a library.

➻ Make sure to select the Item tool before trying to drag or copy a picture box, text box, or line to a library.

➻ If you check the Auto Library Save option in the Application Preferences dialog box, QuarkXPress automatically saves libraries any time you change them.

➻ You can reposition the elements in a library by selecting them and moving them to a new location.

➻ Element labels let you view selected groups of library elements.

➻ Use multiple libraries to keep manageable the number of elements in any one library.

➻ You can move or copy elements between libraries.

Linking to Source Files

In This Chapter

➡ Updating links to source graphics

➡ Understanding Publish and Subscribe and how subscribed objects and links differ from standard objects and links

➡ Updating links to subscribed objects

➡ Exporting text

Document elements such as text and graphics may change, and you need to ensure that your document contains the latest version of all elements. In addition, you sometimes need to make sure that any changes you make to text in a document are made to the original text files because you may want to use the same text in other documents. Both of these problems can be solved with a process known as *linking*. QuarkXPress supports several types of links, all of which are detailed in the sidebar "Understanding Links."

QuarkXPress offers features that address several linking issues, but in some areas, it offers no support at all. QuarkXPress is particularly adept at two kinds of graphic links: static links and Publish and Subscribe (dynamic) links. QuarkXPress is weak, however, at making text links.

Working with Graphics Links _____

You can bring graphics into QuarkXPress documents in two ways: You can import them through the File ➪ Get Picture menu or use the Macintosh clipboard to copy a graphic from another Mac application directly into QuarkXPress. Both methods have their advantages:

➥ The primary advantage to using the import method is that you can create a link to the original graphic in case the graphic is changed or moved.

Understanding Links

QuarkXPress supports several types of links to source files, particularly graphics. The terms used to describe links can be confusing, especially since people tend to use the word "link" generically, no matter what kind of link they are referring to. Links in QuarkXPress fall into two classes: static links to files and dynamic links to objects.

Static links are the standard links common to most publishing programs. When you import a graphics file, QuarkXPress records the location of the file and its date and time stamp. The next time you open a document, QuarkXPress looks to see if the graphic is in its expected location and if its date and time stamp has changed (if so, the graphic itself has been changed in some way since the last time Quark checked the file upon opening the document). QuarkXPress makes these checks for two reasons: First, by linking to the original graphic, QuarkXPress needs to make only a low-resolution image for use on-screen, which keeps the document size manageable and screen-redraw time quick. (When printing, QuarkXPress substitutes the actual high-resolution graphic.) Second, by checking the links, QuarkXPress gives the layout artist the opportunity to use the latest version of a graphic. You can choose for QuarkXPress to do one of the following: always load the latest version of a graphic; ignore any updates to a graphic; or ask you to decide whether or not to update the graphic. If the graphic is not where QuarkXPress expects it to be, the program asks you to find the graphic.

Dynamic links are possible with a new capability offered by System 7 via Publish and Subscribe. Dynamic links differ from static links in two significant ways: First, they are links to *objects* (called *editions*), not entire files. You might, for example, have a link to a range in a spreadsheet or to part of a graphic. Second, the links can be updated any time, not just when you open a document. Dynamic links are managed through a System 7 technology called Apple Events that lets programs communicate with each other and share objects among them in the background without user intervention or management.

There are two basic types of dynamic links: *live* (automatic) and *manual:*

- With live dynamic links, there is regular communication between QuarkXPress and the program that created the object. If the linked object is changed in its original program, the new version is automatically sent to QuarkXPress, which automatically updates the object in the layout document to which it is linked.

- With manual dynamic links, either the publisher or the subscriber must update the link by clicking the Send Edition Now button (in the publishing program) or Get Edition Now button (in the subscribing program).

Either way, the subscriber always has the option of launching the original program with the original file so that modifications can be made.

☞ The primary advantage to using the clipboard method is that you can copy into a document graphics that QuarkXPress ordinarily cannot import. The Mac clipboard translates them to a format (PICT) that QuarkXPress can read. (Note that the PICT format has limits on terms of output resolution and of the image controls that QuarkXPress can apply to it; see Chapters 7 and 20 for details.)

When you open a QuarkXPress document, QuarkXPress checks the links to any imported graphic. These links are created automatically when you import the file; no special effort on your part is needed. QuarkXPress looks for two things: Is the file where it is supposed to be, and has the file changed since the last time it was accessed? (QuarkXPress looks at the file's date and time stamp to determine the second factor.)

If the file is missing or has been modified, QuarkXPress displays the alert box shown in Figure 24-1. You can select Cancel, which tells QuarkXPress not to worry about the problem, or you can choose OK to invoke the Missing/Modified Pictures dialog box, shown in Figure 24-2. (A file might be missing because the file was deleted, moved to a different disk [perhaps for backup], or renamed.)

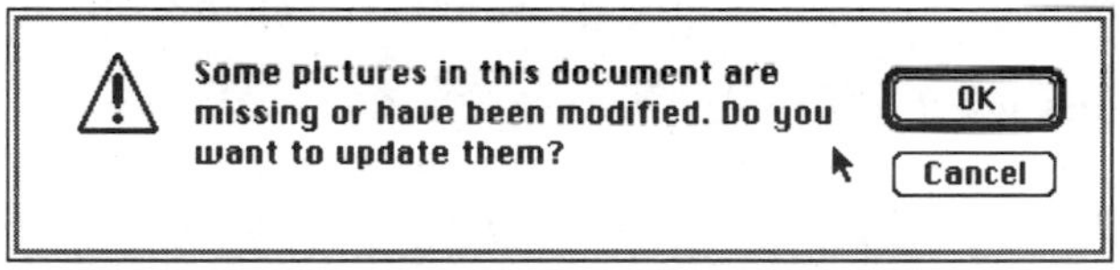

Figure 24-1:
QuarkXPress warns you if files are missing or have been modified.

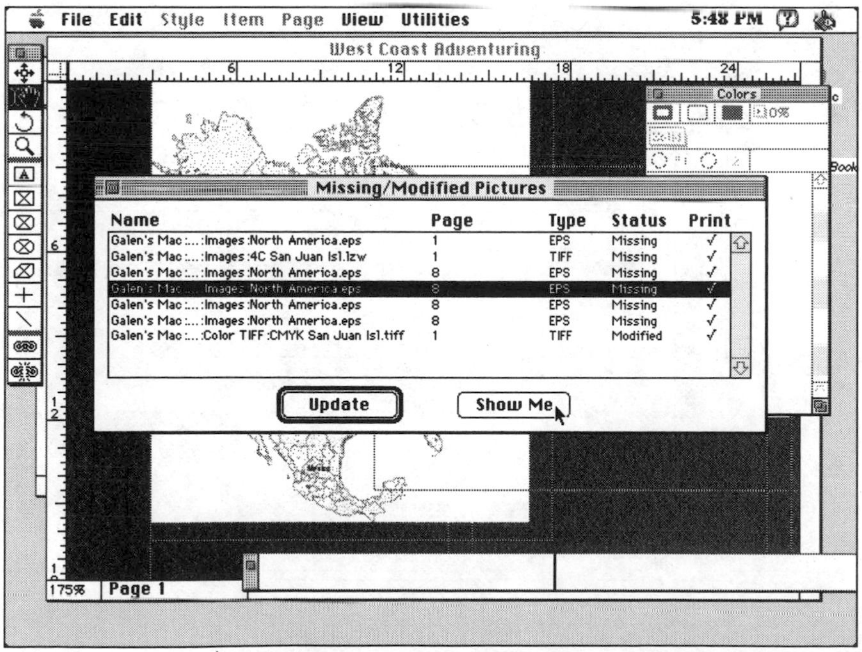

Figure 24-2:
The Missing/ Modified Pictures dialog box.

If you have set your general preferences (Edit ⇨ Preferences ⇨ General, or ⌘Y) so that the Auto Import Picture option is Off, QuarkXPress will not alert you to missing pictures.

The Missing/Modified Pictures dialog box (see Figure 24-2) gives you several pieces of information about the graphics that are missing or have been modified. These include:

ߚ The full file name, including the last known location.

ߚ The page that each graphic appears on. A dagger (†) with the page number indicates that it appears in the adjacent pasteboard.

ߚ The type of graphic format, such as TIFF or EPS.

ߚ The graphic's status (OK, Missing, or Modified). OK appears only after you update a graphic.

ߚ The graphic's print status. If a check mark appears, the graphic will print; by unchecking a graphic, you can suppress its printing. You toggle between having a check mark and not having one by clicking under the Print column in the row for the desired graphic. (Chapter 26 covers printing issues in more detail.)

When you update a graphic, QuarkXPress checks the folder in which the graphic was located to see if other missing graphics are in it (because a common reason for missing graphics is that they have been moved). If it finds other missing graphics, it displays the dialog box shown in Figure 24-3, which gives you the chance to simultaneously update all the missing files in that folder.

Figure 24-3:
QuarkXPress checks for other missing files in the folder from which you update a file, giving you the option to let it automatically update the other files.

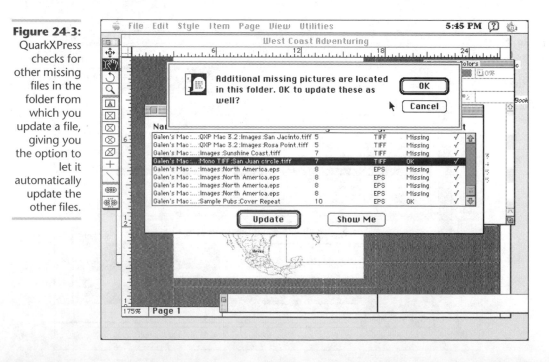

If you need to see the graphic to remember which graphic a file name refers to, select the file name and then choose Show Me in the Missing/Modified Pictures dialog box. QuarkXPress displays the screen version of the graphic on the page on which it occurs. You should be in a normal (100%) or reduced view so that you can see enough of the image when QuarkXPress displays it.

If you don't update files when you open your document (by selecting Cancel in response to the alert box or by not making selections in the Missing/Modified Pictures dialog box), you still see the graphics in your document, as Figure 24-2 shows. What you see is a low-resolution copy of your graphic that QuarkXPress creates when importing a graphic. This low-resolution copy is not appropriate for printing and should not be used in place of the real thing. It exists only to show you what graphic you placed in case you don't remember the graphic by name.

If you decide not to update a graphic link when you first load your document, you can do so later through the Utilities ⇨ Picture Usage dialog box (see Figure 24-4). This box works the same way as the Missing/Modified Pictures dialog box. You can use the Picture Usage dialog box to substitute new graphics for missing graphics because QuarkXPress doesn't know (or care) whether the new links are to the same graphics.

Figure 24-4:
The Picture
Usage dialog
box.

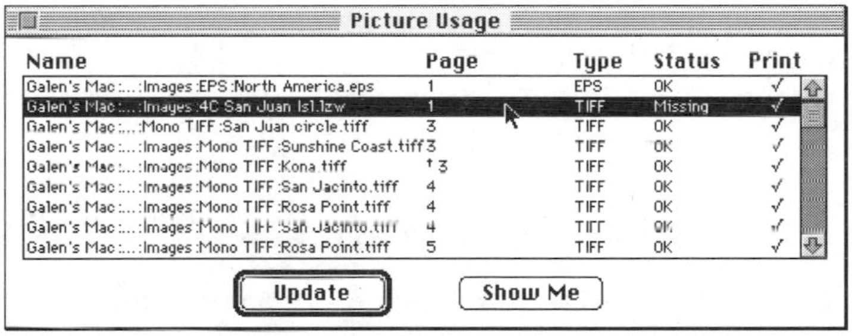

Updating missing graphics

To update the link to a missing graphic, select the file name and then choose Update. Then move through the drives and folders available through the Find *file name* dialog box, shown in Figure 24-5. QuarkXPress uses the standard Mac dialog box to search for missing graphics. In Figure 24-5, the file is located in a different directory than the one it was imported from. If you choose OK, you update the link to the graphic and return to the Missing/Modified Pictures dialog box. You see confirmation of your selection in the dialog box and can update any other files. After you've found the file, it will no longer be labeled "Missing," but it may be labeled "Modified" if the newly located file is more recent than the original. Click the Update button again in the dialog box to update the link to the file.

Figure 24-5:
Search for
missing
graphics in
the Find *file
name* dialog
box.

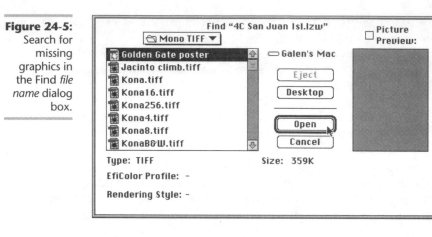

Note that only files that match a particular file type (in Figure 24-5, TIFF) appear in the Find *file name* dialog box's file list. You cannot use this dialog box to replace one type of file (say, TIFF) with another (say, EPS). The way to perform this kind of change is to simply use File ⇨ Get Picture and load the new image into the appropriate picture box.

QuarkXPress can determine whether DOS or Windows files transferred to the Mac are of the appropriate file type for display in the dialog box. You do not have to manually edit the file type in a program like ResEdit or DiskTop, nor do you have to use a translation program to add the file type for, say, TIFF or EPS.

Updating modified graphics

The process for updating a modified graphic is simpler than updating a missing graphic because QuarkXPress already knows where the graphic is located. To update a graphic, select the file name and choose Update. QuarkXPress prompts you with a dialog box and asks you if it is OK to update the file. (You can also cancel the update through this dialog box.) If you choose OK, QuarkXPress creates a new low-resolution screen representation and updates its link to the modified graphic. You also see the graphic's status change to OK.

Only if you have selected On (verify) as the option for Auto Picture Import in the General Preferences dialog box (Edit ⇨ Preferences ⇨ General, or ⌘Y) will you be prompted to update modified pictures.

Deleting a missing graphic's link

If a graphic is missing because you no longer want to use it and have deleted it from your Mac, you can remove the link to it by either cutting the box or boxes that contain the picture or by clearing the picture from any boxes that contain it. (The Item tool must be active to cut a box; use ⌘X or Edit ➪ Cut. The Content tool must be active to clear a box; use Edit ➪ Clear.) Use the Show Me feature in the Missing/Modified Pictures or Picture Usage dialog box to find these boxes.

Finishing the update process

When all missing or modified graphics are updated, their names disappear from the Missing/Modified Pictures dialog box. Whether you were working with missing or modified graphics (or both), you may be puzzled about how to leave the Missing/Modified Pictures (or Picture Usage) dialog box because it does not offer an OK button. To close the dialog box, click the close box in the upper-left corner of the dialog box.

It's possible to complete all of these steps without any of the updates taking place. If you do not save your document, none of the updates are saved.

Working with Publish and Subscribe Links

System 7 brought with it a powerful feature called *Publish and Subscribe* that lets you create *live links* directly between applications. This feature ensures that when you make changes to text or graphics in the program in which you originally created them, the text or graphics are instantly and automatically updated in other programs that use them. Through object embedding, you can launch the application that created the graphic in QuarkXPress and work on the graphic.

Windows users may recognize Publish and Subscribe as similar to Microsoft's OLE (which stands for Object Linking and Embedding and is pronounced like the Spanish word *olé*) capability. OLE and Publish and Subscribe accomplish the same thing. The main difference is that the user of a source application on a Mac must explicitly publish a file to make it available for subscribing, whereas the user of a Windows source application needs only to copy or cut a graphic or text to put it in the Windows clipboard for linking. Another difference is that

OLE is implemented on both the Mac and on Windows, so that some programs (like Microsoft Excel) can have cross-platform links, but Publish and Subscribe is a Mac-only feature. Unfortunately, QuarkXPress supports OLE only in its Windows version, so you cannot have such cross-platform links.

Creating live links

The first step to creating a live link is to create an *edition*, which is the result of publishing all or part of a file in its originating program. This edition file contains the link to the original file and program as well as a copy of the data itself (so that if the original file is lost, you will still have a static image of it).

STEPS: **Publishing and Subscribing to an Element**

Step 1. Select the element(s) in the originating program that you want to publish. Some programs, like Excel, require that you select the element(s); others, like Photoshop, require that you publish the entire file. Figure 24-6 shows the dialog box in Excel, and Figure 24-7 shows the dialog box in Photoshop. Both are accessed via Edit ⇨ Create Publisher.

Step 2. Most programs offer publish options that determine file format and degree of information published. For example, in Figure 24-6, we clicked the Options button to get the Publish Options dialog box (below it), which lets us determine the file format and the resolution. In Figure 24-7, Photoshop's options (choice of PICT, TIFF, and EPS) are in the main publish dialog box.

Because QuarkXPress can subscribe only to graphics, make sure that you publish your data as graphics (for example, the published Excel data will be used as a picture, not as a textual table). Also, make sure that you publish the data in PICT or EPS format — QuarkXPress cannot subscribe to other formats.

Step 3. In QuarkXPress, create or select the picture box that you want to put the edition into. Then choose Edit ⇨ Subscribe To. The dialog box is similar to the Get Picture dialog box, as Figure 24-8 shows. The subscribed-to graphic even has the appropriate color profile applied to it by the EfiColor XTension if the format is PICT.

If your picture box already has a graphic in it, you must have the Content tool active to use Subscribe to place a new graphic in the box. If no graphic is in the picture box, either the Content or Item tool may be active.

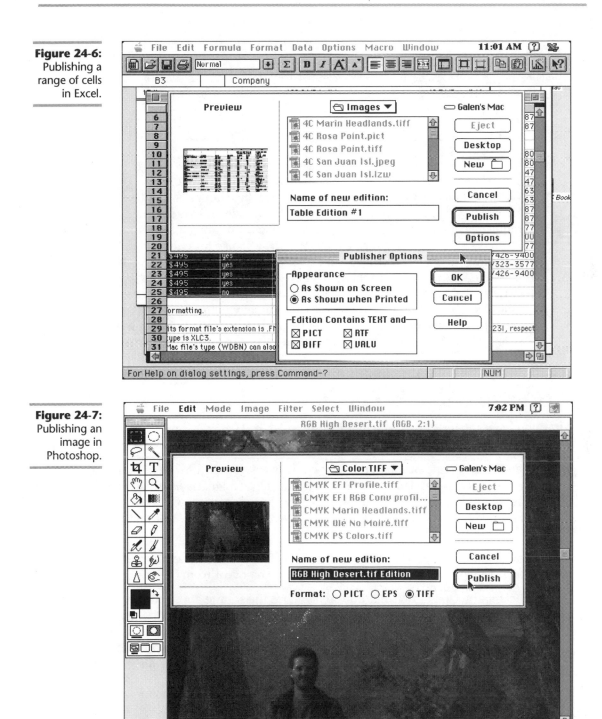

Figure 24-8:
Subscribing
to an edition.

 We don't believe Publish and Subscribe's live-link feature is significantly useful for most QuarkXPress users to be worth the hassle and system memory requirements. QuarkXPress's own graphic-links updating features handle most of what Publish and Subscribe offer. We do see a use for people publishing changing data, such as prices from an Excel table, but because the data must be published as a graphic, users must choose between printing data graphically (when they'd most likely want to format the data in QuarkXPress so that it looks like the rest of their document) or manually reimporting the updated data when it is changed (of course, someone will have to tell them that it has changed, or they will have to check themselves before finalizing their layout).

Updating live links

After you have subscribed to an edition, you can control when it is updated via Edit ⇨ Subscriber Options (see Figure 24-9). Your options are as follows:

- ⊶ The Get Editions portion of the dialog box offers you the choice of Automatically or Manually. The default option is Automatically, which means that whenever the source object is altered, the new version will be placed into QuarkXPress. No matter which you choose, you can click the Get Edition Now button to update the link to the source.

- ⊶ Clicking the Cancel Subscriber button breaks the link to the edition. The current image remains in your document unless you remove it from the picture box.

- ⊶ Clicking the Open Publisher button launches the source application so that you can modify the source object. Note that the application will likely not appear over your current application. If you use the System 7 task list (the list of open applications you get at the far right of the menu bar), you will see the application and be able to select it, bringing it to the foreground with the linked file already loaded.

 If the Content tool is active and you double-click a subscribed-to picture, the Subscriber Options dialog box automatically appears.

The publishing program has a menu item called Publisher Options (in the Edit menu) to cancel the publisher (shown in Figure 24-10 for Photoshop), which deletes the edition file. If the publisher is canceled, a static copy of the last version will be retained in your document. Figure 24-10 shows this dialog box, which is similar to the Subscriber Options dialog box.

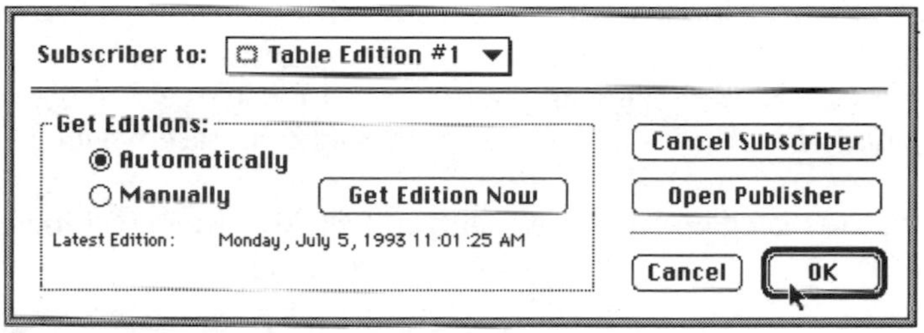

Figure 24-9:
Using the Subscriber options, you control when linked files are updated, and you can also sever a link (cancel a subscription).

> **Subscriber to:** ☐ Table Edition #1 ▼
>
> ┌─ **Get Editions:** ──────────────────┐
> │ ● Automatically   │   [Cancel Subscriber]
> │ ○ Manually   [Get Edition Now]   │   [Open Publisher]
> │ Latest Edition: Monday, July 5, 1993 11:01:25 AM │
> └───────────────────────────────────────┘
>   [Cancel] [**OK**]

Figure 24-10:
Publisher options include control over when linked files are updated and when a published edition is deleted (canceled).

> **Publisher to:** ┌────────────────────────────────┐
>   │ ☐ **RGB High Desert.tif Edition** │
>   │ 🗁 Other   │
> ┌─ **Send Editions:** 🗁 Images   │   [Cancel Publisher]
> │ ● On Save   🗁 QHP Mac 3.3   │
> │ ○ Manually   🗁 IDG Books   │
> │ Latest Edition: 🖙 Galen's Mac   │
>   │ ▓ **Desktop**   │   [Cancel] [**OK**]
>   └────────────────────────────────┘

 You can locate the edition file by clicking and holding the mouse over the file name at the top of either the Subscriber Options or Publisher Options dialog box; the folder hierarchy will display, as shown in Figure 24-10.

Launching source applications

A simpler way to use the Subscribe feature is to launch the application that created a graphic used in a QuarkXPress layout. To do this, you don't have to use Publish. Any graphic imported into QuarkXPress — via Edit ⇨ Subscribe To or File ⇨ Get Picture — may have its originating application launched so that you can work on the graphic.

To launch an application, use the Edit ⇨ Subscriber Options (either the Content or Item tool may be active), as shown in Figure 24-9 and select the Open Publisher button. If the Content tool is active, you can double-click the picture box to get this dialog box. Select Open Publisher to load the program with the source file open in it. Note that the application will likely not appear over your current application. Use the System 7 task list (the list of open applications you get at the far right of the menu bar) to select the application and bring it to the foreground.

 You can locate a file by clicking and holding the mouse over the file name at the top of the Subscriber Options dialog box; the folder hierarchy will be displayed.

The other options in the dialog box are irrelevant, and clicking them will have no effect.

Working with Text

QuarkXPress offers fewer features for text links than it does for graphics links. Its text-link features are essentially limited to export capabilities.

Loading the latest text

One of the few omissions in QuarkXPress is the ability to link text so that you can keep versions of your source text current with your layout. This ability is particularly handy if you want to ensure that your layout uses the latest version of text that changes periodically, such as a price list. Unfortunately, even with the Publish and Subscribe capabilities, you cannot get around this omission because QuarkXPress treats subscribed objects as graphics, not as text.

The only workable option is to reimport changed source text. Before you perform this task, first select all the old text with Edit ⇨ Select All and then delete or cut it.

Exporting the latest text

Fortunately, QuarkXPress offers a way to save changed text in your document to a word-processing file. This feature is beneficial if you need to use the text in other documents or just want to ensure that all versions of text are the same throughout the office.

To export text, you must first select the text with the Content tool. You can highlight specific text to export, or you can just make sure that your text cursor is active in a story that you want to export. After you are ready to export, invoke the Save Text dialog box, shown in Figure 24-11, by selecting File ⇨ Save Text.

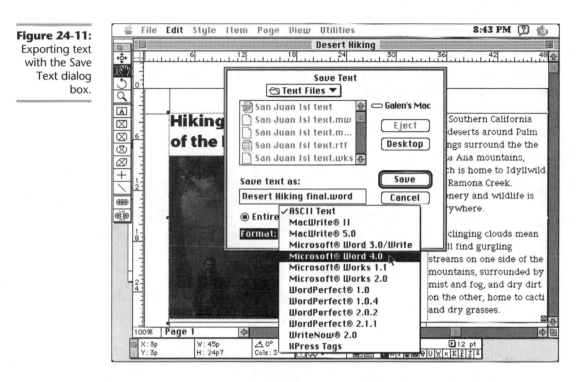

Figure 24-11:
Exporting text
with the Save
Text dialog
box.

The dialog box gives you the following options, which you can do in any order before clicking the Save button:

- ☞ Choose the disk and folder that you want to save the text file to.

- ☞ Choose Entire Story (obscured in Figure 24-11 by the pick list of file formats) if you want all the text in the current chain saved (this is easier than remembering to use ⌘A or Edit ⇨ Select All before invoking the dialog box). Choose Selected Text (also obscured in the figure) if you want to save just the highlighted text (if no text is highlighted, this option is grayed out).

- ☞ Pick the format to save in. When choosing the format, pick your word processor's native format unless you want to export the text for use in other QuarkXPress documents. In that case, use the XPress Tags format, which includes all the codes needed to bring over style tags and formatting.

 Not all programs (or all versions of a program) support all formatting available in QuarkXPress, but most Mac programs support the vast majority of formatting features. Only QuarkXPress's own XPress Tags format retains all QuarkXPress formatting.

Another way to export text is to copy it to the Mac clipboard and paste it into your word processor or other program. But text copied via the clipboard loses all formatting, including such character formatting as font and size and such paragraph formatting as indentations and leading. Special symbols may be lost if you use a different typeface in your word processor than in the QuarkXPress document because not all fonts have all characters available.

Summary

⇥ QuarkXPress checks the status of graphics files when it opens a dialog box, letting you update links to missing or modified graphics.

⇥ Graphics brought into QuarkXPress via the Mac clipboard are copied directly into the document and thus have no links to their source.

⇥ You can update missing or modified links later (rather than right after loading a document) via the Picture Usage dialog box.

⇥ QuarkXPress checks to see if updated graphics are in a supported file format; those that are not are marked in the Picture Usage dialog box.

⇥ QuarkXPress supports live links via System 7's Publish and Subscribe technology. It can have live links that are automatically updated or manually updated, depending on the user's selection.

⇥ QuarkXPress treats all subscribed objects — even text — as graphics, so you must select a picture box for import. You cannot edit subscribed text objects in QuarkXPress.

⇥ Canceled (severed) links leave a copy of the subscribed object in your document as a graphic.

⇥ The Save Text dialog box lets you save parts of a story or an entire story in several word processing formats.

⇥ Exporting text in the XPress Tags format lets you use that text in other QuarkXPress documents with all style and formatting information retained.

⇥ Avoid using the clipboard to copy text from QuarkXPress to your word processor because most character formatting is lost.

Using QuarkXPress in a Workgroup

CHAPTER 25

In This Chapter

•➔ What common elements can be put in a common location and shared by multiple users

•➔ How to share document and general preferences — including kerning, colors, and spelling exceptions — with other documents

•➔ How to create common libraries and graphics

•➔ How to share styles, H&J sets, and master pages among documents

•➔ What to watch for in transferring files between Macintosh and Windows versions of QuarkXPress

•➔ File-transfer tools

Working Together Effectively _____

Publishing is rarely a single-person enterprise. Chances are that the creators of your text and graphics are not the same people who do your layout. And in many environments, the chances are high that many people are involved in layout and production.

By its very nature, publishing is a group activity, and so publishing programs must support workgroups. Yet a Mac is a *personal* computer, so it's easy to work on a Mac without worrying about how your setup and work style might affect others. QuarkXPress lets you create your own balance between the individual and the workgroup.

The key to working effectively in a workgroup environment is to establish standards and make sure that it's easy to stick to them. A basic way to accomplish this task is to place all common elements in one place so that people always know where to get the standard elements. This practice also makes it easy to maintain (to add, modify, and delete) these elements over time — which is essential because no environment is static.

⚭ If you don't use a network, keep a master set of disks and copy elements from the master set in a folder with the same name on each person's Mac. Update these folders every time a standard element changes on the master disk.

⚭ If you do use a network, keep a master set of disks (networks do go down, so you'll want your files accessible when that happens) and create a folder for your standard elements on a network drive accessible to all users. Update this folder whenever a standard element changes on the master disk.

Sharing with Other Mac Users

Some standard elements can easily be accessed from a common folder because QuarkXPress can import certain elements that are stored outside QuarkXPress documents. These elements include graphics files, libraries, kerning tables, and spelling dictionaries.

Other elements reside within documents and templates and cannot be saved in separate files. These elements include edited tracking tables, style sheets, hyphenation-exception dictionaries, H&J sets, color definitions, master pages, and picture-contrast specifications. But style sheets, H&J sets, and color definitions can be appended (imported) from one document to another, and there is a workaround to copying master pages among documents (described later).

When working in a document, all changes that you make via the preferences dialog boxes, the hyphenation dictionary, the kerning and tracking tables, color definitions, and picture-contrast specification are saved with the document as part of its preferences. If you want to use them in another document, you may be out of luck and have to re-create them in that other document. The following sections explain what you can standardize on.

Preference files

When no document is open and you change these preferences (except for picture-contrast specifications, which may be defined only for specific graphics, not globally), the modified settings are stored in a file called XPress Preferences that resides in the Mac folder containing QuarkXPress. If you keep the XPress Preferences file current with all your preferences, you can apply these preferences to all previously created documents by opening them and selecting the Use XPress Preferences button. Figure 25-1 shows this dialog box, which is invoked automatically if QuarkXPress detects a difference between QuarkXPress's preferences and the documents. (Newly created documents always use the most current XPress Preferences settings.)

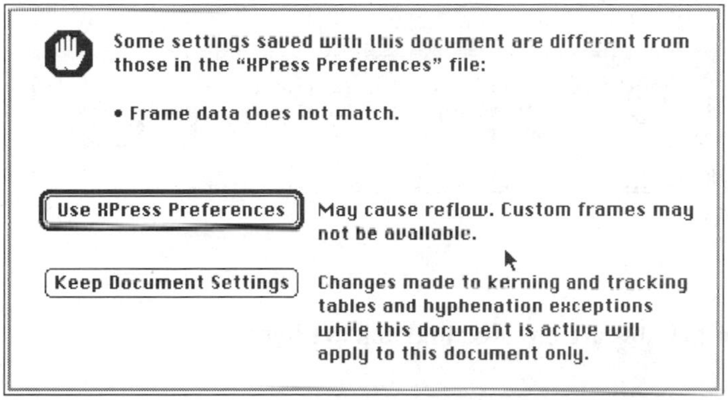

Figure 25-1:
You can apply master preferences to existing documents through this dialog box.

> ✋ **Some settings saved with this document are different from those in the "XPress Preferences" file:**
>
> • Frame data does not match.
>
> [**Use XPress Preferences**] May cause reflow. Custom frames may not be available.
>
> [**Keep Document Settings**] Changes made to kerning and tracking tables and hyphenation exceptions while this document is active will apply to this document only.

Unfortunately, you cannot use System 7's alias feature to use an XPress Preferences file stored in a folder other than the one in which QuarkXPress resides. On a network, being able to use this technique would mean that everyone could share the same XPress Preferences. But because QuarkXPress cannot load an XPress Preferences file from other locations, you cannot use this technique.

Instead, the best that you can do is to have a master copy of the XPress Preferences file and copy it to each user as it is updated (either manually or via a network backup program). If you provide every user with the same copy of the Preferences file, make sure that everyone understands *not* to change the global preferences without permission because everyone else will be affected. For example, if someone changes the EfiColor settings on the global copy and that copy is distributed to the rest of the staff, everyone's EfiColor settings will be changed. (Ironically, QuarkXPress for Windows lets you use a preferences file stored in a different location or even on a network server just so that administering preferences in a workgroup is not a headache.)

Quark does sell a network version of QuarkXPress called Quark Publishing System that supports full network interaction among users. This product is aimed at large companies like magazine publishers.

  Preferences are covered in detail in the Chapter 4.

EfiColor profiles

When you open a document, QuarkXPress checks to see whether an EfiColor profile was used that is not in the current Mac's EfiColor database. Figure 25-2 shows the dialog box that appears if it finds missing profiles. You will need to add the profile before printing if you want that particular color calibration applied. But if you intend to move the document back to the system that has the missing profile, don't worry — the reference to missing profile is retained.

Figure 25-2:
QuarkXPress
alerts you if a
document uses
an EfiColor
profile not
available on the
current Mac.

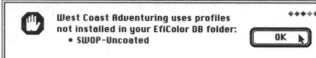

West Coast Adventuring uses profiles
not installed in your EfiColor DB folder:
• SWOP-Uncoated

OK

EfiColor profiles are covered in detail in Chapter 22.

Kerning tables

Like changes to tracking tables, changes to kerning tables are part of a document's preferences unless made when no document is open. But, unlike tracking tables, QuarkXPress provides a method to export and import kerning tables, so that you can move kerning information among documents.

After you have changed kerning values for a particular face, you can export the new values as a text file that can be imported into other documents. Figure 25-3 shows the Kerning Values dialog box (accessed via Utilities ⇨ Kerning Table Edit). At the bottom of the dialog box are the Export button, which creates the kerning file, and the Import button, which loads in previously created kerning files.

If you choose Export, another dialog box appears that lets you select the name and location of the kerning file. (The dialog box actually appears on top of the Kerning Values dialog box. In Figure 25-3, we modified the screen image to show both dialog boxes simultaneously.)

Importing kerning tables gives you a similar dialog box. When you select a kerning table to import, its values will display in the Kerning Values list in the Kerning Values dialog box. Figure 25-4 shows the dialog box for importing kerning files.

Note that the values in the Kerning Values dialog box have not yet been made part of the current document's preferences (or the QuarkXPress default preferences, if no document is open). You must select each pair whose values you want to apply and click Replace to make them part of the current preferences. When done, be sure to click OK to save the changed kerning table.

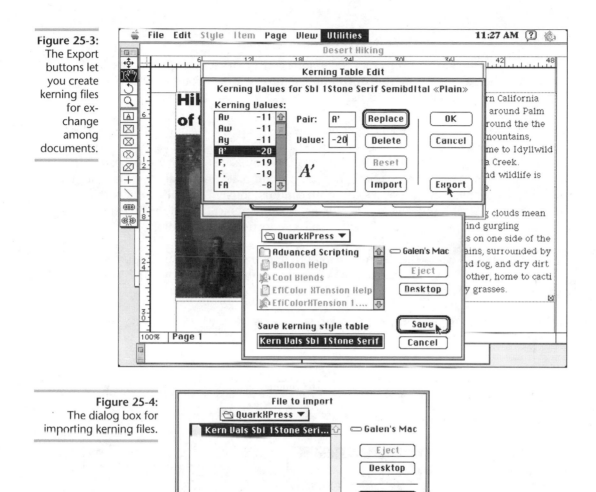

Figure 25-3:
The Export buttons let you create kerning files for exchange among documents.

Figure 25-4:
The dialog box for importing kerning files.

By periodically exporting kerning tables and then importing them into QuarkXPress when no documents are open, you can update the global preferences set in XPress Preferences so that all future documents use these new kerning values.

Kerning and tracking tables are covered in detail in Chapter 12.

Color definitions

It's not unusual to want to keep color definitions consistent across documents. This consistency helps you ensure that corporate-identity colors, if you have them, are used instead of someone's approximations.

You can import colors created in other documents through the Append button in the Colors dialog box (accessed via Edit ⇨ Colors), as shown in Figure 25-5. After you click the Append button, a dialog box will appear so that you can search for the file with the color definitions that you want. (Note that this second dialog normally appears over the first; we moved it in Figure 25-5 to show both simultaneously.) All colors defined in the other document but not defined in the current documents will be imported from the other document. Any trapping settings are also imported for each color.

Any colors whose names match in both documents will not be imported into the current document, and QuarkXPress will not alert you that such conflicts were avoided.

Color definition is covered in detail in Chapter 21.

Figure 25-5: You can import colors defined in other documents via the Append button in the Colors dialog box.

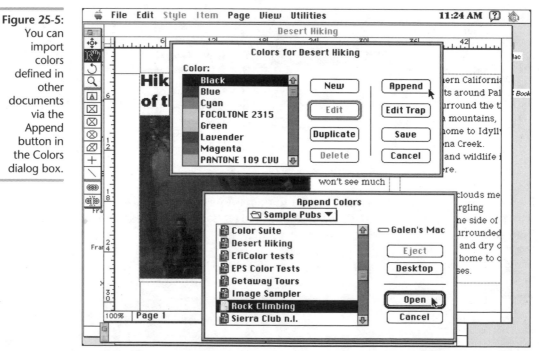

Spelling dictionaries

So that you can add words to the built-in auxiliary spelling dictionary, QuarkXPress requires that you create an auxiliary dictionary (via Utilities ⇨ Auxiliary Dictionary) or open an existing one. Figure 25-6 shows the Auxiliary Dictionary dialog box. Any number of documents can use the same dictionary.

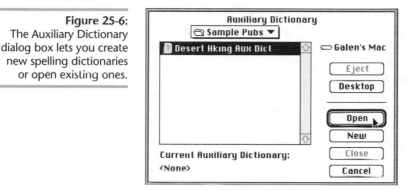

Figure 25-6:
The Auxiliary Dictionary dialog box lets you create new spelling dictionaries or open existing ones.

 If you create a new auxiliary dictionary (via the Create button), the words in the current dictionary (if the document has one) will *not* be copied into the new dictionary.

Unfortunately, you cannot create your own auxiliary dictionaries by using a word processor to edit or merge together multiple auxiliary dictionaries, so it is easy for auxiliary dictionaries to differ widely among documents and different people's Macs. Because spell-checking is not part of the actual layout and production, the lack of consistency among auxiliary dictionaries should not have a major effect on your documents as most spell-checking should occur in word processors before text is imported.

 Sometimes, you will want to remove an auxiliary dictionary from a document. You just have to click the Close button in the Auxiliary Dictionary dialog box.

Auxiliary dictionaries are covered in detail in Chapter 17.

Graphics and text files

Perhaps the most obvious elements to standardize are the source elements — the text and graphics that you use in your documents — especially if you have common elements like logos that are used in multiple documents.

The simplest method of ensuring that the latest versions of these common elements are used is to keep them all in a standard folder (either on each Mac or on a network drive). This method works well when first using a text or graphic element, but it does not ensure that these elements are updated in QuarkXPress documents if the elements are changed after being imported.

For text files, there is no easy solution to this problem because QuarkXPress has no text-link feature. But you can put common text contained in a QuarkXPress picture box into a library, which should handle most needs, such as mastheads, postal information, and standard sidebars (for example "How to contact the company").

For graphics files, either Publish and Subscribe or regular links — when combined with the approach of keeping common elements in a common location — can ensure consistency across documents.

 File links are covered in detail in Chapter 24.

Libraries

QuarkXPress libraries are a great aid to keeping documents consistent. Because libraries are stored in their own files, common libraries can be put in common folders. You can even access them across the network. If you want, you can keep an alias to a library elsewhere on the network on your Mac's local drive.

For many people, libraries offer more flexibility than just linking to graphics files because all attributes applied to graphics and their picture boxes are also stored in the library.

Graphics in libraries also retain any links — either regular import links or Publish and Subscribe links — so you don't have to worry about this information being lost for graphics stored in libraries.

 Libraries are covered in detail in Chapter 23.

Templates

In the course of creating documents, you are likely to evolve templates that you want to use over and over. QuarkXPress can save a document as a template. The only difference between a template and a document is that a template forces you to use Save As rather than Save in the File menu so that you do not overwrite the template but instead create new documents based on it.

Although the optimum approach is to design a template before creating actual documents, the truth is that no one can foresee all possibilities. Even if you create a template (and you should) with a style sheet, H&J sets, and master pages intended for use in all new documents, you can expect to modify your template as work on real documents brings up the need for modifications and additions.

Whether or not you use templates, you will still need to transfer basic layout elements like styles and master pages from one document to another. QuarkXPress offers import capabilities for styles (and the related H&J sets), and we have devised a way to copy master pages from one document to another even though QuarkXPress does not directly offer this capability (see "MasterPages" later in this chapter).

 QuarkXPress (versions 3.2 and later) now supports the use of templates over a network. Each time a template is accessed, the user accessing it is given a local copy. Thus, multiple users can access the template simultaneously, and even a single user can have several copies of the same template open at once.

Styles

The Style Sheets dialog box (accessed via Edit ⇨ Style Sheets) includes the Append button to let you import styles from other QuarkXPress documents and templates. Figure 25-7 shows this dialog box as well as the Append Style Sheets dialog box that it invokes.

Figure 25-7:
The Style
Sheets
dialog box
lets you
import styles
from other
documents
via the
Append
button.

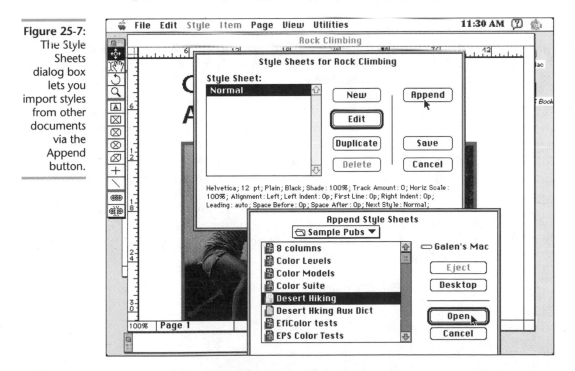

All styles from the other document whose names do not match those of the current document will be imported. If there are styles whose names are the same in both documents, QuarkXPress will prompt you to skip them or give them new names (it adds an asterisk [*] to the end of the style name for such imported styles). (Figure 25-8 shows the dialog box that alerts you to the duplicate names.)

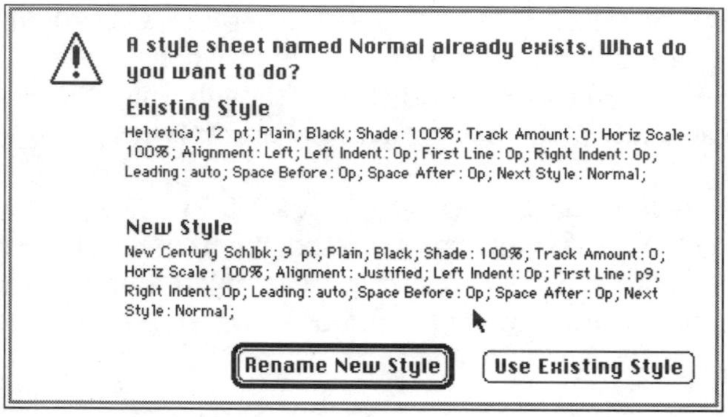

Figure 25-8:
If an imported style uses the same name as the one in your current document, QuarkXPress alerts you to prevent accidental overwriting of the current style.

> ⚠ **A style sheet named Normal already exists. What do you want to do?**
>
> **Existing Style**
> Helvetica; 12 pt; Plain; Black; Shade: 100%; Track Amount: 0; Horiz Scale: 100%; Alignment: Left; Left Indent: 0p; First Line: 0p; Right Indent: 0p; Leading: auto; Space Before: 0p; Space After: 0p; Next Style: Normal;
>
> **New Style**
> New Century Schlbk; 9 pt; Plain; Black; Shade: 100%; Track Amount: 0; Horiz Scale: 100%; Alignment: Justified; Left Indent: 0p; First Line: p9; Right Indent: 0p; Leading: auto; Space Before: 0p; Space After: 0p; Next Style: Normal;
>
> [**Rename New Style**]   [**Use Existing Style**]

You can import from several documents by clicking Append after importing styles from a document; this action reinvokes the Append Style Sheets dialog box. After importing, make sure that you click the Save button in the Style Sheets dialog box to save the imported styles in the current document (or in the general preferences).

If you want to modify the existing styles (whether in your default settings or in a document) with those from another document, import the new styles and let QuarkXPress change the names (adding the asterisk) and then delete the original styles and rename the newly imported versions with original names.

If an imported style uses an H&J set not in the current document, QuarkXPress will replace the reference to the H&J set in the style to the current document's Standard H&J set. There is no warning that a different H&J was used by the imported style. Because you can import H&J sets from documents, we suggest that you first import the H&J set (as described next) and then import the style.

By importing styles with no document open, you copy all new styles into your global defaults (those stored in the XPress Preferences file covered earlier). This technique is a handy way of bringing new styles into your default settings without affecting existing styles.

Style sheets are covered in detail in Chapter 6.

H&J sets

Importing H&J sets is similar to importing styles: use the Append button in the H&Js dialog box (accessed via Edit ➪ H&Js). Figure 25-9 shows the H&Js dialog box and the Append H&Js dialog box that appears after you click the Append button to find the desired documents.

You can import H&J sets from several documents by clicking Append after importing styles from a document, which reinvokes the Append H&Js dialog box. After importing, make sure that you click the Save button in the H&Js dialog box to save the imported styles in the current document (or in the general preferences).

If an H&J set that you are importing has the same name as an H&J set in your current document, QuarkXPress warns you and gives you the option to rename the duplicate H&J set name or skip it. The dialog box is similar to the one shown in Figure 25-8.

If you want to modify the existing H&J sets (either in your default settings or in a document) with those from another document, rename the H&J sets in the other document when importing them, delete the original H&J sets, and then rename the newly imported versions with original names.

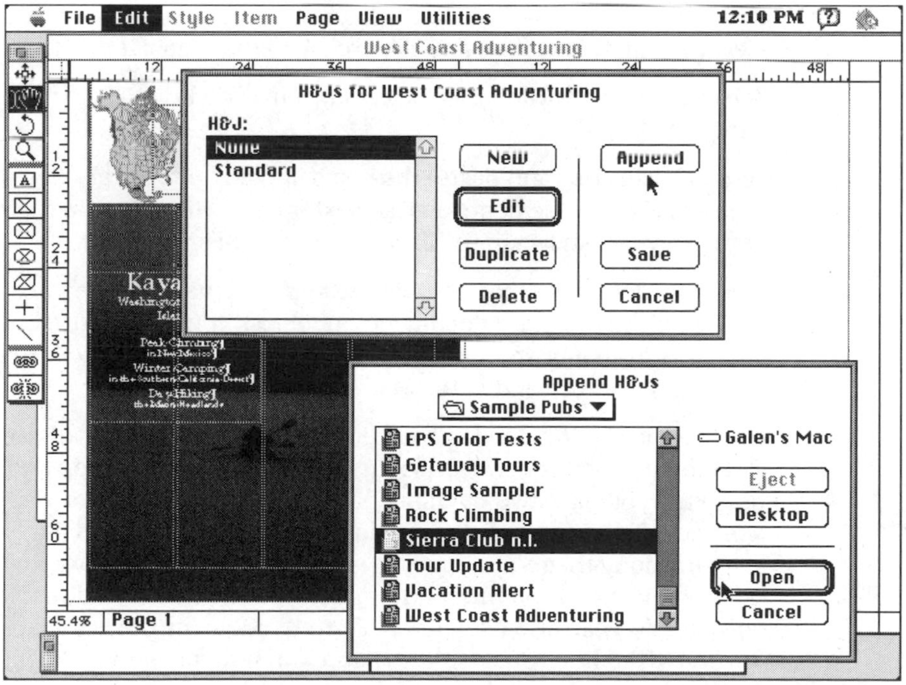

Figure 25-9:
The H&Js dialog box lets you import H&J sets from other documents via the Append button.

By having no document open and importing H&J sets, you are copying all new H&J sets into your global defaults (those stored in the XPress Preferences file covered earlier). This is a handy way to bring new H&J sets into your default settings without affecting existing H&J sets.

H&J sets are covered in detail in Chapter 13.

Master pages

Moving master pages between documents is tricky because QuarkXPress offers no feature that explicitly performs this task. But you can use QuarkXPress libraries as a way station for master pages that you want to move from one document to another. Here are the steps:

STEPS: Copying Master Pages Across Documents

Step 1.   Open a library with File ⇨ Open (⌘O) or create a library with File ⇨ New ⇨ Library (Shift-⌘N).

Step 2.   Open the document with the master page that you want to copy and display that master page (via Page ⇨ Display). We recommend that you change the view to something small, like 25 percent so that you can see the full page.

Step 3.   Select the Item tool and then select all items (via Edit ⇨ Select All or the shortcut ⌘A).

Step 4.   Drag (or use copy and paste) the items into an open library and release the mouse. All of the elements on the master page will appear in their own library box, as shown in the library window in Figure 25-10.

Step 5.   Open the document that you want to copy the master page into. You don't need to close the other document, but unless you intend to get other elements from it or work on it later, go ahead and close it to reduce clutter both on the screen and in the Mac's memory.

Use the View ⇨ Windows menu item to manage how pages display. Tile Documents creates nonoverlapping windows (one at the top and one at the bottom if you have two documents open); Stack Documents overlaps the windows. The names of all open documents also appear so that you can switch among them. You can also resize windows manually by clicking and holding the mouse on the window's resize box (in the window's lower right corner). You can also use View ⇨ Fit to Window (or the keyboard shortcut ⌘0 [zero]) to have QuarkXPress figure out how small to make the page to fit in its window.

Step 6. Insert a new blank master page in the second document.

Step 7. Drag (or copy and paste) the library item containing the first document's master-page elements into the new master page (this master page is at the bottom of Figure 25-10).

Step 8. Rename the new master page so that you can remember what it is. Now you're done.

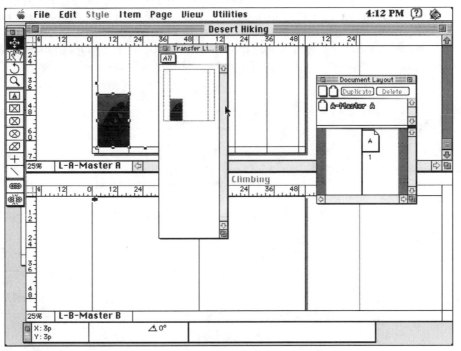

Figure 25-10: Dragging all master-page elements into a library is the first major step in copying master pages across documents. You then can move the elements from the library to a new master page in another document.

Master pages are covered in detail in Chapter 5; libraries are covered in Chapter 23.

Mixed Mac/Windows Environments

This entire section covers differences between the Mac and Windows.

As a cross-platform application, QuarkXPress will appeal strongly to all sorts of users who find that they deal with "the other side." This includes corporate users whose various divisions have standardized on different platforms, service bureaus whose clients use different machines, and independent publishers or layout artists who deal with a range of clients.

QuarkXPress differences

Quark did a good job in making its Macintosh and Windows versions compatible. And with Version 3.3 on both systems, Quark offers functionally identical programs. With the earlier versions, the files are transportable, but not all features are supported. Figures 25-11 and 25-12 show the two platform versions with the same document. You can even open files directly across a network, as Figures 25-13, 25-14, and 25-15 show.

Figure 25-11:
QuarkXPress for Macintosh looks very much like QuarkXPress for Windows (shown in Figure 25-12).

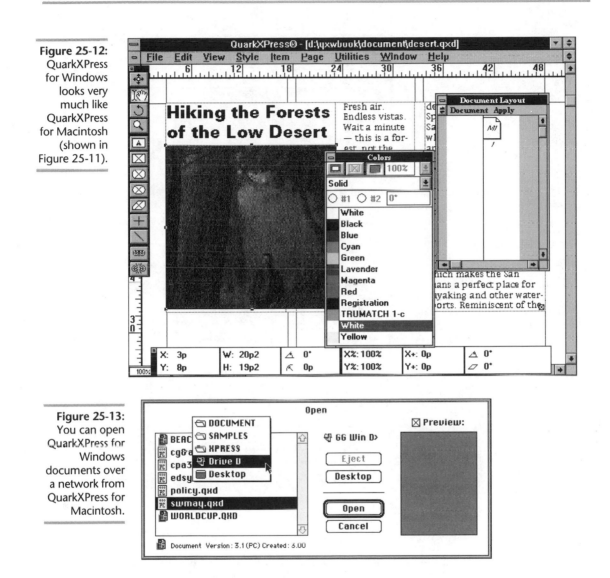

Figure 25-12: QuarkXPress for Windows looks very much like QuarkXPress for Macintosh (shown in Figure 25-11).

Figure 25-13: You can open QuarkXPress for Windows documents over a network from QuarkXPress for Macintosh.

Supported formats

Macintosh Version 3.3 can read Windows Version 3.1 and 3.3 files; Windows Version 3.3 can read Macintosh 3.0, 3.1, 3.2, and 3.3 files. (There was no Windows Version 3.2.)

Mac Versions 3.1 and 3.2 can read Windows Version 3.1; Windows Version 3.1 can read Mac Version 3.2 (but not Mac Version 3.1).

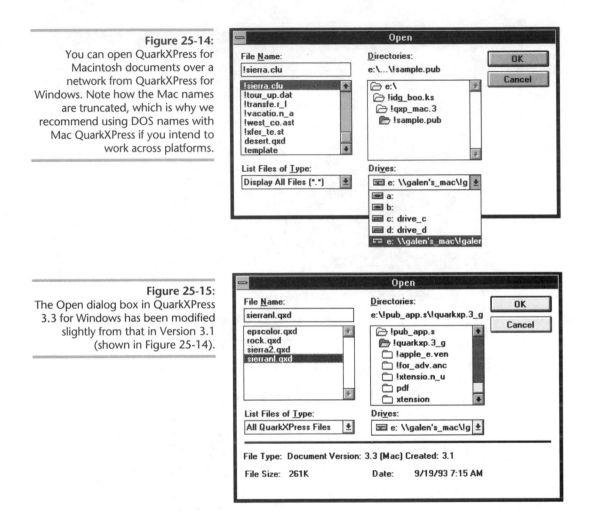

Figure 25-14:
You can open QuarkXPress for Macintosh documents over a network from QuarkXPress for Windows. Note how the Mac names are truncated, which is why we recommend using DOS names with Mac QuarkXPress if you intend to work across platforms.

Figure 25-15:
The Open dialog box in QuarkXPress 3.3 for Windows has been modified slightly from that in Version 3.1 (shown in Figure 25-14).

Which elements transfer

The following elements may be transferred across platform, with any limits noted:

- ↪ Any graphics not supported by the platform version are replaced during printing with their PICT preview images. However, the graphics links are retained, so if you move the document back to the originating platform, the original graphics will again be available for printing.

- ↪ Color definitions not supported on one platform are translated to their CMYK equivalents. Colors may be imported across platforms. With Version 3.3, the two versions support the same color models; Mac Version 3.3 supports several Pantone variants not offered in Windows Version 3.1.

- ๛ Styles are retained. They may also be imported across platforms.

- ๛ H&J sets are retained. They may also be imported across platforms.

- ๛ Hyphenation exceptions are retained.

- ๛ Document preferences are retained, but the XPress Preferences file (called XPRESS.PRF in Windows) cannot be shared across platforms.

- ๛ Cool Blends and other XTensions must be present on both platforms if you are moving documents that use XTensions' features. If you don't have an XTension on, say, Windows and try to load a Mac document that uses that XTension's capabilities, you will get an error message saying that the document may not be loaded. (An exception is Mac Version 3.2 with EfiColor transferred to Windows Version 3.1, as described later in this section.)

- ๛ Kerning data exported from the Mac may be imported into Windows. However, we do not recommend doing this kind of transfer because the font characteristics on the two platforms are different enough that you should customize the kerning on each separately.

- ๛ Some PICT previews from the Mac and some Windows metafile previews on Windows will not translate correctly when transferred. You must reimport or update the link to the graphic to generate a new preview.

- ๛ Although the Windows version does not save preview images for the Open dialog box, such previews created on the Mac are retained even if the document is moved to Windows and back.

 When transferring files from Mac Version 3.2 to Windows Version 3.1, EfiColor profile information is removed once the file is saved in Windows. If the file is moved back to the Mac, the Profile option in the Style menu is grayed out; you must use the Utilities ⇨ Profile Usage option to globally reapply profiles. Quark fixed this problem by issuing a patch to Windows QuarkXPress that upgraded the version to 3.12 (available on CompuServe in DTPFORUM). With this upgrade, the EfiColor information is preserved, even though Windows Version 3.12 does not support EfiColor. With Version 3.3, Windows QuarkXPress fully supports EfiColor, and files may be exchanged freely with no loss of EfiColor information.

Which elements don't transfer

The following elements cannot be moved across platforms:

- ๛ Libraries.

- ๛ Auxiliary dictionaries.

- Flipped graphics will not print or display correctly when moved to Windows. When transferred back to the Mac, all graphic settings for such pictures (such as flipping and sizing) are lost.

- Custom frames created by the Frame Editor on the Mac. These are replaced with solid frames when imported into Windows Version 3.1. When moving files between Version 3.3, these custom frames are preserved for display and printing, even though Windows QuarkXPress continues not to include a Frame Editor of its own.

 Our *QuarkXPress for Windows Designer's Handbook* (IDG Books Worldwide, 1992) details how to use the Windows version of QuarkXPress.

Platform differences

There are also some general differences between Windows (and DOS) and Macintosh themselves that will add a few bumps along the road to cross-platform exchange.

File names

The most noticeable difference between Windows and Macintosh is the file-naming convention. Macintosh files follow these rules:

- Names are limited to 31 characters.

- Any character may be used except for colons (:), which are used by the Macintosh system software internally to separate the folder name (which is not visible on screen) from the file name.

- Uppercase is considered to be different than lowercase, even for the same letters (a file named "FILE" is seen as a different file than "file" or "File").

Windows files follow these rules:

- Names are limited to 8 characters.

- Names may have an extension of up to 3 characters, which is often added automatically by programs to identify the file type. A period separates the file name from the extension: FILENAME.EXT.

- Names may use any characters except for most punctuation: pipes (|), colons (:), semicolons (;), periods (.), commas (,), asterisks (*), equal signs (=), plus signs (+), brackets ([and]), less-than symbols (<), greater-than symbols (>), question marks (?), slashes (/), and backslashes (\), which are all used by DOS to separate parts of paths (file locations, such as drives and folders) or to structure commands. A period may be used as the separator between a file name and an extension.

❧ Case does not matter: "FILE," "file," and "File" are all considered to be the same name. If you have a file named "FILE" and create or copy a file named "file," "FILE" will be overwritten.

When you bring Mac QuarkXPress files and any associated graphics to Windows, you'll have to translate the Mac names into names that are legal on Windows. This rule applies not only to the QuarkXPress document but also any associated files, including kerning tables, libraries, graphics, and auxiliary dictionaries.

If you rename these files, either on the Mac before transferring or on the PC while transferring, you'll find that within the QuarkXPress document itself, the original names are still used. When QuarkXPress tries to open these files, it will look for them by their original Mac names.

 The simplest way to assure that you won't have problems with transferred files looking for incompatible names is to use the DOS naming convention even on your Mac files. This suggestion may gall Mac users, but it will save everyone a lot of headaches. (The Mac has no problem handling Windows file names because Windows file names don't violate any Mac file-naming rules.)

Don't forget the file extensions: QXD for documents and QXT for templates. (Other QuarkXPress extensions are QXL for libraries, QDT for auxiliary dictionaries, and KRN for kerning tables — but the two versions cannot read these types of each other's files.) Typical extensions for cross-platform graphics are TIF for TIFF, EPS for Encapsulated PostScript, AI for Adobe Illustrator files, and PCT for PICT. Files in other formats (not supported on the Mac) are PCX for PC Paintbrush, BMP and RLE for Microsoft bitmap, MAC or PNT for MacPaint, GIF for Graphics Interchange Format, CGM for Computer Graphics Metafiles, WMF for Windows metafiles, CDR for CorelDraw, PLT for HPGL plots, CT for Scitex, and DRW for Micrografx Windows Draw.

Font differences

Although the major typeface vendors like Adobe Systems and Bitstream offer their typefaces for both Windows and Macintosh users, these typefaces are not always the same on both platforms. Cross-platform differences are especially common among typefaces created a few years ago when multiplatform compatibility was not a goal for most users or vendors.

Differences occur in three areas:

- The internal font name — the one used by the printer and type scalers like Adobe Type Manager — is not quite the same for the Mac and Windows version of a typeface. This discrepancy will result in an alert box listing the fonts used in the document that are not on your Mac (or PC). The solution is to use the Font Usage dialog box or the Find/Replace dialog box (covered in Chapter 17) to replace all instances of the unrecognized font name with the correct one for the current platform.

- Even if typefaces use the same internal names, the font files' tracking, kerning, and other character width information may be different on the two platforms, possibly resulting in text reflow. The solution is to check the ends of all your stories to make sure text did not get shorter or longer.

- Symbols do not translate properly. Even when created by the same vendors, the character maps for each font file differ across platforms because Windows and the Macintosh use different character maps. This problem is complicated by the fact that some vendors didn't stick to the standard character maps for any platform or didn't implement all symbols in all their typefaces. The solution is to proofread your documents, note the symbols that are incorrect, and then use the Find/Change dialog box to replace them with the correct symbol. (Highlight the incorrect symbol and use the copy and paste commands to put it in the Text field of the Find/Change dialog box rather than trying to figure out the right keypad code in Windows or the right keyboard shortcut on the Mac.)

 To minimize font problems, use a program like Altsys's Fontographer (214/680-2060) or Ares Software Corp.'s FontMonger (415/578-9090) to translate your TrueType and PostScript files from Mac to Windows format or vice versa. (Both programs are available in both Mac and Windows versions.) This will ensure that the internal font names, width information, and symbols are the same on both platforms.

Transfer methods

Moving files between Macs and Windows PCs is easier now than ever before, thanks to a selection of products on both platforms that let each machine read the other's disks. Here is a brief summary of the major products:

- DaynaFile, from Dayna Communications (801/269-7200). This external Mac drive lets a Mac read DOS 5.25-inch and 3.5-inch floppies, so that you can copy files back and forth. Most PCs today have 3.5-inch floppies, so there is increasingly less need for such a product. Also, Teac and other manufacturers now offer a PC drive that accepts both 3.5-inch and 5.25-inch floppies, which can ease the transition to 3.5-inch disks for PC users still using the 5.25-inch disks.

- Apple File Exchange, which comes on Apple Computer's System software for each Mac. This utility lets you use 3.5-inch DOS disks in an Apple SuperDrive (the high-density 1.4MB drives; it does not work with 800K drives).

- Macintosh PC Exchange, from Apple Computer (408/996-1010). This utility lets you use DOS disks in a SuperDrive and lets the Mac recognize files immediately and know which applications are compatible with each type of DOS file. Unlike Apple File Exchange, you don't need to use a program to copy the files — you can just use the standard drag and drop techniques. It also can automatically add the right Mac icon and file-type information to a DOS file transferred to the Mac based on the DOS file's extension.

- DOS Mounter Plus, from Dayna Communications (801/269-7200). This utility is similar to Macintosh PC Exchange, except that it also works with other types of media, such as SyQuest and tape drives, and over NetWare IPX networks.

- AccessPC, from Insignia Solutions (415/694-7600). This utility is similar to DOS Mounter, except that it also includes Mastersoft's Word for Word translators.

- MacLinkPlus/Translators Pro, from DataViz (203/268-0030). Like AccessPC, this utility includes file translation (DataViz's own translators), as well as Apple's Macintosh PC Exchange. The version called MacLinkPlus/PC Connect includes a serial cable through which you can connect a Mac to a PC (making sort of a two-computer network). And the version called MacLinkPlus/Easy Open/Translators is the same as MacLinkPlus/Translators Pro without including Macintosh PC Exchange.

- Mac-in-DOS, from Pacific Microelectronics (415/948-6200). This utility is similar to Apple File Exchange — except that it runs on DOS and Windows PCs, using their 1.4MB 3.5-inch drives to read from and write to Mac 1.4MB disks.

- Mac-to-DOS, from PLI (510/657-2211). This is similar to Mac-in-DOS.

- MacDisk, from Insignia Solutions (415/694-7600). Like AccessPC and DOS Mounter for the Mac, this driver lets you insert a Mac disk into a PC and have it read by DOS without stopping to run a program. However, it does not map extensions when saving from a PC to a Mac disk, nor does it work with 800K (Mac) and 720K (DOS) disks. A utility bundled with the MacDisk driver lets you format Mac disks and view the original Mac file's full name.

Another method of transferring files is to use a cross-platform network — if you are using one. For small networks, you can use Farallon Computing's Timbuktu and PhoneNet PC combination (510/814-5000), which lets the Mac be a server to PCs and other Macs. Miramar Systems' Personal MacLAN Connect (805/966-2432) lets a Windows PC be a server to Macs and other PCs. Both of these are based on Apple's AppleTalk protocol but also support NetWare IPX. They can work over several types of network wiring, including Ethernet and LocalTalk. For larger networks, you'll likely want to use networks based on Novell's NetWare IPX protocol and on Ethernet wiring; you'll need a consultant or in-house network manager to set such large networks up.

Extension maps

The Macintosh assigns a hidden file to each file; this hidden file tells it which icon to display for the file and which program to launch if you double-click the file. Windows and DOS files have no such hidden files, so they will appear as either TeachText or DOS binary files when you move them to the Mac. To load these files into QuarkXPress (or other Mac applications), you must first load your application and then use the File ⇨ Open command.

AccessPC, DOS Mounter Plus, Macintosh PC Exchange, and Personal MacLAN Connect can be set to create these hidden files automatically based on the DOS file's extension, which means that you can double-click the transferred files. Figure 25-16 shows a sample extension map in DOS Mounter Plus.

Be warned that not all Mac applications will display TeachText or DOS binary files, under the mistaken assumption that the files couldn't possibly be compatible files missing only their hidden file information. You'll have to use a program like Apple's ResEdit program to create the hidden file — and at this point, you need a Mac guru to show you how to use ResEdit because a mistake could corrupt your file irreparably. Fortunately, Mac QuarkXPress doesn't suffer from this problem.

Figure 25-16:
An extension map automatically assigns a DOS file the correct Macintosh file-type information. Several programs offer this feature during file transfer.

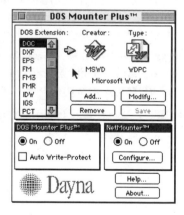

Summary

- ➥ Put common elements in common locations, whether or not you use a network. Consistency, when made part of your process, is consistency likely to be implemented.

- ➥ Export modified kerning tables and import them into QuarkXPress when no document is open. This technique will make them part of your default preferences so that they are used by all future documents.

- ➥ Use the Append buttons in the Colors, Style Sheets, and H&J Sets dialog boxes to import other documents' settings in the current document or in the general preferences (if no document is open).

- ➥ When you create a new spelling auxiliary dictionary, any words in the current dictionary are *not* copied into it, so that you cannot build new auxiliary dictionaries based on existing ones nor can you create auxiliary dictionaries in a word processor.

- ➥ Use libraries to store common picture and text boxes, including their contents, if they are also used often. For text boxes, use placeholder text on which you apply special effects that you want to use in other documents.

- ➥ Libraries maintain all links — including Publish and Subscribe links — to graphics in them.

- ➥ Use libraries as a way station to transfer master pages from document to another. Although you cannot directly copy or import master pages, you can select all their elements, move them into a library, open a new document, and move those elements from the library into a blank master page to duplicate the original document's master page.

- ➥ Use the DOS conventions for file naming even for your Mac files. This practice assures smooth file transfer between the Windows and Mac versions of QuarkXPress.

- ➥ Use a font-translation program to translate your Mac fonts to Windows format (or vice versa) to ensure that fonts are compatible and identical on both platforms. Otherwise, symbols may not map correctly, spacing might differ, and document's font names may not match the system's font names.

- ➥ Choose a DOS disk-mounting utility or a network-transfer product that maps DOS extensions to Mac file types.

Printing and Output

After you create a document, the work is not over — you need to print or output the document in preparation for publication. It's no surprise that QuarkXPress offers a wide range of features to control the output process, from laser printers to imagesetters. At first, these controls may seem daunting, but you'll soon realize that you don't have to use most of them for routine tasks, such as printing a proof copy to a laser printer. And once you've determined the advanced settings for high-end output devices like imagesetters, you'll rarely need to change them.

Keep in mind that how you prepare your document will affect how it prints. Make sure that you've read Chapters 3, 14, 18, 20, 21, and 22 to understand the implications for printing issues like font selection, picture-box settings, image controls, and color settings.

With your document's elements set up to take advantage of your final output device, you're ready to take advantage of the chapter topics in this section: how to set up your printer, how to work with color files, and how to prepare documents for output by a service bureau.

Printing Techniques

In This Chapter

- ➠ Choosing the right printing device
- ➠ Specifying options used in imagesetters, such as registration marks and color separation
- ➠ Printing color separations
- ➠ Working with service bureaus

Which Printer Is Right for You? ____

Choosing the right printer (the hardware type, not the nice people who put ink on paper) is an important part of the publishing process. QuarkXPress documents can be printed on a wide variety of printers, from dot matrix printers to imagesetters. Here is a very simple overview of your choices:

- ☞ **Dot matrix printers** print by applying dots of ink, pressed by pins through inked ribbons, to form images on paper. You measure the resolution (clarity of the image) produced by dot matrix printers by the number of pins they have; the higher the number of pins, the better the image quality. (Chances are, if you have a dot matrix printer, it has either 9 or 24 pins and produces between 72 and 144 dots per inch.) The Apple ImageWriter is a dot matrix printer. If you're a publisher, you won't want to use a dot matrix printer for printing rough proof copies because of their relatively slow speed and low output quality, and we definitely don't recommend their use for final pages.

- ☞ **Inkjet printers** print by ejecting dots of ink onto paper. The appearance of images printed on inkjet printers is generally smoother than that of those printed on dot matrix printers. The reason is that the dots of ink applied to paper by inkjet printers tend to blend together, instead of remaining separate dots as on a dot matrix printer. The Hewlett-Packard Deskwriter is an inkjet printer. Although the appearance of pages produced by inkjet printers is a step above that of dot matrix printers, the image quality is still not sufficient for professional publishing. Inkjet printouts are, however, useful for proofing copy and the placement of graphics.

↪ **Laser printers** print by making a laser-light impression of the page image on a drum, adhering toner to that image, and then transferring the toner image to paper. The output quality from a laser printer is one step above that of inkjet printers, largely because laser printers print at a higher resolution (typically between 300 and 600 dots per inch). The Apple LaserWriter is a commonly used laser printer. Pages produced on a laser printer are great for proofing. Some people use laser output for their camera-ready pages; whether or not doing so is a good idea is a judgment call. Laser output is very useful for proofing work before you send it to your service bureau. It is also adequate for documents such as correspondences, simple newsletters, or price sheets. But laser output does not have a high enough quality for high-end publications such as newspapers and magazines. If you want your document to have a polished, professional appearance, we recommend that you have it produced on an imagesetter.

↪ **Imagesetters** are high-end output devices that produce your document pages on film or photo paper, ready to be printed. Imagesetter resolution ranges between roughly 1200 and 4000 dots per inch. When you send a document to a service bureau, it is output on an imagesetter. The Linotronic 300 is an example of an imagesetter. Pages produced on an imagesetter and then printed professionally have a professional look that is well worth the small expense involved. We strongly recommend outputting your final pages to an imagesetter.

Getting Ready to Print

When you are ready to print a QuarkXPress document, first make sure that the Page Setup dialog box is set up the way you'd like it to be. This dialog box lets you change the size of the document and control the way that it prints. It also lets you specify paper size, the orientation of images on the page, and the page image size.

To display the Page Setup dialog box, choose File ⇨ Page Setup (or use the keyboard shortcut Option-⌘P). Figure 26-1 shows the dialog box.

Figure 26-1:
The Page
Setup dialog
box.

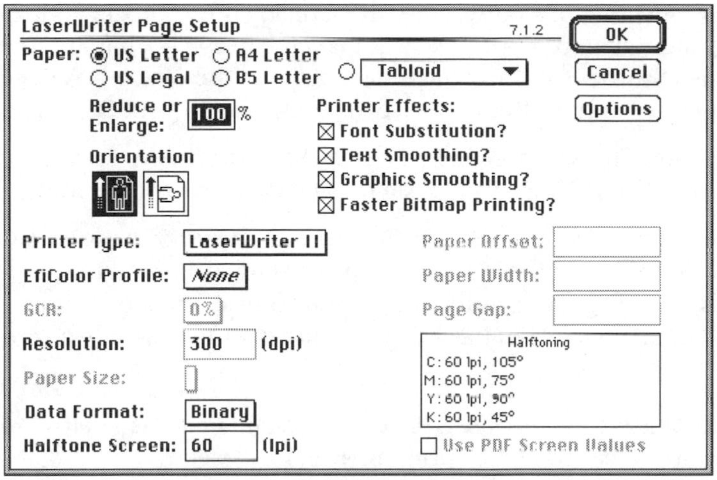

Options you can set in the Page Setup dialog box (File ⇨ Page Setup, or Option-⌘P) include the following:

- ∞ **Paper:** Choose the size of the paper that will be used in the printer. The size of the paper you will be using does not always correspond directly to the trim size of your final document. Note that if you select a printer that is able to print on nonstandard pages, the Paper Size area of the dialog box becomes active so that you can specify the size of the paper.

- ∞ **Reduce or enlarge:** You can scale an image before you print it by entering a value between 25% and 400%. Printing at reduced scale is particularly useful if your document's page size is large and if you can get by with a reduced version of the document for proofing purposes.

- ∞ **Orientation:** Click on the icon that looks like a portrait to get vertical orientation of the document. The horizontal icon produces pages with a landscape orientation.

- ∞ **Printer effects:** If you want the printer to substitute non-PostScript fonts (New York for New Century Schoolbook, Geneva for Helvetica, Monaco for Courier), check the Font Substitution box (leaving it unchecked means that the printer will print bitmap versions of the non-PostScript fonts instead). To smooth the printing of bitmap fonts, check Text Smoothing. To improve the look of printed bitmap images, check Graphics Smoothing. To print bitmap images faster, check Faster Bitmap Printing.

∽ **Options:** Selecting this button displays a dialog box that lets you select additional printing controls — such as flipping the image — that are provided by Macintosh System software; the exact entries in the dialog box depend on the version of the LaserWriter driver version installed in your System folder.

∽ **Printer type:** This is a pop-up menu that lists the printers for which a printer description file (PDF) is available in the QuarkXPress printer folder.

∽ **Use PDF Screen Values:** Checking this box tells QuarkXPress to use the Screen Set Values defined in the PDF file for the selected printer. If this box is not checked, the program uses its own default values. This box is grayed-out if the printer you have selected has a PDF file that does not include a screen value setting.

 The Resolution, Paper Offset, Paper Width, and Page Gap fields are designed for setting specifications when printing to an imagesetter.

∽ **Resolution:** Select the dpi (dots per inch) at which the imagesetter will be printing the document. The minimum resolution for most imagesetters is 1,270 dpi. Note that setting resolution within QuarkXPress does not override the actual settings of the imagesetter.

∽ **Paper Offset:** Entering a measurement value in this field shifts the image that will be printing on the imagesetter to the right (by the distance specified) on the imagesetter's paper or film.

∽ **Paper Width:** The value you enter here should match the actual width of the roll of paper loaded in the imagesetter.

∽ **Page Gap:** Because imagesetters generally output to paper that is on a roll, you need to tell QuarkXPress how much gap should be left between pages.

Printing Options

After the page is set for printing, you are ready to actually print the document. To print a document, select File ⇨ Print (or the shortcut ⌘P) to open the Print dialog box, which is shown in Figure 26-2. Change any options and choose OK, and QuarkXPress sends your document to the printer.

The top left corner of the dialog box gives the name of the printer selected in the Chooser, which you access via the Apple menu. The page setup options include the following basic and advanced options.

Figure 26-2:
The Print
dialog box.

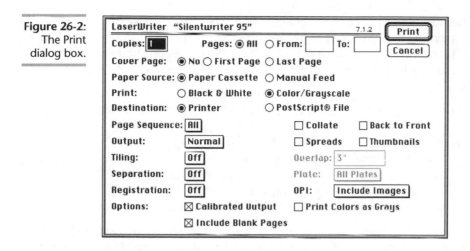

LaserWriter "Silentwriter 95"			7.1.2	Print

Copies: [1]   Pages: ⦿ All ○ From: [ ] To: [ ]   Cancel

Cover Page: ⦿ No ○ First Page   ○ Last Page

Paper Source: ⦿ Paper Cassette ○ Manual Feed

Print: ○ Black & White   ⦿ Color/Grayscale

Destination: ⦿ Printer   ○ PostScript® File

Page Sequence: [All]   ☐ Collate   ☐ Back to Front

Output: [Normal]   ☐ Spreads   ☐ Thumbnails

Tiling: [Off]   Overlap: [3"]

Separation: [Off]   Plate: [All Plates]

Registration: [Off]   OPI: [Include Images]

Options: ☒ Calibrated Output   ☐ Print Colors as Grays
               ☒ Include Blank Pages

Basic options

It's likely that for most printing jobs, you only need to worry about the first two settings in the Print dialog box: Copies, which lets you specify how many copies of your document print, and Pages, which lets you specify whether all pages print or just a selected range of pages.

If you use the From and To options to select a range of pages to print, and you use the QuarkXPress section-numbering feature to create multiple sections in your document, you must enter the page numbers exactly as they are labeled in the document. (The label for the current page appears in the lower-left corner of your document screen.) Include any prefix used and enter the labels in the same format (letters, roman numerals, or regular numerals) used in the section whose pages you want to print. Alternatively, you can indicate the absolute page numbers by preceding the number with a plus sign (+).

For example, suppose that you have an eight-page document with two sections of four pages each. You label pages one through four as AN-1 through AN-4 and label pages five through eight as BN-1 through BN-4. If you enter BN-1 and BN-4 in the From and To fields of the Print dialog box, QuarkXPress prints the first four pages in the section that uses the BN- prefix. If you enter +5 and +8, QuarkXPress prints document pages five through eight — which again includes BN-1 through BN-4.

Other options that frequently come in handy are:

- **Cover Page:** This lets you specify whether a cover page prints. The options are First Page and Last Page, which determine where the cover page falls in the output tray. The cover page includes the document name and the date and time printed.

∞ **Thumbnails:** If you check Thumbnails, QuarkXPress prints reduced versions of the document pages, printing eight pages per sheet. This feature is handy when you want to take a layout sample or storyboard to a meeting without having to bring a large stack of sheets. (This option is available only with PostScript printers.)

∞ **Page Sequence (All Pages, Odd Pages, and Even Pages):** These settings let you control which pages are output. This is useful if you want to do duplex (two-sided) copying and thus need the even and odd pages separated. Note that these settings do not override the settings for the Pages option (at the top of the dialog box). If you select a range of pages in the Pages option and then choose All Pages, Odd Pages, or Even Pages, QuarkXPress applies that option to the range. So, for example, you can print all odd pages from page 3 through page 78.

∞ **Collate:** Check this option to keep pages in sequence when you print multiple copies of a document. When Collate is set at the default — which is unchecked — QuarkXPress prints all requested copies of one page, then all copies of the next page, and so on. This method speeds printing time significantly.

∞ **Back To Front:** If you check this option, QuarkXPress reverses the printing order of the document pages. When you output a document to a printer whose pages print face up, the document is in order when done printing.

∞ **Spreads:** Checking the Spreads box tells QuarkXPress to print facing pages as contiguous output (assuming that your paper size allows it or you output to an imagesetter that uses a roll of RC paper or film).

You may not want to use the Spreads option when outputting to an imagesetter if you have bleeds because there will be no bleed between the spreads. If you use traditional perfect-binding (square spines) or saddle-stitching (stapled spines) printing methods in which facing pages are not printed contiguously, do not use this option.

∞ **Include Blank Pages:** If you uncheck this option, QuarkXPress suppresses the output of blank pages. The default setting is checked, but you'll probably want to change this setting if you use the All option for Pages.

Advanced options

QuarkXPress offers several advanced printing options designed for publishing users. Options not available for non-Postscript printers (such as color options) are grayed out in the Print dialog box.

- **Tiling:** QuarkXPress gives you three *tiling* options: Off, Manual, and Auto. Tiling takes an oversized document and breaks it into several pieces, called *tiles,* that you then reassemble. You can use this option when creating posters, for example. If you choose Off, no tiling occurs. If you choose Auto, QuarkXPress determines where each tile breaks. If you choose Manual, you decide where the tiles break by repositioning the ruler origin in your document. For all pages selected, QuarkXPress prints the tiled area whose upper-left corner matches the ruler's origin. Repeat this step for each tiled area. Choose the Manual tile option if certain areas of your document make more logical break points than others. No matter whether you choose Auto or Manual tiling, you can select the amount of tile overlap by entering a value in the overlap field. You can enter a value between 0 and 6 inches.

- **Separation:** If you check this option, QuarkXPress prints a separate sheet (usually a film negative) for each color. QuarkXPress makes separate sheets for the colors that you specify in the Plate list box. (Color options are covered in detail in the next section.)

- **Registration:** If you check this box, QuarkXPress prints registration marks. (Printers use registration marks to determine where to cut pages when they trim the paper used on the press to the page size actually used in the printed document.) When you output color separations, QuarkXPress also includes a color bar in the output, so that the printing press operator can check that the right colors are used with the right negatives. If you check Registration, you have the added option of selecting Centered or Off Center registration marks. Centered is the default. Use Off Center when your page size is square or nearly square. Choosing Off Center makes it easy for the press operator to tell which sides of the page are the left and right sides and which are the top and bottom sides, thus reducing the chances that your page will be accidentally rotated.

- **Calibrated Output:** This option was added in version 3.2. When this box is checked, QuarkXPress calibrates for the printer it is set to. When the box is unchecked, the printer calibration curves are reset to straight lines. (Calibration curves change how the color and gray values in a file are printed.) If you are using EfiColor, there's no need to check this option because EfiColor performs calibration.

- **Print Colors as Grays:** If you check this box, QuarkXPress translates colors to gray values. This feature is handy for printing proof copies on noncolor printers. It is also helpful if you have a color image that you cannot otherwise convert to gray scale for use in a black-and-white document. If this option is unchecked, colors might appear as solid whites or blacks if printed to a noncolor printer.

Choosing Output Screening Angles

Normally, you'd probably never worry about the screening angles for your color plates. After all, the service bureau makes those decisions, right? Maybe.

If you have your own imagesetter, or even if you're just using a proofing device, you should know how to change screen angles for the best output. If you're working with spot colors that have shades applied to them, you'll want to know what the screen angles are so that you can determine how to set the screening angles for those spot colors (see the "Special Considerations for Spot Colors" sidebar in Chapter 21).

Screening angles determine how the dots comprising each of the four process colors — cyan, magenta, yellow, and black — or any spot colors are aligned so they don't overprint each other. The rule of thumb is that dark colors should be at least 30 degrees apart while lighter colors (for example, yellow) should be at least 15 degrees apart from other colors. That rule of thumb translates into a 105 degree angle (also called –15 degrees; it's the same angle) for cyan, 75 degrees for magenta, 90 degrees for yellow, and 45 degrees for black.

But those defaults sometimes result in moiré patterns. With traditional color-separation technology, a service bureau would have to manually adjust the angles to avoid such moirés — an expensive and time-consuming process. With the advent of computer technology, modern output devices, such as Linotronic imagesetters, can calculate angles based on the output's lpi settings to avoid most moiré patterns. (Each image's balance of colors can cause a different moiré, which is why there is no magic formula.) Every major imagesetter vendor uses its own proprietary algorithm to make these calculations.

Before the introduction of PDF files that contain printer-specific information, these values were not available to programs like QuarkXPress. But because QuarkXPress (version 3.2 and later) can read them, they now are. The optimized settings are calculated by the printer's PDF file, which should be available from the printer manufacturer. Many of these PDF files also come bundled with various programs, including QuarkXPress.

When in the Page Setup dialog box (File ⇨ Page Setup), you check the Use PDF Screen Values box to use the optimized values for your target printer (use the Printer Type pop-up list to select it) and the lpi setting specified in the Halftone Screen field, as the figure on the next page shows.

File　Edit　Style　Item　Page　View　Utilities　　　　　2:45 PM ⑦

LaserWriter Page Setup　　　　　　　　7.1.2　　　[**OK**]

Paper: ○ US Letter　○ A-4 Letter
○ US Legal　○ B5 Letter　○ [**Tabloid** ▼]　　[Cancel]

Reduce or Enlarge: [100] %

Orientation

Printer Effects:　　　　　　　[Options]
☒ **Font Substitution?**
☒ **Text Smoothing?**
☒ **Graphics Smoothing?**
☒ **Faster Bitmap Printing?**

Printer Type: [Linotronic]　　　**Paper Offset:** [0"]

EfiColor Profile: [SWOP-Coated]　**Paper Width:** [8.5"]

GCR: [75%]　　　　　　　　　　**Page Gap:** [0"]

Resolution: [1270] (dpi)

Paper Size: [ ]

Data Format: [Binary]

Halftone Screen: [110] (lpi)

Halftoning
C: 108.503 lpi, 70.017°
M: 108.503 lpi, 19.983°
Y: 115.455 lpi, 0°
K: 128.289 lpi, 45°
☒ **Use PDF Screen Values**

Halftoning
C: 110 lpi, 105°
M: 110 lpi, 75°
Y: 110 lpi, 90°
K: 110 lpi, 45°
☐ **Use PDF Screen Values**

100%　Page 1

X: 0.5"　W: 2.764"　△ 0°　X%: 100%
Y: 1.014"　H: 1.792"　∠ 0°　Y%: 100%

Color Separations

With its built-in color separator, QuarkXPress offers the controls that you need to handle both four-color and spot-color printing, as well as printing that mixes the two. See Chapter 21 for details on how to define colors and an explanation of the difference between four-color and spot-color printing.

When you turn on Separation in the Print dialog box, you can choose which colors have plates printed. You can print plates for the four process colors (cyan, magenta, yellow, and black) and for any colors defined as spot colors in the Edit ➪ Colors menu. Colors translated to process colors in the Edit Colors dialog box do not display (see the next section). If the Colors palette is visible, you can quickly scroll through the list of colors defined for your document, but the Colors palette does not distinguish between spot colors and colors created through process colors.

The default setting of All Plates (selected in the Plates pop-up menu, shown in Figure 26-3) works for most jobs. Although a long list of colors appears, plates are output only for those colors actually used on each page. Thus, if you use yellow, black, and magenta on page two but use cyan, yellow, magenta, and black on page three, QuarkXPress outputs three plates for page two and four plates for page three. The only exception is that QuarkXPress always prints a plate for black, even if you do not use black in your document. Because press operators expect a black plate for each and every page (if for no other reason than they need the piece of negative on their presses), QuarkXPress makes sure that they get it.

If you do not select All Plates, you can select only one color at a time for printing. You typically select plates one at a time if you want to proof (whether on a color or black-and-white printer) specific color plates or if you need to reprint a plate whose negative was lost or damaged.

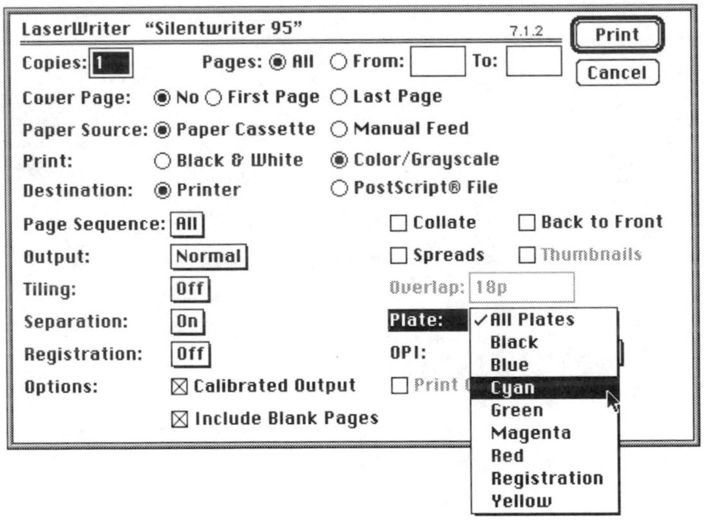

Figure 26-3:
The All Plates pop-up menu in the Print dialog box.

Spot colors and separations

It's very easy to accidentally use spot colors such as red and Pantone 111 (say, for picture and text box frames) in a document that contains four-color TIFF and EPS files. The result is that QuarkXPress outputs as many as six plates: one each for the four process colors, plus one for red and one for Pantone 111. You might expect the red to be separated into 100 percent each of yellow and magenta (which is how red is printed in four-color work). And maybe you expect QuarkXPress to separate the Pantone 111 into its four-color equivalent (11.5 percent yellow and 27.5 percent black). So why doesn't QuarkXPress do this?

By default, each color defined in QuarkXPress — including red, green, and blue that are automatically available in the Edit ⇨ Colors menu — is set as a spot color. And each spot color gets its own plate, unless you specifically tell QuarkXPress to translate the color into process colors. You do so by checking the Process Separation box in the Edit Color dialog box, described in Chapter 21. Check the Process Separation box to make sure that extra plates aren't printed unexpectedly.

If your work is primarily four-color work, either remove the spot colors such as blue, red, and green from your Colors dialog box or edit them to make them process colors. If you make these changes with no document open, they become the defaults for all new documents.

If you do some spot-color work and some four-color work, duplicate the spot colors and translate the duplicates into process colors. Make sure that you use some clear color-naming convention, such as Blue P for the process-color version of blue (which is created by using 100 percent each of magenta and cyan).

The same is true when you use Pantone colors (and Trumatch, Focoltone, Toyo, and DIC colors). If you do not check the Process Separation box in the Edit Color dialog box (choose Edit ⇨ Colors ⇨ New), these colors are output as spot colors. Again, you can define a Pantone color twice, making one of the copies a process color and giving it a name to indicate what it is. Then all you have to do is make sure that you pick the right color for the kind of output you want.

You still can mix process and spot colors if you want. For example, if you want a gold border on your pages, you have to use a Pantone ink because metallic colors cannot be produced via process colors. So use the appropriate Pantone color, and don't check the Process Separation box when you define the color. When you make color separations, you get five negatives: one each for the four process colors and one for gold. That's fine because you specifically want the five negatives.

Outputting with EfiColor

By using the calibration options of the EfiColor XTension (see Chapter 22), you can ensure the truest output of your colors. The actual calibration used in the output is determined by the EfiColor profiles applied to images as they are imported or while they are laid out. For colors defined in QuarkXPress, the calibration is determined by the color model and related settings chosen in the Edit Color dialog box.

When preparing files for output to a color printer or for color separation to be printed on a standard web offset press, you have a few options that influence the results:

- Ensure that the Calibrated Output box is *unchecked* in the Print dialog box (File ⇨ Print, or ⌘P). The EfiColor calibration handles these needs, and having QuarkXPress do its own limited calibration is unnecessary (QuarkXPress's calibration is meant to adjust the dot gain for different output devices, which anticipates the inevitable slight splotching that occurs on a printing press).

- If outputting four-color positives or negatives for eventual output on a printing press, you could change the GCR (gray component replacement) amount in the Page Setup dialog box (File ⇨ Page Setup, or Option-⌘P). The amount can vary from printer to printer, but it's usually 75 percent. This option will be grayed out unless you have selected an EfiColor profile and a printer that supports color separations.

 What GCR does is replace the grays created by mixing cyan, magenta, and yellow (these grays are created when converting an image from RGB to CMYK) with grays created from shades of black. The higher the GCR level, the sharper the grays. But if you make the level too high, you'll lose some of the soft, naturalistic gray tones that you get from having other colors mixed in. Unless you dislike your output, leave these settings alone. Rely on an image-editing or retouching program to do any serious GCR work — EfiColor's five settings of 0, 25, 50, 75, and 100 percent are insufficient.

- You can check the Use PDF Screen Values (which appears as Use EfiColor Screen Values) box. If the box is unchecked, QuarkXPress uses its own values. If the box is checked, it uses the printer driver's values (PDF is the printer description file) or EfiColor's values. Those values appear in the list above the check box. If your printer driver uses special screen angles for optimized color separations (minimizing moirés), check the PDF option. If you're outputting to a color printer, check the EfiColor option. Otherwise, leave the box unchecked.

Figure 26-4 shows the Page Setup dialog box, in which many of these options are available. Note that the dialog box may differ from the one on your Mac because we used the PostScript Level 2 driver (released in late spring 1993) here, which offers a different layout and a few added options compared to the Level 1 driver.

 When printing to a proofing printer (such as a color thermal printer), set your profile to the final target printer (such as web offset) so that EfiColor can give you a good estimation of what the final output will look like. If you calibrate your output to the proofing printer, EfiColor will adjust the colors accordingly, and those adjustments will likely not represent what adjustments it makes when you do your final output.

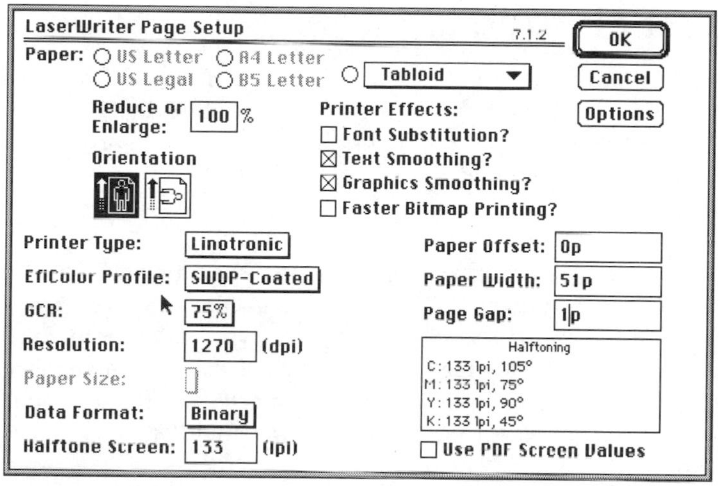

Figure 26-4:
The Page Setup
dialog box
contains several
output
calibration
options,
including
EfiColor profile,
gray compo-
nent removal
(GCR), and
screen values.

LaserWriter Page Setup 7.1.2 [OK]

Paper: ○ US Letter ○ A4 Letter ○ [Tabloid ▼] [Cancel]
○ US Legal ○ B5 Letter

Reduce or [100] % Printer Effects: [Options]
Enlarge: □ Font Substitution?
Orientation ☒ Text Smoothing?
☒ Graphics Smoothing?
□ Faster Bitmap Printing?

Printer Type: [Linotronic] Paper Offset: [0p]

EfiColor Profile: [SWOP-Coated] Paper Width: [51p]

GCR: [75%] Page Gap: [1p]

Resolution: [1270] (dpi) Halftoning
C: 133 lpi, 105°
Paper Size: [ ] M: 133 lpi, 75°
Y: 133 lpi, 90°
Data Format: [Binary] K: 133 lpi, 45°

Halftone Screen: [133] (lpi) □ Use PDF Screen Values

Fixing Your Fiery Output

Even though you have the EfiColor XTension, when you print to an EFI Fiery Print Server that has been calibrated with EFI's Fiery Print Calibrator, your QuarkXPress document can look terrible. Here's the reason and a solution to fix the problem.

The Fiery profile shipped with the EfiColor XTension contains a file, called 'rcur,' stored in the fiery500 profile folder. This file is not required after the Fiery has been calibrated and will cause EfiColor XTension users to encounter "double calibration" (in other words, awful colors). To prevent double calibration, follow these steps:

1. Using the Finder, locate the "EfiColor DB" folder. For most EfiColor XTension users, this will be at the root level of the System folder.

2. Open the "fiery500" folder.

3. Select the file named "rcur" and rename to "rcur.ignore."

You can now use your EfiColor software with a calibrated Fiery.

Supported elements

QuarkXPress color-separates any colors that you define in QuarkXPress. Thus, if you use colors for text, frames, backgrounds, or other such elements, QuarkXPress produces plates for them. The plates are output either as part of the process-color plates or separately as spot colors, depending on how you defined the colors. But QuarkXPress might not color-separate imported images the way that you expect.

 With EfiColor (available since version 3.2) installed, QuarkXPress can color-separate RGB files, such as TIFF, PICT, PCX, and JPEG images. On its own, QuarkXPress can only color separate certain types of color image files: those in the CMYK version of TIFF; those in an EPS file created by an illustration program that can specify color information properly; and those in the DCS (Document Color Separation) format, which is a form of EPS.

For EPS files that use spot colors, the spot color must be defined in QuarkXPress (in the Edit Color dialog box) using the same name as used in the EPS file. For example, if you define a color called Bright Orange in CorelDraw, define the same color — using the same values — with the same name in QuarkXPress. Likewise, if you use Pantone 111 in an Adobe Illustrator document, make sure that you define Pantone 111 in QuarkXPress.

 With version 3.3, QuarkXPress will define the colors for you when you import a color EPS file.

Service Bureau Issues

Service bureaus are great: they keep and maintain all the equipment, know the ins and outs of both your software and your printing press requirements, and turn around jobs quickly — at least most of the time. Working with a service bureau involves commitment and communication between both parties. They need your business; you need their expertise and equipment.

To ensure that you get what you want (fast, accurate service) and that the service bureau gets what it wants (no-hassle clients and printing jobs), make sure that you both understand your standards and needs. As the customer, keep in mind that the service bureau has many customers, all of whom do things differently. Service bureaus likewise must not impose unreasonable requirements just for the sake of consistency because customers can have good reasons for doing things differently.

Paying attention to a few basic issues can help you establish a productive relationship with your service bureau.

Collecting for Output

If you've ever had the experience of giving a QuarkXPress document to a service bureau, only to be called several hours later by the person who is outputting your document because some of the files necessary to output it are missing, you will love the Collect for Output feature that was added in version 3.2. This command, which you access by choosing File ⇨ Collect for Output, copies all of the text and picture files necessary to output your document into a folder. It also generates a report that contains all the information about your document that a service bureau is likely ever to need, including the document's fonts, dimensions, and trapping information. This powerful new feature gives you two very useful things to take to your service bureau: a file that contains everything used by your document, and a report listing all the specifications of the document. Figure 26-5 shows a Collect for Output report.

Figure 26-5:
A Collect for
Output
report.

```
  File  Edit  Style  Item  Page  View  Utilities

                              Sample report

REQUIRED XTENSIONS: None
ACTIVE XTENSIONS: Help publisher

DOCUMENT FONTS
EXTERNAL NAME:        INTERNAL NAME          PS FILENAME
Lucida Bright         LucidaBright           LucidBri
Helvetica             Helvetica              Helve
Helvetica Compressed  Helvetica-Compressed   HelveCom
Helvetica Black       Helvetica-Black        HelveBla
Times                 Times-Roman            TimesRom
Symbol                Symbol                 Symbo
QFontA-Plain          QFontA-Plain           QFonAPla
GarthGraphic-Italic   GarthGraphic-Italic    GarthGralta

GRAPHICS
(EDGE VALUES MEASURED FROM TOP-LEFT OF PAGE)
PATHNAME

TYPE    PAGE    SIZE    BOX ANGLE  PIC ANGLE  SKEW   XSCALE  YSCALE   TOP EDGE  LEFT EDGE  DPI   TYPE
Leatherface:Desktop Folder:Gold Sphere with Note
TIFF    1       147K    0°         0°         0°     100%    100%     5.486"    1.146"     72    RGB
Leatherface:Documentation:Switching:SCREEN.TMP
TIFF    3       67K     0°         0°         0°     56.7%   56.7%    2.124"    1.542"     72    RGB

STYLE SHEETS
        Normal
        Body Copy
        Title
        Heading 1
        Heading 2
        Italic body
        Heading 3
H&JS
        Standard
COLORS
        Black
        Blue
        Cyan
        Green
        Magenta
        Red
        Registration

125%   Page 2
```

The Collect for Output features ensures that your service bureau has all the necessary files and information to output your document correctly. It places a copy of the document and all picture files into a specified folder and it creates a Report file containing document statistics.

STEPS: Using Collect for Output

Step 1.   Choose File ⇨ Collect for Output to display the Collect for Output dialog box.

Step 2.   If a picture file is missing or has been modified, the Missing/Modified Pictures alert is displayed. Click List Pictures to display the Missing/Modified Pictures dialog box.

Note that if you click OK, and continue with Collect for Output without updating missing or modified pictures, Collect for Output will be unable to collect all the necessary files to output your document correctly.

Step 3.   Select each modified picture and click Update to automatically update the picture file. Select each missing picture and click Update to display the Find dialog box. Locate the missing picture file, select it, and click Open.

Step 4.   Click OK in the Missing/Modified Pictures dialog box to continue with Collect for Output.

Step 5.   If the document hasn't been saved during this session, or if any pictures have been updated, an alert is displayed asking "OK to save document before continuing with Collect for Output?" Click Save to continue.

If the document has never been saved, the Save as dialog box appears. Enter a name in the Save current document as field and click Save to continue.

Step 6.   Enter a name in the Report Name field of the Collect for Output dialog box. The default name is the name of the document with the word "report" added.

Step 7.   Select the drive and folder to which you want to save your files.

Or click New Folder to create a new folder for the document and picture files to be placed in. Enter a name for the folder in the Create a folder named field and click Create.

Step 8.   Click Collect in the Collect for Output dialog box.

STEPS: Using the Collect for Output Report File

Step 1.   Collect for Output creates a document statistics Report file and places it in the same folder as the copy of the document and the picture files. The Report is in XPress Tags format and it contains the following information:

- Document name, date, total pages, width, height

- The document's original location and the location to which it is copied

- Version of QuarkXPress, file size, required XTensions, active XTensions

- A list of any necessary EfiColor Profiles (if the EfiColor XTension is active)

- Names of the fonts used (remember that copying fonts is potentially a violation of copyright law)

- Pictures used (size, box/picture angle, skew, pathname, type, fonts in EPS, location in document)

- Resolution of pictures

- The names of style sheets and H&Js

- Each color created and information to reproduce custom colors

- Trapping information

- Color plates required for each page.

Step 2. QuarkXPress provides an Output Request Template to contain the Report file (it is placed in your QuarkXPress folder when you install the program). Open the template (File ⇨ Open) and customize the template to suit your needs.

Step 3. Click on the text box on the lower half of the template and choose File ⇨ Get Text

Step 4. Select the Report file, check Include Style Sheets, and click Open.

Tip: Include Style Sheets is available if the XPress Tags filter was in your QuarkXPress folder when you launched QuarkXPress.

Step 5. Save the new document. Review the report file to confirm that the correct colors, separations, pictures, fonts, and so on, are used in your document.

We strongly recommend using the Collect for Output feature. It ensures that your service bureau has all the necessary files and information to output your document correctly.

Sending documents versus output files

Now that you have Collect for Output, do you give the service bureau your actual QuarkXPress documents or do you send an EPS file? The answer depends on several things:

∽ A document file, even if the graphics files are copied with it, takes less space than an EPS file created from your document, which means fewer disks or cartridges to sort through and less time copying files from your media to theirs.

∽ A document file can be accidentally changed, resulting in incorrect output. For example, a color might be changed accidentally when the service bureau checks your color definitions to make sure that spot colors are translated to process colors. Or document preferences might be lost, resulting in text reflow.

∽ The service bureau cannot edit an EPS file. So the service bureau can't come to your rescue if you make a mistake such as forgetting to print registration marks when outputting the EPS file or specifying landscape printing mode for a portrait document.

Basically, the question is whom do you trust more: yourself or the service bureau? Only you can answer that question. But in either case, there are two things that you can do to help prevent miscommunication: provide the Collect for Output file and report to the service bureau and also provide a proof copy of your document. The service bureau uses these tools to see if its output matches your expectations — regardless of whether you provided a document file or EPS file.

Determining output settings

A common area of miscommunication between designers and service bureaus is determining who sets controls over line screens, registration marks, and other output controls. (Document-specific controls are covered earlier in this chapter; related global settings are covered in the preceding chapter.) Whoever has the expertise to make the right choices should handle these options. And it should be clear to both parties who is responsible for what aspect of output controls — you don't want to use conflicting settings or accidentally override the desired settings.

For output controls on gray-scale images (covered in detail in Chapter 20), the layout artist should determine these settings and specify them on the proof copy provided to the service bureau.

If the publication has established production standards for special effects or special printing needs or if the job is unusual, we recommend that the layout artist determine the settings for such general controls as the registration marks (set in the Print dialog box) and the printer resolution (set in the Printer Setup dialog box).

But for issues related to the service bureau's internal needs and standards, such as how much gap between pages, we recommend that the service bureau determine their own settings. If you are sending the service bureau EPS files instead of QuarkXPress documents, you will have to enter such settings in the Printer Setup dialog box before creating the file, so be sure to coordinate these issues with the service bureau in advance.

Issues related to the printing press (such as which side of the negative the emulsion should be on), should be coordinated with the printer and service bureau. Again, let the service bureau enter this data unless you send EPS files.

In all cases, determine who is responsible for every aspect of output controls to ensure that someone does not specify a setting outside his or her area of responsibility without first checking with the other parties.

 Smart service bureaus do know how to edit an EPS file to change some settings, such as dpi and line-screen, that are encoded in those files, but don't count on them doing that work for you except in emergencies.

Ensuring correct bleeds

When you create an image that bleeds, it must actually print beyond the crop marks. There must be enough of the bleeding image that if the paper moves slightly in the press, the image still bleeds. (Most printers expect ⅛ inch, or about a pica, of *trim* area for a bleed.) In most cases, the document page is smaller than both the page size (specified in QuarkXPress through the File ⇨ Document Setup option) and the paper size, so that the margin between pages is sufficient to allow for a bleed. If your document page is the same size as your paper size, the paper size limits how much of your bleed actually prints: any part of the bleed that extends beyond the paper size specified is cut off. (This problem derives from the way PostScript controls printing; it has nothing to do with QuarkXPress.)

Make sure that your service bureau knows that you are using bleeds and whether you specified a special paper or page size because that may be a factor in the way the operator outputs your job.

Using the EPS Bleeder Utility

The PostScript language automatically strips out any part of a page outside the page boundaries, but printers need images that bleed to extend beyond these boundaries so that in case there is some slippage during printing, there are no gaps on bled images. The standard way to compensate for this problem is to use a page size larger than the actual size, but this method causes problems when printing proof copies to laser printers because such printers take only standard-size paper. It's also easier to lay out a document on the actual page size that you will output to because it is easy to see where the margins and boundaries actually are.

The EPS Bleeder shareware utility, contained on the enclosed XTensions and Scripts Sampler disk, takes EPS files output by QuarkXPress, Adobe Illustrator, Aldus FreeHand, Adobe Photoshop, Aldus PrePrint, Aldus TrapWise, and Aldus PressWise and adds the appropriate bleed area. This addition ensures that the bleeds won't get cut off when output to an imagesetter but lets you use standard-size pages during proof output.

Follow these instructions to use EPS Bleeder:

1. Set the bleed margins by double clicking the EPS Bleeder utility. The figure below shows this dialog box. The default setting is 9 points (⅛th of an inch), which is standard for most printers. If you want to be extra safe, use a larger number. You can set each side's bleed value differently, but there's rarely a reason to do so. (Click the Reset button to go back to the 9-point defaults.) When set, the margins are retained until changed again.

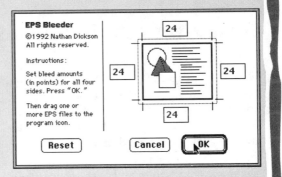

2. Create an EPS file for each page in your document by selecting File ⇨ Save Page as EPS, or use the shortcut key Option-Shift-⌘S. Pick any of the Mac options in the Format pop-up list.

3. Drag the EPS files onto the EPS Bleeder icon; it will process each file.

4. Give the EPS files to the service bureau or department outputting your files. Let them know that the file is a text-only-format EPS file (which means that it cannot be placed in an illustration or layout program).

If you like the utility and use it regularly, note that it is shareware, for which you should send a $10 registration fee to Nathan Dickson, 8640 Seabright Dr., Powell, OH 43065.

Sending oversized pages

If you use a paper size larger than US letter size (8.5 × 11 inches), tell the service bureau in advance because the paper size might affect how the operator sends your job to the imagesetter. Many service bureaus use a utility program that automatically rotates pages to save film because pages rotated 90 degrees still fit along the width of RC paper and film rolls. But if you specify a larger paper size to make room for bleeds or because your document will be printed at tabloid size, this rotation might cause the tops and/or bottoms of your document pages to be cut off.

We've worked with service bureaus who forgot that they loaded this page-rotation utility, so the operator didn't think to unload it for our oversized pages. It took a while to figure out what was going on because we were certain that we weren't doing the rotation (the service bureau assumed we had) and the service bureau had forgotten that it was using the rotation utility.

Summary

➼ You can use dot-matrix, inkjet, and laser printers for proofing jobs that ultimately will be output to PostScript imagesetters.

➼ If you want to print a selected range of pages from a document that has multiple sections, use the exact page-numbering scheme (including the prefix) for the desired section when you specify pages to print. An alternative is to use absolute page numbers, indicated with a plus sign (+) before the page number.

➼ Avoid using the Spreads option if you output to negatives and use bleeds across the spread.

➼ Check the Process Separation box in the Edit Color dialog box for any spot colors that you want separated into process colors. Otherwise, the spot colors print on their own plates.

➼ Give your service bureau a proof printout of your document, with colors, shades, and graphics marked. Also turn in the document's Collect for Output file and report.

➼ Make sure that your paper size is big enough to provide a trim area for bleeds.

PART IX

Extending QuarkXPress

Quark's designers realized several years ago that no program could handle everyone's needs, so they added a capability called XTensions to QuarkXPress. This feature lets other software companies create new features for QuarkXPress that become part of QuarkXPress. This approach is a powerful one now used by many high-end publishing tools, from Adobe Photoshop to Aldus PageMaker.

And with version 3.2, Quark added yet another way to extend the capabilities of QuarkXPress: scripts. Apple's System 7 lets programs talk to each other. With the right software, you can have QuarkXPress work automatically with other programs to, for example, exchange data. These scripts can also be used wholly within QuarkXPress to automate labor-intensive tasks. All it takes to create your own scripts is some proficiency in programming or a willingness to learn.

This section does more than explain the theory behind XTensions and scripts: it covers in detail 16 XTensions (15 of which are included on the disk accompanying this book) and six scripts (including one written just for this book and whose source code is included so that you can use it as a starting point to write your own).

Adding New Capabilities

***

In This Chapter

- ➔ Where to find XTension programs, which add new functions to QuarkXPress

- ➔ Tours of sample XTensions

- ➔ How to use Apple Events and Frontier scripting to automate tasks in QuarkXPress

- ➔ Tours of sample scripts

***

The Power of Extensibility

QuarkXPress is designed to let you add new capabilities, not just use existing capabilities by writing scripts or macros based on the program's own features. QuarkXPress lets you add capabilities in two ways:

- ∞ Buying XTensions, which are add-on programs from Quark and dozens of other companies. These programs integrate themselves into QuarkXPress itself. In fact, several QuarkXPress 3.2 and 3.3 features are actually XTensions bundled with the program. These features include the file-import capabilities, EfiColor (described in Chapter 22), the tracking and kerning editors (described in Chapter 12), Cool Blends (described in Chapter 21), and Font Creator (described in Chapter 14).

- ∞ Writing scripts via Apple Events and UserLand Frontier to let QuarkXPress work with other programs. Scripts let you use the internal functions of many programs to do the work, like mail merge, that QuarkXPress can't do by itself. Because writing scripts is a form of programming, chances are that it will be done mainly in large organizations or service bureaus seeking to automate common tasks.

In both cases, there are nearly unlimited possibilities for extending QuarkXPress's capabilities. The rest of this chapter details the basics and offers several examples to show you the possibilities of what you might do yourself.

An XTensions Sampler

There are more than a hundred Mac XTensions available — ranging in price from free to $6,000 — to handle everything from importing specialized file formats to creating sophisticated tables; from setting hyphenation preferences to supporting multilingual spell-checking. The rest of this section covers some example XTensions organized by their basic functionality. The 🖪 icon indicates the free XTensions that are included in the accompanying XTensions and Scripts Sampler disk. The 🖪 icon indicates that a demo version (in which the print and save functions are usually disabled) of an XTension is included on the disk.

Layout

- BoxSwitch: It converts text boxes into picture boxes and vice versa.

- Notes: Lets you add comments to your document, sort of like electronic Post-Its.

- PiXize: Gives you extra control over how pictures are sized and managed.

- Special Effects: Provides customized text boxes and vertical column rules.

Multipurpose

- Bobzilla: Finds widows, orphans, and overflowed text; lets you move around pages through a pop-up menu; sharpens output of TIFF files; and adds rotation and scaling controls to the step-and-repeat function.

- SpeedOpen: Lets you turn off the dialog box that appears when you open a document whose preferences don't match QuarkXPress's own preference settings.

- Stars and Stripes: Lets you create custom underlines for text and starburst shapes for picture boxes.

Text and Tables

- Dashes and SpellBound: Dashes provides sophisticated controls over hyphenation; versions are available for 29 languages. SpellBound provides finer control over spell checking; versions are available for 11 languages.

- IndeXTension: Lets you create indexes in a QuarkXPress document.

- Tableworks Plus: Lets you create and edit sophisticated tables, including multipage ones.

Output

- BureauManager: Lets you be assured of giving a service bureau all needed files, including fonts, for each document.

- ⇨ Calibration: Lets you manage ink gain in halftone printing to ensure accurate reproduction on a printing press.

- ⇨ ColorManager: Gives you control over the use of color in documents, as well as easily accessible information about your document's color usage.

- ⇨ Printer's Spreads: Lets you output pages in the order a printer needs them on the printing plates, as well as control the placement of elements on pages to account for the effects of staple binding.

All XTensions covered here are available directly from the developers as indicated in the descriptions that follow. The best source for XTensions, however, is XChange, an independent users and developers group that both develops its own XTensions and serves as a clearinghouse between users and XTensions developers. XChange membership is $99 per year in the U.S. and $149 per year in other nations. XChange members get a discount on some XTensions and a monthly demo disk. XChange can be reached at the following locations: P.O. Box 270578, Fort Collins, CO 80527; (303) 229-0656 or (800) 788-7557; fax (303) 229-9773; CompuServe 75300,2336; AppleLink XChange.CO.

Another source of XTensions or demo versions is an on-line service, such as America Online or CompuServe, that has a desktop publishing forum. You'll often find free or shareware XTensions on these services that may offer just the features you need for less than the price of a more complete commercial product.

Quark also makes some of its own XTensions directly available. An example of such an XTension is Cool Blends for Windows which lets QuarkXPress for Windows 3.1 users work with Mac files that use Cool Blends.

The selection of XTensions for QuarkXPress for Windows is smaller but growing. Some XTensions must be installed on all systems that will open a document using their features. For example, you need to have the Cool Blends XTension installed to open a document using one of its special blend patterns, even if that document was created on someone else's system. So cross-platform users should know whether an XTension they want to use must reside on all computers, and if so, they need to make sure that the XTension is available for both Macintosh and Windows versions of QuarkXPress.

General XTension notes

The following apply to all XTensions:

- ⇨ XTensions must be installed in the same folder as QuarkXPress.

- ⇨ Each XTension takes up system memory, so put unused XTensions in a different folder (QuarkXPress creates one called Other XTensions automatically when you install it). Also put infrequently used XTensions in this folder when not in use.

∞ When installed, XTensions add themselves to the regular QuarkXPress menus, add their own menus, or add their own palettes — or a combination of these. You'll also usually see an icon or logo for each XTension appear when you load QuarkXPress. The icon reminds you that the XTensions are being loaded as well.

∞ XTensions usually have a special icon when viewed in a folder, as Figure 27-1 shows (in the second, third, fourth, and fifth columns). Sometimes they won't, but don't panic. This icon is the same as the icon import filters (as shown in the fourth column), as import filters are actually XTensions.

Layout XTensions

BoxSwitch

The BoxSwitch XTension does just one thing, but it's a real time-saver: it converts text boxes into picture boxes and vice versa.

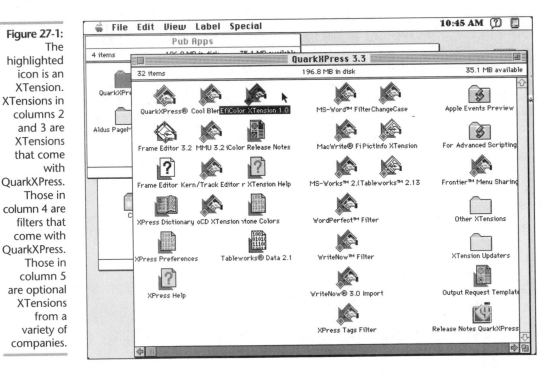

Figure 27-1: The highlighted icon is an XTension. XTensions in columns 2 and 3 are XTensions that come with QuarkXPress. Those in column 4 are filters that come with QuarkXPress. Those in column 5 are optional XTensions from a variety of companies.

Using the XTension is so simple that we didn't need to include a screen image of it. The XTension adds an option to the bottom of the Item menu: Convert Text Box to Picture Box (if a text box is selected) or Convert Picture Box to Text Box (if a picture box is selected). The XTension is smart enough to warn you that any pictures or text in the box you are about to convert will be lost after the conversion, and it gives you the option of canceling the operation.

BoxSwitch does have a limitation: it converts all picture boxes, no matter their original shape, into rectangular text boxes. It does not support QuarkXPress 3.3's polygonal text boxes. Likewise, it converts a polygonal text box into a rectangular picture box.

Available on the enclosed disk, as well as from on-line services. Developer: Lepton Technologies (contact XChange for details on other Lepton XTensions at P.O. Box 270578, Fort Collins, CO 80527; (800) 788-7557, (303) 229-0620, fax (303) 229-9773).

Notes

 The Notes XTension lets you add nonprinting notes to your documents (see Figure 27-2). Notes are associated with a piece of text, which means that notes are deleted if you delete the text that contains the note markers. Also, notes are limited to 255 characters each.

Make sure that the Notes palette is visible (use View ⇨ Show Notes Information). To find note markers in your text, make sure that invisible items are made visible (use View ⇨ Show Invisibles or ⌘I).

If a document containing notes is edited by someone who does not have the Notes XTension, the notes are retained even if that person saves the document. However, the notes will not be visible until you open the document with a version of QuarkXPress that uses the Notes XTension.

STEPS:	**Creating Notes**
Step 1.	Select the Content tool and the text box that you want the note to be associated with. Put the pointer at the spot in the text (if there is any in the text box) that you want the note marker to be; whenever you move the pointer to that location in the future, the note will display.
Step 2.	Type the note into the palette or paste text copied from the Mac clipboard. (Use ⌘C or ⌘X to copy or cut, respectively; use ⌘V to paste.)

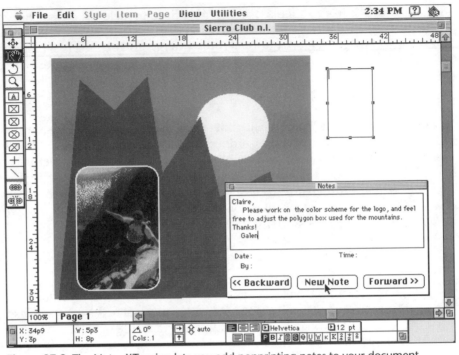

Figure 27-2: The Notes XTension lets you add nonprinting notes to your document.

Step 3.   Click the New Note button to save the note.

Step 4.   The date, time, and creator of the note are added automatically. The creator name is the same as the Mac's network identity (which you set in the Sharing Setup control panel as the owner name), even if you are not using a network.

 Note markers look like a vertical line with a triangle attached to the bottom, as shown in Figure 27-3. These can be hard to spot in text, so use the techniques outlined later to find specific notes.

 If you have notes not associated with a particular block of text, create a new text box anywhere on the page, select the Content tool, and create a note. Any time you select that text box with the Content tool active, the note will appear. Because there is no printing text in the text box, it will not affect your final output. An easy way to remind yourself that this box contains a note is to put several spaces before and after the note marker; this technique makes it easy to see the marker (see Figure 27-3).

Figure 27-3:
The note
marker
indicates
where a
note is
embedded
in text.

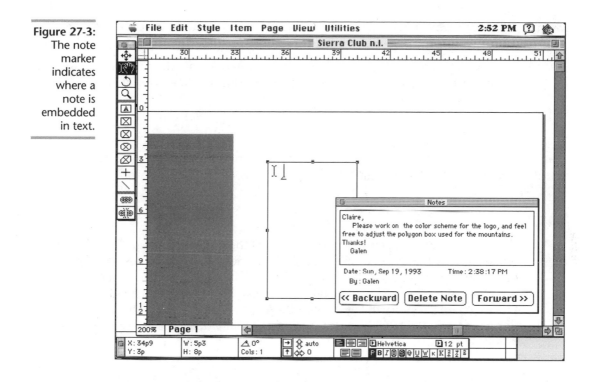

STEPS: Finding Notes

With the Content tool active, select the text box containing the note marker(s).

While you can move the pointer through the text until a note appears, it's easier to use the <<Backward and Forward>> buttons in the Notes palette. These buttons moves your pointer from note to note.

STEPS: Modifying Notes

Select the note with the Content tool active, either by moving the pointer to the note marker or using the <<Backward and Forward>> buttons on the Notes palette. Note that the Forward>> and <<Backward buttons do not move the pointer from one text box to another; they move among notes within the current text box.

Step 2. To change a note, edit the text in the Notes palette and then click the Edit Note button. The date, time, and creator are updated automatically.

Step 3. To delete a note, click the Delete Note button or delete the note marker in the text. Note that the New Note button becomes Delete Note when a note marker is selected.

Available on the enclosed disk, as well as from on-line services. Developer: Quark, 1800 Grant St., Denver, CO 80203; (303) 894-8888.

PiXize

 This utility resizes a picture box to the size of the image it contains. This feature comes in very handy after importing an image because QuarkXPress does not automatically size the picture to fit the box it is imported into, nor does it automatically size the box to match the original dimensions of the imported image. There's a shortcut key in QuarkXPress to do the former (Option-⌘F), but none to do the latter — unless you install the PiXize XTension. PiXize also comes in handy if you resize an image and want the picture box to grow to fit the new dimensions.

To size a picture box to the image, select the picture box with the desired image and use Utilities ⇨ Resize to Picture, as Figure 27-4 shows. Note that the keyboard shortcut Option-⌘R shown in the menu item does not work.

 PiXize will make a picture box bigger to fit an image's dimensions, but it will not make a picture box smaller.

Available on the enclosed disk, as well as from on-line services. Developer: Corder Associates, P.O. Box 26006, Phoenix, AZ 85068; (602) 993-8914.

Special Effects

 This XTension simplifies the creation of special text boxes by adding a floating palette that lets you produce the following three effects: simulate rounded corners on text boxes, cut out part of the top of a text box (perhaps so you can insert a banner), and automatically add vertical rules between columns within a text box. Special Effects also creates a new preferences dialog box to control the settings for these three options.

Figure 27-4:
The PiXize
XTension's
Resize to
Picture
option
enlarges a
picture box
to be the
same size as
the image
within it.

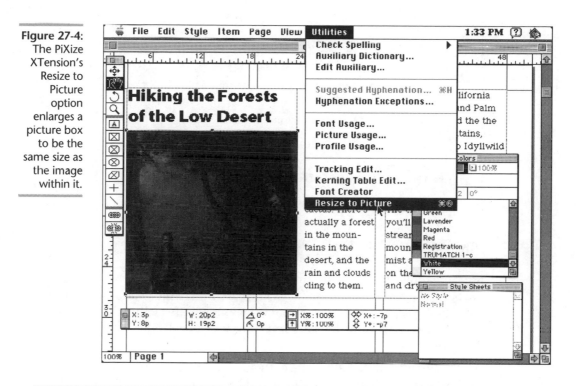

STEPS: Setting Defaults

Step 1. With Special Effects installed, a new menu item appears in the Utilities menu: • Effets Speciaux ("Special Effects"; the XTension was developed in France, so its menu options are in French).

Step 2. To show the Special Effects palette, select Montrer Palette ("Show Palette"). You can hide the palette by clicking its close box or selecting the Cacher Palette option (Utilities ⇨ • Effets Speciaux ⇨ Cacher Palette).

Step 3. To set the options for corner radius, frame width, cut values, and intercolumn rule settings, select the Paramètres ("Settings") option (Utilities ⇨• Effets Speciaux ⇨ Paramètres). Figure 27-5 shows the resulting dialog box. The five types of settings are, from top to bottom, for rounded-rectangle boxes, reverse rounded-rectangle boxes, diagonal-corner boxes, cut-top boxes, and intercolumn rules.

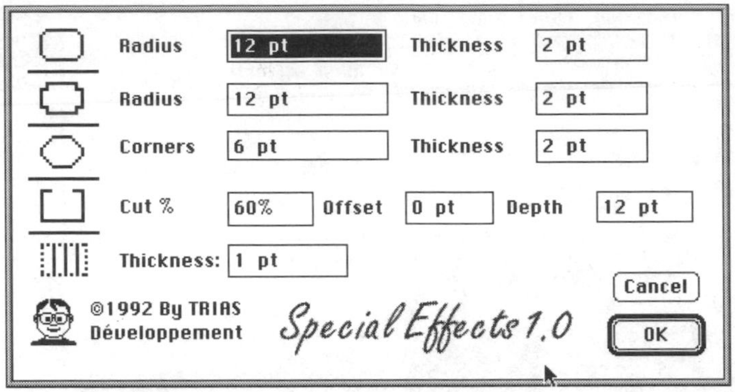

Figure 27-5:
The Special
Effects
preferences
dialog box.

	Radius	12 pt	Thickness	2 pt
	Radius	12 pt	Thickness	2 pt
	Corners	6 pt	Thickness	2 pt
	Cut %	60%	Offset	0 pt	Depth	12 pt
	Thickness:	1 pt		

©1992 By TRIAS
Développement   *Special Effects 1.0*

Cancel

OK

STEPS: Creating Special-Effect Text Boxes

After creating a text box with the Text Box tool, select any of the five tools in the Special Effects palette, as shown in Figure 27-6 (which shows a box that has had the top cut and intercolumn rules applied). Note that the Content tool must be active and the text box selected before the palette will display any of its tools.

For the three tools that affect the corners, Special Effects puts a picture box with the desired shape behind the current text box and groups them together; to ensure that the picture box's frame and corners print properly, make sure that the text box background is set to None (via Item ⇨ Modify, via ⌘M, by double-clicking the text box, or via the Colors palette). The box and frame settings can also be modified these ways.

After one of the corner tools has been used on a text box, all three tools disappear from the palette when that text box is later selected.

For the top-cut tool, Special Effects puts a text box in the center of the select text box's top. This new box can be modified like any other text box; it also is grouped to the original text box.

For the intercolumn rules, Special Effects draws orthogonal rules between columns and groups them to the text box. They can be modified like any other line, but changing the text box's number of columns will not cause the lines to be changed accordingly. Instead, you must delete the rules and use Special Effect's intercolumn rule feature again.

A demo version is available on the enclosed disk. The full version is available from the developer: TRIAS Développement, 89 rue du Maréchal de Lattre de Tassigny, BP 53, F-91702 Sainte Geneviève des Bois Cedex, France; 33 (1) 69-46-21-90, fax 33 (1) 60-15-89-10.

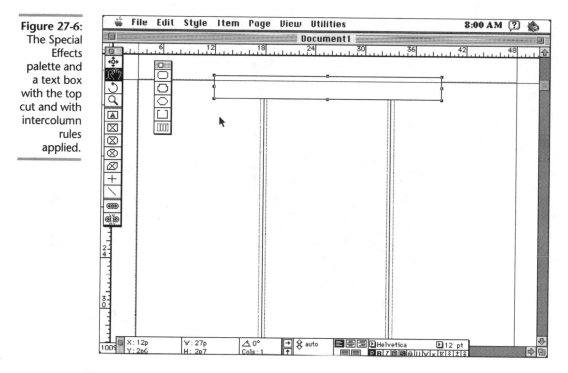

Figure 27-6:
The Special
Effects
palette and
a text box
with the top
cut and with
intercolumn
rules
applied.

Multipurpose XTensions

Bobzilla

First, there was Bob, then Son of Bob. Now there's Bobzilla. All three are collections of must-have add-ons. The first two have been integrated into Bobzilla, which adds new step-and-repeat tools. Altogether, Bobzilla adds four capabilities; the earlier versions provide three features: a pop-up list of pages for easy movement from one page to another (à la PageMaker's row of page icons), the capability to search for widows and orphans and other typographic no-no's, and optimal printing of TIFF files.

STEPS:	Using Go-to-Page

Step 1. Hold the mouse down on the Page field at the bottom left of the QuarkXPress window (to the right of the percentage field). A pop-up menu of your document's pages (including master pages) will appear, numbered as they are in the document (including any section prefixes).

Step 2. Move the pointer to the desired page and release the mouse button. Figure 27-7 shows an example.

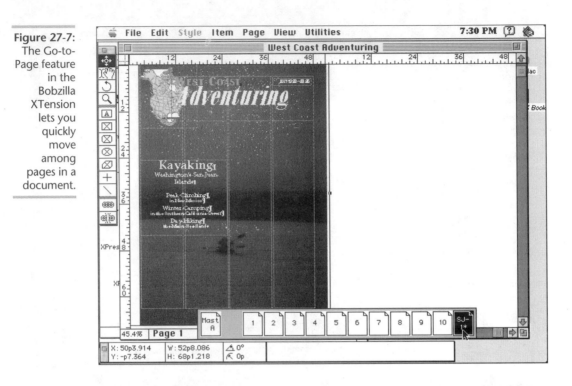

STEPS: Using Line Check

Step 1.   Tell the Line Check XTension which attributes to search for by selecting Utilities ➪ Line Check ➪ Search Criteria. Figure 27-8 shows the dialog box. Select or deselect the ones that you seek. (These criteria become the defaults for all documents until changed.) Note that you usually will not need to search for automatic or manual hyphenation unless you are proofing hyphenation as a quality-check step. Also, a widow — the last line of a paragraph that begins a column — will be found only if the line is less wide than the line. (Lines that fill the column width will not be seen as a widow, although, technically, they are.)

Step 2.   Click the Count button, then click OK. You must do this before Line Check can move to any problem areas that you have just told it to search for.

Step 3.   Use Utilities ➪ Line Check ➪ First Line to begin the search. The violation will be displayed, as shown in Figure 27-9 (text that overflows its text box, at right).

Step 4.   Use Utilities ➪ Line Check ➪ Next Line or the shortcut ⌘; to find the next violation.

Figure 27-8:
The Line Check feature lets you find several types of typographic violations in your document.

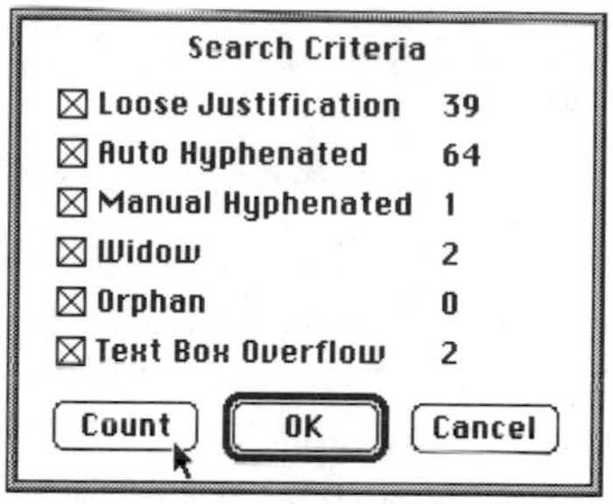

Figure 27-9:
After the Line Check settings have been defined, you can step through each violation found.

STEPS: **Using Super Step and Repeat**

Step 1. Select a box or line and then Item ⇨ Super Step and Repeat.

Step 2. Fill in the desired settings. Options include moving the repeated elements incrementally vertically and/or horizontally, rotating them incrementally, scaling them incrementally, changing the frame width incrementally, and changing the box background shade incrementally. For options beginning with "End," all such settings are based on the selected box's or line's values, and the settings for the repeated elements between the first (the original) and the last (the end) will be calculated automatically. Figure 27-10 shows an example of a picture box that repeated 6 times; the settings are shown in the dialog box at the left of the screen image, while the results are shown at right. You can also set the point in the box from which linear and rotation motion are calculated (through the Vert. Origin and Horiz. Origin pop-ups). Checking the Scale Contents check box ensures that the box's contents are reduced or enlarged with the box if you specify the end box's scale to be something other than 100%.

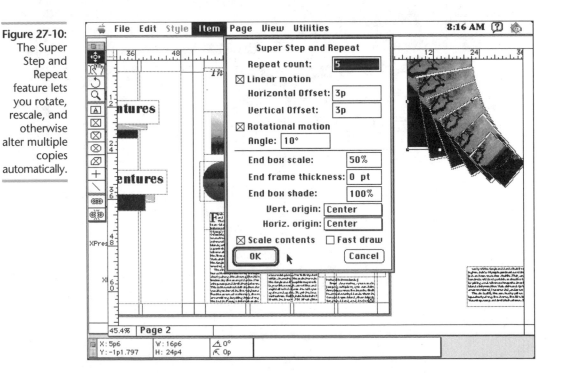

Figure 27-10: The Super Step and Repeat feature lets you rotate, rescale, and otherwise alter multiple copies automatically.

Check the Fast Draw box when doing complex actions for boxes that will overlap. With this option selected, QuarkXPress will display the results only after calculating each new box. If unchecked, each box is drawn after it is calculated, which takes longer overall. Note, however, that text may not reflow properly around boxes created with the Fast Draw option checked. Save, close, and reopen the document, or use the Item ⇨ Send to Back and Item ⇨ Bring to Front options to rearrange the box's layering.

Another Bobzilla XTension, Full Resolution Output tells QuarkXPress to send the picture's full TIFF information to the printer. Normally, QuarkXPress adjusts the TIFF data to match the resolution of the printer, but this can cause areas of flat color — such as a consistent black — to have unwanted halftoning (dot patterns).

STEPS:	**Using Full Resolution Output**
Step 1.	Select a TIFF image.
Step 2.	Select Item ⇨ Full Resolution Output. (A check mark will appear next to this option to show that it is enabled the next time you select the image and the Item pull-down menu, as Figure 27-11 shows. Selecting it again disables the option.)
Step 3.	Repeat this step for all images whose output you want to be at full resolution.

This feature can increase print time because of the added information. Use it only where you have large areas of flat colors, which is likely to occur more often in computer-generated art than in scanned photographs.

Available on the enclosed disk, as well as from on-line services. Developer: Quark, 1800 Grant St., Denver, CO 80203; (303) 894-8888.

SpeedOpen

This handy XTension is one you'll almost never notice — and that's the whole idea. It lets you tell QuarkXPress to turn off a dialog box that many users find annoying: the one that appears when you open a document whose preferences don't match QuarkXPress's own preference settings (see Chapter 4).

Figure 27-11: Applying the Full Resolution Output minimizes halftoning in solid-color areas of a TIFF file.

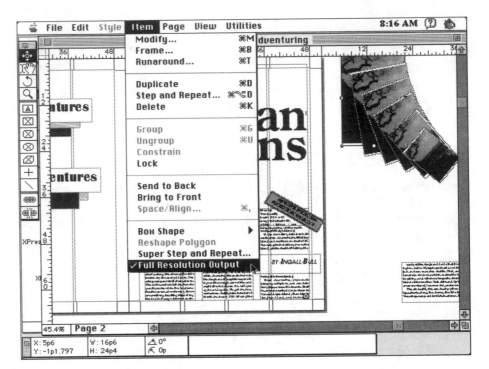

With SpeedOpen installed, a new option appears in the Utilities menu: SpeedOpen. That menu in turn has two options: Settings and Hyphenation Language. The Settings option is the one that you'll use most of the time. Figure 27-12 shows this dialog box. The first set of options lets you tell QuarkXPress what to do when a document's preferences don't match QuarkXPress's: retain the document's, use QuarkXPress's, or prompt you for each document (which is what happens if you don't install this XTension).

Figure 27-12: The settings dialog box for the SpeedOpen XTension.

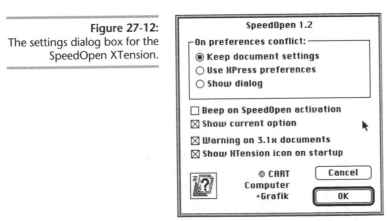

Three other options in this dialog box control SpeedOpen's feedback to you:

- ☞ If you check Beep on SpeedOpen Activation, SpeedOpen will beep any time that it opens a document whose preferences don't match QuarkXPress's; this is to remind you that you are using SpeedOpen.

- ☞ If you check Show XTension Icon on Startup, the SpeedOpen icon will move across the QuarkXPress logo when you first launch QuarkXPress; this is meant to remind you that you have installed this XTension.

- ☞ If you check Show Current Option, SpeedOpen will display the information box shown in Figure 27-13. This feature tells you whether SpeedOpen altered the document's preferences to give you a chance to change your settings and reopen a particular document if you don't want to apply whatever defaults you specified in the SpeedOpen settings dialog box. If you hold the Option key, this information box will continue to display after the document is loaded; otherwise, it will disappear.

Figure 27-13:
SpeedOpen will display a document's preference status if you check the Show Current Option box in the settings dialog box.

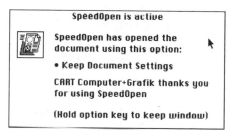

The other option in the settings dialog box, Warning on 3.1x Documents, lets you control whether a dialog box (shown in Figure 27-14) displays when you open documents from QuarkXPress versions earlier than 3.2. This dialog box reminds you that if you save the document in version 3.2 or later, you will not be able to open it in version 3.1 or earlier. (Note that this XTension had not been updated at press time to issue this warning for version 3.2 files being opened by version 3.3; look on CompuServe's DTPFORUM and other on-line services for an update.)

The other Hyphenation Language option in Utilities ⇨ SpeedOpen is normally grayed out. It will appear, however, if you have opened a document that was hyphenated under a different language than the one used in your current system. For example, if you are publishing in English and receive a document from a colleague whose QuarkXPress is set for French, this option will be available. If enabled, selecting this option displays the dialog box in Figure 27-15, which lets you apply the current system's language defaults to the document (by clicking OK) or leaving the original defaults (by clicking Cancel).

Figure 27-14: SpeedOpen has an option to display a warning dialog box if you open documents from older versions of QuarkXPress.

You opened a document created by an older version of QuarkHPress. If you save this document, it can not be opened in the older version anymore.

OK

Figure 27-15: You can change a document's hyphenation language to be that of the current system if the document was created in a different language.

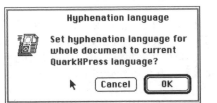

Hyphenation language

Set hyphenation language for whole document to current QuarkHPress language?

Cancel   OK

Available on the enclosed disk, as well as from the developer: CART•Computer+Grafik, Hammer Landstrasse 113, D-41460 Neuss, Germany; phone 49 (2131) 159-703, fax 49 (2131) 159-788.

Stars and Stripes

This XTension adds two features: starburst-shaped picture boxes and custom underlines (the "stripes" in the XTension's name).

STEPS: Creating Starburst Boxes

Step 1. Double-click the Starburst tool (under the Line tool) to set the starburst settings: number of spikes (between 5 and 40), random spikes (if checked, they will be of varying lengths; otherwise, they will be equal in length), and depth (how far from the center to the edge the rays begin, from 10 to 90 percent; a shorter number means shallower spikes). Note that you must define these settings before creating the picture box. You cannot change these settings after the box is drawn, but you can use the Item ⇨ Reshape Polygon option to adjust each spike manually.

Step 2. Draw a rectangle in which the starburst will appear. Figure 27-16 shows an example starburst and its settings.

Step 3. Adjust the runaround settings (Item ⇨ Runaround) if you get strange text wrap; the Manual setting should fix most problems.

Step 4. Place any pictures in the box, apply any frame or background settings, or adjust text inside the box as needed (if you checked the Invert box in the Runaround Specifications dialog box).

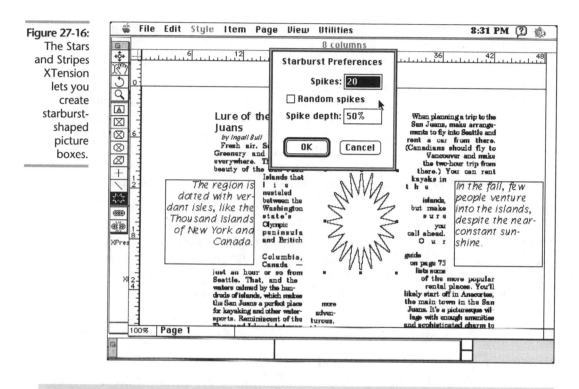

STEPS: Creating Custom Underlines

Step 1a. To create a custom underline for one-time use, select the text to underline and then select Style ⇨ Type Styles ⇨ Underline Styles ⇨ Custom to get the Underline Attributes dialog box. The menu path is shown in Figure 27-17.

Step 1b. To create an underline style that can be applied whenever desired, select Edit ⇨ Underline Styles, which brings up a dialog box similar to the standard Style Sheets dialog box, in which you can create a new underline style or edit an existing one. Either way, you will get the dialog box shown in Figure 27-18, with the addition of a field for the underline style name. Just as with style sheets, you can export underline styles to other documents and import them from other documents. (Chapter 6 explains this process in detail.)

Step 2. Enter the underline attributes (see Figure 27-18 for an example). The width is the underline's thickness, and the offset is the underline's position relative to the baseline (a negative number moves the underline down, a positive number moves it up).

Step 3.   To apply an underline style, select the text to apply it to and then use Style ⇨ Type Styles ⇨ Underline Styles and select the underline style from the list below Custom.

Step 4.   To remove underlines (either a one-time custom underline or an applied underline style), use Style ⇨ Type Styles ⇨ Remove Custom Underline. If you try to remove the custom underline by applying a normal underline (Style ⇨ Type Styles ⇨ Underline, or ⌘U) to the text, you will *add* the normal underline, not substitute it for the custom underline. Selecting Styles ⇨ Type Styles ⇨ Custom Underlines ⇨ Default will replace the custom underline with whatever is defined as the default underline style.

If you open a document that uses custom underlines on a system that does not have the Stars and Stripes XTension, the custom underlines are temporarily removed from the document. When you open the document on a system that has the XTension, the custom underlines are reinstated.

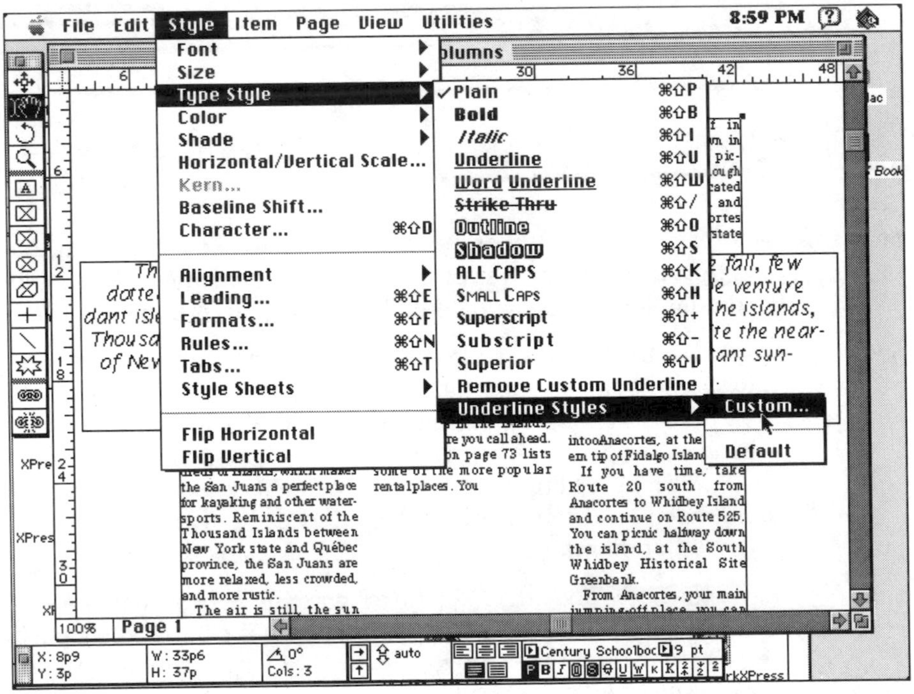

Figure 27-17:
The Stars and Stripes XTension lets you define custom underlines, both for one-time use and as underline styles for repeated use.

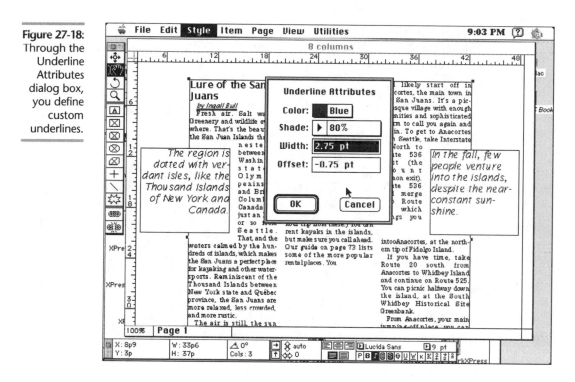

You may experience problems, such as incorrect on-screen text display and system crashes, when working with a document that uses custom underlines on a system that does not have the Stars and Stripes XTension.

Available on the enclosed disk, as well as from on-line services. Developer: Quark, 1800 Grant St., Denver, CO 80203; (303) 894-8888.

Text and Table XTensions

Dashes and SpellBound

Although QuarkXPress provides good hyphenation and spell-checking features, these features can be enhanced, which is exactly what Dashes and SpellBound do. These two XTensions are available as a bundle, and together, they provide fine typographical control in a variety of languages, ranging from American English to Nynorsk Norwegian, from Swahili to Swiss German, from Canadian French to Russian. Both XTensions have their options in a new menu called H&Sp, which appears to the left of the Utilities menu (see Figure 27-19).

Figure 27-19:
The Dashes
and
SpellBound
XTensions
share the
H&Sp menu.

Unlike QuarkXPress's hyphenation dictionaries, Dashes uses linguistic hyphenation rather than algorithmic hyphenation, so that it is more accurate. Dashes works with QuarkXPress's hyphenation settings (see Chapter 13 for details), but adds to them. When active, it inserts discretionary hyphens into words based on its rules. Because QuarkXPress gives precedence to discretionary hyphens over its algorithmic decisions, this feature ensures that Dashes's hyphenation decisions take precedence. (You insert a discretionary hyphen in QuarkXPress via ⌘-.)

STEPS: Using Dashes

Step 1.   Set up the Dashes hyphenation rankings via H&Sp ➪ Dashes Configuration. The dialog box in Figure 27-20 will appear. The Maximum Ranking Allowed option lets you determine how your words will be hyphenated. There are five levels (0 to 4); the number you enter is the last permissible level for Dashes to try. The lower the number, the more easily the hyphenated word will be understood. Setting 3 is a good default. The sidebar "Understanding Hyphenation Rankings" explains the levels.

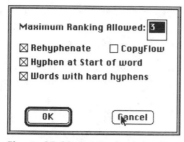

Figure 27-20: Set Dashes's hyphenation rules with configuration dialog box.

Step 2. In the same dialog box, determine how words with hyphens embedded or hyphenated by QuarkXPress's hyphenation algorithm are handled. By checking the Rehyphenation box, you let Dashes rehyphenate words that already contain discretionary hyphens. By checking Hyphen at Start of Word, you let Dashes place a discretionary hyphen at the beginning of a word that should not be hyphenated (this is how QuarkXPress knows *not* to hyphenate a word). You should uncheck this box only to prevent hyphens being accidentally inserted between a punctuation mark (such as an open parenthesis) and such a word, which can be an unwanted side effect of this option. By checking Word with Hard Hyphens, you let Dashes insert discretionary hyphens into words for which you have typed a hyphen (usually compound words like *best-seller*).

Step 3. If you are using North Atlantic Publishing's CopyFlow import XTension, check the CopyFlow box to have text imported with CopyFlow hyphenated.

Step 4. To apply Dashes's hyphenation, use H&Sp ⇨ Insert Hyphens and select from Selection (for highlighted text), Story (for all paragraphs in the current story that have Auto Hyphenation set in their H&J set), or Document (for all text in the document). Use H&Sp ⇨ Remove Hyphens to undo any Dashes hyphenation in text and revert to QuarkXPress's own hyphenation.

Step 5. Use H&Sp ⇨ Suggested Hyphenation for a selected word to see Dashes's recommended hyphenation (this feature is similar to QuarkXPress's feature accessed by Utilities ⇨ Suggested Hyphenation, or ⌘H).

Step 6. You can add your own hyphenation exceptions via H&Sp ⇨ Edit Hyph Exceptions and share hyphenation settings with other documents and users via the Export Hyph Settings and Import Hyph Settings options in the H&Sp menu.

Understanding Hyphenation Rankings

Linguistically, some hyphenations are better than others because where they break gives the reader a better indication of what the full word is, making comprehension easier. Dashes supports five levels of hyphenation ranking and lets you determine the levels to allow. The rankings are as follows, in order of most preferred to least preferred:

0. At word boundary: at the natural break in a compound word, such as *rail-road*.

1. At prefix or suffix: at the addition of a standard modifier, such as *pre-release* or *develop-ment*.

2. Within root: inside the root portion of a word, such as *docu-mentary* or *mas-terful*.

3. Within a suffix or prefix: outside the root portion of a word, such as *documentar-ian* or *masterful-ly*.

4. At a single letter: such as *A-sia* or *foli-o*. This kind of hyphenation is considered typographically unacceptable by most publishing professionals.

STEPS: Using SpellBound

Just as Dashes refines QuarkXPress's hyphenation, SpellBound refines its spell checking. For example, it can detect words that should be capitalized but aren't, it can spell-check words using ligatures like *fi* (such as in *final*) and it can use as many as five auxiliary spelling dictionaries at once. Figure 27-21 shows the menu options for SpellBound; like Dashes, they appear in the H&Sp menu.

Step 1.   Set up the auxiliary spelling dictionary or dictionaries by using the H&Sp ⇨ Edit Aux Spell Dictionary. These dictionaries, like QuarkXPress's equivalents (see Chapter 17), contain lists of words that the spelling checker may not know about, such as scientific or industrial terms. To prevent being asked whether such unusual words are correct, add them to an exception dictionary. By having the ability to have up to five auxiliary dictionaries at once, you can set up dictionaries for different reader levels, different topics, and the like, and combine them when appropriate.

Step 2.   Set up the spelling exception dictionary via H&Sp ⇨ Edit Spell Exceptions to make SpellBound flag correctly spelled words that don't meet your house style. For example, if you enter *disc*, SpellBound will flag all occurrences of *disc* so that you can correct them to the more common *disk*. (Of course, you can accept the spelling *disc* when SpellBound flags it; for example, this feature lets you make sure that you use the common *disk* except for those times when referring to laser discs or other optical discs, for which the *c* variant is common.)

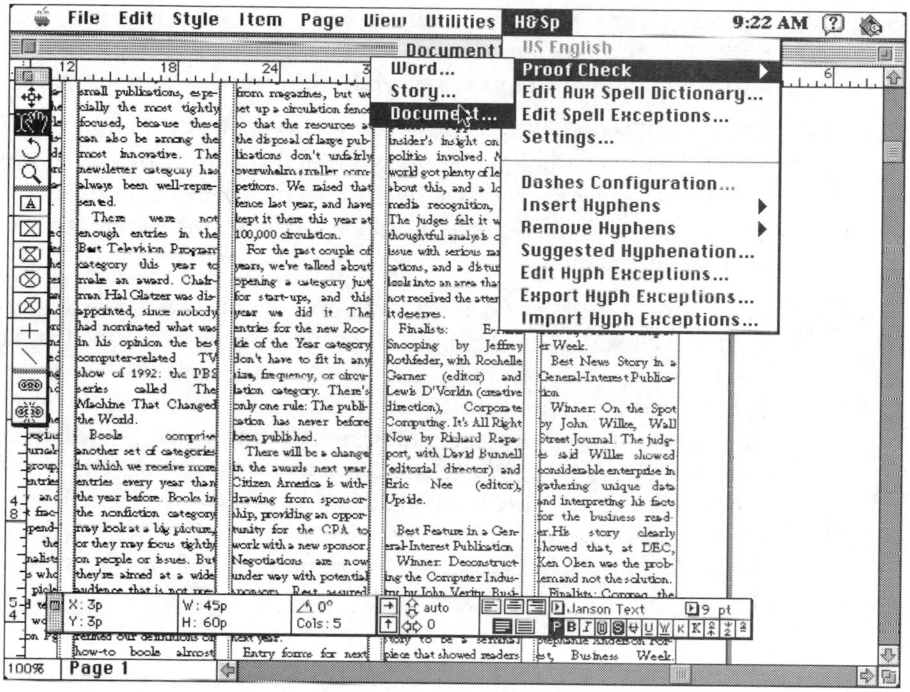

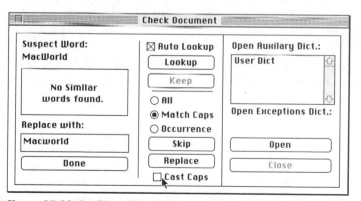

Figure 27-21: You select what part of a document that you want to spell-check with the SpellBound XTension through the H&Sp menu, not the Utilities menu.

Figure 27-22: SpellBound lets you control how text is replaced or skipped during spell-checking, as well as what auxiliary and exception dictionaries are used.

Step 3.   To spell-check, use H&Sp ➪ Proof Check and select from Word, Story, or Document, as desired. If SpellBound finds a word that it suspects is misspelled (or miscapitalized), it will display the dialog box in Figure 27-22.

Step 4.   Open any desired auxiliary dictionaries by clicking the Open button at the right of the Check Document dialog box. Open a spelling-exception dictionary by holding the Option key while clicking the Open button.

Step 5.   When SpellBound finds a suspect word, it displays it in the field at the upper left of the Check Document dialog box. If the Auto Lookup box is checked, it will display suggested alternatives in the box below the suspect word. Otherwise, click the Lookup button if you want SpellBound to suggest correct alternatives.

Step 6.   Either select the desired alternative, enter your own in the Replace With field and click the Replace button, or click the Skip button. If you use Replace, make sure that the Cast Caps box is checked if you want SpellBound to ensure the capitalization of the replacement word matches that of the suspect word; if unchecked, the capitalization will match whatever is in the Replace With field. If you use Skip, you have three options (in the center of the dialog box): All, to skip all further occurrences of the suspect word no matter how they are capitalized; Match Caps, to skip only further occurrences capitalized the same way; and Occurrence, to skip only this occurrence of the suspect word.

You can still use QuarkXPress's spelling checker in the Utilities menu. SpellBound does not change how that spelling checker works, so make sure that users standardize on one or the other to avoid the use of different spelling dictionaries (preferably SpellBound because of its more complete options and finer control).

Dashes and SpellBound cost $200 each when purchased separately or $300 for the two bundled together from the developer: CompuSense Ltd., Avondale House, The Square, Ballincollig, Cork, Ireland; 353 (21) 871-394, fax 353 (21) 874-513.

IndeXTension

QuarkXPress offers few business-document features like indexing, opening the door for XTension developers to fill the gap. IndeXTension adds the ability to add index entries to your document and generate a simple index. IndeXTension adds several options near the bottom of the Utilities menu.

The demo version of IndeXTension (on the enclosed disk) allows only 20 entries.

STEPS: Adding Index Entries

Step 1.   Use Utilities ⇨ Indexing Preferences to set up the defaults for IndeXTension. Figure 27-23 shows the dialog box. Marker Highlighting controls how the index marker codes display on screen; we suggest using a color because that is the most visible method. If your publication is distributed across several document files, make sure that Index Auto-Sorting is set to Off; you'll have to manually sort the index from each of the documents later. You can also assign a shortcut key for adding index entries.

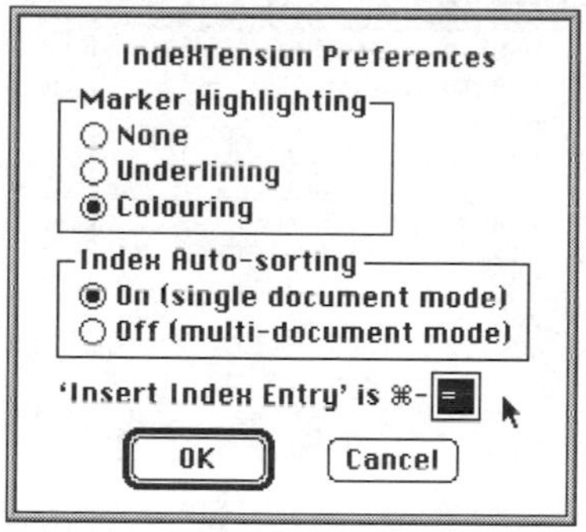

Figure 27-23: Set display and shortcut key preferences for the IndeXTension utility with this dialog box.

Step 2.   When you are ready to add index entries, select Utilities ⇨ Show Index Markers. This option ensures that you will see the index entries on-screen, but your text flow will temporarily be incorrect as text flows to make room for the embedded index entries.

Step 3.   Highlight the text to be added to the index and use your index-entry shortcut defined in Step 1 or use Utilities ⇨ Insert Index Entry. The highlighted text will change to the index highlight color defined in Step 1; the code <$I will precede it and the code > will follow it. Figure 27-24 shows an example of indexing in operation (the text *British Columbia* is being added to the index). Note that highlighted text will not print, so that if your index entries are based on actual text in the document, copy it first and use the copied text for the index entry.

Step 4.   For multilevel entries, separate the levels with semicolons. (You can edit the index entries that you have created just like any other text in your document.) For example, in *<$ITravel;California;camping;tent>*, the overall entry would be *Travel*, the next level would be *California*, the next level *camping*, and the final level *tent*.

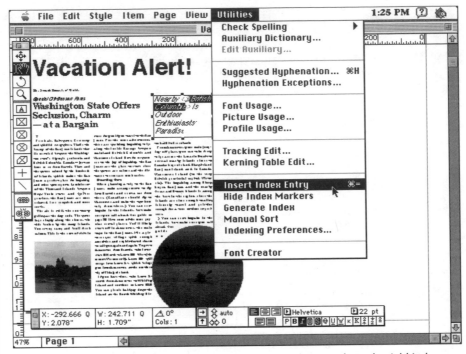

Figure 27-24: To add an index entry, highlight the desired text and use the Add Index Entry option in the Utilities menu. The text color will change, and the index marker codes will appear around it.

Step 5. When you finish entering index entries, hide the index codes via Utilities ⇨ Hide Index Markers. The document's text will now flow normally, and the index entries will be changed into nonprinting hidden text (this XTension thus requires the use of QuarkXPress 3.1 or later).

Steps 3 and 5 work differently when it comes to hidden text. If you select text and choose Utilities ⇨ Insert Index Entry, the selected text is bracketed with colored, hidden text, but the selected text itself is not colored and will not be hidden when you choose Hide Index Markers. If, on the other hand, you select an insertion point and choose Insert Index Entry, the text that you then type will be colored and hidden. Even more confusing, if you choose Insert Index Entry and paste text from the clipboard, the pasted text will not appear colored, but it will hide when you choose Hide Index Markers and will reappear when you choose Show Index Markers.

Step 6. For multidocument indexes, make sure that the page numbering for each document is different (for example, document 1 may be numbered from pages 1 to 49, so that document 2 should start on page 50) or that each document has a separate section prefix (such as *A-* for document 1, *B-* for document 2, etc.). In either case, use Page ⇨ Section to set up page numbering.

Follow the instructions in Step 7, and then cut and paste each document's index into one text box. The use Utilities ➪ Manual Sort to realphabetize the entries and remove duplicates.

Step 7. Create a text box in which to flow the index. Then select Utilities ➪ Generate Index. The index will appear, sorted alphabetically. Each sublevel will be indented via tabs, one more unit than the previous sublevel. A tab will precede the page number, so you can, for example, set up your style sheet to make that tab flush-right with a dot leader.

A demo copy is available on the enclosed disk. The full version, developed by Vision's Edge, costs $99 and is available from XChange, P.O. Box 270578, Fort Collins, CO 80527; (303) 229-0656.

Tableworks Plus

This XTension from Npath Software is almost a full program in its own right. With it, you can create sophisticated tables, such as those used in feature charts, conference calendars, and the like. Do make sure that you have enough memory allocated to QuarkXPress if you're planning to work on complex tables (with more than 600 cells) — we find 4500KB to be a good setting.

 To set a program's memory, click its icon and then get the Info dialog box via ⌘I or File ➪ Get Info. In System 7.1, change the Preferred Size settings at the bottom of the dialog box, as shown in Figure 27-25. In earlier versions, change the Current Size settings.

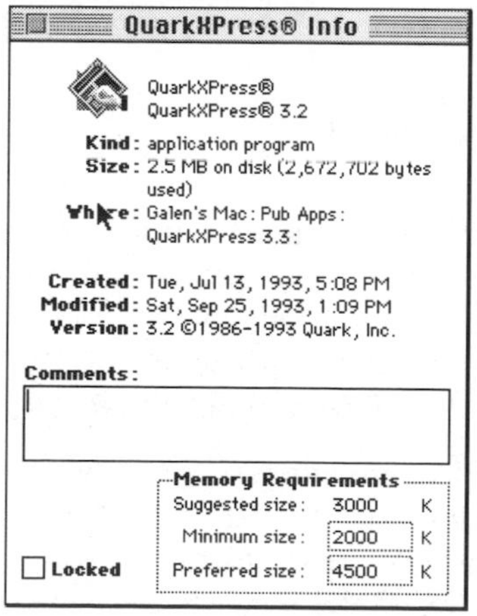

Figure 27-25:
Increase the amount of memory used by QuarkXPress when using Tableworks Plus for complex tables.

QuarkXPress® Info

QuarkXPress®
QuarkXPress® 3.2

Kind: application program
Size: 2.5 MB on disk (2,672,702 bytes used)
Where: Galen's Mac : Pub Apps : QuarkXPress 3.3 :

Created: Tue, Jul 13, 1993, 5:08 PM
Modified: Sat, Sep 25, 1993, 1:09 PM
Version: 3.2 ©1986-1993 Quark, Inc.

Comments:

☐ **Locked**

┌─ Memory Requirements ─┐
Suggested size: 3000 K
Minimum size: 2000 K
Preferred size: 4500 K

When Tableworks Plus is active, the Tool palette will have two added items below the Line tool: the Table tool and the Cell tool. Use the Table tool to add a table and the Cell tool to adjust a table. You'll also have a new menu — Table — added to the right of the Utilities menu. Figure 27-26 shows the modified QuarkXPress interface.

Because Tableworks Plus is so powerful, we do not describe every feature. Instead, we run through the creation of a large specification chart based on an Excel spreadsheet.

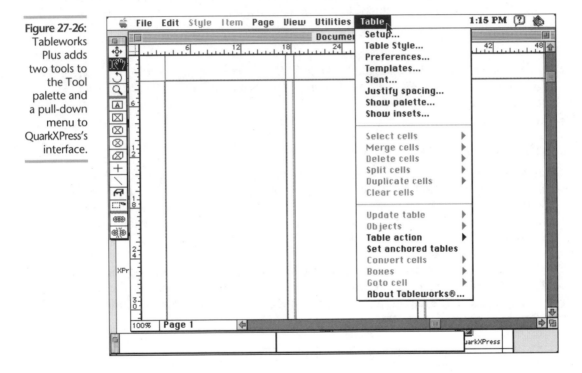

Figure 27-26: Tableworks Plus adds two tools to the Tool palette and a pull-down menu to QuarkXPress's interface.

STEPS: Using Tableworks Plus

Step 1. Because neither Tableworks Plus nor QuarkXPress imports spreadsheet files directly, we saved our Excel spreadsheet in text format, making it a tab-delimited file because that matches Tableworks Plus's default settings. (We also could have saved the spreadsheet as CSV, or comma-delimited, and then set Tableworks Plus to handle that format.)

Step 2. We set up our basic parameters via Table ⇨ Preferences and Table ⇨ Style dialog boxes. Figures 27-27 and 27-28 show these dialog boxes. For the preferences dialog box, selecting an option displays a brief description of the option's effects at the bottom of the dialog box. For our project, we used the preferences dialog box to set the table to size automatically along the horizontal axis (width) but require manual confirmation, and we used the Default Table Style dialog box to set alternating column shading at 10 percent blue, 1-point black lines around cells, and a 2-point black frame around the table. (The Line Scripts button opens a dialog box that lets you customize lines even more.)

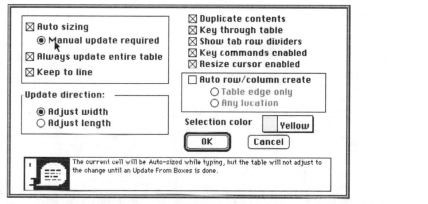

Figure 27-27: You set Tableworks Plus basic settings in the preferences dialog box.

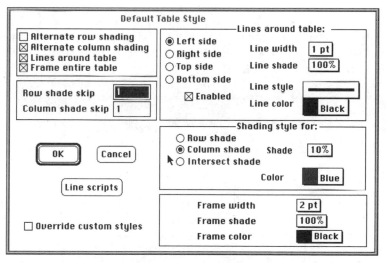

Figure 27-28: You set other basic settings in the Default Table Style dialog box.

Step 3. Because we knew that the table would be several pages wide, we used the Document Layout palette to create a multipage spread, as shown in Figure 27-29.

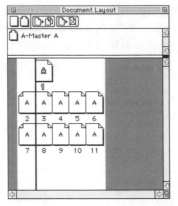

Figure 27-29: When importing a table that is several pages wide, make sure that you create a multiple-page spread wide enough to contain it via the Document Layout palette.

Step 4. We used the Table tool to draw a table box. Doing so automatically invokes the New Table Setup dialog box (see Figure 27-30). We didn't worry about the size of the box because we wanted to adjust the table setup before importing the table file. But we did position the table's origin and left side where we wanted it since Tableworks Plus will grow a table from those points.

You can also use Table ▷ Setup and fill in the table dimensions to have Tableworks Plus create the box. But we have found that this approach does not let you import text from other text boxes or from text files, despite the Import button being active.

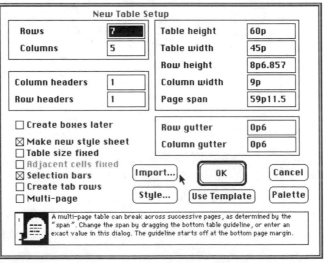

Figure 27-30: The New table Setup dialog box lets you determine table dimensions.

Step 5.   In the setup dialog box, we selected the Make New Style Sheet check box so that any table-specific formatting would be saved in its own QuarkXPress styles. We did not select the Multipage option because that affects only tables multiple pages *deep*, not wide; we knew that our table was wider than a page. If you select this option, Tableworks Plus will force the table to be the width of the current page, so select it only if you're sure the table will fit. You can always go back later into this dialog box and turn Multipage on if it needs to be activated.

Step 6.   Because we were importing an existing spreadsheet (saved as text), we clicked the Setup Then Import button, which results in the import dialog box (see Figure 27-31). We selected Include Headers option because we wanted the top row of the imported text to be the header and the left column to be the header column of the Tableworks Plus table. We selected Auto Grow because we wanted Tableworks Plus to figure out the actual number of rows and columns based on the imported file. We did not check the Preserve Style option because we wanted to apply our own text formatting. Finally, we chose Text File from the Source pop-up list to indicate we wanted to import a file; selecting Text Box (you must have first selected a text box, otherwise this option is grayed out) lets you import tabbed text from a text box in the current document, which is handy for converting old QuarkXPress tables into Tableworks Plus tables. (The sidebar "Subscribing to Spreadsheet Tables" describes another import method that requires extra software.)

By selecting Setup Then Import rather than Import, we can have Tableworks see the number of rows the imported file has. To have this happen, select the file to import and click OK. Then click Setup to return to the New Table Setup dialog box to see what the adjusted settings are and to make any desired

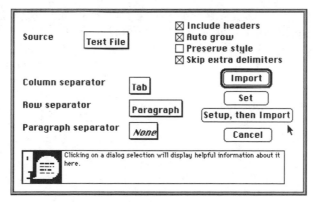

Figure 27-31: The import dialog box gives you several ways to handle file import. Here, it is set for importing a text file.

adjustments. (Our adjusted settings are shown in Figure 27-32.) To actually import the file, click the Import button to return to the import dialog box and then click Start Import button. (You can move between these two dialog boxes.) If we had clicked Import rather than Setup Then Import, Tableworks Plus would have sized the rows automatically and we would have made any adjustments after the file was imported.

New Table Setup

Rows	44	Table height	66p
Columns	50	Table width	225p
		Row height	1p6
Column headers	1	Column width	4p6
Row headers	1	Page span	

☐ Create boxes later

☒ Make new style sheet | Row gutter | p3
☐ Table size fixed | Column gutter | p
☐ Adjacent cells fixed
☒ Selection bars   Import...   **Start Import**   Cancel
☐ Create tab rows
☐ Multi-page   Style...   Use Template   Palette

Clicking on a dialog selection will display helpful information about it here.

Figure 27-32: By using the Setup Then Import option in the import dialog box, you can return to the New Table Setup dialog box to fine-tune settings before actually importing a file.

Step 7. Use the Tableworks Plus palette (see Figure 27-33) to apply text and cell formatting to the imported table (if it does not display, use Table ⇨ Show Palette). You can also use QuarkXPress's Measurements palette to apply formatting to text and to cells (which are just text boxes as far as QuarkXPress is concerned).

Step 8. Use the appropriate options in the Table pull-down menu to merge, split, or delete cells. Other options include anchoring a table to a specific text or rectangular picture box and having a table automatically resized based on its contents.

Make sure that anyone editing a QuarkXPress document with a Tableworks Plus table in it also has the Tableworks Plus XTension; otherwise, text will reflow and table formatting may be lost.

Tableworks Plus is available for $299 and TextLinker for $89 from the developer: Npath Software, P.O. Box 523, Isaquah, WA 98027; (206) 392-7745.

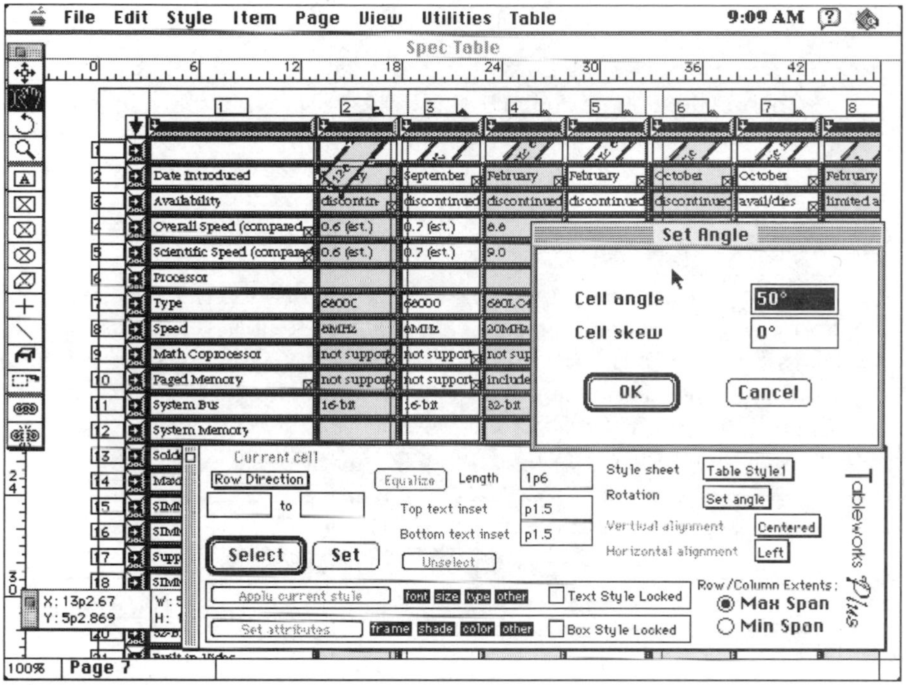

Figure 27-33: The imported file and the Tableworks Plus palette with which you can modify cells and text formatting.

Subscribing to Spreadsheet Files

Tableworks Plus has a Subscribe To option in its Source pop list in the import dialog box that is available only if you have installed Npath's TextLinker XTension, which lets QuarkXPress link to text files and Excel spreadsheets. (Without TextLinker, QuarkXPress supports Subscribe only with graphics, and it cannot Publish elements for use in other programs.) You can use this option to link directly to Excel or Lotus 1-2-3 spreadsheets, to Word tables, or to FileMaker Pro databases (or to any tabular data in a program that has a Create Publisher or similar option to make edition files). Chapter 24 explains how the Subscribe mechanism works.

☞ After the data has been published, use the Table tool in QuarkXPress to draw a table box and then select the Import button in the New Table Setup dialog box.

☞ If you want to preserve the original formatting for an Excel file, select the Preserve Styles option (this will slow import considerably). Supported formatting includes row and column sizes, lines, font, type size, type style, colors, and background shades. Note that the Preserve Styles option has no effect with other publishers, like Microsoft Word. If the option is unchecked, the Excel formatting is ignored.

⥁ Change the Source option to Subscribe To and find the edition file you want to subscribe to. The figure below shows the dialog box. Once imported, the table will appear with an "S" in the upper left corner to indicate a subscribed-to table.

You can also edit the subscribed-to table with Tableworks Plus as if it were any other table.

In addition to the need for TextLinker, the use of Subscribe requires a lot of system memory. We recommend at least 12MB, but preferably 16MB. Also, you'll probably need to increase the amount of preferred memory for the source application. For example, we had to switch the amount of preferred memory for Excel from the default of 2048KB to 3200KB. (See the beginning of the Tableworks Plus section in this chapter for instruction on how to change memory settings.)

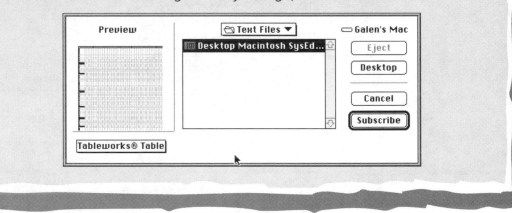

Output XTensions

BureauManager

Making sure that the service bureau has all the needed materials to output your documents can be a real hassle, especially if you are using XTensions and uncommon fonts. QuarkXPress's new Collect for Output feature (see Chapter 26) ensures that graphics files and text files are copied along with your document, and it creates a report showing which fonts and XTensions are used, but it does not collect the fonts or create a job sheet for the service bureau. The BureauManager XTension does. BureauManager creates a new menu, called BM, to the left of the Utilities menu.

STEPS: Preparing Files for a Service Bureau

Step 1. Set up which document elements are to be copied to the disk or cartridge to be sent to the service bureau via BM ➪ Mover ➪ Move Defaults. Figure 27-34 shows the dialog box. It's best to check all the options but Delete Originals because you should retain a copy of what you send the service bureau on your own system. (If you are archiving materials, you may want to check Delete Originals; everything but fonts and preference files are deleted.) The Move EPS Fonts option tells BureauManager to include fonts used by your document's EPS files. The AutoFind option tells BureauManager to look for any files that are missing. You set up the search path via BM ➪ AutoFind defaults. Checking Report and Special Instructions tell BureauManager to copy these documents, which it creates if Create Document Report is checked; these documents contain information for the service bureau about your document. You can choose what report format to have created by using the pop-up list in the Report field.

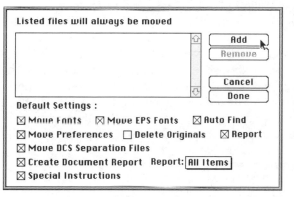

Figure 27-34: With the BureauManager XTension, you set up which elements related to a QuarkXPress document are moved with the document, such as when sending files to a service bureau.

Step 2. Set up the report format via BM ➪ Report ➪ Report Setup. Figure 27-35 shows the Report Setup dialog box. Select the report name from the Report pop-up list; use Rename Report to change the name of one of the reports. The default, All Items, includes all data from the nine options listed in the scroll box at left. For each option, a series of suboptions appears as a set of check boxes at right. You can customize the contents of a report by selecting options and suboptions. We suggest that you use the Misc Report1 and Misc Report2 reports to set your company's report preferences and rename them something more meaningful to you.

Figure 27-35: In the Report Setup dialog box, you tell BureauManager what details about the document to record in the service-bureau report.

Step 3. Set up the document's special instructions for the service bureau via BM Í Instruction Defaults. Figure 27-36 shows the Special Instructions Setup dialog box. Enter the contact information at the bottom of the dialog box. In the Titles scroll box, there are six options for setup instructions: Print Medium, Resolution, Film Setting, Priority, Screen Lines, and Trapping. Select each in turn and choose the appropriate instruction for the bureau from the Items scroll box. You can add your own items by entering the text in the field at the top of the middle column and then clicking the Insert button. Click Replace to substitute the text in that field with the selected item. Click Remove to delete the selected item. Click the Save button to save your changes for this document.

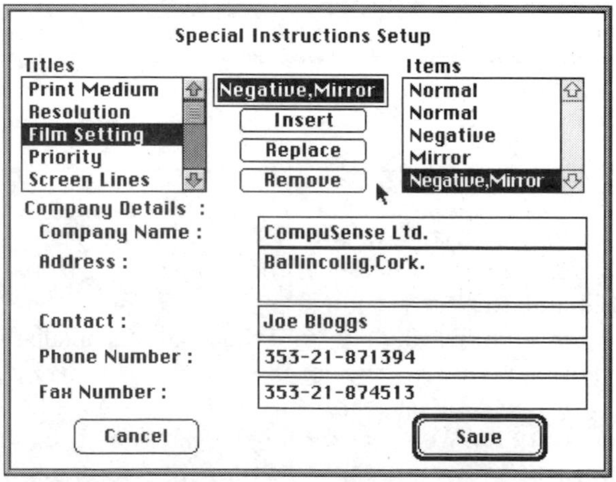

Figure 27-36: In the Special Instructions Setup dialog box, you tell BureauManager what instructions to give the service bureau for outputting your document.

Step 4. To move files for transfer to the service bureau, select BM ⇨ Mover ⇨ FileMover, ensure that the desired options are checked, and select the document to be moved. If you want just to move the fonts used by a document (perhaps to ensure that a colleague has the same set of fonts), use BM ⇨ Mover ⇨ FontMover.

Step 5. To create a report independently of moving files, use BM ⇨ Report File Report. This creates a text file based on the settings in the Report Setup dialog box. Figure 27-37 shows such a report imported into the document for which it refers.

BureauManager costs $129 and is available from the developer: CompuSense Ltd., Avondale House, The Square, Ballincollig, Cork, Ireland; 353 (21) 871-394, fax 353 (21) 874-513.

Figure 27-37:
A sample Bureau-Manager report.

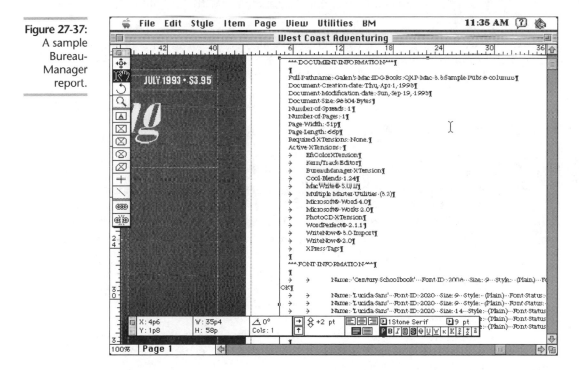

Calibration

Designed for use by service bureaus and in-house publications departments, this XTension lets you calibrate printing from QuarkXPress to ensure the best reproduction of your documents. Essentially, it lets you lighten gray levels that print darker than specified (say, a 20 percent background that actually prints at 25 percent), and darken grays that print lighter than specified. To use this XTension, you will need a reflective densitometer to scan your output sample; Calibration uses the results of that scan to compare the actual output against the original file and then adjust the output for all future documents. This calibration should be run with every output device that you use with QuarkXPress.

STEPS: Calibrating Printers

Step 1.   Open the document Calibration Test included with the Calibration XTension and print it to your printer(s).

Step 2.   Use the densitometer to make gray-scale readings from the output (for example, compare the swatch labeled "80%" with the densitometer's actual density readings for that swatch).

Step 3.   Open the Printer Calibration dialog box (Utilities ⇨ Printer Calibration) and select the printer that you want to calibrate, as shown in Figure 27-38. (These are the printers whose names appear in the Page Setup dialog box's Printer Type pop-up list.)

Step 4.   Make sure that the High Freq setting matches that in the Page Setup dialog box for your printer. You can change the Low Freq setting, but if you do, change the screen values (Style ⇨ Other Screen) for each swatch in the Calibration Test document's Low Frequency swatches to match the new setting before printing and using the densitometer. Examine the density and coverage curves (use the pop-up Format menu to switch between the two) and compare them against the actual densitometer readings. (You can use either method, depending on how your densitometer portrays the data or on what you are most comfortable using. The coverage method is more intuitive for many people because it is based on percentages of black desired. For example, if your 10 percent black boxes print at 15 percent, you'd want to adjust the output value down, to perhaps 7 percent to compensate for the unwanted dot gain.)

Step 5.   By selecting each point in turn on the curves for low and high frequency, adjust the density or coverage curves to match what you would like the printer to output. For example, if the density at 80% should be 0.62 rather than the 0.69 indicated on the curve, move the pointer until the density setting at the bottom right of the dialog box says 0.62. (Figure 27-39 shows this change being made.) Note that you can reset the curves by clicking the No Gain button.

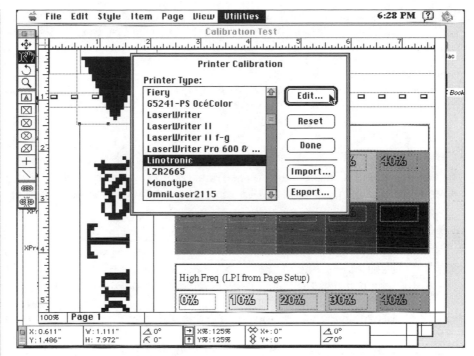

Figure 27-38: The Calibrations XTension lets you adjust output density for your printers.

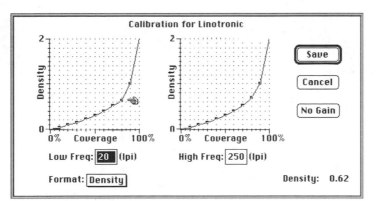

Figure 27-39: By editing the density or coverage curves, you adjust the printer's output to match your specifications.

Step 6.   Click the Save button to save the changes. The printer name will now have an asterisk in front of it to indicate an altered calibration. Click the Reset button to undo the changes.

Step 7.   Output the sample again and remeasure it with the densitometer. If the output values don't match your desires, repeat steps 3 to 7 until they do.

Step 8.   If there are several QuarkXPress users with the same printers, use the Export and Import buttons to transfer the calibrated settings to them.

Available on the enclosed disk, as well as from on-line services. Developer: Quark, 1800 Grant St., Denver, CO 80203; (303) 894-8888.

ColorManager

The ColorManager XTension lets you see how color is used throughout your document and manage that usage. It adds a Color menu to the right of the Utilities menu.

STEPS: Checking Color Usage

Step 1.   Use Color ⇨ Color Usage to display the Document Color Usage dialog box, which shows the colors used in the current document for text, lines, frames, backgrounds, and pictures. Like QuarkXPress's Font Usage and Picture Usage dialog boxes, you can use this dialog box to search and replace colors throughout a document, as well as shades. You can also replace a color with a process (CMYK) version by selecting the On radio button in the Process Separation field. Figure 27-40 shows the dialog box.

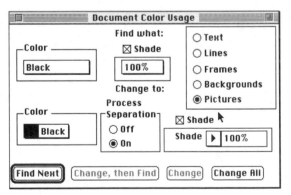

Figure 27-40: The ColorManager XTension includes a dialog box to find and replace colors and shades used in a document.

Step 2.   Use Color ⇨ Color List to see the colors used in a document and to display their constituent color values. It also shows whether a color is a spot or process color. Figure 27-41 shows the Document Colors dialog box and the list of color percentages displayed for the selected color.

Step 3.   You can print or save to disk a report of color usage via Color ⇨ Color Report.

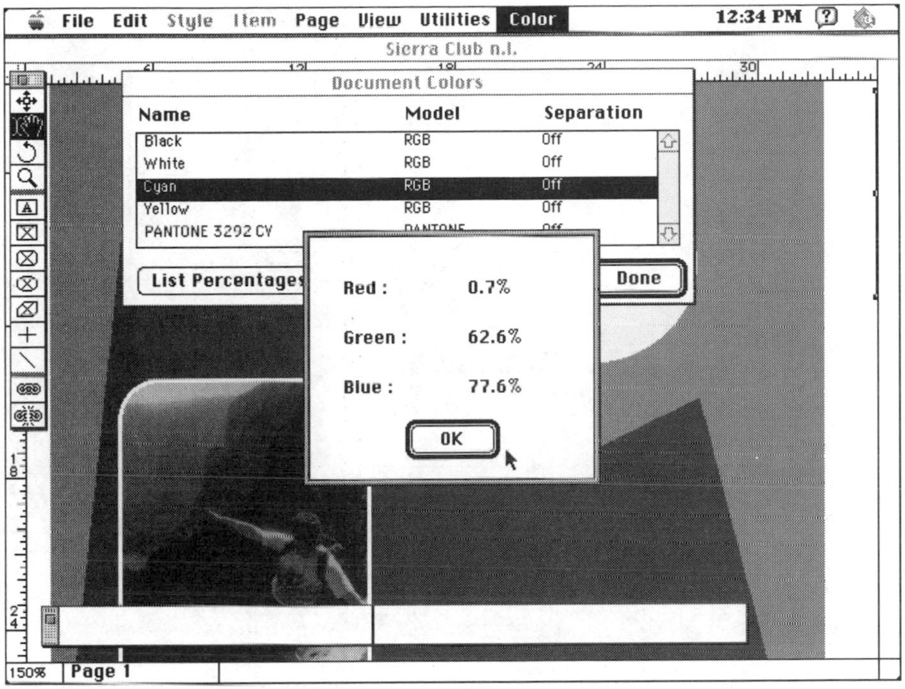

Figure 27-41: The Document Colors dialog box gives more information about colors than QuarkXPress's Colors palette, without showing colors defined but not used in the document.

STEPS: Working with EPS Files

Step 1. With Version 3.3, QuarkXPress imports the colors in an EPS file. But if you're using version 3.2, or if you are a version 3.3 user who wants to know which colors came from which EPS files, use the Color ⇨ EPSF Usage option to get a list of colors in the document's EPS files. Figure 27-42 shows the EPS Color Usage dialog box, the list of colors for the selected EPS file, and the values for that color (accessed by clicking the Create and Edit button). By clicking the Create or the Create and Edit buttons, you can add the color to QuarkXPress's Colors palette. (If the color already exists, the Color Exists box will be checked.)

Step 2. Use Color ⇨ EPSF Report to print or save to disk a report on color usage in a documents EPS files.

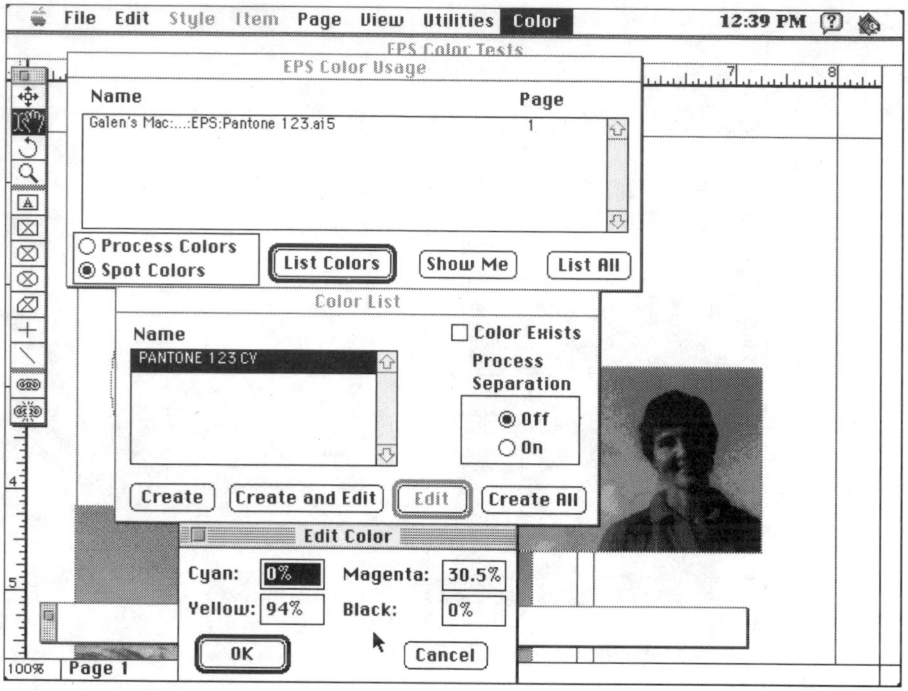

Figure 27-42: Color-Manager's EPS Color Usage dialog box lets you see what colors are defined in a document's EPS files and import those colors into QuarkXPress as well as adjust their values.

STEPS: Working with Output

Step 1. With Color ⇨ Screen Angles, you can quickly change the CMYK screen-angle values for four-color printing (see Figure 27-43). There's usually no reason to change the defaults unless you are using nonstandard colors instead of CMYK in process-color printing or you are using spot colors in combination with CMYK process colors and want to adjust the screen angles so that the mix of colors prints well; your printing service should advise you on the appropriate settings.

Step 2. The Color ⇨ File Mover option will copy your document and any linked graphics. But with QuarkXPress 3.2's Collect for Output feature, this task no longer needs to be accomplished by an XTension.

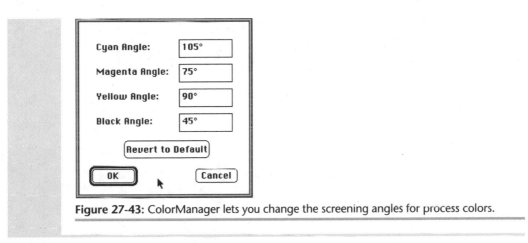

Figure 27-43: ColorManager lets you change the screening angles for process colors.

ColorManager costs $149 and is available from the developer: CompuSense Ltd., Avondale House, The Square, Ballincollig, Cork, Ireland; 353 (21) 871-394, fax 353 (21) 874-513

Printer's Spreads

 This XTension solves two problems common to people who publish newsletters, catalogs, and other documents that are staple-bound ("saddle-stitched," in publishing parlance).

One problem is arranging the pages so that they appear in the order the printer needs them. Designers arrange pages sequentially, but because of how pages are arranged on the printing press, a printer must rearrange that consecutive order. Almost everyone who works with printers knows about page-imposition forms that show you how to rearrange pages accordingly; Printer's Spreads will rearrange the pages for you. (Figure 27-44 shows a page-imposition sheet for a 16-page saddle-stitched document.) If your documents are square-bound ("perfect-binding," in publishing parlance), you won't benefit from Printer's Spreads.

The other problem is that, for documents 24 pages long or longer, a printer typically needs to offset pages to compensate for the effects of saddle-stitching's V fold. The pages at the center of the publication (where you can see the staples) have a wider gutter than those nearest the cover because the fold of the paper with so many pages in between causes a smaller gutter on those pages. Figure 27-45 shows the effect. Printer's Spreads will actually move all text and picture boxes on each subsequent spread a little to the outside margin to compensate for the V fold's effects. The creep is incremental: if you set the value at 1 point, the center spread has no creep, the next spread has 1 point of creep, the following spread has 2 points, and so on.

The demo version of this XTension bundled with this book is limited to 8-page documents.

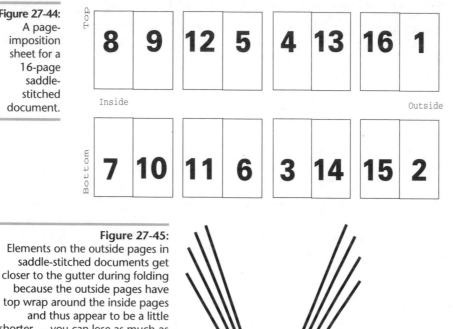

STEPS: Rearranging Pages

Step 1. Make sure that your document has an exact multiple of 4 pages (4, 8, 12, and so on). Add or delete blank pages as necessary. The document should also be set for facing pages and two sides per page.

Step 2. If any text or picture boxes have an upper left corner that falls outside the page margin, group them with another box that falls completely within the page margin. (Elements that originate outside the page's upper left corner are considered to belong to the previous page by QuarkXPress, so that Printer's Spreads won't know to move them with their pages. Grouping them to an element wholly within the page fixes that problem.)

Step 3. Save your document.

Step 4. Use Utilities ➪ Printer's Spreads ➪ Reorder Pages to invoke the reordering dialog box, as shown in Figure 27-46. This figure also shows the page numbers for a sample 8-page document so that you can see later how the pages are rearranged.

Step 5. If you are using QuarkXPress's automatic page-numbering feature, check the Convert Page #'s box to have automatic page numbers maintained when the pages are rearranged. If this option is not checked, QuarkXPress's automatic numbering will cause the page numbers to be incorrect, since the page order has changed. (For example, when page 5 moves to page 1, QuarkXPress would renumber page 5 to page 1. Checking this box prevents that occurrence.)

Step 6. Enter the amount of creep in points. Your printer can tell you the appropriate value for the number of pages and type of paper you are using. A positive number moves the elements away from the gutter; a negative number moves them toward the gutter (which you would do if you wanted to alter the creep value to a lesser amount later).

If you are setting page creep, make sure that you have set your general preferences (Edit ➪ Preferences ➪ General, or ⌘Y) so that the Master Page Items option is set to Keep Changes. Otherwise, the creeping will not be made.

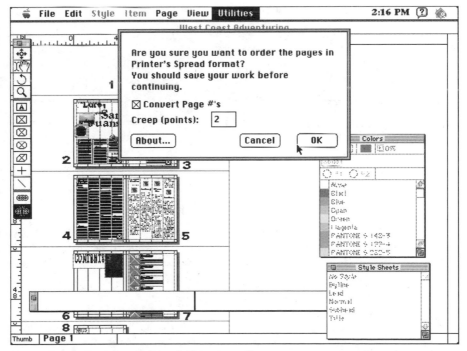

Figure 27-46: The Printer's Spreads XTension will rearrange pages into the order used on a printing press, as well as compensate elements' positions for gutter lost in saddle-stitched documents. The numbers show the original page numbers (compare them to the arrangement in Figure 27-47).

Similarly, if you will not set creep amounts, make sure that the Master Page Items option is set to Delete Changes.

Step 7.   Click OK. Then enter a new file name for the rearranged document (which ensures that, if there is a problem during rearranging or if you later decide to add pages and want to redo the rearranging, you have your original version). Click OK to start the process. When Printer's Spreads is done, the document will reappear in the new arrangement, as Figure 27-47 shows.

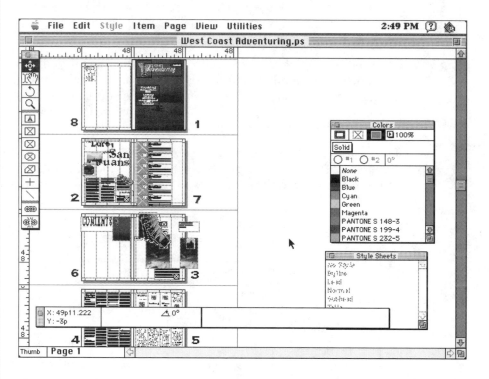

Figure 27-47: The rearranged page order for the document in Figure 27-46.

There will be an extra, blank page at the front that you should not print. It exists only to ensure that the document's first real page to be printed starts on the left. If you delete this page, QuarkXPress will move all the pages up one in the page order, destroying the appropriate arrangement.

Although you can use the Utilities ⇨ Printer's Spreads ⇨ Back to Normal option to reverse the rearrangement of pages for printing, we recommend that you instead open the original document. The reason is that, for documents that used QuarkXPress's automatic page numbering, the Printer's Spreads' Back to Normal option does not renumber the pages back to their original numbers. It's also often faster to reopen the original document.

STEPS: **Setting Creep Amounts**

Step 1. If you don't set the creep amount when rearranging the page order — or if you want to change the creeping values later — you can do so with the dialog box shown in Figure 27-48, which you access via Utilities ➪ Printer's Spreads ➪ Creep/Uncreep.

Step 2. Enter the creeping value. A positive number moves elements toward the outside of the page; a negative number moves them toward the gutter.

> How much creep do you want to add?
> Use a negative value to lessen the current creep.
>
> ☐ Convert Page #'s
> Creep (points): [2]
> [About...]   [Cancel]   [OK]

Figure 27-48: The Creep/Uncreep dialog box lets you increase or reduce the creep amounts for a rearranged document.

If you are setting page creep, make sure that you have set your general preferences (Edit ➪ Preferences ➪ General, or ⌘Y) so that the Master Page Items option is set to Keep Changes. Otherwise, the creeping will not be made.

If you are modifying the creep amount for a previously creeped document, note that the creep amounts are additive: rather than replacing it, any new creep amount is added to the previous creep amount. Thus, if the original creep was 4 points and you use the creep/uncreep dialog box to set a 1-point creep, the result is a 5-point creep.

A demo copy is available on the enclosed disk, as well as from on-line services. The full version is available for $179 from the developer: Corder Associates, P.O. Box 26006, Phoenix, AZ 85068; (602) 993-8914.

Introduction to Scripts

Scripts are essentially custom programs — sort of like XTensions — that let you automate existing functionality or add your own. To show the capabilities of this new feature, QuarkXPress comes with scripts written in UserLand's Frontier language; scripts can also be written in Apple's AppleScript language.

Applications must support System 7's Apple Events to be scriptable; QuarkXPress and Claris FileMaker Pro are examples of programs that support Apple Events.

A runtime version of UserLand Frontier is bundled with QuarkXPress, so that you can run scripts created with the Frontier language. To run AppleScript scripts, you'll need the AppleScript extensions, available from Apple individually or as part of System 7 Pro.

Installing scripts

When you install QuarkXPress, you have the option of checking the Apple Events Scripting box, which installs everything you need to run Frontier scripts. If you did not check that box during installation, you can manually install the necessary files by copying the contents of the Apple Events Scripting Disk into the folder that contains QuarkXPress. Make sure that the Frontier Menu Sharing XTension is in the QuarkXPress folder.

 We suggest that you create a folder called Scripting and put all relevant files in it, rather than use the Apple Events Preview and For Advanced Scripting folders that QuarkXPress creates. The runtime Frontier files are all in the Apple Events Preview folder.

 If you are using a full copy of Frontier rather than the runtime version, apply all actions described in this section for Runtime.root to the Frontier.root file instead. Also, be sure to copy the QuarkXPress.Frontier document from the For Advanced Scripting folder into Frontier.root by double-clicking QuarkXPress.Frontier. We suggest that you move this file, which tells the full version of Frontier how to interact with QuarkXPress, to the same location as your other scripts.

The Runtime.root file bundled with QuarkXPress comes with several Frontier scripts loaded into it. In QuarkXPress version 3.2, you cannot remove these scripts. (Version 3.3 has a script called Menu Editor to remove them.) In either version, you can add new scripts by double-clicking the scripts or dragging them onto Frontier Runtime; this action causes Frontier to put a copy of the script into either Runtime.root. Once copied into Runtime.root, you can remove the original script files from your hard disk (but keep them on a floppy disk or other backup medium as a safety backup). Figure 27-49 shows the dialog box that confirms a script has been copied into Runtime.root.

AppleScript scripts cannot be executed from Frontier, and thus they cannot be executed from within QuarkXPress (because Apple has no menu-sharing XTension for AppleScript like UserLand has for Frontier). However, you can write what are essentially your own applications that you double-click to control QuarkXPress and/or other applications.

In Figure 27-49, note the horse-and-cowboy icon that designates Frontier script files and the stylized "S" that designates AppleScript script files.

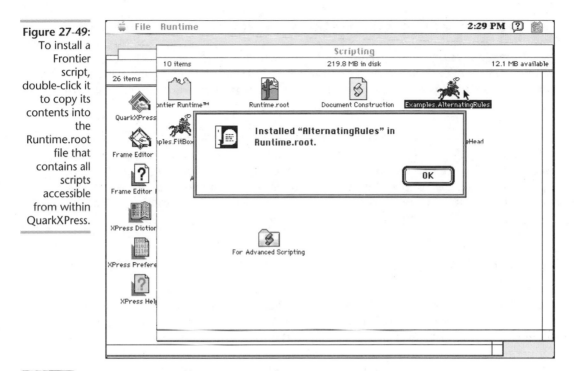

Figure 27-49:
To install a
Frontier
script,
double-click it
to copy its
contents into
the
Runtime.root
file that
contains all
scripts
accessible
from within
QuarkXPress.

If you use the full version of Frontier, you can manage the contents of its
Frontier.root file, including deleting unwanted scripts.

Using scripts

To run Frontier scripts within QuarkXPress, Frontier must be active. You can double-
click the Runtime.root or Frontier Runtime files (which QuarkXPress puts in the Apple
Events Preview folder) to start Frontier. An easier way — if you use scripts a lot — is to
use System 7's alias feature to put an alias (File ⇨ Make Alias from the Finder) of
Runtime.root in the Startup Items folder in the System Folder. That way, Frontier will be
active whenever you load QuarkXPress. Note that the first time you load Frontier, you
will be asked to register it by entering your name, company (optional), and initials. You
can tell that Frontier is active because a new menu, Scripts, will appear to the right of
the Utilities menu. The scripts are listed in order of installation.

Frontier Runtime takes 2 megabytes of system memory, in addition to the 3
megabytes that QuarkXPress prefers and the memory taken by other System
software and XTensions.

A Tour of the sample scripts

The XTensions and Scripts disks contains five sample Frontier scripts from Quark to show you examples of scripting's capabilities. (If you have a full version of Frontier, you can edit them to fit your specific needs.) All will appear in the Scripts menu after you install them, as explained earlier.

Note that it can be difficult to know when these scripts are finished — they work more slowly than applying a format or using a feature manually. On a Centris 610 or slower Mac, the slowdown can be noticeable; on faster Macs, it is often not perceptible. The speed of a script also depends on how well it was programmed. Expect the cursor or box to flash while a script is running. Some scripts issue dialog boxes to indicate that they are complete, but some do not.

Alternating rules

For text boxes consisting entirely of one-line paragraphs — such as tables — this script lets you put gray backgrounds behind alternating lines. This element can aid readability, especially on wide tables. While you can accomplish the same thing by having two styles (one with the background, one without), this script is much easier to use because you don't have to apply the styles yourself. But this script only applies 40 percent black backgrounds. (A new version planned for release after this book went to press will allow user-defined shades.) Also, we found that it performed erratically, sometimes not putting rules behind all lines it should have. Figure 27-50 shows the dialog box and the resulting formatting. The number of continuous rows indicates the pattern for the alternating rules; choosing 2, for example, would mean that two consecutive lines have a background, the next two do not, the next two do, and so on.

Fit box to text

This script shortens a text box to fit the amount of text in it. (It will not enlarge a box whose text does not fit.)

Guide locking

This script locks guides if they are unlocked and unlocks them if they are locked. Figure 27-51 shows the dialog box for changing unlocked guides to locked. (Locked guides cannot be moved with the mouse, which prevents accidental changes to their location.)

Import EPS colors

Although the latest version of QuarkXPress imports the colors defined in EPS files, it does not import those color definitions for EPS files already placed in earlier versions of QuarkXPress. If you want those definitions imported, use the Import EPS Colors script.

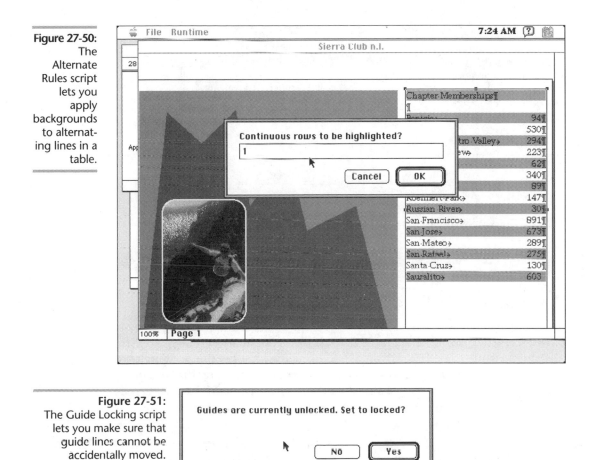

Figure 27-50:
The Alternate Rules script lets you apply backgrounds to alternating lines in a table.

Figure 27-51:
The Guide Locking script lets you make sure that guide lines cannot be accidentally moved.

To import the definitions for a particular EPS file, select the file and then Scripts ⇨ Import EPS Colors. You will get the dialog box shown in Figure 27-52. Click the Current button. (If you click Other, you can select another EPS file from your hard disk or network. That EPS file will replace the selected one, and its colors will be imported — just like doing a File ⇨ Get Picture.)

To import the color definitions for all EPS files in the document, make sure that no box is selected (one way to deselect any boxes is to click on the pasteboard outside the boundaries of the current page). You will get the dialog box shown in Figure 27-53.

In either case, Pantone colors in the EPS files defined using the Pantone color model are imported as Pantone colors. All other colors — including Trumatch, Pantone ProSim, and Pantone Uncoated — are imported as spot colors defined as CMYK mixes. If you want any imported EPS colors to separate into CMYK, use Edit ⇨ Color to edit the color definitions so that the Process Separation box is checked (see Chapter 21 for details).

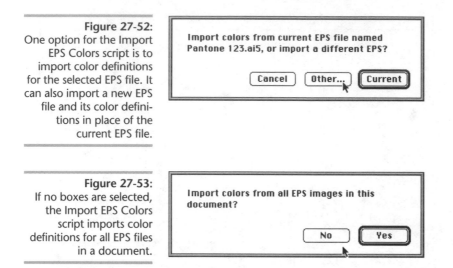

Figure 27-52:
One option for the Import EPS Colors script is to import color definitions for the selected EPS file. It can also import a new EPS file and its color definitions in place of the current EPS file.

Figure 27-53:
If no boxes are selected, the Import EPS Colors script imports color definitions for all EPS files in a document.

Reverse head

This script puts a black bar behind the current line of text and changes the text color to white. It is handy for creating table titles, but you could also create a style that accomplishes the same thing. The advantage to using the script is that it figures out all the settings for the rule size and position for the text — something that often requires trial and error when done in a style sheet. By using this script and then using the resulting text to create a style from, you can eliminate that trial and error.

Creating scripts

Because scripting involves a detailed knowledge of programming with Apple's mechanism for sending commands among applications (called Apple Events) and a detailed knowledge of the capabilities of the program (like QuarkXPress) being scripted, we do not detail the creation process here, but we do provide an overview.

When you install scripting with QuarkXPress, a document called "Chapter 4 – Advanced Scripting" is included in the For Advanced Scripting folder. This 130–page manual covers the details of the QuarkXPress scripting commands and syntax in the two supported scripting languages: UserLand Frontier and Apple AppleScript. To get a feel for the languages, open one of the Frontier scripts provided with this book or the Document Construction sample AppleScript script supplied with QuarkXPress (in the For Advanced Scripting folder). Pages 2.02 – 2.10 of the QuarkXPress scripting manual is also a good place to look because it shows the same script in both the AppleScript and Frontier languages.

To create your own scripts, you'll need a full version of Frontier or the AppleScript Editor. You can get Frontier from UserLand at (415) 369-6600. The AppleScript Editor is available from Apple at (800) 776-2333 or as part of System 7 Pro. Frontier is a more powerful scripting environment, and Frontier scripts have the added advantages of being accessible from with QuarkXPress via the Scripts menu. AppleScript is less powerful but simpler to learn.

Examining a sample script

To show the basics involved in scripting, Kelly M. Kordes of Quark created a simple script called Raise Trademark Symbols with the help of some of Quark's scripting experts: Marc Grabowski, Sid Little, and Dave Shaver. The script changes the positions of any ® and ™ characters in a document so that they are raised. This script is bundled with this book (on the accompanying disk), and the script code is also bundled (and reproduced later in this section). The code is AppleScript, but the principles hold true for Frontier scripts as well.

Planning the script

Kordes is not a professional programmer. As she explains, "I don't know anything about programming. I understand the AppleScript syntax and capabilities. I know the theory of Apple Events and how all the objects in QuarkXPress act. I can write very nice lines of AppleScript that accomplish one specific task. But when it comes to making loops, If/Then statements, etc., I'm totally lost." This statement underscores the fact that anyone writing moderate to complex scripts should have a programming background. If your scripting needs are less ambitious, you may be able to write your own scripts if you follow these guidelines:

1. Think of a task that can't be done automatically in QuarkXPress. Character-based formatting tasks are good candidates for scripts. The Raise Trademark Symbols script is a good example of addressing such a need. Looking for legal symbols is difficult because they're small and you never know when they'll pop up. Use Edit ⇨ Find/Change is inefficient because you can't handle both variants of the trademark symbol at the same time. (The ® symbol means the trademark has been registered with the U.S. Patents and Trademark Office, and the ™ symbol means that the trademark registration is pending.) Plus, if you want to use QuarkXPress's superior feature rather than superscripts for these symbols, you can't use Edit ⇨ Find/Change because this tool doesn't support the superior character attribute. (Chapter 14 explains the difference between superscripts and superiors.)

2. Write in English how the script should work. For Raise Trademark Symbols that explanation was: Look at every character in every text box in the active document; when an ® or ™ is found, change its Type Style to Superior or Superscript.

3. Look at other scripts and try to find all the necessary parts. Find one that looks at the active document in QuarkXPress (easy, most of them do that). Find one that looks at every text box on every page (got that). Find a script that looks at every character and isolates specific characters (found one, but not sure how to isolate symbols).

4. Paste it all together in the AppleScript Editor. All the variables are wrong and the loops are out of context.

5. Start the hard work of editing the pieces you've assembled. Make sure you do, in fact, have all the pieces you need. Make the variables consistent. Create a dialog box with buttons and attach routines to those buttons. Then determine the ASCII character values of ® and ™ (the shareware PopChar control panel can do this task for you; it's available on CompuServe; most word processors, including Microsoft Word, also have functions to insert special symbols that will display the ASCII character values). Add the finishing touches, such as making sure that if you run the script more than once on the same document that the previous changes to ® and ™ aren't undone. If you're new to scripting, expect to need help from someone experienced. (It was at this stage that Kordes brought in Grabowski, Little, and Shaver, who each helped her with a different problem.)

That's how to write a script: figure out what you want, look at examples, and then beg for help. Looking at examples is one of the best ways to figure out how to write a script. But you will need to experiment until you get it right. The key is that you need a lot of time dedicated to scripting.

Understanding the script code

First, the *tell* statement lets the script know which application's Apple Events terminology to use, which ensures that the script and the application are speaking the same language. *Tell* is the verb, *application* is the object; the object is referenced by name.

```
tell application "QuarkXPress® 3.2"
```

The *activate* AppleScript command simply brings QuarkXPress to the front so that you can see the script running.

```
activate
```

The *if* statement uses the *exists* verb to see if a document is open. If not, it goes directly to the *else* statement below and displays an alert with the message: "You must have a document open to run this script."

```
if exists (document 1) then
```

This *tell* statement references the frontmost document; the index value of the frontmost document is always 1.

```
tell document 1
```

The *set* statement assigns the results of a dialog box to the variable *x*. *Display dialog* is an AppleScript command that brings up a dialog box with the message in quotes and the buttons assigned within the brackets. *Default button 1* references the first button, *Superior*, by index value; this command adds a border to the button and makes it respond to the Return key. (These two lines are actually one line; this character (¬) is used to indicate line breaks which are made for readability.)

```
set x to display dialog "Select a Type Style for ® and ™" buttons {"Superior",¬

        "Superscript", "Cancel"} default button 1
```

If the user clicks the Superior button, the script goes through the following routine. This line looks for every occurrence of ™ and ® in every story in the active document. The script then looks at all the styles turned on for the character and makes sure that the superior character attribute is on and the superscript attribute is off. This task is different from applying the Superior type style to the character. If the script simply change the type style, superior would toggle on and off each time that you ran the script.

```
if button returned of x = "Superior" then

    set style of every character of every story ¬

        where (it is "™") or (it is "®") to ¬

            {on styles:{superior}, off styles: {superscript}}
```

If the user clicks Superscript, the script goes through the following routine. The lines are similar to the Superior routine.

```
else if button returned of x = "Superscript" then

    set style of every character of every story ¬

        where (it is "™") or (it is "®") to ¬

            {on styles:{superscript}, off styles: {superior}}
```

```
                    end if

               end tell
```

Because there is no way to indicate that an AppleScript is running (no clocks or spinning wheels), most scripts have a dialog box that indicates that they are finished. The box requires the user to click OK to complete the script. The end messages can also report information such as how many characters were changed.

```
          display dialog "This script was completed successfully."

     else
```

This is the alert that displays if you don't have a document open when you launch the script.

```
              display dialog "You must have a document open to run this script."

          end if

     end tell
```

 This script may not work if you have early versions of AppleScript. To get it to work, you need to recompile the code in your version of the AppleScript editor. The code is on the accompanying disk.

 This script is written to look for QuarkXPress 3.2. Change *3.2* with *3.3* and recompile the script after you upgrade to QuarkXPress 3.3.

Summary

- ◆ XTensions let you add features unavailable in QuarkXPress itself.

- ◆ XTensions take up memory, so install only those you need. Remove occasionally used XTensions from the QuarkXPress folder until they are needed.

- ◆ Scripts can automate repetitive tasks, including those that require work among applications (such as updating values from a database).

- ◆ Writing scripts requires some programming abilities.

Real-World Techniques

X PART

Because QuarkXPress can do so much, it can be hard to see how all its capabilities fit together. The skill in using a program like QuarkXPress is first understanding the relationships between its tools and your tasks and then figuring out the relationships among those relationships.

That series of relationships may sound confusing, but it all comes down to understanding how to select the right set of tools to accomplish your goals for each specific document. After you understand the implications for using one tool or how another tool might be used, you'll be able to simplify your work and push QuarkXPress even harder.

This section shows several actual publications designed by experienced QuarkXPress users. Instead of focusing on a specific type of task, like the other sections in this book do, this section's chapter shows the steps — related or not — that the designers had to follow to produce their documents. By seeing how they combined techniques, you'll understand how you can do the same.

Designers' Examples

In This Chapter

➹ Examples of actual designers' work to show their techniques

➹ How to use a flexible grid for a design-intensive layout like that in a magazine

➹ How to create an engaging table of contents

➹ How to style type for use on a cover illustration

➹ How to use placeholders in design

➹ How to use spot color cost-effectively without losing design impact

➹ How to produce high-impact documents printed only in black and white

Seeing Is Believing

There's no better teacher than experience, so we asked several designers to share their experience using QuarkXPress on real-world documents to show how the many techniques explained in this book work together.

The rest of the chapter contains a representative sample of documents divided into three sections: magazines, covers, and newsletters. Despite the fact that they were done by different people to service different editorial and design needs, you'll probably notice that underlying all of these works are simplicity in design and effective use of the tools that QuarkXPress provides.

Magazines

Feature

An eye-catching design is critical to enticing readers to sample a publication's contents, and *Macworld* has pioneered the use of Macintosh-based tools to produce inviting illustration and a rich design that avoids the stereotypes of cold, simplistic computer-generated artwork. *Macworld* also uses a variety of tools — for example, both QuarkXPress and Aldus PageMaker, both Adobe Illustrator and Aldus FreeHand, and both Adobe Photoshop and Fractal Design Painter, among others — in creating its pages. The magazine's features show off a lot of the magazine's design approaches because lengthy articles give the designers the opportunity to use multiple techniques within the overall design framework.

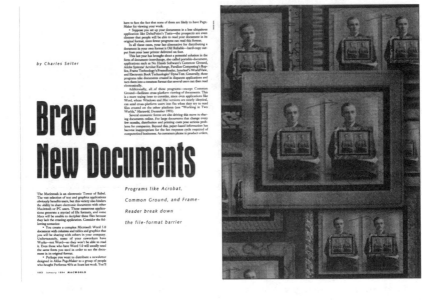

Designers: Leslie Barton and Dennis McLeod
Publication: Macworld
Company: International Data Group

The magazine's design offers a flexible grid that allows different numbers of columns and column sizes from feature to feature. By having a standard grid, similar to the grid shown in Figure 28-1, the magazine's design director can be assured that the entire package will be cohesive; by letting individual designers have options within that structure, the design director can be certain that the appropriate creative flexibility is available to keep the reader engaged. Every standard element — body text, sidebar, screen image, diagram, table, and caption — must take up an integral number of columns, but the

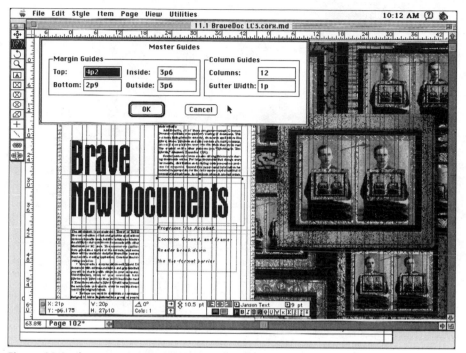

Figure 28-1: The master guides grid shows the options designers have for placement of standard elements. Here are the settings for *Macworld*. Note that the master guides are set up in master pages; the dialog box to create them has been placed on this document page to show the settings used.

number per element is up to the designer. To create the grid, the designer uses Page ⇨ Master Guides in the document's master page (or pages, if there are several). After the basic elements are laid out, the grid display can be turned off via View ⇨ Show Guides.

The document also has a text box with each line so that the designers and copy editors can quickly tell how many lines under or over the text is or what the depth of an element is in terms of lines. When working with editors, designers and copy editors can thus give the editors their requests in a common language: the number of lines, rather than the depth in picas (how designers often think of it) or the character count (how editors often think of it). The text is in a special color (Nonrepro Blue, defined as 33.7 percent red, 41.5 percent green, and 100 percent blue in the RGB color model) that does not photocopy, and the lines are hairline ruling lines defined in the numbers' style. The Nonrepro Blue color is not set to color-separate, so the line-depth guides using that color will not print on the CMYK plates. Figure 28-2 shows the nonreproducible line numbers.

Figure 28-2:
To produce
the non-
reproducible
line numbers
(at left), the
designer
created a
special color
(via Edit ⇨
Colors, as
shown at
top) and set
a ruling line
below the
numbers to
indicate the
baseline of
each line
(via the
Paragraph
Rules dialog
box, as
shown
below).

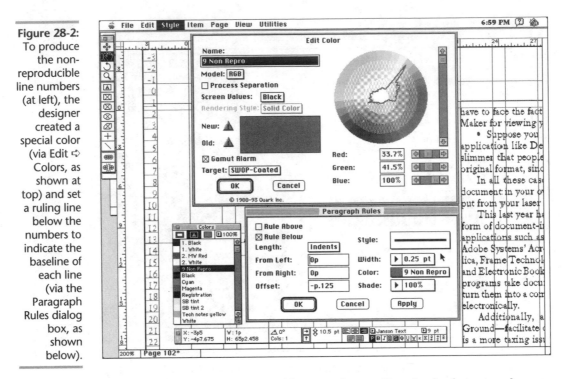

The *Macworld* design relies on a core set of fonts — Janson Text for body text and Syntax for sidebar text, caption text, and subheads — to keep the look unified. Similarly, certain colors used throughout — such as Macworld Red and Tech Notes Yellow — are standardized. But the designer can create custom tints for sidebar backgrounds for each feature, based on the overall color scheme (see Figure 28-3).

Tables are a common element in any magazine (see Figure 28-4). For straightforward tables, QuarkXPress's tab features suffice. The designer sets up the tabs (via Style ⇨ Tabs, or Shift-⌘T) for each column based on the needs of the content. This requires a fair amount of give and take to ensure that the tab settings result in readable but not space-wasting margins. Also, the designer needs to account for extra margins between columns that break across a page. For more complex needs, a designer turns to an XTension like Tableworks Plus (see Chapter 27 for details on this XTension).

In tightly leaded text (*Macworld* uses a leading of 10.5 points for its 9-point text), the settings for subscripts, superscripts, and small caps are important because there is little room for these elements' size and position, but they must be distinct enough from the standard body text to be discernible by the reader. *Macworld* uses different settings, shown in Figure 28-5, for these elements than we recommended in Chapter 4. Although our settings work well for most documents, each document's font, size, and leading

Figure 28-3: Although there are several types of elements, the use of just two main typefaces and standard colors ensures a consistent look and feel.

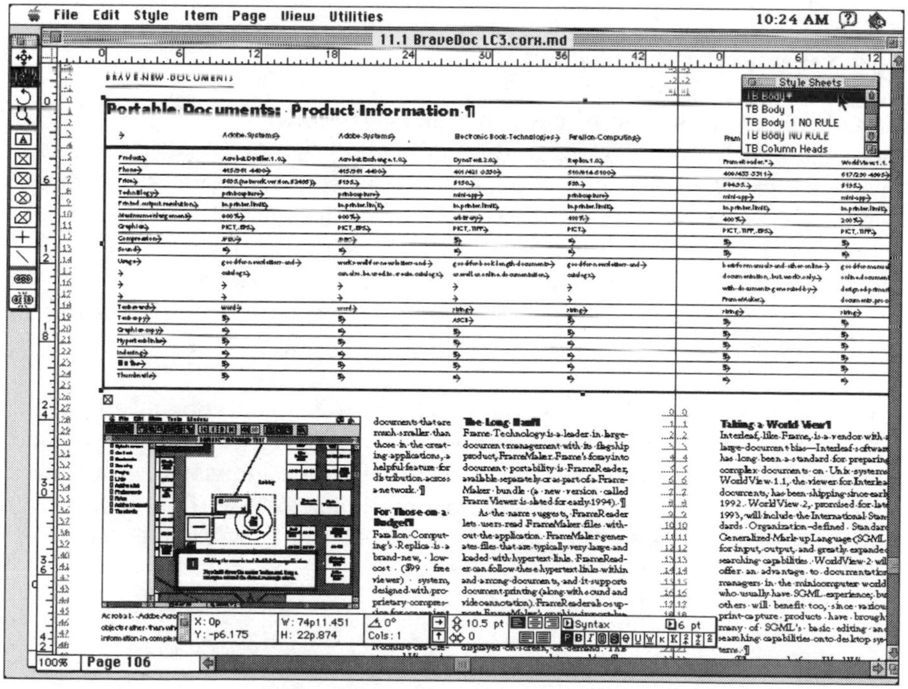

Figure 28-4: To set up tables, the designer uses QuarkXPress's tab settings to define the appropriate settings for each table. Although the basic type specs are in the table style, the tables differ too much for the tab settings to be pre-defined in that style.

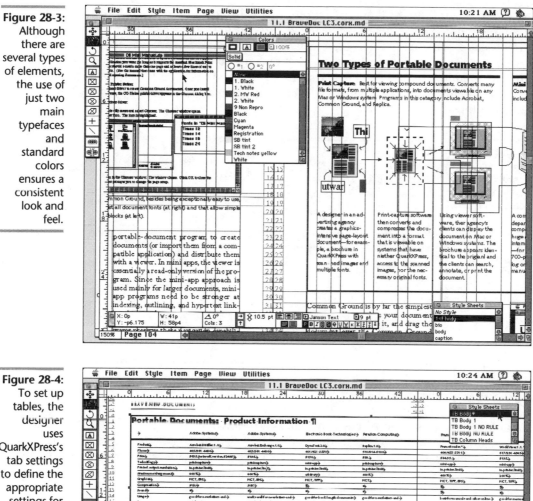

together may require further customization. The biggest difference is that subscripts are moved down only 15 percent in *Macworld*'s settings (versus 30 percent in ours) — a direct result of the magazine's tight leading. *Macworld* also uses a slightly smaller size for superscripts and subscripts (60 percent versus 65 percent) for two reasons: these are rare elements, so readability is less important, and the tight leading favors smaller sizes to eliminate the possibility of subscripted or superscripted text running into adjacent lines.

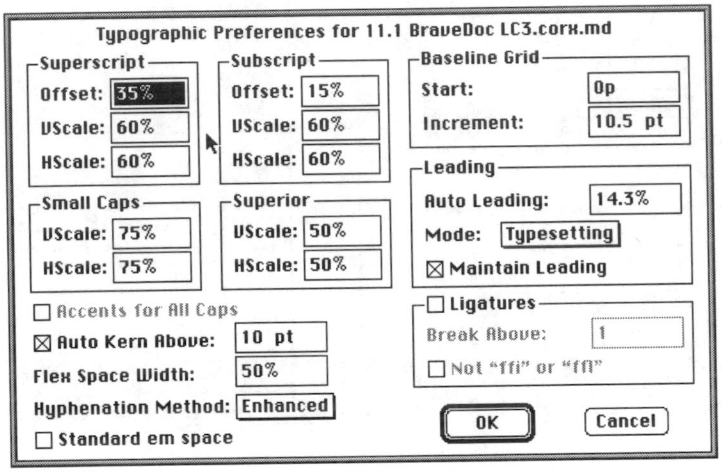

Figure 28-5:
Macworld's typographic preferences. Because of the tight leading, the magazine moves subscripts down very little.

Table of contents

A table of contents must be both engaging and informative. *IEEE Software*'s format is a good example of one that succeeds at doing both. This is particularly important for a magazine like *IEEE Software*, which is aimed at technical readers covering many subdisciplines who may bypass editorial content that does not directly apply to their immediate interests. By making the presentation engaging, the magazine helps keep its readers abreast of multiple subdisciplines and thus better prepared for dealing with their complex projects. The magazine's design-oriented layout contains several techniques that a designer can use to work effectively with QuarkXPress.

The designer uses gradient backgrounds behind the contents' masthead information — the staff and contributors information in the box at right and the postal and circulation information in the box at bottom — to provide color and visual interest to solid text blocks that could otherwise distract from the use of a portion of the cover's color image (see Figure 28-6). The page numbers, magazine logo, and contents title also use

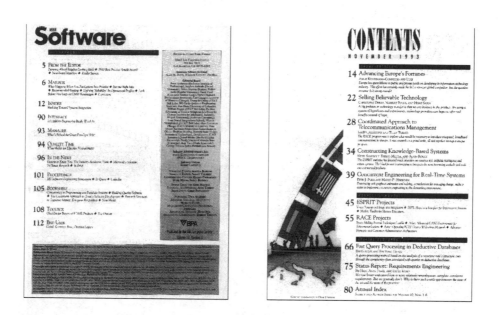

Designer: Dirk Hagner
Publication: IEEE Software
Company: IEEE Computer Society

color to enhance the page's vitality. To get the linear blends, the designer defines a series of colors that complement the cover repeat's colors in QuarkXPress's Colors dialog box (Edit ➪ Colors). He then uses the linear blend feature in the Colors palette to create the gradient.

The designer substitutes a diamond-shaped special symbol in place of the standard circle bullet to add visual accent (see Figure 28-7). In this case, the symbol is from the Zapf Dingbats font, so the designer takes advantage of a QuarkXPress shortcut: entering Shift-⌘Z and then U (the letter that maps to the diamond character). The shortcut changes the font to Zapf Dingbats just for the next character.

Because a table of contents' basic elements are the same for each issue, the designer locks (Item ➪ Lock) the text and picture boxes whose positions don't change (see Figure 28-8). This technique ensures that they are not inadvertently moved when working with other elements. The locked elements can still be modified via Item ➪ Modify, or they can be unlocked (Item ➪ Unlock) and moved with the mouse.

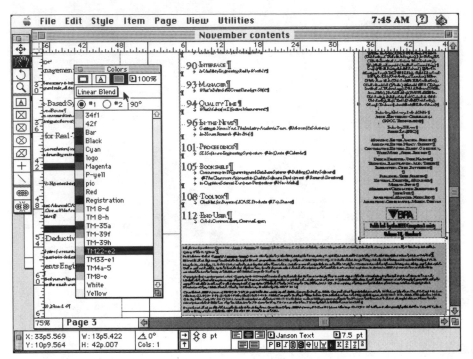

Figure 28-6: Using QuarkXPress's color-definition and linear-blend features, the designer can create backgrounds whose colors work well with the cover image. The highlighted picture box (the vertical one) appears to have no blend; it does, but to speed screen redraw, QuarkXPress disables the blend on-screen for selected items.

Black bars with lightly colored text — called reversed-out text — create a bold effect that makes it easy for a reader to find major groupings. In this contents spread, the designer uses the effect to highlight the magazine's different kinds of features and its departments. To produce this effect, the designer created a style whose paragraph settings put a black rule below the text; the rule's width is 4 points more than the text's point size, which allows for 2 points of space above and below the text. The style also sets the character's baseline position to –12.5 points, which moves the text down into the ruling line, creating the reversed-out text effect. Figures 28-9 and 28-10 illustrate the process used to create reversed-out text.

Figure 28-7: Using symbols for bullets adds a visual accent, and QuarkXPress's Shift-⌘Z shortcut lets you switch to Zapf Dingbats for just the next character, thus saving time.

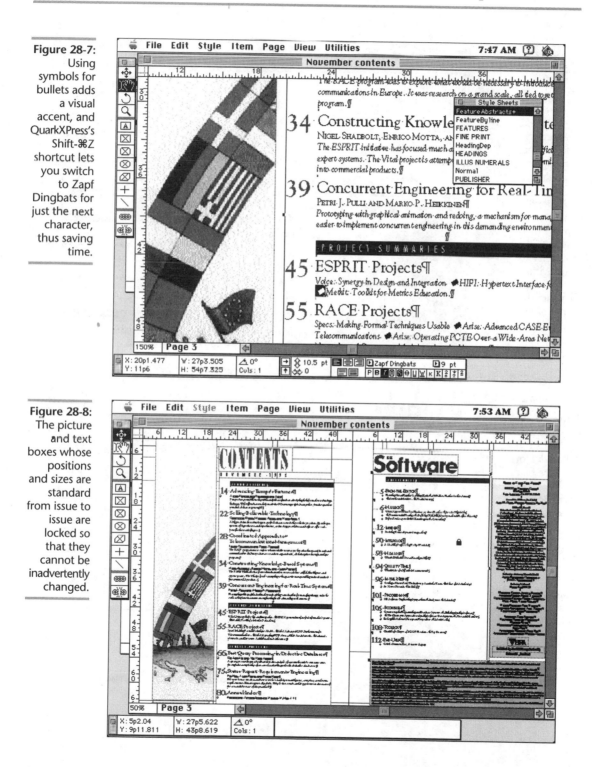

Figure 28-8: The picture and text boxes whose positions and sizes are standard from issue to issue are locked so that they cannot be inadvertently changed.

Figure 28-9: In the first step to producing the reversed-out text effect, the designer sets a ruling line in the paragraph style; the line's width is more than the text's point size to provide a gutter within the line for the text.

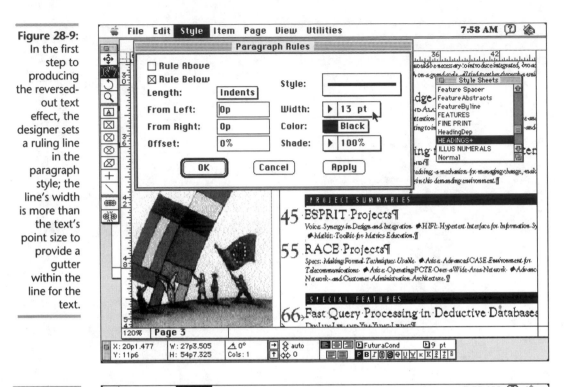

Figure 28-10: The designer shifts the baseline of the text down to move the text into the line that was defined to be below it for a reversed-out text effect. He also used a user-defined color (P-yell) for the text.

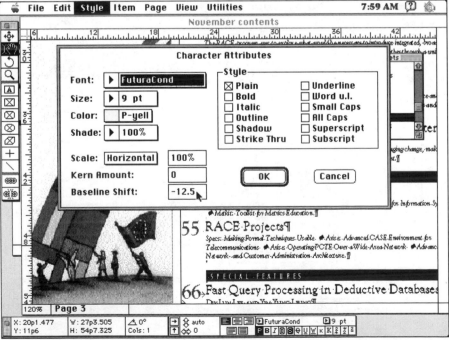

Covers

Magazine cover

It's too easy when using computers to create art that looks, well, like it was created on a computer. *IEEE Software* does almost all of its production electronically, but its staff does know when to use traditional tools. The cover illustrations are first sketched out by hand and then scanned in. The resulting file is brought into Photoshop, where it is cleaned up and enhanced. This method of producing art preserves the natural-media feel and is often faster than starting from scratch in a program like Fractal Design Painter, which offers natural-media creation tools. After the Photoshop work is done, the file is saved in CMYK TIFF format and imported into QuarkXPress.

Designer: Dirk Hagner
Publication: IEEE Software
Company: IEEE Computer Society

The type is created using QuarkXPress's text tools, and the logo is an EPS file that is imported into its standard position. (The designer has a template with the boxes for the logo and date locked in place.) After the EPS file is placed, the designer uses the Colors dialog box (Edit ⇨ Colors) to convert the logo's Pantone color from spot to CMYK. (Colors for the cover type are either defined in CMYK to begin with in the same dialog box or defined as Pantone and then converted to CMYK.) The cover is then ready for output.

The cover also uses other techniques that are not so obvious at first glance. For example, all the type is a shade of the Pantone color used in the logo. The issue date, as shown in Figure 28-11, is 60 percent of Pantone 1385. There's also a faint drop shadow on the main title. This design element was created by duplicating the text box containing the title, removing the small text, changing the text color to black, and positioning the text box 2 points to the right of the original text box. The original text box was then moved to the front (Item ➪ Bring to Front), causing a faint right-facing drop shadow. Figure 28-11 shows the two text boxes. A third set of effects is used on the title text: it is highly condensed (70 percent) and tracked (15 units), and the second line is actually smaller (80 points versus 96 points) than the first line. The magazine uses this style for each cover, as well as similar artwork, to reinforce its personality.

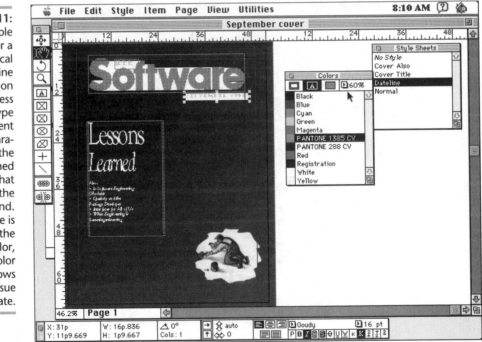

Figure 28-11:
This simple cover for a technical magazine relies on QuarkXPress for the type placement and separation of the scanned image that forms the background. All the type is a shade of the logo's color, as the Color palette shows for the issue date.

Insert cover

The most effective design is usually a bold, simple one. Consider a magazine insert detailing a conference. The insert is not meant to be detailed; instead, it is a gallery of pictures meant to capture the fun spirit of the conference. The rationale is simple: as an insert to a publication for those who sell Pacific Mutual insurance, the editors and designers know that a change of pace from immediate business advice is likely to get reader interest — which means more people will be aware of the conference and may want to attend the next year. The insert's vacation gallery approach lends itself to a simple treatment that relies on the images to convey the casual meaning.

Designers: Robert Francisco and John Frick, Jr.
Publication: Field News
Company: Pacific Mutual Life Insurance

In designing this insert, the trick was simulating elements until they had been scanned in. This technique allowed the designers to experiment with several feels quickly, without making the scan of dealing with the slowdown that using such large images creates. For example, although designers knew they would use a scan of brown postal paper for background, they simply put a placeholder picture box with a similar color (Focoltone 2177) behind the document. They also made this color a spot color, so that in case it was not removed before printing, the color would not be separated onto the CMYK plates. Similarly, they put picture boxes with solid white backgrounds as place-holders where the stamp illustrations would appear. Finally, they did the same with a TIFF file with the stamp cancellation image.

Using placeholders lets designers work before all the elements are in, which can be a time and money saver if it prevents redoing scans sent out to a service bureau because of a design change made after the document's look has become more solid. Also, for designers who don't have access to high-end scanners or use traditional stripping methods for their color artwork, using placeholders lets them design the document in a realistic environment and then output just the plate holding the type (the black plate here). Using a color proofing device, the designers can then show the printer where the art elements go more effectively than relying on just keylines. Figure 28-12 shows an attractive, yet simple, cover.

Figure 28-12:
This simple cover for a conference magazine insert relies on a textured background stripped in by the printer over which a roughed-out postmark and the cover type is placed.

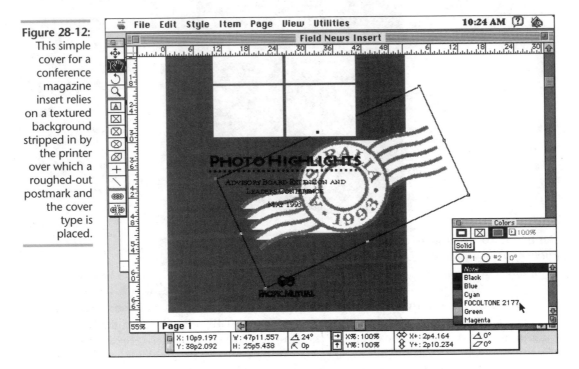

Newsletters

Spot-color

Unlike magazines, newsletters often use color sparingly, and typically in the form of spot color. Pacific Mutual's *Advance* newsletter is a good example of how to use spot color on a simple publication. Aimed at the company's financial service advisers, this newsletter is meant to be simple and authoritative. But it's not meant to be dull, so the designers use spot color to provide visual enhancement without compromising the newsletter's inherent seriousness.

Designers: Robert Francisco and John Frick, Jr.
Publication: Advance
Company: Pacific Mutual Life Insurance

The newsletter uses a standard color (Pantone 187) for several elements, which provides visual variation within a conservative structure appropriate for the newsletter's audience. Figure 28-13 shows part of *Advance's* front page. The drop cap, the pull-quote (except for the rules above and below), the continued line, the border of the "Inside This Issue" box, and the 20 percent background of that box all use the color. Not visible is the use of the color in the logo.

Figure 28-13 also shows the use of separate text boxes to achieve a visual effect: the oversized quotation marks in the pull-quote. Although this effect could have been achieved by changing the size and baseline position for the two quotes, it's frankly faster to keep these elements in a library or on a pasteboard and manually position them relative to the quote's text. Sometimes, quick-and-dirty is more preferable than sophisticated.

Figure 28-13:
This simple newsletter shows how spot color can be a unifying element that still provides visual interest. Spot color is fairly inexpensive when used this way.

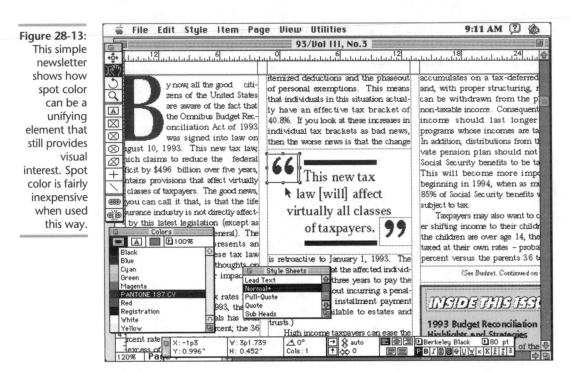

Black-and-white

Although QuarkXPress is renowned for its color, it's equally adept at black-and-white publications. The Computer Press Association's *Network News* is a good example of such a newsletter. In this case, spot-color is not cost-effective because the association is a nonprofit that has chosen to produce a high number of complimentary copies for distribution to opinion leaders in its field in order to attract new members and to help stimulate discussion throughout its industry. Although it uses none of QuarkXPress's color features, the newsletter uses many of its layout, design, and text features.

Because it has no color, the newsletter uses gray backgrounds, black rules of varying thicknesses, and contrasting headline and body text fonts to provide visual interest and subtlety. For example, its pull-quotes use rules above and below, with a 10 percent shade behind the quote. Creating these pull-quotes requires the layout artist to make a text box with a 10 percent black shade and two 1.5-point rules. To ensure that these three pieces don't get moved apart, the designer groups them with QuarkXPress's Group command (Item ⇨ Group, or ⌘G), shown in Figure 28-14. Once the pull-quote positions have been finalized, the designer also locks them using the Lock command (Item ⇨ Lock).

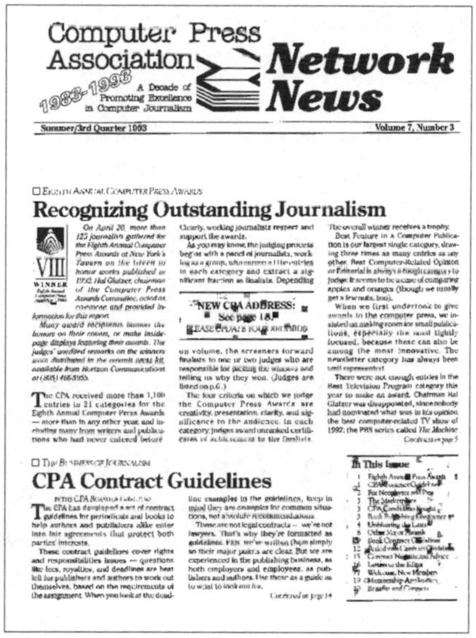
Computer Press Association
1983–1993
A Decade of Promoting Excellence in Computer Journalism
Network News
Summer/3rd Quarter 1993
Volume 7, Number 3

Eighth Annual Computer Press Awards

Recognizing Outstanding Journalism

NEW CPA ADDRESS: See page 18

CPA Contract Guidelines

In This Issue

Designer: Galen Gruman
Publication: Network News
Company: Computer Press Association

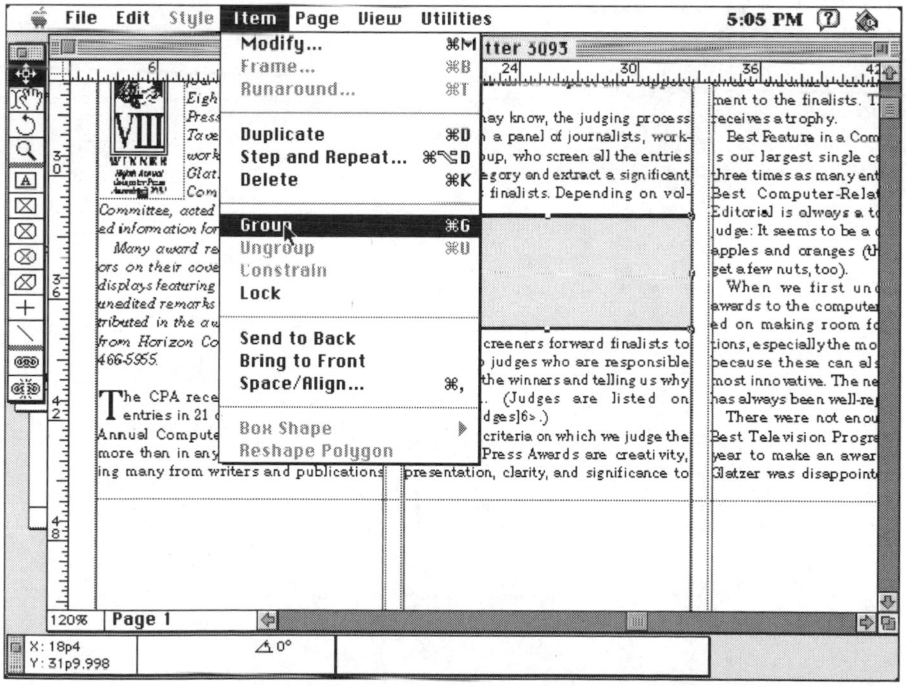

Figure 28-14: By grouping the rules and the shaded box that form a pull-quote, the designer can prevent inadvertent repositioning of the pull-quote's elements.

The pull-quotes also use horizontally and vertically centered text to provide a different visual shape for each pull-quote (because each line breaks differently, each pull-quote's text has a different contour). The horizontal centering is accomplished in the style for the pull-quote, but the vertical centering is achieved by modifying the text box (through the Text Box Specifications dialog box, via Item ⇨ Modify, or ⌘M). Because vertical centering must be set for each text box, the designer keeps a preformatted empty one in a library so that all he must do is alter the text in (and sometimes the vertical depth of) the pull-quote. Figure 28-15 shows the dialog box and the library.

In addition to pull-quotes, the newsletter's design uses horizontal rules to border the tops and bottoms of other elements such as sidebars and the masthead's date and issue information. In the case of the masthead, the designer chose to make the rules part of the paragraph style rather than place rules above and below the text box containing the date and issue information, since the rule positions are related to the text size and depth, not to the depth of the text box. He then groups the rules with the text box. Figure 28-16 shows how the rules are defined (using Edit ⇨ Style Sheet ⇨ Edit ⇨ Rules). Notice that the rule lengths are set at Indents rather than Text. This setting was specified because the text is indented 6 points on either side, but the rule is supposed to go the full width of the text box (which has no indent). In this option, Indent refers to the box's settings, not the text's.

Figure 28-15:
Because vertical centering must be applied to each pull-quote's text box, the designer has created an empty version and placed it in a library to prevent the need for creating each pull-quote from scratch.

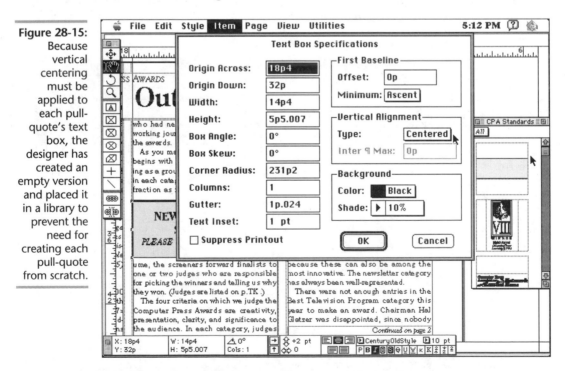

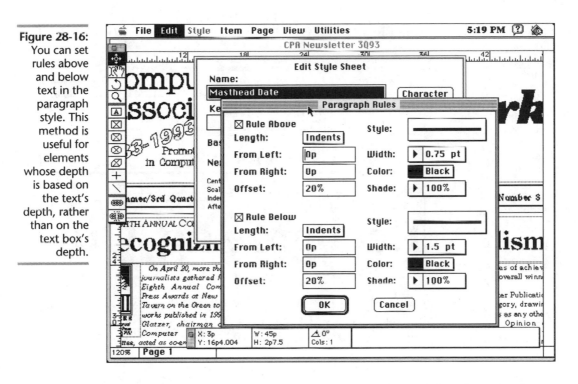

Figure 28-16:
You can set rules above and below text in the paragraph style. This method is useful for elements whose depth is based on the text's depth, rather than on the text box's depth.

The newsletter also uses a box character to lead the kicker for each headline. But the standard fonts have no such character. The character in the Symbol PostScript font has an unwanted drop shadow, and the one in the Wingdings TrueType font is a wider rectangle. To create a square box, the designer uses the Wingdings character but changes the horizontal scale (via Style ➪ Horizontal/Vertical Scale) to make it square (he rescales it to 75 percent of its original width, as shown in Figure 28-17). This task can be time-consuming if the character is needed often, in which case the designer uses a font-editing program like Altsys Corp.'s Fontographer or Ares Software's FontMonger to create the desired character in a new symbol font. (Using one of these utilities is, in fact, what the designer ultimately did because the newsletter also uses a corporate icon as a bullet character.)

Figure 28-17:
To create a
square box
from a
rectangular
symbol
character, the
designer uses
the scaling
feature to
condense the
rectangle
horizontally
into a square.

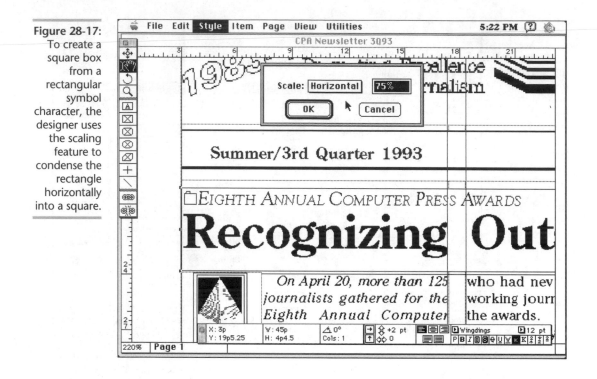

Summary

→ Using a flexible layout grid gives the designer a framework in which to work without imposing uniformity. Similarly, using a standard set of fonts and colors promotes a sense of identity.

→ Black-and-white publications can use shades of gray to give the sense of visual continuity and variation usually provided by color.

→ You can set up nonprinting guides and production information using a spot color.

→ Dingbats and other symbols can add interest to a layout, and QuarkXPress offers shortcut methods for selecting symbols and dingbats.

→ Applying the scaling features to text or special characters can result in pleasing variations or in new special characters.

→ Combining rules and colored type lets you define reversed-out banners for titles; you can then tell QuarkXPress to create a style based on your settings.

→ You can simulate final colors or artwork in QuarkXPress to try out a design concept before committing time and money to execute it.

Appendixes

Chances are you're not going to read this book from cover to cover. Perhaps you have used earlier versions of QuarkXPress and you want to know what the new features are. Or maybe you use this book as a reference (we certainly hope you do — it's designed to be a reference you can count on for years after you've read it as a primer or tutorial). For any way you are using the book, there are simply some types of information that need to be presented in multiple ways.

For example, if you're looking for the new QuarkXPress features, checking each page for the icon that highlights them is a great deal of work. Or if you have a specific technical question in mind, it would be nice to see that question and its answer rather than looking in several places for the details. We believe you should be able to get that sort of information quickly, but without compromising the detail and scope of the main body of the book.

That's where this section comes in. The three appendixes help you quickly and easily find commonly sought information. The first appendix reminds you how to reinstall QuarkXPress so that you can change options, such as adding or removing filters and XTensions. The second appendix summarizes all the new features and indicates which version of QuarkXPress introduced them. The final appendix — based on Quark's internal documents — lists the most common technical support queries that Quark gets and provides the answers to them.

Reinstalling QuarkXPress

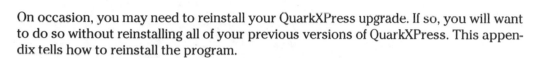

On occasion, you may need to reinstall your QuarkXPress upgrade. If so, you will want to do so without reinstalling all of your previous versions of QuarkXPress. This appendix tells how to reinstall the program.

The QuarkXPress Updater (version 3.2 or above) comes to you preserialized with your serial number (the same as the number on the disk label). You can also use this Updater program as an Installer. To reinstall QuarkXPress, take the following steps:

1. Disable all virus checkers, screen savers, and other INITs. You perform this task by moving these INIT files from the System Folder onto the desktop. (If you are using System 7, simply restart your Macintosh with the Shift key held down to disable System Extensions and then skip to step 3.)

2. Restart the Macintosh.

3. Insert QuarkXPress Program Disk 1 Updater disk into the disk drive.

4. Double-click on the disk icon; the QuarkXPress Updater icon is displayed.

5. Double-click on the QuarkXPress Updater icon to launch it.

6. The following message is displayed: "To begin updating QuarkXPress, click OK. You will be asked to locate your current version of QuarkXPress." *Do not click OK and do not QUIT.*

7. Hold down the Option key and click OK.

8. At this point, the following message is displayed: "Install QuarkXPress As." Follow the instructions displayed on-screen to complete the installation process.

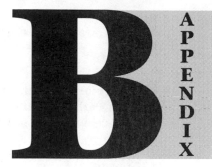
What's New in QuarkXPress

Compared to the version 3.1 of QuarkXPress, version 3.2 added significant new features, particularly in the area of color handling. QuarkXPress 3.3, released less than six months after version 3.2, fine-tuned the program even further.

The new QuarkXPress features are covered in depth throughout this book and are denoted with the [NEW 3.3] icon. But experienced users may also want to get a quick feel for the new features that have been added. That's where this appendix comes in. It summarizes the new features and cross-references the chapter that covers each one in detail.

Like the rest of the book, this appendix is divided into functional areas, so you can locate information by the task that you're trying to accomplish. If a new feature affects more than one area, it is covered in each area, sometimes with additions or modifications to address the separate interests of each area.

Part I: Interface

 Backup: QuarkXPress now offers automatic backup options in the Application Preferences dialog box. See Chapters 3, 4, and 24.

 Saving files: QuarkXPress now offers automatic file saving. See Chapter 3.

Color application: You can now select a color from the Colors palette and drag it onto a text or picture box to change its background color. See Chapter 18.

 Color calibration: With the EfiColor XTension installed, you can set up the default color calibration based on your monitor type in the Application Preferences dialog box. You can also set up the default calibration applied to imported images in the EfiColor Preferences dialog box. See Chapters 4 and 22.

Color removal: When colors are deleted in the Edit Color dialog box, QuarkXPress now gives you an option to substitute another color in any element that uses the deleted color. See Chapter 21.

 Documents: QuarkXPress supports multiple open documents, and full cut, copy, and paste among them. It also has altered the menu sequence for creating new documents to File ➪ New ➪ Document. See Chapter 8.

 Document Layout palette: The Document Layout palette has been redesigned (differently in the two versions) to simplify creation, deletion, and alteration of master pages. See Chapter 5.

 Keyboard Template: A keyboard template has been added to the QuarkXPress package. It provides visual reminders of keyboard functions. See Chapter 6.

 Image display: In the Application Preferences dialog box, you can now set the resolution for color and gray-scale TIFF images by the number of colors (such as 8-bit for color or 256 levels for gray-scale). If you set the color depth to 32-bit, you can output 24-bit color images to a QuickDraw printer without losing any resolution. See Chapter 4.

 Icon deselection: When the Item tool is selected, you can deselect any selected items by pressing the Tab key. See Chapter 2.

 Next Style: The Style dialog box now includes a "Next" option which lets you apply the next style (in the list of styles) to a paragraph. See Chapter 6.

 Libraries: Libraries are now opened via File ➪ New ➪ Library (keyboard shortcut Option-⌘N), rather than through the Utilities menu. See Chapters 8 and 23.

 Measurement units: QuarkXPress now supports hundredth-inch measurements in dialog boxes and rulers. See Chapter 8.

 Missing graphics: If several graphics files are missing and the user updates a graphic from a directory in which there are other missing graphics, QuarkXPress automatically updates those graphics as well. See Chapter 24.

 Multiple monitors: QuarkXPress can now be set, through the Application Preferences dialog box, to automatically display a large document across several monitors if you have multiple monitors installed on your Mac. See Chapter 4.

Page grabber hand: This option has been removed from the Application Preferences dialog box because this feature is now always active. See Chapter 4.

 Quotes: The Application Preferences dialog box includes a new option for Smart Quotes, which includes a choice of several languages' typographic quotation marks. See Chapters 4 and 17.

 Scrolling speed: In the Application Preferences dialog box, you can set the speed of scrolling through a document. See Chapter 4.

 Templates: QuarkXPress now supports the use of templates with multiple simultaneous users across a network. See Chapter 25.

 Text editing: In the Application Preferences dialog box, you can set QuarkXPress to allow drag-and-drop editing of text. See Chapters 4 and 17.

 Text sizing: Holding the ⌘ key while resizing a text box also resizes the text in the box proportionally. See Chapter 9.

 Trapping settings: The trapping settings have been moved from the Application Preferences dialog box to their own Trapping Preferences dialog box. See Chapter 4.

 Typographic settings: QuarkXPress refined several typographic options:

- ꙳ In the Typographic Preferences dialog box, you can set QuarkXPress to retain accent marks on capitalized letters if the All Caps attribute is applied to lowercase text. Such accents are often removed in European typesetting. See Chapter 4.

- ꙳ The Typographic Preferences dialog box has been redesigned to make setting ligatures easier, but the same results are available in version 3.1. See Chapter 4.

- ꙳ In the Typographic Preferences dialog box, you can choose whether QuarkXPress determines the size of an em space by making it equivalent to the letter *M* (the new option) or to two zeroes (the previous method). See Chapters 4 and 12.

- ꙳ The Leading Mode option has been renamed Mode, and it has been grouped with the Auto Leading and Maintain Leading options under a heading called Leading. To make room, the Flex Space Width and Auto Kern Above options have been moved to the left side of the dialog box. See Chapters 4 and 12.

↝ The Application Preferences dialog box includes a new option for Smart Quotes, which includes a choice of several languages' typographic quotation marks. See Chapters 4 and 17.

 Undo: The Undo command is now available after deleting multiple items.

 Version settings: In the Application Preferences dialog box, QuarkXPress now offers an option to save a user-specified number of previous versions of documents. See Chapters 4 and 24.

 Views: The new Ctrl-V keyboard shortcut lets you change views quickly by highlighting the value in the view percentage field at the bottom left of the QuarkXPress window. See Chapter 8.

 Window sizing: QuarkXPress has added several options for controlling the display and size of document windows:

↝ In the Application Preferences dialog box, you can set documents to display full-screen, but this display size obscures the window's close box with the Tool palette. See Chapter 4.

↝ The View menu has new Tile Documents and Stack Documents options to arrange multiple windows on screen.

Part II: Document Preparation _____

 Document Layout palette: The Document Layout palette has been redesigned (differently in the two versions) to simplify the creation, deletion, and alteration of master pages. See Chapter 5.

 Import formats: Newly supported formats are PhotoCD images and QuarkXPress for Windows 3.1 documents (in version 3.2), and JPEG-compressed and PCX bitmap images and QuarkXPress for Windows 3.3 documents (in version 3.3). Version 3.3 also added the capability to import spot-color definitions from imported EPS files. See Chapters 7, 21, and 25.

 Templates: QuarkXPress now supports the use of templates with multiple simultaneous users across a network. See Chapter 25.

Part III: Page Layout

Document Layout palette: The Document Layout palette has been redesigned (differently in the two versions) to simplify the creation, deletion, and alteration of master pages. See Chapter 5.

Picture boxes: You can now slant (skew) and flip (mirror) text and picture boxes. See Chapter 18. The Cool Blends XTension, which allows several types of blended box backgrounds, is now bundled with QuarkXPress. See Chapter 21.

Text boxes: QuarkXPress supports polygonal text boxes. It also now lets you slant (skew) and flip (mirror) text boxes. See Chapter 9. The Cool Blends XTension, which allows several types of blended box backgrounds, is now bundled with QuarkXPress. See Chapter 21.

Text sizing: Holding the ⌘ key while resizing a text box also resizes the text in the box proportionally. See Chapter 9.

Part IV: Typography and Text

Accented characters: In the Typographic Preferences dialog box, you can set QuarkXPress to retain accent marks on capitalized letters if the All Caps attribute is applied to lowercase text. Such accents are often removed in European typesetting. See Chapter 4.

Indents: The Indent Here character (⌘\) now remains in effect when an indented paragraph breaks across a column or box. See Chapter 15.

Indents align with text: Left and right text indents now indent from the margin of the text box, as you would expect. Before version 3.3, the text would also indent the specified indent amount from the edge of any picture box placed on top of the text box.

Kerning: Kerning pairs defined in the Kern/Track Editor may now include spaces. See Chapter 12.

Kern to Space: The Kern/Track Editor now lets you use an en space as one of the characters in a kerning pair. See Chapter 12.

Multiple master fonts: With the bundled MMU XTension, QuarkXPress supports Adobe's Multiple Master Type 1 PostScript font format. When the XTension is installed, the Font Creator option in the Utilities menu lets you create Multiple Master variants directly within QuarkXPress. See Chapter 14.

 Paragraph breaks: In the Paragraph Formats dialog box, the settings for Keep with Next ¶ and Keep Lines Together have been enhanced to work with multiple-line subheads. See Chapter 13.

 Preference settings: The Typographic Preferences dialog box has been redesigned to make setting ligatures easier, but the same results are available in version 3.1. Also, the Leading Mode option has been renamed Mode, and it has been grouped with the Auto Leading and Maintain Leading options under a heading called Leading. To make room, the Flex Space Width and Auto Kern Above options have been moved to the left side of the dialog box. See Chapter 4.

 Two-character tab fillers: Tab-fill characters can now be two characters. This feature is useful if, for example, you want to use a period and a space for filling leader space. See Chapter 16.

 Quotes: The Application Preferences dialog box includes a new option for Smart Quotes, which includes a choice of several languages' typographic quotation marks. See Chapters 4 and 17.

 Tabs: QuarkXPress lets you use any two characters in the Paragraph Tabs dialog box — rather than just one — as a leader. See Chapter 16.

 Text editing: In the Application Preferences dialog box, you can set QuarkXPress to allow drag-and-drop editing of text. See Chapter 4.

 Text effects: You can now slant (skew) and flip (mirror) text. See Chapter 9.

Text sizing: Holding the ⌘ key while resizing a text box also resizes the text in the box proportionally. See Chapter 9.

Space defaults: In the Typographic Preferences dialog box, you can choose whether QuarkXPress determines the size of an em space by making it equivalent to the uppercase letter *M* (the new option) or to two zeroes (the previous method). See Chapter 4.

 Vertical text scaling: In the Style menu, you can select a Scale option that now allows you to scale text vertically, in addition to horizontally. See Chapters 12 and 15.

Part V: Graphics and Images _____

 Blends: The Cool Blends XTension, which allows several types of blended box backgrounds, is now bundled with QuarkXPress. See Chapter 21.

 Color application: You can now select a color from the Colors palette and drag it onto a text or picture box to change its background color. See Chapter 18.

 Color calibration: With the EfiColor XTension, QuarkXPress supports the color calibration of imported images, colors defined within QuarkXPress, and printed documents. See Chapters 4, 21, 22, and 26.

 EPS output: QuarkXPress can now save individual pages in several new variants of EPS: DCS (Document Color Separations) version 2.0 with either PC or Mac previews, or standard EPS with a PC preview. It continues to support standard EPS with a Mac preview. See Chapter 11.

 Import formats: Newly supported formats are PhotoCD images (in version 3.2) and JPEG-compressed and PCX bitmap images (in version 3.3).

 Missing graphics: If several graphics files are missing and the user updates a graphic from a directory in which there are other missing graphics, QuarkXPress automatically updates those graphics as well. See Chapter 24.

 Shades for TIFF images: You can apply a shade to a gray-scale TIFF image. See Chapter 20.

 Spot-color import: QuarkXPress now imports spot-color definitions in EPS files. See Chapters 7 and 21.

Part VI: Color Publishing _____

 Blends: The Cool Blends XTension, which allows several types of blended box backgrounds, is now bundled with QuarkXPress. See Chapter 21.

 Color application: You can now select a color from the Colors palette and drag it onto a text or picture box to change its background color. See Chapter 18.

Color calibration: With the EfiColor XTension, QuarkXPress supports the color calibration of imported images, colors defined within QuarkXPress, and printed documents. See Chapters 4, 20, 21, 22, and 26.

 Color models: QuarkXPress version 3.2 added three variants of the Pantone color model: uncoated, process, and ProSim. QuarkXPress version 3.3 also added two other color models: Toyo and DIC (Dainippon Ink & Chemical), which are popular in Japan. See Chapter 21.

 EPS output: In the Save Page as EPS dialog box, QuarkXPress can now save individual pages in several new variants of EPS: DCS (Document Color Separations) version 2.0 with either PC or Mac previews, or standard EPS with a PC preview. It continues to support standard EPS with a Mac preview. See Chapter 11.

 PICT output: With the 32-bit color option selected in the Application Preferences dialog box, QuarkXPress can accurately print 24-bit color PICT images on non-PostScript printers. See Chapter 4.

 Spot-color import: QuarkXPress now imports spot-color definitions in EPS files. See Chapters 7 and 21.

 Removal: When colors are deleted in the Edit Color dialog box, QuarkXPress now gives you an option to substitute another color in any element that uses the deleted color. See Chapter 21.

Part VII: Managing Documents _____

 Documents: QuarkXPress supports multiple open documents. It also has altered the menu sequence for creating new documents to File ⇨ New ⇨ Document. See Chapter 8.

 Document Layout palette: The Document Layout palette has been redesigned (differently in the two versions) to simplify the creation, deletion, and alteration of master pages. See Chapter 5.

 Templates: QuarkXPress now supports the use templates across a network with multiple simultaneous users. See Chapter 25.

Version settings: In the Application Preferences dialog box, QuarkXPress now offers an option to save a user-specified number of previous versions of documents. See Chapters 4 and 24.

Part VIII: Printing and Output _____

 Color calibration: With the EfiColor XTension installed, QuarkXPress can calibrate the output of color elements to match the output device's capabilities. This feature includes the ability to select from several gray-component-removal (GCR) settings when printing. See Chapters 4, 22, and 26.

 EPS output: In the Save Page as EPS dialog box, QuarkXPress can now save individual pages in several new variants of EPS: DCS (Document Color Separations) version 2.0 with either PC or Mac previews, or standard EPS with a PC preview. It continues to support standard EPS with a Mac preview. A related new option is the ability to save the EPS files in binary or ASCII format. See Chapter 11.

 OPI compatibility: QuarkXPress supports version 1.3 of the Open Prepress Interface standard. See Chapter 26.

 Changes to the Print Dialog Box: Four new selections — Low Resolution, Blank Pages, Calibrated Output, and Print Status — are included in the Print dialog box. See Chapter 26.

 Collect for Output: This new feature copies your document and all of its associated picture files into a folder and creates a detailed report about every aspect (fonts and so on) of the document to give to your service bureau. See Chapter 26.

 Printer support: QuarkXPress now supports PPD (PostScript Printer Definition) version 4.0 or greater files, which contain information about a printer such as dot-gain calibration or tray settings. If QuarkXPress sees both a PPD and a PDF (Printer Description File), it will use the PPD. See Chapter 26.

Part IX: Extending QuarkXPress __

 Scripts: QuarkXPress now supports scripting via AppleScript and UserLand Frontier scripts. See Chapter 27.

Most-Frequently Asked Questions about QuarkXPress

If you have questions about QuarkXPress, chances are that other users have been asking those same questions. We've compiled this appendix by talking to Quark's Technical Support Department. They've supplied us with the most commonly asked questions they receive on a daily basis *and* their answers to those same questions.

By the way, Quark offers free technical support for the first 90 days after you register the product. After the first 90 days, you can purchase additional technical support, which includes a subscription to Quark's newsletter *Expressions*, as well as fax, mail, and phone support.

The authors thank Quark, Inc., for giving us permission to share with you these questions and answers. Some of the answers given in this appendix are taken directly from Quark's FaxFacts — faxable sheets of information sent to users who call with common questions. FaxFacts are a copyright of Quark, Inc., and are excerpted here by permission.

Note: Some of the situations described in the questions that follow may no longer apply because of subsequent releases of QuarkXPress.

Q: When I print blends with QuarkXPress, sometimes I get a banding effect. What can I do to get rid of, or at least lessen, that effect?

A: First, check the calibration of your output device. Because blends are composed of a series of shades, incorrect calibration settings can cause banding. On an imagesetter, make sure that the laser exposure intensity is correctly set by printing an acceptable 100% screen and accurate screen tints. If you need to further adjust the calibration, you can use a software calibration utility (such as the Quark Calibration XTension bundled with this book) to remap screen tint values and get more accurate output. You should be aware, however, that software calibration utilities actually decrease the number of gray levels that you can reproduce. Relying too heavily on software calibration can increase your chances of banding.

Similarly, if you select the Use Calibrated Output option in the QuarkXPress Print dialog box, blend quality on some low-resolution printers will suffer. That's because the Printer Description Files (PDFs) for such printers as the Apple LaserWriter contain modified calibration curves.

When you are satisfied with the accuracy of your printer's screens, you're ready to do some calculations and find out the optimum settings for your blend.

1. Find out the resolution of your output device. As an example, we'll use a device that prints at 1,200 dots per inch (dpi) and 60 lines per inch (lpi).

2. Calculate the percentage change in your blend. If you are using different percentages of one color, simply subtract the lower percentage value from the higher. A blend from 80% black to 30% black, for example, would yield a 50% (80% – 30%) change.

   If your blend consists of two colors, find the process color (CMYK) values for each one and use the process color that changes most to calculate the percentage change in your blend. For instance, let's say you are blending a dark teal (C-100%, M-10%, Y-30%, K-50%) and a reddish brown (C-50%, M-100%, Y-100%, K-0%). Because the greatest change occurs in the values for Magenta, you would use 90% (100% – 10%) for your percentage change value.

   For our sample calculation, we'll use a blend between 90% red and 30% red, which yields a change of 60 percent.

3. Calculate the number of steps you need for a smooth blend using this formula:

   $$(dpi/lpi)2¥ \text{ percentage change of the blend}$$

   Because of a limit imposed by PostScript, this number cannot be greater than 256. If it is greater, just use 256 in your subsequent calculations. If you're using the QuarkXPress blend feature, the number of steps are automatically calculated for you as long as you have specified dpi and lpi values in your Page Setup dialog box. If you're using a drawing program, specify this number as the number of steps in your blend. Example: (1200/60)2 | 0.6 = 240 steps.

4. Calculate your blend factor by dividing the length of your blend (in inches) by the optimum number of steps in your blend. Generally, if the blend factor is greater than .03, the blend will band. If our blend is twelve inches long, for example, our blend factor would be (12/240) = .05, which would cause banding. Changing the length of the blend to seven inches would bring the blend factor down to .029, which is acceptable. Generally, the smaller the blend factor, the less the chance of banding.

Adjust your variables (dpi, lpi, and blend length) to get your blend factor as low as possible. Even if you do, you probably won't get a perfect blend. However, minor banding that appears on your prepress output will usually diminish or vanish altogether by the time your publication comes off the press. Thanks to on-press dot gain, the smearing and expanding of dots can smooth some imperfections of a blend.

Q: Whenever I try to import a picture using the Get Picture dialog box, QuarkXPress crashes. What's going on?

A: The presence of Norton Directory Assistance has been known to cause QuarkXPress to crash when importing pictures. The symptoms of this incompatibility are as follows: If QuarkXPress 3.2 and the EfiColor XTension are used in conjunction with Norton Directory Assistance, QuarkXPress will run smoothly until you import a picture via the Get Picture dialog box, at which time the application will crash — and will continue to crash until either Norton Directory Assistance or the EfiColor XTension is disabled.

Another sign of this problem is the Type field in the Get Picture dialog box. If Norton Directory Assistance and the EfiColor XTension are both enabled, the file-type name listed in the Type field appears bolded, colored, or reversed out. If you notice any of these symptoms, click Cancel, save the document, and disable either Norton Directory Assistance or the EfiColor XTension.

If you still experience problems, they may be related to other factors, such as a shortage of memory or a corrupt picture file.

Q: QuarkXPress doesn't seem to recognize the clipping paths I've saved with my DCS file. When I color-separate the image, it prints only the image's bounding box. What's the problem?

A: Quark fixed this problem when it released an updater to version 3.2, called updater 3.21. If you're running version 3.2 and don't have the updater (which is available from Quark and on on-line services like CompuServe in the DTPFORUM), it is recommended that you convert the DCS file to an EPS file. Otherwise, the DCS file's CMYK plates may not color-separate correctly when they are downloaded to the printer.

Q: How do I anchor a text box or picture box to other text?

A: You can anchor a box to text so that the box acts like a character and flows with the text, which is helpful if you have a picture or a block of text that should stay with its associated text. You can edit the contents of an anchored box as you would any other picture box or text box.

To anchor a box, take the following steps:

1. Select the Item tool and click on the picture box or text box that you want to anchor.

2. Choose Edit ⇨ Cut (⌘X) or Edit ⇨ Copy (⌘C).

3. Select the Content tool and place the Text Insertion bar where you want to anchor the box.

4. Choose Edit ⇨ Paste (⌘V).

   Tip: The anchored box is displayed with three handles for resizing it. If the text overflow symbol appears when you paste the box, the anchored box is too large to fit in the text box or column. You can resize the text box or column to display the anchored box. Then resize the anchored box.

   Tip: If Auto Leading is specified for a paragraph, the line spacing is relative to the largest character on the line. An anchored box is treated as a character and will affect the line spacing in an auto leaded paragraph if the anchored box is larger than the text.

   Tip: When you anchor a nonrectangular box, it becomes rectangular; anchored boxes also lose any specified Box Skew or Rotation.

To change the vertical alignment of an anchored box, do the following:

1. Click on the anchored box with the Item tool or the Content tool.

2. Choose Item ⇨ Modify (⌘M) to display the Anchored Text/Picture Box Specifications dialog box.

3. Click Baseline in the Align with Text area to align the bottom of the anchored box with the baseline of the line of text.

   Click Ascent in the Align with Text area to align the top of the anchored box with the ascent of the largest character in the line of text.

4. Click OK.

To change the baseline shift of an anchored box, do the following:

1. Activate the anchored box by highlighting it with the Text Insertion bar.

2. Choose Style ⇨ Baseline Shift to display the Baseline Shift dialog box.

3. Enter a positive value in the Baseline Shift field to shift the anchored box up; enter a negative value to shift it down.

4. Click OK.

Q: How do I write an Apple Events script?

A: The ability to automate your Macintosh with scripts is derived from a System 7 feature called Apple Events. However, there is no such thing as an Apple Events script. You can write Frontier scripts or Runtime scripts with UserLand Frontier or you can write AppleScripts or Applets with AppleScript. Any of these scripts can be used to automate tasks in QuarkXPress.

To write scripts, you need the following:

- ☞ Macintosh System 7.0 or greater.

- ☞ A scripting application such as UserLand Frontier, available from UserLand Software, Inc., (415) 369-6600; or AppleScript, available from the Apple Programmer's and Developer's Association (APDA), (800) 282-2732.

- ☞ The documentation, included with your scripting application, that teaches scripting language. Familiarize yourself with the scripting language before attempting to write scripts for QuarkXPress. (The scripting software developers provide support at varying levels.)

- ☞ A basic understanding of programming (including concepts such as loops, conditional processing, if-then-else constructs, and variables) gained through writing HyperTalk scripts or macros, or from working in programming languages such as C, BASIC, or Pascal.

- ☞ The following documentation, provided with QuarkXPress:

    - *A Preview of Apple Events Scripting with QuarkXPress*, a booklet that introduces the concepts behind Apple Events and documents how to use Frontier Runtime and the sample scripts included with QuarkXPress.

    - *Apple Events Scripting with QuarkXPress*, a QuarkXPress document on the Apple Events scripting disk that provides the reference material necessary to write scripts for QuarkXPress.

 See Chapter 27 for more details.

Q: In the Print dialog box, there is an option called "Calibrated Output." What does it do?

A: When the Calibrated Output option is checked in the Print dialog box, QuarkXPress uses the printer calibration settings defined for your selected printer. These settings reside in a file called the Printer Description File (PDF), which printer manufacturers create so that their printers and QuarkXPress work better together.

So what's printer calibration? Printer calibration is a method of compensating for screen tint inaccuracies. For instance, if you set a screen to a 40 percent density value in QuarkXPress, an inaccurate printer might print the screen with a 45 percent density value. Such a problem can make screens look too dark and can even affect the quality of linear blends.

To help printers and imagesetters output screens more accurately, Quark distributes a free XTension called the Quark Calibration XTension (included on the disk bundled with this book). It lets you view the calibration settings from the PDF of any printer and modify those settings. Taking the previous example, you could change the settings for the printer so that every time QuarkXPress was set to output a 40 percent screen, it would send a lower density value to the printer to compensate for the difference in screen tints. That way, even if the density of your printer is too high, your screens would still come out correctly.

Think of the Calibrated Output option in this way: you have a friend who is always fifteen minutes late. In order to keep dinner reservations at 6:00, you compensate by telling him to meet you at 5:45. He shows up at 6:00, and everything works out fine. QuarkXPress can do the same type of compensation for printers that don't print correct screen densities.

If the Calibrated Output option is unchecked, QuarkXPress makes no compensations. Thirty percent screens are processed as having 30 percent density, 40 percent screens are processed as having 40 percent density, and so forth. Sometimes, if you want to match the output of another software program that doesn't have calibration capabilities, it's better to leave this option unchecked.

If you decide to test the Use Calibrated Output feature, keep in mind that unless you make your own settings with calibration software, selecting Use Calibrated Output might not produce output that is different from uncalibrated output. Only a few printers, such as LaserWriters, have PDFs that use a modified calibration curve as a default. The PDFs for many printers leave calibration up to the user. If, for example, you don't set calibration for your Linotronic imagesetter, the output will be the same, whether or not you've selected Use Calibrated Output.

Q: What do I do when I get an alert that says "This document requires minor repairs"?

A: When you open a damaged document, QuarkXPress alerts you and reports the extent of the damage. The damage is usually in the document's internal file structure and is probably not caused by anything you did.

If you get an alert that says, "This document requires minor repairs," the only option is to click Repair it. The repair process is transparent; you cannot determine exactly what caused the damage. Although repairing a document will not move or delete any items or pages, it may affect text formatting and colors applied to items. After a document is repaired, check for the following:

- Missing colors, style sheets, and H&Js that were defined in the document. If the repair process deletes a specification, items with that specification applied are handled as follows:
  - Items and text with a deleted color applied are changed to black.
  - Paragraphs with a deleted style sheet applied are changed to Normal.
  - Paragraphs with a deleted H&J applied are changed to the Standard H&J.
- Color list, style sheets list, and H&J list re-created entirely according to the application default lists.
- Missing local formatting applied to characters or paragraphs.
- Font substitution.

  Tip: If the "document requires minor repairs" alert displays often, it may be because you are generating documents from a damaged template. You can open the template, repair the new document, and resave it as a template (File ➪ Save As).

  Tip: Document damage can result from system failures. To enable yourself to recover the last saved version of a document after a system failure, use the Auto Backup feature (Edit ➪ Preferences ➪ Application Preferences, or Option-Shift-⌘Y) in QuarkXPress.

Older documents and extremely complex documents may become damaged beyond repair. If this is the case, you'll see this alert: "This document is damaged and cannot be fixed. Try dragging document pages to a new document to recover them."

The "cannot be fixed" alert gives you two options:

- Click Abort Open to cancel opening the document. You will not be able to use the document.
- Click Open Document Anyway if you want to attempt to recover the pages by dragging thumbnails.

Tip: To recover pages by dragging thumbnails, create a new document with the same page size (File ⇨ New). Hold the Option key and choose View ⇨ Windows ⇨ Tile Documents to tile the documents in Thumbnails view. Click on the pages in the corrupt document that you want to recover and drag them to the new document. If the document is severely damaged, thumbnail drag will only create another damaged document. Usually one item on one page is damaged. Try selectively dragging pages to isolate the page with the damaged item.

Tip: If you can isolate the page containing the damaged item, you may want to recover the remaining items on that page. To do so, switch to any View other than Thumbnails, select the Item tool, and drag one item at a time to the new document. Save the new document after dragging each item (when you drag the damaged item, it may cause a system crash).

Q: How do I drag pages between documents?

A: The Thumbnails view allows you to drag copies of pages between documents. Dragging thumbnails is also helpful for recovering pages of damaged documents. The document you are dragging pages from is referred to as the "source document"; the document you are dragging pages to is referred to as the "target document."

Preparing for thumbnail drags requires the following steps:

1. Open the source document and the target document (File ⇨ Open).

    Tip: You cannot drag pages from a source document with a Page Size specified that is larger than the target document. You cannot drag pages from a facing-page document to one with nonfacing pages.

2. Hold the Option key and choose View ⇨ Windows ⇨ Tile Documents to automatically specify Thumbnails view for both documents and arrange them in horizontal tiles on-screen.

    Tip: You can access the Windows submenu by holding the Shift key and clicking on the document title bar. To tile documents in Thumbnails view, hold the Option and Shift keys, click on the document title bar, and choose Tile Documents.

To drag thumbnails, do the following:

1. Select any tool and highlight the page(s) you want to move in the source document.

    ↪ To move one page, click on the page.

    ↪ To move a range of pages, hold the Shift key and click on the first page and the last page in the range.

    ↪ To select nonsequential pages, hold the Command key and click on each page.

2. Drag the pages from the source document to below page one in the target document. (You cannot drag pages on top of page one.)

3. Delete page one of the target document (Page ⇨ Delete).

   Tip: The style sheets, colors, and H&Js specified in the source document are copied to the target document. Text reflow may occur if the XPress Preferences differ between the documents.

The pages will bounce back and an alert will display if you try to drag pages to a document with a smaller Page Size specified or if you try to drag pages from a facing page document to a nonfacing page document.

Q: How do I select the right EfiColor profile for imported pictures?

A: The Profile Usage dialog box (Utilities menu) lists all the EfiColor profiles used in a document. When you transfer documents between computers, the Profile Usage dialog box enables you to keep track of the profiles required for each document. Also, if you want to change a profile assigned to a particular picture or a group of pictures, you can use the Profile Usage dialog box. If you want to change a single picture's profile, you can use the Profile command (Style menu).

To verify or globally change EfiColor profiles assigned to pictures, follow these steps:

1. Choose Utilities ⇨ Profile Usage to display the Profile Usage dialog box.

2. Click on the profile that you want to change. (Pictures will be listed in the Objects column.)

3. Click Show First.

4. Click Replace or Replace All. The Replace Profile dialog box is displayed. (The name of the missing profile is grayed out.)

5. If you clicked Replace All in step 4, choose a different profile from the EfiColor Profile pop-up menu to replace all occurrences of the profile assigned to pictures in the document. If you clicked Replace in step 4, choose a different profile to change the profile assigned to the selected picture displayed in the upper left corner of your document window.

To change picture profiles on a picture-by-picture basis, do the following:

1. Select the picture whose profile you want to change.

2. Choose Style ⇨ Profile to display the (RGB Picture or CMYK Picture) Profile dialog box.

3. Choose a new profile from the EfiColor Profile pop-up menu.

   This change has the same effect as reimporting the picture and assigning a new profile in the Get Picture dialog box, but you won't lose your scaling, cropping, or rotation settings.

EfiColor profiles

∞ Profiles are named according to their devices or printing processes for easy identification.

∞ When importing a picture, you assign a profile that corresponds to the device or printing process designated for the picture. If the picture was scanned on an HP ScanJet IIc, choose HP ScanJet IIc from the EfiColor Profile pop-up menu in the Get Picture dialog box (File menu). On the other hand, if the picture was color corrected and separated for production on an offset press using SWOP inks, choose SWOP-Coated from the EfiColor Profile pop-up menu. If you do not know the device or printing process designated for a picture, you can choose a default profile from the EfiColor Profile pop-up menu.

∞ Profiles are stored in your EfiColor DB folder in your System folder.

   Tip: Changing EfiColor profiles is like changing fonts. When you use Font Usage to replace a font, you change the design and might cause text reflow. When you use Profile Usage to replace a profile, you change the color output of a document.

The Default Profiles area of the EfiColor Preferences dialog box determines the default displayed in the EfiColor Profile pop-up menu in the Get Picture dialog box when you select RGB or CMYK pictures. However, PICTs always default to the Apple 13" profile because PICT is a native Macintosh format.

Cachet, a color editing application from Electronics for Imaging, Inc. (EFI), also accesses the EfiColor DB folder for information about color devices. You can assign a profile to a picture in Cachet and maintain the profile association when you import it into QuarkXPress.

 See Chapter 22 for more details.

Q: How do I transfer QuarkXPress documents that contain graphics between platforms?

A: The first task is to transfer the graphics to the other platform. Once transferred, you need to be aware of potential on-screen display and output problems.

Transferring files

- ✆ Shared networks or floppy disks should be used to transfer graphics. To read PC-formatted disks with the Macintosh, the Macintosh must have either the Apple File Exchange application or an INIT such as DOS Mounter currently running.

- ✆ Naming conventions must be followed if you want to move graphics between platforms. Use the eight-character naming convention and include the correct three-character extension (for example, .EPS for an Encapsulated PostScript file, .TIF for a TIFF file, and so on). If you do not name Macintosh graphic files according to these conventions, the file names will not be displayed within QuarkXPress for Windows. If you do not name Windows graphic files according to these conventions, the file names will not be displayed within QuarkXPress for Macintosh.

- ✆ TIFF files that are generated properly should transfer smoothly between platforms. With the exception of the eight-character naming convention, TIFFs are designed to be platform-independent.

On-screen display and output

- ✆ EPS files created on the Macintosh can be previewed in QuarkXPress for Windows. Use the original Macintosh application to save a PC version of the illustration, or, if you have a PC version of the application, use it to open and save the illustration with a PC preview. Windows applications use TIFFs to preview illustrations on-screen; illustrations saved as TIFFs preview correctly on the Macintosh.

- ✆ Special characters used in EPS files must exist in the character sets of both platforms. Most of the characters not included in the basic 127 ASCII character set will not map properly between platforms.

PICT and Metafiles

PICT files contained in QuarkXPress for Macintosh documents that are opened in QuarkXPress for Windows are converted to Metafiles (a comparable PC-based format). As these files are incorporated directly into the document, there is no problem outputting them. Metafiles contained in QuarkXPress for Windows documents that are opened in QuarkXPress for Macintosh are converted to PICTs.

PICT files can contain object-oriented (mathematically defined) information as well as bitmap information. Occasionally, PICTs with object-oriented information may not display or print correctly on the PC. If the PICT represents a TIFF or EPS picture, reimport the picture. Otherwise, try re-creating the picture using a different application or using a different format on the Macintosh. The same problem can occur with Metafiles that include object-oriented and/or bitmap information when you move them from the PC to the Macintosh. The same solutions apply.

Graphics paths

If you plan to output a document after moving it to a new platform, check the Picture Usage dialog box (Utilities menu) to make sure that the paths to high resolution pictures and the names of those files are current. You will see an alert if you try to print a document with missing or modified pictures.

 See Chapter 25 for more details.

Q: I get PostScript errors and virtual memory (VMerror) errors when I try to print my documents. What can I do?

A: Many errors are caused by insufficient memory in the RIP (raster image processor) of the printer. Typical error messages include: "Limitcheck," "VMerror," and "The document is okay but cannot be printed." While the ideal solution is to add more memory, you can choose certain options to increase the amount of memory available in your printer for processing documents.

1. With a QuarkXPress document open, choose Page Setup from the File menu.

2. The numbers visible just to the left of the OK button in the Page Setup dialog box indicate the version of Laser Prep (or LaserWriter extension under System 7.x) currently in use. You should be using version 6.0.1 or higher with System 6.0.x or LaserWriter version 7.1.1 or higher with System 7.x.x. If you are not, install it now. To do so, follow these steps:

   a. Quit QuarkXPress.

   b. Insert the Macintosh Printing Tools disk (System 6.0.5 or greater) or the Printing disk (System 7.x.x) into your diskette drive.

   c. Double-click on the "Apple Color" folder to display its contents. (This step is needed only for System 6.0.x users.)

   d. Drag both the "Laser Prep" file and the "LaserWriter" driver file to your System folder. (The System 7.x.x LaserWriter extension incorporates the Laser Prep file within it, and does not use a separate Laser Prep file.)

   e. Drag the "Print Monitor" file to your System folder as well.

   f. Launch QuarkXPress. Open your document and choose Page Setup from the File menu.

3. Uncheck all four printer effects: Font Substitution, Text Smoothing, Graphics Smoothing, and Faster Bitmap Printing.

4. Click Options.

5. Check Unlimited Downloadable Fonts.

6. Click OK to close the Options dialog box; then click OK to close the Page Setup dialog box.

7. Attempt to print the file again.

8. If you are unsuccessful, reimport any graphics and attempt to print again.

9. If you are still unsuccessful, attempt to print the document in rough (Output) mode by clicking the Rough button in the Print dialog box (File Í Print). Graphics are not printed. If the document prints in Rough mode, the problem is related to the graphic.

10. If you are still unsuccessful, consult technical support for the illustration program or Quark Technical Support for tips to reduce the complexity of graphics.

Q: I get virtual memory (VM) errors when printing QuarkXPress documents with Adobe Illustrator graphics. What can I do?

A: Occasionally when you are printing a complex document (one that contains long paths, streamlined objects, blends, masks, and/or patterns), Adobe Illustrator or Adobe Separator will generate an error message. Typical error messages include: "Limitcheck," "VMerror," "The document is okay but cannot be printed," "Please use the Chooser to select a printer," and "-8133."

These errors occur when the document is too complex to be printed with the memory currently available on the printer. Installing additional memory into the printer (if possible) will help; however, there are several other things that you can try to reduce the number of printing problems

Working in Adobe Illustrator, try the following tips. Work with a copy of your original file, not the original itself.

ℂ Choose Preferences from the Edit menu. If you are working in Adobe Illustrator 88, set the Split Path Resolution to 5080; this is the maximum setting and will split long paths automatically. If you are working in Adobe Illustrator 3.0, check Split long paths on Save/Print. You may see a series of horizontal lines across your illustration; they indicate where the paths are divided, but they do not print.

ℂ If patterns and/or custom colors are being used, make sure to check under the Style menu for these items and delete all unused patterns and custom colors; deleting these unused elements will simplify the document. (To avoid virtual memory errors, use no more than three patterns in a single document.)

- ↪ Flatness under the Paint menu can be increased to approximately 4 or greater for a laser printer (8 for an imagesetter). This option should be used carefully, however, since it will alter the appearance of the illustration if set too high.

- ↪ Blends may have to be replaced by new blends that contain fewer steps.

- ↪ Use a printer with more RAM, or print at a lower resolution (1200 vs. 2400, for example).

If the document still does not print, it may have to be done in sections that can then be stripped together for printing.

Patterns require a lot of memory. Here are some tips for creating memory-efficient patterns.

- ↪ Use the background as one of the pattern's colors or as solid objects in a pattern rather than drawing the background as a separate object.

- ↪ Group objects within the pattern tile with common paint attributes to make a pattern print faster.

- ↪ Make the tile smaller by reducing the number of its objects.

- ↪ Use objects with simple paths, or decrease the number of points on a path when you draw a pattern object.

- ↪ Remove any detail too small to appear in the final printed output.

If you have further questions, call Adobe Technical Support.

Q: How do I handle trapping on a "rich black"?

A: To create depth in a publication, you can use rich black (also called *superblack*). Rich black is a color you create by combining a 100% process black ink with a percentage of one or more of the other process colors (typically, printers use 100% process black with 40% process cyan). Because this rich black is made up of more than one process ink, the possibility for misregistration is high.

For this reason, trapping is handled differently on a rich black. If the foreground object spreads into the rich black background, all process colors except process black will spread (according to the trap value). If the rich black background chokes into the foreground object, then only the process black plate will choke. These trapping and choking settings keep the background process colors from showing through in the event of misregistration.

Example #1: No common process colors

White (100%) text (or object) on a rich black (100%K, 40%C) background

White text would automatically knock out of any background color, but in the case of a rich black, the white text would spread into the process cyan plate while the white text would simply knock out the process black plate.

Example #2: Common process colors

Cyan (40%) text (or object) on a rich black (100%K, 40%C) background

Cyan text would normally spread into a process black background and the process black plate would knock out, but since Rich Black also has an equal component of process cyan, the cyan type merely knocks out of the process black plate. Because the percentage of process cyan is the same in both the object and the background, there is no knock out, spread, or choke on the process cyan plate.

Example #3: Common process colors of differing percentages

Cyan (60%) text (or object) on a rich black (100%K, 40%C) background

Though process cyan is common to both colors, the differing percentages would cause the process cyan of the object to spread into the process cyan of the background. The same would hold true even if the object percentage were lighter than the background percentage.

Example #4: Some common/some uncommon process colors

Color (40%C, 100%M) text (or object) on a rich black (100%K, 40%C) background

There is no spread or choke on the process cyan plate. The process black plate knocks out, and the process magenta component spreads into the process black plate.

Example #5: Darker color chokes lighter color

Rich black (100%K, 40%C) background to choke to White (100%) type (or object)

In this case, the white type would merely knock out the process cyan plate while the process black plate would choke into the white type. (Note that this trap setting would have to be made manually. It would not occur naturally.)

See Chapter 22 for more details

Q: How do screen values work?

A: Color separations create continuous-tone images by laying cyan, magenta, yellow, and black patterns on top of one another. Each layer (called a plate) is made up of many dots repeated at a certain number of lines per inch (called frequency) and set at a certain angle. When combined, the four layers create tiny rosette patterns that trick your eye into seeing colors in the image, not the pattern itself. If the frequency and angle of each plate are not set correctly, the combination of individual patterns creates distracting patterns. Screen values refer to the frequency of the screens and the angle at which those screens are set on each color plate.

Color separations are created by taking a number of dots, squares, or lines, arranging them in a repeating pattern for each color plate and then overprinting the colors to create a continuous-tone image. (In four-color separations, those colors are cyan, magenta, yellow, and black, or CMYK.) Screen frequencies and angles determine how the colors overprint each other.

The frequency of each plate measures the quantity of its dots, squares, or lines. A common measure of frequency is lines per inch. As a general rule, the higher the frequency, the higher the quality of a four-color image. But the quality of an image's color also depends on screen angles.

In order to combine the four process colors and make them look like continuous color, each plate must print at a distinct angle. If they did not, the colors would directly overprint each other, and the results would look like eight-day-old coffee. By varying the angles, the patterns only partially overprint each other, and their combination tricks the eye into thinking that it sees only one color.

If the screen values are not what they should be, output will suffer, and you'll see problems such as moiré patterns, which are undesirable, repetitive patterns of geometric shapes that run through your colors. They are most visible in areas of solid color or in colors that are difficult to reproduce, such as flesh tones. Moiré patterns are tricky to avoid because the combination of CMYK dots is a geometric pattern. It takes precise screen settings to rid your image of moiré.

Traditionally, professional printers created manual separations that made accurate continuous-tone images at certain screen frequencies and angles. Then, with the advent of PostScript, publishers started to print color separations from the desktop, and they discovered that the old screen values didn't work very well with new systems. That's because PostScript is a mathematical representation of an image, and it plots coordinates on a grid made up of squares. These squares do not match exactly the patterns of traditional methods, so that using traditional angles and frequencies results in printing problems such as inaccurate color and moiré patterns. To address that issue, Adobe utilized Rational Tangent Screening that uses new, more PostScript-friendly screen angles and frequencies. That made for better output, but it was still not accurate enough to satisfy high-end users.

Now there are several companies that have come up with new angles and frequencies to make PostScript output more precise. Linotype-Hell uses its High Quality Screening (HQS) algorithm to determine accurate screen values. Agfa-Compugraphic GS/BIS has Balanced Screening Technology (BST), which uses a lookup table to determine screen values at most frequencies. Purup uses Purup ColorScreens. These screen value systems are used in the respective companies' imagesetters and are generally proprietary.

Adobe also developed a new set of values called AccurateAngles, which works with PostScript Level 2. Adobe licenses the AccurateAngles technology, and some imagesetters now give you the option to use the information. Quark is also addressing the screen value issue by releasing a QuarkXTension called QuarkPrint. With it, you can manually set both screen angles and screen frequencies for the individual color plates of any print job.

By understanding and correctly using available technology, you can get professional-quality color output with QuarkXPress. Any of the systems mentioned above will give you better output than traditional angles; further research can tell you which one is best-suited for your color documents. If you use service bureaus, shop around and ask which technologies they use, and then select the one that suits you best.

 See Chapter 20 for more details.

Index

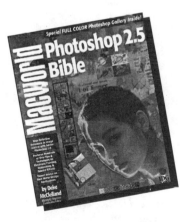

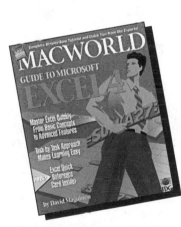

Macworld Guide To Microsoft Works 3

by Barrie Sosinsky

Macworld Guide To Microsoft Works 3 is your definitive guide to mastering Works' individual modules and integrating them effectively to produce powerful documents. A step-by-step approach, expert tips, and task-oriented examples teach you to use Works in the context of your own particular needs. You'll master word processing, database, spreadsheet, draw, charting, and communications modules. Then find out how to use the macro recorder and to share data between programs.

Learn how to use Works for business publishing, with templates, or running on a network. A special section even shows you how to use Works on the road with your PowerBook. And you'll also receive special instructions for using the program with System 7. 434 pages.

Book   **ISBN: 1-878058-42-8**   **$22.95 US/$29.95 Canada**

Macworld Guide to Microsoft Word 5/5.1

by Jim Heid

Just like a travel guide, *Macworld Guide To Microsoft Word 5* is well-illustrated, organized for quick reference, and packed with tips from a knowledgeable insider. You can start your excursion through Word 5.1 with basic editing and formatting techniques, or jump directly to more advanced formatting with frames and sections.

Want to improve your accuracy through Word's built-in spelling, style, and grammar checkers? Create footnotes, tables of contents, and indexes? Save keystrokes with Word's glossary features? Just turn right to the appropriate chapter for complete, easy-to-follow instructions. You'll even learn to exchange information with other programs and to customize Word to design your own stationery, menu commands, and keyboard shortcuts. 408 pages.

Book   **ISBN: 1-878058-39-8**   **$22.95 US/$29.95 Canada**

Order Form

Order Center: (800) 762-2974 (8 a.m.-5 p.m., PST, weekdays) or (415) 312-0650

For Fastest Service: Photocopy This Order Form and FAX it to : (415) 358-1260

Quantity	ISBN	Title	Price	Total

Shipping & Handling Charges

Subtotal	U.S.	Canada & International	International Air Mail
Up to $20.00	Add $3.00	Add $4.00	Add $10.00
$20.01-40.00	$4.00	$5.00	$20.00
$40.01-60.00	$5.00	$6.00	$25.00
$60.01-80.00	$6.00	$8.00	$35.00
Over $80.00	$7.00	$10.00	$50.00

In U.S. and Canada, shipping is UPS ground or equivalent.
For Rush shipping call (800) 762-2974.

Subtotal _____

CA residents add applicable sales tax _____

IN residents add 5% sales tax _____

Canadian residents add 7% GST tax _____

Shipping _____

TOTAL _____

Ship to:

Name _____

Company _____

Address _____

City/State/Zip _____

Daytime Phone _____

Payment: ❏ Check to IDG Books (US Funds Only)   ❏ Visa   ❏ MasterCard   ❏ American Express

Card # _____   Exp. _____   Signature _____

Please send this order form to: IDG Books, 155 Bovet Road, Suite 310, San Mateo, CA 94402.
Allow up to 3 weeks for delivery. Thank you!

BOBMW

IDG Books Worldwide License Agreement

By opening the accompanying disk package, you indicate that you have read and agree with the terms of this licensing agreement. If you disagree and do not want to be bound by the terms of this licensing agreement, return the book for refund to the source from which you purchased it.

The entire contents of these disks and the compilation of the software contained therein are copyrighted and protected by both U.S. copyright law and international copyright treaty provisions. The individual programs on these disks are copyrighted by the authors of each program respectively. Each program has its own use permissions and limitations. You may copy any or all of these programs to your computer system. To use each program, you must follow the individual requirements and restrictions detailed on the following installation page of this book. Do not use a program if you do not want to follow its licensing agreement. Absolutely none of the material on these disks or listed in this book may ever be distributed, in original or modified form, for commercial purposes.

Disclaimer and Copyright Notice

Installing the Macworld QuarkXPress 3.2/3.3 Bible Bonus Software Disk

The Bonus Software disk that comes free with this book contains scripts, utilities, and extensions that you can use with QuarkXPress. Chapter 27 contains descriptions and instructions for using this software.

Before you can use the files contained on the disk, however, it's necessary to install the file. Follow the steps below to complete a successful installation of the disk.

Installation Steps

Installing the disk is a pretty simple procedure. Start your Macintosh and follow these steps to install the QuarkXPress Bible disk to your hard drive.

1. Insert the disk into your drive. The QuarkXPress Bible window appears on your screen.

    Note: Double-click the **READ ME** icon for information about the files on the disk.

2. Double-click the **QuarkXPress Bible Freebies.sea** icon. When a window appears in the middle of your screen, click the **Continue** button.

3. When the Save dialog box appears on the screen, select the hard drive on which you are installing the software and then click the Save button. Installation creates a folder called **QuarkXPress Bible Freebies** on your hard drive and installs the files within that folder.

4. When the **Installation was successful!** dialog box appears on the screen, click the Quit button. The installation is complete.

5. Eject the disk from your drive and store it in a safe place.

Open the **QuarkXPress Bible Freebies** folder to examine its contents. Notice that this folder contains three additional folders — **Scripts, Utilities,** and **XTensions.** These folders contain files that you can use with QuarkXPress.

IDG BOOKS WORLDWIDE REGISTRATION CARD

RETURN THIS REGISTRATION CARD FOR FREE CATALOG

Title of this book: MW QuarkXPress Bible

My overall rating of this book: ❏ Very good [1] ❏ Good [2] ❏ Satisfactory [3] ❏ Fair [4] ❏ Poor [5]

How I first heard about this book:

❏ Found in bookstore; name: [6]

❏ Advertisement: [8]

❏ Word of mouth; heard about book from friend, co-worker, etc.: [10]

❏ Book review: [7]

❏ Catalog: [9]

❏ Other: [11]

What I liked most about this book:

What I would change, add, delete, etc., in future editions of this book:

Other comments:

Number of computer books I purchase in a year: ❏ 1 [12] ❏ 2-5 [13] ❏ 6-10 [14] ❏ More than 10 [15]

I would characterize my computer skills as: ❏ Beginner [16] ❏ Intermediate [17] ❏ Advanced [18] ❏ Professional [19]

I use ❏ DOS [20] ❏ Windows [21] ❏ OS/2 [22] ❏ Unix [23] ❏ Macintosh [24] ❏ Other: [25]_____
(please specify)

I would be interested in new books on the following subjects:
(please check all that apply, and use the spaces provided to identify specific software)

❏ Word processing: [26]

❏ Data bases: [28]

❏ File Utilities: [30]

❏ Networking: [32]

❏ Other: [34]

❏ Spreadsheets: [27]

❏ Desktop publishing: [29]

❏ Money management: [31]

❏ Programming languages: [33]

I use a PC at (please check all that apply): ❏ home [35] ❏ work [36] ❏ school [37] ❏ other: [38]_____

The disks I prefer to use are ❏ 5.25 [39] ❏ 3.5 [40] ❏ other: [41]_____

I have a CD ROM: ❏ yes [42] ❏ no [43]

I plan to buy or upgrade computer hardware this year: ❏ yes [44] ❏ no [45]

I plan to buy or upgrade computer software this year: ❏ yes [46] ❏ no [47]

Name: _____ Business title: [48] _____ Type of Business: [49]

Address (❏ home [50] ❏ work [51] /Company name: _____)

Street/Suite# _____

City [52] /State [53] /Zipcode [54]: _____ Country [55]

❏ **I liked this book!** You may quote me by name in future IDG Books Worldwide promotional materials.

My daytime phone number is _____

IDG BOOKS

THE WORLD OF COMPUTER KNOWLEDGE

☐ YES!

Please keep me informed about IDG's World of Computer Knowledge.
Send me the latest IDG Books catalog.